Comparative Urban Planning Law

Comparative Urban Planning Law

An Introduction to Urban Land Development Law in the United States through the Lens of Comparing the Experience of Other Nations

James A. Kushner
Professor of Law
Southwestern University
School of Law

CAROLINA ACADEMIC PRESS
Durham, North Carolina

ISBN 0-89089-206-7
LCCN 2002114902

Carolina Academic Press
700 Kent Street
Durham, North Carolina 27701
Telephone (919) 489-7486
Fax (919) 493-5668
www.cap-press.com

Printed in the United States of America

Contents

Table of Cases

Principal cases are indicated by italic type.

Preface

Each year, and for more than a decade, I have been traveling to Europe to participate in the Traveling Land Use Seminar sponsored by the Property Law Forum at the University of Southern California (U.S.C.) Law School, led by comparativist George Lefcoe. The seminar takes place in different cities each year and during the seminar we study the city with city officials and local university professors, tour new projects with developers and city officials, and meet to compare the American experience. After a few years, I found that I was extending my trips to visit more cities, and taking additional trips during school holidays or during sabbaticals, to retrace the steps of my earlier trips to view completed and mature projects. Without a conscious curriculum modification, I found myself frequently introducing experiences from abroad in my classes in Land Use Law and Housing and Community Development Law. The response of my students has been extraordinary. Students are engaged by discussions of alternative strategies, cultures, and experiences, and are more willing to critically look at American policy through international comparisons. As part of my travels, I try to capture my experiences through photography, and gradually I have generated various slide shows on topics such as European social housing, brownfield redevelopment, sustainable and green architecture and planning, and transit-oriented development. The slide shows of my latest trip are now an annual event at my school, not simply with my land use students, but particularly with first year students who are now eagerly looking toward land use law. I have also taken the shows and my international comparisons that I have published,[1] and found receptive audiences at schools of law, planning, and geography at U.C.L.A., U.S.C., the Universities of Dortmund in Germany and Utrecht in the Netherlands.

As a result of the success of my efforts at injecting international experiences into the teaching of housing, redevelopment, and land use law, I set out to produce a set of mate-

1. James A. Kushner, *A Comparative Vision of the Convergence of Ecology, Empowerment, and the Quest for a Just Society*, 52 U. Miami L. Rev. 931 (1998); James A. Kushner, *Growth for the Twenty-First Century: Tales from Bavaria and the Vienna Woods—Comparative Images of Urban Planning in Munich, Salzburg, Vienna, and the United States*, 29 Urb. Law. 911 (1997), *reprinted as modified*, 6 Southern California Interdisciplinary L. J. 89 (1997); James A. Kushner, *Planning for Downsizing: a Comparison of the Economic Revitalization Initiatives in American Communities Facing Military Base Closure with the German Experience of Relocating the National Capital from Bonn to Berlin*, 33 Urb. Law. 119 (2001); James A. Kushner, *Social Sustainability: Planning for Growth in Distressed Places—the German Experience in Berlin, Wittenberg, and the Ruhr*, 3 Wash. U. J. L. & Pol'y 849 (2000), *published in* Evolving Voices in Land Use Law Ch. 13 (Germany) (Washington University Journal of Law & Policy 2000); James A. Kushner, *A Tale of Three Cities: Land Development and Planning for Growth in Stockholm, Berlin, and Los Angeles*, 25 Urb. Law. 197 (1993).

rials that would allow a systematic study of the range of issues that would be stimulating to students and fun to teach. Written judicial opinions are very much an American and an English tradition, and the written opinions from non-American or non-Britain and its former empire members, are not typically translated. Thus, I have relied most heavily on my own narrative on the American planning law comparison and the use of edited excerpts from law and interdisciplinary literature that typically focus on comparing planning issues from a non-American jurisdiction with the American experience.

It should be understood that this book does not attempt to present a summary of the current laws and policies affecting land development and urban planning throughout the world. Instead, the idea is to offer contrasting experiences, particularly legal, and to offer a sufficiently diverse view of a problem to appreciate the value of looking to the experiences of other lands and to receive an expansive sense of strategies and mechanisms to comprehend and influence the impacts of alternative law and policy. Some of the readings have been chosen—not because they reflect the current law of the jurisdiction described, but because it best underscores the relationships I seek to highlight, the interface between alternative comparative laws and systems, and the efficacy of public policy.

The narrative summary of American land use law running throughout the book is accurate and contemporary and I am committed to maintaining it. However, it is highly abbreviated so as to permit the appropriate balance with comparative materials. The narrative also frees the instructor from having to spend a significant portion of class time describing the American law affecting each issue. Instead the materials should allow class time to be centered on larger and more focused policy questions arising from contrasts and comparisons. The narrative also allows students in advanced classes who lack the benefit of having taken a basic land use law class to catch up and enjoy the class with greater confidence.

The materials can be used to teach a basic land use law course in a law, planning, geography, or other urban issues class by the instructor who prefers a heavy policy orientation, or it could be used to teach an upper division class or seminar that can be even more policy focused with less attention to the basic American planning jurisprudence. It is my hope you will agree that these materials are compelling, raising critical questions about planning and planning law alternatives. The book notably includes many readings designed to create controversy in the classroom, excitement, incitement, entertainment for the reader, and a generally accessible *reader* for any student of urban issues, urban sprawl, and urban development. For many years I have taught a seminar on Housing and Community Development in which I stress social equity issues: homelessness, affordable housing access, economic development, transportation, housing discrimination, segregation, and urban revitalization. After many classes, along with the students, I went home saddened by the awful suffering of those struggling within and those struggling to enter the government's "safety net," and the frustration of reform. What I discovered was that if, without ignoring or masking reality, I could introduce a theme of optimism, and present readings and ideas that offered hope, that students became more engaged. Curiously, I noticed this change at the same time I was introducing comparisons from other nations. This result was particularly enhanced where I was able to present images of European social housing and brownfield revitalization. I have focused on this theme of optimism and I have sought to offer through these materials a sense of my own optimism for the future, for an enhanced quality of urban life through intelligent planning and policy formation, and legal mechanisms that embrace these goals. Most importantly, I hope that this book reflects my belief that through the tools of planning and planning law employed throughout the world, that efficacious instruments have been provided for transforming and improving the human environment and experience.

This project could not have been undertaken without an extremely long list of friends and colleagues, including developers, city officials, and academics abroad that have welcomed me to their communities and have provided me with an extraordinary education. It was also supported by financial assistance from Southwestern University School of Law and my friend and dean, Leigh H. Taylor. I must also thank Linda Whisman, the Director of Southwestern's Law library and her fabulous research and acquisitions staff that scour book lists and periodical indexes for international and comparative land use scholarship, continually adding to our extraordinary specialty collection. Southwestern's library, which happens to be the most beautiful law library in the world, housed in the world-renowned Art Deco Bullocks Wilshire building in Los Angeles, was the recipient of the Donald G. Hagman Memorial Collection which contains much of Don's incredible collection of comparative land use and zoning materials. I would also like to thank Dean Matthew Spitzer of the U.S.C. Law School for the wonderful support and treatment I received during my visit in 2002 and Associate Dean Scott Altman, who supported me and my plan to teach these nontraditional materials, allowing me a laboratory to test drive the book. I know that the book is much better for the effort. There are so many exciting discussion topics for each chapter that classes were never boring. The materials are so keyed to current events that students would come to class with agenda proposals based on newspaper stories or the interface with their personal study of a foreign land use system. I structure the class around each student choosing a topic and analyzing the problem or question by comparison of the American experience with that of another nation, typically comparing problems in an American city and a foreign city, looking to local and national legal and planning environments and solutions.

I also want to thank my students who are my inspiration as well as my hope for the future. The students in my Housing and Community Development Law Seminar at Southwestern University School of Law who have written their research papers on comparative planning topics have engaged me and informed me of the intricacies of the law and policies of other nations. In addition, since the 1980s, I have employed an army of assistants researching the real estate and land use laws and experiences of every region of the world. I also want to thank the receptive students in Jan van Weesep's urban geography class at University College at Utrecht University, the planning students of Klaus Kunzmann and Ben Davy at Dortmund University, and those of Tridib Banerjee at U.S.C.'s School of Policy, Planning, and Development, who have convinced me that there is a very wide and receptive audience to the ideas contained in this volume. I also wish to thank the students in the U.S.C. Masters of Real Estate Development German Planning and Development class of Susan H. Kamei that I taught in and accompanied to Berlin and the Ruhr in 1999. I also wish to thank the students in my class on Comparative Land Use at the U.S.C. Law School during my visit in 2002, who enthusiastically and appreciatively put up with the inaugural test flight of these materials.

Finally, and without a doubt, the most significant reason why this book has been published is because of Keith Sipe and the incredible family of Carolina Academic Press. Keith has suffered through three editions of my textbook on Housing and Community Development Law, putting up with my co-authors, a who's who of prima donna problem authors who think contract submission dates are "advisory." Nevertheless, when I came to him with an idea for a book for a course that no school offers, and no discipline teaches, he instantly agreed to publish. I have been heartened by the number of teachers in urban affairs, urban planning, geography, as well as state and local government, and land use who are enthusiastic about the project and would gladly teach such a course but for the lack of materials and the rather exhausting undertaking to collect and contrast not just more than one system, but a taste of the world.

Although before this project my work has largely centered on the United States and Europe, I have sought to include comparisons and materials from Asia, Africa and the Americas, I have sought to include the questions of sustainability, globalization, and the local, regional, national, and international perspectives affecting social equity. I hope Keith is rewarded for his courageous underwriting of projects that may not carry a promise of financial success but are simply interesting. If you have any questions or comments e-mail me at jkushner@swlaw.edu. If you have written, or have read a piece that should be included in the next edition, please send me a citation. Anyone who can send me a citation to a current updated discussion of any jurisdiction described or discussed in the book will be thanked when I include it in the next edition. If you have any complaints contact Keith. Although I have been collecting and editing materials for several years, I wrote the textual materials while living at University College at Utrecht University in the Netherlands and in trains crossing Germany in 2001, and completed the final edit after teaching each chapter at the U.S.C. Law School during my spring visit in 2002. Of course this project would not have happened without the support of my family who with relatively good cheer leave me to my projects.

Los Angeles

2002

List of Copyright Permissions

The author gratefully acknowledges permission to reprint the following materials:

American Bar Association Environmental Lawyer for permission to reprint from Jon Owens, *Comparative Law and Standing to Sue: A Petition for Redress for the Environment*, 7 Environmental Lawyer 321 (2001) and Stephanie Yu, Note, *The Smart Growth Revolution: Loudoun County, Virginia and Lessons To Learn*, 7 Environmental Lawyer 379 (2001). Copyright © 2001 by the American Bar Association. Reprinted by permission.

American Bar Association Forum Committee on Affordable Housing and Community Development Law for permission to reprint from Janet Ellen Stearns, *Urban Growth: A Global Challenge*, 8 Journal of Affordable Housing and Community Development Law 140 (1999). Copyright © 1999 by the American Bar Association. Reprinted by permission.

American Bar Association Section of Local Government Law for permission to reprint from Eric M. Braun, *Growth Management and New Urbanism: Legal Implications*, 31 Urban Lawyer 817 (1999) and Nico Calavita, *Urbanization, Public Control of Land Use and Private Ownership of Land: The Development of Italian Planning Law*, 16 Urban Lawyer 459 (1984) and James A. Kushner, *Growth for the Twenty-first Century—Tales from Bavaria and the Vienna Woods: Comparative Images of Planning in Munich, Salzburg, Vienna, and the United States*, 29 Urban Lawyer 911 (1998), printed as modified, 6 S. C. Interdisciplinary L.J. 89 (1997) and James A. Kushner, *A Tale of Three Cities: Land Development and Planning for Growth in Stockholm, Berlin, and Los Angeles*, 25 Urban Lawyer 197 (1993) and Enrico Riva, *Regulatory Takings in American Law and "Material Expropriation"in Swiss Law—A Comparison of the Applicable Standards*, 16 Urban Lawyer 425 (1984) and Shelley Ross Saxer, *Planning Gain, Exactions, and Impact Fees: A Comparative Study of Planning Law in England, Wales, and the United States*, 32 Urban Lawyer 21 (2000) and Jan van Weesep, *Comment: A Perspective on Housing Privatization in Eastern Europe*, 29 Urban Lawyer 595 (1997). Copyright © 1984, 1993, 1997, 1998, 2000 by the American Bar Association. Reprinted by permission.

Boston College Environmental Affairs Law Review for permission to reprint from Jay Wickersham, *Jane Jacob's Critique of Zoning: From Euclid to Portland and Beyond.* Reprinted from 28 B.C. Envtl. Aff. L. Rev. 547 (2001) © by Boston College Law School.

The Canadian Tax Foundation Enid Slack & Richard Bird, for permission to reprint from *Financing Urban Growth Through Development Charges*, 39 Canadian Tax J./Revue Fiscale Canadienne 1288 (1991). Reproduced with the permission of the Canadian Tax Foundation from, Enid Slack & Richard Bird, "Financing Urban Growth Through Development Charges," (1991) vol. 39, no. 5 *Canadian Tax Journal.* 1288–1304.

Colorado Journal of International Environmental Law and Policy for permission to reprint from Clay Fong, Comment, *Taking It to the Streets: Western European and Amer-*

ican Sustainable Transportation Policy and the Prospects for Community Level Change, 7 Colorado Journal International Environmental Law and Policy 463 (1996).

Columbia-VLA Journal of Law and the Arts for permission to reprint from Barbara Hoffman, *Law for Art's Sake in the Public Realm*, 16 Columbia-VLA Journal of Law and the Arts 39 (1991) and Nicole B. Wilkes *Public Responsibilities of Private Owners of Cultural Property: Toward A National Art Preservation Statute*, 24 Columbia-VLA Journal of Law and the Arts 177 (2001).

John C. Dernbach, for permission to reprint from *Sustainable Development as a Framework for National Governance*, 49 Case W. Res. L. Rev. 1 (1998).

Robert C. Ellickson and Yale Law Journal for permission to reprint from *Controlling Chronic Misconduct in City Spaces: Of Panhandlers, Skid Rows, and Public-Space Zoning*, 105 Yale Law Journal 1165 (1996). Reprinted by permission of The Yale Law Journal Company and William S. Hein Company from *The Yale Law Journal*, Vol. *105*, pages *1165–1248*.

Emory International Law Review for permission to reprint from Jon A. Stanley, Comment, *Keeping Big Brother Out of Our Backyard: Regulatory Takings as in International Law and Compared to American Fifth Amendment Jurisprudence*, 15 Emory International Law Review 349 (2001).

Georgetown Journal on Poverty Law and Policy for permission to reprint from Todd Schneider, Note, *From Monuments to Urban Renewal: How Different Philosophies of Historic Preservation Impact the Poor*, 8 Georgetown Journal on Poverty Law & Policy 257 (2001). Reprinted with permission of the publisher, Georgetown Journal on Poverty Law & Policy © 2001.

Georgia Journal of International and Comparative Law for permission to reprint from Kirby Mitchell, Note, *Rescuing Prague's Past: A Survey of Legislative Attempts at Architectural and Historical Preservation in Prague*, Czech Republic, 24 Ga. J. Int'l & Comp. L. 523 (1995).

Carmen G. Gonzalez and Denver University Law Review for permission to reprint from Carmen G. Gonzalez, *Beyond Eco-Imperialism: An Environmental Justice Critique of Free Trade*, 78 Denv. U. L. Rev. 979 (2001). Reprinted by permission of *Denver University Law Review*.

Harvard International Law Journal for permission to reprint from Aya Gruber, Recent Development, *Public Housing in Singapore: the Use of Ends-Based Reasoning in the Quest for a Workable System*, 38 Harvard International Law Journal 236 (1997). Copyright © 2001 by the President and Fellows of Harvard College and the Harvard International Law Journal.

Harvard Law Review for permission to reprint from Note, *Making Mixed-Income Communities Possible: Tax Base Sharing and Class Desegregation*, 114 Harvard Law Review 1575 (2001) Copyright © 2001 by the Harvard Law Review Association.

Hastings Women's Law Journal for permission to reprint from Dana Young, Note, *The Laws of Community: The Normative Implications of Crime, Common Interest Developments, and "Celebration,"* 9 Hastings Women's Law Journal 121 (1998). Copyright © 2001 by University of California, Hastings College of Law. Reprinted from 9 Hastings Women's Law Journal, page 121 (1998), by permission.

Indiana International and Comparative Law Review for permission to reprint from Brian Gardiner, Comment, *Squatters' Rights and Adverse Possession: A Search for Equi-*

table Application of Property Laws, 8 Indiana International and Comparative Law Review 119 (2000).

Journal of the American Planning Association for permission to reprint from Ernest R Alexander, *Alexander Responds*, 67 Journal of the American Planning Association 97 (2001), vol. 67, No. 1; Ernest R Alexander, *Netherlands Planning: The Higher Truth*, 67 Journal of the American Planning Association 91 (2001), vol. 67, No. 1; Timothy Beatley, *Dutch Green Planning More Reality Than Fiction*, 67 Journal of the American Planning Association 98 (2001), vol. 67, No. 1; Emery Roe & Michel van Eeten, *The Heart of the Matter: A Radical Proposal*, 67 Journal of the American Planning Association 92 (2001), vol. 67, No. 1; and Michel Van Eeten & Emery Roe, *When Fiction Conveys Truth and Authority: The Netherlands Green Heart Planning Controversy*, 66 Journal of the American Planning Association 58 (2000), vol. 66, No. 1 (Winter 2000). Reprinted by permission of the *Journal of the American Planning Association*, vols. 66, 67 (2000–2001).

Journal of Land Use and Environmental Law for permission to reprint from Mark Fenster, *Community by Covenant, Process, and Design: Cohousing and the Contemporary Common Interest Community*, 15 Journal of Land Use and Environmental Law 3 (1999). Copyright © by the Journal of Land Use and Environmental Law.

Kansas Journal of Law & Public Policy for permission to reprint from Jeffrey M. Euston, *Clinton's Empowerment Zones: Hope for the Cities or a Failing Enterprise?*, 2 Kansas Journal of Law & Public Policy 140 (1994).

Norman Karlin and Pacific Institute for Public Policy Research for permission to reprint from Norman Karlin, Zoning and Other Land Use Controls: From the Supply Side, 12 Southwestern University L. Rev. 561 (1981), *reprinted in* Resolving the Housing Crisis: Government Policy, Decontrol, and the Public Interest (M.B. Johnson ed. Ballinger Publ. 1982). Reprinted by permission of the Pacific Research Institute.

Deborah Kenn and Brooklyn Journal of International Law for permission to reprint from *One Nation's Dream, Another's Reality: Housing Justice in Sweden*, 22 Brooklyn Journal of International Law 63 (1996).

Jane E. Larson and Georgetown Law Journal for permission to reprint from *Free Markets Deep in the Heart of Texas*, 84 Georgetown Law Journal 179 (2000). Reprinted by permission of the publisher Georgetown Law Journal © 2000.

George Lefcoe, for permission to reprint from *How Taxes Affect Urban Design-And How to Make Them Do a Better Job of It*, 4 Real Estate L.J. 244 (1976) and *When Governments Become Land Developers: Notes on the Public-Sector Experience in the Netherlands and California*, 51 Southern California Law Review 165 (1978).

Bill McKibben for permission to reprint from *Curitiba*, in Hope, Human and Wild: True Stories of Living Lightly on the Earth Ch. 2 (1995). Reprinted by permission of William KcKibben and the Watkins/Loomis Agency.

Pace International Law Review for permission to reprint from Donald C. Dowling, Jr., *Forum Shopping and Other Reflections on Litigation Involving U.S. and European Businesses*, 7 Pace International Law Review 465 (1995).

Pacific Rim Law & Policy Journal for permission to reprint from Chang-Hee Christine Bae, *Korea's Greenbelts: Impacts and Options for Change*, 7 Pacific Rim Law & Policy Journal 479 (1998) and C: Kam Wing Chan, *Infrastructure Services and Financing in Chinese Cities*, 7 Pacific Rim Law & Policy Journal 503 (1998) and William Chapman, *"The Best Laid Schemes...": Land-Use Planning and Historic Preservation in Cambodia*, 7 Pacific Rim Law & Policy Journal 529 (1998) and Mark T. Kremzner, *Manag-*

ing Urban Land in China: The Emerging Legal Framework and its Role in Development, 7 Pacific Rim Law & Policy Journal 611 (1998) and Jeffrey Patterson, *Testing the Partnership Model of Growth Management*, 7 Pacific Rim Law and Policy Journal 721 (1998).

Laura M. Padilla and the Wisconsin Women's Law Journal for permission to reprint from *Single-Parent Latinas on the Margin: Seeking a Room with a View, Meals, and Built-In Community*, 13 Women's Law Journal 179 (1998).

Katharina Richter and the Arizona Journal of International and Comparative Law for permission to reprint from *Compensable Regulation in the Federal Republic of Germany*, 5 Arizona Journal of International and Comparative Law 34 (1988) Copyright © 1988 by the Arizona Board of Regents. Reprinted by permission.

Neal Alison Roberts and Macmillan Publishers for permission to reprint from The Reform of Planning Law: A Study of the Legal, Political and Administrative Reform of the British Land-use Planning System 188–195, 250–261 (1976)

Bernard H. Siegan and the California Western School of Law—Law Review, for permission to reprint from *Non-Zoning is the Best Zoning*, 31 California Western Law Review 127 (1994).

Southern California Law Review for permission to reprint from Geoffrey Graber, Note, *Choosing the Chosen: The Validity of Racial Restrictions on the Alienation of Property in Israel and the United States*, 73 Southern California Law Review 437 (2000) and George Lefcoe, *When Governments Become Land Developers: Notes on the Public-Sector Experience in the Netherlands and California*, 51 Southern California Law Review 165 (1978). Reprinted with permission of the Southern California Law Review.

Temple International and Comparative Law Journal for permission to reprint from James A. Wells, Comment, *Exporting SLAPPs: International Use of the U.S. "SLAPP" to Suppress Dissent and Critical Speech*, 12 Temple International and Comparative Law Journal 457 (1998).

U.C.L.A. Law Review for permission to reprint from Donald G. Hagman, *The Single Tax and Land-Use Planning: Henry George Updated*, 12 UCLA L. Rev. 762 (1965). Originally published in 12 UCLA L. Rev. 762. Copyright © 1965, The Regents of the University of California. All Rights Reserved.

United Nations University Press for permission to reprint from Voula Mega, *The Concept and Civilization of an Eco-society: Dilemmas, Innovations, and Urban Dramas*, in Cities and the Environment: New Approaches for Eco-societies 47 (Takashi Inoguchi, Edward Newman, and Glen Paoletto eds. 1999).

University of Miami Law Review for permission to reprint from Barbara Arco, Comment, *When Rights Collide: Reconciling the First Amendment Rights of Opposing Parties in Civil Litigation*, 52 University of Miami Law Review 587 (1998) and James A. Kushner, *A Comparative Vision of the Convergence of Ecology, Empowerment, and the Quest for a Just Society*, 52 U. Miami L. Rev. 931 (1998).

Vanderbilt Journal of Transnational Law for permission to reprint from Clifford Larsen, *What Should Be the Leading Principles of Land Use Planning? A German Perspective*, 29 Vanderbilt Journal of Transnational Law 967 (1996).

Virginia Environmental Law Journal for permission to reprint from Robert Cervero, *Growing Smart by Linking Transportation and Urban Development*, 19 Virginia Environmental Law Journal 357 (2000) and Oliver A. Pollard, III , *Smart Growth: The Promise,*

Politics, and Potential Pitfalls of Emerging Growth Management Strategies, 19 Virginia Environmental Law Journal 247 (2000).

Washington University Journal of Law & Policy for permission to reprint from Wilton Hyman, *Empowerment Zones, Enterprise Communities, Black Business, and Unemployment*, 53 Washington University Journal of Urban and Contemporary Law 143 (1998) and James A. Kushner, *Social Sustainability: Planning for Growth in Distressed Places—the German Experience in Berlin, Wittenberg, and the Ruhr*, 3 Washington University Journal of Law & Policy 849 (2000).

West Group for permission to reprint from James A. Kushner 2 Subdivision Law and Growth Management Ch. 10 (2d ed. 2001).

William and Mary Law Review for permission to reprint from Douglas W. Kmiec, *Inserting the Last Remaining Pieces into the Takings Puzzle*, 38 Wm. & Mary L. Rev. 995 (1997). Copyright © 2001 by the William and Mary Law Review.

Yale Journal of International Law for permission to reprint from Matthew A. Light, Note, *Different Ideas of the City: Origins of Metropolitan Land-Use Regimes in the United States, Germany, and Switzerland*, 24 Yale Journal of International Law 577 (1999).

Yale Law & Policy Review for permission to reprint from James A. Kushner, *Growth Management and the City*,12 Yale Law & Policy Review 68 (1994). Reprinted by permission of Yale Law & Policy Review, Vol. 12, No. 1, pp. 68–92.

Comparative Urban Planning Law

When one is immersed in his own law, in his own country, unable to see things from without, he has a psychologically unavoidable tendency to consider as natural, as necessary, as given by God, things which are simply due to historical accident or temporary social situation.... To see things in their true light, we must see them from a certain distance, as strangers, which is impossible when we study [the] phenomena of our own country. That is why comparative law should be one of the necessary elements in the training of all those who are to shape the law for societies....[1]

1. Pierre Lepaulle, *The Function of Comparative Law*, 35 Harv. L. Rev. 838, 858 (1922), as quoted in Clifford Larsen, *What Should Be the Leading Principles of Land Use Planning? A German Perspective*, 29 Vanderbilt J. of Transnational Law 967, 970 (1996) .

Chapter 1

Introduction

> "Men come together in cities," said Aristotle, "in order to live: they remain together in order to live the good life." Only fragments of this purpose are fulfilled in the modern world; but a new pattern of the good life is emerging, partly by pressure from within, partly by reaction against the disordered environment, the wry, dehumanized purposes, the ugly barbarisms that still prevail in the world at large.
>
> Lewis Mumford, The Culture of Cities 492 (1938)

City Life

Americans typically perceive that the quality of life in the United States leads the developed nations. Indeed, for many, travel abroad is largely designed to confirm that claim. Returning voyagers are quick to point out how they missed the comforts and conveniences of their world. The typical traveler explores the tourist world of old city centers, historic landmarks and shopping streets. The tourist rarely observes the life of the typical urban dweller. For those who explore public transit and wander some of the residential districts, some startling contrasts are often identified. In most European cities, and many of the world's urban centers, public transit is very convenient, comfortable, and inexpensive, and gets you just about anywhere you care to go. Where the subway, tram, or bus stops, there are usually a cluster of shops and restaurants. It is possible to leave the tram, pick up some groceries and walk several blocks to one's home. The journey to work, a concert, a restaurant, a coffeehouse, or a shopping center, are all but a stroll or a tram ride away. Evermore comfortable and speedy also are the intercity trains that can transport riders to the center of another capital or population center in the time it takes to find the entrance of the freeway, autobahn, or turnpike in the automobile world.

Another startling contrast is that not only are destinations walkable, they can be reached through streets that are attractive, often tree-lined, and interspersed with urban parks, both large and small, that make the journey pleasant. Transit only expands the range of this pedestrian lifestyle.

In America's population centers, the typical lifestyle is automobile centered. It is necessary for most people to drive to each and every destination except for the few who happen to live close to some place. As America's suburbs have developed, most require a drive to school, work, shopping, library, or exercise at the park. The elderly, the young, and the disabled, unable to drive, are captive in their homes and dependent on others for mobility. Americans, long sold on the benefits of the quiet country life, and committed to preserving the low-density subdivisions that define suburban sprawl, and despite being content with the car-centered culture, nevertheless long for the main street of their childhood, nostalgic descriptions from literature and film, or the charming locale of a past vacation. City life is pursued in a few tourist-supported neighborhoods in cities like New York, Chicago, Baltimore, Miami, Pasadena, or Philadelphia, and is often newly constructed by creative developers in places called Horton Plaza in San Diego, Universal City Walk in Los Angeles, the new Disney park addition in Anaheim, or the casino hotels of Las Vegas.

City life is not just about access for the affluent. Indeed, some of the harshest impacts of low density, automobile-dominant sprawl development fall on the poor and working class as major employment centers are not served by convenient public transit, rendering automobile ownership a condition of employment.

Another stark reality in American communities is the impact of taxation policies on development patterns. Public facilities such as parks, libraries, schools, streets, and sewer and water systems are typically the responsibility of local government. As supporting businesses move with the population to the suburbs of separate taxing agencies, central cities with lower income communities often suffer a decline in revenue, translating into declining resources for schools, transit, police, and the delivery of other municipal services; the cycle encourages even more suburban migration and urban decline. In the suburbs these forces generate "Nimbyism" or "not in my backyard" policies that seek to exclude development that will demand additional costly supporting infrastructure, such as apartments and affordable housing because they attract children who require costly schools and demand more costly services than for example a Wal*mart that demands little in services but generates property and sales taxes sought to subsidize the high costs of building the utility, road systems, city services, and other infrastructure that sprawl demands. The result is not simply congestion, but class segregation and dramatic unmet housing and service needs of those of lower income.

What is extraordinary in America, in addition to its expanse of resources, is the extraordinary sense of civic optimism:

> Eternal change is certainly the hallmark of American urban history, which, as we shall see, is the story of a series of urban ideals—some mundane, some high-minded, some wonderful, some wrongheaded, some elitist, some popular—that were often interrupted by unforseen events, interruptions frequently accompanied by calamitous consequences. What is surprising is the continuing sense of public optimism throughout. Despite the setbacks, urban expectations go on unabated. Sometimes the past is impatiently discarded, sometimes it's resurrected, sometimes it's ignored, but throughout the making and unmaking of cities, there is evidence of a constant striving to correct and improve, of an attempt finally to get it right.
>
> Witold Rybczynski, City Life 34 (1995).

The subject of this book is an exploration of the laws and policies affecting planning and city development. The focus is comparing the American experience with the other Nations of the World. Why is Vienna different from Los Angeles? How is adequate affordable housing generated in an expensive society like Sweden? How is it that relatively poor so-called "emerging," "developing," or "under-developed" nations," as in the case of Curitiba, Brazil, have attained a significant measure of urban success. This book is designed to offer insights into these phenomena and an explanation to those discerning travelers who observe striking contrasts between various destinations. At the same time, this book offers an introduction to the official planning and development approval process and should be valuable to the public official, the citizen that seeks to participate in the development process, and a stimulating reader for the student of urban planning, geography and the law of land development.

This book will also explore alternatives to current American planning policy. Those alternatives range from the regulatory society to the more free market deregulated laissez faire model. A powerful central component to many contemporary planning regimes is the notion of sustainability. The basically environmental-oriented concept looks at the quality of air and water, seeks to reduce dependency on oil and non-renewable resources, and seeks to develop communities that are not based on pollution generation but upon an ethic of pedestrianization, protecting flora and fauna, and encouraging community and architectural design that seeks greater efficiency and self-sufficiency. Voula Mega offers a vision of the eco-society:

Voula Mega, *The Concept and Civilization of an Eco-society: Dilemmas, Innovations, and Urban Dramas,*

in Cities and the Environment: New Approaches for Eco-societies 47 (Edited by Takashi Inoguchi, Edward Newman, and Glen Paoletto 1999)

. . . . The city is a dynamic and complex socio-economic and human eco system, a place of encounters, challenges, sociability, confrontation, dialectics, and emotion. According to Aristotle, the city is "built politics": there is high interaction between its form and the political values predominating in its governance. Vitruvius wanted the city to be solid, beautiful, and useful. Levi-Strauss proclaims it to be the human invention "par excellence." Jacobs defines the city as a settlement that consistently generates its economic growth from its own local economy, and Mumford defines it as the form and symbol of an integrated social relationship. Preceding all of them, Alcaeus suggested in the seventh century BC that "not houses finely roofed nor the stones of walls well built nor canals nor dockyards make the city, but men able to seize their opportunities." This last definition reminds us of the one given by Geddes: "City is a dramatic action."

Europe is first and foremost urban. According to the European Commission's *Green Paper on the Urban Environment* (hailed as the first sign of interest in cities on the part of the European Union), as we move towards the twenty-first century cities will continue to be the main centres of economic activity, innovation, and culture. Cities are increasingly strong on the European scene, they compete more, but they also collaborate more. They all want to win the battle of sustainable development and to become more attractive to people and capital. But cities are becoming more ambivalent: there are cities that include but also exclude, that assemble but also divide, that integrate but also disintegrate, that enrich but also impoverish, that fulfil but also drain potential. Turning problems into opportunities is a paramount challenge for all actors and decision-makers. . . .

Sustainability has been the most popular and emblematic term in recent years. "Sustainable development" succeeded the concepts of holistic, integral, or endogenous development. The principle of urban sustainability links cities to the destiny of the planet. It projects them onto the world stage of the future. The concept has been defined more and more as a process and not as an end-point, as a journey rather than a destination. It

1. Karl Marx Hof. One kilometer-long social housing in Vienna, Austria was the first mixed use community, containing shops, restaurants, and schools, it's own rail station, and attractive park landscaping

might be a journey to Ithaca. According to the European Commission, environmental sustainability cannot be envisaged without social equity and economic sustainability. It has been defined as "equity extended into the future." The Charter of European Sustainable Cities describes sustainability as a creative, balance-seeking process extending into all areas of local decision-making. A healthy environment, social cohesion and economic efficiency, harmonious co-evolution, based on an active citizenship, are the pillars of urban sustainability.

The achievement of an eco-society presumes an urban regeneration and renaissance. Cities should not simply invest in a better environment, but should be recreated as Civitates, places of civilization. Expressions like "the martyr city" or even "urban genocide" are significant, but the city at least has the capacity to renew itself. Urban renaissance is needed to bring back harmony to cities often suffering from schizophrenia and a deep divide between the historic core and the dispersed-homes, dispersed-jobs, overwhelmingly car-dependent satellite suburbs. The renaissance cannot be perceived without an overall rethinking of the city, its form, and its functions.

The last UN Summit of the century, Habitat II (Istanbul, 3—14 June 1996), preceded by the first World Assembly of Cities, offered a panorama of the problems and challenges of our rapidly urbanizing world. Dissemination of practices and sustainability indicators were suggested as two important instruments for a qualitative leap forward. The development of indicators is linked to the search for a new measure of progress. Indicators can measure the success of one course of action and even stimulate action, but they do not indicate what kind of action to take. Decision-makers can avail themselves of a large choice of instruments for urban intervention, and good practice guides can inspire them. Moreover, they should be able to define actions which lead to a targeted goal....

Cities are networks of networks and at the same time the poles of global networks. Society is based on networks (networks of every thing) and local actors constitute the diversified poles of the global networks. Technology, information, and markets are global, but people are local. Information technology provides the infrastructure for the integration of the global system. The space of flows (global) is in interaction with the space of places (local) and the cities gain an increasingly dual (global—local) function. Competition is geographically uneven and new technologies have the power to shrink distance and to extend geographical distribution. Both the vanishing city and the omnipotent city are possible, depending on the actors and the policies....

* * *

Trouble on the Commons

The American city is too often anything but the romantic European town or capital. The former home of the rich, struggling to keep city services up with burgeoning demand as the poor and service-dependent concentrate in the city center. One significant inhibition to urban revival is the environment of homeless, beggars, and other street people that make a community colorful but undesirable. Although a full discussion of the problem of homelessness is beyond the scope of this chapter and though a solution might be as simple as having a national housing program to produce needed affordable housing, the subject is raised to symbolize the need to address the negative aspects of the declining city. The issue of street misconduct offers an opportunity to talk about the future of the city from the standpoint of one of its negative symbols.

Robert Ellickson has looked at one manifestation of urban decline, the rising problem of street misconduct. He describes the contemporary specter of aggressive solicitation of alms, the homeless who take over stoops, benches, and parks metaphorically symbolizing mean streets in the semi-abandoned central city. Whether the solution involves regulating behavior, addressing poverty and unmet public services, or the undertaking of a coherent affordable housing policy, the problem of street misconduct raises an interesting debate about the causes of urban problems and their solutions:

Robert C. Ellickson, *Controlling Chronic Misconduct in City Spaces: Of Panhandlers, Skid Rows, and Public-Space Zoning,* 105 Yale L.J. 1165 (1996)

To the bewilderment of pedestrians in the 1980s, panhandlers, aimless wanderers pushing shopping carts, and other down-and-out individuals appeared with increasing frequency in the downtown areas of the United States. During the same period, in an apparent paradox, the Skid Rows of most U.S. cities were in sharp decline. While New Yorkers were encountering more panhandlers in their subway system, their city's most famous Skid Row—the Bowery—was fading from view. While the number of homeless campers occupying Palisades Park in Santa Monica rose, fifteen miles away, Los Angeles's Skid Row east of Spring Street was losing population.

By the early 1990s, the increased disorderliness of the urban street scene had triggered a political backlash. Commentators began to report that the urban populace was suffering from "compassion fatigue." Even in the nation's most liberal cities, mayoral candidates campaigned for greater control of street misconduct, and city councils passed crackdown ordinances. In New York, San Francisco, Washington, D.C., and countless other cities, these legal measures, coupled with a general hardening of pedestrians' attitudes, began to reduce the incidence of disorderly behavior in public spaces. In 1994 alone, voters in Berkeley, Santa Monica, and Santa Cruz—three of the most politically liberal municipalities in California—compelled their local officials to take steps to limit street disorder...

These open-access public spaces are precious because they enable city residents to move about and engage in recreation and face-to-face communication. But, because an open-access space is one everyone can enter, public spaces are classic sites for "tragedy," to invoke Garrett Hardin's famous metaphor for a commons. The media are quick to report the gravest problems of the streets, such as armed robberies, drug trafficking, and drive-by shootings. This Article focuses on problems that by comparison seem trivial: chronic street nuisances. Chronic street nuisances occur when a person regularly behaves in a public space in a way that annoys—but no more than annoys—most other users, and persists in doing so over a protracted period. Two hypothetical examples of street nuisances recur during the analysis that follows. The first involves a panhandler, by assumption a mild-mannered one, who repeatedly stations himself on a sidewalk in front of a particular restaurant. The second involves a mentally ill bench squatter who, morning after morning, wheels a shopping cart full of belongings to a bench in a downtown plaza, stretches out a sleeping bag on the bench, and dozes there intermittently until dark. The street behavior in both cases is assumed to result in a net decrease in the use of these public spaces. Because the panhandler's presence inhibits pedestrians, the sidewalk is less used and the restaurant's business suffers; although the bench squatter himself contributes to the daytime population in the plaza, the average headcount falls because fewer pedestrians wish to linger there.

Chronic street nuisances pose practically knotty and normatively perplexing questions about the management of public spaces. Most courts have held that a city can prohibit more aggravated nuisances, such as aggressive panhandling and overnight sleeping in parks not designated for camping. Conversely, there is universal agreement that every person, no matter how scorned, is entitled, assuming he behaves himself, to walk on every public sidewalk and to sit on every bench in every public park. The examples of protracted panhandling and bench squatting fall in the baffling normative terrain that lies between these easier cases.

Most of the legal scholars who have written on street misconduct have come at the topic from one of three angles: hyper-egalitarianism, free speech libertarianism, and criminal defense. Each of these is a pertinent, but overly narrow, perspective....

Notable and forceful advocates of controls on street misconduct are relatively more prominent in the literature beyond the law reviews. Urbanologist Jane Jacobs and criminologist Wesley Skogan have both stressed that maintaining the invitingness of streets, sidewalks, and parks is essential to the viability of an urban neighborhood. The well-known "broken windows" thesis of James Q. Wilson and George L. Kelling also sounds this theme. Wilson and Kelling assert that the persistence of a minor disorder not only disturbs a neighborhood on its own account, but also, like an unrepaired broken window, signifies that social controls are attenuated at that locale. Passersby, sensing this diminished control, become prone to committing additional, perhaps more serious, criminal acts. According to Wilson and Kelling, unchecked street misconduct thus has a multiplier effect.

A specialist in property law approaches the issue of street order as a problem not of speech or of crime, but of land management. Many lawmakers and scholars have treated municipal lands as an undifferentiated mass. City spaces, however, are highly diverse in character and are subject to hugely varied demands. A central normative thesis of this Article is that a city's codes of conduct should be allowed to vary spatially—from street to street, from park to park, from sidewalk to sidewalk. Just as some system of "zoning" may be sensible for private lands, so may it be for public lands...

This term ["homeless"] is commonly applied to all poor people—including those who reside in permanent dwellings—who chronically make heavy use of the streets. Because the term often crops up in litigation and policy discussions, I conclude this part with some linguistic housekeeping on the differences between the "homeless" and "street people."

The nouns customarily used to describe down-and-out street people have moved with the spirit of the times. Before the 1980s, street people were usually saddled with a negative label, such as "vagrant," "derelict," "bum," "drifter," or "beggar." In the 1980s, activists encouraged journalists and scholars to relabel street people as the "homeless," a term that had been used with reference to street people only sparingly during prior decades. In the mid-1980s, the universal adoption of the term "homeless" helped engender more empathy for street people. Whenever possible in this Article, however, I refer to "street people" (or "panhandlers" or "bench squatters"), not to the "homeless." "Homeless" is an unduly ambiguous word and implies policy solutions that are inapt.

Ordinary speakers tend to attach the "homeless" label to individuals whose lives meet at least one of three quite different criteria: persons who spend the night in an emergency shelter; persons who spend the night on the "streets" (e.g., in vehicles, railroad stations, parks, and other spaces not designed for residential use); and panhandlers, daytime bench squatters, squeegee men, can collectors, and other active "street people." To be sure, the members of all three groups share a number of attributes. They tend to be destitute, socially isolated, and at most episodically employed. They also tend to be heavy users of public spaces.

Nevertheless, the composition of these three groups overlaps far less than is popularly thought. For example, although pedestrians may assume that a panhandler sleeps in a shelter or on the streets, studies indicate that, in most cities (but seemingly not in New York), a large majority of panhandlers have "regular access to a permanent dwelling" and thus fail to meet the scholarly definition of the homeless. Conversely, only a small fraction of the street and shelter homeless engage in panhandling.

The label "homeless" also has fostered misguided policies. The word implies that the problems of the people so labeled can be solved with bricks-and-mortar—with "housing, housing, housing," as Robert Hayes and other advocates were still saying in the late 1980s. By the early 1990s, there was broad agreement that this policy response was largely off target, and the new mantra became "therapy, therapy, therapy." Brendan O'Flaherty persuasively argues that the new policy fix is no better than the old. Singling out persons labeled "homeless" for special benefits and burdens tends to entrap them in a marginal status. O'Flaherty would treat them like everyone else, not as members of a special class....

[I]n step with the increase in the population of unmarried males, the number of federal and state prisoners ballooned from 196,000 in 1970, to 316,000 in 1980, and to

740,000 in 1990. This trend may have reduced violent street crime by incapacitating more offenders. On the other hand, it also may have increased the number of street people. State-prison inmates have a median age of about 30. The median age of homeless persons is higher, in the late 30s. The increase in incarceration brought in its wake a jump in the number of prisoners being released at an age when they were ripe for becoming homeless. On release, these individuals, handicapped by low job skills, adverse prison influences, and likely employer discrimination, become prime candidates for the street. By getting tough on violent crime and drug offenses in the 1970s, the United States may have increased levels of minor street misconduct in the 1980s and 1990s....

Some scholars, judges, and advocates apparently believe that provisions of the Federal Constitution tightly and uniformly constrain city policies in all open-access public spaces. This monolithic conception is reflected in Justice Roberts's famous dictum in Hague v. CIO: "wherever the title of streets and parks may rest, they have immemorially been held in trust for the use of the public and, time out of mind, have been used for purposes of assembly, communicating thoughts between citizens, and discussing public questions. Such use of the streets and public places has, from ancient times, been a part of the privileges, immunities, rights, and liberties of citizens." Justice Roberts's sweeping characterization of the uses of streets and public places is descriptively false. For example, most cities treat street pavements primarily as transportation corridors, and thus give transportation functions priority over citizens' efforts to use those pavements for parades, gatherings, solicitations of drivers, and other speech activities that interfere with traffic flows. Justice Roberts's broad dictum is also suspect as a statement of constitutional doctrine; the municipal priorities just mentioned have long been held not to violate the First Amendment.

Charles Tiebout has indicated the theoretical advantages of enabling people of disparate tastes to "vote with their feet" among local governments that offer distinct packages of public goods and taxation policies Consumer sovereignty is also served by the provision of an array of physical and social environments within a single political unit. Manhattan is interesting partly because of the striking variations among its neighborhoods—Wall Street, Greenwich Village, Chinatown, the Theater District, Harlem, and so on. This part contrasts informal and formal methods of "zoning" public spaces to add to the richness and diversity of urban life.

A Hypothetical Division of City Public Spaces into Red, Yellow, and Green Zones

As a mental experiment, imagine that it would be desirable for a city to have three codes, of varying stringency, governing street behavior. Borrowing from the system of traffic signals, let's call these codes Red, Yellow, and Green. Each of the city's public spaces would be assigned to a zone paired with just one of these colors. (Who is to do this zoning will be addressed shortly.) As with a traffic signal, Red would signal extreme caution to the ordinary pedestrian; Yellow, some caution; and Green, a promise of relative safety. It must be stressed that these color codes are chosen with an eye to pedestrians of ordinary tastes, not to those inclined to engage in nuisance behavior. This usage is consistent with the phrase "Red Light District," which connotes disorderliness to an ordinary citizen, but not necessarily to a brothel patron.

In Red Zones (say, 5% of a city's downtown area), normal standards for conduct in public spaces would be significantly relaxed. The rule would hardly be "anything goes," of course; even in these places, violence to person or property, for example, would be subject to sanction. But many sidewalk behaviors that would be considered disorderly in the rest of the city would not violate Red-Zone rules-of-the-road. In these relatively rowdy areas, a city might decide to tolerate more noise, public drunkenness, soliciting by prostitutes, and so forth. More pertinently for the topic at hand, chronic panhandling and bench squatting would be permitted in a Red Zone. Red Zones, in short, would be designed as safe harbors for people prone to engage in disorderly conduct.

Yellow Zones would comprehend, say, 90% of a city's downtown public spaces. The city's civic center, plazas, central business district, and other principal agoras would be placed under this large umbrella. The applicable code of conduct would aim to make a Yellow-Zone space serve as a lively mixing bowl. As mentioned, a city would have to walk a fine line to achieve this objective. On the one hand, the city could not control its Yellow-Zone spaces so tightly that the flamboyant and eccentric would be kept out; on the other hand, it would have to curb street misbehavior enough to make the great majority of citizens willing to enter these spaces without hesitation. A Yellow Zone's rules of public decorum therefore would be stricter than a Red Zone's rules. There would be constraints on excessive noise, drunkenness, and other disorderly conduct. For present purposes, let's assume that chronic (but not episodic) panhandling and bench squatting—permitted in a city's Red Zones—would be prohibited in its Yellow Zones.

Green connotes unusually pleasant environmental conditions. In Green Zones, the remaining 5% of downtown, social controls would be tailored to create places of refuge for the unusually sensitive: the frail elderly, parents with toddlers, unaccompanied grade-school children, bench sitters reading poetry. To accomplish this goal, the Green-Zone code would be relatively strict in its regulation of mildly disruptive activities such as radio playing, walking a dog, leafleting, and street performances. Let's also suppose that even episodic panhandling and bench squatting would be banned in these locations. A large Green Zone would offer real respite from the ordinary hurly-burly of the streets. A city might also create scattered pockets of refuge, perhaps around all bus stops.

To summarize: Under the hypothetical regime, chronic panhandling and bench squatting would be permitted only in 5% of downtown public spaces (the Red Zones), but episodic panhandling and bench squatting would be permitted in 95% downtown public spaces (all but the Green Zones)....

Unchecked street misconduct creates an ambience of unease, and for some, of menace. Pedestrians can sense that even minor disorder in public spaces tends to encourage more severe crime. City dwellers who perceive that their streets are out of control are apt to take defensive measures. They may use sidewalks and parks less, or favor architectural designs that discourage leisurely stays in public spaces. In particular, they may relocate to more inviting locales. As modes of travel and communication improve, individuals have ever greater choices. Shoppers can switch to enclosed malls, employers can move to suburban industrial parks, and universities can shift activities to satellite branches....

* * *

Notes and Comments

1. *Criticism.* For criticism of Professor Ellickson's proposal, see Stephen R. Munzer, *Ellickson on "Chronic Misconduct" in Urban Spaces: Of Pandhandlers, Bench Squatters, and Day Laborers*, 32 Harv. C.R-C.L. L. Rev. 1 (1997).

2. *Criminalization.* Many communities have addressed homelessness and activities described as street misconduct through regulation, criminalization, and de facto policies of expulsion. Some communities have adopted ordinances that make aggressive

solicitation or solicitation in certain places such as outdoor restaurants, banks, and transit stops a crime after objection is lodged. Some communities in a sense follow Ellickson's suggestion and exclude the ostensibly homeless from certain tourist and shopping areas. This is reflected in Vancouver running the homeless from "Robsonstrasse," its prestigious shopping street, San Francisco declaring Golden Gate Park as off-limits for the poor, or Los Angeles assuring that urban redevelopment includes no public furniture that is attractive to the homeless. Anastasia Loukaitou-Sideris, *Privatization of Public Open Space*, J. Regional Sci., May, 1993, at 131, 153–54, cited in James A. Kushner, *Growth for the Twenty-First Century: Tales from Bavaria and the Vienna Woods—Comparative Images of Urban Planning in Munich, Salzburg, Vienna, and the United States*, 29 Urb. Law. 911, 946 (1997), *reprinted as modified*, 6 S. Cal. Interdisciplinary L.J. 89, 124 (1997). Policies that deny the homeless housing, welfare, medical services, school access or the right to vote are constitutionally suspect. *See generally* No Homeless People Allowed (1994) (report by the National Law Center on Homelessness & Poverty on anti-homeless laws, litigation, and alternatives in 49 United States cities); Maria Foscarinis, *Downward Spiral: Homelessness and its Criminalization*, 14 Yale L. & Pol'y Rev. 1 (1996); Maria Foscarinis, Kelly Cunningham-Bowers & Kristen E. Brown, *Out of Sight—Out of Mind?: The Continuing Trend Toward The Criminalization of Homelessness*, 6 Geo. J. Poverty L. & Pol'y 145 (1999).

3. *Aggressive Solicitation.* The Los Angeles "aggressive solicitation" ordinance was enjoined as being in violation of the First Amendment as the federal trial court found the ordinance content-based discrimination. *Los Angeles Alliance for Survival v. City of Los Angeles*, 987 F. Supp. 819 (C.D. Cal. 1997), on appeal the Ninth Circuit certified the question of the ordinance's validity under state law to the California Supreme Court, which ruled that the ordinance was not content-based. 993 P.2d 334 (Cal. 2000). The Ninth Circuit conformed to the ruling but nevertheless affirmed the grant of the initial injunction despite the content-neutral characterization as free speech concerns outweighed government interests. 224 F.3d 1076 (9th Cir. 2000). *See also* Andrew D. Leipold, *Targeted Loitering Laws*, 3 U. Pa. J. Const. L. 474 (2001).

4. *Homeless Assistance.* With passage of the Stewart B. McKinney Homeless Assistance Act, Pub. L. No. 100-628, 102 Stat. 3230 (1988), *codified at*, 42 U.S.C. §§ 11301–11489 (1994 & Supp. V 1999), Congress resolved to provide federal resources to provide shelters and services for the homeless. While the legislation has generated a massive expansion in shelter capacity, unfortunately, the program has led to "shelterization," shelters becoming a permanent component to housing the poor, with no real permanent solution to the lack of decent housing and communities. *See generally* Michael A. O'Connor, *Homeless: A Local View of the McKinney Act*, 23 Clearinghouse Rev. 116 (1989); Florence Wagman Roisman, *The Lawyer as Abolitionist: Ending Homelessness and Poverty in Our Time*, 19 St. Louis U. Pub. L. Rev. 237 (2000) (advocating a litigation and legislation objective of the abolition of homelessness).

5. *Altering Urban Design.* Altering urban design may generate a land use pattern that mitigates many of the negative externalities associated with urban sprawl low density development. Transit policies that assure access to employment and shopping centers could drastically alter both opportunities for seeking employment and greater mobility to allow workers a greater choice or residence. The development of an adequate supply of affordable housing integrated with working class housing would also diminish the excessive unmet demand for housing that has so oppressed the poor by imposing excessive inflated rents. The combination of inflated rents resulting from the failure of government to support a meaningful housing policy, together with

urban policy that has favored the destruction of single room occupancy housing and the demolition of older housing under urban renewal and code enforcement programs has contributed to homelessness and an environment in which even many workers are rendered poor, trapped in neighborhoods inaccessible to the variety of opportunities that most Americans take for granted. In cities such as Baltimore, Detroit, and St. Louis, that have been bypassed by recent immigrant population growth and facing job and population decline, vacant low income housing stock is referred to as "undercrowding." Low rent fails to compensate for the lack of economic opportunity and jobs and the increasing blight of escalating scattered adbandonment and the demolition of scattered houses in an increasing number of blocks. James Cohen, *Abandoned Housing: Exploring Lessons from Baltimore*, 12 Hous. Pol'y Debate 415 (2001).

City Life in Developing Nations

One might assume that the best government and the best urban planning is found only in advanced industrialized and developed western Nations. The assumption may be misplaced. Bill McKibben argues that the United States has a lot to learn from the simple and intelligent solutions from our developing neighbors:

Bill McKibben, *Curitiba*, in Hope, Human and Wild: True Stories of Living Lightly on the Earth

Ch. 2 (1995)

The first time I went there, I had never heard of Curitiba. I had no idea that its bus system was the best on earth, that it had largely solved the problem of streetchildren that plagues the rest of South America, or that a municipal shepherd and his flock of thirty sheep trimmed the grass in its vast parks. It was just a mid-size Brazilian city where an airline schedule forced me to spend the night midway through a long South American reporting trip. I reached my hotel, took a nap, and then went out in the early evening for a walk—warily, because I had just come from crime-soaked Rio. But the street in front of the hotel was cobbled, closed to cars, and strung with lights. It opened onto another such street, which in turn opened into a broad and leafy plaza, with more shop-lined streets stretching off in all directions. Though the night was frosty—Brazil stretches well south of the tropics, and Curitiba is in the mountains—people strolled and shopped, butcher to baker to bookstore. There were almost no cars, but at one of the squares a steady line of buses rolled off, full, every few seconds....

From time to time over the next few years, I would see Curitiba mentioned in planning magazines or come across a short newspaper account of it winning various awards from the United Nations. Its success seemed demographically unlikely. For one thing, it's relatively poor—average per capita income is about twenty-five hundred dollars. Worse, a flood of displaced peasants has tripled its population to a million and a half in the last twenty-five years. It should resemble a small-scale version of urban nightmares like São Paulo or Mexico City. But I knew, from my evening's stroll, it wasn't like that, and I wondered why....

Curitiba is among the world's great cities. Not for its physical location: there are no beaches, no broad bridge-spanned rivers. Not in terms of culture or glamour: it's a fairly provincial place. But measured for "livability"—a weak coinage expressing some optimum mix of pleasures provided and drawbacks avoided—I have never seen any place like it. In a recent survey 60 percent of New Yorkers wanted to leave their rich and cosmopolitan city; 99 percent of Curitibans told pollsters that they were happy with their town.... It has slums: some of the same shantytown *favelas* that dominate most Third World cities have sprouted on the edge of town as the population has rocketed. But even they are different, hopeful in palpable ways. They are clean, for instance—under a city program a slum dweller who collects a sack of garbage gets a sack of food from the city in return.

And Curitiba is the classic example of decent lives helping produce a decent environment. One statistic should underline the importance of this place to the world. Because of its fine transit system, and because its inhabitants are attracted toward the city center instead of repelled out to a sprawl of suburbs, Curitibans use 25 percent less fuel per capita than other Brazilians, even though they are actually more likely to own cars.... It came from designing a city that actually meets people's desires, a city that is as much an example for the sprawling, decaying cities of the First World as for the crowded, booming cities of the Third World. A place that, at the very least, undercuts the despair that dominates every discussion of the world's cities, where half of human souls now reside....

[In] 1940 there were 125,000 residents. By 1950 the number had jumped to 180,000, and by 1960 doubled to 361,000—the explosive, confident growth that marked the entire country was underway in Curitiba as well. And with many of the same effects: traffic downtown started to snarl, and the air was growing thick with exhaust. It was clear that the time had come to plan; and as in almost every other city, planning meant planning for automobiles.

Curitiba's official scheme called for widening the main streets of the city to add more lanes, which would have meant knocking down the turn-of-the-century buildings that lined the downtown, and for building an overpass that would link two of the city's main squares by going over the top of Rua Quinze de Novembro, the main shopping street. Any American living in a city that has undergone urban renewal or been cut off from its waterfront by a belt of highway would recognize the plan in an instant; in one form or another, it's how urban areas around the globe have been reconfigured for the auto age....

... [I]t was a good thing that Jaime Lerner had visited Paris as a young student and especially that he had grown up loving the mix of people in Curitiba. Because Lerner, through a chain of political flukes, found himself the mayor of Curitiba at the age of thirty-three. Brazil in the early 1970s was ruled by the military, and the local governor was not interested in appointing anyone who might turn out to be a political rival. He picked Lerner, who took the job despite his repugnance for the army. All of a sudden his friends and colleagues were pulling their plans out of the cupboards. All of a sudden they were going to get their chance to remake Curitiba not for cars but for people. "I was born on the street of the central railroad station," says Lerner. "My father he had a shop in this street, and we lived in the back of the business. I used, since six, to play in the street. Since my childhood I had everything from the street.... I never could forget this street, which was a Street like other streets that everyone has in his life. But a Street is the synthesis of the whole city, the whole society."

And so the story of Curitiba begins with its central street, Rua Quinze—the one that the old plan wanted to obliterate with an overpass. Lerner insisted instead that it should become a pedestrian mall, an emblem of his drive for a human-scale city. "I knew we'd have a big fight," he says. "I had no way to convince the storeowners a pedestrian mall would be good for them, because there was no other pedestrian mall in Brazil. No other in the world, really, except maybe Munich. But I knew if they had a chance to actually see it, everyone would love it." To prevent opposition, he planned carefully. "I told my staff, 'This is like a war.' My secretary of public works said the job would take two months. I got him down to one month. Maybe one week, he said, but that's final. I said, 'Let's start Friday night, and we have to finish by Monday morning.'" And they did—jackhammering up the pavement, putting down cobblestones, erecting streetlights and kiosks, and putting in tens of thousands of flowers."

It was a horrible risk—he could easily have been fired," says Oswaldo Alves, who helped with the work. But by midday Monday the same storeowners who had been threatening legal action were petitioning the mayor to extend the mall. The next weekend, when offended members of the local automobile club threatened to "reclaim" the street by driving their cars down it, Lerner didn't call out the police. Instead, he had city workers lay down strips of paper the length of the mall. When the auto club arrived, its members found dozens of children sitting in the former street painting pictures. The transformation of Curitiba had begun.

But this was not some romantic revolution, a cultural protest of the sort so common in the wake of the sixties and so evanescent. Even this small victory was possible only because Lerner and his architect friends had thought so carefully about the future of the city. They had, among other things, carefully replotted the city's traffic flow, not only to make the downtown function without cars on its main street, but also to direct growth throughout the city. Instead of buying up buildings and tearing them down to widen streets, planners stared at the maps long enough to see that the existing streets would do just fine—as long as they were considered in groups of three parallel avenues. Traffic on the first avenue would flow one way, into town. The middle street would be devoted to buses, driving in dedicated lanes so they could move more quickly. A block over you'd find motorists heading out of town. No highways in the city—three streets still scaled to human beings. And more important, once the planners had designated five of these "structural axes" leading out from the center of town like spokes in a wheel, they could begin to tinker with zoning. Along these main routes, high-density buildings were permitted the apartments that would hold the commuters eager to ride the buses. Farther from the main roads, density decreases.

From the observation deck on the top of the city's television tower, you can see the results spread out below you not a ring of high-rises choking the downtown, but orderly lines of big buildings shading off into neighborhoods along each of the axes; a city growing on linear lines that removed congestion from the center, and kept a mix of housing and hence, of incomes—throughout the city. "Every city has its hidden designs old roads, old streetcar ways," says Lerner. "You're not going to invent a new city. Instead, you're doing a strange archaeology, trying to enhance the old, hidden design. You can't go wrong if the city is growing along the trail of memory and of transport. Memory is the identity of the city, and transport is the future."...

Transport in the case of Curitiba means buses. Though larger Brazilian cities were investing in subways and though "there were always people trying to sell them to us as the modern way," Lerner and his team decided the subways were too expensive—that they were stuck with buses. They also decided that buses needn't be stuck in traffic. They quickly designed the system of express lanes that sped travel to and from the downtown, and ridership began to take off. In 1974 the system carried 25,000 passengers a day; by 1993 the number was 1.5 million—or more than ride the buses in New York City each day. The route network looks like a model of the human brain. Orange feeder buses and green buses traveling in constant loops through the outer neighborhoods deliver passengers to terminals, where they catch red express buses heading downtown or out to the factories on the city's edge.

In an effort to increase speed even further, the red express buses were replaced in the late 1980s by silver "direct line" buses on the busiest streets. The buses move faster not because they have bigger motors but because they were designed by smarter people. Sitting at a bus stop one day, Lerner noticed that the biggest time drag on his fleet was how long it took passengers to climb the stairs and pay the fare. He sketched a plan for a glass "tube station," a bus shelter raised off the ground and with an attendant to collect fares. When the bus pulls in, its doors open like a subway's, and people walk right on (or, in the case of wheelchairs, roll right on). A year after the "speedybuses" went into service, the city did a survey: 28 percent of the passengers were new to the system, commuters who had parked their cars because of the new convenience. In 1993 Curitiba added another Lerner innovation—extra-long buses, hinged in two spots to snake around corners and able to accommodate three hundred passengers. Five doors open and close at each stop, and on busy routes at rush hour one of these behemoths arrives every minute or so; twenty thousand passengers an hour can move in one direction. There is a word for this kind of service: subway.

Amazingly, the city doesn't need to subsidize its bus service. The fleet is purchased and owned by private companies; the government assigns routes, sets fares, and pays each contractor by kilometer traveled. For about thirty cents, you can transfer as often as you want; and the whole network turns a profit. A few years ago, to help celebrate Earth Day, Curitiba lent New York several of its loading tubes and special buses. Brazilians installed the system in five days, and for a couple of months the buses plied a loop from the Battery to South Street Seaport and back. The *Daily News* reported "looks of bewilderment" at the "space age pod" donated by the Third World to the absolute epicenter of world finance, but by all accounts passengers loved the system. Still, it seems to have disappeared into some bureaucratic maw. The New York City bus system has seen ridership fall 42 percent in the last twenty years and is only now beginning to experiment with "innovations" like stopping every third block instead of every second one. The "realistic hope," according to a recent Transit Authority report, is that ridership will fall only 7 percent this decade. I understand why; I never rode the buses when I lived in New York. I could walk faster than a rush-hour bus in midtown, and the rest of the day they rarely came; the windows were so scratched that once you were on board you had to peer owl-eyed to see if your stop was approaching. But in Curitiba I rode every day, pushing my daughter's stroller onto the bus, finding my way more easily than in Manhattan despite my pidgin Portuguese. *The bus* serves *you*, and not the other way around; you feel in control of the city, not a victim of its tie-ups and bottlenecks and ancient every-day-repeated traffic jams....

Cheapness is one of the three cardinal dictates of Curitiban planning. Many of the city's buildings are "recycled." The planning headquarters is in an old furniture factory; the gunpowder depot became a furniture factory; a glue plant was turned into the children's center. An old trolley stationed on the Rua Quinze has become a free babysitting center where shoppers can park their kids for a few hours.

The city's parks provide the best example of brilliance on the cheap. When Lerner took office for the first time in 1971, the only park in Curitiba was smack downtown—

the Passeio Püblico, a cozy zoo and playground with a moat for paddleboats and a canopy of old and beautiful *ipé* trees, which blossom blue in the spring. "In that first term, we wanted to develop a lot of squares and plazas," recalls Alves. "We picked one plot, we built a lot of walls, and we planted a lot of trees. And then we realized this was very expensive."

At the same time, as luck would have it, most Brazilian cities were installing elaborate flood-control projects. Curitiba had federal money to "channelize" the five rivers flowing through town, putting them in concrete viaducts so that they wouldn't flood the city with every heavy summer rain and endanger the buildings starting to spring up in the flood plain. "The bankers wanted all the rivers enclosed," says Alves; instead, city hall took the same loan and spent it—on land. At a number of sites throughout the city, engineers built small dams and backed up the rivers into lakes. Each of these became the center of a park; and if the rains were heavy, the lake might rise a foot or two—perhaps the jogging track would get a little soggy or the duck in the big new zoo would find itself swimming a few feet higher than usual. "Every river has a right to overflow," insists parks chief Nicolau Kiupel, who became known as "Nicolago."

Mostly because of its flood-control scheme, in twenty years—*even as it tripled in population*—the city went from two square feet of green area per inhabitant to more than a hundred and fifty square feet per inhabitant. The official literature always points out, with understandable pride, that this figure is four times the World Health Organization standard of twelve square meters. From every single window in Curitiba, I could see as much green as I could concrete. And green begets green; land values around the new parks have risen sharply, and with them tax revenues.

The entire city government runs on a $250 million budget, or about $156 per capita, compared with, say, $807 per person in Dallas or $1,179 per person in Detroit. The municipal obsession with parsimony would amaze anyone used to traveling in the developing world, where visitors are invariably taken to huge and ostentatious showplace buildings in an attempt to prove the modernity and power of the government—in an attempt to show that they're as good as anyone else. In Curitiba, by contrast, I spent a typically dusty day with two of the local public housing authority officials, who were busy setting up a program that allowed newly arrived peasants to build tiny houses of their own for the price of two packs of cigarettes a month. After we looked over dozens of these new homes, the officials took me by a grand edifice that I'd noticed on the horizon—it turned out to be a school, built by Brazil's federal government (a government that may lead the world in corruption and inefficiency). Perched above a *favela*, the school had a lovely basketball court, just like you might find in a prosperous suburban high school in the United States. But dust was an inch thick on the parquet floor, and none of the classrooms were in use, either—in part because there were no desks, chairs, or other furnishings. "Someone ate up the in-between money," says one of the housing guys. "When I think of what we could do if we had the cash that went into this place..."

Simple is brother to cheap, and it's another of the mantras Curitiba's builders chant regularly. "The cities of the future will not be scenarios from Flash Gordon, as some people imagine," says Lerner. ("Nor scenarios from Blade Runner, as others, tied to an overpessimistic view, may fear.") Instead of supermen, their heroes will likely be people like João "Janguinho" Jorge, who was sitting on a sprung desk chair in a cluttered room off the bus repair station on the outskirts of the city when I interviewed him. He began his transit career in 1967 as a fare collector; by the time that Lerner's fancy new express buses came along, he was a top driver, one of those selected to train on the new equipment that Volvo was producing. On a regular bus, it doesn't make much difference where you stop—the passengers will just walk a few steps to board. But with the tube stations, the bus has to be in just the right place, or the openings on the tube won't align with the bus doors. Volvo was planning on installing an elaborate optical computer system.

"I said, 'Let's try a stripe painted on the pavement,'" recalls Janguinho. "And they said it wouldn't work. But I said, 'Let me try it once, I'll *see* if it works.' And it did." It's the kind of solution that gets you noticed in Curitiba; everyone kept telling me I had to go interview Janguinho, who was promoted to driving instructor and is now working on the one defect of superlong double-hinged buses: "If there's an accident ahead of you and you have to back up to get around it, it's kind of like driving a serpent."

"It's very hard to understand simplicity," says Lerner. "Simplicity needs a kind of commitment. You have to be sure of yourself. If you're not, you'll listen to the complexity-sellers, and the city is not as complex as they would like you to believe."...

Along with frugality and simplicity, Curitiba stresses speed. When Lerner ripped up the main street and reassembled it as a pedestrian mall over a single weekend, he set a precedent his administrations have followed ever since. "Public work is always linked to easygoing work in people's minds," he says. "With speed comes credibility." The city's showcase Opera House, a steel-and-glass birdcage set dramatically in an abandoned stone quarry next to a spectacularly lit waterfall, was built in a month; one big park was carved out in twenty days because officials feared it was about to be invaded by slums....

Christine Braga helped implement the city's voluntary, and highly successful, recycling program within a matter of months after it was first suggested. "It was like during a war," she says fondly. "We didn't have any time to make researches then. We had to establish it and implement. It's been going since 1989, and we only started to finally collect the data last year...."If you say, 'I'll need three months for this part, and three months for this part, and three months for this,' he says, 'Okay, you have three months. Total.' We used to say he consulted with oracles to set the dates, but to tell you the truth, everything comes out finished."...

Curitiba now has a "twenty-four-hour street," a block-long covered arcade near the city center with shops and restaurants that never close. It grew out of Lerner's realization that "million-dollar structures remain vacant in off-peak hours, while the pressure for space is a major factor in urban tension." And the creativity is contagious. Planners from other cities spent a few days in the city last year for an exercise. For a while they stayed stiff and formal, more interested in speechifying than in sketching. Eventually, though, they met the mayor, who told them his secret of creativity: "You have to have fun. All my work, all my life, we have fun. We're laughing all the time. We're working on things that make us happy." Before they went home, one team of visitors designed a "toy factory," a big canvas tent that can move from one poor neighborhood to another, where children could be taught to make toys from recycled trash. The favorite toy? A plastic mineral water bottle laid on its side and decorated to look like a tube station for the speedybus.

The fact that the toy factory was quickly set up and still travels about the city helps explain another of the reasons Lerner has such dedicated colleagues. There are bright designers and architects the world over, but most of them labor in university departments; they have to scratch for years to get their best projects built. It's true that a senior architect in Curitiba's planning department may make three or four hundred dollars a month, which doesn't go much further than three or four hundred dollars in

2. Ikitelli Başak. Without subsidies, Istanbul, Turkey created a city. Şehir Residence for 500,000 occupants financed through a system of increasing prices on middle income flats so as to subsidize units for those of lower income and recent immigrants.

America. “Sometimes we are down because of the money,” says city planner Liana Vallicelli. “But then along comes some beautiful project. It’s possible to see these things actually get done.”

And what makes for high morale, says Lerner, makes for effective government as well. “You have to begin the game. You don’t have to have all the answers before you start—you can’t be such smart guys. To start is important.”...

Lerner—and Curitiba—seems to have shed ideology in the name of constructive pragmatism. Building things to human scale may be an ideology of sorts, but it’s outside of the political dialogue. In the argument between private and public that occupies center stage in America, for instance, Curitiba persists in choosing from column A and column B, entirely according to success. It gave buses priority over cars, which sounds vaguely liberal, but it let private companies run the buses—when the speedybus system was installed, the city spent *$4.5* million putting up tube stations, and the private companies spent *$45* million buying buses. On the other hand, it told the bus companies what fare they could charge.

Life without political fetishes seems necessary to the free wheeling creativity of the place. Consider trees, for instance. The city began from the position that it liked them, liked them a lot. It planted trees all over town: one of Lerner’s first slogans was, “We provide the shade, you provide the water.”...

It sounds vaguely authoritarian, and yet from any high spot in town you see puffs of trees everywhere you look. Many streets are totally canopied, tunnels of green. And as the trees have grown, so has their popularity. We stopped to look at some sidewalk trees—*Coorticaeria*, gorgeous trees but the wrong ones to have planted along the street, since they have begun to drop branches on the power lines, and their roots are cracking the pavement. “But we can’t just take them down,” Edison says. “People would go crazy.” In a solution that seemed to me very Curitiban, they had planted other trees all up and down the street. In seven or eight years they would be high enough to really shade the sidewalk, and only then would the chainsaw crew be sent out for the problem trees.

In a world of cities, states, and nations increasingly whip sawed by the demands of business, perhaps the best example of the value of Curitiba's independence is its Industrial City. When Lerner took over as mayor for the first time, he realized that the city needed industry: its traditional role as a governmental and financial center couldn't support the population boom that was clearly coming, and also couldn't underwrite the aggressive programs he had in mind. He could have simply offered huge tax breaks to anyone who promised jobs. Instead, acting quickly before speculators could run up the price, the city used eminent domain to purchase about forty square kilometers of land seven miles from downtown seven miles *downwind* of downtown. The government put in streets and services, housing and schools, and linked the area solidly to the bus system, building a special "worker's line" that ran to the biggest poor neighborhood. It also enacted a series of regulations stiff laws on air and water pollution and on the conservation of green space. (Only six square miles are actually available for building factories, and almost as large an area has remained planted in trees.) "What we've found is that regulation *attracts* good industries, the kind we want," says Oswaldo Alves. Foreign corporations were among the first to see the advantages; Volvo built a factory, lured in part by the chance to work out improved bus designs with city planners. And new businesses continued to arrive throughout the 1980s, drawn as much by the quality of life for executives fleeing São Paolo as by the ease of doing business with the nearby Southern Cone countries of Argentina and Paraguay. Even in the teeth of Brazil's endless recession and inflation, the number of jobs continued to increase. By 1990 there were 346 factories in the Industrial City, generating fifty thousand direct jobs and one hundred and fifty thousand indirect ones—and 17 percent of the entire state's tax revenue.

The boom in business, the constant rezoning, the speed with which decisions are made—anywhere else in Brazil, and most places in the world, these conditions would have led to corruption on a massive scale. Influence undoubtedly carries some weight in Curitiba: groups of businessmen keep the pressure on to rezone the streets where they have buildings, for instance. But by all accounts the problem is relatively small, as far as I could tell because most people have bought into Lerner's image of the city as a whole. "People do come in to complain," says Liana Vellicelli, the city planner, when asked about it. "A neighborhood politician may say, 'This street is really important. Can you do something for it?' Or someone may say, 'You've put an express bus down my street. I can't live there anymore.' And we say, 'It's for the city.'" The attitude feeds on itself; companies out in the Industrial City, for instance, have begun to fund hundreds of slots in the municipal day-care centers near their plants. And in turn the companies have begun to thrive, Vermont-style, on the city's image, even though that image has been created only in the last two decades. "Our best marketing is to say that we are from Curitiba," one executive told the Brazilian newsmagazine *Veja* last year. "The fact that our product is Curitiban gives it a certain charisma to consumers from other regions," said another....

In 1990 the number of streetchildren in Curitiba had increased to about five hundred nothing like the tens of thousands that roam the larger cities of Brazil, but clearly heading in that direction. She opened a shelter with activities ongoing all day in an effort to keep the children off the streets. "Not like school, because they won't go to school," she says. "They need a lot of love." And if they don't find it at the shelter, they can go to one of thirteen "support houses," where a pair of houseparents raises eight or ten of the streetchildren. If you want to call them orphanages, I suppose you could; it goes to show that intent and attitude are what really matter. Many boys from the street have been enrolled in the newsvendor program; you see them piling out of trucks at dawn, selling newspapers supplied at a discount by the publisher. They have a dormitory of their own, and half their earnings are saved for them till they are old enough to leave. Other kids, wearing special vests, carry bags for shoppers at the roving street markets that the city sponsors. When the new Botanic Garden was inaugurated a couple of years ago, boys from nearby slums tore up most of the flowerbeds. Instead of posting police, the city hired the children as assistant gardeners.

Two years later the number of streetchildren had dropped to about two hundred. "We know them all by name, and we talk to them constantly, trying to find a program they'll join," says Mrs. Lerner. "The most important thing in the programs is food," she adds—important not just because the kids are hungry, but because all over Brazil children will sniff glue to ward off hunger pangs. "My office spends more on food than on anything else. I remember once my husband came by, and he asked the children, 'What do you like best about the program? Your teacher? The games?' And he was very surprised when they all started shouting, 'The snacks, the snacks.'" When kids are lacking parents, or they're afraid to go home and get beaten again, paternalism is what they need. Food is what they need. Love is what they need. They come out differently if they get it.

The city doesn't wait for kids to become homeless, either. Lerner said from the start of his career that his two priorities were the environment and children, and a large percentage of the municipal budget goes to education, beginning with the city's day-care centers, which are free to children three months or older. The centers run eleven hours a day, allowing parents to get to and from work, and serve three meals and a snack. The federal government runs the elementary and high schools, but in Brazil school lasts only half a day; and even if there were jobs, federal law prohibits Brazilians from working until they're fourteen. So there are long hours to be filled each day. Upper-class kids take music lessons or go to the sports center. Poor kids hang out, or they did until the city inaugurated a system of "PIA"centers—*pia* is Indian slang for small child and also stands for Childhood and Adolescence Integration Program. Christine Braga took me to one of them in a *favela* called Sabara near the Industrial City.

It occupied a typical plot of *favela* land—a steep patch of bare dirt leading to a sour drainage ditch. The slope, however, wasn't eroding away: the twelve- and thirteen-year-old boys in the program, under the leadership of a grizzled older man named Oswaldo, had planted bed after bed of vegetable crops in the soil. Onions, lettuce, parsley, tomato, spinach, cabbage, broccoli, pumpkin, popcorn. Orange trees, tangerine trees. Oswaldo had grown up a peasant farmer and was passing on to the gang of skinny boys his pleasure in the work. "They come spontaneously," he says—attendance at the PIA is voluntary. "But when I explain the importance of the vegetables, the flowers, and when they see the plants growing, they can know the importance of their jobs." Sidney, Gilberto, Claudio, Wilimar, Marcio, another Marcio, Allesandro, Lindomar, Fabio, and Gilmar clustered around me, insisting I take down their names. "They fight sometimes, especially Lindomar," notes Oswaldo. "I tell them they have to go home for the day, and that stops it right there." In one corner of the plot, row after row of potted marigolds sat under black mesh screening to protect them from the sun. The PIA gets the seed from the city and in turn sells the flowers back for use in the parks—the boys make a small amount of money. "My mother is sick and I want to help support the house," says Claudio. "My grandmother is trying to build a house," adds Fabio, "and I want to buy some bricks." Every one of them wore his orange PIA cap, the brims so tattered they were peeling back. Everyone but Willmar. "Mine's at home—my mother's washing it today," he explains....

A couple of blocks away, a line of women waited outside a tiny community center. A garbage truck had just pulled up, but it wasn't carrying garbage; it was carrying food. For three years now the city has been buying surplus food from farmers in the surrounding countryside and trading it for bags of garbage—six kilos of trash bought a sack of rice, potatoes, beans, and bananas. For a kilo more, some eggs. The program began in 1989 when an outbreak of leptospirosis, a rat-borne disease, was noted in the slums. Because the streets are narrow and unpaved, the garbage trucks hired by the city couldn't get up them to collect trash, which was piling up in the favelas. Lerner's team made a few quick calculations: how much would it cost to pay the garbage haulers (a private concern) to collect the trash from the crowded slums? When they had a figure, they determined how much food they could buy for that sum and then let the slum dwellers collect the trash themselves and bring it down out of the favelas to the trucks. Along the way, the program manages to support small farmers who might otherwise have to abandon their fields and migrate to town....

To learn from Curitiba, the rest of the world would have to break some long-standing habits—the habit of finding answers in the rich countries, for instance. "People can't imagine there's a city in Brazil with all the facilities," says the director of the city's housing authority. "When I visit America, people are convinced that when I come home, I have to take a jeep from the airport through the jungle, like Tarzan." Residents of the First World "say, 'Curitiba is a Third World city, what can it teach us?'" sighs Lerner. "People in the Third World say, 'We're a First World city.'"...

* * *

Notes and Comments

1. What were some of the planning initiatives that Curitiba undertook? Are these initiatives transferrable to advanced westernized cities? Why do they seem so strange to the way contemporary American policies are designed and implemented?

2. Consider the problems and challenges facing American and European communities and consider whether the approaches and philosophy behind Curitiba's success could be employed effectively. What would change if Jaime Lerner or a forward thinking planner were the mayor of your city? Can you identify any inexpensive and simple solutions to contemporary planning challenges from green space and the need for affordable housing, to recreation, traffic congestion, the lack of pedestrian-friendly streets, or the need for childcare services?

The next chapter will introduce the traditional institution of zoning, the dominant institution controlling urban design in most developed Nations.

Chapter 2

Zoning

A Man knocked at the heavenly gate;
His face was haggard and old.
He stood before the Man of Fate
For admission to the fold.

"What have you done," Saint Peter asked,
"To gain admission here?"
"I've been in the zoning business, Sir,
For many and many a year."

The pearly gates swung open wide;
Saint Peter touched the bell.
"Come in and choose your harp," he said,
"You've had your share of Hell."

Richard F. Babcock & Charles L. Siemon, The Zoning Game Revisited 255 (1985) (quoting Wis. A County Code Administrators' Newsletter, Jun., 1977)

Zoning refers to the device that is used by most modern cities to implement the urban design adopted in the form of a comprehensive plan. While plans call for various housing types and all the supporting commercial, industrial, and open spaces, it is the zoning process that assigns a use to each parcel of land in the community. In the American version of zoning, uses must typically be segregated, that is, within a district all uses must be compatible and typically identical. For example residential districts are separated from manufacturing and as well from commercial shopping and employment centers. *Chrinko v. South Brunswick Township Planning Bd.*, 187 A.2d 221 (N.J. Super. Ct. Law Div. 1963) (mixed use PUD sustained as meeting uniformity standard in equal treatment of all developers). Even within residential zones, single family detached housing on large lots would be separate from those on smaller lots and both would be located at a distance from multifamily housing, with apartments for workers and the less affluent far from the condominiums or suburban detached houses of the affluent.

The United States Supreme Court, placed its imprimatur on the institution of zoning in the landmark case of *Village of Euclid v. Ambler Realty Company*, 272 U.S. 365 (1926). Zoning refers to regulation on the type of use, the maximum height, and the regulatory limits on the bulk of land such as requiring setbacks from the street or between neighboring structures. In approving a developing community's zoning restrictions of undeveloped land, the Court suggested that the underlying rationale for zoning was the avoidance of nuisance. For example, separating polluting manufacturing from residential districts is a noble aim of zoning. Unfortunately, the Court chose not the example of segregating polluting uses from areas of habitation, but instead explained its ruling from the standpoint of separating tenements of the poor, which the Court characterized as simply places where people make real estate investments, from the homes of those real estate investors. While the Supreme Court may have believed that *Euclid* was a tool to avoid the unliveable conditions that can come from too many tenements amidst too many factories, what it licensed was permission to isolate the poor and working class not just from the affluent, but from the access necessary to compete in the search for employment opportunities, and the infrastructure such as recreation, convenient and economical shopping, or quality schools and employment training so essential to city life. Two years later the high Court in *Nectow v. City of Cambridge*, 277 U.S. 183 (1928), invalidated a zoning classification where a parcel of property was zoned residential because it was adjacent to a manufacturing plant in a district that was becoming primarily industrial. The result was a fair one as the residential zone left the owner with no feasible use for the property as it could not be used for non-residential use; given the character of the neighborhood there would be little market or economic return if housing were developed. The lesson of *Nectow*, however, is that zoning is suspect only where it denies an investment opportunity or a reasonable economic use to the owner. That zoning may make it impossible for senior citizens to have the freedom of mobility or for the poor to gain employment has alluded American courts.

The next excerpt by Matthew Light contrasts the zoning schemes encountered in The United States, Germany, and Switzerland. The notes after the reading will describe more fully the American zoning system and will describe the flexibility built into that system through the use of special permits, exceptions, and variances.

Matthew A. Light, Note, *Different Ideas of the City: Origins of Metropolitan Land-Use Regimes in the United States, Germany, and Switzerland,*

24 Yale Journal of International Law 577 (1999)....

[N]ational regimes of land-use regulation—the whole body of a country's institutions, laws, and jurisprudence that regulates building and development—can be understood only in the context of distinct political and legal regimes. National land-use regimes do not arise in response to universal laws of the market that exert the same influence at any location on the planet. Rather, land-use regimes differ from country to country. They are embedded in a complex, historically developing framework of ideology, law, and culture. If land-use controls regulate the physical shape of the communities we live in, then it is history itself that regulates what kind of community we view as wholesome, normal, and desirable—our ideas of what "the city" and "the good city" mean.

Much thinking about land-use topics in the United States seems to be predicated on the unspoken assumption that metropolitan development can only follow the pattern it has taken in the United States since World War II, namely that of business and residential expansion on the urban periphery, "dispersed in a pattern that can only be served by the single occupant auto." In fact, however, other countries have selected, and continue to pursue, radically different land-use regimes. By examining such alternatives to American policies, we are forced to confront the fact that much of what we take for granted about the American metropolitan scene can be traced to concrete political choices. Ultimately, the comparative approach helps demonstrate that Americans, like other peoples, have a particular idea of the good city; that our idea arises out of our history, culture, and legal doctrine; and that this idea can be recognized in many aspects of a country's regime of land-use regulation....

[W]hile American land-use policies aim at the safeguarding of private life, German and Swiss policies aim at the shaping of public space. American policies feature fragmented decision-making, concentrated in municipalities, and focus on the protection of single-family residences. German and Swiss laws, by contrast, involve all levels of government in concert and are devoted to preserving a certain urban form: The compact city.

American land-use controls are marked by a few particularly noteworthy characteristics: the comparative weakness of overt involvement by state and federal government in local land-use controls; the corresponding delegation of land-use regulatory power to municipalities; the reliance on zoning as the preeminent method of local land-use controls and the relatively weak links between zoning and comprehensive land-use planning; and the ubiquitous use of zoning to effect the separation of "incompatible" residential and non residential uses—and particularly the protection of single-family homes from "lower" uses....

The other key feature of the American regime that distinguishes it from its German and Swiss counterparts—and that justifies a national-level comparison—is America's reliance on municipal zoning as the preeminent tool of metropolitan land-use regulation. Western European observers are frequently perplexed by the fact that zoning appears to exist in the absence of highly developed national (or even state) policies on land-use *planning*. To be sure, planning is not absent from the American scene. Indeed, the Standard State Zoning Enabling Act—the product of a commission appointed by then-Secretary of Commerce Herbert Hoover, and still the basic source of zoning power in most states—calls for zoning regulations to be "made in accordance with a comprehensive plan"

Yet the early and continuing tendency among American courts has been to hold that this requirement is met merely by demonstrating the existence of a zoning law itself, as the putative end product of a planning process. In most jurisdictions, no separate plan for the town's development has been required to uphold a zoning law. In addition, such land-use planning remains largely restricted to the local municipal, or at most the regional metropolitan, level. State enabling acts typically provide for weak regional planning boards; frequently, municipalities can simply refuse to participate in these boards. Moreover, the enabling acts usually specify that the plans drawn up by these boards are to be advisory rather than legally binding. In short, American land-use planning is weak and usually optional....

Land-Use Regimes in Germany and Switzerland

German and Swiss land-use regimes diverge from the American model along every dimension that was explored above. Fundamentally, they stem not from a glorification of private life, as in the United States, but rather from a subordination of private life and private property to a certain model of the normatively desirable community. The German and Swiss regimes give government full control over the location and extent of future development. And government employs this power so as to preserve the hegemony of important towns over their surrounding smaller towns, villages, and countryside.

In addition, the German and Swiss systems share a common structure involving all levels of administration: a federal government that frames the broad outlines of land-use policy and identifies the objectives of land-use controls; German states (*Länder*; singular, *Land*) and Swiss cantons that provide relatively detailed plans for the use of the

3. Margarethenhöhe. The beautiful and earliest social-employee housing built by Krupp in Essen, Germany

territory under their jurisdiction; and, finally, regional and local administration of these plans, including zoning and direct control over individual land parcels. In both countries the basic system of land-use controls is laid out in a federal law.

The Land-Use Regime of Germany

Thus, in Germany, The federal *Bundesraumordnungsgesetz* (Federal Land-Use Law, hereinafter BROG) sets out the goals of land use regulation and the means of their implementation in a general and nonhierarchical manner. The BROG requires each German *Land* to formulate a program and comprehensive plans for its own territory. This state-level planning (*Landesplanung*) is intended to produce a development program (*Landesentwicklungsprogramm*) with a lifespan of about fifteen years. This program divides the territory of the state into regions; for example, the relatively large German *Land* of Bavaria is divided into eighteen planning regions. Within each of these regions the government assigns a particular status to the various cities, towns, and villages within the state, based on their size and importance.

These designations do not simply *describe* a particular settlement; rather they *prescribe* a particular status for it. The designations reflect the so-called "central cities" approach prescribed by the BROG, which is derived from the work of German planners in the 1930s. These planners believed that "a community is interwoven with the surrounding area for which the community provides the source of services and facilities." Under the influence of this principle, the *Länder*, as part of their activities under the BROG, have usually chosen to categorize all settlements as main, middle, or subordinate centers, or as non-centers.

What turns on this distinction is the right to future development of the center (or non-center):

> [Main centers] are intended to offer a full range of educational and cultural opportunities, health care, housing, shopping, and economic opportunity. Other categories of centers will only be allowed to offer jobs and services to accommodate the needs of the surrounding population. Communities that are not designated as centers will typically receive only minimal public investment funds and *will not be allowed to grow* beyond replacement of existing housing stock.

In other words, the location of development is ultimately determined by the *Land*, in conformity with national policy.

In addition, restrictions on development cannot be evaded by moving out of town altogether, as they can be in the United States. To begin, in contrast to the United States, nearly all German land lies within the territory of a municipality. This means that it is not possible, as it is in the United States, for a developer to evade the zoning plan of a municipality by relocating her building activities a mile or two beyond the city limit. More fundamentally, the use of nonurban (i.e., primarily agricultural) land, which has received the legal designation of *Aussenbereich*, or "outside area," is regulated with great strictness in Germany. Under German law, building on such land is essentially limited to construction ancillary to agricultural activities. In short, in Germany there is no escape from regional land-use regulation and national land-use policy.

Finally, in further contrast to the United States, the power of the federal government and *Länder* also extends to the control of land-use regulation enacted by local government. Under the German Federal Building Code, each municipality is required to draw up zoning plans (*Flächennutzungspläne*) and, at the most detailed level, building plans (*Bebauungsplane*), that regulate individual subdivisions. These plans are subject to higher-level review. For example, the *Land* of Schleswig-Holstein reviews "[local] development plans, which are drafted for a period of five years, and may disapprove the plans if they do not meet federal and state planning goals." Thus, Germany's land use regime is both more hierarchical and more comprehensive than America's. Do Germans tolerate these restraints on the use of private property because they are more left-wing than Americans, as evidenced by Germany's strong labor unions and historically Marxist left? No. Rather, German land-use controls represent a consensus on what constitutes the model of the good urban life. This model is embraced not just by the concededly rather social democratic Germans, but by their decidedly free-market neighbors, the Swiss.

The Land-Use Regime of Switzerland

The Swiss Federation's power to implement a national land-use policy is derived from a constitutional amendment adopted only as recently as 1967. By this amendment the Swiss federal government was empowered to enact legislation to establish basic principles with respect to the development and settlement of the nation and the use of land, and in particular the creation of zoning regulations by the cantons. Under the constitution, the federation is also authorized to promote and coordinate the land-use regulation activities of the cantons. As can be readily observed, this range of powers corresponds closely to that exercised by the federal government of Germany.

On the strength of this new constitutional provision, the Swiss government later enacted land-use legislation, known as the *Bundesgesetz über die Raumplanung* (RPG) of 1979. Like the German BROG, the RPG establishes general rules to which all levels of government must adhere. In addition, the RPG allocates responsibilities among different levels of government. Thus, the federation's duties include consultation with the cantons, regular reporting on the current land-use situation, and (more substantially) the elaboration of certain *Sachpläne*, plans over specific policy areas.

As to the cantons, the RPG directs them to produce development programs (*Richtpläne*), similar to those of the German *Länder*, in which the cantons are to report on the current condition and development of population, traffic, and so forth. The cantons must specify the time framework for the implementation of their program, and the *Richtpläne* are also to be reexamined and, if necessary, reworked every ten years. The cantons must also designate which areas are most suitable for agriculture or are deserving of protection because of their beauty, cultural significance, or susceptibility to environmental problems. In addition, the cantons are directed to produce more specific use plans, or *Nutzungspläne*, which actually carve up their territory into several different use zones; these plans are normally drawn up by the communes (i.e., municipalities) on the orders of the cantonal governments. The main use zones are the building zones (*Bauzonen*), the agricultural zones (*Landwirtschaftszonen*), and the conservation zones (*Schutzzonen*).

Because it prohibits urbanization of agricultural zones, the RPG ensures that agricultural land is protected, while land available for development is contained and monopolized by existing centers. In addition, the RPG specifies that building zones can encompass only land that is already developed or whose necessary development is foreseeable within a span of fifteen years. Thus, it becomes clear that it is new *development* that the RPG views as the proper object of restraint and suspicion.

As for the cantons, they use their land-use powers in accordance with the same broad goals as those underlying the RPG. For example, the 1985 *Baugesetz* (Building and Planning Code) of the canton of Bern provides a useful illustration of the actual implementation of the national policy on the cantonal level.

Within the canton of Bern, planning and zoning responsibilities are meticulously divided and coordinated among different levels of government. Thus, the cantonal administration itself is responsible for the publication of reports on land use, for the delineation of agricultural land, for the establishment of cantonal development plans when the communes or the regions fail to safeguard interests broader than their own, and for the development plans required by the RPG.

Below the cantonal level, the regions and communes of the canton of Bern also play an important role in land-use regulation. These "regions" are groups of communes agglomerated for the purposes of land-use control. As Zaugg explains, "the region in the sense of land-use planning law is a space that is characterized and limited by geographic features...and by economic relationships and interdependence." The regions are responsible for land-use regulation tasks that require coordination among the member communes. They also serve as an intermediate level and liaison between the cantonal government and the communes.

Finally, at the most local level, the municipalities are bound by the federal constitution and legislation and by cantonal legislation. However, it is also the communes that actually zone their own territory and regulate subdivision development and actual buildings. In addition, they are responsible for supplying authorized developments with public utilities and roads and for the consolidation of building areas. Thus, the example of Bern demonstrates how Swiss and German land-use law integrates all governmental bodies into an effort to pursue a national policy....

The German and Swiss Regimes: Goals

The German and Swiss land-use laws share a number of objectives. Broadly speaking, the laws are formulated to prevent destabilizing social change. Swiss and German policies evince a refusal to treat land-use regulation in the American manner, as essentially a matter of regulating private property rights; in contrast, Swiss and German laws assume that land-use regulation is an important way of maintaining the social order.

This broad goal of maintaining social stability is instantiated in more specific policy objectives. These include the stabilization of small cities' populations by preventing large-scale migration for economic reasons; the prevention of sprawl and the preservation of the appearance of both cities and countryside; and the promotion of commercial agriculture and especially family farmers. Let us consider these concerns in turn, using examples drawn from both Germany and Switzerland.

First, by closing off the overwhelming mass of agricultural land to development through the legal categories of *Aussenbereich* in Germany and *Landwirtschaftszone* in Switzerland, existing cities in effect receive a monopoly of most nonagricultural economic activity, and population growth is directed to existing centers. The designation of towns as "centers" of different ranks, or as non-centers, also serves this goal. That is, by restricting development in minor centers and non-centers, German policy discourages people from moving to areas where, by definition, housing, jobs, and services will not be provided. Like the strict controls on building in the *Aussenbereich* and in the *Landwirtschaftszonen*, the policy of "center" designation thus appears to stem from a desire to limit internal migration and keep people where they already are.

Some support for this characterization of the goals of German land-use policy can be found in recent German history. The policy of using land-use controls to contain internal movement was born as a result of a substantial increase in migration during the early post-World War II years, when areas of The Federal Republic near the inter-German border began to suffer economic decline after being cut off from their traditional markets that were now located in the German Democratic Republic. In consequence, land-use controls, in conjunction with various forms of federal aid to depressed areas, have come to be viewed as an important means of preventing "massive population movements causing the under-utilization and decay of older infrastructure and a concomitant increase in demand for new infrastructure."

Second, Swiss and German concern is not just with migration of persons between cities; it is also with migration of persons, and businesses, from towns into the hinterland. An important principle of the BROG requires the territory of Germany to be developed so as to construct "a balanced relationship between populated areas and rural space." Stripped of the pleasing rhetoric, this policy means that existing downtowns receive a monopoly of most economic functions in order to prevent development from spilling out into the countryside. Again, the goal can be described at its highest level of generality as preservation of the traditional compact city.

Swiss law also uses national policy to preserve urban cores. For example, Bernese law discourages the development of large shopping centers outside existing downtowns by requiring municipal authorization and supervision of any such projects. This prohibition is unapologetically intended, in part, *to protect such downtowns from competition*. The Bernese model of city development calls for "decentralization of settlement and economy," in other words, the preservation of numerous viable population centers. It is worth noting in this context that U.S. courts have frequently been confronted with the anti-competitive implications of comprehensive plans designed to protect downtown merchants. While such plans have generally withstood litigation, the fact that the issue is raised at all indicates how controversial and sometimes offensive downtown-protection can seem in an American legal context.

In Switzerland, it appears, the legal community takes a different view of this issue. Zaugg writes that "[R]estrictions on trade and commerce are permissible when based on regulatory grounds (*polizeilichen Gründen*), on considerations of social policy, and on measures undertaken by the cantons in the immediate context of land-use planning." Thus, the goal of providing the cheapest prices to consumers at the point of purchase is implicitly subordinated to the goals of land-use planning.

The Swiss also use numerous other policies to favor high-density settlements. To begin, development is supposed to take into account the need for providing public transport. Bernese law thus requires the provision of public transit to small towns, so that people who do not live within walking distance of a train station will have access to a bus line. In addition, Swiss towns are intended to remain attractive and accessible to pedestrians. The law requires that towns be provided with bicycle and pedestrian paths, trees, and green spaces. Such provisions aim to make the dense settlement pattern called for by Swiss law seem desirable rather than burdensome.

The corollary of this policy of entrenching towns is draconian restrictions on the development of the countryside. Accordingly, Bernese law contains guidelines that preserve land for agricultural use and try to maintain the attractiveness of the landscape. Small building zones are avoided, as they tend to lead to destruction of the countryside. In addition, remarkably, all building zones are to be separated by "green" zones (which cannot be developed) so as to prevent the "excessive agglomeration of built-up areas" ("*die übermässige Zusammenballung überbauter Gebiete*"). This ensures that Swiss towns and villages maintain their separate physical identity. Clearly, regulating the appearance of the landscape is an important goal of Swiss and German policy.... Finally, it should not be forgotten that the protection of the countryside and the protection of downtowns are necessarily linked. Thus, in Switzerland, the decline of the family farm has provoked increased pressure on the Swiss government to permit more placement of residences and businesses in agricultural areas....

How effective have German and Swiss land-use policies been in achieving their ends? On the one hand, German and Swiss policies appear to have had some success in meeting their stated objectives of preserving the compact city. The beauty of the German landscape, free of clutter and scattered residential development, is one prize of the country's land-use policies. Another achievement is the preservation of vibrant urban cores, producing a country of livable and prosperous medium-sized cities. As a result, German land-use policies have drawn approbation elsewhere in Europe.

On the other hand, Swiss and German policies should not be romanticized: They entail serious costs that Americans would probably find intolerable. As one might expect, because of the scarcity of available land, "Germany ranks last among western European countries in the percentage of the population that own their own home." Germany also pays for its successes with "a high degree of bureaucratic control, loss of local government control over land-use policy, and severe restrictions on individual private property rights." In addition, the insistence on extremely detailed public supervision of development has had to be modestly revised in the former German

Democratic Republic in order to deal with urgent housing and infrastructure problems there.

Finally, the argument that Germans and Swiss (and more broadly, Europeans) are committed to containing metropolitan growth does not mean that there are no large—and sprawling!—metropolises in Europe. Indeed, there is much evidence that trends in Europe and elsewhere in the developing world to some extent mirror those in the United States toward greater suburbanization of metropolitan populations and greater reliance on the automobile. But what is important to observe, and what this Note has tried to demonstrate, is that public policy in Europe has not endorsed these trends, and has had some success in containing them.

In conclusion, to restate national objectives at the highest level of generality, the American policy of *separating* putatively incompatible uses can be contrasted with the German and Swiss policy of *combining* uses that are understood to complement each other. Such a policy might be called one of urban compression....

There is, in fact, some reason to think that the American approach to building cities reveals a rejection of ideas about traditional city form that may be more extreme than in any other country. In other words, German and Swiss attitudes toward the city may be more typical of attitudes in most Western countries. Two English-speaking countries with close cultural links to the United States furnish support for this claim. Our northern neighbor Canada, despite its cultural and historical closeness to the United States, has adopted an urban policy emphasizing "gradual expansion of the urban envelope... seeded by higher-density 'nodes' where office, retail, and residential land uses occur in healthy mixes." Likewise, the United Kingdom has had a succession of national land-use policies since the 1940s. These have emphasized maintaining the existing distribution of regional populations and surrounding central London with a greenbelt of non-urbanizable land. Notably, the first of these policies was enacted by the post-World War II Labour Party government in an atmosphere of "informed agreement among rational men of good will" and was seen as being relatively uncontroversial. The policies of these two countries, otherwise so similar to the United States, seem to suggest that there is something unusual and radical in the U.S. willingness to forego similar policies....

If German and Swiss land-use regulations place the individual in the center of a managed landscape and a restrictive community, American land-use regulation seems to reject this idea of a socially situated self. If German and Swiss land-use policies reflect a dogged determination to control the modern town and make it conform to an inherited idea of the well-made community, American land-use controls represent a willingness to experiment with unprecedented forms of urban life.

* * *

Notes and Comments

1. Would American land development planning and control be improved with participation by the state or federal government? What is the cost of allowing each town to determine its own design? What would be the costs involved with conversion to a more hierarchical system? Is the American system a function of its history and culture, including reverence for property owners rights and a romance with the automobile? Can and should the American system be modified?

2. For an excellent decription of the German Planning Process, see Thomas J. Schoenbaum, *Planning and Land Development Law in the Federal Republic of Germany*,

54 Tul. L. Rev. 624 (1980). For another interesting discussion of German planning from the standpoint of the development rights of landowners, see George Lefcoe, *The Right to Develop Land: The German and Dutch Experience*, 56 Or. L. Rev. 31, 35 (1977) (noting that the United Kingdom and Sweden have abolished the right to develop).

3. Within the general zoning scheme is a system that allows for flexibility and discretion in the development process. Zoning itself appears quite rigid in specifically defining the types of structures and uses permittted with each district. The early American zoning ordinances contained several components that allowed for some flexibility in the application of the zoning scheme. It was also recognized by the zoning designers that cities lacked the resources to survey every parcel of land to determine if the zoning was compatible with the land and with the surrounding developed community. Chapter 7 will discuss the notion of excessive regulation and the doctrine of takings under American law. Generally, a zoning classification that precludes the development of any economically viable use constitutes a taking and the government must compensate the owner. *Lucas v. South Carolina Coastal Council*, 505 U.S. 1003 (1992). To avoid the compensation problem, zoning ordinances provide that an excessively regulated land owner may seek a variance from the strict application of the law. *Otto v. Steinhilber*, 24 N.E.2d 851 (N.Y. 1939). The following notes describe the labyrinth of exceptions. Another way of looking at the system is that the scheme provides a series of alternative strategies to landowners to achieve their development objectives.

4. *Special Use Permits.* Zoning districts usually provide for certain uses as of right, meaning, uses that the owner will be permitted to pursue subject to compliance with other local health and safety regulations. For example, a developer would still have to comply with subdivision, site plan, or planned unit development (discussed in Chapter 3), environmental review, and obtain building and other permits. Within those districts, ordinances typically provide for additional uses that might be located within the district under a provision calling for special use permits, special exceptions, or exceptions. *Jones v. City of Carbondale*, 576 N.E.2d 909 (Ill. App. Ct. 1991). To obtain such a permit an administrative hearing is held before a zoning board, board of appeals, or legislative body acting in an administrative capacity for the purpose of determining if there are adequate reasons for denying the permit. For example, a residential community may well be served by houses of worship, a gas station, a convenience store, or the obligatory Starbucks coffee café. In the special use permit proceeding it is assumed that the owner can develop the special use subject to the regulating body demonstrating a valid justification for denial. The justification should be grounded in environmental, infrastructure capacity, meaning supporting facilities such as water, sewer, and roads, or questions of the need for the use and whether it is adequately served. For example, a community that might be well-served by a gas station may not want a second or a third, particularly on the same corner where the character of the neighborhood might be altered. A special use permit for the second or third station may properly be denied. Some communities may permit a second station to provide the possibility of competitive prices for consumers. Similarly, where a community contains churches, parking capacity may be exceeded and at some point good planning would call for denying further special uses. Nevertheless, special uses or exceptions are consistent with the zoning ordinance and are not disfavored as are variances.

5. *Variations.* Zoning ordinances may provide that the zoning administrator of the regulating community has the discretion to allow minor variations or an exception to a zoning requirement where compliance would cause a problem or difficulty for a project. These exceptions or variations are most often applied in the case of lot set-backs or sideyard requirements and exception authority is typically provided to allow variations

of up to 10 percent from the ordinance standard or some other percentage limit set by the local ordinance. *E.g.* Los Angeles Mun. Code § 12.28 (adjustments and slight modifications of up to 20 percent).

6. *Variances.* The concept of the variance was to provide a safety valve to prevent confiscatory regulation where a parcel of land, because of its unique, typically topographical characteristics or because of the character of the district, is zoned in a classification that is not a realistic development opportunity. *See generally*, Jonathan E. Cohen, Comment, *A Constitutional Safety Valve: The Variance in Zoning and Land-Use Based Environmental Controls*, 22 B.C. Envtl. Aff. L. Rev. 307 (1995). For example, in *Nectow*, the United States Supreme Court invalidated the residential zoning of a parcel that was adjacent to a large manufacturing plant and not economically developable as a site for a residence. If the same case were brought today the courts would rule that the case was unripe, for the landowner should have sought a variance to permit some reasonable use. The variance gives the regulating body the opportunity to correct mistakes in the specific zoning classification as applied to particular parcels of land.

Because variances provide for the use of property that is inconsistent with the character of the zoned district, they are not easily obtained. Indeed, because of the easy abuse of the variance process that allows regulating communities to approve pet projects and the variance process places extraordinary power in the hands of communities to offer special treatment to favored developers, some states have abolished use variances. Cal. Gov't Code § 65906 (allowing only bulk or area variances); *Bradley v. Zoning Bd. of Appeals*, 334 A.2d 914 (Conn. 1973); *Leah v. Board of Adjustment*, 37 S.E.2d 128 (N.C. 1946); *Swain v. Board of Adjustment*, 433 S.W.2d 727 (Tex. Civ. App. 1968); *Board of Supervisors v. Rowe*, 216 S.E.2d 1999 (Va. 1975).

Variances are divided into two types: (1) Use variances that permit the owner to conduct a use that is not provided for within the zoning district, and (2) area variances that allow a modification in the building envelope but not the use. For example, the need to have relief from a rear yard setback because a steep hill makes compliance cost prohibitive.

In the case of use variances, the courts generally require the demonstration that the application of the current zoning classification imposes a hardship. *Otto v. Steinhilber*, *supra*. By comparison, the courts apply a more lenient standard for area variances requiring only that they present practical difficulties to the developing landowner. *Wolf v. District of Columbia Bd. of Zoning Adjustment*, 397 A.2d 396 (D.C. 1979). New Jersey, on the other hand, allows variances for any good reason, such as where a use might provide affordable housing or some other use of benefit to the community. *Burbridge v. Governing Body*, 568 A.2d 527 (N.J. 1990) (aesthetic benefit); *DeSimone v. Greater Englewood Hous. Corp. No. 1*, 267 A.2d 31 (N.J. 1970) (need for low income housing). The wider use of variances places a heavy burden on zoning officials and local legislators to avoid conflicts of interest and the appearance of impropriety and raises the potential for corruption in the making of gifts or campaign contributions. Jesse Dukeminier & Clyde L. Stapleton, *The Zoning Board of Adjustment: A Case Study in Misrule*, 50 Ky. L.J. 273 (1962).

Most states also require that the owner could not recover a reasonable rental or return on the property, *Baker v. Connell*, 488 A.2d 1303 (D.C. 1985); *Graziano v. Board of Adjustment*, 323 N.W.2d 233 (Iowa 1982), insist that the proposed use not be detrimental to the community, *Carman v. Zoning Bd. of Adjustment*, 638 A.2d 365 (Pa. Commw. Ct. 1994), require that the problem giving rise to the need for the variance is unique to the applicant's parcel and not reflect a general area topographical problem that should be dealt with through replanning and rezoning. *Topanga Ass'n for a Scenic Community v. County of Los Angeles*, 522 P.2d 12 (Cal. 1974). *See* Osborne M. Reynolds, Jr., *The "Unique Circumstances" Rule in Zoning Variances—An Aid in Achieving Greater Prudence and Less Leniency*, 31 Urb. Law. 127 (1999). Finally, the courts reject variances where the alleged hardship was self-imposed by the applicant. *Klehr v. Zoning Bd. of Appeals*, 320 N.E.2d 498 (Ill. App. Ct. 1974) (subdivision by owner retaining substandard lot); *Hoffman v. Harris*, 216 N.E.2d 326 (N.Y. 1966) (converted to multifamily and then sought variance to permit it). Some courts require that the owner first seek to sell the lot to a neighbor or another before seeking a variance, *Puritan-Greenfield Improvement Ass'n v. Leo*, 153 N.W.2d 162 (Mich. Ct. App. 1967), and courts might not allow a variance to a landowner that holds title to the adjacent lot, preferring a merger of the lots and protection of the uniform zoning scheme. *Brum v. Conley*, 572 A.2d 1332 (R.I. 1990).

7. *Conditional Use Permits.* Although these names of special use or conditional use permits and even special exceptions are often interchangeable from the ordinance of one community to another, I here use the term conditional use permit to connote an ordinance that singles out a specific use for special administrative review. For example, zoning for uses that permit the sale of alcohol, involve controversial issues such as location of landfills, prisons, or perhaps regulation of the siting of adult businesses, may generate permit procedures where the zoning board or city council can review the site and identify and hopefully mitigate, through the imposition of conditions, any adverse impacts that the proposed use may present. This type of ordinance may apply to all zoning districts and is typically found in enactments not within the zoning ordinance but under police power regulations specific to the regulated use. *Goat Hill Tavern v. City of Costa Mesa*, 8 Cal. Rptr. 2d 385 (Ct. App. 1992). *See generally* Roslyn Mack, Comment, *Bringing Down the Walls of State Preemption: California Cities Fight for Local Control of Alcohol Outlets*, 3 African-American L. & Pol'y Rep. 295 (1997).

8. *Zoning Interpretation.* Occasionally, a dispute may arise over the interpretation of a zoning ordinance or a comprehensive plan as it applies to a particular property. The dispute may arise from vagueness as to specifically which parcel was intended to be the dividing line between use districts. Where such an interpretation problem arises, ordinances frequently assign the job of interpretation to the zoning administrator of the community. There may typically be an administrative appeal to a board of zoning appeals or a similar body. As with most such administrative review, the question is whether the decision was arbitrary and whether findings made are supported by substantial evidence in the record.

9. *Zoning Amendment.* A direct method of altering the existing zoning classification is to obtain an amendment to the zoning ordinance. There are two types of zoning amendments. First, and the most common, is when an ordinance seeks to change the zoning classification from one use or other restriction, such as height or bulk, to another classification. An ordinance amendment may seek to change residential zoning to commercial, agricultural to residential, single-family to multi-family, or might ask that the same single-family homes be permitted in a zone that permits more or fewer units to the acre. *Bartrum v. Zoning Comm'n of Bridgeport*, 68 A.2d 308 (Conn. 1949). The less common zoning amendment is an amendment to the text of the zoning ordinance that defines what is permitted within the classification. *Western Land Equities, Inc. v. City of Logan*, 617 P.2d 388 (Utah 1980). *See e.g.*, Julian C. Juergensmeyer & Thomas E. Roberts, Land Use Planning and Control Law 184–85 (1998). For example, an ordinance might provide that the maximum height of buildings in a particular zoning district is to be set higher or lower, or that coffee bars that serve *cappuccino* are a permitted

use in residential zones. *Swarthmore Co. v. Kaestner*, 266 A.2d 341 (Md. 1970) (overlay). Re-zoning ordinances whether they amend the text or the more typical map amendment constitute legislative enactments in the majority of jurisdictions. *Arnel Dev. Co. v. City of Costa Mesa*, 620 P.2d 565 (Cal. 1980). The city council may disfavor the zoning amendment as it places the politician in the seat of the administrator creating controversy and competing with other urgent legislative needs. The number of potential zoning amendment applications tend to tie up the capacity of the legislative body and its zoning committee. For this reason the general rule is that legislative bodies enjoy a presumption that zoning or zoning amendments are correct, and the challenger enjoys a very heavy burden to demonstrate that the classification is arbitrary, discriminatory, or perhaps constitutes a taking. *McGowan v. Cohalan*, 361 N.E.2d 1025 (N.Y. 1977) (rezoning); *BAC, Inc. v. Board of Supervisors*, 633 A.2d 144 (Pa. 1993) (zoning ordinance). In some communities, legislative bodies defer to the position of the representative of the district containing the site, establishing an agreement to leave development to the local neighborhood. *Gautreaux v. Chicago Hous. Auth.*, 265 F. Supp. 582 (N.D. Ill. 1967) (allowing aldermen to veto public housing sites resulted in racial segregation in violation of Title VI); Beth Shuster, *One Zoning Law, Two Outcomes; Politics: The L.A. Council Recently Voted to Close a Synagogue But, Using the Same Rule, Allowed a Sex Club to Remain Open. Homeowners Question the Rationale*, Los Angeles Times, Nov. 11, 1997 (each council member a mayor of sorts in their district). This practice may avoid disputes and reduce the workload of the legislative body, but it may tend to disrupt a plan for the community and result in neighborhoods utilizing the power to exclude unwanted land uses. Although there are many honorable public servants committing their time for the public good, the rezoning process can become, like the variance, a discretionary device that places extraordinary power, and the potential for corruption, in the hands of the politician. Some developers may prefer to pursue a variance application as it does not go to the legislative body but to the administrative board of zoning adjustment. *Pittsburgh Trust for Cultural Resources v. Zoning Bd. of Adjustment*, 604 A.2d 298 (Pa. 1992). In some instances because of the public hearings and local media coverage, that zoning amendments may receive more public attention than administrative agency deliberations. This is not always the case and a variance application can become a cause celebré. Shuster, *supra*.

Because of the potential for an abuse of discretion arising from the presumptive validity of zoning amendments, some jurisdictions have established or altered the rezoning scheme to impose a more exacting standard on the legislature.

Under Maryland's "change or mistake" rule, zone changes are permitted only where the applicant can demonstrate that the existing zoning classification is the result of a mistake in the original planning and zoning process or that there has been such a significant change in the circumstances under which the current zoning scheme is rendered obsolete. *Howard County v. Dorsey*, 438 A.2d 1339, 1345 (Md. 1982). Several states have followed Maryland's lead. *Zoning Comm'n v. New Canaan Bldg. Co.*, 148 A.2d 330 (Conn. 1959); *Hayden v. City of Port Townsend*, 613 P.2d 1164 (Wash. 1980). Maryland also uses zoning hearing examiners and treats the process more as an administrative proceeding which many claim is less political with discretion exercised more professionally.

The Oregon Supreme Court in *Fasano v. Board of County Commissioners*, 507 P.2d 23 (Or. 1973), in addressing the standard of review indicated that rezonings would be treated in two different ways. Where a zoning amendment reflects a true legislative policy shift as in the case of a zoning text amendment, or involves the implementation of that policy through the amendment of a vast number of parcels or acreage, as in the case on a development intensity reduction or a large area of the community, such as where an urban growth boundary is established, the court would continue to apply the traditional presumption of legislative correctness. However, where the zoning amendment was a map amendment altering the classification on a limited number of parcels, the court would characterize such an amendment as an administrative ruling and would not apply the traditional presumption. Thus the legislative body's decision must be nonarbitrary and the decision must be supported by findings which in turn are supported by substantial evidence in the record. A few states have followed Oregon in recharacterizing the zoning process as administrative. *New Castle County Council v. BC Dev. Assocs.*, 567 A.2d 1271 (Del. 1989); *Board of County Comm'rs of Brevard County v. Snyder*, 672 So. 2d 469 (Fla. 1993); *Golden v. City of Overland Park*, 584 P.2d 130 (Kan. 1978); *Fleming v. City of Tacoma*, 502 P.2d 327 (Wash. 1972). The court in *Fasano* went on to say that in reviewing the substance of the rezoning decision the legislative body and reviewing court should look to the plan, the need for plan consistency, and the need that is the basis for the application.

One consequence of characterizing the zone change as administrative is that the zoning process is then removed from the initiative and referendum process whereby citizens can take over the zoning process when they believe that the legislative body is not acting in pursuit of the public interest and will. *Arnel, supra.* Many growth management and smart growth measures have been established in spite of the legislature, through the initiative process under which citizens place measures on the ballot by obtaining voter signature petitions. David L. Callies, Nancy C. Neuffer & Carlito P. Caliboso, *Ballot Box Zoning, Initiative, Referendum and the Law*, 39 Wash. U. J. Urb. & Contemp. L. 53 (1991).

In addition to the traditional rezoning models presented, a variation of the theme is that when communities enjoy the discretion to grant or deny a rezoning, compromise often takes the form of some condition or conditions that the owner agrees to place on the property in exchange for rezoning. This may frequently occur where the legislative body is willing to allow a particular use but is concerned that changing the classification will in the future allow conversion to a less attractive now permitted use. Communities may impose aesthetic or landscaping conditions to buffer certain uses and may ask that an owner execute covenants to restrict certain activities that may occur on the property. For a complicated intellectual exercise compare the discussion below on contract zoning whereby many jurisdictions will invalidate rezoning agreements based on a contract to rezone entered into with the landowner.

10. *Judicial Challenge.* Judicial challenge for most developers would be a strategy of last resort as project profits are reduced by litigation costs, yet judicial standards have been established so that the over-regulated, as well as the citizen concerned with unenforced norms, enjoys access to court. The following is a brief list of favorite litigation strategies.

A. *Substantive Due Process.* Due process generally refers to the requirement of fair procedures. *Mullane v. Central Hanover Bank*, 339 U.S. 306 (1950) (notice and hearing). Most commonly this refers to procedural due process discussed below. Substantive due process refers to the ultimate decision made on the merits. Was the legislative decision arbitrary and unreasonable. *Nebbia v. New York*, 291 U.S. 502 (1934). The federal courts generally limit substantive due process protection to certain identified fundamental rights, such as access to the administration of justice, *Boddie v. Connecticut*, 401 U.S. 371 (1971), procreation and questions of procreative freedom, *Planned Parenthood v. Casey*, 505 U.S. 833 (1992), and have not extended the strict scrutiny model of judicial review to zoning and other land uses contexts. *City of Cleburne v. Cleburne Living Cen-*

ter, 473 U.S. 432 (1985) (see however the discussion on regulating the occupants of land in Chapter 12, where *Cleburne* is reproduced). State courts however have been willing to invalidate excessively restrictive zoning. The exclusionary zoning cases where state courts have invalidated efforts of exclusive suburbs to make development of affordable housing impossible are based on this doctrine. Exclusionary zoning is discussed in Chapter 11 in the context of securing housing.

B. *Takings*. Takings challenges may take five different forms. First are the cases where government physically occupies one's land due to government-caused flooding or where a new highway may block a landowner's access. *Loretto v. Teleprompter Manhattan CATV Corp.*, 458 U.S. 419 (1982). Second, is the traditional claim that regulation denied the possibility of developing an economically viable land use. *Lucas, supra.*; *Nectow v. City of Cambridge*, 277 U.S. 183 (1928). Third, are claims that permit conditions are excessive and far exceed any reasonable mitigation measures based on the impact of the project. *Dolan v. City of Tigard*, 512 U.S. 374 (1994). Fourth, regulation may be challenged under the ad hoc balancing standard that compares the character of the regulation the economic impact, including whether reasonable investment-backed expectations of the landowner were thwarted. *Penn Cent. Transp. Co. v. New York City*, 438 U.S. 104 (1978). Finally, taking claims may be based on excessive time delays from the government's failure to efficiently pursue and process the rezoning or other permit generating procedure. *City of Monterey v. Del Monte Dunes*, 526 U.S. 687 (1999); Kimberly Horsley, Comment, *The Abnormality of Normal Delay*, 28 Pepperdine L. Rev. 415 (2001). The takings doctrine will be discussed in Chapter 7.

C. *Equal Protection*. Equal protection, a component along with due process, of the fourteenth amendment to the U.S. Constitution, requires equality in the administration of the governmental land use regulatory process. James A. Kushner, Government Discrimination (1988 & Supp. 2002) (also available as a Westlaw on-line treatise). The classic violation involves invidious disparate treatment of landowners or applicants based on racial or ethnic characteristics or upon one's status such as disability, gender, citizenship, or sexual orientation. An alternative model would allow protection where the local government treats an application disfavorably because of vindictiveness towards the applicant or landowner. This vindictiveness may arise from prior tension or conflicts with public officials, political differences, or just a personal dislike. The United States Supreme Court in *Village of Willowbrook v. Olech*, 528 U.S. 562 (2000), has stated that a plaintiff may raise an equal protection claim even where they may be a unique class of one, as where the regulator imposes a development condition that has not been applied to other similarly situated applicants. The equal protection doctrine and other forms of land use discrimination will be discussed in Chapter 12.

D. *Spot Zoning*. Spot zoning is a theoretical relative of equal protection. The spot zoning characterization of rezoning refers to the image that is created when parcels of a different use designation surround a small parcel that has been rezoned. To be invalid spot zoning, the change must establish a conflict with the use designation contained in the comprehensive plan and must be found to have been undertaken largely to benefit the interests of the landowner rather than providing a benefit to the community. *Woodland Estates, Inc. v. Building Inspector of Methuen*, 358 N.E.2d 468 (Mass. Ct. App. 1976); *Randolph v. Town of Brookhaven*, 337 N.E.2d 763 (N.Y. 1975).

E. *Contract Zoning*. Contract zoning is a designation that typically results in the automatic invalidation of the zone change or rather the compact, agreement, or ordinance reflecting the agreement. *Bayliss v. City of Baltimore*, 148 A.2d 429 (Md. 1959). Theoretically, contract zoning is condemned because it is an agreement by the local legislative body that is interpreted to establish a legally binding agreement to change the zoning in exchange for the landowner engaging in or refusing to engage in certain behavior on the land. The agreement is seen as a bargaining away of the local government's police power—the power to regulate matters of health, safety, welfare or morals. *State ex rel. Zupancic v. Schmenz*, 174 N.W.2d 533 (Wis. 1970). The contract zoning dilemma is that it is often difficult to distinguish contract zoning from the generally acceptable practice of conditional rezoning. *Collard v. Incorporated Village of Flower Hill*, 421 N.E.2d 818 (N.Y. 1981). For example, if the city says we will rezone a parcel to commercial use if the owner executes a restrictive covenant that will preclude conversion of the property to a gas station, the agreement appears to be a contract. In some jurisdictions, the city might refuse to act on the rezoning but say they would reconsider the matter in light of the owner executing a restrictive covenant described above. It might appear that the characterization is a matter of form, but states do not agree on the definition of contract zoning so contracts or conditions may be identified depending on the jurisdiction. Nolan M. Kennedy, Jr., Note, *Contract and Conditional Zoning: A Toll for Flexibility*, 23 Hastings L.J. 825 (1972). See Chapter 3 for a discussion of development agreements as distinguished from, or as an exception to, contract zoning).

F. *Plan Consistency*. Although all states do not insist on zoning classifications being in strict consistency with the designated community character indicated in the comprehensive plan, a growing number do. Mark Stanton Thomas, Comment, *Urban Planning and Land Use Regulation: The Need for Consistency*, 14 Wake Forest L. Rev. 81 (1978). The effect of strict consistency is to require that before exceptions from the plan and its conforming zoning ordinances are permitted, the community must initiate the comprehensive plan amendment process, requiring that a scientific process consider community needs and anticipated future demand together with the capacity of existing facilities and services, to justify the community design choices to coordinate demand and supply projections. In some jurisdictions, consistency is easily insulated through a pro forma concurrent plan amendment altering the designated use for a parcel. This type of spot planning should be as suspect as spot zoning, yet there are few reported appellate cases. Joseph F. DiMento, *Taking the Planning Offensive: Implementing the Consistency Doctrine*, 7 Zoning & Plan. L. Rep. 41, 46 (1984). Some states have sought to reduce the opportunity for spot planning by placing a limit on the number of planning amendments permitted. For example, California allows a local government a maximum of four amendments a year to what the California statute refers to as the "General Plan." Cal. Gov't Code §65358 (permitting additional amendments for single residential developments containing 25 percent affordable housing).

11. *A Note on Prior Nonconforming Uses*. At the inception of American zoning, certain development had already occurred and not necessarily in conformity with the adopted plan and zoning. To make a preexisting inconsistent use illegal would be unfair to the landowner who invested in good faith, expose the regulating body to takings liability, and would discourage the adoption of zoning and planning. Instead, ordinances recognize these inconsistent uses as "prior nonconforming uses" and allow them to continue operation despite the adoption of inconsistent land use regulation. *Conforti v. City of Manchester*, 677 A.2d 147 (N.H. 1996). The designers of the ordinances expected that over time the nonconforming uses would be eliminated and the plan would ultimately define the built city. To that end, ordinances typically provide that upon destruction of a significant portion of the structure, in the event that remodeling or maintenance costs exceed a set portion of the structure's value, such as 40 percent, or if the use is discontinued, that the nonconforming use will lose its immunity from the current zoning stan-

dard. *Granger v. Board of Adjustment*, 44 N.W.2d 399 (Iowa 1950). Unfortunately, these prior nonconforming uses are often of great value for they may offer the landowner a monopoly status in the community. The use may be insulated from competition where it is the only hotel, restaurant, store, or high density housing or commercial center. Such a monopoly status encourages the landowner to maintain the building annually so that it never falls under the ordinance provision that prevents a major renovation. Some jurisdictions make an exception to nonconforming use protection where there is a significant health or safety concern, and may allow the application of a new ordinance to a preexisting use, as in the case of red light abatement laws that may cause adult entertainment to be closed in some neighborhoods. *Alexander v. City of Minneapolis*, 698 F.2d 936 (8th Cir. 1983); *County of Cook v. Renaissance Arcade & Bookstore*, 522 N.E.2d 73 (Ill.), *appeal dismissed*, 488 U.S. 882 (1988); *FW/PBS, Inc. v. City of Dallas*, 648 F. Supp. 1061 (N.D. Tex. 1986), *aff'd*, 837 F.2d 1298 (5th Cir. 1988), *modified on other grounds*, 493 U.S. 215 (1990). *Contra Ellwest Stereo Theaters, Inc. v. Byrd*, 472 F. Supp. 972 (N.D. Tex. 1979) (adult business protected as prior nonconforming use).

There are also laws in some jurisdictions that have attempted to phase out nonconforming uses by giving them an amortization period. *Collins v. City of Spartanburg*, 314 S.E.2d 332 (S.C. 1984). This period of use is designed to assure the landowner that a significant portion of the lost value is enjoyed by the landowner. For example, some states may allow a set period, such as five years, *Grant v. Mayor of Baltimore*, 129 A.2d 363 (Md. 1957), while others may allow continued use until the owner has fully depreciated the asset under the income tax laws of the state or federal government. Where amortization laws are enforced, courts often differ as to the validity of the law as to whether the subject parcel is a nonconforming use or a nonconforming structure. *City of Los Angeles v. Jones*, 295 P. 14 (Cal. 1930). For example, if the structure is a home previously used for a commercial use but easily convertible to a residence, the reasonable amortization period is likely to be upheld. Where, however, the structure is nonconforming, amortization laws may prove excessive and unenforceable. *Id.* Should a landowner construct a multifamily housing project or an expensive manufacturing plant, local government will likely not be able to enforce an ordinance that requires only single-family detached homes in the district. *Cf. La Mesa v. Tweed & Gambrell Planning Mill*, 304 P.2d 803 (Cal. Ct. App. 1957 (amortization best based on physical life of nonconforming building).

12. *A Note on Conflicts of Interest.* The discretion accorded to the various land use regulatory authorities offers an opportunity for unethical conduct. Applicants or potential applicants may seek to obtain the obligation of government officials, and public officials may bow to the opportunity to exact compensation for government action. Although bribery is not unknown in the development community and the occasional public scandal receives intense media attention, most local public officials involved in regulating land development are honest and hardworking. Indeed, perhaps the worst indictment that might be addressed at zoning officials is that they did their jobs well, carried out the letter and intent of the planning and zoning ordinances, as well as the will of their constituents, yet ultimately executed a failed plan. There are beautiful and well-planned suburban subdivisions throughout America that have afforded the majority, and particularly the affluent, a pleasant bucolic existence. A criticism of American planning is that the low density can be efficiently served only by private automobiles and highways. The automobile-based plan renders access to work, school, recreation, shopping, and other destinations almost impossible for most unless they have access to an automobile.

Despite my testimonial for local public officials, there is the appearance of impropriety that arises from the receipt of campaign contributions by officeholders and candidates for public office. The courts have upheld the right to make and receive campaign contributions, *Woodland Hills Residents Ass'n v. City Council*, 609 P.2d 1029 (Cal. 1980), even where an applicant for zoning consideration has made a contribution to a member or members of the local legislative body that is acting on a legislative rezoning application, or in the capacity of an administrative appeals board. *Snohomish County Improvement Alliance v. Snohomish County*, 808 P.2d 781 (Wash. Ct. App. 1991) (campaign contributions received by members not an impermissible ex parte communication). There exists an opaque line between the reality of politics and the situation where a campaign contribution might be interpreted as a *quid pro quo* for benefit dispensed. Regardless of judicial definitions of morality in government, it is disturbing to note that the most significant campaign donors in local elections are land developers and other contractors who benefit through city business or permits. Ron Curran & Lewis MacAdams, *The Selling of L.A. County*, L.A. Weekly, Nov. 22–28, 1985, at 24, 26.

Beyond the contributions and bribery questions, it is common for conflicts of interest to arise on the part of both legislators and administrators. This is particularly the case in the typical community where the local officials are part-time employees or serving officials. It is frequently those who are actively involved in development that understand government and its processes and are attracted to public service. Engineers, like attorneys, architects or planners, may serve local government and there is a possibility that an associate at their firm is employed on a project or with a client that comes before the local agency. Such employment conflicts, as well as a personal stake in an ongoing matter pending before a board or legislative body likely requires recusal of the official and the obligation not to lobby other members. *Clark v. City of Hermosa Beach*, 56 Cal. Rptr. 2d 223 (Ct. App. 1996); *Bossert Corp. v. City of Norwalk*, 253 A.2d 39 (1968) (commission member's law firm represented opponent).

There is another distinction between legislative and administrative officials in that administrative officials are to be neutral and objective while elected politicians need not be. A member of the city council may run for office on a plank of halting a development proposal and if victorious need not avoid participation in decisions of the project. *Schauer v. City of Miami Beach*, 112 So. 2d 838 (Fla. 1959) (applying conflict of interests regulations applying to administrative board members to legislators where zoning characterized as quasi-judicial). A planning commission or zoning board of adjustment member, however, would have a conflict if they had been involved or publicly announced a position with regard to a specific matter before them. *Winslow v. Town of Holderness Planning Bd.*, 480 A.2d 114 (N.H. 1984) (disqualification of planning board member who had spoken in favor of project before becoming a member). The more theoretical question arises where an activist legislator, who can vote on a legislative rezoning application, but if sitting as an appeals board on a subdivision, variance, or other administrative application that has been acted upon by the planning commission. The legislature acts in an administrative agency capacity and thus the activist may have a conflict for such a decision. *See Schauer*, *supra*. For the same political reasons that courts give legislators immunity, they are likely to extend it where elected officials act on administrative matters. *See generally* Patricia E. Salkin, *Legal Ethics in Land-Use Planning*, 30 Urb. Law. 383 (1998).

13. *A Note on Non- Euclidean Zoning*. *Euclidean* zoning refers to the traditional three dimensional building envelope established under the traditional zoning ordinance legitimated in *Euclid v. Ambler Realty* and based on regulation of the use, height, and bulk limits on the parcel. *Euclidean* zoning could also be seen as a play on Euclid, the father of plane geometry, in that classic zoning is a regulation based on plane mea-

surements. Most communities now regulate land in part through non-*Euclidean* regulatory measurements.

A. *Floating Zones.* Floating zones are zones that exist only in the text of the zoning ordinances rather than being mapped. *Rodgers v. Village of Tarrytown*, 96 N.E.2d 731 (N.Y. 1951). Thus, a planned unit development ordinance that allows a certain form of development such as mixed use commercial and residential may be mapped at the time that a specific development proposal is advanced. *Woodland Manor Assocs. v. Keeney*, 713 A.2d 806 (R.I. 1998). From an economic standpoint, the policy carries the benefit that the developer should be able to acquire the property at a lower cost than if a more intensive zoning district had been placed on the zoning map prior to attempts to acquire the land. To be sustained, the floating zone should have specific standards defining where it is appropriate to place such a use. *Lutz v. Longview*, 520 P.2d 1374 (Wash. 1974) (cannot leave to planning commission). Most ordinances require a certain minimum parcel size and may set forth other requirements or conditions. *Rodgers v. Village of Tarrytown, supra.*

B. *Performance Zoning.* Communities are experimenting with the use of performance standards as compared to traditional zoning ordinances. Lane Kendig, Performance Zoning (1980); Frederick W. Acker, Note, *Performance Zoning*, 67 Notre Dame L. Rev. 363 (1991). For example, ordinances may set maximum noise or pollution standards, *City of Rochester v. Superior Plastics, Inc.*, 480 N.W.2d 620 (Mich. Ct. App. 1992) (sustaining noise standard zoning), or may simply define ratios of parking, or the ratio of height to the bulk area. These latter ratios are called floor area ratios (FAR) and explain how city centers can be built and planned for despite the development of skyscrapers. *Broadway, Laguna, Vallejo Ass'n v. Board of Permit Appeals*, 427 P.2d 810 (Cal. 1967) (describing FAR). A downtown, like Los Angeles, with a 6:1 FAR would allow a landowner to build up to six floors on the total parcel. This leaves the owner free to build 12 floors on half the lot, leaving the remainder as parking or a public square. Ordinances may also award a density bonus for being accessible to public transport, for including affordable housing, for creating a public shopping or recreation arcade, or for other reasons. *Montgomery County v. Woodward & Lothrop, Inc.*, 376 A.2d 483 (Md. 1977). In addition, developers can typically purchase or lease development rights from other district owners who have not utilized their full FAR ratio-permitted development. James T.B. Tripp & Daniel J. Dudek, *Institutional Guidelines for Designing Successful Transferable Rights Programs*, 6 Yale J. Reg. 369 (1989). *See also* Margaret Giordano, Note, *Over-Stuffing the Envelope: The Problems with Creative Transfer of Development Rights*, 16 Fordham Urb. L.J. 43 (1988); Madeleine A. Kleiner, Note, *The Unconstitutionality of Transferable Development Rights*, 84 Yale L.J. 1101 (1975). Through such bargaining a developer can assemble sufficient land to permit an ever-taller skyscrapper. Assuming that the FAR average is maintained throughout the downtown, there should be sufficient street, water, sewer, and other facilities necessary to sustain the city and allow for comprehensive planning.

C. *Timing.* Many growth management schemes contain an element of timing, such as statutes and regulations that require concurrancy of adequate facilities as a condition for development approvals. Fla. Stat. Ann. § 163.3180 (concurrency); *Dateline Builders, Inc. v. City of Santa Rosa*, 194 Cal. Rptr. 258 (Ct. App. 1983) (sustain sewer extension timing to assure adequate capacity); Brenna Durden, David Layman & Sid Ansbacher, *Waiting for the Go: Concurrency, Takings, and the Property Rights Act*, 20 Nova L. Rev. 661 (1996).

In addition to regulating development, governments often are involved as developers or involved in a public-private partnership. Chapter 16 discusses urban revitalization strategies such as urban renewal where the government becomes more intensively involved in the development process. The Netherlands presents the planned community with extensive involvement of government in land development:

George Lefcoe, *When Governments Become Land Developers: Notes on the Public-Sector Experience in the Netherlands and California*,

51 Southern California Law Review 165 (1978)

The Division of Labor Among Levels of Government in the Netherlands

a. *Central Government*: To appreciate the division of labor among the levels of government with respect to planning policy and land development activity, some aspects of the Dutch political system require explanation. Due partly to the constitutional autonomy of municipalities embodied in the Constitution of 1848 and the Municipal Act of 1851, and partly to the realities of Dutch politics, Dutch localities exercise a relatively free hand in their land development activities. Dutch municipalities, not unlike their U.S. counterparts, are delegated autonomy with respect to matters of "local concern." But, as in the United States, local powers may be curtailed in the name of national or regional policy. Any number of policies—from housing supply to conservation of open space—could be invoked to support a far greater central government involvement in land development than actually exists.

Local governments depend for their revenues almost entirely upon the central government. Cities receive 37 to 40% of their annual budgets from the central government's Municipal Fund—roughly akin to general revenue sharing in the U.S.—and another 45 to 55% for specific programs, most of them mandated by the central government. Through the discreet use of the power of the purse, the central government could insist that municipalities dance whatever tune the central government decided to play. Why this has not happened, and why the central government has played a secondary role in land development policy, may be determined through an examination of Dutch politics.

At the national level power over localities is diffused among several ministries. No one political party is able to hold a clear majority of Parliament. Hence, a coalition designates the twenty-five ministers and state secretaries (sub-ministers) that constitute the cabinet. Ministers come from several parties; their only responsibility to the Prime Minister or their fellow ministers is contained in the precise agreement to which the coalition parties happened to assent when they formed the government. With respect to all other issues, each minister freely acts on his own concerning the activities of the ministry he governs. The minster of Housing and Physical Planning need not come from the same party as the Minister of Finance. And the finance minister need not have the same allegiance as the Minister for Culture, Recreation, and Social Work, who dispenses many of the categorical grant programs. It should not be surprising then to find that physical planning at the national level is regarded as, at most, establishing a general, somewhat permissive framework for local authorities.

The Dutch Prime Minister is not in a position to impose strong central government planning policies. He is something more than an equal among equals, but he enjoys none of the authority of an English Prime Minister. Usually, he heads an unsteady coalition. In addition, even if no party could amass a majority, members of the Dutch Parliament, like members of the United States Congress, are perfectly free to dissent from the position their leaders in the cabinet assume. In fact, party loyalists suspect a party member once he becomes a cabinet minister. Party leaders in Parliament sometimes oppose their former cohorts who assume ministerial duties.

Political parties in the Netherlands not only divide along traditional political lines, but also reflect very deep class and religious cleavages. On the political continuum there are the Labor (socialist), Liberal, and Anti-Revolutionary (conservative) parties, and a number of successful splinter parties. There is also a Christian Democratic Party which reflects a merger between the Catholic and Christian Historical Parties. Forty percent of the Dutch regard themselves as Roman Catholic, forty percent as Protestant, and the remainder as nonbelievers or adherents to other faiths. This dual political-religious split is exemplified by the fact that there are numerous union organizations; one is Catholic, one is Protestant, one is secular, and there are also three associations of manufacturers.

To give some examples of how difficult it is to organize a politically-cohesive majority in the Dutch milieu, consider the position of farmers—a predominantly conservative bloc—who have usually split their votes almost evenly among Catholic, Christian Historical, and Anti-Revolutionary Parties. Businessmen are overwhelmingly anti-Labor Party, but divide their votes among the other major parties and a score of minor parties as well. There is far more political cohesion at the local level where socialist-led left-of-the-center coalitions govern the largest cities.

While the positions of Prime Minister, cabinet ministers, and party politicians in Parliament will strike an American as quite familiar, resembling the positions of the President and the Congress, the Dutch have an institution not paralleled in the United States, a Council of State. This group, with no more than twenty members, is an adjunct of the cabinet, formally appointed by the Crown. They are usually elder statesmen, many of them former officeholders. With respect to administrative review, they perform in a manner akin to our [U.S.] Supreme Court, except that most of their work is advisory. Prior to submitting legislation to Parliament or ratifying a treaty, the cabinet sends it to the Council for comment. To carry out administrative functions, the Council divides itself into sections to supervise the work of each ministry. The Council also has an administrative disputes section that forms a part of the national judiciary. Of special relevance to our topic, the Council of State acts in the place of the Crown in hearing appeals from the provincial level of government arising out of municipal plans. It also reviews municipal expropriation (condemnation) decisions.

Theoretically, the executive branch of the Dutch central government is the Crown. Although the Queen does have a more active place in governmental affairs than, say, her English equivalent, she has no base of power sufficient to support an active land policy at the national level.[195]

The key staff functions of the executive branch are carried out by general secretaries, a cadre of senior civil servants known collectively in the Netherlands as the *administration*. When the government changes hands only the twenty-five or so cabinet members leave. All the rest of the ministerial personnel remain intact from one coalition to the next. As Professor Weil describes, "There is a deep tradition of loyalty by the officials to their political superiors." By maintaining this position of loyalty to whatever government is in power, the civil service has assured its own survival as well as a high level of

195. ...The Queen's role in the political process is crucial when coalitions are difficult to form because she designates the person charged with trying to form a ruling coalition.

competence in the daily affairs of government. At executive levels they are almost all university-trained, and the profession is regarded as among the best a university graduate can attain. They have a near monopoly of information on public affairs and enjoy high status.

Almost all legislation is initiated by the cabinet. Although the Parliament must give its approval, its main function is as critic and collaborator. In recent years members of Parliament have become more vocal as critics and have amended proposed laws far more than in the past, indicating the assumption of a changing and more important role.

The central government has promulgated three reports on physical planning, the most recent one in the form of an options paper—not a "national plan" but a "national policy." Some reasons for such a modest role can be hypothesized. Since the contemplated horizon for a national physical plan far exceeds the expected life-in-office of any given coalition, it is appropriate for the national plan, such as it is, to direct itself to generalities and leave plenty of room for subsequent changes. It would not stretch the imagination to suppose that these reports are devised by the *administration*, particularly the civil servants in the housing and physical planning ministry, and that they are far from eager to assume a dictatorial or controversial stance. Too intransigent a stance could be incompatible with their tradition of political loyalty to the party in power.

b. *Provincial government*: The current burden of fulfilling the central government's planning goals is mainly on the provincial governments. The country is divided into eleven provinces. Each has an elected assembly, known as the Provincial Council, and a chief executive, the Queen's Commissioner. The council members (totaling 39 to 83, depending upon the size of the province) serve 4-year terms. The commissioner or chief executive is formally appointed by the Crown, but actually is appointed by the cabinet on the recommendation of the Minister of the Interior. His appointment is for an indefinite period, and he is paid by the central government.

The daily administration of provincial affairs falls on a Provincial Executive, composed of six members of the council elected for 4-year terms, and the Queen's Commissioner. Provincial government is far less important than municipal; the province serves in part as an administrative arm of the central government, but it also has independent legislative authority in some areas. Five-sixths of provincial budgets come from the central government; the total expenditure of the provincial level is only five percent of the total municipal budget each year.

In physical planning and land development the provincial governments have important work, mainly as reviewing or supervising agencies. They must approve all municipal budgets. Given that 90% of municipal revenues comes from the central government, this would seem a ministerial task at best. A sizable portion of the remaining 10%, however, can come from the municipality's activities as land developer. There is no statutory limit on the municipality's land acquisitions debt except for provincial scrutiny. While the provincial executive does not enjoy a line-item veto, it can remand the entire budget. The provincial executive must also approve each expropriation separately, both as to purpose and price, for cities with populations under 100,000.

The provincial council is supposed to develop broad structure plans for all land developments within its boundaries and to review each local *bestemmingsplan* (destination plan—a merger of a general plan, a development plan, and a zoning ordinance) in light of the provincial regional plan. Provincial discretion in exercising its review powers is limited by law and practice through a system of appellate review to the Crown (actually, to the Council of State and the cabinet).

c. *Municipal government*: The official governing body of the municipality in the Netherlands is the municipal council (*gemeenteraad*), composed of from seven to forty-five members depending on the size of the city. These councilpersons are elected at large every 4 years by a system of proportional representation. The council is the legislative body that enacts all laws and passes on the annual budget. The day-to-day administration, however, is handled by two to six members of the council, elected by their peers, chosen for the same period as the council. They are called aldermen, or *wethouders*, and in the big cities they serve full time and are salaried.

Each town also has a mayor or burgomaster. This official is appointed by the cabinet. In the cities with populations over 50,000 the post is one of considerable prestige. The mayor is the chief executive, in charge of police and fire departments, chairing the meetings of the council (of which he is not a member) and of the executive committee (College of Burgomaster and Aldermen, or *Burgemeester en Wethouders*).

Big cities active in land development usually have one alderman who chairs a council committee concerned with the topic and who works directly with the civil servants in the city charged with carrying out council policy as it affects real estate. Although the council committees are often inactive, the *wethouder* or alderman, the full time councilperson assigned to supervise the real estate department, will often take a major role in land development policy.

Cities have a number of ways they may organize the staff functions of real estate development. Article 252 of the Municipal Corporations Act authorizes localities to establish a special municipal real estate department entirely separate from the city's other administrative departments. Sometimes, though, especially in the case of larger cities, this real estate enterprise, or *grond bedrijf*, is located within an existing municipal department. How the city views its real estate operation—the objectives it seeks to pursue and the scale of operation it has in mind when establishing its real estate operation—may be gleaned from where it chooses to locate the function.

In Eindhoven, the *grond bedrijf* is part of the Municipal Housing Department. In Amsterdam, a city that has expanded its developed area by successive large-scale mixed-use developments, the *grond bedriff* is within the Public Works Department. In Rotterdam it is part of the City Development Department (much like Los Angeles County's Department of Community Development, which oversees county renewal projects). In a small village, the *grond bedrijf* may be handled part-time by someone regularly employed in the public works department. Wherever located in the local government hierarchy, the *grond bedrijven* are responsible for the purchase, sale, and leasing of municipal property both in undeveloped areas on the urban fringe and properties in the inner city as well....

Even though the proposed project conflicts with the existing *bestemmingsplan,* [destination plan—a merger of a general plan, a development plan, and a zoning ordinance] a municipality may proceed under article 19 of the 1962 Physical Plan Act. This article allows the Burgomaster and Wethouders to issue a building permit even if the application conflicts with the statutory plan in force, so long as a new plan is being prepared to which the proposed development conforms. Article 19 was modeled after article 20 of the post-World War II Reconstruction Act, which allowed rebuilding when old plans were obsolete and the locality had been unable to update them because of the war.

Considerable development is done by localities who stretch the legislative intent behind article 19. Instead of incurring the delays and costs of *bestemmingsplan* preparation, many cities simply go through the motions of preparing a new plan while proceeding full speed ahead with their development projects, knowing full well the plans will never be completed although the project will. Once the area is fully developed, the National Physical Planning Act makes the *bestemmingsplan* plan optional.

In an area that is fully developed no *bestemmingsplan* is needed because the Dutch presume that built-up areas will remain largely as they are. There is no right to redevelop in existing towns, only a right to build to the predominant scale of development. Scale enlargement is presumptively prohibited absent a *bestemmingsplan*; scale continuity is a matter of right even in the absence of a *bestemmingsplan*. But article 19 affords localities a shortcut for achieving a change in scale without an approved *bestemmingsplan* by allowing development to proceed if it is in accord with a prospective plan though the new plan has not been completed or formalized.

In practice, then, a community willing to cooperate with a private developer can evade the legal requirements for plan enactment—the public review, provincial approval, and possible appeals to the Crown. There are other shortcuts the community may take when the municipality wants land developed quickly. Besides the *bestemmingsplan* Dutch cities have rather detailed building codes, and the planning law requires compliance to be certified and a permit issued prior to the commencement of construction. The building permit process is complicated in the Netherlands, involving as many as ten separate city department heads to review construction plans. Expediting is possible, however; in Leiden, the housing department has organized a one-stop procedure by bringing all the separate departments to one reviewing table.

Moreover, it is not unheard of for city public works department heads to approve construction before the formalities of permit approval have been concluded. Builders, especially on public land, proceed in reliance on those informal go-aheads. City officials are seldom troubled by this. When municipal land is involved, the city has entered a detailed construction contract with the developer and can obtain relief under the contract even if it is estopped from protesting noncompliance with the building permit procedures.

Another source of flexibility is that the Burgomaster and Wethouders are expressly authorized in most *bestemmingsplannen* to waive planning requirements when those standards do not serve to facilitate the best use of the site. The proper scope of this discretionary authority has been subject to litigation, and the courts have attempted to draw some boundaries around it. Nonetheless, it is widely used, and the boundaries are often exceeded, especially when the city officials know they can reach the developer through a development contract or ground lease.

In drafting a *bestemmingsplan* for an area where development is imminent, the locality has the option of omitting many of the details customarily included in such plans. As in American planned unit development zones, densities, permissible uses, and open space requirements are listed as percentages of the project area, but no detailed site plans are drawn until a developer comes forward with his own specific plans for the site. The developer has the final say on whether houses are to be clustered or located on separate parcels and whether open space is to take the form of recreational areas shared by the community or big front yards for each house. Known as a global *bestemmingsplan*, this type of ordinance can be invoked whether the city owns the land or not. Most city officials, however, are more comfortable knowing that they have the ultimate control of being the land owner if negotiations pursuant to a global *bestemmingsplan* should falter.

The major advantage of the global *bestemmingsplan*, the planned unit development, and other similar arrangements is their flexibility: the city and the developer are not committed to a plan that may prove unmarketable a few years later. Market research techniques are simply inadequate to assess long-range land use needs. Perhaps the advantages and risks of combining flexible planning techniques with public land ownership can be seen in the following example.

Suppose a particular site-100 acres—half of which is nearly level, half of which slopes steeply. It is zoned for three units to the acre, R-1. Suppose further that the jurisdiction badly needs housing for moderate-income elderly people. The developer has often been accustomed to cutting mountain slopes, knows the costs, and regards a mountain side as nothing but a useless obstruction to family living. Imagine, too, that the developer's experience has been as a builder of houses for families; he has never built projects for elderly residents anywhere.

What are the options? Should the mountain be saved, making available a planned unit development zone in which the developer could cluster all his houses on that portion of the lot not covered by the mountain? Or, since the property is zoned for three units to the acre, should the developer be allowed to build a standard residential subdivision and blast the mountain away? Suppose the planning staff reports that this area is too remote from job centers to make good family housing because it will increase the number and length of commuting trips. Nonetheless, the family units proposed here will market well but at the expense of an older, declining neighborhood in an urban core eight miles away. How, in our panoply of controls, do we save the mountain *and* provide housing for the elderly? The simple answer is that we do not.

In the Netherlands the local government would own the site and would probably enact a global *bestemmingsplan* that prescribed some acreage density but left the rest to negotiation between the builder and the head of the municipal real estate department. Most likely, the mountain would be preserved intact, and the elderly housing would be built. All of that would come to pass in about the same time that California local governments, in a parallel situation, would still be conducting public hearings at which area residents would most likely protest any form of housing except one-family on large lots, while insisting that the mountain be saved anyway.

But would the same happy Dutch ending be repeated in the typical American municipality if it established a land development agency? One possibility is that the mountain would be saved and the elderly housing built, but that many of the units would go unsold because the city planning staff had overestimated the market for such units. Another possibility is that the mountain would come down and the 300 houses for families would go up. Perhaps the mayor's sister-in-law, a licensed real estate broker, would procure an exclusive listing to sell the 300 houses, and the developer would donate $3500 to the mayor's re-election fund...

* * *

Notes and Comments

1. Does the Netherlands experience suggest that local autonomy and well-planned communities are compatible?

2. Is the real issue the underlying cultural ethic toward preservation, the environment, and land use?

The following chapter looks to the administrative process by which individual project proposals are reviewed as compared to the planning and zoning function.

Chapter 3

Administrative Subdivision Regulation

> "I trained in England, and coming back to this country was a real culture shock. The first zoning ordinance I ever read, I read after I came back here, after I had my degree in planning and had worked in planning for two years. They don't have subdivision regulations or zoning ordinances in Great Britain. Then a lightbulb went off inside my head: *This is why America looks the way it does!* The law is the major problem with the development pattern. Developers don't fight it, they go with the flow."
>
> James Howard Kunstler, The Geography of Nowhere 263 (1993) (quoting Randall Arendt).

Project Review

Although many communities engage in planning when they enact a comprehensive plan and follow that adoption with implementing consistent zoning, it is the administrative process leading to the acquisition of building permits that looks at the specific proposal and the capacity of infrastructure as well as the appropriateness of the project and the site. For most American communities, it is the subdivision review process that takes the first hard look at environmental impacts and the adequacy of supporting facilities and services and any adverse impacts generated by the proposal. Because American housing development is skewed by market demand toward a small rather affluent market target, most development takes the form of individually owned detached single family homes. The process by which a larger parcel of land is divided into separate parcels or individually owned condominium units is referred to as subdivision and it is this process through which amendments to the project are made and conditions on facilities investment and site design are made. *See* James A. Kushner, Subdivision Law and Growth Management (2d ed. 2001 & Supp. 2002).

In communities reviewing typically commercial or industrial development not involving the subdivision of land, it is typical to find the enactment of site plan ordinances that provide for a mirror image discretionary administrative review process that can impose modifications and other conditions. *Friedman v. Planning Comm'n of Rocky Hill*, 608 A.2d 1178 (Conn. 1992).

As with other administrative review procedures related to zoning, the standards applied must be enacted by ordinance or in some instances regulations, *Goldstein v. Plan-*

ning Bd., 639 A.2d 1161 (Law Div. 1993), and the decision of the reviewing body must not be arbitrary, capricious, or otherwise not in accordance with law. *Mansfield & Swett, Inc. v. Town of W. Orange*, 198 A.2d 225 (N.J. 1938); *Helmick v. Town of Warrenton*, 492 S.E.2d 113 (Va. 1997). The basis for the decision must be included in findings which must be supported by substantial evidence in the record. *Pocono Green, Inc. v. Board of Supervisors*, 568 A.2d 612 (1990); *Batch v. Town of Chapel Hill*, 387 S.E.2d 655 (N.C. 1990) (competent evidence). This scrutiny should be contrasted with the extreme deference that the courts accord to legislative enactments such as rezonings or replanings. *Garat v. City of Riverside*, 3 Cal. Rptr. 2d 504 (Ct. App. 1991) (plan and initiative amending it); *Norbeck Village Joint Venture v. Montgomery County Council*, 254 A.2d 700 (Md. 1969) (rezoning). Nevertheless, planning commissions and those bodies engaging in administrative appellate review exert a dramatic control on development and courts often apply nearly a presumption of correctness due in large part to the separation of powers tensions between state courts and local and regional government. *Blakeman v. Planning Comm'n*, 206 A.2d 425 (Conn. 1965); *Coscan Washington, Inc. v. Maryland-Nat'l Capital Park Comm'n*, 590 A.2d 1080 (Md. Ct. Spec. App. 1991).

While American planning appears driven by perceptions of market preference and the preferences of local politics, the British system may be driven by long-standing development patterns and the steady hand of the planning bureaucracy:

Neal Alison Roberts, The Reform of Planning Law: A Study of the Legal, Political and Administrative Reform of the British Land-use Planning System

188–195 (1976)

Reforming the Control Process

The title of this [reading] is *not* "reforming plan implementing" because that would imply that there was in fact a causal relationship between the development plans, in their shiny new armor, and the day-to-day decision-making process at the local level on planning applications. Since such a supposition is tenuous to say the least, we will start the discussion from the premise that we are investigating a bureaucratic process dealing with applications on a case-by-case basis. While there are frequent attempts to lump all public-development decisions together under the rubric of 'planning control,' we will leave aside the decision-makers in charge of their own public purse and concentrate on the area where public officials attempt to control the use and development of land which is not directly in their ownership. Britain's attempt to control private development piece by piece is at the heart of the system, and if policy is not being realistically formulated in the structure plans, then, if it exists at all, it must be within the process of development control.

By returning to the local and particular decision we have come full circle from the idea of strategy and policy in an abstract sense to an arena of very concrete particularised decisions. We are back to particularised rights in relation to specific parcels of land, with personal property interests being affected by the decisions. The rather hazy, over-generalised nature of structure plans, and the intra-government disputes which seem to be looming on the local planning horizon, point to the fact that the attempts to re-arrange radically the approach to planning attempted under [planning legislation] legislation have not particularly altered the importance of the individual caseworker's decision. We are back, then, to the problems...with the reorganisation of local government, and the time-consuming development of structure plans, the problems of the ability to man the casework part of the process are in even more serious doubt.

Positive Purposes in Negative Process

Compared with the lofty aims of the development plans, and the positive development ideas present in, say, the arranging of a New Town or the compulsory purchase and comprehensive redevelopment of land, development control is concerned solely with what one can *not* do on one's land. Although some 80 per cent of the 615,000 applications received in 1972 were permitted, development control is the focus for the criticism of those who cannot expand their homes, build their shops, find inexpensive homes to buy, or stop their neighbours from erecting an ugly addition to their property. Since the development-control caseworkers can only negotiate—they cannot force owners to build or develop in some way that the owner does not desire or think profitable—they often find it very difficult to convince themselves or the public of the value of their work. While there is some hope of using planning conditions to mold development more positively, this is not the usual procedure....

First, we have to take as an article of faith the proposition that a review by a local-government employee will prohibit more development that the 'public' would consider 'bad' than it will development that they would consider 'good'. The reason this has to be accepted on faith is that nowhere in the legislation are the criteria of 'goodness' or 'badness' of deciding on a particular development actually laid out, and no studies have been made (or perhaps are possible) which can show that this piece-by-piece review is having beneficial results. Perhaps Lewis Keeble, writing almost fifteen years ago, expressed the tenets of the faith most lucidly:

> As always with statutory planning, a great deal of the greatest success cannot be seen on the ground, but consists in the prevention of evils. If one were to add up the total amount of good done by preventing damage to quietness, privacy, safety and general pleasantness in residential areas through excluding unsuitable uses, it would add up to a total sufficient alone to justify the whole elaborate code of legislation and the large and unwieldy planning machine which is operated.

In order to accept this almost religious sentiment, we have to return to those goals mentioned previously which form the underpinning of the planning legislation. We must accept the notions of the 'goodness' of physical order, the idea of constraint of urban areas, the provision of 'amenity': in a phrase, the garden mentality. At the particularised level the judgement which the caseworker exercises has to be guided by what he or she thinks does not offend the public consciousness. In the words of the Parliamentary Secretary to the Ministry of Town and Country Planning, in the first years of the Act's implementation: 'If a man seeks to build an isolated home in the countryside it is clear that he is entitled to do so, so long as it does not affront the eye, absorb farm land or create some other public mischief.' It is this concentration on the nuisance quality of development which, in fact, the caseworker must ultimately fall back on. In the same way that a court can weigh the competing claims in a neighbourhood and eliminate a land-use that is a nuisance, when reviewing an application the caseworker must look to the particular surroundings, weigh the claims against notions of the planning legislation's aims (which, as we have seen, include conservation or amenity), and reach a conclusion.

At the start of an analysis of the control process it should be borne in mind that a number of commentators do not accept this fundamental creed at all. Apart from the growing number of journalists who criticise the green belts for depriving people of cheap housing land, there is a body of academic opinion which holds the view that the underpinnings of the planning system were, in fact, geared to the protection of the affluent and upper-middle class and that the aggregate effect of the control decisions has been to deprive the great mass of people of homes, gardens, jobs, or even accessible amenities. Peter Hall's massive two-volume work on the containment of urban England is perhaps the most erudite exposition of this view:

> The main theme underlying [the ideas of urban containment and what I have called the garden mentality] is the undesirability of rapid or profound change. This is not surprising as a slogan for a group which was securely in possession and which felt a threat to the status quo.... This was easier because as possessors they could manage the political system.... [The policies lead to small cramped housing but] perhaps only a few yards from the new estate, at most perhaps a mile or two, the open countryside extends un-interruptedly. Here and there stand meticulously preserved villages or isolated cottages, long since deserted by their original agricultural owners and bought by the more fortunate citizens of exurbia... Rural England was of course always a place of segregation, of social status, where the social hierarchy was finely but firmly drawn. By and large, it has remained so. The more prosperous members of the old county society, joined by selected newcomers from the cities, have sought to defend a way of life which they regarded as traditionally their right. The weapon they have used, and it has been a powerful one, is conservationist planning.

Perhaps, with this dispute as to the purpose of what the caseworker is doing in mind, we can proceed to the way in which he approaches the refusal or granting of a planning application. It must be remembered that, compared with his colleagues in structure-plan work at the county level, for example, the caseworker in the new district planning authority is of a markedly lower calibre. He has less academic training, fewer professional qualifications and a lower salary. Further, it is generally conceded that, with each new set of recruits, it is rarely the man with the top qualifications who takes a position in development-control work. There may be many factors to explain this phenomenon, but a crucial one is the character of the work itself. The mundane parcel-by-parcel review, the servicing of the development clientele, simply is not of the type that stimulates or attracts the recent graduate. In Harrison's words:

> Younger planners would perhaps rather work on more academic tasks where they can be insulated from the real political processes and can also retain illusions about the social and economic benefits of planning. The limits encountered in implementation can be ignored and there is no need to face up to the real image of planning with the public.

It is no wonder, then, that the caseworkers feel like second-class citizens in their jobs.

Turning to the job itself, we must start by looking at how the process functioned under the old local-government system and from there we can proceed to how it will function under the new system. Under the old system, with all the planning power located in the counties, it would seem likely that at least the location of casework would be clear. As it happened, however, the counties, although they were prohibited from delegating away all their planning functions, worked out with the old local districts a series of bilateral agreements to delegate the casework of development control and enforcement. Various types of districts entered into such agreements. Various sizes of districts could enter into such agreements with the counties, and all boroughs of more than 60,000 population could insist on such a delegation agreement. Some counties relied heavily on delegation, while eleven counties had no such system at all. The delegation agreements allowed a flexible arrangement between the counties and districts, but with the counties always maintaining the final say and always receiving notification of all planning applications. It also led to a great many conflicts between the upper and lower tiers, a duplication of effort and a lack of speed in processing. The old process, described at length in Professor Mandelker's study of green-belt application processing in East Sussex, starts with informal contact between the caseworker in the local council and the prospective developer. After this consultation, and various advice as to the best way to submit an application, the developer submits an application for planning permission. The caseworker both views the site and talks with various people in his department, and reaches a personal decision on the 'goodness' of the development. Under the statute, the local authority 'Shall have regard to the provisions of the development plan, so far as material to the application, and to any other material considerations.'

This leaves the caseworker reasonably free to reflect what he thinks is the view of the 'public' and in particular what the views of members of the local council's planning committee might be. The caseworker makes up the recommendation on the application in a short paragraph or two and submits this, along with similar recommendations on a long series of applications, to that committee. These recommendations tend to be automatically approved *pro forma* unless a particular political complaint has been made to one of the council's planning committees, in which case there might be a short discussion. Although there may not be contentious issues in the great majority of the cases, it is the caseworker's decision which is actually the controlling one. As Mandelker said: 'In the counties which I visited, the planning committee followed the advice of its technical officers in at least 95% of the cases.'

The existence of the delegation agreements meant that the wise developer would make his preliminary consultation with both the county and district officers. When the application came in, copies were sent to both levels of local government and the county would decide whether this was a matter that was to be decided by them or left to the districts. While there are a number of different models for liaison between the two levels—joint efforts, successive review, or mixed application review teams—a fairly typical one would be the situation in the city borough of Rye. There the County Area Planning Officer would consult with the Borough (district-level) Surveyor on the site and help to formulate the recommendations to the Town Planning Committee. The Town Planning Committee would either approve or not approve that recommendation at one of its meetings every six weeks and this decision, in turn, would be ratified by the entire Borough Council. Under this particular delegation agreement, in cases where the planning committee and the full council disagree the county makes the final decision. In an unpublished study by Graham the relationship between the county and the borough was explored and the supremacy of the county's role was underlined. The county could call in any important planning applications, and the caseworker could pay close attention to important matters. Also, due to the small economic base of the borough, any major disagreement which might result in an inquiry or a compulsory purchase order had to have the backing of the county, or else the cost could conceivably endanger the financial position of the small borough. Graham goes on to point out that, since the old development plan merely said about the town of Rye 'the county will continue to be predominantly agricultural, residential and recreational in character' and the town map for the area only covered existing use up until 1967, the case-by-case decisions depended very much on the particular views of the caseworkers. He found that in some cases the town map was pointed to as the primary reason for a decision, while in others it was ignored completely.

This then leads to the crucial question: under the old system what was the basis of the decision? Graham points to the personal feelings of the development-control caseworkers. Mandelker states that 'as the departmental liaison between the county and district councils, the area officers' judgment on the individual application will often be controlling,' and he goes on to say that 'the technical planning officer appears to predominate. Vagueness in the county development plan and in the green belt concept allows him to use a wide degree of discretion in reaching his decision.'

McLoughlin, in an extensive survey of seventeen local authorities, framed a questionnaire which revealed that the caseworkers themselves felt that the development plan really was the most important factor in their decisions, followed by 'local policies, the site and its surroundings, precedent, experience and common sense and personal judgement and philosophy,' but in his own analysis the 'written matter of development plans' (like the structure plan) ranked well below the inputs of the personal site view or an up-to-date local town map. What this means, then, is that the very 'technical' task of reviewing a particular application for development is in reality a very subjective process, not capable of being defined in terms of standards, but only a matter of subjective revelation from the caseworkers.

Influences on the caseworkers: Politics, Central Government and Law

There are three external influences which must figure dramatically in the caseworkers' general approach, the first being the role of political opinion, either ideological or party-political, the second being the views and influence of central government, and the third being law. Political views exert their influence at the juncture between the caseworkers' recommendations being presented in the planning committee's agenda (either the county or delegated to the district) and their recommendation to the entire council. According to most of the studies undertaken, and my own interviews, the personal view of the committee chairman is usually the key ingredient in approval. The control officer will often keep very close control over the information coming to the chairman and the view he expresses. Since, by definition, the chairman is an elected and thus an 'amateur' planner, the caseworker attempts to create a relationship which requires him to act as an interpreter or teacher to the chairman. Graham described how in Rye the discussion at committee meetings was always guided by the chairman and caseworkers acting in concert. In Dennis's study, when his group of fairly provocative residents attempted to supply information directly to the committee members and bypass the antagonistic caseworkers, they were met with statements like:

> Look, the proper and decent thing to do is to write to the planning department. The chairman [of the planning committee] has asked you to write through the paid officials.... Any normal decent transaction should be done through the officials. The officials advise on policy. The councillors generally, not always, but generally, accept the advice of the officials.

Dennis goes on to criticise this attempt at information control, and makes rather stirring pleas for local democracy, but this leads to the second aspect of the relationship between party politics and caseworkers' decisions.

In Britain the unified centralised nature of the political process guarantees any individual government figure at the local level a certain level of anonymity. While local issues are the caseworker's bread and butter, his elected counterpart on the planning committee knows that his political future will, to a large extent, reflect national party performance, *not* local issues. It is this anonymity which, in part, led to the recent local government scandals. The representatives are interested in the occasional application, but they know that they will not be held responsible at the local polls....

[note this excerpt was written in English, the English spellings are retained unless they were confusing, in which case the editor has translated the word into American; this minimal change is not in any way a criticism of Professor Roberts' fine work].

Notes and Comments

1. Would the enactment of more specific objective standards at the state or local ordinance level improve plan implementation at the project review stage? The standards are likely to be effective in some communities but might be less likely to impact performance where local politics rule. For a discussion of obtaining development permission in Amsterdam, see George Lefcoe, *The Right to Develop Land: The German and Dutch Experience*, 56 Or. L. Rev. 31, 46–58 (1977).

2. The pioneer comparative land use scholar, Donald G. Hagman, warned that comparisons with the English system are problematic, focusing not on planning but the balkanization of home rule control:

> It is not entirely fair...to compare the English system with American law. England's smaller territorial area renders it more amenable to unified control than America. The English also have the advantage of a form of government possessing more centralized direction on the national level. In assessing the American experience one must remember the predominant role of state government in planning and development control law, and the consequent babble of diverse state procedures. Until state practice is harmonized, the English system will continue to influence and impress Americans, if only for the virtue of its uniformity.

Donald G. Hagman & Steven Pepe, English Planning Law: A Summary of Recent Developments, 11 Harv. J. Legis. 557, 593 (1974).

3. In the United States, the subdivision and site plan review typically requires consistency between the proposal with both the comprehensive plan, *Town of Lebanon v. Woods*, 215 A.2d 112 (Conn. 1965), and the zoning ordinance. *Christofaro v. Town of Burlington*, 584 A.2d 1168 (Conn. 1991) (subdivision consistency with zoning); *Walsh v. Town of Orano*, 585 A.2d 829 (Me. 1991) (site plan zoning consistency). This requires that developments follow the zoning scheme that is typically low density. *Board of County Commissioners of Cecil County v. Gaster*, 401 A.2d 666 (Md. 1979) (reprinted below). The newer planned unit developments and some forward looking urban planning schemes are calling for mixed uses on the same parcel. *Cheney v. Village 2 at New Hope, Inc.*, 241 A.2d 81 (Pa. 1968). Offices, parking, retail, and a mix of residential tenures and costs can generate inviting pedestrian streets with outdoor entertainment and walkable neighborhoods. Andrés Duany, Elizabeth Plater-Zyberk & Jeff Speck, Suburban Nation: The Rise of Sprawl and the Decline of the American Dream (2000).

4. The American development law bifurcates the subdivision process. At the same time that a developer must pursue permits through the subdivision process, states and the federal government regulate the marketing and sale of subdivision parcels. 2 James A. Kushner, Subdivision Law and Growth Management § 9:10 (2d ed. 2001). Under the Federal Interstate Land Sales Full Disclosure Act, subdivisions that are marketed interstate must make

certain disclosures, register, and meet certain standards. 15 U.S.C. § 1701-20. Unfortunately, homes or building sites are sometimes marketed by unscrupulous developers or by those with ambitions that exceed financing and market demand. The availability of services or amenities such as recreation facilities, schools, police and fire protection, or even essential infrastructure such as roads, water, sewers, and flood control may be advertised but not delivered. Exceptions, such as where prospective purchasers visit the parcel for a free or discount vacation, 15 U.S.C. § 1702(b), or where marketing is limited to the state where the subdivision is proposed render the regulations imperfect. *Olsen v. Lake Country, Inc.*, 955 F.2d 203 (4th Cir. 1992) (per curium) (use of television advertising took development out of single-family exemption); *Giralt v. Vail Village Inn Assocs.*, 759 P.2d 801 (Colo. Ct. App. 1988) (mailing two letters by certified mail to prospective condominium purchasers, met jurisdictional use of mails). State laws often mirror the federal standard. The Digest of State Land Sales Regulations (Stuart M. Bloch & W. Ingersoll eds. 1981). Criminal and civil penalties and damages are available under the various laws, *Adams v. Hyannis Harborview, Inc.*, 838 F. Supp. 676 (D. Mass. 1993), and the federal statute allows a 7-day "cooling off" period to allow a purchaser to timely back out of a contract. 15 U.S.C. § 1703(b). The cooling off period was demonstrated in the movie and play of David Mamet, "Glengarry Glen Ross," where Al Pacino's character, Ricky Roma, lies to a prospect that he would not submit the contract until Monday, but when the prospect sought rescission on Monday the 3-day cooling off period under the drama's statute had run. Jack Lemmon's character, Shelley "The Machine" Levene, demonstrates the use of "birddogs," the use of phony references to serve as satisfied customers. *United States v. Judd*, 889 F.2d 1410 (5th Cir. 1989) (fake testimonials and promises of nonexistent mineral rights).

The following case reflects many of the issues that are encountered in the review of subdivision and other development proposals in the United States:

Board of County Commissioners of Cecil County v. Gaster

401 A.2d 666 (Md. 1979)

....Cecil County (the county) is located in the northeast corner of Maryland, at the head of the Chesapeake Bay, on the east side of the Susquehanna River and immediately adjacent to the States of Delaware and Pennsylvania. It has a land area of 352 square miles and a 1970 population of 53,291 people. It is cut in two by the Chesapeake and Delaware Canal. The Northeast, Elk, and Bohemia Rivers, all of which are navigable, separate parts of the county from other parts. It is traversed by two major highways running from the Baltimore metropolitan area to other populous areas of the Northeast. Because of their close proximity, portions of the county may be called a bedroom community for Wilmington, Delaware, and Philadelphia, Pennsylvania. Wilmington is situated in New Castle County, the northernmost of the three Delaware Counties. Cecil County's numerous miles of waterfront are inviting to many people in the Wilmington and Philadelphia metropolitan areas. Indeed, it was said by the engineers for appellees in a letter of transmittal to the county's planner:

> [W]e feel that the project should be considered in terms of growth potential for Cecil County. Residents would be located within easy commuting distance of available jobs in both Cecil and New Castle Counties. Additionally, the project represents the creation of a recreation-oriented community unavailable in the majority of housing developments.

Appellees, Gerald Gaster et al. (Gaster), own a tract of land comprising 174.3 acres located between Oldfield Point Road and the Elk River in what is known as Elk Neck. The area in question is zoned "Shoreline Recreational-Residential Zone R-R." It is located in the same election district as Elkton, the county seat.

Gaster presented to the Cecil County Planning Commission (the commission) a preliminary subdivision plan for what he called "Chesapeake Coves." He contemplated development of 408 lots for single family dwelling units, together with associated roads, water and sewer facilities, and recreational areas. The commission notified Gaster that it "ha[d] disapproved said plat as not being in conformance with the Cecil County Subdivision Regulations." It went on to say:

The Commission's disapproval is based primarily on the following:

1. A purpose of the Subdivision Regulations (Section 1.1) is to legislate the intent of the County's Comprehensive Plan by providing for substantial conformance to the Plan. The Planning Office is required by the Subdivision Regulations to check the Preliminary Plat as to its substantial conformity with the Plan (Section 4.1.7) and the Planning Commission must review the Plat with regard to such conformity (Section 4.1.9). The Commission also reviews the Plat in light of the impact on existing and proposed roads and the feasibility of a subdivision in the area with regard to total number and size of lots and effect on the school district (Section 4.1.21).
2. The Preliminary Plat of Chesapeake Coves specifies a density of 2.3 units per acre, whereas the Comprehensive Plan indicates that residential developments in the subject area "may be approved for density up to 1.0 units per acre". Therefore the Chesapeake Coves Preliminary Plat cannot be said to meet the substantial conformance requirements of the Subdivision Regulations.
3. Neither is the substantial conformance requirement met with respect to the Plan's provision that access to and from development tracts shall be through roads having capacity and alignments sufficient to protect public safety. The addition of more than 400 dwelling units represented by Chesapeake Coves would mean a 73% Increase in traffic on Oldfield Point Road, which has poor vertical and horizontal alignment, poor sight distances, and narrow width. This road is not programmed for reconstruction before 1990.
4. Finally, review of the Preliminary Plat in accordance with the provision in the Subdivision Regulations requiring consideration of impact on the school district concluded that the increased school enrollment from Chesapeake Coves would be beyond the capacity of the schools to absorb.

Gaster appealed to the Cecil County Board of Appeals, as the commission advised him he might do. It reversed. It found the conclusions of the commission were "factually correct and would be sufficient to defeat (the) appeal if they were, in fact, applicable to the development in question." It explained:

> The Board finds, therefore, that in so far as the regulations of the Planning Commission permit the rejection of a subdivision plan on the grounds herein above stated, the same exceed the authority given by the enabling act and are consequently invalid.
>
> The Planning Commission argues, however, that the provisions of 3.08 of Article 66B when read in conjunction with the provisions of Section 3.2 of the

> Subdivision Regulations, permits the Board to reject the subdivision on grounds of non-compliance with the presently existing Cecil County Master Plan. The Board feels that the short answer to this contention is the fact that while the Master Plan constitutes a useful, effective, and necessary guideline in the planning and zoning area, it does not have statutory effect until implemented by the Zoning Ordinance. The Board does not feel that the Master Plan can be used to override the existing criteria as set forth by the Cecil County Zoning Ordinance for the R-R zone in which the subdivision is located and with which criteria the subdivision complies in its entirety.

The commission and the Board of County Commissioners of Cecil County appealed to the Circuit Court for Cecil County....

Before we get into the legal background for this particular controversy, a word should be said relative to planning and zoning generally. Zoning did not come into Maryland easily. Prior to the enactment of Chapter 672 of the Acts of 1970, planning and zoning authority for non-charter counties (in the absence of a local law as to a specific county) was found in Maryland Code (1957) Art. 66B, §§ 10–37.... In it provision was made for a planning commission which was granted the power to prepare and adopt a master plan. No approval of the plan by the local legislative body was required. Once such a plan had been adopted, then under § 18 "no street, square, park or other public way, ground, or open space, or public building or structure, or public utility, whether publicly or privately owned, [was permitted to] be constructed or authorized in the municipality [a term defined in § 10 as including or relating to counties] or in such planned section and district until the location, character, and extent thereof sh[ould] have been submitted to and approved by the commission...." By §§ 21 to 23 power was granted the local legislative body of counties to adopt zoning regulations. Title 3, found in §§ 24 to 30, provided for subdivision control....

Section 3.05 concerns the general powers and duties of the planning commission.... [I]t is "to make and approve a plan which shall be recommended to the local legislative body for adoption...." It directs that the plan contain certain elements, including a land use element "which shall show proposals for the most appropriate and desirable patterns for the general location, character, extent and interrelationship of the manner in which the community should use its public and private land at specified times as far into the future as is reasonable"; a transportation element showing "proposals for the most appropriate and desirable patterns for the general location, character, and extent of the channels, routes, and terminals for transportation facilities, and for the circulation of persons and goods at specified times as far into the future as is reasonable"; a community facilities element showing "proposals for the most appropriate and desirable patterns for the general location, character, and extent of public and semipublic buildings, land, and facilities for specified times as far into the future as is reasonable," and "the planning commission's recommendation for land development regulations to implement the plan...."

The purpose of a master plan is set forth in § 3.06:

> The plan shall be made with the general purpose of guiding and accomplishing the coordinated, adjusted, and harmonious development of the jurisdiction, and its environs which will, in accordance with present and future needs, best promote health, safety, morals, order, convenience, prosperity, and general welfare, as well as efficiency and economy in the process of development; including among other things, adequate provisions for traffic, the promotion of

> public safety, adequate provision for light and air, conservation of natural resources, the prevention of environmental pollution, the promotion of the healthful and convenient distribution of population, the promotion of good civic design and arrangement, wise and efficient expenditure of public funds, and the adequate provision of public utilities and other public requirements.

The procedure to be followed for a planning commission to recommend adoption of a master plan is found in § 3.07. After the required hearings it must certify "[a]n attested copy of the plan or part of the plan... to the local legislative body." Section 3.08 provides that after adoption of the plan by the local legislative body "no street, square, park or other public way, ground, or open space, or public building or structure, or public utility, whether public or privately owned, shall be constructed or authorized in the jurisdiction... until the location, character, and extent of such development shall have been submitted to and approved by the commission As consistent with the plan...." (Emphasis added.)....

The provisions relative to subdivision control are contained in §§ 5.01–5.08. The county argues that the 1970 amendments to Art. 66B require enactment of subdivision regulations which would implement the master plan and that avoidance of congestion of population is one of the permitted purposes of subdivision regulations. Gaster says that "the accuracy of that argument is not supportable by either the law or the legislative history." We disagree. Section 5.02 provides that when a local legislative body shall have adopted the transportation element of the plan of the territory within its jurisdiction and shall have duly filed a copy of the plan in the office of the clerk of the circuit court, "then no plat of a subdivision of land within such territory or part shall be filed or recorded until it shall have been approved by the planning commission and such approval entered in writing on the plat by the chairman or secretary of the commission." Then § 5.03(a) goes on to provide:

> Before exercising the powers referred to in § 5.02, the planning commission shall prepare regulations governing the subdivision of land within its jurisdiction. Those regulations may provide for the adequate control of shore erosion; the control of sediment and the protection from flooding; the proper arrangement of streets in relation to other existing planned streets and to the master plan; the adequate and convenient placement of public school sites and of open spaces for traffic, utilities, access of firefighting apparatus, recreation, light and air and the avoidance of congestion of population, including minimum width and area of lots....

We believe the second section of § 5.03(a) should be read as follows:

> These regulations may provide for
>
> 1. the adequate control of shore erosion;
> 2. the control of sediment and the protection from flooding;
> 3. the proper arrangement of streets in relation to other existing planned streets and to the master plan;
> 4. the adequate and convenient placement
>   (a) of public school sites and
>   (b) of open spaces for
>   (1) traffic,
>   (2) utilities,

(3) access of fire-fighting apparatus,

(4) recreation,

(5) light and air and

5. the avoidance of congestion of population, including minimum width and area of lots.

The clause "the avoidance of congestion..." does not relate to "the adequate and convenient placement of...open spaces."

Section 5.03(c) provides for submission of the proposed subdivision regulations to the local legislative body for adoption and that when they shall have been "adopted by the local legislative body, a copy thereof shall be certified by the commission to the clerk of the circuit court in which the jurisdiction is located for record." It is clear to us that the adoption of subdivision regulations is required once a transportation plan has been adopted and that those regulations are authorized to take into consideration "the avoidance of congestion of population."

Section 5.04 provides that when a planning commission has approved a subdivision plat it "shall by virtue of such approval, be deemed to be an amendment of or an addition to or a detail of the plan and a part thereof." It goes on to provide that the commission may from time to time "recommend to the local legislative body amendments of the zoning ordinance or map or additions thereto to conform to the commission's recommendations for the zoning regulation of the territory comprised within approved subdivisions."

In the argument relative to the apparent conflict between the county's zoning ordinance and the subdivision regulations the parties seem to have lost sight of § 1.2 of the subdivision regulations providing that in any instance where "any provisions of th[o]se regulations conflict with any other provision of law, whether set forth in th[o]se regulations or contained in any restrictions covering any of the same subject matter, that provision which is more restrictive or imposes a high standard or requirement shall govern. Such determination shall be made by the Planning Commission." Cecil County, Maryland, Subdivision Regulations § 1.2 (April 15, 1976)....

There are three integral parts of adequate land planning, the master plan, zoning, and subdivision regulations. The need for subdivision regulations as a part of that planning is well illustrated by the case here. As it is put in 4. R. Anderson, *American Law of Zoning* § 23.03 (2d ed. 1977), "[Z]oning ordinances are not calculated to protect the community from the financial loss which may result from imperfect development. Some of these purposes are sought through the imposition of subdivision controls." 4 A. Rathkopf, *The Law of Zoning and Planning* Ch. 71 § 2 (4th ed. 1979), gives reasons for subdivision control:

> Planning enabling acts and the requirements for plat approval are based upon the realization that homes are no longer generally constructed one at a time for individual owners, resulting in a gradual development which can be controlled by zoning ordinances and local health, building, plumbing, and electrical codes alone. Vacant lots suitable for single homes in already developed communities have all but disappeared. The great increases in population and the unprecedented demand for homes has necessarily resulted in opening up undeveloped land in outlying areas, and the development thereof by large numbers of homes which may be said to be built all at one time. Where such development takes place without restriction other than zoning restrictions, it is the

> developer who designs the community in respect to the number, length, width, condition, and location of streets. The developer also determines where the newly arrived inhabitants of the community shall reside, without consideration of the necessity for, or existence of, schools, fire protection, parks, playgrounds, and other public facilities. If subdivisions develop too rapidly, or before the community is ready for the added burdens which an increased population imposes, and without adequate control, the result too often is the creation of deteriorating neighborhoods which create a blight upon the community and a drain upon the municipal purse....

When Cecil County adopted its zoning regulations providing for rural zones and for lot sizes and density in such zones it was not contemplating that all undeveloped area would become developed area. The county simply was specifying the size of lot it regarded as compatible with the rural zone. It might well have specified a smaller sized lot but for the fact that the necessity for driving a well and providing adequate sewage disposal through a septic tank system dictates a certain minimum size. It was not contemplated that numerous homes would be built, yet had the county provided in a rural area that no homes could be built other than on a farm it then would have been impossible for a farmer to convey out a lot to his son or daughter. On the other hand, had the county required a very substantial sized lot as a minimum, *e.g.* five or ten acres, it would have been guilty of poor land use, of failing to carefully husband one of our irreplaceable and disappearing natural resources, namely, land devoted to agricultural production.

The General Assembly certainly contemplated some change from the previously existing scheme of planning and zoning when it decreed that in the counties covered by Art. 66B approval of the master plan by the local legislative body was required and that subdivision regulations should be adopted by such body. How can a county effectively plan for capital expenditures for roads, schools, sewers, and water facilities if, without regard to preexisting plans, a developer, as proposed here, might place a settlement of 1,200 or more people in the middle of a previously undeveloped area, a settlement which would overtax school facilities and which would necessitate improvement of a road whose reconstruction had not been contemplated before 1990? Planning would be futile in such situations....

In the case at bar we see no basic conflict between the zoning regulations and the subdivision regulations. If there were a conflict, the subdivision ordinance in this instance provides that the more restrictive provision shall prevail. Moreover, Art. 66B, § 3.08 specifies that once a master plan has been adopted by the local legislative body "no street...shall be constructed or authorized...until the location, character, and extent of such development shall have been submitted to and approved by the commission as *consistent with the plan....*" (Emphasis added.) It must be remembered that the board of appeals found the factual conclusions of the commission to be correct. Thus, it follows that if this proposed subdivision were approved, the streets contemplated in it would be spewing traffic out onto a county road "which has poor vertical and horizontal alignment, poor sight distances, and narrow width [, a] road...not programmed for reconstruction before 1990." Given the provisions of § 3.08, this in itself was a sufficient basis for the disapproval of the subdivision plat by the commission....

In sum, Cecil County has validly used the planning tools placed in its hands by the General Assembly to provide for orderly growth for the county.

* * *

Notes and Comments

1. *Gaster* demonstrates the interplay between the comprehensive plan, zoning, and the administrative project review.

The following materials look at the problems of application timing and vested rights. At what point should a developer have the right to complete a project without a change in standards?

The Vesting Problem

Vesting refers to the point in the development process where the law recognizes the developers' interest as an entitlement, that is, a property right to proceed so that attempts to alter the regulatory environment constitute property deprivation. *Western Land Equities, Inc. v. City of Logan*, 617 P.2d 388 (Utah 1980). Because vesting involves a state recognized property interest it is constitutionally protected from confiscation under the takings clause. *Mays-Ott Co. v. Town of Nags Head*, 751 F. Supp. 82 (E.D.N.C. 1990). The battle has been drawn between developers desiring early vesting and regulators and environmentalists seeking a later vesting point. The developer's equitable claims are based on an argument that significant resources and often unrecoverable investments are made in reliance on the laws and standards in existence at the commencement of the project. The environmentalist argues that it is typically only after a project is proposed and an environmental assessment completed that the impacts of the proposal are understood and environmental concerns and facilities capacity measured so that public policy proposals can be adjusted to the conditions. Early vesting, they argue, will result in many ill-planned projects obtaining approval despite projects presenting a drain on the limited infrastructure capacity or imposing significant environmental degradation, a condition that was unknown to regulators before a development proposal was advanced.

Even where developers were unable to achieve early vesting in the courts, *Avco Community Developers v. South Coast Regional Comm'n*, 3 P.2d 546 (Cal. 1976), legislators were swayed by arguments that late vesting would increase development costs and render housing costs affordable only to the affluent. Michael M. Shultz, *Vested Property Rights in Colorado: The Legislature Rushes in Where...*, 66 Den. U.L. Rev. 31 (1988). State legislatures have enacted streamlining legislation designed, if not to provide early vesting, to offer developments a fast track where bureaucratic delay is kept to a minimum. N.Y. Gen. City Law § 32; Tex. Local Gov't Code Ann. § 212.003; Brian W. Blaesser & Franklin G. Stearns, *The Importance of "Process" in Smart Growth Initiatives: Ballot Box Versus Streamlining*, 52 Land Use L. & Zoning Dig. 3 (Jun. 2000). Under such statutes, boards have a set number of days to decide project proposals or applications may be automatically approved. *Leavenworth Properties v. San Francisco*, 234 Cal. Rptr. 598 (Ct. App. 1987); *Cardinale v. Ottawa Regional Planning Comm'n*, 627 N.E.2d 611 (Ohio Ct. App. 1993).

The challenge of this chapter is to identify a development process that is fair, equitable, and assures environmental sustainability.

The following excerpt describes the range of vesting points that courts and legislators have established:

2 James A. Kushner, Subdivision Law and Growth Management

Ch. 10 (2d ed. 2001).

Vested Development Rights

Vested rights refers to the status enjoyed by a property developer when the law prevents government from interfering with development previously approved through the devices of changed planning, zoning, or other more restrictive land use controls.

When rights vest is a complicated issue, one that differs among states and situations. Vesting is particularly important in that local government must be empowered to create and modify strategies so as to effectively carry out land use policy to protect public health, safety, and welfare and to successfully and adequately plan for the changing future. For the same reason, vested rights are typically ruled to be personal and not enjoyed by the transferee of land. With regard to subdivision approval, while a minority of jurisdictions provide for a vesting of rights at the time of preliminary plat application, the majority establish vesting only upon preliminary [subdivision] tract approval, with others requiring substantial expenditures in reliance on a permit....

Estoppel is a form of vested rights in that government may be estopped from interfering with already approved projects or projects which have progressed to a point where the hardship from investment of time, capital, and resources forecloses the change of rules. Estoppel differs from vested rights in that estoppel is based on the representation by government, often through a permit, that the developer may invest and proceed with development, and on the developer's good faith reliance upon that representation. Nevertheless, a promise of future subdivision approval is an ultra vires agreement unenforceable against public officials.

Vested rights is a creature of state rather than federal law. In states such as California, which at common law does not follow the concept of estoppel in land use controls, vested rights must be found. While rights do not vest under common law until all permits are granted and the developer commences substantial construction, state statutes offer vested rights to certain tentative tract subdivisions approvals. Absent early vesting statutes, rights do not vest until long after developer reliance on representations of government that the developer may proceed. An exception to late vesting may exist if application disapproval is made in bad faith to halt the process pending the subsequent enactment of more rigorous conditions for development. Similarly, a building permit may not be denied in anticipation of a law change nor by legislation enacted to frustrate a particular developer's plans.

Vested rights or rights protected by equitable estoppel are not immutable but are subject to waiver. Vested rights may be lost through abandonment, recoupment, or an overriding benefit to the public. In addition, vested rights may be extinguished by exercise of the police powers in furtherance of a legitimate public goal....A municipality may be estopped to change a previously approved plat as lot purchasers rely on established streets and frontage. A finding of a vested right to proceed with development may not exempt a development from a subsequently enacted timing-based permit limit imposed as a growth control measure, as courts may distinguish the timing of development from the right to develop. Despite vesting, such rights may be impaired by legislation enacting police power regulation where reasonably necessary to prevent a danger or nuisance to the public....

Zoning or planning maps indicating permitted or projected development patterns constitute neither representations of the right to develop, thereby invoking estoppel, nor any guarantee that action will or may be taken, and thus rights will not vest based upon written studies, comprehensive plans, or maps. Zoning changes following tentative subdivisions tract approval, however, may not apply to such plans.

The majority of states follow the rule that subdivision rules may not be changed following tentative or preliminary tract approval. Some jurisdictions may protect ancient subdivisions or subdivision applications not yet acted upon. The tract approval thus establishes both the point that rights vest and when the developer may rely on the representation of permission and hold the community to estoppel. Communities adopting subdivision regulations for the first time may grandfather and exempt previously zoned parcels. Plats filed under platting laws prior to subdivision ordinances or regulations and remaining undeveloped are subject to subsequently enacted subdivisions regulations. A minority of jurisdictions, including California, do not, through their common law, foreclose the modification of subdivisions regulations. California by statute accords vested rights to certain tentative tract subdivisions approvals. Some states may deny protection when the change in law was pending or where the reasons for retroactive application are compelling.

It is possible under the taking cases such as... [*Lucas v. South Carolina Coastal Council*, 505 U.S. 1003 (1992) and *Penn Central Transportation Co. v. City of New York*, 438 U.S. 104 (1978)]...that zone changes reducing the intensity of development to a point whereby no economic use of the property is possible are not justified by important societal needs. Nevertheless, zoning itself is subject to change, and while such changes could thwart investment-backed expectations, warranting the payment of damages or invalidation, zoning does not present any representation that government may not subsequently change the rules, and no rights vest upon the promulgation or maintenance of the zoning districting of a parcel or property. In addition, there is no vested right to a variance or the availability of a variance procedure. Certainly, developers obtain no vested rights, despite expenditures or improvements, based on a mere application for a zone change to a higher intensity use, and owners of adjacent land enjoy no vested rights in the maintenance of a particular zoning classification. Nevertheless, owners may enjoy vested rights in previously granted variances from zone changes or attempted modifications or extinguishment of ancient variances, and municipalities may be estopped from undertaking zone changes devised solely to frustrate a landowner. Some courts will protect landowners from zone changes after substantial reliance on a recent landowner's requested rezoning. Yet, a rush to project commencement with knowledge of a likely zone change may be deemed bad faith so as to deny any estoppel or vested rights....

The comprehensive plan, as in the case of highway or urban renewal plans, does not create vested rights, and is not a representation of actions that the government will permit without interference. Nevertheless, once tentative tract subdivision approval is granted, the project may be exempt from subsequent changes in the comprehensive plan....

Jurisdictions have not typically defined the vesting of rights on the submission of a plat and application and such is not a form of government permission upon which estoppel might be based. Nevertheless, some jurisdictions do provide protection in the form of grandfathering pending applications, thus exempting them from new regulations. To allow vested rights on the filing of a subdivision application would frustrate the ability of government to regulate regardless of public need for controlling land use.

A landowner's acceptance of an amendment extending the termination date of a conditionally approved subdivision may constitute acquiescence in the failure to approve the plat unconditionally, thereby allowing the application of conditions authorized by planning law after the amendment. Even without vesting, many jurisdictions will scrutinize zone changes designed to frustrate development involved in subdivision approval disputes....

The general rule is that preliminary or tentative tract approval established the vesting or rights and the point of estoppel in land use cases....

As most jurisdictions use tentative or preliminary tract approval for vesting purposes, the final subdivision plat approval or precise planned unit development approval is somewhat irrelevant for vesting purposes. Nevertheless, a significant number of jurisdictions provide vesting upon final tract approval. Perhaps, in some jurisdictions, where changes are brought about by third party entities such as the state legislature, the courts, or other administrative agencies, final tract approval might supply a vesting point. Statutes may protect approved subdivisions from revocation where individual lots have been mortgaged.

Often, subdividers receiving final tract approval are given a period of time to obtain a building permit during which time the project is protected from zoning amendments. Reasonable conditions short of prohibiting the use may be attached to such grandfathered permits....

....Some states grant vested rights by statute as of the date of building permit application. Vesting may not occur, however, unless the permit application is consistent with all land use regulations, including applicable zoning and building code requirements. Other communities, while not denying full vested rights to applications, may nevertheless limit regulatory change applicability to measures pending at the time of permit application. A few jurisdictions follow a rule that protects expenditures made before a permit is obtained but in reliance of the probability of permit issuance. While the majority of jurisdictions allow zoning and other planning modifications following permit issuance, and a few establish vesting upon permit issuance, most preclude an estoppel finding absent issuance of a building permit. Some states provide a grace period allowing the developer to proceed under a building permit, thereby providing an exemption from zoning and other regulatory changes: a vested right during the grace period.

Projects with permits may nevertheless be subject to a building moratorium if there exists a substantial question of a threat to public health by construction. Despite earlier vesting, building permits may be revoked if necessary to prevent a threat to public health or if the original issuance was violative of law, at least where the landowner has not in good faith and without knowledge of the illegality made expenditures in reliance of the permit. Once a building permit is issued and work commenced, however, both vested rights and procedural due process may restrict the power to revoke a permit....

In federal courts, and in some states, including California, except for the availability in certain cases of statutory vesting at tentative approval, vesting occurs upon issuance of a building permit together with substantially commencing construction. This is similar to the even more restrictive Massachusetts statutory rule requiring construction commencement within six months and proceeding to completion.

In the majority of jurisdictions, rights vest at the latest upon the commencement of substantial construction undertaken in good faith reliance in the form of expenditures made or liabilities incurred upon a government permit to proceed. Many courts interpret "good faith" to mean the objective standard of whether actions taken were those of a reasonable landowner under the circumstances. Mere knowledge of a pending regulatory change is typically insufficient to find objective bad faith. A landowner will not acquire a vested right in development where the purview of the permit has been exceeded. While substantial construction would clearly be sufficient reliance in estoppel jurisdictions, substantiality varies. While some states require more than the purchase of land or the commencement of actual physical construction, other jurisdictions might require far less, such as incurring liabilities, or expensive site preparation.

Further problems are present by the definition of "substantial construction." In California, Maryland, and Pennsylvania, for example, site preparation, grading, utilities installation and even laying the foundation may not qualify. Substantiality appears to be somewhere between the ground and the roof. While building completion would clearly be sufficient, other communities follow differing degrees of project progress to find substantiality. In some states, development rights will not vest until site excavation is completed. Professor Mandelker identifies the majority rule to be a "set quantum" of expenditures to constitute substantial reliance, recognizing that other jurisdictions look to a ratio of expenditures to total project cost, or a balancing test with expenditures a factor in the equation....

Phased developments, where different sections go through the approval process at different times either to pace facilities and service capacity expansion or to reflect the developer's financial capacity, or the anticipated market demand, present different vesting problems. Generally, each section or phase is treated as a separate project following the jurisdiction's vesting or estoppel rules....

* * *

Notes and Comments

1. California has legislatively advanced the vesting point in subdivision regulation from the common law building permit plus substantial construction. Cal. Gov't Code § 66474.2 provides that only regulations and standards in place or pending at the time the tentative subdivision application is filed control the application's review. Cal. Gov't Code § 65961 precludes imposition of building permit conditions that could have been imposed at tentative tract approval. Cal. Gov't Code §§ 66498.1 to 66498.7 provides for "vesting tentative maps that vest, along with the approval of building plans at tentative subdivision approval. *Kaufman & Broad Cent. Valley, Inc. v. City of Modesto,* 30 Cal. Rptr. 2d 904 (Ct. App. 1994). Development rights may also vest through development agreements executed between developers and regulating communities. David L. Callies, *Developers' Agreements and Planning Gain,* 17 Urb. Law. 599 (1985); Daniel J. Curtin, Jr. & Scott A. Edelstein, *Development Agreement Practice in California and Other States,* 22 Stetson L. Rev. 761 (1993).

The following excerpt describes the German law of regulatory takings that protects vested development plans:

Katharina Richter, *Compensable Regulation in the Federal Republic of Germany,*

5 Arizona Journal of International and Comparative Law 34 (1988)

BauGB § 39 provides for compensation for expenses incurred in reliance on an existing *Bebauungsplan* [approved development plan]. Payment for such damages (*Ver-*

trauensschaden) is based on an equitable estoppel concept which focuses on the unfairness of the government's action when changing the regulations governing a property. BauGB § 39 provides as follows:

> Property owners or other persons with legal interests in the use of the property who, in reliance on an existing zoning plan have made improvements in preparation for the development of their property for any use permitted by the specific zoning plan, may, to the extent the improvements lose in value as a result of a change, expansion, or repeal of the existing zoning, demand reasonable compensation in money. This includes any exactions, expenses or improvements previously required by federal or state law for improvement of the property.

A claim for compensation under BauGB § 39 requires:

1. an existing, legally valid Bebauungsplan;
2. payment only for actual expenses; and
3. good faith reliance on the existing Bebauungsplan in making the expenditures.

BauGB § 39 permits money compensation for actual, out-of-pocket expenses incurred in preparation of development. These could include items such as architectural, engineering, or surveying costs, drainage and grading plans, costs of a building permit, or interest costs for financing the development project. Also included are any development fees or the value of exactions previously paid to the municipality for improvement of the property.

BauGB § 39, however, strictly limits the situations in which preparatory development costs will be compensated. For example, preparatory costs must have been expended for the development of a use specifically permitted in the *Bebauungsplan*. If the use would only have been permitted by obtaining a variance, BauGB § 39 does not apply. Only actual expenditures are compensable; loss of future profits, the purchase price of the property, and loss of property value are not compensable. Loss of value, however, might be compensable pursuant to BauGB § 42....

Most important for recovery of preparatory, pre-development expenditures is the criterion that a *Bebauungsplan* must be legally existing at the time the costs are incurred. Expenditures based on a *Bebauungsplan* that has been declared unconstitutional or void on procedural grounds cannot be the basis of a claim for compensation pursuant to BauGB §39. Given the fact that so many *Bebauungspläne* have been declared invalid on minor procedural grounds in the past few years, this can be an insurmountable barrier to compensation for some property owners.

Finally, the reliance on an existing *Bebauungsplan* must be justified. Reliance is not justified if the property owner has actual knowledge that the *Bebauungsplan* may be amended or repealed in the near future. Thus, once a municipality has given public notice of its intention to amend or repeal the *Bebauungsplan*, subsequent expenditures made in reliance on that plan are no longer compensable under BauGB § 39. Additionally, reliance cannot be based upon a land use designation in a *Flachennutzungsplan*, since, unlike a *Bebauungsplan*, such plan does not give the owner any legal rights to a particular land use.

A claim for compensation pursuant to BauGB § 39 is somewhat similar to a vested rights claim. In the United States, if a property owner "has performed substantial work and incurred substantial liabilities upon a permit issued by the government, he acquires a vested right to complete construction in accordance with the terms of the permit." In most U.S. jurisdictions, a valid building permit must have been issued prior to the zone change to establish a vested right to a previously permitted use. Pre-development costs for items such as feasibility studies, market surveys, soil surveys, and drainage plans, which are incurred prior to the issuance of a building permit, usually do not establish a vested right.

A few jurisdictions in the United States, however, have recognized that such pre-development costs often constitute a substantial and necessary part of large-scale development projects, and courts, therefore, have been willing to find a present right to the planned use based on an equitable estoppel standard without the requirement of a building permit. In such U.S. jurisdictions, a municipality may be estopped from changing regulations when a property owner.

1. in good faith, and
2. in reliance upon some act or omission of the government,
3. has made such a substantial change in position or has incurred such extensive obligations and expenses that it would be highly inequitable and unjust to destroy the right he acquired.

The legal principle underlying BauGB § 39 is comparable to the equitable estoppel standard recognized in the United States. No permit or governmental assurances are required beyond the designation in the *Bebauungsplan* itself. Further, unlike a vested rights or equitable estoppel claim in the United States, BauGB § 39 does not give a German property owner the right to proceed with the planned development of the land. Instead, if the municipality wishes to change the zoning so as to preclude the use, it must pay for the actual pre-development costs which the property owner has expended in preparation of the previously permitted use.

Compensation for pre-development expenditures may only be paid in money. It is usually to be paid in a lump sum; however, the property owner can request compensation to be paid in installments including interest. Although compensation is limited to actual costs incurred, there is no limit to the amount payable....

* * *

Note on The Great Mall of China

On April 23, 1992, McDonald's opened its world's largest restaurant on the corner of China's busiest shopping street in the capital city of Beijing. 700 seats occupied this two-story 28,000 square foot restaurant, which could serve up to 50,000 customers a day making it eight times larger than the average McDonald's in the United States. Furthermore, 95 percent of the food is produced in China.

McDonald's is called "Maidanglao" in Chinese and a Big Mac is uttered "Juwuba." However amusing the names of the items on the menu may be, the prices are not. In 1992 a hamburger, regular french fries, and a small soda cost approximately $1.81 in U.S. dollars. The average per capita income of a Beijinger is $31 U.S. dollars a month.

The Beijing McDonald's is a "50-50 joint venture with a powerful Beijing government conglomerate who runs over 1,000 other enterprises in China." Robert Benjamin, *Beijing Gets First Taste of McDonald's*, The Houston Chronicle, April 23, 1992, at sec. A page 27. Beijing McDonald's Food Co. Ltd. is a capitalistic Chinese corporation half-owned by McDonald's and half-owned by the Chinese government. Many believe that McDonald's could not have secured this prime location in Beijing without the desire of the communist party leaders. In addition, Chinese officials are quite likely to personally profit from this joint venture. Robert Novak, *Big Mac capitalism Finds Tiananmen Home*, Chicago Sun-Times, July 18, 1993, at Editorial page 35.

November 21, 1994 marked the beginning of a long war between McDonald's and the Beijing municipal government. Beijing's city government asked McDonald's to vacate its largest restaurant in the world to make room for the Oriental Plaza, which would be an office, retail, cultural, entertainment, and residential complex. Reuters, *Golden Arches May be Falling in Beijing*, The Financial Post, Nov, 22, 1994, at sec. 1 page 16. This complex was a joint venture between Chinese and Hong Kong firms. It was planned by a Hong Kong tycoon, Li Ka-shing, who allegedly had connections with Chinese officials and the power to drive McDonald's out of its prime location. Beijing officials stated that McDonald's would be allocated a space within the $1.2 billion Oriental Plaza. Amy Chew, *McDonald's Seeks Meeting on Beijing Eviction*, South China Morning Post, Nov. 29, 1994, at sec. News page 1.

McDonald's believes it has a legal right to remain at the location due to a 20-year land use agreement signed between McDonald's and Beijing city officials. The Beijing government essentially broke the 20-year contract with the American food outlet and told the restaurant to "make way for the bulldozers." China's laws and regulations change on a regular basis which makes many foreign companies reluctant to invest or open shops in the Asian nation. *Beijing Serves Up a Surprise for McDonald's*, The Plain Dealer, Nov. 29, 1994 at sec. Editorials & Forum page 9B.

After two years of resisting an eviction order by the Beijing government, on December 2, 1996, McDonald's finally agreed to close the restaurant and vacate the premises. Reuters, *McDonald's to Move Beijing Restaurant*, The New York Times, Dec. 2, 1996, at sec. D page 2 col. 4 Due to breaching the land use agreement, Beijing paid McDonald's $12.3 million in compensation for lost business and for ordering the restaurant to vacate its prime site in the city's capital. *Beijing Paying McDonald's Millions for Vacating Store*, The Orlando Sentinel, Dec. 25, 1996, at sec. Business page B5.

McDonald's restaurant was the last building to be demolished in the area and was continuing to do business while all the other surrounding buildings were demolished. Meanwhile, McDonald's signed an agreement with the Beijing city government to move its restaurant to a temporary site about 150 meters from its original location until the Oriental Plaza was completed. *McDonald's Finally Moves Disputed Beijing Store*, The Reuter European business Report, Dec. 1, 1996, at BC cycle.

The Oriental Plaza has had many problems besides the difficulties in evicting McDonald's. *Last "Take-Away" for Beijing McDonald's*, Agence France Presse, Dec. 2, 1996, at International News. The project had to be re-submitted for approval because the local Beijing government had not gotten the final approval from the State Council, which is part of China's central government. *China Moves Earth to Save Beijing Relics at Oriental Plaza Site*, Agence France Presse, Nov. 27, 1994, at International News. Initially, the architectural blueprint exceeded height regulations. The revised plans that were approved by the State Council in May of 1996 will cover approximately 8.2 million square feet, of which 2.8 million square feet will be below ground level. *Last "Take-Away" for Beijing's McDonald's*, Agence France Presse, Dec. 2, 1996, at International News.

About a month after the eviction, excavation crews found 20,000-year-old stone tools and fossilized bone fragments 40 feet below the ground of the former McDonald's restaurant. A university professor stated, "This is the first time Paleolithic artefacts have been found in Beijing." As a result, the Oriental Plaza project was delayed to allow for more archaeological excavations. *20,000-Year-Old Relics Found Under Beijing's McDon-*

ald's Site, Agence France Presse, January 5, 1997, at International News. But the delay was for a good cause. Developer Li Ka-shing agreed to build a 4,300 square foot museum underneath the giant complex in order to provide a home for the artifacts. This agreement was reached after construction was temporarily halted due to protests from several academics requesting that the Stone Age remains be protected. *Delay-Plagued Oriental Plaza Gets Underway in Beijing Again*, Agence France Presse, May 6, 1997, at Financial Pages.

Besides the evicted McDonald's restaurant, as of September 1997, the 34 other McDonald's outlets in Beijing were all forced to pay legal and illegal fees to the local government. Daniel J. Curtin, Jr. & Christine M. Treat, *Land Use in the People's Republic of China*, 21 State & Local L. News 3 (Summer 1998) (ABA state and local government law section newsletter); Ian Johnson, *Fees to Go? McDonald's Pays in Order to Stay in Beijing*, Asian Wall Street Journal, Sept. 8, 1997, at sec. A page 21 col. 1; Joe McDonald, *They Deserve a Break Today: Government Soaks McDonald's, Mayor's Report Shows*, Pasadena Star-News, Sept. 10, 1997, at B4 (including fees for "spiritual civilization"). Such fees pay for repairing air-raid shelters and spreading Communist Party propaganda. Daniel J. Curtin, Jr. & Christine M. Treat, *Land Use in the People's Republic of China*, 21 State & Local L. News 3 (Summer 1998) (ABA state and local government law section newsletter, noting that propaganda involved telling the Chinese people to be more gracious) ; Ian Johnson, *Fees to Go? McDonald's Pays in Order to Stay in Beijing*, Asian Wall Street Journal, Sept. 8, 1997, at sec. A page 21 col. 1. The propaganda include telling people to be more gracious and to plan their future families. The fees also pay for flowers for city streets, river dredging in a city with only one relatively small river, and employee and public safety activities. Some fees, which are charged in addition to taxes, are not unusual but are excessive. Trash collection charges range from \$600–\$12,000 U.S. dollars per year, \$4.30 per parking space for traffic safety, and \$1.20 per employee for public tree planting. Joe McDonald, *China Puts Bite on McDonald's Fast-Food Chain Must Pay Fees for Flowers, Dredging*, The Toronto Star, Sept. 10, 1997, at sec. Business page B9. Ironically, McDonald's restaurants are partially state-owned companies who must still pay these excessive fees. This mall story is not to be confused with the Changping Shopping Center on the outskirts of Bejing near the Great Wall. Edmund Mander, *Newman Plans 'Great Mall of China,'* Shopping Center Today, Apr. 1997, at 45.

Early vesting can have a negative effect on planning in that some developers may sit on entitlements and permits pending a more favorable market, while late vesting may encourage developers to progress diligently. The following excerpt describes how anti-vesting can be used to encourage development:

Mark T. Kremzner, *Managing Urban Land in China: The Emerging Legal Framework and its Role in Development,*

7 Pacific Rim Law & Policy Journal 611 (1998)

The conversion of land into a commodity does not ensure that its productive potential will be harnessed. Owners of land use rights frequently hold land for speculative purposes, lack the capital to develop it, or may be unsure of how and when they want to develop land. This is considered neither desirable nor productive under China's urban land law regime. A survey of national and local legislation as well as central government circulars suggests that productive uses of urban land are those that result in the reclamation or improvement of land and the construction of desirable projects with "high demand," such as affordable housing, manufacturing enterprises, and infrastructure facilities. The emphasis on avoiding waste and using land productively is a norm with a long history in China and continues to be expressed in national and local laws. For example, the 1982 Constitution imposes an affirmative duty on all organizations and individuals to ensure that land is used rationally, and the Land Management Law directs all levels of government to implement policies to develop and rationally use land.

To ensure that land is not wasted or lies idle, there are provisions in several key urban land laws that allow land use rights to be withdrawn by the SLA if development is not undertaken in a timely manner or if it is abandoned. The Land Management Law stipulates that land use rights may be revoked if the land is not used for two successive years according to the approved use. The 1990 Urban Land Use Right Regulations have a slightly different provision and specifies the sanctions that may be imposed. It requires the holder of a land use right to develop or utilize the land in accordance with the schedule and conditions specified in the land use right grant contract (*tudi shiyongchuan churang hetong*). Failure to comply could result in punishment ranging from the issuance of a warning and imposition of a fine to loss of the land use right without compensation. The 1995 Real Estate Law and the Urban Development Procedures revised this approach on discouraging land idleness. Both require development to begin within one year of the start date set forth in the granting contract, otherwise an idle land fee (*tudi xianzhi fei*) equivalent to not more than twenty percent of the original grant fee may be imposed. If development upon granted land does not start within two years of the start date, then the land use rights may be recovered by the state without compensation.

Land speculation has been a particularly troublesome issue for central level authorities. Speculative activities make it difficult for urban planners in the MOC to control development and urban growth, and for authorities in the SLA to control real estate prices in areas adjacent to development projects. Secondly, government authorities, particularly those at the central level, are unable to tap into the revenue from gains earned in speculative deals. Finally, speculation is an activity that is widely associated with the evils and excesses of capitalism. While talk of controlling speculation and terminating the get-rich-quick schemes of real estate developers is politically popular, the results have been less concrete. Many government and Party authorities at all levels have personal or economic interests in land deals. They receive kickbacks or share profits with construction and real estate companies that develop and sell urban properties.

At the 1993 National Land Conference, delegates concluded that fiscal measures should be employed to discourage land speculation and recapture lost revenues. The Land VAT Regulations and accompanying implementing rules impose a progressive tax on the revenue or other consideration realized on the net gain from the assignment or resale of land use rights and other real property. The costs and expenses incurred in "land development," "construction of new buildings," and "obtaining and selling the property" are deductible.

The 1995 Real Estate Law also contains measures to discourage land speculation by barring assignments (i.e. sales, leases, or mortgages) of granted land until at least twenty-five percent of the total amount of investment or contracted development is completed. For large tracts of land where infrastructure is to be installed, all development work agreed to in the land use grant contract must be completed fully before the land use rights may be assigned, unless the land use right grant contract or allocation document provides that development work may proceed in discrete stages. Under the Urban Development Procedures, a commensurate level of funds may be invested for each particular stage of a development project according to the schedule in the grant contract or allocation document. Thus, when a particular stage of a project is completed, it may be assigned.

* * *

Notes and Comments

1. Under American land planning ordinances, permits typically carry a termination date, requiring that substantial work be undertaken within a period of so many days or months. The failure to exercise such rights can require the applicant to proceed again through the permit application process, but where final subdivision approval has been granted and a developer fails to timely commence work under a building permit, the applicant continues to enjoy the vesting of rights granted under state statute or judicial constitutional interpretation, but must comply with any new building permit requirements such as increased administration application fees. Where subdivisions are approved but undeveloped for years, even the earlier vesting rights may expire requiring an entire new subdivision application.

The following chapter looks at the financing of infrastructure to support proposed development. The limits on imposing development conditions on developers is a central issue in the subdivision or other administrative review proceeding leading to development permit.

Chapter 4

The Financing and Development of Infrastructure: Facilities and Services Necessary to Support Development

> Los Angeles may be a reluctant metropolis, but it is not an inadvertent one. The Los Angeles area is a large metropolis today mostly because the fathers of the growth machine built the economic infrastructure required to sustain it—water and power, ports and airports, freeways and railways, and so on. Far superior to that in most other American metropolitan areas, this infrastructure has shaped the growth of the Los Angeles region for decades.
>
> William Fulton, The Reluctant Metropolis 99 (1997)

4. The Marble Road. Even the best planned cities can succumb to a lack of sustainability. Excessive urban sprawl and deforestation led to the loss of access to the sea for Ephesis, Turkey.

Communities must be served with roads, water, electrical power, sewers, libraries, schools, police and fire protection, health care, recreation, parks, flood control, and other services and facilities. When America's suburbs were first built it was believed that property tax revenues would allow the financing of supporting facilities and services. The costs of constructing and maintaining facilities skyrocketed while the ability to raise taxes was politically limited; some states made increased tax revenues a challenge as taxpayers approved measures that restricted the ability to increase property taxes or impose new taxes. In California, voters enacted Proposition 13 which generally capped real property taxes at one percent of value. *See Nordlinger v. Hahn*, 505 U.S. 1 (1992) (Proposition 13 sustained over equal protection claim). Today, most communities believe that new development should finance the cost of expanding the supply of infrastructure and that increased taxation is synonymous with bad government.

Developers are responsible for the improvement and development of the project parcel and where supporting infrastructure is called for, the developer may be required to dedicate land to the local government for a school site, *City of Carbondale v. Brewster*, 398 N.E.2d 829 (Ill. 1979), *appeal dismissed*, 446 U.S. 931 (1980); *Jordan v. Village of Menomonee Falls*, 137 N.W.2d 442 (Wis. 1965), *appeal dismissed*, 385 U.S. 4 (1966), park, *Hoepker v. City of Madison Planning Comm'n*, 563 N.W.2d 145 (Wis. 1997), sewer treatment facility, *Sarasota County v. Taylor Woodrow Homes, Ltd.*, 652 So. 2d 1247 (Fla. Dist. Ct. App. 1995), or for street widening. *Sparks v. Douglas County*, 904 P.2d 738 (Wash. 1995). On-site development conditions may involve reserving land for open space or parks, *In re Denio*, 608 A.2d 1166 (Vt. 1992), as well as to buffer the project from surrounding uses, *Ayers v. City Council*, 207 P.2d 1 (Cal. 1949). The inclusion of amenities including recreational facilities such as athletic fields, tennis, golf, skateboard, or swimming facilities are often planned both for marketing attractiveness to homebuyers as well as land use regulators. The following text describes the two leading United States Supreme Court rulings on development exactions:

First in *Nollan v. California Coastal Commission*, 483 U.S. 825 (1987), the United States Supreme Court restricted the authority of government to impose conditions on discretionary permits, such as subdivision, site-plan, variance, conditional rezoning, and use permit approvals. When the Nollans sought a permit to tear down a small beach bungalow and replace it with a larger home, the coastal commission conditioned the permit on the provision of a lateral easement running north and south on the sandy beach between a sea wall and the home.

As a background to the dispute, California, pursuant to its constitutionally established public trust doctrine, grants the right to the public to use the waters and beaches of the state regardless of ownership. The sea wall erected in front of the Nollan property was designed to halt beach erosion. Below the wall on the seaward side of the wall, the public had access only during low tide for portions of the year. Thus, without the requested easement on the leeward or land side of the wall, the public could not walk along the beach from the public beach on the north to another on the south except for limited times.

According to Justice Scalia, the coastal commission offered three reasons for the permit condition: (1) protecting the public's ability to see the beach, (2) assisting the public in overcoming the "psychological barrier" to using the beach, and (3) preventing congestion on public beaches. In addition, Justice Scalia in fn. 6 identifies what he characterizes as a fourth "made-up" purpose, that of avoiding boundary disputes. Justice Scalia also noted that the commission identified a fifth interest, to advance a comprehensive program to provide continuous public access along the beach. Justice Brennan in his dissent argues in addition that the condition would (6) avoid the reduced public access resulting from restricting visual access, (7) would contribute to resolving the increased need for facilities due to development, including the movement of private development closer to public beach property.

Any discussion of whether the condition denied economically viable use of land was dicta as the Court invalidated the condition for lack of an "essential nexus." What Justice Scalia meant by essential nexus is that the condition must substantially serve a legitimate state police power interest. According to the majority, the first offered interest, protecting the public's ability to see the beach, was simply not served by a lateral easement. Justice Scalia offered in dicta that a condition for the Nollan's to construct and maintain an expensive viewing platform, offering public access would meet the essential nexus test. Justice Scalia simply did not understand how a lateral easement would assist the public in overcoming the "psychological barrier" to using the beach resulting from development, the second offered interest. Justice Scalia did not even address the third interest, implicitly not understanding how an easement would prevent congestion on public beaches. Justice Scalia believed the interest of avoiding boundary disputes to be pretextual. Finally, Justice Scalia apparently rejected the alternate interest of advancing a comprehensive program to provide continuous public access along the beach as it was a tautology: the easement served the interest of having an easement. Justice Brennan's argument that the condition would avoid the reduced public access resulting from restricting visual access, contribute to resolving the increased need for facilities due to development, including the movement of private development closer to public beach property, was ostensibly just another variation on the "psychological barrier" argument rejected by the majority.

The essential nexus standard actually appears identical to the traditional substantive due process standard under the Fourteenth Amendment that looks to whether legislation is arbitrary and capricious or fails to serve a valid police power interest as encountered in Chapter 2 in *Euclid* and *Nectow*. The standard would also appear to be identical to the taking clause "public purpose" inquiry, where the Court defers to legislative findings that a condemnation action serves a legitimate state interest.

Second, in 1994, the Court sought to further refine the constitutional standard in *Dolan v. Tigard*, 512 U.S. 374 (1994). The Dolans applied to the City of Tigard for a permit to reconstruct and double in size their A-Boy Hardware store in Tigard from its current 9,700 square foot structure to one with 17,600 square feet. In addition, the current gravel parking lot would be improved to a paved 39-space lot. A second phase of the project would include an additional structure as a site for additional complimentary businesses and another parking lot enlargement.

The Dolan store sits on a 1.67-acre lot. While the front of the lot is on Main Street, the rear of the lot lies along a creek within a 100-year floodplain.

At issue in the case was the city's condition imposed on the permit that the owner dedicate approximately ten percent of the property along the creek for improvement as a storm drainage system and a pedestrian/bicycle pathway.

First, applying the *Nollan* essential nexus test, the Court had no problem finding that the condition served legitimate interests in protecting against flooding and providing relief to congested streets and parking facilities in the city. There was also no doubt that the redevelopment would generate additional automobile and truck trips and that the parking lot improvement would increase surface water runoff and exacerbate flooding problems.

The Court established standards to assure that the exactions or permit conditions imposed on developers were not extortionate but were related to the need for infrastructure generated by the proposed project.

The Court renamed and adopted the general and near universal rule under prior state law that the conditions imposed bear a rough proportionality to the demand for infrastructure. Second, the regulating agency must make an individualized determination to assure compliance with the rough proportionality standard. The Court refused to adopt either the very demanding Illinois test that the need for the permit condition be uniquely attributable to the proposed project or the deferential reasonable relationship test adopted by a few state courts. The Court renamed the rational nexus, or what it refers to as the reasonable relationship, test as the rough proportionality test for fear that the adopted test would be confused with the Fourteenth Amendment rational basis test.

Although the city estimated that the redevelopment would generate 435 additional trips per day and the Court acknowledged that no precise mathematical calculation is required, the Court wanted additional findings in the record to support the dedication of a pedestrian path. The Court also demanded a quantified estimate of the flood control capacity needed to accommodate the increased runoff and how it related to the extent of the floodplain requested to be dedicated.

The dissent argued that the majority failed to provide deference similar to legislative deference for development review standards and suggested that the majority is reenacting a version of strict substantive due process where the court second guesses the policy decisions of local or state government.

Due to these rather vague judicial rulings, communities are now focusing on impact fees to finance new development. Impact fees typically are computed by taking the cost of each facility improvement and dividing it by the number of dwelling units or square footage of commercial or industrial projects to be served. Impact fees have been used to finance both traditional infrastructure and an ever-wider array of community service needs such as the financing of affordable housing, mass transit, job training, daycare, or the provision of public art. The following decision of the California Supreme Court is an example of judicial application of the United States Supreme Court rulings in *Nollan* and *Dolan*:

Ehrlich v. City of Culver City

Supreme Court of California
911 P. 2d 429 (1996)

ARABIAN, Justice....

Between 1973 and 1975, plaintiff acquired a vacant 2.4-acre lot on Overland Avenue in Culver City and obtained city approval to develop the site as a private tennis club and recreational facility. At plaintiff's request, the city amended its zoning and general plan ordinances governing uses on the property from a split zone R-1 (single family residential) and C-2 (retail commercial) to C-3 (commercial). A specific plan was also adopted by the city providing for the development of a privately operated tennis club and recreational facility. A report prepared by city planning officials in 1974 recommending approval of the development permit recognized that "the need for additional tennis facilities in this city is a real one"; the planning commission resolution recommending approval likewise observed that "[t]he proposed zoning of the property in conjunction with the specific plan will provide a suitably located area within the City for additional tennis club facilities in the form of a private tennis club." From 1975 to 1988, plaintiff alone or through others, operated the sports complex—consisting by then of a swimming pool, five tennis courts, racquetball courts, and weight training and aerobic facilities—on the site.

In 1981, in response to financial losses, plaintiff applied to the city for a change in land use in order to construct an office building on the site; that application was abandoned after the city planning commission recommended against approval on the ground that the existing sports and tennis club provided a needed commercial recreational facility within the city. The club continued in operation under a series of managers until August 1988, when plaintiff closed it as a result of continuing financial losses. The following month, he again applied to the city for an amendment to the general plan, a zoning change and amendment of the specific plan to allow construction of a 30-unit condominium complex valued at $10 million....

...In April 1989, the city decided not to purchase the property. At the same time, the city council disapproved plaintiff's application based on concerns over the loss of a recreational land use needed by the community. In the meantime, plaintiff obtained a demolition permit and tore down the existing site improvements. The still useful equipment, including the tennis court lights, nets, and lockers, he donated to the city.

Following the rejection of his application, plaintiff entered into discussions with members of the city council and city staff in an attempt to restructure the project. He asserts that he was informed the project would not be approved *unless* he agreed to build new recreational facilities for the city. In response, plaintiff apparently raised the possibility of constructing four new municipal tennis courts. During this time period plaintiff filed, but did not serve, a petition for writ of mandate and complaint for damages commencing this lawsuit. Following a closed-door meeting Ostensibly to discuss the pending litigation, the city council voted to approve plaintiff's application conditioned upon the payment of certain monetary exactions. In lieu of the construction of four tennis courts as a condition of approval, the city required the payment of $280,000 "to be used" as stated in the ratifying ordinance, "for additional [public] recreational facilities as directed by the City Council." The minutes of the city council meeting state that the $280,000 fee was to be used "for partial replacement of the lost recreational facilities..." occasioned by the specific plan amendment. The amount of the fee was based upon a city study which showed that the replacement costs for the recreational facilities "lost" as a result of amending the specific plan would be $250,000 to $280,000 for the pool, $135,000 to $150,000 for the paddle tennis courts, and $275,000 to $300,000 for the tennis courts....

...The site was subsequently developed and residential units were sold to the public....

Under this view of the constitutional role of the consolidated "essential nexus" and "rough proportionality" tests, it matters little whether the local land use permit authority demands the actual *conveyance* of property or the *payment* of a monetary exaction. In a context in which the constraints imposed by legislative and political processes are absent or substantially reduced, the risk of too elastic or diluted a takings standard—the vice of distributive injustice in the allocation of civic costs—is heightened in either case....

...[P]laintiff and several supporting amici curiae insist that because the club was a *privately* operated facility, accessible only by dues-paying members, a zoning change withdrawing the parcel from such private recreational use could not have a cognizable *public* impact as a matter of law....

The assumption that, because property is designated for private recreational use, it lacks public value and that its subsequent withdrawal has no public impact is flawed as a matter of logic. Although privately owned and operated, plaintiffs health club was a business establishment, accessible to the public on the payment of a membership fee. The opportunity of Culver City residents to use such private recreational facilities created a *public* benefit by enlarging the availability of such facilities. Without such a facility, residents would have to travel farther, wait longer, and put up with other inconveniences and restricted choices in their recreational pursuits. Thus, the fact that a recreational facility is privately rather than publicly owned does not erase its value to the public....

There thus exists a potential basis *in logic* for a connection between a social need generated by plaintiffs condominium project and the $280,000 mitigation fee imposed by the city....

Applying the Heightened Standard in This Case

We come, then, to the application of the combined *Nollan-Dolan* "essential nexus" and "rough proportionality" test to the facts in the record before us. Like the high court in *Dolan*, we will conclude that, although the city's findings with respect to the relationship between the monetary exaction and the withdrawal of a parcel of land within Culver City restrictively zoned for private recreational use satisfies the essential nexus standard, the present record is inadequate to support the requirement that plaintiff pay a recreational fee of $280,000 for the desired permit. We conclude instead that although the city may be able to justify a monetary exaction in *some* amount, what that figure is we are quite unable to say on this record.

We have no doubt as to the city's legitimate authority to impose development impact fees for park and recreational purposes. Nor is there any genuine dispute that the $280,000 fee, which the city has committed to the purchase of additional recreational facilities, will substantially advance its legitimate interest in correcting a demonstrated deficiency in municipal recreational resources. Unlike *Nollan*, where the high court found no logical connection between the commission's demand for a lateral easement across the owner's property and the purported governmental purpose of enhancing visual access, the "essential nexus" in this case is plain.

We must next decide whether there is a "rough proportionality" between the public impact of the land use change and the recreational fee. The *Dolan* court, in an effort to balance the government's legitimate need to impose reasonable exactions against the property owner's right to be free of undue burdens, formulated an intermediate standard of review and a corresponding evidentiary burden on local government. "[G]eneralized statements as to the necessary connection between the required dedication and the proposed development" are constitutionally insufficient, according to the court. As noted, however, the *Dolan* majority also rejected the claim that the government "demonstrate that its exaction is directly proportional to the specifically created need" as being more than the Fifth Amendment demands.

In both *Nollan* and *Dolan*, the court conceded that the development project at issue would have negative effects that the city could mitigate using its police power. It found insufficiently substantial, however, the connection between those effects and the required public dedications. Similarly, the record before us in this case is devoid of any individualized findings to support the required "fit" between the monetary exaction and the loss of a parcel zoned for commercial recreational use. The city argues that its $280,000 recreation fee is warranted as partial compensation for the loss of some $800,000 in recreational improvements that were formerly located on plaintiffs property. But in this case it is error to measure the lost recreational benefits by the lost value of plaintiffs health club. The loss which the city seeks to mitigate by levying the contested recreational fee is not the loss of any particular recreational facility, but the loss of property reserved for private recreational use....

...The city may not constitutionally measure the magnitude of its loss, or of the recreational exaction, by the value of facilities it had no right to appropriate without payment.

This is not to say, however, that *some* type of recreational fee imposed by the city as a condition of the zoning and related changes cannot be justified. The amount of such a fee, however, must be tied more closely to the actual impact of the land use change the city granted plaintiff. Although we are unable to discern, on this record, the precise value or the economic cost of these impacts, several possibilities suggest themselves. One such possibility is likely to be the additional administrative expenses incurred in redesignating other property within Culver City for recreational use. The city's director of human services, who opposed the abandonment of a recreational use restriction on plaintiffs property, stated that to "permit this type of recreational development elsewhere would...involve arduous and costly rezoning and public hearings." It would be reasonable to require plaintiff to contribute toward defraying these anticipated rezoning costs, so that the city does not have to bear them itself or pass them along to future private developers seeking to construct recreational facilities.

More generally, the city's approval of plaintiffs condominium project may have given rise to public costs in the form of a diminished ability to attract private recreational development. If the city can show that it would have to incur greater costs to attract a developer of suitable private recreational facilities because plaintiffs parcel is no longer reserved for such a recreational use, it may consider these costs to be a part of the impact of plaintiffs project, and would be constitutionally permitted to impose such an exaction. Such a fee would enable the city to induce private health club development by offering monetary incentives roughly proportional to the land use incentive it relinquished when it removed the recreational use restriction from plaintiffs property.

Of course, the city could not constitutionally require plaintiff to dedicate the same amount of land for *public* recreational facilities. It could, however, require plaintiff to transfer, so to speak, the restricted land use designation at the Overland site to a comparable parcel plaintiff owns within the city, thus returning the city to the status quo as it existed prior to approval of the condominium project, that is, with a similar parcel of vacant land reserved for recreational use as an inducement to the development of private recreational facilities. If the city decides, however, that such a restricted land use transfer is impracticable, it may surely levy an in-lieu exaction to accomplish the same objective. Such a fee would serve the same purpose as do all development fees: providing the city with a means of escaping the narrow choice between denying plaintiff his project permit altogether or subordinating legitimate public interests to plaintiff's development plans....

Kennard, Justice, concurring and dissenting....

I dissent from the judgment insofar as it concludes that a city may impose a mitigation fee for the "loss" of private recreation facilities when property on which such facilities were located is redeveloped for a different use....

Because Ehrlich's proposed construction of 30 townhouses on his land would have increased the community's housing stock and thus the number of its residents, City could reasonably impose a fee to offset the increased demand on public recreational facilities attributable to the increase in population resulting from the development. City did exactly this by imposing a $30,000 "parkland" fee....

The $280,000 recreational mitigation fee that City imposed on Ehrlich was designed not to offset the increased demand on public recreational facilities caused by the addition of 30 residential units, but instead to compensate for the "loss" of the private recreational club that had previously existed on the property. The distinction is crucial.

* * *

Notes and Comments

1. Prior to *Dolan*, states adopted various tests to judge the reasonableness of development permit conditions and exactions. They ranged from the highly deferential "reasonableness" standard attributed to California, *Associated Home Builders v. City of Walnut Creek*, 484 P.2d 606 (Cal. 1971); *Grupe v. California Coastal Comm'n*, 212 Cal. Rptr. 578 (Ct. App. 1985), to the least deferential test associated with Illinois, whereby the need for the condition had to be uniquely attributed to the landowner's project. *Pioneer Trust & Sav. Bank v. Mount Prospect*, 176 N.E.2d 799, 802 (Ill. 1961). Whatever test adopted by different states, whether it was called a nexus, reasonable nexus, or reasonableness, most courts demanded some rational basis or debatable basis to say that the development generated a need for the exaction.

2. While some courts continue to wonder whether impact fees are subject to *Dolan* review, *Homebuilders Ass'n v. City of Scottsdale*, 930 P.2d 993, *cert. denied*, 521 U.S. 1120 (1997); *Ehrlich, supra.*, others continue to review fees under state statutory or court-established standards. In *St. Johns County v. Northeast Fla. Builders Ass'n*, 583 So. 2d 635 (Fla. 1981), the Florida Supreme Court, prior to *Dolan*, applied what has come to be called the "dual nexus" test in reviewing a school impact fee. The county established the fee program that charged each new single-family home $448 for the building of new schools. The fee was based on a study prepared by an expert that estimated the number of children likely to reside in the homes planned for the county. Based on an estimate of 0.44 children per household and estimating that each new home generated the need for $2,899 in new school capacity based on the number of housing units and the costs of school construction needed to accommodate the projected population, and by deducting $2,451 reflecting existing taxes and revenue sources available, the calculation resulted in the set impact fee.

The developer in *St. Johns* challenged the fee on four bases. First, that as many homes would have no children attending public school, that the fee was in fact a tax that had not met the state standards for imposition of taxes. The court rejected this argument as the fee was based on the capacity to serve the educational needs of the entire county and homes received that benefit whether the service was utilized or not. Similarly, homes enjoyed fire services whether they suffered a fire or never had the occasion to call the fire department.

The second challenge was based on the claim that the school impact fee violated the state constitutional guarantee of free public schools. The court rejected the claim finding that the provision does not mean that parents are exempt from paying any costs of maintaining public schools. Traditionally, schools are funded primarily through local property taxes assessed on property owners.

Third, the developer claimed that the local impact fee ordinance was preempted under state law. The court found adequate power to enact the impact fee within the home rule powers enjoyed by local government in Florida.

Finally, the court rejected a claim that the raising of impact fee revenues and turning them over to the school district constituted an unlawful delegation of power. The court rejected the claim, finding that the fundamental policy decisions are made by the county with the discretion of the school board sufficiently limited.

There are several other requirements of valid impact fee programs that are mentioned or suggested by the decision in *St. Johns*. First, the fee ordinance must be imposed throughout the county and may not be imposed only in a section of the school district. This is a requirement of uniformity that may be established in many jurisdictions. Second, the revenues collected under the impact fee ordinance must be earmarked and the funds must be timely expended or refunded.

A question not yet addressed by the courts is what happens when the next level of infrastructure expansion capacity exceeds current demand generated by the project? What should be the responsibility of the developer? Where a new elementary school is required to accommodate the anticipated population increase and a development that would generate but half the demand for classrooms, *Dolan* would suggest that the developer cannot be required to finance the entire school. In jurisdictions allowing a denial of the plat or permit for inadequate school capacity, the developer may have to suffer a project denial, be required to scale back the project to be within existing school capacity, or enter into a voluntary arrangement whereby the developer would fund the expansion with an agreement of the school district or regulating governmental unit to reimburse the developer as additional developments are subsequently approved and school exactions or impact fees collected. Similarly, whether a city demands one acre of open space for every 1,000 occupants of a development or five acres would appear to reflect a policy determination established under local regulatory and master planning. Of course state legislation can preempt such a determination.

A second requirement of valid impact fee programs that are mentioned or suggested by the decision in *St. Johns*, is that the revenues collected under the impact fee ordinance must be earmarked in a separate fund for the purpose of school construction and may not be placed in a fund with general revenues. The commingling with general tax revenues could result in invalidation as the fee would be characterized as a tax.

Finally, the impact fee revenues must be expended within a set limited period of time for the purposes collected or refunded to the developer. Under the county ordinance, the fees had to be expended within six years.

Despite a history of individualism in approaching land use regulation, there has been a virtually unbroken pattern of state courts and legislatures simply adopting *Dolan* as the sole standard for the validity of permit conditions. Perhaps the greatest impact of *Dolan* is the generation of uniform standards on permit conditions, providing greater predictability and a richer developed jurisprudence. Other than the outcome in *Nollan* and

Dolan, however, it is not possible to point to the results of reported cases and see a different outcome from application of the prior state standards. *See also Homebuilders Ass'n v. City of Beavercreek*, 729 N.E.2d 349 (Ohio 2000) (following the Florida model).

3. Another vehicle for financing infrastructure is the special assessment. *Holmes v. Concord Fire Dist.*, 625 So. 2d 811 (Ala. Civ, App. 1993). Under the special assessment, landowners are charged a fee for a period of years equal to the cost of retiring bonds used to front the costs of capital improvements. *Bauer v. City of Olathe*, 894 P.2d 823 (Kan. 1995). At one time most suburban communities used assessments to finance new schools, parks, fire stations, and other facilities. The scheme has become less popular because creation of the district is voluntary and the assessments added to mortgage, tax, insurance, and maintenance obligations makes assessments unattractive to neighborhoods and home purchasers. *See generally* 1 James A. Kushner, Subdivision Law and Growth Management §6:33 (2d ed. 2001); Marc N. Melnick, *New Avenues for Special Assessment Financing*, 25 Urb. Law. 539 (1993).

4. A variation on the traditional special assessment district is the facilities benefit assessment district, endorsed in *J.W. Jones Companies v. City of San Diego*, 203 Cal. Rptr. 580 (Ct. App, 1984). San Diego County sought to plan for adequate infrastructure in the generally undeveloped county area and to shift the primary burden of financing facilities to developers and new residents. The financing device created to implement the county's comprehensive plan was the Facilities Benefit Assessment. Challenging the use of the FBA was the developer of North University City an area to be developed with 23,130 residential units with 698 acres of commercial and industrial uses. Based on an estimated $55 million for streets and parks, nearly $27 million would be charged to the developer and approximately the same amount would be raised through the FBA. The remaining amount, just under $2 million, would be paid by the city and other sources. The developer made several legal challenges to the FBA: (1) As the charge was made to recoup the cost of public improvements made to specially benefit the property, the court found that the FBA was not a tax or assessment subject to Proposition 13 which would have required super-majority referendum approval by voters, (2) The court rejected an equal protection claim based on the exemption of already developed properties, as the court found such properties not similarly situated for they did not generate the need for the new proposed facilities. All undeveloped properties were treated similarly with an FBA assessment.

The FBA differs from the traditional special assessment in several respects.

a. The tradition assessment is charged to properties specially benefitted based either on an allocation to owners based on the front footage of the parcel in relation to the total frontage in the benefitted district or the percentage of assessed valuation of each parcel. Under the FBA, the assessment is equally divided between each dwelling unit.

b. Under the traditional special assessment, payments are made annually over a period, such as ten years, to pay off bonds sold to finance the facility. Under the FBA, the assessment is paid at the time of building permit application. By comparison, if the financing technique was an impact fee, the fee might be due upon subdivision approval. Under the FBA, the develop can await market demand for units and avoid the higher carrying costs associated with impact fees.

c. Unlike the traditional special assessment, the scheme does not consider the location of an assessed parcel and thus proximity and contiguity to the facility is not essential.

d. Under the traditional special assessment all properties benefitted are equitably assessed for the benefit enjoyed. Under the FBA, developed properties are exempt. Although a court might treat an FBA in a developed community differently, in the generally undeveloped community in *J.W. Jones*, no defect was found.

The FBA is similar to the traditional special assessment in that funds collected are earmarked and spent solely for the purpose for which the assessment was imposed. Both are enforced through lien foreclosure.

5. Mello-Roos bond-financed assessment districts are similar to traditional special assessment districts in that the assessments are not charged at the time of building permit application but paid over a multi-year period along with property taxes. Thus, the device is not as unpopular with developers who avoid the front-end fees and are able to price homes at a lower more competitive level. Buyers, however, are often very unhappy when they realize the real monthly home payment costs include taxes, insurance, mortgage insurance premiums, and now special assessments. Paul S. Clark & Janet T. Davidson, *The Mello-Roos Community Facilities Act of 1982: A Flexible Tool For Financing Infrastructure Improvements in Newly Developing Areas*, 10 Cal. Real Prop. J. 19 (Summer 1992).

6. *BIDs*. A variation on the special assessment district is the Business Improvement District, or "BID." BIDs are typically undertaken as a mini-redevelopment strategy to enhance the attractiveness of commercial districts. Rather than placing administration within an existing or newly created governmental service district, BIDs are administered by private, non-profit boards made up of district business owners. BIDs allow businesses in a specific neighborhood to increase the level of services provided by government. The BID might provide additional security, valet parking, or maintenance, as well as the "calming" of streets, expansion of public pedestrian spaces, installation of attractive lighting, or widening of sidewalks for landscaping and outdoor cafes and dining. Traffic "calming" refers to strategies to reduce automobile traffic. In Europe, calming is often connected to making streets available for pedestrians. Suzanne H. Crowhurst Lennard & Henry L. Lennard, Liveable Cities 98 (1987) (Dutch "Woonerf" not so much an auto-free policy as a traffic reduction or calming scheme often calling for the mixed use of streets by pedestrians, children, and residents' automobiles); Eran Ben-Joseph, *Changing the Residential Street Scene: Adapting the Shared Street (Woonerf) Concept to the Suburban Environment*, 61 J. Am. Plan. A. 504 (1995). *See also* Donald Appleyard, Liveable Streets (1981). BIDs are often authorized by statute. *E.g.*, Cal. Sts. & High. Code §§36601–36651; *Foote Clinic, Inc. v. City of Hastings*, 580 N.W.2d 81 (Neb. 1998). *See generally* Richard Briffault, *A Government for Our Time? Business Improvement Districts and Urban Governance*, 99 Colum. L. Rev. 365 (1999); David J. Kennedy, *Restraining the Power of Business Improvement Districts: The Case of the Grand Central Partnership*, 15 Yale L. & Pol'y Rev. 283 (1996) (BIDs can be used to generate profits for business and cause gentrification, which may displace or exclude the less wealthy and adversely affect adjacent areas or the larger community without citizen or area resident participation); Daniel R. Garodnick, Comment, *What's the BID Deal? Can the Grand Central Business District Serve a Special Limited Purpose*, 148 U. Pa. L. Rev. 1733 (2000). The BID is responsible for turning Times Square around. Josh Getlin, *Ball Has Dropped on Seedy Times Square—Renovation: New Yorkers Agree Area is Now Safer, but They're Torn Over Whether it's Better*, Los Angeles Times, Dec. 30, 1998, at A1.

The following excerpt discusses infrastructure finance in The Netherlands as compared to the American experience:

George Lefcoe, *When Governments Become Land Developers: Notes on the Public-Sector Experience in the Netherlands and California*,

51 Southern California Law Review 165 (1978)

.... Customarily, American cities use one of five means of paying for public works. First, some jurisdictions "pay as they go" by utilizing current tax revenues even for major public improvements. Wary of debt, they only build what they can afford in the building year. Economists criticize the use of current revenues for anything other than current operating expenses on the theory that if an improvement has a long life, it should be financed over that life for two reasons. First, the jurisdiction's books better reflect its actual wealth position when payments for long-term improvements are also long-term. Second, debt financing shifts the burden of payment from taxpayers in the year of construction to taxpayers likely to benefit from the project over its entire life. In any event, the debate over this type of financing has become moot since very few jurisdictions have the financial capacity these days to cover long-term investments out of current tax receipts.

Second, some cities finance construction projects through general obligation bonds. These bonds pledge the full faith and credit of the municipality to the bondholders and are usually paid out of the general fund.

Third, there are revenue bonds. For repayment, revenue bondholders must look only to the net income of a particular project, usually the one for which bonds are floated in the first place.

Fourth, special assessments are used to finance capital improvements. For Street lighting or the undergrounding of utility wires, many jurisdictions form a special district and levy an assessment against properties in that district on the theory that since these properties are benefitted in a special way by the public improvement, they ought to be burdened with its debt. Redevelopment area improvements are seldom, if ever, financed in this way for two reasons. First, in a depressed area further taxes work an even greater hardship on already hard-pressed property owners. Second, the redevelopment improvements often do nothing to benefit property in its existing use. Redevelopment improvements usually contemplate widespread demolition of currently existing structures in favor of new land uses. Trying to support such assessments legally would be difficult when site values for the proposed new land uses are uncertain at best.

Fifth, there are "hybrid" bonds, securities that merge the characteristics of general and revenue bonds. For example, the bonds issued by local housing authorities are supported primarily out of housing authority revenues (subsidy contracts with the federal government) and also carry, as a back-up, the full faith and credit guarantee of the federal government to hold bondholders harmless against loss.

Finally, there is tax increment financing. When a redevelopment plan is officially adopted by a local government, the property values within the project area are ascertained. In each succeeding year property taxes are levied as before, for the benefit of all taxing agencies. The assessed values, as they appeared on the tax rolls in the year before the project boundary was established, are multiplied by whatever tax rate the local government mandates for the city as a whole. As values rise in the project area, property owners are taxed on the increased value just as they would be if their properties were located outside it. The increment in tax yield attributable to any increase in assessed values may be utilized, however, by the redevelopment agency to support bonded indebtedness incurred to improve the project area....

Haagse Beemden (*Hedged Meadows*)

....This case study starts with the plan as a given and explores how municipalities finance their expansion plans. Specifically, this case study will examine: what types of off site improvements (roads, parks, schools) are included when a Dutch municipality develops pursuant to a *bestemmingsplan*; how the costs of these improvements are allocated between the project area and the municipality as a whole; how the costs are divided among prospective land uses within the project area; and who bears the deficit if land uses within the area cannot support the level of cost assigned to them.

The *Haagse Beemden* (Hedged Meadows) development area in the town of Breda contemplates 14,000 dwellings for 43,600 inhabitants on an area of 831 hectares[258] to be built over a 19-year period—quite an expansion for a town of fewer than 120,000. The plan provides for a regional shopping center, neighborhood centers, and housing of all types (one-family, row, and multi-family). It also contemplates medical facilities, schools, parks, churches, and a community center. Indeed, within its boundaries there is room for every urban land use need; only industrial facilities are left out of this planned development zone.

How does a locality in the Netherlands determine the mix of public and private land uses at a site, the kinds and quality of public facilities to be provided, and the amount of open space to be reserved for parks and roads? To some extent we may assume that the more experienced town planning departments "work backward" by estimating the price they might be able to realize for various types of developed land and then making sure all public facilities costs can be supported from those proceeds. But we can also assume that the very rationale for a local government's embarking upon a development scheme is to set aside land for middle-income housing and for certain types of public amenities.

Dutch municipalities have considerable discretion in deciding what kinds of infrastructure are needed, but they are often guided by planning standards prepared by the National Institute for Physical Planning and Housing. Thus, for example, for every 1000 low-rise or one-family dwelling units and every 4000 high-rise multi-family units the Institute recommends one elementary school containing twelve classrooms on a lot of 5000 square meters. For every 8.5 elementary schools, one school is supposed to have a swimming pool. For each new resident, two square meters of space are to be reserved for service stations and auto repair garages.

Although few localities follow these standards in minute detail, most towns use them as a rule of thumb. The unfortunate result is that many urban expansion plans seem to be cut from the same mold. Each neighborhood contains space for exactly the same functions as are provided in every other neighborhood. In the United States our proliferation of autonomous local school districts has given us somewhat more variety in school design and location, but this is more than offset by our ubiquitous private-sector chain stores—from K-Mart to McDonald's.

258. 831 hectares is approximately 2000 acres.

Within each municipality, Dutch expansion areas are often uniform in appearance because the city itself is responsible for installing all infrastructure, from paving the roads to landscaping the fire station. Efficiency and predictability argue for a high degree of repetition in the design of all public facilities.

Private Dutch contractors argue that cities could save money and look less alike by allowing the private sector to do the work of grading, filling, paving, landscaping, and the like. If the contractors are right, these putative savings would often be sizable. The cost of making land ready for development—especially in the populous western part of the country—can run as much as twenty times the acquisition cost of farm or undeveloped acreage. These *bouwrijpmaken* costs are high because the water table is high—only sixty centimeters below the land in some cases. According to some commentators, the reason that much of Holland's "green heart" remains agricultural is not because of extraordinary farm productivity or stringent land use controls; it is simply due to the high cost of developing on wet land.

Local government officials are mindful of the challenge of the private sector, but often remain unpersuaded to contract the task away because they fear private contractors do shoddy work, leaving the municipality later with the task of repairing sidewalks that buckled badly or streets so unstable that they come to resemble roller coasters. Few private contractors have been willing, thus far, to meet the municipal challenge by promising to correct defects should they appear years after construction is completed.

Also important is whether the costs are allocated to the project area or to the entire municipality or are shared partly within the district or partly without. In most localities costs are either borne by the planned area or picked up in whole or in part by the municipality. But in Breda the costs of some public works are apportioned among adjoining project areas when the facilities are to be shared by those areas.

Breda makes an allocation for the costs of holding land, presumably based on the interest rate it would have to pay on borrowed capital. It attributes no cost to lost property taxes, however. This omission scarcely matters in the Netherlands where property tax rates are negligible and farms are entirely exempt from the tax. Were Breda located in California, the foregone property tax revenues (at something like twenty percent of gross income) would be less readily dismissed from a calculation of the opportunity cost of holding land.

Another aspect of cost allocation peculiar to Holland concerns sewage treatment. Since 1969, when the Surface Water Pollution Act was adopted, water polluters pay fees in accordance with the amount and type of waste material they are expected to discharge. These fees are used for the construction and maintenance of new and improved sewage treatment plants, and they are the only revenue source that the town will allow to be used for sewage treatment facilities. The Crown has prohibited municipalities from assessing the capital costs of sewage facilities—except for trunk lines and hookups—to any other land user or private developer. Strict adherence to the "polluter pays" principle has resulted in polluters polluting less than was originally expected. Rather than pay the tax, they have cut down on their waste discharges. As a consequence, the Dutch seem to have overbuilt their sewage treatment facilities because their planning assumed a continuation of prepollution tax discharge levels.

The final step in the cost-allocating process is the apportionment of costs among the various types of land users. The city must allocate its costs, roughly 65 Dfl. (Dutch florin) / square meter, to that portion of the land area to be sold for development, approximately 4.25 million square feet. Land retained by the Town Public Works Department is dedicated free of charge to the city; its proportionate share of the *bouwrijpmaken* tab is shifted to other land users in the area. Not *all* publicly owned sites in the project are carried on this cost-free basis—only the parks, plazas, parking areas, streets, sidewalks, and bike paths are financed in such a way. Other public or quasi-public users pay, including schools, churches, medical centers, and neighborhood centers. But these are subsidized by the expansion plan to some degree; they pay 90% of the weighted average land cost, 90% of 66 Dfl./square meter [editor's note—About $30 or 30 Euro divide Guilder by two], or 59 Dfl./square meter. Land to be used for athletic fields, playgrounds, folk gardens, and cemeteries are marked at 28 Dfl./square meter—an even better break.

These below-cost prices are sustained largely from the sale of land for a regional shopping center. The center pays 197 Dfl./square meter-2.75 times actual cost. Neighborhood retailers are billed 98 Dfl./square meter—1.5 times actual cost.

The land use implications of this pricing system would be immediately clear to any American suburbanite visiting a recently built Dutch suburb for the first time. For example, there is never more than one regional shopping center in each marketing area. Americans are accustomed to seeing stiff competition among regional shopping centers. In addition, there is more open space—bike paths are everywhere, as are plazas and parks. In many American cities a bike path is, more often than not, just a line painted on a highway three feet from the curb—a suicide lane at busy intersections. In Dutch suburbs bike paths often run through parks and can be used to navigate to almost any point in town. It would seem fair to conclude that the Dutch have conferred a limited-area monopoly and exacted a monopoly land price from the shopping center developer that they use to underwrite the costs of open space.

* * *

Notes and Comments

1. Contrast the American system of infrastructure finance with that of The Netherlands. Is one system superior? Is the American system and the Dutch system hiding who exactly pays for improvements? What is the most equitable way to distribute municipal services and raise the costs of system administration? Does the Dutch system argue for land banking by local government?

2. Would the Dutch system of having commercial developers subsidize housing and supporting infrastructure pass scrutiny in the United States? Under *Dolan*? *Cf. Volusia County v. Aberdeen*, 760 So. 2d 126 (Fla. 2000) (refusal to permit school impact fee imposition on housing restricted to senior citizens). Does the city's land ownership permit setting prices and avoiding the appearance of an exaction? Although taking arguments are often technical, establishing a unique jurisprudence, there are other clauses where the Court has not allowed form to control over substance. In *South-Central Timber Dev., Inc. v. Wunnicke*, 467 U.S. 82 (1984), the State of Alaska sold timber conditioned on the buyer having the timber milled in the state. The challenger claimed that the in-state preference violated the commerce clause. The state argued that as the state was the seller that it enjoyed a "market participant" exemption. The Supreme Court ruled that the ability to impose conditions on the timber buyer allowed the Court to treat the state as if it were a market regulator. Could it be argued that the sale of city land, presumably at a price in excess of market price, or where the sale is conditioned on buyer exactions or expensive conditions be treated as a permit condition under *Dolan*?

Great Britain and Wales offer another view of developer-funded infrastructure with which to compare to the United States experience:

Shelley Ross Saxer, *Planning Gain, Exactions, and Impact Fees: A Comparative Study of Planning Law in England, Wales, and the United States,*

32 Urban Lawyer 21 (2000)

A large discount store chain, Company X, decides to build a new superstore in a suburban community located within commuting distance from an urban employment center. Company X conducts studies of the local demographics and determines that the income level and age of the population will support a decent profit margin after land purchase and capital improvements. Hearing that Company X is targeting this particular community, competing Company Y conducts its own study and also discovers that this particular county is an attractive area for new development. However, the two largest cities located in this county have differing views about new development. City 1 is anxious to promote new land development projects, while City 2 is a slow growth community seeking to preserve open space, agriculture, and a rural living style. Both cities realize that new development will generate tax revenue and jobs, but they also realize that new development will require additional infrastructure, such as sewers, roads, sidewalks, police and fire services, schools, libraries, etc. Who should bear the burden of these new infrastructure needs, and how should they fit into the planning process? Historically, these external costs fell on the community, while the development benefits accrued only to the developer, investors, and landowner. Increasingly, in both the United States and in England and Wales, private land developers, rather than public agencies, are bearing these externalities. This article explores the issues that arise when governments shift the burden of these externalities back on the developer and compares the processes by which the United States and England and Wales have attempted to accomplish this shift in externalities.

Externalities exist where someone makes a decision to use a resource without taking into account the full effects of the particular activity because some of the costs fall on others and are external to the decision maker. For example, the developer may not take into account infrastructure needs when conducting its project cost accounting to determine sales or leasing prices. Therefore, the entire community will, necessarily, subsidize the developer and the developer's targeted consumer. Because the community may bear the burden of these externalities, local governments have had to struggle with the financial pressures associated with new development. In each country, local governments may feel the financial pressure to permit new development as a way of increasing local revenues, while avoiding increases to local taxes in order to finance continuing infrastructure needs.

To deal with these externalities, communities in the United States and England and Wales have attempted to restrict development or force the developer to internalize the externalities in exchange for development permission. U.S. jurisdictions use exactions, impact fees, and, sometimes, linkage fees to transfer the burden of adverse development impacts to the developer. England and Wales use the concept of planning gain to extract planning conditions or planning obligations from developers before granting development rights. Planning gain is a term applied whenever, in connection with a grant of planning permission for development, the local planning authority seeks to impose on the developer an obligation to carry out works not included in the development for which planning permission has been sought or to make some payment or confer some extraneous right or benefit in return for permitting development to take place.[6]

The term "planning gain" has been applied to both legitimate government planning processes and to questionable government attempts to extract benefits from developers, not necessarily related to the burdens imposed by the development, but which are instead "the price of planning permission." Because of the high level of government involvement in this process of accounting for development externalities, public and private abuse is a concern in the United States and in England and Wales. In the United States, we continue to search for a definition of what constitutes a regulatory "taking" of private property under the Fifth Amendment, while in England and Wales "here is scope both for unhealthy collusion between planning authorities and large developers and for planning authorities to make developers provide benefits as a condition of planning permission in a way which would not stand examination by the Secretary of State."

Marketplace competition may be one way to control public abuse by restricting government regulation and relying on the market to distribute the benefits and burdens of land development. However, such market forces among developers are more likely to occur in England and Wales, where land development opportunities are limited, than in the United States....

In contrast to the competition that occurs in England and Wales, market competition for land development in the United States is more likely to occur among municipalities than private developers. In the United States, municipalities compete for tax revenue and attempt to avoid the externalities by shifting them to a nearby municipality or forcing the developer to internalize any infrastructure burdens. Recently, several U.S. scholars have proposed that government zoning regulation be limited through market-oriented approaches to land-use management such as common-law nuisance and restrictive covenants. Nevertheless, in current U.S. law and practice "the very 'localness' of local government means that there is no concept of equalisation of revenues and resources between local authorities, such as is practised in England and Wales." The British government has recently committed itself to giving the market more of a role in land-use planning with the 1998 publication of a document detailing the changes intended to modernize its planning system.... The government now appears to accept the view that "market forces are distorted if commercial developments are not required to bear their own external costs."

Difficult legal issues arise in these countries when the government acts to distribute development burdens. In the United States, the legitimacy of government practices is resolved based on the federal constitution, specifically the Fifth Amendment's prohibition against the "taking" of property without just compensation, the Equal Protection Clause, substantive due process, as well as by reference to differing state laws and state constitutions. In England and Wales, the misuse of planning authority is controlled by reference to guidance papers published by the Secretary of State for the Environment, the Town

6. ... The term has also been defined as "a process under which developers make voluntary contributions to the local planning authority in order to overcome some legitimate planning object to their proposed development." ...

and Country Planning Act 1990, the "section 106 planning obligation" under the section 12 provisions of the Planning and Compensation Act 1991, and judicial restrictions on local planning authority power to impose conditions in exchange for granting permission. However, after the House of Lords' decision in *Tesco Stores, Ltd. v. Secretary of State for the Environment* in 1995, their lordships appear "willing to go further than the U.S. courts would permit in upholding the right of a local planning authority to take into account, when determining a planning application, an offer from a developer that went beyond what was reasonably necessary for the development proposed."...

Land development typically creates additional burdens on the existing infrastructure of the geographic area in which it occurs. If the developer does not internalize these externalities through the use of exactions, impact fees, linkage fees, or planning obligations..., the local geographic constituencies must absorb the adverse effects. These burdens will impact the local authority permitting the development as well as its citizens, who must potentially deal with either an increase in local taxes to improve the infrastructure or a decrease in the service or efficiency of the existing infrastructure. Therefore, local authorities will often condition permission to develop on the developer's willingness to internalize these burdens. However, in the United States a local authority may be limited in its efforts to have the developer internalize these burdens under the "unconstitutional conditions" doctrine. The "unconstitutional conditions" doctrine provides that "even if a state has absolute discretion to grant or deny a privilege or benefit, it cannot grant the privilege subject to conditions that improperly 'coerce,' 'pressure,' or 'induce' the waiver of constitutional rights." This issue arises "whenever a government seeks to achieve its desired result by obtaining bargained-for consent of the party whose conduct is to be restricted." England and Wales have a similar constraint on governmental power when "the requirement to provide a benefit [is] being unilaterally imposed by the planning authority."...

In many instances, the local authorities involved in granting or denying permission for new land development, along with its citizens, will be the only ones affected by the development's impacts. Development may create new infrastructure needs such as roads, traffic signals, sewers, schools, libraries, parks, and other public services. The United States and England and Wales attempt to make the developer realize and internalize these costs or impacts when proposing new development. For example, in England and Wales, and in some parts of the United States, developers may be required to consider impacts on affordable housing needs and employment training when a developer changes a site from an industrial use to a replacement use, such as a superstore. In addition, a developer may be required to offset negative impacts by providing a benefit to the community. A controversial case in England, *R. v. Westminster City Council, ex p. Monahan*,[39] involved the demolition of historical buildings in Covent Garden to make way for new offices. The Westminster City Council gave permission for this development in order to generate funds to rehabilitate the nearby Royal Opera House. The Council's action was upheld by the High Court following the Covent Garden Community Association's challenge. Another case in England, *R. v. Plymouth City Council ex p. Plymouth and South Devon Co-operative Society*,[42] allowed the planning authority to consider the provision of a bird hide and a tourist center as benefits that could be used

39. [1990] 1 Q. B. 87.
42. [1993] 67 P. & C.R. 78.

to offset the adverse impact of allowing two superstores to be located in a community where the local plan only allowed for one....

In England and Wales, commentators refer to development impacts and offsets as planning losses and planning gains. Planning loss refers to the structural impact of the development on the community, and planning gain refers to the compensation offered by or required from developers in England and Wales to offset these impacts. Local authorities in the United States use exactions and impact fees to offset these planning losses. Planning gain, exactions, impact fees, and linkage fees are all local government devices requiring developers to internalize the external costs created by new development projects which would otherwise burden the local community and its citizens. "Exactions are requirements that local governments impose as conditions to their grants of permission for a building or subdivision." Admittedly, this process of trading benefits for permission to create adverse impacts may be susceptible to public corruption through abuse of the process. This can be effectively controlled, however, by using the reasonableness principles developed in England and Wales to avoid corruption of the process by the excessive influence of large developers which may outweigh the community's concept of an acceptable development plan....

[I]n England and Wales, a landowner generally has neither the right to develop nor the right to receive compensation for planning restrictions on either new or existing land uses. "Unlike the case in the United States where development rights have been conceptualised as interests in land capable of protection under the constitution, English law does not recognise a "'right' to develop."

In contrast to England and Wales' failure to recognize a landowner's right to develop, some United States authorities and commentators have explicitly referred to the right to develop as one of the sticks in the bundle of property rights....

In the United States and England and Wales, permission to pursue development projects may be conditioned on the developer offering, agreeing, or being required to either restrict the development in some way or to offset any adverse impacts by internalizing the external costs generated by the project. In England and Wales, these restrictions or offsets, popularly referred to as "planning gain," need to be "material considerations" in order to be taken into account in deciding whether to grant planning permission. By examining the degree of the relationship of the "material consideration" to the proposed development's impact and assuring that the decision is reasonable, England and Wales attempt to prevent both private and public abuse of the planning permission process and the planning gain concept. Similarly, the constitutional protection of property rights in the United States limits public abuse of regulatory authority to require developers to internalize external costs through exactions, impact fees, and linkage fees by examining the degree of the relationship between the condition sought and the development's impact. Finally, bargaining between the developer and the local authority is currently protected from abuse by the "material consideration" determination in England and Wales and by the "reserved powers clause" in the United States that prevents local government from bargaining away its police power....

While land-use planning in the United States is a local government function, which varies in nature from state to state, the planning system in England and Wales has national uniformity because of its central government agency, the Department of the Environment. Limited development is permitted "as of right" by national legislation and planning permission applicants have a right of appeal to the Secretary of State. However, local control is dominant in England and Wales, because most "development requires planning permission, and the local authority has wide discretion in deciding whether or not to grant such permission." Although there is, of course, no Fifth Amendment in England and Wales to protect property owners, Parliament is still guided in its legislative action by the principle that "property should not be taken away without compensation." But, similar to the treatment of property rights under the Fifth Amendment, there is generally no right to receive compensation for a diminution in property value when planning permission is denied. Nevertheless, if a "refusal results in the land being 'incapable of reasonable beneficial use in its existing state'" there may be a right to compensation for the existing use value.

The decision to grant or deny planning permission requires local authorities to take into account only material considerations and ensure that the decision is not unreasonable. This principle resembles the U.S. requirement that the state can only use police power to promote legitimate state interests. The test to determine what constitutes a material consideration is whether it serves a planning purpose and whether the planning purpose is one that relates to the character of the use of the land. Local planning authorities must consider the relevant development plan and must give the planning permission application "unbiased consideration on *planning* grounds." Local authorities must also evaluate planning conditions to determine if they are "material considerations" in order to consider them in the grant of planning permissions. A planning condition is valid if it meets the test advanced in the *Newbury* case[231] by fulfilling a planning purpose, being "fairly and reasonably related to the development for which planning permission is granted," and being "clearly reasonable." The Secretary of State, in D.O.E. Circular 11/95 dated July 20, 1995, entitled, "The Use of Conditions in Planning Permissions," states that the power to impose conditions allows development to proceed, when it might otherwise be stopped, but cautions that planning objectives "are best served when the power to add conditions is exercised in such a way that 'the conditions are clearly seen to be fair, reasonable and practicable.'"

When a developer offers to alleviate an adverse impact, the benefit will conform to the local development plan because it directly reduces an undesirable impact. However, when a developer offers to compensate the local community for an adverse impact, considering this offer tends to subvert development plan policies. Some commentators have suggested that deciding whether or not a benefit offered by the developer is a material consideration should depend on "whether it alleviates or compensates for the development's adverse impact." As a proposed reform to the existing planning gain process, this classification would allow the local authority to treat a benefit, which alleviates an adverse impact, as a material consideration. However, if the benefit is intended to compensate the local community for an adverse impact, it would not be considered as material in the planning permission decision unless it is similar enough in kind to the impact. It has also been proposed that local authorities should be allowed to explicitly provide for the acceptance of certain types of compensatory benefits in their development plans. Although these compensatory benefits would still need to be proportionate to the adverse impacts addressed, including them in the local development plan would eliminate a major objection to treating compensatory benefits as material considerations.

Concerns remain that allowing compensatory benefits will permit adverse environmental impacts to occur in exchange for the benefits, and that including them in the development plan merely pushes the "problem of collusion back from the planning application stage to the development plan approval stage." However, in England and Wales,

231. ...Newbury D.C. v. Secretary of State for the Environment [1981] A.C. 578.

as well as in the United States, land-use regulation can be seen as analogous to nuisance law in that both seek to control harm to, or interference with, the property rights of others. In some circumstances, nuisance law allows a land use that constitutes a nuisance to continue, but forces the user to internalize the costs of the nuisance activity by paying damages. Therefore, compensatory benefits or exactions should be allowed in cases where the judiciary would refuse to enjoin nuisance activity, but would require the user to pay damages for the adverse impacts of the activity....

* * *

Notes and Comments

1. Does the arguably more deferential review of British exactions result in a material difference? Is the American land ethic, including the right to develop or exploit one's land generate a different regulatory system? Perhaps politics and the local political system affect the development process so that developers are treated about the same on both sides of the water? Of course a property rights-sensitive United States Supreme Court could prevent individual states from instituting policies that are too communitarian, or designed to promote the public good at the expense of landowners as in *Nollan*.

2. Does the inter-municipality competition to develop tax generating uses and exclude service-consuming non tax-generating LuLus (locally unwanted land uses) argue for the Minneapolis-St. Paul regional tax-sharing concept?

The following excerpt describes a proposal for tax sharing on the regional level:

Note, *Making Mixed-Income Communities Possible: Tax Base Sharing and Class Desegregation*,

114 Harvard Law Review 1575 (2001)

This Note articulates and defends a proposal to regionalize the local property tax to promote greater integration of different income groups within a metropolitan area. Under the current regime, local taxes—particularly the property tax—finance a number of public services, including schools, police, fire protection, and sanitation. It is well known that this system creates dramatic disparities in the level of services different municipalities can afford. However, this Note focuses on another effect of the current regime, namely the powerful incentive for municipalities to prohibit land uses that dilute the local tax base. A wealthy locality will rationally seek to prevent construction of multifamily units and other low-income housing, because the residents of such housing would consume more in local services than they would contribute in taxes.

This fiscal calculus is by no means the only reason that suburban municipalities seek to exclude the poor, but it is one of the most prominent ones. The hostility of wealthy suburbs to low-income residents contributes to poverty concentration in the inner cities and, more recently, in the inner ring of metropolitan suburbs. This geographic isolation creates a self-perpetuating cycle of poverty that compounds the burdens of poverty alone. There are few jobs in the ghetto, and opportunities for economic and educational advancement are limited. Residents of these communities often become socially isolated from the rest of society, both because it is difficult for them to break out, and because nonghetto residents will not move into the decaying neighborhoods.

Policy responses to the plight of the urban poor generally adhere to one of two strategies: enrichment or deconcentration. Enrichment approaches seek to provide direct assistance to the ghetto to combat crime, decrease unemployment, and heal fractured communities. Deconcentration approaches, of which this Note's regional taxation proposal is one, seek to help the poor by increasing their mobility, thus allowing them to escape the ghetto's concentration effect. After all, if concentration effects are strong enough, they may cancel out the benefits of any direct aid to poor communities....

The proposal in this Note also differs from prior attempts to deconcentrate urban poverty. Most past efforts have focused on forcing suburbs to reduce exclusionary zoning—that is, the use of municipal zoning power to prevent the construction of housing suitable for lower-income residents. Due to intense opposition from suburban municipalities, these inclusionary zoning efforts tend to require a complex system of administrative and judicial oversight to ensure that low-income units are actually constructed. However, to the extent that fiscal concerns motivate exclusionary zoning, a system that eliminates the fiscal motive may prompt suburbs to relax their zoning laws voluntarily. Thus, the advantage of this Note's proposal is that, once adopted, it would create an incentive for municipalities to participate more willingly in deconcentrating poverty in the region....

By setting minimum lot sizes and banning multifamily housing, a municipality can effectively screen entrants for socioeconomic status. This practice is known as "exclusionary" zoning because its primary goal is to exclude lower-income persons from the area. "Fiscal" zoning is a type of exclusionary zoning motivated by a desire to preserve or increase a municipality's tax base/local services ratio. Because there are also many nonfiscal reasons for desiring to exclude the poor from one's neighborhood, it is reasonable to suppose that most exclusionary zoning rules are motivated by a mix of fiscal and nonfiscal concerns.

Whatever their motivations, exclusionary zoning rules are often thought to be both damaging to the poor and inefficient. Setting efficiency considerations aside for the moment, there is little doubt that the distributive effects of exclusionary zoning are regressive. In addition to the already-mentioned distributive implications of income segregation, exclusionary zoning has other independent effects on the poor. The restriction of land use to single-family lots, if widespread, dramatically reduces the amount of land available for multifamily construction. This artificial restriction raises the price of unrestricted land, thereby making apartment housing more expensive than it otherwise would be. This increase in price, in turn, forces apartment dwellers to consume less housing as well as to pay more for the housing they do consume. In contrast, the same ban on multifamily housing artificially depresses the price of restricted land, effectively subsidizing single-family homes....

The problem of externalized social costs, the phenomenon of jurisdictional competition, and the inability of municipalities to act in concert are all functions of the fragmentation of regional authority among autonomous jurisdictions. Proponents of fiscal autonomy and exclusionary zoning often argue that such a system enhances efficiency and promotes free choice by allowing individuals to select among different packages of social services from competing municipalities. This argument traces back to an influential article by Charles Tiebout entitled A Pure Theory of Local Expenditure.[60] Tiebout

---

60. Charles M. Tiebout, *A Pure Theory of Local Expenditure*, in Readings in Urban Economics 513 (Matthew Edel & Jerome Rothenberg eds., 1972).

hypothesizes a world in which households are freely mobile and jurisdictions differ in the type and quantity of public services they are best able to provide. To achieve optimal size, jurisdictions compete for households, and households choose among jurisdictions based on the tax rate and the bundle of services that the jurisdictions offer.

Tiebout's model has been widely criticized for its unrealistic assumptions, which limit its applicability to the real world. In particular, critics have demonstrated that the model does not tend toward equilibrium as long as the assumption of free mobility remains in place. Because local revenues are based on taxes rather than some sort of uniform user fee, the wealthy contribute more to local revenues than do the poor residing in the jurisdiction. Thus, the poor always have an incentive to migrate into wealthy jurisdictions, and the wealthy always have an incentive to leave jurisdictions in which poor residents predominate. Without restrictions on mobility, the poor would therefore end up chasing the wealthy from suburb to suburb in an endless game of "musical suburbs." Bruce Hamilton, among others, has addressed this problem by adding exclusionary zoning to the model, an addition that reduces the model's instability by restricting the mobility of the poor and makes the model more reflective of modern-day conditions....

One way to create a system that removes the fiscal incentive to segregate by income would be to pool property taxes from the entire metropolitan area into a common fund, so that no municipality's budget depended on the amount of taxable property within its borders. This Note proposes that the fund be divided among jurisdictions in direct proportion to the share of the regional population that each contains....

Because revenues under the proposal are tied to the population rather than to the tax base, municipalities should be fiscally indifferent to the wealth of entrants into the jurisdiction. Moreover, because the marginal cost of providing a public service decreases as the number of people in the jurisdiction increases, jurisdictions would likely compete for residents. Yet unlike in the competition envisioned by Tiebout, municipalities would seek to attract residents regardless of their income. In this way, the proposed regime will highlight an incentive for economies of scale that is currently obscured by the fiscal advantages of excluding the poor.

Under the new regime, exclusive jurisdictions would have to decide whether to remain exclusive or to begin allowing lower-income housing within their borders. If they choose to remain exclusive, they will be forced to pay for their exclusionary preference with a relatively small public services budget. In response, the wealthy may decide to opt out of the public system of local services and send their children to private schools or hire private security guards to police their streets. They should not be forbidden to do so: it would be sufficient to require them to pay the same amount of local taxes as those who do take advantage of public services. Such a rule would be consonant with current practice, because no one is entitled to withhold taxes for public services he does not consume.

In addition to redistributing property tax revenue from wealthy jurisdictions to poor ones and equalizing their levels of social services, regionalization of the tax base is likely to have important secondary effects on the housing market. First, property values in each municipality are likely to increase or decrease depending on whether the municipality's tax-rate-to-services ratio used to be higher or lower than the regional average. In most metropolitan regions, the standardization of the tax rate will mean that central cities and working-class suburbs will experience a significant decrease in their property tax rate, whereas the tax rate in exclusive suburbs will increase. High-density jurisdictions in and around the urban core will receive a much higher proportion of the regional revenues than will less populous low-density jurisdictions at the periphery of the region. Thus, a rise in property values in poor populous jurisdictions, accompanied by a corresponding decline in suburban property values, would be expected. Although many suburbanites are sure to perceive the shift as an assault on their property, the change would take place on the heels of decades of federal subsidies to the suburbs in the form of home mortgage interest deductions and highway construction grants....

Regional tax base sharing of the type proposed in this Note has never been adopted in any metropolitan region,[90] but if implemented, it would inevitably have far-reaching effects.

The final economic argument against the proposal considered here involves its effect on nonresidential property. Given a population-based disbursement of regional revenues, the presence of industrial property in a jurisdiction ceases to be a tax advantage and actually decreases the municipality's revenues by taking up space that could be used for residences. Thus, under the proposal, industrial property may replace multifamily housing as a locally undesirable land use (LULU). This local effect may result in sub-optimal amounts of space dedicated to industrial development if each jurisdiction would prefer such development to occur elsewhere. Alternatively, however, a jurisdiction may believe that industrial development within its borders will attract employees to locate there in order to minimize commute time, thereby increasing the local population. In that case, some industrial development may remain a fiscally attractive proposition for municipalities. As is the case with other elements of the proposal, this element's efficiency or inefficiency is difficult to demonstrate theoretically, and it cannot be tested empirically until it is tried.

The last category of objections to the proposal is potentially the most devastating because it consists of claims that the proposal will fail to achieve its stated goals. First, it may be argued that the proposal does not address income segregation at the neighborhood level. Just as central cities now have wealthy and poor neighborhoods, each suburb, although motivated to attract residents regardless of wealth, might try to segregate them in discrete neighborhoods within the jurisdiction. After all, eliminating the fiscal advantages of income segregation leaves intact the nonfiscal incentives for such segregation on the block and neighborhood levels. Admittedly, the inability of the proposal to encourage desegregation on those levels is a serious shortcoming. Nevertheless, the proposal is likely to result in much greater proximity between different income groups simply because it will reduce the homogeneity of municipalities. Moreover, the proposal creates a greater possibility of fiscally stable mixed-income neighborhoods, even though it stops short of mandating their creation.

Whereas the first ineffectiveness claim focuses on the neighborhood level, a second claim takes a supraregional perspective and asserts that the wealthy will be able to escape regional redistribution by leaving the region. They may do so by migrating either outside the boundaries of the metropolitan region or into other metropolitan regions that have not adopted regional tax-base sharing. The first alternative, however, is limited by the wealthy household's tolerance for commuting, the cost of relocation, the state's ability to redefine metropolitan boundaries to include new territories, and zoning rules that preserve rural land for agricultural use or open space. The second alternative is limited by the costs of relocation, the extent to which people perceive cities as non-

90. The most ambitious existing program, in force within the Twin Cities area of Minnesota, redistributes 40% of the growth in the commercial industrial property tax base. See [Myron Orfield, Metropolitics 87–90 (1997)] (describing the Twin Cities program).

fungible, and the likelihood that other regions will adopt regional tax-base sharing. It is likely that some families will be undeterred by these costs and risks, but it is even more likely that the vast majority of homeowners will remain exactly where they are. The cost of inter-regional migration is much higher than the cost of moving to another jurisdiction within the same region, so an analogy to white flight in the face of racial desegregation is less appropriate than it might otherwise appear....

* * *

Notes and Comments

1. Would the author's proposal tend to retard urban sprawl or might it exacerbate urban sprawl?

2. In his book, Inside Game-Outside Game: Winning Strategies for Saving Urban America (1999), David Rusk, the former mayor of Albuquerque, argues that regional tax base sharing and urban growth boundaries are the key to urban revitalization and regional stability.

Does the following excerpt suggest that Canada has found an effective alternative? Does Canadian policy follow the American or British model?

Enid Slack & Richard Bird, *Financing Urban Growth Through Development Charges,*

39 Canadian Tax J./Revue Fiscale Canadienne 1288 (1991)

Municipalities in Canada, as everywhere, face increasing financial pressures as rising demand for local services confronts declining provincial government assistance to municipalities and local pressure to limit property tax increases. New developments require large capital outlays. Historically, such investments were financed from property taxes, water and sewer rates, grants from other levels of government, and borrowing. In some provinces, however, municipalities have become increasingly reluctant to go into debt for any purpose and have been relying almost exclusively on current revenues. High interest rates in the 1970s coupled with provincial restrictions have made borrowing less desirable for municipalities. Municipalities are thus turning more and more to the private sector to finance the infrastructure costs of new development.

Development charges, known in British Columbia as development cost charges (DCCs) and elsewhere in Canada as lot levies (and in the United States as exactions and impact fees) are charges per lot (or per area) imposed on developers to finance the off-site costs of development.[2] Such charges are also sometimes applied in cases of redevelopment. Generally, charges are levied to finance the building of water supply systems, sewage treatment plants, trunk mains, and roads, but they have also been used to finance such services as libraries, parks, recreation centres, and schools....

British Columbia

Under the BC Municipal Act, local governments are entitled to levy DCCs to pay for services in specific developments where there is an approval of subdivision or a building

2. On-site services (sidewalks, water, sewers, roads, street lighting, and do forth) are always the responsibility of the developer.

permit authorizing construction, alteration, or extension of a building or structure. Once collected, the funds must be placed in separate DCC reserve fund of each purpose for which the charge was levied.

DCCs may be levied to pay for the capital costs of providing parkland and providing, constructing, altering, or expanding sewage, water, drainage and highway facilities (other than off-street parking facilities) to service, directly or indirectly, the development for which the charge is being imposed. The DCC thus applies only where a development imposes new capital cost burdens on a local government, and the funds can be used only to pay the costs and debt charges on debt incurred for that development.

Church properties, buildings that contain less than four self-contained units for residential use only, and cases where the value of the work does not exceed $50,000 are excluded from the charge. In addition, no charge is applicable where there is no new capital cost burden on the municipality or where a DCC was previously paid on the development (unless new capital costs are imposed on the municipality).

The DCC is payable at the time of the approval of the subdivision or the issue of the building permit, as determined by the municipality. In some instances, the charge may be paid in installments over a period of years.

DCCs may vary with respect to different zones or different defined or specified areas, different uses, different capital costs as they related to different classes of development, and different sizes or different numbers of lots or units in a development. Charges must, however, be the same for all developments that impose similar capital cost burdens on the municipality. Also, as part of the determination of the charge, the municipality is required to consider future land use patterns and development, the phasing of services, the provision of parkland, whether the impact of the estimated development cost charge is excessive relative to the capital cost of the standards maintained for existing services, whether it will deter development, and whether it will discourage the construction of reasonably priced housing or serviced land. The rationale for the magnitude of the charge has to be made available to the public on request. The province's inspector of municipalities must be satisfied both that the charge is related to the capital costs attributable to projects included in the bylaw and that the local government has considered the impact of the charge before a DCC is imposed.

The Municipal Act also permits a local government to require an owner to provide "excess" or extended services (roads, water, and sewer and drainage systems) beyond his own lands, in which case the municipality collects charges form subsequent property owners connecting to or using the excess or extended services and repays the owner (including an interest component as determined by bylaw).

In summary, although the legislation governing DCC's in British Columbia is fairly specific about which types of capital costs are eligible, it is quite vague about how the services related to the development since charges can be levied to cover the capital costs incurred to service *directly* or *indirectly* the development to which the charge is applied....

The method of calculating DCCs is specified in individual municipal bylaws, which differ greatly in detail. In the more detailed bylaws, engineering estimates are made of the actual and projects costs of service provision. Costs are sometimes apportioned between existing residents and the new development, where the service provided will result in benefits to both groups. In some cases, efforts are made to differentiate service needs by type of development to provide a basis for charging different levies on different types of properties. The DCC is generally differentiated by zones of areas of the municipality to reflect the fact that different services are provided in different parts of the municipality. In addition, charges often vary by the type of dwelling unit—single-family, multiple residential, and so forth....

...most municipalities levy charges on some services, but few levy on all the services possible in law. In most municipalities, the charge is differentiated according to the location of the property in the municipality, the housing type (single-family, multiple-residential, and so forth), or both, but there are significant differences in the degree of variation. For example, one municipality may differentiate only according to urban and rural areas whereas another may differentiated according to ten specific areas. Similarly, housing unit types range from 2 to over 40 categories.

Charges vary considerably also in amount. In the small cities, towns, and villages, the levy tends to be fairly small, exceeding \$1,300 only in one town (Sidney, which is part of the Capital Regional District and which is experiencing significant growth). The DCC is largest in some parts of the townships of Langley and Richmond and the districts of Surrey and West Vancouver, all of which are contained in the Greater Vancouver Regional District (GVRD), have significant populations, and are generally fast-growing....

British Columbia and Ontario Compared

Even though it is difficult to compare the use of development charges across provinces when there is such variation within provinces, a few general observations can be made. First, the BC legislation restricts municipalities in terms of the services they can levy for to water, sewers, roads parks, and drainage. In Ontario, the new legislation is broader and, indeed, municipalities already levy charges for such services as recreational and cultural facilities and administration. In addition, school boards in Ontario can now levy for the growth-related capital costs of new schools.

Second, municipalities in British Columbia can levy for parks and open space, and over half of the municipalities that levy development cost charges do so. Where a developer has provided parkland, the development cost charge is reduced accordingly. In Ontario, since under the Planning Act developers are required to set aside 5 percent of their land for parks, there were no development charges for parks until the 1989 Development Charges Act.

Third, local DCCs in British Columbia must be approved by the provincial inspector of municipalities before they can be implemented. Municipalities in Ontario do not require such approval (although they are subject to appeal at the Ontario Municipal Board). School boards, under the new legislation in Ontario, are required to obtain provincial government approval for development charge funds.

Fourth, most municipalities in both provinces differentiate charges by the type of housing unit. The designation of specific charges for specific zones is much more prevalent in BC municipalities than in Ontario, however.

Fifth, municipalities in both provinces are allowed to levy on all forms of property—residential, commercial, and industrial. Most of the municipalities surveyed in British Columbia levy on residential and commercial property, and many do so on industrial property as well. In Ontario, only a few municipalities levied on commercial and industrial property in the past, but that is changing.

Finally, in both provinces, nothing precludes municipalities from negotiating other exactions with developers as part of the approval process, and this procedure appears to be widespread in both provinces.

The Economics of Development Charges

The literature of the incidence of development charges is limited and reaches no clear conclusion about who bears the burden of lot levies: new-home buyers, all homebuyers, developers, or pre-development landowners. The answer depends on such factors as whether the levy is uniform or non-uniform across municipalities, the demand and supply condition in the market for new housing, and whether the existence and magnitude of the levy are known to the developer prior to the undertaking of the development.

In the absence of a development charge, a developer will charge what the market will bear. The extent to which imposing a development charge results in higher prices for new housing depend, in part, on whether the charge is uniform or non-uniform across municipalities. In the case of a non-uniform development charge, in which a charge is levied in one municipality only, the developer in that location will be unable to raise the price of new housing in that location because his competitors in nearby locations are unaffected by the charge and will not raise their prices. In contrast, in the case of a uniform development charge, in which developers of new houses in all locations are charged the same amount per lot, while the precise extent to which the charge can be passed on to new-home buyers depends on demand and supply conditions, new-home buyers are most unlikely to escape the charge. The simplest case to analyze, and the one implicitly assumed in most of the literature, is a uniform development charge across municipalities (for example, over a housing submarket). In this case, developers will try to pass the levy on to new-home buyers by charging a higher price for new houses or by reducing the quality or size of the houses built. Develops at the margin will not bear the burden of the charge in terms of reduced profits because, in a competitive market, they are already earning profits at levels that just compensate for their costs and risks relative to their uses of their investments capital. Rather than bear the charge, they will not develop the land.

The extent to which a charge is reflected in higher prices for new housing depends, however, on the supply and demand conditions for new housing. For the developer to be able to pass on the levy fully to new-home buyers, the demand for new housing in those locations has to be fairly inelastic. In other words, new-home buyers have to be relatively insensitive to price and willing to pay more to live in those communities. Such a market might exist, for example, in a community with "unique characteristics, such as historic institutional, or scenic attributes, located within a larger market area." Generally, the demand for housing tends to be relatively inelastic in highly desirable markets (such as Toronto and Vancouver) where there are few close substitutes, and in small urban areas where competition is limited. Under these circumstances, the levy will be passed on to consumers. Studies of development charges that have estimated demand and supply elasticities suggest that they type of market most often encountered is one characterized by a rather elastic supply and an inelastic demand....

Development charges have potential advantages in terms of the efficient use and provision of public services. In particular, properly designed development charges could in principle be used to cover two parts of a three-part tariff: the capital cost of constructing the facility and the capital cost of extending the service to a particular neighbourhood (where this latter cost is based on location, density, and distance, for example). However, development charges do not reflect the short-run marginal costs of using facilities, which has led Snyder and Stegman to question the efficiency potential of development charges. In both Canadian cases discussed in this paper, some effort is made to design charges to reflect the capital costs of particular facilities, but in only a few instances are those costs related to the specific costs of development in particular locations....

Municipalities in British Columbia and Ontario have been levying charges on developers for some years to recoup the growth-related costs of development. Financial pressures on municipalities coupled with the philosophy that growth should pay for itself has made this device an attractive revenue source for municipalities.

Development charges may be an important source of revenue for some municipalities, but they are not a large source. Moreover, because charges are limited to the "growth-related capital costs" of development—and are being increasingly placed under public scrutiny to ensure that they do relate to those costs—they seem even less likely to produce significant revenues in the future. If municipalities are seeking new sources to supplant property taxes, they should look elsewhere.

New-home buyers probably bear the burden of development charges rather than developers, an outcome which may in some respects be considered both fair and efficient (if not always politically popular). But new-home buyers are also paying property taxes, which are used to finance both existing and future services in the municipality. Moreover, a shift from general revenues to development charges means that existing residents enjoy a windfall gain: past generations have partly financed their services and they are not responsible for financing the services of new residents. Views from this perspective, the equity of development charges seems questionable, as does the efficiency of the particular "average cost" charging systems now used in Canada.

Development charges can be made more equitable and efficient, of course. In particular, they could reflect the true marginal cost of services by being determined on a development-by-development basis (as well as on the basis of housing type) because the cost of services varies by the type and location of development. In addition, if new-home buyers are to bear the burden of the growth-related costs of new development, then their property taxes (and user charges) should presumably be adjusted so that they are not also paying for existing and future residents. The adjustment could be made, for example, by reducing the charge to compensate for the debt-financing component of user fees and property taxes.

Finally, it is worth emphasizing that in an important sense what is really going on is the substitution of private for public borrowing. Canadian municipalities, particularly in Ontario, are generally run in a fiscally conservative fashion, partly by choice and partly in response to strong provincial controls on local borrowing. The traditional case of borrowing for local public capital facilities is not accepted, and municipalities tend to pay for everything out of current revenues (including, of course, provincial grants) to the extent possible. One consequence of this policy is the increasing reliance on development charges discussed in this paper: in effect, public sector borrowing is replaced by private sector borrowing (by developers and/or new-home buyers). This substitution seems unlikely to be economically efficient, however, given the greater riskiness and generally higher transactions costs of private sector borrowing. As with the earlier discussion of equity and efficiently, the more closely one looks at the development-charge approach to financing municipal infrastructure, the less attractive it becomes.

* * *

Notes and Comments

1. Having looked at the infrastructure finance systems of several nations, discuss the strengths and weaknesses of each system and propose a more equitable or efficient system. Does equity demand that new development finance the cost of capital facilities expansion, or should capital costs be shared by all taxpayers? Why should existing residents pay for the cost of growth and new development? Particularly if the new development tends to be high-end homes for the affluent? What is the impact of shifting from public to private financing of facilities? Should the market determine the scope and design of new development or should it be a matter of public policy?

The following reading describes infrastructure financing in the People's Republic of China. What unique problems are presented by developing Nations with tremendous demand for affordable communities for large populations?

Kam Wing Chan, *Infrastructure Services and Financing in Chinese Cities*,

7 Pacific Rim Law & Policy Journal 503 (1998)

China finances local government in a fundamentally different manner from most other countries, especially in the case of municipal government. In most other countries, cities do not raise enough money from local taxes to finance their expenditures, so higher levels of government must issue grants to make up the difference. In China, this flow is reversed. On average, cities collect more in taxes than they spend and can remit substantial funds upward to the central government. Formally, these upward remittances consist of tax revenues that either belong to the central government or are shared between central and local governments. Continually renegotiating the base upon which taxes are shared, however, destroys any real concept of ownership of tax revenue. This means that, for China, it is inappropriate to distinguish between "locally-raised revenue" and "revenue from external sources"....

Undoubtedly, China has made great strides in providing urban infrastructure services, as seen in the growth in per capita provision of most types of service in almost all of the cities in the last ten years. The supply of gas and bus services has grown fastest, both nationwide and in the five cities studied. Despite these improvements, many urban infrastructure services[82] still fall short of the demand.

These shortfalls will worsen as urbanization proceeds. In the past ten years, actual urban population growth rate averaged about five percent per year. This trend will likely continue, and the urban population will more than double, from the 359 million in 1996 to about 750 million by the year 2010, making China a predominantly urban society. Rising per capita income, especially in the cities, will also fuel the demand for better urban infrastructure services. Such growth poses critical issues of financing infrastructure maintenance and investments, necessary for economic growth and a better quality of life.

The Asian Development Bank has estimated that to meet the increased demand, China would need to invest more than $500 billion over the next ten years to improve

82. Notably in water supply, public transportation, telecommunications, electricity supply, sanitation and fire services.

its transportation and communications infrastructure alone. Most of these investments will have to favor urban centers. At present, urban governments in China have insufficient budgetary autonomy for raising revenues and allocating expenditures. This often leads to heavy reliance on ex-budgetary sources, as in the case of financing urban infrastructure services. These practices are often erratic and fraught with problems from both efficiency and equity points of view.

Currently, funds for urban construction in China, and all the cities visited, come from taxation levied largely on enterprises, and from asset (land) sales. Urban households, who benefit from many municipal services, in general have not paid the full costs of the services. In line with the principle of making the users pay, more revenue needs to be raised from users' fees and taxes, especially from the household sector. The recent consumer boom in major cities indicates that the average urban household can pay significantly more for housing and municipal services than generally perceived.

More fundamentally, a stable system of local taxes (and user charges) needs to be implemented. Based on a redefinition of the role of local governments, these local levies should directly relate to the benefits generated by municipal services. International experiences and local conditions suggest that China should consider taxing land, and residential and business property, to create a stable, lasting source of local government revenue for most urban centers in coming years. A tax on immobile or largely immobile factors has many advantages as a local tax. Such a tax generally takes the form of an annual or quarterly charge, calculated as a percentage of the land or residential property value.[85] This type of tax has only a minor undesirable distortionary effect. Generally, it places the burden on those with a greater ability to pay. The taxes also tie closely to the benefits accrued to taxpayers.[86] As the city develops, land/property values will increase, along with the revenue base of town government. A stable system will reduce incentives for the hasty sale of state assets, such as land and housing, and the overuse of users' fees, such as road tolls and multiple fees on new urban construction.

While all levels of government, including those of cities visited, recognize the importance of financing, management is equally crucial and should not be overlooked. The neglect of management, traditionally a weak point in most socialist economies, is a legacy of the conventional physical planning mentality where expansion (construction) overshadows efficiency (better management). Management includes regulating demand to reduce excessive and wasteful use. For example, piped water consumption, underpriced in most cities in China, is excessive in many places, even in the face of general water shortages. One may persuasively argue that China should raise urban water rates, especially considering today's actual, not officially reported, urban incomes.

Similarly, better management can increase the efficiency of use of most urban facilities. An obvious case is the use of urban roads and the lack of any effective traffic management. In fact, among the five cities visited in Shandong and Guizhou, only one (Guiyang) has created a separate entity to look after the day-to-day maintenance of infrastructure services. In other cities, this task falls to the urban construction authorities, who at times seem more interested in building facilities than in making them work.

...[T]he average growth rates in urban infrastructure service provision are overstated because they do not take into account the growing segment of urban residents

85. Contrast this tax with the one-time lump-sum approach of many places in China which charge a relatively hefty "infrastructure capacity expansion fee" (*zengrong fei*).

86. In the form of increased property value because of better urban services, for instance.

registered as "temporary" households. This group includes the "floating population," whose size has grown from a few million in the early 1980s to about 100 million by 1994. While not entitled to government-provided urban services, these people cannot be totally and effectively excluded from sharing some of the services, such as roads, public transportation, and water supply. In any case, dividing the population within cities into those with urban entitlements and those without will inevitably exacerbate social conflict. This discrimination against new migrants from the countryside reflects a strong urban bias in the overall approach.

On a per capita basis, service provision varies significantly between cities (even considering only the "full-status" urban population). Political and economic factors, often differences in revenue, tip the balance in favor of larger centers. Besides being inequitable, this systematic bias is also inefficient because it distorts fair competition between urban centers and regions. Moreover, this bias underlies the significant hierarchical brain drain from the countryside to small centers and to larger metropolises, as has happened in many Third World countries. The depletion of well-educated human resources in areas outside major metropolises harms long-term national development. To fully exploit the nation's potential, China must ultimately have a more decentralized pattern of urban development.

Finally, for the same service, urban residents in new projects and those in existing structures pay different charges. The unavailability of long-term borrowing has forced many local governments not only to sell assets, but also to impose most of the costs of investment on the taxpayers they catch, often owners and occupants of new developments. This practice unfairly penalizes current and future generations that cannot, like previous generations, avoid paying. These huge initial costs also impede the development of China's fledgling housing market.

* * *

Notes and Comments

1. How does the lack of long-term infrastructure financing affect the pace and quality of development, including economic development? Would there be an impact on affordable housing?

2. Although the various systems of infrastructure finance are neutral, the impact of the systems may be all but neutral. American infrastructure finance, particularly when comparing the minimal expenditure on mass transit as compared to the enormous federal, state and local road budgets, contains an unstated bias in favor of decentralization, sprawl and suburban development. Robert Cervero, *Growing Smart by Linking Transportation and Urban Development*, 19 Va. Envtl. L.J. 357 (2000). The limits on financing discourage development of affordable housing and thus the suburbs get richer and the central cities suffer tight budgets that must balance the need for more services and the loss of tax revenues as commerce and the affluent migrate to the city's edge. Jerry Frug, *Geography of Community*, 48 Stan. L. Rev. 1047 (1966). Centralization may be a far more efficient urban development policy, emphasizing pedestrianization, expanding park systems, and creating cities that appear more European than current American urban design.

Centralization is first about the density necessary to establish efficient public transit and the establishment of a pedestrian-accessible city where destinations are attractive walks from transit stops. It is also about the effect of centralizing a region's cultural resources, university, and intellectual life. David Rusk argues that suburbs are dependent on central cities and where revenues and regulation is shared on a regional basis including cities and suburbs that urban stabilization is achievable. Scholars differ on the state of the developed city. David Rusk, Inside Game/Outside Game: Winning Strategies for Saving Urban America (1999). Some believe that sprawl is efficient and satisfies the market. Peter Gordon & Harry W. Richardson, *Are Compact Cities a Desirable Goal?*, 63 J. Am. Planning Ass'n 232 (1997). Many other lament the death of cities as regional economic life moved toward the edge. Joel Garreau, Edge City: Life on the New Frontier (1991); James Howard Kunstler, The Geography of Nowhere: The Rise and Decline of America's Man-Made Landscape (1994).

3. An added complication in generating central city revitalization is that central city investment often generates housing, schools, or other facilities that are all minority-occupied, exacerbating racial concentrations and segregation demographic patterns. Being challenged by civil rights organization, the cost and difficulty of development on brownfields, and the burgeoning suburban population has generated greater investment in suburban infrastructure.

Taxation

The taxation of real property can have significant impacts on patterns of development. For example, a tax based on the front footage of land resulted in Amsterdam's narrow houses and efficient use of space, and a tax on the number of floors resulted in false windows that made two floors look like one in Madrid's Gothic Quarter. Real property tax considerations motivate many local politicians and planning commissioners in making planning and zoning decisions. The exclusion of affordable housing or other uses seen to attract expensive municipal services such as schools, and the outright competition between towns to attract tax-generating jobs or sales and the attractive sales tax results in "Big Box" retailers and dramatic second generation shopping malls take precedence over people. William B. Fulton, The Reluctant Metropolis: The Politics of Urban Growth in Los Angeles (1997); Marlon Boarnet & Randall Crane, *L.A. Story: A Reality Check for Transit-Based Housing*, 63 J. Am. Plan. Ass'n 189 (1997) (tax considerations discourage local planning of housing around Metrolink light rail stations).

Capital gains taxation under income tax laws also impacts urban development patterns. As income is only taxed when a gain is realized, such as the time of sale, and property is subject to a property tax based on what is actually developed, there is an incentive to hold onto land that has appreciated so as to avoid the capital gains tax. This is particularly the case where the land is generating rents from parking, storage, or an antiquated manufacturing shop. The effect is to underuse urban land, thus encouraging developers to look to the urban fringe. The pattern is one of leap-frog development, leaving many parcels for infill development, tax revenues lower than necessary and a loss of economic activity and vitality for the city? Should cities utilize a system like that suggested by Henry George, where land is taxed based on its highest use rather than actual use, thus discouraging waste and unproductive land, and favoring development and redevelopment at the maximum density allowed, bringing economic activity and the financing to support expanded municipal services? What might be the drawbacks of such a system? Might beautiful landmarks be destroyed where a more efficient higher intensity use could replace it?

Don Hagman, the dean of comparative land use writers for too short a portion of the last quarter century, described the tax alternative advanced by Henry George:

Donald G. Hagman, *The Single Tax and Land-Use Planning: Henry George Updated,*

12 UCLA L. Rev. 762 (1965)

The ideas and energy of Henry George, born 125 years ago, spawned a politico-economic movement of world-wide proportions. Even today, dedicated Georgists work with zeal and, in some countries, with a degree of success. In the United States, George's idea of land-value taxation sparks cyclic waves of interest as each generation wonders why so idyllic a scheme has not been adopted as a cure for societal ills....

As you know, the theory of land-value taxation is relatively simple. Each year we will determine the amount of funds needed to provide governmental services and then levy a tax only on land. As an example, one of the offers to purchase a site in the center of New Chicago has been made at $2 million for a 500 square foot site. This amount will be the market value of the site against which we will apply the tax rate. As development occurs the value of that site and others will increase. We expect that the value which is *added* to sites in New Chicago each year by development will be much more than the taxes needed to support the municipal government. Theoretically, therefore, the entire city budget can be paid for by recapture of the unearned and undeserved yearly increment in land values.

Moreover, a land-value tax will prevent the undesirable speculative holding of land. As you know, one-fifth to one-seventh of the land in the United States, even in central cities, is held out of productive use by speculators. The land-value tax will avoid this because it will make it an economic necessity to put the land to immediate use. Land prices will be kept low and increased taxes will make the price even lower, thereby encouraging development of the land.

On the other hand, since there is no tax on buildings, investment in them will be very attractive and will increase the demand for land, thereby pushing the price up. Thus, land will still be priced high enough to encourage intense use, discourage underuse, and prevent sprawl—the latter, as you know, causing undue extension of public facilities which raises costs. Building will in fact be encouraged to the point where the density of occupancy will be reduced.

We will not have to bother with special assessments, since increases in site value resulting from public improvements will be automatically reflected in the market value to which the tax is applied. The continually expanding supply of buildings, which will be built on cheap land not held out of the market for speculative reasons, will keep rents low. Increases in taxes will not be shifted to the tenant. Buildings will be remodeled and will be well maintained because taxes will not be increased where improvements are made, as is customary in the United States, thereby penalizing persons who improve their property. Under such a system, slums will not be permitted to develop. Moreover, manufacturing concerns will seek outlying areas, away from the commercial and residential districts, because proximity to the center of things is not of great interest to them, and they will seek the lowest site valuations. This is just one example of how a land-use planning principle can be accomplished by land-value taxation. An additional benefit will be that, when and as it becomes necessary to acquire land for public purposes, the low land values will permit acquisition at modest prices....

Land-value taxation, as a movement, began with Henry George. The concept of a single land-value tax did not originate with George, however; the ingredients of his ideas are often traced to the Physiocrats (French 1750–1790), Ricardo and Mill. The movement reached its zenith in 1910–1920. In the United States, the Pittsburgh-Scranton experiment and the Houston experiment were initiated during that period. While the former experiment is still viable, the latter experiment lasted only a few years. With the exception of developments in Hawaii in the 1960's, there was no extension of land-value taxation in the United States since the early experiments. Early experiments begun in other countries, however, notably in France, Denmark, Germany, Australia, New Zealand and Canada, were continued and in some instances expanded in scope....

In any event, this movement itself expired in the middle 1920's....

Law as a Bar in the United States

While George was able to generate a political force in his own country for land-value taxation, the movement made less headway in the United States than in several other areas of the world. There were many reasons for this, but, in addition to those other reasons, it was clear that state constitutional provisions requiring uniformity in taxation presented a barrier in many states....

* * *

Notes and Comments

1. For an argument for Smart Growth taxation arguing that Henry George taxation could stimulate Smart Growth and urban revitalization, see Thomas Gihring, *Incentive Property Taxation: A Potential Tool for Urban Growth Management*, 65 J. Am. Plan. Ass'n 62 (1999).

Professor Lefcoe makes some very interesting observations on the land development impacts of income taxation policy and the interplay between income taxation and other forms of taxation:

George Lefcoe, *How Taxes Affect Urban Design—And How to Make Them Do a Better Job of It*,

4 Real Estate L.J. 244 (1976)....

Assume for a moment that we had an urban design policy for America, or an outline for a national growth policy in the United States that Congress might conceivably endorse. We could then ask quite usefully whether our tax systems supported those goals or frustrated them. Moreover, if there were such consensus on policy, as there is in other countries, possibly lawyers would seldom be asked to talk about the impact of taxes on design. Where the directions for urban growth are clear and widely accepted and the role of the public in aesthetic controls is settled, lawyers have litttle function in planning. In Australia, the Netherlands, and Germany, for instance, these questions are reserved largely for economists, business people, planners, and architects. But since there is no consensus in this country, attorneys step in as advocates and mediators. And while they are not usually expected to look at tax policy in the light of planning and design goals, they sometimes need to consider how taxation might affect the quality of the urban environment.

In our tax systems at the local level, we are more concerned with averting corruption than with achieving lively or even livable space. Of all values implicit in our taxing system, the single most important value is that like cases be treated alike, and, as a corollary, that the assessor should have as little discretion as possible in carrying out his task. The impact on design can be exasperating, even if it is inevitable.

Whether it's a billboard or an architectural monument—the Seagram Building to take a much-publicized example—the tax assessor's task is to appraise them on the same basis. For both types of structures, since they are relatively unique, an appraisal based on the market approach—recent sales of similar property—is often impracticable. As an alternative, in the case of a newly built structure, the assessor naturally looks at what the owner paid to build it. Billboards are cheap to build, architectural monuments are dear. So, the billboard is probably underassessed, and the Seagram Building or comparable structures hit too hard.

The assessor could try to use an income approach to value by trying to guess what the property would yield in annual rents. But this is a far more difficult and speculative task. Billboard companies, for instance, receive much of their revenue in the form of "barter": from the airlines, they receive tickets to peddle; from the radio stations, advertising time, which they may assign to other users. The new office building is no easier to assess on an income basis. It can take five years before the building achieves full occupancy. Even then, the assessor who uses a capitalized income method of appraisal must determine whether the lease prices are about right, and whether the operator's claimed expenses are reasonable. How much safer to rely on construction costs, and not income, as the basis for appraisal!

Our tax systems, to the extent that they influence urban design, have conflicting impacts. What the local property tax thwarts, the federal income tax encourages. Spare not a second thought on the seeming inequity of the ways the billboard operator and the Seagram Building are taxed, for the federal income tax rights the balance. Seagram's depreciation, based on actual construction costs, is sufficient to shelter all the income produced from the building and $360,000 a year besides, while the billboard operator pays federal income taxes on every penny, whether received in cash or goods. Moreover, property taxes are deductible from income for federal tax purposes, thus halving the local tax bite for a taxpayer in the 50 percent bracket.

In one respect, not the tax itself, but the administration of the local real property tax in the United States has been criticized sharply. Inner-city suburbs here have been found to be grossly overassessed. A recent study found that properties in some blighted neighborhoods bore an effective tax rate higher—by as much as ten times—than "upward transitional neighborhoods" of the same city. The consequence is that owners in poor areas are left with little cash to make improvements. Even owner-occupants, who have a tendency to spend more on improving their properties than absentee owners, simply lack the means; as much as 25 percent of their gross receipts goes to pay property taxes. These assessment practices are illegal, yet persistent....

Decisions about where and what to build are determined by so many planning and market factors that any effort at tracing the impact of taxes on design is bound to be frustrated. In Australia, the Netherlands, and Germany, however, certain taxes reinforce articulated urban values. We cannot prove for sure that Amsterdam or Sydney owes its shape and form to a particular set of tax policies. But we can see in the policies that exist there and in other cities as well that the tax does express clear public preferences about how a city ought to look and where it ought to grow.

In Sydney, the property tax is based on the unimproved value of the land. Advocates for this "single tax," whose spiritual founder is Henry George, contend that by taxing land heavily and exempting improvements, landowners are encouraged to develop. Under this system, a property owner pays the same tax on a vacant lot as on a developed property. This amounts to an annual levy against speculators and helps clear the way for developers. What we should expect to see, then, if we look at Sydney, is a densely developed area....

Not all the tendencies which site-value taxation reinforces are benign. Because such taxation encourages intense development, vacant parcels are swiftly built, instead of remaining vacant or being paved for parking lots, while their owners await a propitious time for development. Parking lots may be ugly, but they are also useful; Sydney's new Opera House, for example, suffers for want of parking.

A more serious problem with site-value taxation is that it continues to encourage development even where densities are already uncomfortably high. If Sydney depends too much for a city its size on its one center, taxes may have been among the factors to blame only the center city seems capable, thus far, of attracting both the rich professionals from the northern suburbs and the working classes from the south and west. Planners in Sydney are now trying, as are planners in large cities all over the world, to limit the density of development, and to find some means of orderly decentralization....

An interesting issue is whether site-value taxation has had any impact at all on the limited extent of development at these suburban stations. Edgardo Contini of Victor Gruen & Associates contends that the property-tax assessment practices in some American cities impede such development here. When a transit system is built, such as San Francisco's BART, major institutions such as banks seek to purchase sites around the major stops with the intention of holding the site until after the transit system has been operating for a while and its full commercial potential has become apparent. However, the tax assessor can force the purchaser's hand by raising assessments so substantially as to coerce immediate development, at a scale sufficient to meet the tax burden, yet far smaller than would be necessary for the site to serve as a major regional center. If Contini is correct, possibly the Sydney assessor can be cited as having contributed to the premature development of these nodal sites which should have been held off the market.

Sydney has "sprawl." How can sprawl occur in a city subject to a single tax? First, many suburbs have voted against using site-value taxation. Low-density housing is possible even in those that do use site-value taxation because in areas far from the center, land is a bargain and the tax rate reflects that bargain.

Sprawl is also promoted by the state tax system. While New South Wales levies a tax on the unimproved capital value of land, most housing—90 percent or so—is effectively exempt. The exemption is based on the dollar value of the house itself. Luxury housing and apartments are both penalized, in effect, since land on which they are built does not benefit from the exemption. Assuming one-family houses are generally built at lower densities than apartments, the net impact of this tax should be to encourage a concentration of commercial uses and a spread of one-family tracts.

Inner-city suburbs have tended to remain intact, because while land is generally assessed on the basis of the highest potential use and not the current use, an exception is made for owner-occupants of houses, who are assessed as if their homesteads had no value greater than as single-family dwellings. Their moderate taxes give residents in the suburbs-even in the areas zoned for apartments the option of holding on to their houses in spite of potential value. And, the property tax has left owners of Sydney's remarkable Victorian houses sufficient funds for upkeep....

The same factors that yielded a high level of maintenance have also protected owners until recently against having to sell out to so-called higher and better uses. The demand for apartments has increased; and some areas, such as the now-fashionable Paddington, an inner-city suburb of Sydney, have become "gentrified," that is, the professionals and middle class have taken over terrace houses from elderly, poor, and working-class people. As the values of houses increased in Paddington, it became difficult for people of moderate means to hold on. Thus, house after house was sold to middle-class persons. Physically the neighborhood remained the same and even improved. Sociologically, it changed a great deal. The newcomers have saved Paddington from private redevelopment, for they have managed to procure rezoning barring further apartment development. Areas physically comparable, but not as chic, have yet to obtain the rezoning that would assure the safety of their terrace houses from demolition....

Gentrification is fostered in Australia because, at the national level, there are no taxes on capital gains. This adds to the already sizable incentives of urban lot owners to sell, and it has also encouraged considerable amateur speculation in real estate at the edges of suburbia. What the Henry George-type land tax encourages in the way of development is probably more than offset by the exemption of capital gains from the federal income tax in Australia.

In Australia there is more land than could possibly be settled. At the other extreme, in the Netherlands, densities are among the highest in the world, and land has had to be reclaimed from the sea. Amsterdam's four-story, one-room-wide gabled houses that line the canals, represent a careful and balanced use of space: The houses are not too high to block what little sun shines in Amsterdam, yet they are dense enough to crowd 800,000 people into a space that would not happily accommodate one-fifth as many Sydneysiders.

The form of property tax in Amsterdam could not sensibly be a tax on land, since to tax land is to encourage its development. So, Amsterdam levies taxes on the net footage of what is built, that is, on every square meter. Even when new hotels are constructed in Amsterdam, those large and gracious lobbies have to be reconsidered in light of the tax burden they create.[12]

As a caveat, I must add that the Dutch property tax is modest by American standards. Dutch cities depend very little on the property tax, receiving upwards of 80 percent of their revenues from federal revenue sharing. What matters for this discussion is that the local tax expresses a design value manifested in other local laws. It reinforces these laws instead of cutting, however narrowly, across the grain....

Not all the cities in the Netherlands have the same basis for assessing property taxes as the city of Amsterdam. Dutch cities have their choice: They can tax both land and improvements, tax the surface area of the land and exempt improvements entirely, or tax the net floor area. A city that wants to grow, therefore, can encourage development by taxing undeveloped land heavily.

---

12. There is a price to pay for preserving Amsterdam's scale. On the top of most canal houses is a roof beam which must be rigged to bring furniture through upper-story windows; most stairways are too steep and narrow for the purpose. More significant than this minor inconvenience, there is a substantial shortage of housing which has led to an active program of government subsidies. It is so active that the Dutch seem to prefer paying 10 percent of their income for crowded, obsolescent quarters than the 20 to 25 percent (if people were willing to pay that) that would enable developers to provide a quality of housing commensurate with the nation's real wealth.

Preoccupied as we are in the United States with the concept of equal protection, we do not allow each city to select the base which best complements its growth policies. Thus, our cities do not enjoy the planning advantage of Dutch municipalities.

In one respect, though, the national tax system in the Netherlands works against planning policy. As in Australia, there is no tax on capital gains.[14] The owner of a canal house, who sells to an English company for conversion of the residence into office space, pays no tax whatsoever on the transaction. Many a Dutch property owner has found the tax-free sale irresistible.

Anyone who has been to Germany will probably remark about the compactness of the towns and villages. The town line can be seen clearly from a passing car as one moves from the well-spaced concentration of housing immediately into an unimpaired farm and forest area. For once, lines drawn on a planner's map are seen in evidence across the landscape. At the center of each town is a village shopping area, and, while convenience stores are scattered in residential neighborhoods, each town has a discernible retail center, often dominated by family-run restaurants and shops.[17]...

The primary tax raised locally is based on business revenues, the gross receipts of all shops, offices, and factories (with deductions for interest payments, etc.). Although there is also a tax of 2 percent on the capital value of commercial improvements, it is minor compared to the business receipts tax.

Every town and village would like to have its own center for commerce and industry—but only *one* center. Since a city's revenue depends on sales, there is no point in having competition, as far as the city is concerned. If all the shoppers in a region shop at the same central locale, the city can save itself the cost of road, policing, and fire services that otherwise would be spread at two or more locations.

Housing, too, is concentrated, partly due to high land costs. But communities have no reason to encourage tract housing because they receive almost no revenues from it. Housing is exempt from most forms of taxation in Germany—mostly because the country did not want to do anything to discourage the rebuilding of its housing stock after the Second World War.[18] As in the Netherlands, towns in Germany receive more than half their monies from federal revenue sharing, with entitlements based on residents' incomes. Given the relatively even distribution of wealth throughout the country, this system works as an incentive in favor of population, but not as an incentive for large-lot zoning. The town receives its tax sharing whether its residents live clustered in town houses or dispersed in subdivisions. Moreover, for the less affluent towns, there are special subsidies to help meet their governmental operating costs.

---

14. Individuals are not taxed at all, and corporations are taxed at a flat rate of 20 percent, less than half the income rate.

17. The Rhine-Ruhr region probably would resemble the deconcentration of Southern California if there were better transportation, but the German area depends to a considerable extent on a public-transit system ill-suited to commuting and on an even worse road network. "The inadequacy of the road system is most marked within the cities. After 1945 parts of the Rhine-Ruhr cities were rebuilt piecemeal on their old street lines—which in most cases were medieval. The effective result, though it does not seem to have been consciously planned, is to keep the motor vehicle out of the central business districts of the cities." As recently as 1955, two-thirds of all commuter journeys in the Rhine-Ruhr region were made on foot....

18. Tax breaks for those who are saving for home ownership, and the exemption from all but a modest imputed-rent-value tax have probably had the impact of increasing residential densities by increasing the demand for residential land.

The property tax as it exists in the United States makes every local government something akin to a secured lender on every piece of property in its jurisdiction. The local government is assured of a return on all landed wealth, even if the owners of these properties are earning nothing on their investment.

For instance, in the first year after a regional shopping center is built, the local assessor feels perfectly comfortable using construction costs as an appraisal base even though sales levels may be very low. If the center later suffers because of undue competition, the tax assessor can ignore this, too. As long as some shopping centers in the area are doing well, the assessor may argue plausibly that even the center now losing money could be sold at a profit.

Or, take the case of a manufacturer that recently located in the city of Santa Monica. The company lost money last year and consequently paid neither federal nor state income tax. However, the company owns very expensive equipment. Thus, the property tax assessor for the county of Los Angeles valued the building, and particularly the stock, at several million dollars. So this firm, which paid taxes to no other jurisdiction, must pay $60,000 this year to Santa Monica. It is no wonder our city governments tend to take the position that any business locating in a city is a good thing. If the newcomer competes with an existing business to the point that one of them is driven to bankruptcy, the city may remain unconcerned as long as some owner of that property has enough money to keep meeting the property tax payments.

Compare this to the German system. The reliance of German cities on a gross receipts tax causes them to be not unlike preferred or limited partners who are entitled to skim a little of the cream off the top of profitable businesses. As the firm's revenues decline, so also does the city's take.

Through the urban renewal program, American cities have, on occasion, ventured from the safety of their role as tax collector into the troubled waters of equity investment. As land developers, the cities have managed no better and, in many notable instances, considerably worse than private developers. The New York Port Authority's World Trade Center serves as the most wasteful use of land. Even if local governments could be counted on to "make a killing" in real estate, they would fail to satisfy a public that expects more from governments when they act as developers....

* * *

Notes and Comments

1. The intricacies and mysteries of the Internal Revenue Code are beyond the scope of this work. Although there have been significant modifications to the tax treatment of real estate both in the United States and abroad since Professor Lefcoe's article was published, it is an excellent vehicle to appreciate the existence of land use impacts of taxation.

2. For other analyses of the interplay and general impacts of tax on land use, see Edward A. Zimmerman, *Tax Planning for Land Use Control*, 5 Urb. Law. 639 (1973).

3. For an analysis of the incidence and impacts of statutory or court-created property rights on the property tax, see James A. Kushner, *Non-Owner Rights in Real Property and Their Impact on Property Taxes*, 7 Urb. L. & Pol'y 333 (1985).

Chapter 5

The Comprehensive Planning Process

> ....[I]n a metropolitan area the words "comprehensive plan" are meaningless if not self-contradictory when applied to each of one hundred suburbs...."In accordance with a comprehensive plan" is far from being an infallible guide to legitimate municipal decision-making, and in each passing decade as we become cosmopolites in everything but our local political districts the "principle" becomes more fallble.
>
> Richard F. Babcock, The Zoning Game 148 (1966)

The centerpiece of American planning is the comprehensive plan. Charles Haar, *The Master Plan: An Impermanent Constitution*, 20 Law & Contemp. Probs. 353 (1955). Prepared by the best planning officials available, the plan defines the character of the developing community, particularly in the newer edge cities that rise in America. The current dialogue includes discussion of "smart growth" and environmental sustainability, suggesting a more eco-friendly alternative to traditional American sprawl low density development. Yet, while there are an increasing number of reported smart growth initiatives, the existing pattern of detached single-family homes and dispersed shopping all served only by roads and highways is the rule.

American planning law accepts political and planning policy decisions without regard to whether there is access for those without autos, housing for the non-affluent, or whether the town design is consistent with current planning knowledge. In most American towns the only issue on the planning radar is sales tax revenue acquisition. William Fulton, The Reluctant Metropolis: The Politics of Urban Growth in Los Angeles Ch. 10 (1977) ("sales tax canyon"). The mechanism that commits a community to adhere to its plan is the consistency doctrine, statutorily or judicially imposed to require that zoning and land development permit approvals reflect development that is compatible with the comprehensive plan. *Wolf v. City of Ely*, 493 N.W.2d 846 (Iowa 1992). Many states, however, treat the plan as a guide rather than an enforceable standard. *Kozesnik v. Township of Montgomery*, 131 A.2d 1 (N.J. 1997); *Board of Supervisors v. Williams*, 216 S.E.2d 33, 41 (Va. 1975). A plan is also only as effective as the implementation techniques employed. Absent aggressive application of the consistency doctrine limiting development to the plan's requirements, implementation of even a perfect plan will be imperfect.

Witnessing evermore acreage of agricultural land on the urban fringe converted to subdivisions of homes, generating crowded schools and congested roads, many forward looking state legislatures followed a pattern of requiring the comprehensive plan to contain a wide array of elements both to identify environmental impacts and to generate better resource management and more well-reasoned land use planning and development decisions. N.J. Stat. Ann. §40:55D-28; *Twain Harte Homeowners v. County of*

Tuolumne, 188 Cal. Rptr. 233 (Ct. App. 1982). Plans in many states require housing, transportation, recreation, and capital facilities elements, that must be rationally based on planning information and must be internally consistent. *Concerned Citizens v. Calavaras County Bd. of Supervisors*, 212 Cal. Rptr. 273 (Ct. App. 1985).

Current plans, however, continue to be population focused, tax-focused, or infrastructure focused and are rarely based on an urban design form. In the United States it is almost exclusively the advocacy of New Urbanism, an architectural reform movement seeking to create higher density communities served by public transportation with pedestrian-friendly streets, town centers, green pedestrian routes, and utilizing neo-traditional architectural and planning components to place people on walkable streets, porches, and walking paths. See the discussion of New Urbanism in Chapter 11.

American town planning has been driven from market survey information based on the desired housing type and location of those who can afford to purchase the most expensive homes produced. From an economics standpoint many might argue that this is precisely what should happen, producing the most efficient system of housing production. The response is that the low density and pattern or urban design has been imposed by government, often subsidized and typically arbitrary. Robert Cervero, *Growing Smart by Linking Transportation and Urban Development*, 19 Va. Envtl. L.J. 357 (2000) (partially reprinted in Chapter 10).

Most striking may be the American assumption that current planning and development patterns are normatively desirable despite the complete failure of the system to provide access to critical destinations to those without the means of access to a reliable personal automobile. Peter Gordon & Harry W. Richardson, *Are Compact Cities a Desirable Planning Goal?*, 63 J. Am. Plan. Ass'n 232 (1997) (celebrating American sprawl and its popularity). The following excerpt compares the American planning process with the role and function of comprehensive planning under German planning law:

Clifford Larsen, *What Should Be the Leading Principles of Land Use Planning? A German Perspective*,

29 Vanderbilt Journal of Transnational Law 967 (1996)

The passage of the *Raumordnungsgesetz* [The fundamental concept of German land use planning is *Raumordnung*, or the ordering of space, which is established by the legislation entitled *Raumordnungsgesetz* or ROG] was attributable not only to increasing sentiment in favor of its principles, but also to constitutional principles that had not existed prior to the founding of the Federal Republic. Germany's new constitution, the *Grundgesetz*, provided two important underpinnings for the new approach to land use planning. First, federalist principles allowed the federal government to set *Raumordnung's* underlying goals, leaving the states to implement plans to achieve those goals. Second, Germany was established as a social state. Germany's land use planning can be understood only in the context of these constitutional principles.

The *Grundgesetz* provides the basis for the federal-state division of authority that is now a hallmark of German land use planning. This division highlights land use planning's primary goal of equivalent living conditions for all members of society, because, as explained immediately below, certain federal legislative authority may be used only when needed to create equivalent living conditions.

In principle, the German federal legislature, like its U.S. counterpart,[59] has only that legislative authority granted to it by the national constitution.[60] The *Grundgesetz* grants two types of authority to the German federal government. The first type is exclusive authority. Within those fields enumerated by Article 73 of the *Grundgesetz* as being within the exclusive authority of the federal government, the states may legislate only when specifically authorized to do so by federal law. Broad-based land use planning is not listed in Article 73 as an area in which the federal government has exclusive authority.

The second type of federal authority is concurrent authority, *i.e.*, when the federal government "shares" power with the states. This "sharing" is subject to conditions on both levels of government. The states may use their concurrent authority to the extent that the federal government has not used its concurrent authority to legislate. Pursuant to Paragraph 2 of Article 72, the federal government may use its concurrent *authority only to achieve the creation of equivalent living conditions in the country or when the maintenance of legal and economic unity requires federal action.*

The *Grundgesetz* further divides the concurrent authority of the federal government into two types: "full" concurrent authority and "framework" concurrent authority. Article 74 enumerates the areas in which the federal government has "full" concurrent legislative jurisdiction. The federal government may pass detailed legislation in the field, *provided* that the legislative goal is to achieve equivalent living conditions and legal and economic national unity. Again, land use planning is not an enumerated field within the full concurrent authority of the federal government.

The second type of federal concurrent authority allows the federal government to pass "framework laws," or "*Rahmengesetze*," in areas enumerated by the *Grundgesetz*. Although the *Grundgesetz* does not further specify the meaning of "framework law" or the authority of the federal government when acting pursuant thereto, the *Grundgesetz* does state that framework laws may regulate an area in detail only in exceptional circumstances. Once the federal government has passed a law pursuant to its framework authority, the states must pass more detailed implementing legislation. As with federal full concurrent jurisdiction, federal framework concurrent jurisdiction exists only when necessary to achieve equivalent living conditions in the country or to create national political and economic unity. Among the enumerated areas in which the federal government may pass framework laws are the "partitioning of land" and "*Raumordnung*." The main federal legislation in the field of *Raumordnung* is based on this authorization.

Financial provisions of the *Grundgesetz* reinforce the concept that federal activity in a field should be based on the effort to create equivalent living conditions. For example, Article 106 provides that the federal and state governments share the proceeds of sales taxes. The proportions that the federal and state governments receive are determined by a federal law that requires the approval of the *Bundesrat*, the upper house of the legislature that is composed state representatives. One of the leading principles used in determining those proportions provides that the taxes shall be apportioned so as to achieve equivalent living conditions. Similarly, Paragraph 4 of Article 104a allows the federal government, under certain conditions, to provide financial assistance to states, localities, or groups of localities for particularly important investments. One such condition is that investments equalize differences in economic capacity across the country. Finally, as part of its obligation in discharging these responsibilities important to society as a

---

59. *See* U.S. Const. amend. X.

60. "The states have the right to legislate, to the extent that this Constitution does not grant the power to the Federal Government."

whole, the federal government is to finance one-half of each state's expenditures in improving regional economic structures where federal participation is necessary for the improvement of living conditions.

The second underpinning for land use planning and its leading principles in postwar Germany is the establishment of the Federal Republic as a "social state." While disagreeing on the appropriate level of state ownership and the proper amount of control given to workers, all major parties have agreed to move beyond classic liberalism and to provide the state with a role in achieving a social "*Ausgleich*" or equalization.

Article 20, Paragraph 1 of the *Grundgesetz* embodies this social state principle. It reads simply: "The Federal Republic of Germany is a democratic and social federal state." *Grundgesetz* Article 28, Paragraph 1 further requires that the constitutional order of the constituent states correspond to the principles of the republican, democratic, and social state of law as provided by the *Grundgesetz*. The principle of Article 20 is considered so basic to the German constitutional order that *Grundgesetz* Article 79, Paragraph 3 forbids any change to the Constitution affecting the social state principle.

Article 20 does not define the term "social state." Nor does Article 20, in and of itself, generally provide a cause of action for a citizen to claim that the state must act in accordance with its social mandate. Similarly, the Federal Constitutional Court, the Federal Administrative Court, and the Federal Social Court have all held that an individual citizen generally has no right to state benefits, particularly financial ones, unless granted by law. Rather, the Federal Constitutional Court has referred to the social state principle embodied in the *Grundgesetz* as an "open-ended" principle that is both capable of and requires a high degree of shaping.

This open-endedness does not mean that the constitutional commitment to a social state is an empty phrase, especially in determining the basic principles of land use planning. Going beyond the concept of the classic liberal state of law, the social state principle *obliges* the state to actively shape the society. In an early decision, the Federal Constitutional Court stated that the legislature "is constitutionally required to be active in the social arena, in particular to provide for an acceptable balancing of competing interests and the providing of acceptable living conditions for all those who are in need." More specifically, German courts have held that a social state must work toward social justice and security, meet the needs of those in economic distress, and abolish the disadvantages suffered by certain groups and classes of citizens. This obligation has been further interpreted to mean that the legislature is required to reduce the economic gap between rich and poor.

Thus, rather than providing the basis for any particular claim, the social state principle can be seen as providing the general direction and goals toward which the state must strive. This direction is binding not just on the legislature, but on all branches of government. In particular, government ministries are obliged to follow the social state principles when using their discretion in setting the norms for the interpretation of laws.

The social state principle of Article 20 shapes German law not only in its own right, but also in its influence on the interpretation of other provisions of the *Grundgesetz*. Articles 1 through 19 are considered to embody basic rights, or *Grundrechte*, the substance of which may not be infringed upon. For example, Article 1, Paragraph 1 of the *Grundgesetz* provides: "Human dignity is inviolable. To respect it and protect it is the duty of all state authority." The Federal Constitutional Court has interpreted this Article, *in connection with the social state principle of Article 20*, to mean that the state *must* provide a minimum level of benefits necessary for survival because the care of those in need is an "obvious" duty of the social state....

In addition to Article 2, Article 14 of the *Grundgesetz* specifically adds a social component to the ownership of land. Article 14, Paragraph 1 guarantees the right to property (and the right to inherit), but allows the right to be restricted by law. More importantly, Article 14, Paragraph 2 states: "Property entails obligation. Its use should serve the well-being of society." This provision reinforces the concept, inherent in Article 2, that the individual's use of space is inextricably linked to the relationship of the individual to society....

An example of the interplay between the overarching principles of Article 1 and the more specific goals of Article 2 can be found in the goal of creating a balanced, integrated structure of urban and rural areas. Rather than allowing an urban area to expand unchecked, with subsequent overburdening of infrastructure and disappearance of green space, planners attempt to spread urban development and coordinate the building of traffic, supply, and disposal facilities. For rural areas, Article 2 establishes further priorities, such as the creation of a diversified economy, even in those areas where rural population is declining. For all areas, other Article 2 goals include respecting the environment (including ecologically sound agriculture and forestry), providing housing in areas of heavy job concentration, and meeting the needs of the population for recreation in natural surroundings. Because these sometimes contradictory goals are not listed in any order of priority and cannot be pursued simultaneously, Article 2 provides that they should be weighted *in accordance with the principles of Article 1....*

While German practice has always been to emphasize the achievement of "equivalent living conditions" as the chief goal of land use planning, the ROG itself does not define the term. By considering both official and unofficial statements, however, the broad outlines of the policy become relatively easy to discern:

> The designation "equivalent living conditions" is not meant to mean equality in the sense of equalizing. That meaning, in light of the very different structures of the individual regions of the Federal Republic of Germany, is illusionary and not reachable. Rather, this equality means an equivalence in the sense that in each region, especially through the providing of necessary infrastructure, all main activities can be undertaken and at least a minimum level of proper environmental conditions can be achieved. In specific terms, most important are varied work opportunities within a reasonable distance from the home, the possibility of modern living, appropriate environmental policies and the maintenance of natural resources as well as a sufficient supply, through public and private channels, of the populace with goods and services and infrastructure for all levels of needs, within a reasonable distance of the home....

This state involvement in the creation of equivalent living conditions reflects a conviction that market forces, the main engine for growth, will not by themselves create the equivalent living conditions that are the goal of both *Raumordnung* and the social state. Rather, the state must actively guide, even counterbalance, market forces....

The [the Federal Ministry of Land Use Planning, Building, and Urban Development (*Bundesministerium für Raumordnung, Bauwesen und Städtebau* or "BBauM")] plays the major federal role in these activities. Because federal authority in land use planning has been based primarily on the federal government's "framework" competence, the BBauM does not engage in detailed land use planning for the states, nor does it act as a "super ministry" in which all federal activity relating to spatial ordering is planned. Rather, the BBauM is charged with the coordination of federal and state land use planning activities, the issuing of reports on *Raumordnung*, and the review of the general direction and priorities of land use planning....

In providing direction and guidance to the states, the BBauM and its research arm, the Federal Research Institute for the Study of States and Land Use Planning (*Bundesanstalt für Landeskunde und Raumordnung*), provide studies on dozens of issues relevant to land use planning: population growth and structure, local and regional infrastructure, availability of housing and leisure facilities, environmental issues, and many others. For example, the BBauM divides the country into a number of analytical regions based upon criteria such as the number of cities of a certain size and the interconnections among those cities. The living conditions in these regions are then compared. Subsequent state actions are often based on these studies....

While federal legislation establishes the *Raumordnung* framework by designating ultimate goals such as the achievement of equivalent living conditions and methods of coordination and cooperation between and among levels of government, the individual German states are responsible for the implementation of those goals through the planning process....

One such vehicle for steering planning so as to achieve equivalent living conditions is the establishment of a state land use "plan." This plan typically determines long-term goals, often for a period of fifteen to twenty years, although state law provides for modification of the plans before the end of that period. Providing the point of departure for many of the specific decisions made by state and local level planners, the plan considers a vast array of factors that indicate whether the state is achieving its goal that all citizens have access, within a reasonable distance of their homes, to all major public and private infrastructural facilities....

As at the federal level, the state-level quest for equivalent living conditions leads inexorably to another central feature of land use planning: close coordination among different levels of government and between government and other groups. For example, in addition to establishing the state plan, state-level planning officials perform a number of activities in approving and coordinating activities within the state. The state reviews the county (*Kreis*) and free city (*kreisfreie Stadt*) development plans, which are drafted for a period of five years, and may disapprove the plans if they do not meet federal and state planning goals. Local planners wishing to establish plans must also inform state planners, who then notify local officials of the goals of federal and state planning law, both of which are binding on local planning. The actual local plans must be submitted to state planners before the plans may go into effect.

In addition, state planning officials can in certain instances delay, for a period up to two years, building activities that are in accordance with published local plans, yet contrary to new or changed state planning goals....

Establishment of a Central Cities System

Another vehicle employed by state planning to provide all citizens with equivalent living conditions is the federally-mandated central cities system. This system, based on the pioneering work of Walter Cristaller in the 1930s and later refinements by August Loesch, starts with the principle that a community is interwoven with the surrounding area for which the community provides the source of services and facilities. The size of the surrounding area supplied by the city and the array of goods and services offered varies with the size of the city. Briefly summarized, the central cities system channels certain types or levels of development and limited government resources into particular areas, and in so doing, attempts to assure that all citizens have access to a full array of work, social, cultural, and educational opportunities within a reasonable distance of their homes.

... [C]ities and towns are given different designations as "centers" of various levels, or as no center at all, with each designation determining the level of development allowed in that city or town. State law provides that each type of center is to have certain minimal facilities, both private and public, and specifies the type of commercial development allowed. Thus, the smallest designated centers, known as country centers (*ländliche Zentralorte*), meet the basic needs of the town itself and the immediately surrounding community. These centers are to have:

> grade schools [grades 1–4] and, whenever possible, *Hauptschule* [the upper-level of a non-college-preparatory elementary school], playground and sports facilities, open-air swimming pool, kindergarden, medical and dental services, pharmacy, small retail stores, tradesmen and craftsmen, [private] service providers such as branches of credit institutions, as well as local government institutions.

The next-highest level, small centers (*Unterzentren*), are to provide a more complete source of supply for basic needs. As stated above, in reference to the town of Trittau, small centers are to have, in addition to the facilities of a country center:

> full-time local administration, Realschule [a secondary school largely non-college-preparatory], special schools, doctors who specialize, credit institutions, individual state officials or service centers, a [state] employment office, and where size warrants, a technical school, and college-preparatory secondary school.

The next-highest level, middle-size centers (*Mittelzentren*), provide goods and services not only for daily needs, but also for middle-term needs of the city itself and of several surrounding smaller cities. The additional facilities they should contain are:

> Trade and technical schools, college-preparatory schools, other educational facilities, especially those for adult education, general hospitals, doctors in many different specialty areas, larger sports facilities, the offices of lower-level federal and state officials, courts and credit institutions.

The highest designation, main centers (*Oberzentren*), meet not only short-term and middle-term needs, but also long-term needs of the city itself and of its large surrounding area, including middle and small "centers" and rural areas. Main centers have:

> Post-secondary education [universities, technical universities, etc.], hospitals of supra-regional status, stadia, covered swimming pools, theaters, department stores, higher-level or regionally-responsible federal and state officials, courts, insurance and large credit institutions

Main centers are also to have large, diversified industrial bases that are to be further developed.

The law further provides additional designations for cities on the outskirts of other centers and "mixed" designations for cities that provide goods or services at different levels.

The state provides financial assistance to the central cities for these facilities. In addition, in order for the central cities system to help achieve equivalent living conditions, inhabitants of smaller towns must be able to travel to the facilities in larger centers.

5. Kuperbusch-Siedlung. Acqueducts and landscaped drainage ponds built on the revitalized brownfields of the Ruhr at a project designed to integrate the disabled and non-disabled in the community's housing and school in Gelson-Kirchen, Germany.

Thus, state law strives to organize the road and rail system such that larger centers are accessible by road and rail from smaller centers....

In 1989, Article 1 of the ROG was amended to include, among other things, a new "leading principle." Article 1, Paragraph 3 now reads:

> The *Raumordnung* in the Federal Republic is to create and promote the spatial prerequisites for cooperation in the European area.

The addition of this principle parallels the development of *Raumordnung* philosophy in Germany since the 1960s: just as there are certain spatial ordering problems that cannot be solved at the local level, thus requiring the development of *Raumordnung* at the state and national level, so are there European-level modalities that create spatial and habitation structure issues that cannot be addressed exclusively at the national level. Germany's position has thus been to support both cooperation between neighbors and those European-level activities in particular subject areas that affect the ordering of space....

While similar tensions between governmental regulation and total freedom of action exist in any democratic system, land use planning as practiced in Germany could not be applied as easily in the United States. As well as having different histories and population densities, U.S. and German citizens start from widely varying constitutional premises. For example, the German conception of freedom is at once both broader and narrower than its American counterpart. It is narrower in that individual freedom is more clearly linked to and limited by existence in society, and broader in that freedom is not merely the right of the individual to do as he pleases, but also the right of free development of the personality in connection with the social state obligation to provide the conditions necessary for that individual development.

Not surprisingly, Americans and Germans tend to have different mentalities in approaching land use planning issues. For example, U.S. citizens would be unlikely to grant public officials the power to make the sweeping decisions necessary to achieve a principle such as equivalent living conditions. That hesitance would be particularly great when the officials are primarily non-elected and operating at the state level, rather than local and elected. In addition, the German approach of achieving consensus on land use planning issues—through the political means of inclusion of many different groups in *the* decision-making process, but then precluding many private legal challenges to the system—would seem unusual to U.S. citizens accustomed to relying more heavily on the courts to regulate the relation of the individual to government....

* * *

Notes and Comments

1. How would Germany's planning requirement of equivalent living conditions be applied or enforced in the United States? Would the principle provide greater protection than the Equal Protection Clause of the Fourteenth Amendment to the United States Constitution?

The following excerpt describes how planning theory is being applied in the People's Republic of China:

Mark T. Kremzner, *Managing Urban Land in China: The Emerging Legal Framework and its Role in Development,*

7 Pacific Rim Law & Policy Journal 611 (1998)

The Formal Legal Framework for Urban Planning

The Land Management Law, Urban Planning Law, and 1995 Real Estate Law establish an integrated urban planning legal framework that aims to modernize cities, coordinate urban land uses, and regulate the growth of urban areas. To achieve these objectives, these national laws attempt to control the amount of land available for urban development and expansion and the way in which particular parcels of land are used. The legal framework evidences the legacy of central economic planning institutions, where the current urban planning regime originated from. In particular, the legal framework is premised on the belief that plans based primarily upon the interests and instructions of central authorities will be closely adhered to by municipal authorities.

The Detailed and Overall City Plans

All municipal governments are required to formulate two types of urban plans that "scientifically forecast local needs." The detailed city plan (*chengshi xiangxi guihua*) addresses building height, density limits, construction standards, and the particulars of specific proposed development projects, including floor area plans. The overall city plan (*chengshi zongti guihua*) addresses matters such as zoning, land use layout, construction standards, transportation systems and green space. The overall city plan must be coordinated with several other land management plans that have been approved by higher level authorities. These are the national land plan (*guotu guihua*), regional plan (*quyu*), waterway and lowland plan (*jianghe liuyu guihua*) and the overall land utilization plan (*tudi liyong zongti guihua*). The overall city plan must be submitted to higher level authorities for approval, thereafter the detailed city plan may be submitted to the municipal people's government for approval. Upon approval of the overall and detailed city plans, all land within a municipality must be used according to the contents and requirements of the approved overall and detailed urban plans. Overall urban plans are supposed to have a term of approximately ten to twenty years, while detailed urban plans often are revised every several years. In addition to these national urban planning law provisions, there may be locally promulgated rules detailing urban planning procedures and requirements. While many medium and small sized municipalities have little land use legislation, most major cities do.

Land Utilization Plans

China's current urbanization policy seeks to minimize the growth of large urban areas and facilitate the "appropriate development" of medium and small cities. There are two planning systems that operate to help secure this objective. The overall land utilization plans are employed to balance agricultural and non-agricultural land uses and serve to guide the course and direction of urban development on a larger scale. The "land use grant plans" (*tudi shiyong churang jihua*) are more of a micro-management tool, which serve to monitor specific land development and construction projects within a municipality or county....

Each year provincial level governments and the State Council establish quotas on the amount of land use rights that may be granted out by each municipal government....

Urban Planning and Development in Practice

The formal legal framework provides the state with a significant degree of authority to plan urban land uses. However, in practice the central government has not obtained the desired planning and orderly uses of urban land that the formal law seemingly provides. One reason for this is that the interests and objectives of central government officials differ significantly from those of local authorities. This has made it difficult for central authorities to secure the cooperation of local officials and obtain proper enforcement of the formal legal framework.

Central level planning authorities are interested in city and land use plans based on accurate local data. They want to more effectively coordinate urban growth and land use within a broader region. From the perspective of central authorities, urban land planning should ensure that there are sufficient amounts of agricultural land available to supply food to urban centers, and that there are adequate infrastructure facilities for industrial, commercial and residential facilities. Cities with industrial or commercial facilities that succeed in generating new jobs may be allowed to expand and convert agricultural land to urban uses. Those that have succeeded in attracting foreign investment may be allowed to convert agricultural land to urban uses and establish ETDZs or similar types of preferential zones. The formal legal framework is premised upon coordination and cooperation among urban areas. Yet the reality of the economic reform era is that cities and districts within cities are engaged in fierce competition to have domestic and foreign enterprises locate within their boundaries and to be connected to or supplied with infrastructure, systems such as transport networks, power lines and water supplies.

Municipal Party chairs and city mayors pursue their own set of objectives, which coincide little with those of central authorities. Local officials frequently manipulate information fed to higher authorities and tailor the content of city and land use plans to advance their particular economic development and political strategies. The factual information set forth in the overall city plans may be intentionally misleading or erroneous. Figures on the amount of agricultural and urban land are reduced in order to prevent higher level authorities from properly calculating the actual amount of revenue earned from taxes and land use grants. Agricultural yields might be adjusted upward or industrial expansion and employment rates exaggerated to justify, or obtain permission for, conversion of arable land to urban uses. From the perspective of municipal authorities urban planning is about promoting local development, facilitating job growth and increasing the status of their city vis-a-vis other political units. Increased status of a city confers greater administrative authority upon local officials, thus freeing them from some of the restrictions and demands imposed by higher level authorities. As a city expands, so too does the political power base of municipal Party secretaries and city mayors. Thus, for many local authorities urban planning is not about controlling growth and land uses, but merely about growing as rapidly as possible.

Local level urban planning also is significantly more political, and less scientific than called for under the Urban Planning Law. Each municipal Party chair typically assembles a small committee, known as a "small leadership group" (*lingdaoxiaozu*) composed of officials from an array of commissions and local offices. The small leadership group discusses and negotiates a broad range issues such as where particular industries are to be situated, what land is to be utilized for agricultural needs, and the requirements and location of infrastructure (roads, power, water, sewer, etc.) While technical planning factors, such as environmental conditions or proximity to conflicting uses are addressed, these often are not overriding considerations. Commercial or political interests typically prevail. As many frustrated professionals in MOC urban planning departments across China will admit, their technical recommendations often are not followed. Rather, they receive instructions from the small leadership group on how the overall and detailed city plans should be prepared. Afterwards the city plans receive an unofficial approval by the municipal Party secretary, and sometimes the mayor, and are sent upward for approval as required by the Urban Planning Law. In most locales city plans change within a few years, whenever a new municipal Party secretary takes office or other political conditions change.

Municipal officials also exercise a high degree of discretion in enforcing city and land use plans. Investors and developers, both domestic and foreign, will negotiate with municipal officials over such issues as project location, site layout and building design. Beyond the application and permitting stage, compliance with the urban plans is more problematic. Once construction begins, either on a project that has properly obtained all necessary permits or one that has not, enforcement often is a politically charged affair. After obtaining information from an enforcement committee, superior officials may decide not to enforce or prosecute the matter, perhaps because of a personal or political connection with the violator. If the decision is made to enforce, a negotiated solution may be reached that permits the structure or project to continue within prescribed limits. This is such a typical occurrence that developers frequently prepare a site and pour foundations as quickly as possible, knowing that there is a strong likelihood that a settlement can be reached allowing the structure to stand. During the period 1990 to

1995, more than two hundred million square meters of illegally built floor space was constructed. In mid-1995 the Ministry of Construction announced that it would launch a campaign to enforce urban planning in six hundred cities throughout the country.[208] More significant than the official response is the increase in the incidence of private enforcement actions, whereby citizens bring suit to prevent or remedy illegal land uses.

Some of the most serious defects in the urban planning system have been in securing compliance with the land supply plans. Over the past decade so much arable land reportedly has been improperly converted to urban uses that SLA officials have warned the nation is on the brink of becoming dependent upon foreign imports of food. There are several reasons for the breakdown of the land supply regulation system. First, municipal governments have failed or neglected to comply with the land quotas issued to them by higher level authorities. Second, investors and land development companies simply enter into deals with collectives or local officials for the purchase and acquisition of collectively owned land without obtaining approval to requisition, convert and obtain land use rights through the SLA.

In response to these problems, the SLA, in cooperation with the SPC, initiated a series of investigations and campaigns beginning in the mid-1990s. In 1996, the SLA and SPC jointly implemented procedures to limit the issuance of land use permits according to the annual construction use land plan and prohibit any construction not authorized under that plan. To ensure compliance by local officials, the procedures stipulate that any government unit that violates its annual land use plan quota shall have its annual construction quota reduced and the offending government official criminally prosecuted. In April 1997, additional steps were taken when the SLA placed a moratorium on all non-agricultural land uses. Along with the Ministry of Supervision and other central government departments the SLA launched a nationwide investigation to determine whether local and provincial officials were complying and enforcing properly all national land management laws. Significantly, in an effort to ensure the continued flow of foreign capital, the SLA announced that foreign funded development projects would be exempt from the land use freeze.

* * *

Notes and Comments

1. China's planning compared to the German system would be characterized as weak. How would you characterize the planning systems in the United States?

An interesting debate in planning theory is whether planning utilizes fiction in the way that planning-related public relations or propaganda tends to define or marginalize reality. For example, communities tend to emphasize the country or rural secluded private or old-fashioned main street commercial center, but what they may be planning is a staging area for a long commute to ever-more dispersed inconveniently located subur-

---

208. Many of these violations however are not committed by the holders of granted land use rights, but by the holders or occupiers of administratively allocated land use rights, many of whom are state enterprises, central ministries, municipal agencies, and the defense establishment. While administrative allocated land is subject to the requirements of the detailed urban plans, the holders of such land are not required to enter into land use contracts with the SLA detailing uses and construction design.

ban job sites. The following is a discussion of planning theory from a Dutch perspective through the subject of the existence of The Netherlands "Green Heart:"

Michel van Eeten & Emery Rose, *When Fiction Conveys Truth and Authority: The Netherlands Green Heart Planning Controversy*,

66 Journal of the American Planning Association 58 (2000)

Spatial planners are strange characters. They traffic in fiction, and at the same time ask us to take it all seriously. Even more surprising, those of us who are not planners do take them at their word and grant them the authority they crave. This open-eyed reliance on fiction as a basis for public policy is remarkable, to put it mildly, and requires explanation....

The congruence and mutual dependence of fiction and authority are illustrated through a case study of the Dutch Green Heart region. The Green Heart refers to the less urbanized area between the four major Dutch cities of Rotterdam, The Hague, Amsterdam, and Utrecht. The cities and other urban areas that encircle the Green Heart like a horseshoe are called the "Randstad City Ring." The City Ring and Green Heart together comprise the Randstad area, the Netherlands' economic and demographic core.

Recently, the Green Heart planning concept has become the focal point of a major policy controversy. Its dominant feature is the tension between the fictionality of the Green Heart concept and the authority with which it continues to be treated. The concept has been fiercely criticized for its fictional nature. The Green Heart does not exist, according to the critics, and therefore it cannot be used to justify far-reaching policy measures. Surprisingly, however, the concept has been immune to this criticism. Advocates of the concept admit it is fictional, but still maintain that it is the most appropriate basis for policymaking. The two sides in this important controversy have become deadlocked. Our analysis explains why the problematic Green Heart concept persists, even when it is not factually true. We do this by showing how fiction conveys truth, and how truth and authority are welded together in a series of step and forms. It turns out that the critics, although correct about the fictional status of the Green Heart concept, have not gotten to the truth that really matters.

To understand the controversy, we first examine the general practice of Dutch planning. In the Netherlands, spatial planning has been a governmental preoccupation for decades. Its importance is best glimpsed in the rapid expansion of spatial planning itself as a profession and in the elaborate policy system that has blossomed around the planning of buildings, infrastructure, and associated spatial activities. Ideally, spatial planners identify, if not create, options for the planning and development of all kinds of activities, including housing, industry, nature conservation, transport, and recreation. Part of their task is to manage competing claims to space. Conflict resolution is site specific and contingent on variable local considerations, whereas plans and their documentation describe more or less abstract arrangements of functions over a space that has been washed of many of it particulars—by necessity, planners would insist.

Planning concepts are the pivot of spatial planning. Through words and images they articulate the ways in which the desired spatial arrangements are viewed, as well as the nature of the interventions deemed essential. Concepts that demonstrate rather than actions that implement are the planners' most important instrument today, since it is abundantly clear that many societal and governmental actors cannot be regulated by the putatively "binding" plans of spatial planners. Even within such a narrow horizon, planning concepts still influence the ways in which these stakeholders think. Dutch planners have made a virtue of the fact that they persuade rather than direct. And as the role of persuasion has increased, so too has storytelling moved toward the center of planning.

When reading their plans, you cannot fail to notice the peculiarly pictorial nature of the language planners use. Dutch planning is not unique in this respect, as others have demonstrated. Plans are runways where metaphors take off. In the Dutch context, this includes current planning concepts such as the compact city, buffer zones, transport axes, green wedges, blue chambers, and, of course, the Green Heart. An almost literary use of language permeates the documents of planners and, perhaps to an even greater extent, their oral renditions. Anybody who has ever heard planners in action knows that they are skilled storytellers. With a compelling story, colorful images and metaphors that last, they increase the chances of getting their message(s) across and convincing us of likely futures and plausible policy interventions. It is difficult to resist the ethnological comparison of planners and their forums with the practice and rituals of traditional doctors, whose kits include evocative art and incantatory language....

The joint Green Heart/City Ring concept has been central to Dutch planning doctrine for years. Keeping the Green Heart open became a central tenet of national policy in the 1950s, when planners feared a doomsday scenario of metastasizing urbanization filling the open spaces among the existing towns and cities. This scenario still plays an important role in today's controversy, and it is frequently referred to as the "Los Angeles Syndrome." According to the scenario, if the Randstad is allowed to develop spontaneously, the whole region is in jeopardy. The planners' worst nightmare would materialize—a "stone, suburban desert." To prevent this from happening, the planners argue that action needs to be taken and policy choices made, notwithstanding the complexity of the issues. The story line about protecting the right-and-heart structure of the area as a way of averting the doomsday scenario is the dominant narrative driving current Dutch spatial planning.

Fear of uncontrollable suburbanization has led to the acceptance of the proposition that the center of the Randstad should be kept open. In addition to being a barrier to further urbanization, the open area would provide citizens of the Randstad with large parks and recreation sites. In this way, planners see the open center as the function "heart" that keeps the urbanized areas alive and vital.

The Green Heart and City Ring concepts have been directly translated into far-reaching policy choices. One key decision concerns the locations for new housing projects. It is estimated that nearly 1 million new houses will have to be built in the next two decades. The twin concepts set the framework and determine the planning alternatives from which to choose: on the Ring, outside the Ring, or inside the Ring. Inside the city Ring is rejected because of the need to preserve the Green Heart. Building outside the Ring has increased vehicle and congestion problems in the past. So, the logic goes, the most sensible choice is to build on the Ring. Indeed, national planning policy states: Decision: Not outside the ring, not inside the ring into the Green Heart, but intensifying urban areas on the ring."

To preserve the Green Heart, additional restrictions have been established. These severely restrictive policies limit the rights of local governments and market forces to develop housing and industry in the area. Funds are also channeled into projects aiming to reinforce the green features of the Green Heart....

Current policy entails major interventions and high costs. For example, residential construction on the Ring is much more expensive than in the Green Heart. These higher costs could result in less housing being developed, thereby ensuring a persistent shortage. Another example is the investment of approximately 1 billion guilders (about half a billion U.S. dollars) for building an underground tunnel for the highspeed train that runs through their region....

Critics aim mainly at two aspects of the joint concept as it has been used in practice. First, they argue that keeping the Green Heart open is unrealistic and undesirable because of certain societal developments and potentially adverse results. For example, some critics say that housing will find its way into the Green Heart anyway. For the past three decades, the rate of urbanization and economic growth in the Green Heart has been higher than that of the surrounding city....

Second, critics claim the Green Heart concept is fictional and therefore unacceptable as a basis for national policy. If trying to keep the Green Heart open is not a sensible course of action in view of societal development already underway, it is but a short step to question whether there is such a thing as a Green Heart in the first place. If it isn't actually there, why treat it seriously? In any case, why take great pains to keep it open and risk incurring costs that well exceed the benefits?...

The Green Heart does not form an homogeneous unity. This argument is that from the perspective of the physical landscape, there is no recognizable, continuous whole one could call the Green Heart. Instead, the region between the cities displays a wide diversity of landscapes. Moreover, this region is transected by infrastructure: freeways, railroad lines, and high-voltage wires. According to Loezing, "those who want to see the unity of the Green Heart will have to look for it on the maps of the national and provincial planning agencies."

The Green Heart has no firm boundaries. In the current national plan, *Vierde Nota Ruimetelijke Ordening Extra* (VINEX), the Green Heart has been demarcated precisely, with a clear boundary mapped around it....

The Green Heart is scarcely green. According to one of its sharpest critics, the Green Heart is a "biological disaster area where only masochists can find beautiful routes for recreation," and a "motley meadow that, thanks to European Union subsidies, has developed itself into a monotonous and gloomy agricultural industrial zone."...Only a few limited parts of the Green Heart have environmental integrity in terms of an ecosystem: What have been defined as "nature and recreational areas" make up only 3.8% of the Green Heart, which looks pale when compared to a national average of 14.8% and a City Ring average of 16.0%. Of course, there still is the "green" of the rural landscape, and indeed, 83.1% of the area is agricultural land. But this pastoral idyll rings hollow when one realizes that the population density in the Green Heart is 470 people / km2—a figure which is slightly higher than the national average (440 people/km2) of a nation not known for being an unspoiled, rural country.

The Randstad City Ring does not exist...The geographical relationship of the Ring cities to one another—e.g., in terms of commuting between them—does not in and of itself constitute a coherent, continuous "ring." Furthermore, residents have little sense of identity as citizens of the Randstad as a whole. They identify mainly with their city or town, not with something like "the Ring."...

The Green Heart is not so open...Everywhere in the Green Heart one can see urban buildings a short distance away; there is no more visual openness per se....

Fiction, as we all know, can convey higher truths. Indeed, fiction is one of our primary mechanisms for rising above the hurly-burly of minutiae, sense data, and simple factuality in order to say something truthful about what really matters. When this happens, a piece of fiction is true, precisely because it is fiction. This is the case for the Green Heart/City Ring concept....

Let us look at some of the alternatives to the Green Heart and City Ring concepts: Ladder Metropolis, Green Archipelago, and Green Metropolis. Rather than being exclusively oppositional, these alternatives share one thing in common with the Green Heart and City Ring concepts: They all turn out to be the product of the same map reading strategy, which we call the "iconographic gaze." According to Van Alphen, "the gaze is a reading attitude that conflates model and figure in representation, that is an attitude encouraged by 'transparent' realism, effacing any traces of the labor of representation." For example, the Ladder Metropolis concept uses the image of a ladder to read the spatial structure of the western Netherlands. This metaphor is retained as it is transferred from the map surface into the text of planning documents and back again. The Green Archipelago concept both describes and maps green areas in a more or less urbanized sea. Both in words and on the map, the Green Metropolis concept nests the Green Heart and City Ring together into one unit, the metropolis, the green areas of which are like parks on a citymap....

If you want a way out of the controversy, the answer is not to come up with alternatives like those discussed so far. They are all about finding the correct, referentially accurate icon. In this way, they fall victim to the iconographic approach that treats maps as the *sine qua non* of land use planning. This approach will only perpetuate the planning dialogue-of-the-deaf on truth and fiction. Literally, there is no mapping our way out of the deadlock. The significance of this becomes apparent when we realize that an important part of the strategy of the central planning agency continues to be characterized as "planning through consensus building," as evidenced by the so-called "Green Heart Conversations" with experts and stakeholders that the agency organized in 1995.

Instead of more of the same, we offer two solutions. One way out of the controversy is to adopt planning approaches that depend much less directly on maps and cartographic imaging. Obvious candidates include process or learning approaches that rely much more on activities and linkages than on spatial fixedness and identity. One example will have to suffice. A major criticism, you'll remember, has been that the Green Heart has rates of urbanization and population increase greater than those of the Ring cities. This is true, but what about its semiotic opposite, the greening of the urban areas, particularly those of the City Ring? If we are to better plan for the Green Heart's inevitable urbanization, as the critics are demanding of us, then we should also be planning for the greening of the Ring cities, for each entails the other. We would go so far as to say both have to be planned together if they are to make any planning sense. Moreover—and here is our crucial point—if you are planning the variegated greening of the cities, you will be using planning approaches that are *not* predominantly iconographic or even map oriented. Such planning would revolve around focus group needs and preferences, neighborhood environmental initiatives, community tree planting, and home gardening, all of which may have aspects that can be mapped, but none of which are to be evaluated solely or even centrally in terms of their mappability, as the Green Heart has been.

An even more profound way out of the controversy would be to deny the hegemony of the planners themselves....Throughout this controversy, it is the planners who have determined the given, the descriptions, the scenario, the stakes in the controversy, and the wider context in which this all takes place. How to move beyond this hegemony and develop spatial planning into something more useful is the challenge confronting Dutch planning at the beginning of the 21st century.

* * *

Ernest R. Alexander, *Netherlands Planning: The Higher Truth*,

67 Journal of the American Planning Association 91 (2001)

....Iconographic metaphors are the basic language for communicating about space, whether physical or conceptual. To realize this it is enough to look at any other field, from astronomy (e.g., spiral galaxies) to genetics (e.g., the double helix of DNA), to understand that this is a way of conveying meaning that the longest, best, and most detailed text cannot rival. That is why the iconographic metaphor is an intrinsic element—perhaps even the core—of any planning doctrine. In light of the Dutch term for planning, *ruimtelijke ordening* (spatial order) it is surprising that van Eeten and Roe, of all people, seem to forget that space is mainly what this kind of planning is about, and that designing possible futures for space is perhaps the most important thing planners can do. And since the subject of these plans is physical/territorial space, maps are necessary for the two-way translation between the diagramatic abstraction of the metaphor and the concrete realities of geographic location.

But their alternatives to iconographic metaphors and mapping suggest that the authors' problem is less the approach itself as the scale of its application, in terms of governance. Their counterproposal to the "Green Heart"—combining controlled urbanization of the previously reserved "green" area with "the greening of the Ring Cities"—can also be expressed in an iconographic metaphor and spatially mapped. In fact it has been, and while so far this argument has not proved persuasive in the current national debate, it may yet lead to a radical revision of the prevailing doctrine. However, this is not what they advocate. Rather, they propose planning that "would revolve around focus group needs and preferences, neighborhood environmental initiatives,...and home gardening,...none of which are to be evaluated solely or even centrally...as the Green Heart has been."

This leads directly into their normative agenda "...to deny the hegemony of the planners themselves—for example by protecting the heterogeneous local communities which seek control over their own territories." Here van Eeten and Roe have not only forgotten that planning is about space; they have forgotten the essence of what planning is about: averting the "tragedy of the commons," what happens when individual "lords" of their own domains and communities that control their own territories meet their short-term wants and "needs" and pursue their own rational self-interests.

Perhaps a country like the U.S. with its redundancy and resources can afford the luxury of Jeffersonian democracy and local autonomy, which seem to be van Eeten and Roe's nonplanned utopia, although it is debatable whether even there it ever existed or is feasible today. For a small, crowded country like The Netherlands, abdicating "the hegemony" of planning to give "local communities...control over their own territories" is simply impossible in terms of the most basic functional interdependencies which demand planning: coordinating individuals', households', and firms' location and investment decisions with public investments at the metropolitan, regional, and national levels....

* * *

Emery Roe & Michel van Eeten, *The Heart of the Matter: A Radical Proposal,*

67 Journal of the American Planning Association 92 (2001)

....Our approach is different. Greening of the agricultural lands or urban areas adjacent to the three nature reserves has merit in and of itself, apart from whatever effect it would have the nature reserves. The greening of agricultural land could take place through a number of different options. Between two nature reserves could be a housing settlement, the profits from which could be used to purchase even more agriculture land around the housing estate that could, in turn, be improved so that ecological functions were now better off than they were under agriculture. In addition, a different set of the nature reserves could be linked by an office block complex, the profits from which would be used to purchase adjacent agricultural land and resold only to those who would use it for more environmentally friendly or sustainable agriculture purposes, for example, the land would be resold with conditions that it be used for organic agriculture or incorporate soil-enhancing crop rotations. In this way, the Network would end up not only with greener land uses than found now on the agricultural land in question, but also with corridors between them that probably could not have been funded otherwise (i.e., the Network could not compete against the price urban uses would pay for the land in question)....

Such an approach to greening the Green Heart is diametrically opposed to the current strategy of contesting urbanization at every juncture. Not only is the current strategy a losing proposition—urbanization in the Green Heart continues, as do the number of proposals to accelerate it even further—but it also fails to sufficiently recognize the degree to which ecosystem functions and services are being harmed under current land use practices and the high opportunity costs of not taking action now, because there is a real potential for improving ecological functions. Under our proposal, it would be the land developers who pay for the improvement of ecological functions as core to their overall development proposals....

By this point, it should be clear that nothing in the above proposal calls for the devolution of planning to local governments and groups, nor do we call for the end of spatial planning and the advent of unplanned utopias....

* * *

Ernest R. Alexander, *Alexander Responds,*

67 Journal of the American Planning Association 97 (2001)

...Finally, I submit that Drs. van Eeten and Roe's proposal illustrates my assertions concerning iconography in planning, rather than refuting them, as they seem to think. In the article that was the subject of my comment, they advocated the abandonment of mapping or spatial diagrams as a way of conceptualizing and communicating planning ideas, and their analysis (correctly) showing the essential fictitiousness of planning metaphors implied that using such metaphors in planning discourse was wrong.

My comment rejected both these conclusions because (1) some form of graphic presentation (maps or diagrams) is essential for communicating any ideas that have a spatial dimension, as planning concepts and doctrines must have; and (2) the fact that all metaphors are essentially fictions in their relation to reality in no way diminishes their usefulness in conceptualizing and communicating planning ideas.

Their proposal does not dismiss spatial iconography; it just suggests mapping land uses at a different scale and in a different way. Nor does it abjure iconographic metaphors; it just substitutes a different one ("greening") for the ones dominating planning discourse now. As I read it, van Eeten and Roe's proposed substitute for the "Randstad Green Heart" planning doctrine has many intrinsic merits, but disproving my argument is not one of them.

* * *

Timothy Beatley, *Dutch Green Planning More Reality than Fiction,*

67 Journal of the American Planning Association 98 (2001)

...While the critique of the Green Heart concept is certainly accurate in many respects, I have a very hard time accepting the basic notion that it represents a "fiction" in the sense that the authors argue. The landscape qualities of this area are not insignificant, I would argue (I'm actually writing this as I'm traveling though the Green Heart by train), and while virtually everyone I talk with understands the problematic nature of the metaphor (e.g., that intense agriculture is not especially ecological, that significant development has been allowed to occur, for various reasons), there are still important values being pursued here. Among other things, this area is a classic Dutch poldered landscape, interspersed with small towns and villages. The aesthetic and recreational values are real and significant—the ANWB (the Dutch equivalent of the American Automobile Association), for instance, publishes a number of maps laying out bicycle trips in the Green Heart, and indeed many people do bicycle there! It is perhaps not as easy as it should be to get to the Green Heart from cities such as Leiden, but on balance it is amazingly accessible by bicycle, at least by American standards.

I'm not really convinced by many of the other critiques and arguments cited. Being able to see urban buildings in the distance is just a fact of life in a very heavily populated place such as western Holland. Overall population density is higher in the Green Heart than expected in large degree because there are two sizeable cities—Gouda and Alphen aan de Rijn—located in the middle of the Green Heart (and compactly developed cities, for the most part). Moreover, I would argue that the principle of compact cities is in fact the most significant planning concept in the Dutch spatial planning system, at least in recent history....

I also have a difficult time, with Alexander, accepting the notion that we should dispense with maps. In ecological and green planning, mapping is an essential tool not only to convey ecological and spatial relationships but also as a practical and necessary guide for conservation and planning action. However, van Eeten and Roe have done a great service by raising the issue and critically questioning the impacts of maps and mapping. While there is no question that we need maps, it is also certainly true that they have perceptual implications and impacts, and we need to examine and highlight these. The van Eeten and Roe criticism is especially relevant in our contemporary debate about growth management and metropolitan greenspaces planning in the U.S. Many of us argue for urban growth boundaries (UGBs), but there is a definite tendency to see nature and greenspaces as primarily lying beyond the UGB; this is a result, at least in part, of the visual force of maps. Van Eeten and Roe make some good points here, worth considering by planners. Undoubtedly we need to think about greening cities and more urban forms of development—it's not just a matter of designating green areas (on maps) outside of cities.... These are points well taken....

At a still more basic level, I'm not convinced of the merit of allowing the kinds of "trades" the authors seem to have in mind. It sounds like a recipe for increasing sprawl in rural areas—especially given that many of the things for which the authors want to trade development rights are already happening (e.g., innovative sustainable housing, urban ecology, and city greening initiatives). Why not strengthen existing programs, including, for instance, subsidies for organic farming and support for renewable energy production in rural areas?...

* * *

Notes and Comments

1. Does the "Green Heart" controversy suggest a greater truth? That public support and enthusiasm for urban design initiatives takes powerful symbols and images combined with inspired leadership?

2. The Dutch political culture is accustomed to the pursuit of consensus. While the consensus characteristic may accurately reflect a desire to reach a collective agreement among group members, it may mask various forms of coercion and manipulation within the system. *Compare* Johan Woltjer, Consensus Planning: The Relevance of Communicative Planning Theory in Dutch Infrastructure Development (2000) *with* Charles J. Hoch, *Coming to Consensus*, 68 J. Am. Plan. Ass'n 112 (2002) (critical of the consensus image)

3. Does planning matter? For an argument that many African nations have been strructurally damaged by physical and spatial planning schemes imposed by European colonial powers, see Ambe Njoh, Urban Planning, Housing and Spatial Structures in Sub-Saharan Africa: Nature, Impact and Development Implications of Exogenous Forces (1999).

Italy, compared to its northern neighbors, is less of a planned society. The following excerpt describes planning in Italy:

Nico Calavita, *Urbanization, Public Control of Land Use and Private Ownership of Land: The Development of Italian Planning Law,*

16 Urban Lawyer 459 (1984)

The Development of Italian Planning Law

For most of the post-World War II period, Italian planning laws have been passed and administered within the context of a strong centralized state. The central governments had intensive control over local governments. This control was exercised by the Prefect, the state agent in the provinces. The scope of local planning activities was limited by the central government. Master Plans prepared by localities had to be approved by the state, which also had the power to make modifications, leaving very little autonomy to local governments.

The situation changed with the establishment of regional governments, a process started in 1970. The passage of powers from the central government to the regions was completed in 1978, when the regions were given control of approximately 25 percent of the entire national budget. This devolution power was contemplated in the Constitution of 1948 but the DC, fearful that some regions would be run by Communist administrations and would be used to subvert national programs, delayed its implementation.

Article 117 of the Constitution gives the regions the power to legislate in several areas, including urban planning and public works. These legislative powers, however, are "complementary" in the sense that regional councils are limited to legislation within the framework of national legislation. This framework of national legislation controlled local planning before the mid-seventies and now controls both regional and local planning....[48]

Urbanistic Law

At the time of its passage, the 1942 Urbanistic Law represented one of the most advanced pieces of urban planning legislation known in that period; it still represents the backbone of the complex system of Italian urban planning legislation. Laws passed in the postwar period have only modified, amplified and integrated the 1942 Urbanistic Law.

The principal mechanism contemplated by this law to guide the physical development of a locality is the Master Plan *(Piano Regolatore)*. It includes plans for transportation networks and a detailed land use plan. Implementation of the Master Plan is effectuated through Subdivision Plans *(Piani Particolareggiati)*. Height and bulk regulations and procedures for development are contained in the Building Regulations (*Regolamento Edilizio)*. The Urbanistic Law gave local governments the power of eminent domain to secure the areas designated for development in the Master Plan at a cost which did not reflect the increase in value which would result either directly or indirectly from the approval of the Master Plan and its implementation. This provision was considered the backbone of the 1942 law which, it was thought, would permit positive planning and eliminate land speculation. Financial and administrative mechanisms to implement that aspect of the law, however, were never established.

The Urbanistic Law made the preparation of a Master Plan obligatory for all cities included in a list to be approved by the Public Works minister, not later than one year from the approval of the Urbanistic Law. This list, however, did not appear until twelve years later, in 1954. When, finally, the designated cities prepared and adopted a Master Plan, they had to wait many years for approval by the central government.

In part, this failure to implement the Ubanistic Law was the result of a post-World War II anti-planning climate in which the building and reconstruction of the Italian cities damaged by the war took first priority. Because of the fear that planning might slow down the development of Italian cities and of the economy in general, development was allowed to continue on the basis of market logic only, leading to the unrestrained and anarchic development of all major cities.

48. ...It is interesting to note that regional governments have been very active—more in the north and center than in the south—in passing planning related legislation, especially as it concerns environmental protection. One important change from the centralized past is that Master Plans are now approved at the regional level.

Chapter 6

Judicial Review of Land Use Decisions

> Curiously, the distrust that Americans have of government, and of the bureaucracy in particular, has generally been balanced by their implicit confidence in the Judiciary. Once appeals have run their course, legal judgments are usually accepted. However, by directing appeals from local planning decisions to the courts instead of to higher regional planning administrations, American practice magnifies the planning effect of the legal system's invisible web. Furthermore, under the tradition of decentralized authority, any opportunity for administrative planning at a regional scale is all but precluded.
>
> Richard Tseng-yu Lai, Law in Urban Design and Planning: The Invisible Web 169 (1988)

Citizen participation in European land development, despite slight national variations reflecting local cultural experience, is less confrontative than the often hostile environment of the regulatory and political process. In Europe there is a tendency for projects to be generally acceptable to the public as the proposal reflects extensive discussions within and between various governmental authorities and departments. Typically, concerns for historic preservation, the environment, and consistency with community design have been voiced, and the project modified to mitigate adverse impacts. Because of the influence of unions and the political power of environmental groups, local government is frequently very sensitive to environmental issues and projects approved often reflect a realistic balancing of interests and design options. That is not to say that development is not on occasion controversial, but the deference to public decision-making is a testament to the general perception that good ethical government is a sufficient guarantee of rational planning for growth. Citizen participation in the United States tends to be a few moments of a representative number of residents being permitted to address the planning commission, city council, board of supervisors, or planning board, or the submission of comments on environmental impact analyses. Only when all the administrative processes are completed does the truly American brand of citizen participation commence: the lawsuit.

Challenges to new development are brought by neighbors, homeowner associations, competitors, adjacent cities or other neighboring units of local government, as well as environmental organizations, civil rights or consumer organizations. Even developers are frequent litigators, sometimes suing the regulators and claiming civil rights or taking damages, and sometimes suing the neighbors or other challengers as a strategic move to silence opposition. These SLAPP (strategic litigation against public participation) lawsuits, designed to silence those that threaten developers or other powerful interests, have been met with anti-SLAPP legislation that allows for fast-tract procedures to dismiss such litigation before expensive discovery and other proceedings are undertaken. Cal. Code Civ. Proc. §425.16 (early motion to dismiss); N.Y. Civ. Rights L. §70-a; *Dixon v. Superior Court*, 36 Cal. Rptr. 2d 687 (Ct. App. 1994). Tenacious development opponents have on occasion responded to the more aggressive developers with their own countersuits or lawsuits referred to SLAPP-back litigation. In development challenges, a number of issues frequently arise. Elmond Constantini, *SLAPPS/SLAPPback: The Misuse of Libel Law for Political Purposes and a Countersuit Response*, 7 J. L. & Pol. 417 (1991). *See generally* George W. Pring & Penelope Canan, SLAPPS: Getting Sued for Speaking Out (1996); Thomas A. Walldman, *SLAPP Suits: Weakness in First Amendment Law and in the Courts' Responses to Frivolous Litigation*, 39 UCLA L. Rev. 979 (1992).

Standing

The doctrine of standing is an off-shoot of the Article III case and controversy requirement. Article III requires that federal courts are only to exercise power over actual cases and controversies, conversely, judicial rulings must not be advisory opinions. *Hayburn's Case*, 2 U.S. (2 Dall.) 409 (1792). The notion of standing has historically been that the litigant challenger must be personally injured by the challenged behavior. In *Warth v. Seldin*, 422 U.S. 490 (1975), the Supreme Court rejected standing for a number of challengers to alleged exclusionary zoning that precluded the development of affordable housing. The Court ushered in a new generation of restricted federal jurisdiction that would dramatically narrow the entryway to the federal courthouse. The Court ruled that in addition to the Article III-required proof of personal injury, *Allen v. Wright*, 468 U.S. 737 (1984), that it would impose what it calls prudential limitations of litigation, *Warth, supra.*, presumably designed to reduce the jurisdiction of federal courts. First, the Court requires that in addition to real injury, unique to the plaintiff, that the plaintiff demonstrate that the injury was the direct result of the defendant's challenged behavior—the requirement of causation. *Allen, supra.* Second, the plaintiff must demonstrate that the court is able to provide a remedy for the plaintiff's injury—the requirement of redressability. *Lujan v. Defenders of Wildlife*, 504 U.S. 555 (1992) (government aid to another nation not redressable as environmental injury avoidance cannot be ordered by the American court as the project likely to proceed without American assistance). For example, in *Warth, supra.*, a taxpayer of the central city could not sue the exclusionary suburb on the basis that the central city is forced to house all the poor because the cause of the injury is the central city policies of building to meet suburban as well as urban needs. Poor workers seeking housing in the exclusionary suburb in which they work lack standing because they are unable to show that if they prevail that the court could redress their grievance, as the litigant can point to no affordable dwellings that would be built. In addition, the Court has developed the "generalized grievance" doctrine that denies standing to anyone, even if significantly injured, where the injury alleged is suffered by the entire community. For example, an allegation that the government is not obeying the law or constitution is not actionable unless the plaintiff's injury is unique from injury suffered by other citizens. *United States v. Richardson*, 418 U.S. 166 (1974). While the standing doctrine is easily satisfied by alleged over-regulated developers, it is problematic for many poor or environmental or social equity-concerned plaintiffs. Limiting standing to developers, *Village of Arlington Heights v. Metropolitan Hous. Dev. Corp.*, 429 U.S. 252, 260–64 (1977), is also problematic as profit-motivated developers are not motivated to spend precious capital for litigation and affordable housing proposals can easily be rendered infeasible due to unplanned project costs.

Standing presents a litigation hurdle particularly affecting the ability to bring environmental claims based on the global and ecological impacts of programs and projects. Some states provide broader rights of standing, *Citizens for Uniform Laws v. County of Contra Costa*, 285 Cal. Rptr. 456 (Ct. App. 1991) (taxpayer standing); *Southern Burlington County NAACP v. Township of Mount Laurel*, 456 A.2d 390 (N.J. 1983) (standing for individual or group interested in securing low income housing opportunities), and challenges under civil rights laws typically provide broader standards allowing anyone aggrieved to maintain an action. *Havens Realty Corp. v. Coleman*, 455 U.S. 363 (1982) (recognizing standing for fair housing investigators or neighborhood residents). Nevertheless, many states require litigants to demonstrate some special injury, *Nautilus of Exeter, Inc. v. Town of Exeter*, 456 A.2d 407 (N.H. 1995) (neighbors from .6 to 6 miles from proposed hospital expansion to remotely affected for standing), and in federal courts most claims, unless involving a direct regulation and injury to a developer or landowner, *Village of Arlington Heights, supra*, may be problematic. *Warth, supra* (refusing standing to a range of litigants seeking to challenge alleged exclusionary zoning precluding housing for low income workers).

The following excerpt compares the federal American constitutional standing with that provided in a range of Nations:

Jon Owens, *Comparative Law and Standing to Sue: A Petition for Redress for the Environment*,

7 Environmental Lawyer 321 (2001)....

Through such means as narrowly interpreting the "case or controversy" requirement of the United States Constitution, the U.S. Supreme Court recently has increased the obstacles that environmental plaintiffs must overcome in order to demonstrate standing to sue. These limitations on standing primarily have been justified by concerns over deterring frivolous litigation, maintaining the integrity of the adversarial system, and preserving the separation of powers between the judicial and the executive branches.

In contrast, many other nations have promoted greater access to their courts. Countries such as the Philippines use a broad standing doctrine as a means to check and balance the power of the executive branch. Other nations such as Italy, Australia, and the United Kingdom permit experienced environmental organizations to enforce environmental laws. These nations value broad standing and do not allow fears over potential increased litigation and impairment of the adversarial judicial system to impair citizen enforcement of environmental laws. Broad standing to sue also has allowed them to limit the ability of the courts to dismiss cases merely for political reasons....

In this last century, the United States Supreme Court has changed standing to sue from a highly liberalized requirement to a serious constitutional obstacle to public interest litigants. Modern standing requirements pose an especially high barrier to citizen suits that seek to enforce environmental laws through bringing suit on behalf of natural resources, future generations and other entities that are otherwise underrepresented in the political process and voiceless in the judicial system....

Many nations have moved towards granting standing to certain groups based upon their organizational interests, such as protecting the environment. This has allowed groups in both common law and civil law jurisdictions to assume a greater role enforcing and shaping the law.

Common Law Countries

Despite the current American movement towards greater restrictions on standing to sue, other common law countries have moved in the opposite direction over the past two decades. This movement towards broader standing to sue has occurred in conjunction with the gradually increasing role that public law plays in people's lives worldwide.

The United Kingdom has moved towards a more flexible, liberalized approach to standing regarding judicial petitions based upon public laws. Prior to the last two decades, the British standing doctrine generally required that one who sought to enforce the public law must have suffered a special injury apart from the general populace, except for certain situations such as the enforcement of prerogative writs. The landmark case of *Boyce v. Paddington Borough Council* demonstrates this requirement. In *Boyce*, the plaintiff sought standing to challenge an alleged violation of various open spaces statutes. The statutes provided public rights of access to certain open spaces for exercise and recreation and barred the construction of buildings within those spaces. The plaintiff had built residences adjacent to a disused churchyard. The local government erected a screen within the churchyard to prevent the plaintiff from obtaining an easement of light and to preserve the churchyard as an open space. In response, the plaintiff sued to enforce the open spaces laws against the local government. The court required the plaintiff to suffer "special damage" in order to have standing to assert a violation of public law.

This special injury requirement is designed, in part, to promote the production of evidence, which is furthered by litigants with a genuine interest. As noted by one commentator, the impediment is also due to "an innate and traditional British distaste of informers, 'busybodies' and 'snoopers' interfering with matters that do not really concern them." Unfortunately, that distaste had prevented access to the courts to enforce the rule of law and had been used as a device to preserve the status quo.

In the United Kingdom, Section 31(3) of the Supreme Court Act of 1981 commands, "No application for judicial review shall be made unless the leave of the High Court has been obtained in accordance with rules of court; and the court shall not grant leave to make such an application unless it considers that the applicant has a sufficient interest in the matter to which the application relates." Similarly, Order 53 now commands, "The court shall not grant leave unless it considers that the applicant has a sufficient interest in the matter to which the application relates."

In 1982, in International Revenue Commissioners v. National Federation of Self-Employed and Small Businesses Limited ("I.R.C."), the House of Lords construed the requisite interest in a more flexible light than in past years. The British courts now appear to apply the threshold standing requirement as a means to filter out frivolous litigation "by busybodies, cranks and other mischief-makers," rather than to deny those with a valid concern for the law. In I.R.C., the House of Lords granted standing to taxpayers to challenge tax officials' lenient approach to the enforcement of the tax laws against a group of violators.

Since I.R.C., several British cases have demonstrated a general movement towards liberalized standing. For instance, just three years after I.R.C., in *Her Majesty's Treasury v. Smedley*, an appellate court granted a taxpayer standing to challenge the British government's attempt to pay British tax monies to the European Community, which he claimed was impermissible. The Smedley court noted that in light of I.R.C. the rules of standing had been "greatly relaxed" and that the former restrictive rules of standing have been virtually abandoned. Although the court noted that Order 53 would give it broad discretion to dismiss the case if the plaintiff's case were frivolous, the court found no signs of such abuse of the courts and granted standing.

Continuing the trend, in *Her Majesty's Inspectorate of Pollution and Ministry of Agriculture, Fisheries and Food v. Greenpeace Ltd.*, a British court held that the Greenpeace organization had a "sufficient interest" for standing to challenge an agency's decisions regarding the discharge of radioactive wastes. As in Smedley, the court focused on whether the applicant for standing was a serious litigant rather than a "mere" or "meddlesome busybody." Recognizing the national and international integrity of Greenpeace, the court refused to consider it to be a mere "busybody." However, the court did emphasize the fact that 2,500 Greenpeace supporters lived near the site of the dumping and thus would be prone to having a genuine direct interest in the perception of a pollution problem.

In a 1994 case, *Regina v. Secretary of State for Foreign and Commonwealth Affairs ex parte The World Development Movement Ltd.*, a British court considered a petition for standing from a public interest organization to contest an agency's funding of a project in Malaysia. The World Development Movement's organizational goals are to increase trade and poverty assistance to foreign nations. In this case, World Development sought standing to challenge the British government-funded Pergau Dam project. Its huge expense-overruns would cost Malaysians 100 million more pounds for their electricity over the 35-year life of the project than if a more reasonably-priced project had been employed. The court noted that since I.R.C. the British courts had adopted "an increasingly liberal approach to standing...." Therefore, the court granted standing, declining to consider the well-respected non-partisan organization to be "busy-bodies, cranks, or mischief-makers." The court determined the British organization to have "sufficient interest" because it had a genuine concern for ensuring that British taxpayer funds are properly disbursed to where foreign aid is needed most. Additionally, the court noted that if the organization did not have standing, then no one would have standing to ensure that the development funding law was exercised lawfully. The latter factor reflects a view that the agency must be held accountable to the rule of law and prevented from violating its duty to the public, especially when no claimant other than a watchdog organization would have standing to seek redress in the courts. At least one federal appellate court in America has expressed a similar concern....

Since breaking away from the British Empire, Australia, Canada, and India have retained the British common law as a foundation but have each developed their modern legal doctrines independently. Interestingly, these countries have each adopted a liberalized standing doctrine. Their particular national history and needs, however, have shaped the approach that each nation has taken to develop a broad standing doctrine....

As in Australia, Canada also has liberalized its requirements for standing. Beginning in the 1970's, the Supreme Court of Canada began to move away from the restrictive confines of *Boyce v. Paddington*. The Boyce court granted standing to make constitutional challenges against legislation based upon a mere generalized grievance of the litigant. As with Australia, in recent years, territories in Canada have sought legislative reform for standing. For instance, the Yukon Territory's Environment Act, which creates a right to a healthful environment, has abolished the common law special injury requirement for standing in suits against both private parties and against the government for its failure to perform its responsibilities. Similarly, Ontario has enacted the "Environmental Protection Act" and the "Fisheries Act."

The judiciary of India has construed its constitution's protection of the fundamental right to life as including the right to a clean environment. Commentator Martin Lau has observed that plaintiffs charging a violation of this right are not required to demonstrate standing and do not have to support their allegations with scientific evidence. Additionally, others have observed that since the early 1980's, the Supreme Court of India has rejected former British-based restrictions on standing in public interest cases. In particular, any person may bring a violation to a court's attention by writing a letter, which the court then treats as a petition for redress.

Civil Law Countries

Besides those countries in which the *locus standi* doctrine is derived from English or American constitutional law, several other European and South American nations also have embraced a more progressive approach to standing to sue in recent decades. Therefore, it appears that the collective wisdom of the world's nations is moving towards recognition of broad access to the courts to seek redress for violations of public law.

Similar to the United States, Italy employs a tripartite system of government with goals such as providing checks and balances, limiting the power of the courts, and preserving a separation of powers. Professor Douglas Parker, a scholar who has studied the Italian constitutional system, has undertaken an in-depth comparison of standing in the United States and Italy. As in the United States and in other nations, Italian courts have struggled with whether they should grant standing for individuals to assert collective rights, such as those shared by people seeking to enforce a public law. As early as the 1960's, the Italian legislature attempted to grant broad standing to "any person" to enforce the public law. However, the courts initially resisted this attempt by narrowly construing the provision as granting standing only to those who are suffering a special injury.

In response, the Italian legislature instituted a different approach by conferring standing on nationally recognized organizations, which the courts upheld. Although the Italian judiciary's acceptance of broad standing for organizations with a national reputation mirrors the approaches taken in the United States and Australia, the Italian system may exclude local organizations that might actually suffer a more concrete harm but lack the expertise of a national organization.

[S]everal Italian laws grant standing without an "injury-in-fact" (special injury) that the U.S. Supreme Court would require. For instance, the 1970 Workers' Law grants unions standing to challenge violations without requiring the allegation of injury to the union as an organization. As environmental cases are particularly prone to standing difficulties, the Italian legislature's means of conferring standing is of particular importance. Italy's environmental statute was passed in 1986 and confers standing on nationally-certified environmental organizations to intervene in government enforcement proceedings against private parties despite lack of special injury. Their participation in such cases appears to be limited to acting in an amicus curiae role. Additionally, despite lack of special injury, such organizations can bring citizen suits to challenge agency actions that affect the environment. Therefore, the Italian approach values the ability of experienced, competent national organizations to enforce the national environmental agenda through participation in the court system. It appears that this system considers this benefit of civic involvement through the judicial system to outweigh such concerns as placing too much power in the hands of the judiciary and flooding the courts with litigation.

The administrative courts in The Netherlands have recognized broad standing to sue at least since 1975. Observers have noted that in the 1980s and 1990s, the Dutch Supreme Court recognized that impairment of an environmental group's interests created a tort, which allowed such a group to bring suit in a court of law. Along these same lines, a lower Dutch court recognized in a particular case that an organization whose goal was the protection of birds could sue to recover the clean-up costs of an oil spill.

As in Italy, The Netherlands recognizes standing for formally structured organizations to challenge agency actions if the goals of such groups are related to the actions they challenge. Specifically regarding organizations' interests, the 1994 General Administrative Law Act provides that "the general and collective interests for the promotion of which they were established and which they are actually promoted in practice, shall also be regarded as their own interests." Additionally, Dutch law provides that such organizations may participate in agency consultations regarding whether or not to grant permits that affect organizational interests.

Article 24 of Greece's constitution imposes an obligation on the State to protect the natural environment and to take special preventive and corrective measures for its preservation. The Supreme Court of Greece has facilitated citizen enforcement of this constitutional provision by recognizing standing to challenge government actions that affect large portions of Greece's environment. As construed by the Supreme Court of Greece, Article 24 establishes "the fundamental principle of prevention of damage to the natural environment in the interests of ecological balance and of the conservation of this end of natural resources for the benefit not only of the present generation, but also of those who will follow." To implement this constitutional provision, the legislature enacted an environmental impact assessment ("EIA") statute, which requires the government to assess the effects of its projects that seriously impact the environment....

Several nations have instituted greater access to the courts as a means of empowering citizens who seek to oppose governmental corruption and abuse. The Philippines, South Africa, Brazil, and Pakistan are examples of countries that have used liberalized standing to increase democratic participation in the political and legal process....

Pakistan has experienced much internal turmoil since its independence from the British Empire in the 1940's. Since then, it has endured many instances of martial law and five military coups. Despite this, the Pakistani courts have occasionally served a valuable role by opening their doors for important political debate. As noted by one commentator regarding Pakistan, "[j]udicial review can be a precursor of democracy, providing its prerequisite, free expression...." In recent years, Pakistan expanded access to the courts for the protection of constitutional rights as part of a movement toward democratic reform. However, as part of a military coup the military government suspended the constitution of Pakistan in 1999. This suspension leaves the masses in Pakistan without the ability to seek justice in the courts for enforcement of their fundamental rights.

The experience of other nations demonstrates that there are benefits associated with broad standing to sue, such as curbing corruption. Broad standing also equalizes access to the administrative law system by opening it not just to regulated industries but also to those citizens who hope to benefit from effective enforcement of the law. Three concerns generally underpin the United States' standing doctrine: concerns about concrete adversariness and increased litigation; concerns about the separation of powers; and concerns about judicial bias. The experience of other nations demonstrates that fears in the United States that broader standing would result in a breakdown in the adversarial system, increased litigation, and undue judicial interference in executive actions are without merit. Increases in litigation can be controlled by placing prudential limits on standing rather than creating a constitutional barrier to standing. Nations such as the Philippines also demonstrate that standing is a powerful tool that can empower those without voting rights such as children and future generations. A simpler, open-access policy towards standing also avoids the complex American standing test, which some judges have employed to dismiss cases on political grounds....

The U.S. Supreme Court's modern approach to standing does not bode well for the environment. The Court's ruling in [*Lujan v. Defenders of Wildlife*, 504 U.S. 555 (1992)] sets a requirement that the plaintiff show a concrete, particularized harm in order to have standing to protect an endangered species. However, this puts at risk those endangered species that are not "charismatic" or not easily observed. Furthermore, obtaining standing becomes more difficult as a species becomes more endangered and thus more difficult to observe. Ironically, in *Defenders of Wildlife*, the Court also required that the plaintiffs have concrete plans to observe an endangered species in order to establish standing to sue, but it could not make such definite plans due to human interference (namely, a war) in the endangered species' environment....

* * *

Notes and Comments

1. For an analysis of standing to litigate under Italian law, see Douglas L. Parker, *Standing to Litigate "Abstract Social Interests" in the United States and Italy: Rexamining "Injury in Fact,"* 33 Colum. J. Transnat'l L. 259 (1995) (providing broader standing to established national organizations as compared to local and spontaneous organizations).

2. *Exhaustion of Administrative Remedies.* A basic principle of administrative and land use law in the United States is that before one can bring a judicial challenge, all available administrative processes, including appeals must be exhausted as a precondition. *Weinberger v. Salfi*, 422 U.S. 749 (1975). Acts of the planning commission or board of adjustment must be appealed where such review processes exist. *Town Council v. Parker*, 726 N.E.2d 1217 (Ind. 2000). The doctrine of exhaustion also exists under federal administrative law but the doctrine tends not to be raised as most federal litigation challenges raise constitutional claims such takings or due process, or statutory issues such as civil rights legislation-based claims. *McKart v. United States*, 395 U.S. 185 (1969). These claims are typically brought under the general civil rights statute, 42 U.S.C. § 1983, and the United States Supreme Court has ruled that due to the importance of civil rights statutes and the danger that states might attempt to thwart civil rights, that civil rights litigants need not exhaust administrative remedies prior to bringing a federal court action under federal statutory law. *Patsy v. Board of Regents*, 457 U.S. 496 (1982). As the United States Supreme Court's composition became more conservative and increasingly hostile to the continued expansion of civil rights, the Court developed a strategy to reduce the federal court caseload of such challenges, including standing, and expanded a series of procedural hurdles that make federal litigation, at least outside of the civil rights filed, unattractive:

3. *Ripeness.* Another doctrine that has been applied in both administrative as well as constitutional and other litigation is the doctrine of ripeness. *Abbott Laboratories v. Gardner*, 387 U.S. 136 (1967). Ripeness, like standing, arises out of the Article III consideration of the case and controversy. Gene R. Nichol, Jr., *Ripeness and the Constitution*, 54 U. Chi. L. Rev. 153 (1987). Not only must the plaintiff be injured, but the controversy must have developed to the point where the injury is real and the parties are distinct and the record is sufficiently developed. *Renne v. Geary*, 501 U.S. 312 (1991). Some claims, by comparison, may require additional development before the federal

courts will accept jurisdiction. Ripeness is a close relative to the exhaustion requirement as it typically requires additional action before an agency or by the alleged perpetrator. *Williamson County Regional Planning Agency v. Hamilton Bank*, 473 U.S. 172 (1985) (finality doctrine). The problem for the Supreme Court was that its prior decisions did not permit rejection of jurisdiction on the basis of non-exhaustion of administrative remedies. Rather than overruling the nonexhaustion doctrine, the Court simply generated a new requirement that the academy has generally accepted. The doctrine of "finality" was created by the Court in *Williamson*. In *Williamson*, a developer sought to challenge a subdivision decision in federal court alleging a takings clause violation by excessive regulation. The subdivision application had been rejected because the density of the plan violated the zoning ordinance. To raise the takings claim the developer employed Section 1983, the provision that is not subject to exhaustion of administrative remedies. Instead, the United States Supreme Court ruled that rather than the challenger being required to exhaust administrative remedies, that the decision on the allowable development level was not yet "final." This finality doctrine, which requires a developer to exhaust, for example, any available variance procedure, is rationalized by the Court to be more a ripeness problem than one of exhaustion. The doctrine may be far more deceptive than it first appears because there is the assumption than upon pursuit of an available administrative mechanism proposing a specific project and permitting the regulating community to define what level of development it will permit, that the developer-applicant could return to federal court to present the ripened or final challenge. The developer may also be required to pursue a challenge in the state courts under, for example, an inverse condemnation statute that allows lawsuits for excessive regulation. Upon litigating these matters in the state court, the challenger would be foreclosed from relitigating the issues in federal court under the doctrine of res judicata or collateral estoppel, doctrines that prevent the relitigation of the same issue between the same parties. The doctrine of finality may be worse than the doctrine of exhaustion because it may in reality be an abstention doctrine: an absolute bar to federal litigation. The Court has ruled that once a regulatory body has indicated what development would be permitted that a landowner's claim ripens. *Palazzolo v. Rhode Island*, 533 U.S. 606 (2001). The United State Supreme Court, although largely having excluded takings claims from federal litigation, has yet to announce whether it would apply the finality or ripeness doctrines to claims brought under procedural and substantive due process, equal protection, or other civil rights or environmental claims. *Compare Taylor Inv., Ltd. v. Upper Darby Township*, 983 F.2d 1285 (3d Cir. 1993) (substantive due process and equal protection claims arising from use permit denial must be submitted to zoning hearing board before ripe); *Del Monte Dunes at Monterey, Ltd. v. City of Monterey*, 920 F.2d 1496 (9th Cir. 1990) (due process, equal protection, and takings claims require finality through a variance or other submission) *with Restigouche, Inc. v. Town of Jupiter*, 59 F.3d 1208 (11th Cir 1995) (regulation challenge under substantive due process ripe as rule final, but as applied taking claim not final as must submit compensation claim); *Executive 100, Inc. v. Martin County*, 922 F.2d 1536 (11th Cir. 1991) (alleged arbitrary decision ripe as for equal protection and due process claims, but taking requires application for variance).

4. *Abstention*. Many federal court land use challenges are rejected on standing or ripeness grounds but a few may, despite meeting those narrow requirements, be nevertheless rejected under the companion justiciability doctrine of abstention. *San Remo Hotel v. City of San Francisco*, 145 F.3d 1095 (9th Cir. 1998). Abstention is a function of the notion of federalism where the courts attempt to respect the sovereign existence of

both the federal government and the states. Abstention is a judicially created doctrine that states that certain claims may not be litigated because of a conflict or a danger of a lack of respect for sovereignty. *Younger v. Harris*, 401 U.S. 37 (1971). For example, under the *Younger* doctrine, once a state institutes litigation and the proceedings are underway, a federal court, except in the most extraordinary circumstances presenting a necessity, will abstain from allowing federal litigation on the same subject to advance. This doctrine frequently sends state or local public sector attorneys scurrying to state court to preempt any federal challenges.

Under the *Burford* doctrine, where challenges present questions pertaining to the interpretation of intricate regulatory statutes, the federal court will abstain and leave interpretation and administration to the state. *Burford v. Sun Oil Co.*, 319 U.S. 315 (1943).

Pursuant to the *Pullman* doctrine, the federal court will abstain in challenges that turn on the interpretation of state law. *Railroad Comm'n v. Pullman*, 312 U.S. 496 (1941). These doctrines are easily advanced in cases arising from the zoning, subdivision, and planning processes of local government.

5. *Statute of Limitations.* Each state has adopted widely varying limits on when a lawsuit or administrative claim may be instituted. *King County v. Central Puget Sound Growth Management Hearings Bd.*, 979 P.2d 374 (Wash. 1999). In addition, state statutes and local ordinances may establish set periods in which to appeal administrative or other decisions. *City of Portsmouth v. Schlesinger*, 672 A.2d 712 (N.H. 1996). These dates must typically be carefully adhered to or the challenger will be denied court access. For federal litigation, challengers must determine the applicable state statute, typically the state's personal injury statute of limitations, for that is the time limit applied by federal courts in claims brought under Section 1983, covering due process, equal protection, and takings claims. *Wilson v. Garcia*, 471 U.S. 261 (1985).

SLAPP Suits

Some developers have engaged in a strategy of suing project opponents to discourage opposition of their project. These Strategic Lawsuits Against Public Participation or SLAPP suits have the potential effect of discouraging exercise of first amendment rights of speech and to petition the government. The problem of developers or the government using litigation to suppress opposition has become a national problem in the United States:

Barbara Arco, Comment, *When Rights Collide: Reconciling the First Amendment Rights of Opposing Parties in Civil Litigation*,

52 University of Miami Law Review 587 (1998)

Endemic in American society is the reflexive behavior of filing a lawsuit based upon one's perceived notion of having been victimized. This litigious propensity has resulted in overloaded court dockets at both the state and federal levels. Though the Constitution grants all citizens the right to seek redress from a neutral judiciary, discretion should be exercised to ensure that this designated right is not abused. The judiciary and other officers of the court have a corresponding duty to ensure that the system is being properly implemented to promote justice and fairness to everyone....

Illustrative of this dilemma is a modern wave of First Amendment suits which seem to have reached epidemic proportions. These suits, called SLAPPs, an acronym for Strategic Lawsuits Against Public Participation, have proliferated throughout the United States, and have since spilled across its borders to other parts of the globe. The suits pit an individual's right to petition the government for redress against one's rightful access to seek a remedy in court....

Submitted for your approval: A concerned citizen, interested in procuring a safe and healthy community, participates in meetings with a municipal environmental department regarding groundwater contamination allegedly caused by a landfill. These meetings include discussions of the department's rules and regulations concerning landfills. Subsequently, this concerned citizen writes to the department's director and other interested state and federal officials. These letters memorialize the proceedings, including contamination studies and the landfill owner's resistance to monitor the contaminant levels to safeguard the community, and further express gratitude for the department's recognition and consideration of the problem. Riled by these letters, the landfill owner gives the author three options: Provide specific facts and documents in support of the allegations in the letters; formally retract the letters; or brace for formal legal recourse. When no retraction is forthcoming, the citizen is sued. You have now begun your journey into the SLAPP zone.

The situation described above is common among SLAPP suits. George Pring and Penelope Canan, professors of law and sociology, respectively, at the University of Denver, have studied the SLAPP phenomenon extensively over a ten-year period. They characterize a typical SLAPP as a civil lawsuit filed against private individuals or organizations who have spoken out on substantive issues of public interest or social significance. The underlying strategy for these suits is retaliation, aimed at intimidating an individual from engaging in particular behavior believed to be detrimental to the SLAPP filer. The suits tend to have a chilling effect on public participation in governmental decision making.

The majority of SLAPP filers are seeking to protect their own vested economic or property interests. Ironically, targets of the suits are usually individuals or groups who are also seeking to protect their own economic, property, or family interests. Some targets, however, are motivated by a desire to achieve self-gain or revenge, or by other questionable, self-serving goals.

Trademark legal claims of SLAPPs include suits for defamation, tortious interference with business relationships, abuse of process, conspiracy, civil rights violations, and other violations of law such as nuisance. As these causes of action tend not to arise from federal law, most of the suits are brought in state courts. The pattern seems to be the invocation of a claim that the target is infringing on the filer's right to contract freely, and depends, to a great extent, on rights guaranteed under the U.S. Constitution.

The First Amendment provides "the right of the people...to petition the Government for a redress of grievances." When written, the clause was intended to correct evils experienced by the framers of the Constitution and the Bill of Rights that had been imposed by an overly authoritative sovereign....

Since the 1960s, the incidence of SLAPPs has increased dramatically, ultimately becoming a major threat to involved citizens. Prevalence of SLAPPs is particularly evident in the areas of environmental matters ("eco-SLAPPs") and real estate development.

However, their effects can be seen in any area involving political activities, such as "circulating a petition, writing a letter to the editor, testifying at a public hearing, reporting violations of law, lobbying for legislation, peacefully demonstrating, or otherwise attempting to influence government action."

Whatever claims are asserted by the SLAPP filer, their intent is clear: SLAPPs act as a continuing threat to fundamental American values. Though statistics demonstrate that the suits routinely fail in court, they tend to have devastating economic and chilling effects, allowing them to succeed in their underlying purpose—silencing concerned public citizens into submission.

To counteract the chilling effect of SLAPPs, some states have enacted anti-SLAPP legislation. These statutes are designed to protect a citizen's First Amendment right to speak out against impending community development plans without fear of being sued by the developers they oppose as a result. Although the intent of the anti-SLAPP statutes is genuine, problems arise from the statutes' language, which categorizes the activities sought to be protected in broad terms, providing little guidance to the courts applying them.

The difficulty in identifying a SLAPP exists because it requires evaluating the filer's motivation. Thus, the questions raised include: Is the suit a retaliatory reaction, or is it based on a legitimate belief of having been wronged? Can a legislature enact a statute that provides a remedy for a plaintiff who legitimately believes he has been denied a valid economic opportunity or has been defamed, while singling out a true SLAPP filer? Unfortunately, there are no simple answers to these complex questions, though several states have tried to provide answers with varied levels of success.

Currently, in recognition of the essential role that public participation plays in a democracy, eleven states have passed laws directed at suppressing a SLAPP filer's incentive to initiate such suits. These states are California, Delaware, Georgia, Maine, Massachusetts, Minnesota, Nebraska, Nevada, New York, Rhode Island, and Washington. In addition, anti-SLAPP bills have been proposed in Florida, Indiana, Maryland, New Hampshire, New Jersey, Pennsylvania, Tennessee, and Texas, but have been defeated either at the congressional or gubernatorial level....

Professors Pring and Canan have devised a litmus test for determining the efficacy and validity of an anti-SLAPP statute. To provide adequate protection and correspondingly encourage public participation, they believe the law must possess the following characteristics:

It must cover all public advocacy and communications to government, whether direct or indirect and whether in the form of testimony, letters, reports of crime, peaceful demonstrations, or petitions.

...It must cover all government bodies and agents....

...It must set out an effective early review for filed SLAPPs, shifting the burden of proof to the filer and, in so doing, serving a clear warning against the future filing of such suits....

Impliedly, all the anti-SLAPP laws were designed to allow a speedy hearing by a judge and a quick dismissal where applicable, though many of the statutes are not so explicit. The common statutory scheme places the burdens of proof and persuasion on the filer to prove that the target should not be protected. Many of the statutes permit a countersuit by the target for legal fees and some even allow awards of punitive damages in certain situations.

Still, there are some procedural differences among the statutes. The California and Massachusetts laws permit motions to dismiss to be filed within sixty days of service of the complaint. In contrast, for all other suits brought in California, a defendant has only thirty days to file a response, while in Massachusetts, a response must be filed within twenty days. Therefore, a defendant, by asserting that a suit is a SLAPP, can use this procedural benefit to delay responding to an otherwise meritorious claim.

Half the states with SLAPP legislation mandate that courts order a stay on all discovery upon the filing of a motion to dismiss pursuant to their applicable statutes. However, they also allow the courts, upon good cause shown, to order specified and limited discovery. The remaining five states with anti-SLAPP legislation place no stays on discovery, and, except for Nebraska, which provides for an expedited hearing, there are no constraints on a plaintiff prohibiting him from conducting discovery that may enable him to prevail at the eventual hearing....

Some of the statutes require a filer to establish by clear and convincing evidence that the communication giving rise to the action was made with knowledge of its falsity or with reckless disregard of whether it was false. Meanwhile, the statutes of other states couch the burden requirements in terms similar to those imposed by Rule 11 of the Federal Rules of Civil Procedure, requiring that the claim be well grounded in fact and warranted by existing law, or a good faith argument for the extension, modification, or reversal of existing law.

California's statute requires only that the filer establish a probability that he will prevail on the claim. Though not as heavy a burden as proof by clear and convincing evidence, when coupled with the mandatory discovery stay, it constitutes an equally high hurdle to overcome. In negotiating enactment of the bill, Senator Bill Lockyer, Chairman of California's Senate Judiciary Committee, entered into a compromise with Governor Wilson, who had voiced concerns that the "pleading hurdle" proposed—a substantial probability that the filer would prevail—was too high for a plaintiff. The substantial probability test is similar to that which must be overcome to sustain a punitive damages claim against doctors and religious organizations. The governor contended that such a burden was too restrictive. In lowering the standard to a "reasonable probability" of success on the merits, a plaintiff must only present "evidence that substantiates the claim."...

As illustrated by the various statutes, there is an odd reversal of roles between the parties in the SLAPP context in that the laws place the burden of persuasion on the party opposing the motion to dismiss to show the validity of the basis of his claim. Though this approach is similar to that imposed by summary judgment procedures, because of the limits placed on discovery, the non-movant is denied access to the very evidence that the motion specifically requires be produced, and which is instrumental in a summary judgment proceeding, as distinguished from a motion for a judgment on the pleadings. These laws also radically rework the effect of the rules of civil procedure, as the special motions to dismiss require an inquiry into the assessment of the facts and the filer's motives, not merely the more flexible determination of whether a pleading has stated a claim upon which relief can be granted.

Most of the anti-SLAPP statutes provide for the mandatory recovery of reasonable attorneys' fees and costs when a target prevails on a motion to dismiss. Delaware, Maine, Nebraska, and New York, however, give courts discretionary authority to award attorneys' fees and costs to targets who succeed on motions to dismiss.

Ironically, only four states prescribe recovery of attorneys' fees and costs to a successful filer who meets the extraordinary burden imposed and overcomes the motion to dismiss. Nevada simply makes the award mandatory. California places a condition on the imposition of attorneys' fees and costs, mandating an award if the court finds the motion was brought for a frivolous reason or to otherwise delay the proceedings. Nebraska merely makes imposition of fees and costs discretionary once the falsity of the defendant's communication has been established by clear and convincing evidence.

In addition to fees and costs, most of the anti-SLAPP statutes permit a target to recover compensatory damages and, in some instances, punitive damages. The Minnesota and Rhode Island statutes mandate the recovery of compensatory damages if the court determines that the suit was filed to harass, inhibit public participation, interfere with the exercise of protected rights, or otherwise wrongfully injure the target. By contrast, the courts of Delaware, Nebraska, and New York, upon making the same determination, may award compensatory damages at their discretion. Those states that provide for an award of punitive damages in their statutes grant courts the discretion to determine whether such a penalty should be imposed.

California's anti-SLAPP law is silent as to both compensatory and punitive damages, and makes no provision for a cause of action for a prevailing target (a "SLAPP-back").... California's statute is very broadly drawn as to the activity covered, although it places a less demanding burden on a filer, requiring only a demonstration of probability of prevailing on the merits, as opposed to requiring proof by clear and convincing evidence....

Real obstacles exist in researching a pattern for the filing of SLAPPs for several reasons. First, since the original claims are based on actionable torts, those states without anti-SLAPP legislation apply traditional First Amendment and tort analyses in assessing the validity of the allegations. Second, many SLAPP targets retreat from their positions to avoid prolonged and expensive litigation. Third, and perhaps most frustrating, the majority of the decisions are rendered at the trial court level; therefore, there are no published reports of the proceedings and findings....

Anti-SLAPP statutes have been construed most frequently in the courts of California and Massachusetts. California courts have given its statute a very broad interpretation, but have also reached contradictory decisions among the state's appellate districts.

A slander suit arising from a private dispute is not covered by California's anti-SLAPP statute, according to the state's First District Court of Appeal.[114] This is true even where the dispute spawned a prior legal proceeding. In construing the statute and denying the target's special motion to dismiss, that court opined that the statute was narrowly drawn to discourage a type of suit that chills public participation and does not apply to actions concerning matters lacking public significance....

The most frequently filed SLAPPs involve real estate development, zoning, and land use issues. Other favored issues, in descending order, are criticism of public officials and employees, environmental and animal rights protection, civil and human rights, neighborhood problems, and consumer issues. A natural deduction from this pattern is that most of the suits are triggered by contact on a local government level, and only infrequently by activity on the federal level.

To gain access to court, filers claim a judicially cognizable injury, translating the offending political behavior into legalistic tort claims. Typically, the suits allege: defamation (e.g., libel, slander, and business libel), business torts (e.g., interference with contract, antitrust, trade restraint, and unfair competition), process violations (e.g.,

114. Zhao v. Wong, 48 Cal. App. 4th 1114, 1130–33 (Ct. App. 1996).

malicious prosecution, judicial or administrative abuse of process), conspiracy, civil and constitutional rights violations, and other legal violations (e.g., nuisance, emotional harms, trespass, and tax exemption attacks). Defamation is by far the most commonly utilized tort, though several filers utilize the "shotgun pleading" approach, alleging numerous categories of tortious behavior....

The Supreme Court has proclaimed that the right to petition conferred by the First Amendment is one of the "fundamental principles of liberty and justice which lie at the base of all civil and political institutions...." However, it must not be forgotten that a plaintiff in a civil action possesses the same right to petition as does the defendant. This right to petition includes the right of access to courts. It is both illogical and inequitable to grant one right to the exclusion of another.

Rights and duties have corresponding realms of significance. An absolute right to petition for redress of grievances implies the absolute nonexistence of any right to one's reputation or good name if it is implicated in something styled a "petition." Thus, reform geared to protect against SLAPPs necessarily lessens the legal protection for personal and professional reputation....

* * *

Notes and Comments

1. Ms. Arco compares the California, Delaware, Georgia, Massachusetts, Minnesota, Nebraska, and New York anti-SLAPP statutes. In the interest of length and limiting present coverage to the policies behind the anti-SLAPPs, most references to specifics of the various statutes have been omitted. If you wish to highlight the practices within a particular jurisdiction, see the excellent published comment at 52 U. Miami L. Rev. 587, or in WESTLAW at 52 UMIALR 587.

The success of the SLAPP strategy has unfortunately crossed the water:

James A. Wells, Comment, *Exporting SLAPPs: International Use of the U.S. "SLAPP" to Suppress Dissent and Critical Speech,*

12 Temple International and Comparative Law Journal 457 (1998)

Since the 1970s, Strategic Lawsuits Against Public Participation (SLAPPs) have existed in the United States as a mechanism to silence dissent and criticism. SLAPPs are suits usually brought by companies, corporations, and governments against citizens, as individuals or groups, or public interest organizations, that have spoken out against corporate or governmental actions. The primary goal of these lawsuits is to stifle and silence a citizen's or group's criticism. Damage claims are usually inflated to maximize the intimidation factor. This is achieved by dragging SLAPP targets into court based on legal theories that are usually hollow. Once the suit begins, the target is forced to concentrate on defending against a lawsuit, effectively ending the debate over the original issue....

Consequently, this dubious legal maneuver has expanded beyond U.S. borders as opportunistic filers and their attorneys have recognized the utility of the SLAPP. Throughout this decade, the use of SLAPPs internationally has increased with disturbing frequency. Not only are U.S. corporations SLAPPing critical speech in other countries, but foreign domestic corporations, foreign based multinational corporations, and foreign governments have also found the technique useful to silence dissent and criticism.

In the United States, the problem has been recognized, and a significant minority of states have passed anti-SLAPP statutes that provide a layer of protection for the victims of SLAPPs. Unfortunately, most countries are unprepared for dealing with this most recent U.S. export. Countries that are now experiencing the SLAPP phenomena are in a similar position as the individual states in the United States were in the late 1980s, when the states were just beginning to perceive the threat of SLAPPs and formulate ways to contain them....

This survey is not an exhaustive catalogue of every SLAPP in each country, but rather, a sampling of some cases that have achieved infamous notoriety and others that have gone relatively unnoticed. That only three countries were selected for this study does not mean to imply that SLAPPs do not yet exist in other countries and other legal systems; indeed there is evidence of SLAPPs arising in a diverse array of countries including South Korea, Singapore, Pakistan, France, and New Zealand.

SLAPPs in England

David Morris and Helen Steel, members of London Greenpeace, were not aware that they would be making history when they decided to distribute a pamphlet at local McDonald's restaurants that attacked the corporation's cheery facade. Their incisive eight page pamphlet resulted in what was to become the longest trial in Britain, lasting over thirty months. The pamphlet criticized McDonald's marketing strategies towards children, treatment of animals, deforestation and other environmental abuses, food quality and nutritional value, and the corporation's relations with its workers. On the pamphlet's cover was a drawing of a fat corporate executive with an evil sneer on his face, donning a cowboy hat and smoking a cigar. The executive, a symbol of greedy U.S. capitalism, was holding a mask of Ronald McDonald's smiling face on a stick.

The pamphlet, entitled "What's Wrong With McDonald's: Everything They Don't Want You To Know," was not received well by McDonald's. In 1990, several years after publication of the pamphlet, McDonald's filed suit in English courts claiming damage to its reputation. McDonald's named several defendants, most of whom settled the case. Morris and Steel decided to fight it out. The two brazen defendants went through the entire trial without any representation, prepared their case on the subway on the way to court, and relied on pro bono advice from sympathetic lawyers. McDonald's, of course, had some of the most expensive and well trained lawyers in England on its side.

The case concluded in the summer of 1997, with the judge finding for the plaintiff, McDonald's. After the trial, a press conference on the courthouse steps, the defendants handed out copies of the original pamphlet that had started the whole action. Because of the bad press and the fact that the defendants would never be able to pay, McDonald's decided not to have the $98,500 judgment enforced and collected.

The case was unique because the two defendants were not only viewed as extremely sympathetic, they were also extremely vocal. They established a worldwide network of financial and legal support and made continuous press releases to the media. The publicity generated by the trial produced a harsh public relations backlash against McDonald's. It was a classic corporate Goliath against activist David, as McDonald's desire to censor criticism became more transparent throughout the trial, and public support for the defendants grew.

Undoubtedly, this case has all the elements of a classic SLAPP. Morris and Steel were part of a group organized to address environmental concerns. They targeted McDonald's for its environmental and labor abuses and attempted to publicize their views on a corporation that commands more resources than some nations and is prominent in almost every country in the world, including England. Then McDonald's reacted by threatening to sue all the members of London Greenpeace, which was successful in causing all of the other members to settle. McDonald's sued Morris and Steel for damages, although the combined income of the two amounted to [£7500 or less than $12,000 U.S.]. It is evident that McDonald's was employing the classic SLAPP strategy of elongating the litigation to be as expensive as possible for the targets. As it resulted in the longest trial in English history, it seems apparent the multinational corporation had perfected this skill.

McDonald's was so sensitive about the allegations that it sued these two activists from an unknown organization. This can possibly be explained by the fact that the last thing McDonald's wanted was an open public debate delving into its business practices and procedures. The corporation had much more to gain by either silencing the debate or by moving the discussion into a judicial forum where the rules would be stacked in its favor and it could shift the focus from corporate abuses to libelous activists. In other words, McDonald's knew it may lose an open and public political debate, so it went on the offensive and changed the terms of the dispute. Although this lawsuit deserves the SLAPP label, it was definitely not the typical SLAPP. The case went all the way to judgment and the plaintiff actually won, which are both rare occurrences in a SLAPP. Usually filers drop the suit before a judgment is reached, or targets back down and settle. The case attracted massive publicity worldwide where McDonald's came off as the corporate Goliath who spent $16 million suing two broke and unrepresented Davids. The public relations backlash exposed McDonald's strong-arm tactics and brought unwanted attention to the corporation's practices in several politically sensitive areas. The "McLibel Two" had a tenacious resolve to prove their point and went far beyond what most normal people could withstand to support their cause....

SLAPPs in Canada....

One of the most prominent SLAPPs in Canada involved the Lubicon Lake Indian Nation's battle to obtain their ancestral and legal rights of ownership to a territory in Northern Alberta. In 1988, the Alberta government gave a Japanese multinational corporation, Daishowa, the right to build the largest pulpwood plant in Canada, Peace River Mill, directly in the heart of territory claimed by the Lubicon. The next year, the government gave Daishowa a timber lease on an additional 11,600 square miles in northern Alberta. The Lubicon had no say in this agreement.

Friends of the Lubicon (FoL) was created in response to the threat of Daishowa to the Lubicon's ancestral lands. Since 1991 it has conducted a "secondary boycott" aimed at informing companies and consumers that use Daishowa's paper packaging products of the corporation's policies and dissuading them from buying from Daishowa. The goal of the campaign is to prevent Daishowa from acting on the licenses they have to clear-cut the land claimed by the Lubicon. The boycott has effectively dissuaded forty-seven companies in Canada from using packaging products from Daishowa.

The corporation went to the courts and obtained an injunction against FoL's boycott activity, which temporarily enjoined FoL from interfering with Daishowa's business and picketing or threatening to picket customers of the corporation. Unsatisfied, however, Daishowa is taking it a step further by suing FoL for $812 million in damages and seeking an injunction that permanently forbids FoL's secondary boycott activity. Therefore, not only has the tool of the boycott been stifled, but now the group must defend against a giant SLAPP calculated to cripple the volunteer organization and ultimately silence its criticism. Much like the McLibel case in England, Daishowa had been unwilling to engage FoL publicly; rather, its goal was to move the debate into court, where the focus could shift from aboriginal rights and environmental impact to interference with profit. This is a classic motive for filing a SLAPP....

SLAPPs in Australia

Industry and government in Australia have also begun to recognize the utility of the SLAPP in suppressing dissent and opposition. An article in an Australian journal, the Current Affairs Bulletin, surveyed recent Australian SLAPPs. The article discussed a 1991 industry conference on "Pollution Law" in Melbourne, where a paper entitled "Legal Rights of Industry Against Conservationists" was presented. It pointed to the United States' SLAPP as a potentially useful weapon of intimidation against environmental activists.

In one of the more blatant SLAPPs mentioned in the article, several developers had sued the Helensburgh District Protection Society, a local environmental group, for responding to a land use proposition by the Wollongong City Council, which encompassed Helensburgh. The council had requested submissions from the public on its proposition to rezone certain tracks of land as "environmentally protected," which would prohibit development on those tracts. The Society rallied public support for the proposition, published articles supporting the measure, and sent letters directly to the council urging them to adopt the proposal. Developers who had recently been defeated in a bid to develop the same land that was targeted for rezoning SLAPPed the Society for responding to the City Council's request for public input on the proposal, claiming that the Society spread false information about the effects of development. The developers claimed as damages the profits they might have had if they had been permitted to build on that particular land. The Society defended by asserting that they were simply responding to a request for public submissions, an essential part of the political process, and that they had legitimate environmental concerns about the particular land in controversy.

Eventually the developers suspended the legal action against the Society, went above the city council men's heads, and persuaded the Minister of Planning to form an official inquiry into the proposal. When the Society protested this inquiry, the developers threatened further legal action. As of 1994, the developers had not followed through on prosecuting the case, but rather, had decided to keep the case in suspension until the government completes an environmental impact study.

The developers' actions in this case are prototypical of land use SLAPPs in the United States. The Society's communication with the city consisted of attempts to influence the council's decision on a measure that had a direct impact on the developers' economic interests. As a result of losing the political debate, the developers resorted to intimidation to protect their interests and moved the dispute into court....

SLAPP-Backs: SLAPP-backs are commonly looked upon as the solution to SLAPPs. A SLAPP-back is a separate lawsuit initiated by the target against the filer for damages that the target incurred from the filer's original SLAPP. These suits can result in high awards for the target. SLAPP-backs are usually brought on malicious prosecution and abuse of process claims. If a target wins a SLAPP-back, not only does he or she get reimbursed for the expense of being sued, but the benefit that the filer obtained by bringing the original SLAPP is negated....

Canada....

Canada's resident SLAPP expert, Professor Chris Tollefson, has analyzed how Canada could combat SLAPPs. Professor Tollefson pointed out that under section 2(b) of the Canadian Charter of Rights and Freedoms, "freedom of thought, belief, and expression" is protected and that this provision has been broadly interpreted by the Canadian Supreme Court to encompass a variety of forms of speech. Although this provision would seem to provide the protection SLAPP targets need, free speech under the Charter is only protected from government intrusion, and does not protect speech among private parties. This makes developing a response to the SLAPP based on substantive rights difficult.

Despite this obstacle, several recent decisions by the Supreme Court of Canada indicate that the Court is moving in the direction of extending Charter protections to private disputes. Based on these decisions, Professor Tollefson argues that the "public" nature of SLAPP suits and the harm they impose on the public in general should qualify SLAPP targets for protection under the Charter, even if the actual parties are private. He has also made a call for a legislative response to SLAPPs that would establish a statutory right of public participation.... [proposals mirror the American variations of the anti-SLAPP legislation]...

Finally, Professor Tollefson's suggestion of a legal aid service for targets would be especially effective, since the lawyers for the organization would develop substantial expertise in defending targets, and would present a formidable challenge to filers who rely, in part, on the legal inexperience of targets and their attorneys for the success of the SLAPP. In addition, targets would be free to continue their free speech or petitioning activities if they did not have to pay legal fees. Alternatively, if Canadian legislatures are reluctant to establish a legal aid service, then they should allow some form of government intervention on behalf of SLAPP targets—either the governmental bodies with which the targets communicated in petition cases, or attorneys' general offices in free speech SLAPPs.

Australia....

Primarily, Australia does not have a specific constitutional guarantee of the right to free speech or the right to petition the government. Several cases decided from 1992 to 1994 by the Australian High Court have established the foundation of an "implied" right to free speech which may be able to provide more protection for SLAPP targets....

As a result, SLAPP targets whose speech dealt with issues that are in the public interest, but did not deal with the government, may not be able to avail themselves of the potential protections of this new implied right. These targets should try to frame the issues underlying the SLAPP action as implicating governmental interests in some way to be protected as political speech....

England

England is a country that is ripe for SLAPPs. Although libel is only one cause of action among many that filers can choose from, it is the one most subject to abuse in England. Because English libel laws are extremely plaintiff friendly, there is an incentive for filers to SLAPP, as it is more likely that they may actually win their SLAPP based on the substantive law. Such was the case with the infamous McDonald's SLAPP against two environmental activists in London. Even though the McLibel case backfired on McDonald's in terms of public relations, the corporation still won the actual case, albeit for far lower damages than it expected.

A second problem facing targets in England is that, like Canada and Australia, there is no specific constitutionally protected right to free speech or to petition the government. However, much like Australia, several recent cases indicate that freedom of speech is becoming a higher priority in English common law. In addition, England's status as a signatory to the European Convention on Human Rights has forced its courts to reevaluate the right to free speech, especially in the area of libel. This encouraging trend should provide more protection for targets and make the passage of anti-SLAPP legislation a more feasible possibility....

European Convention on Human Rights

The European Convention on Human Rights (Convention), to which England is a signatory, specifically provides for a broad protection of free expression. Article 10 of the Convention states that the right to free expression can only be constrained by restrictions that are "prescribed by law and are necessary for a democratic society," and that there be a "pressing social need" for any law that puts limitations on free expression. This language puts limits on how far laws can impinge on free expression. There are no comparable provisions in English statutory law, nor in the common law....

* * *

Hate Speech

What happens when the First Amendment collides with litigation that may be pursued for a discriminatory purpose? For example, where opponents of a proposed housing project that may house the disabled or members of a race that are in the minority in the community engage in discriminatory behavior designed to block the project and exclude the group protected either under the Equal Protection Clause or a statute such as the Fair Housing Act. Opposition tactics can range from acts of violence, to traditional expressive techniques such as signs, leafleting, or marching. Tactics of the group may also be to go to city hall for protest or public participation, or the ultimate American public participation tactic of bringing a lawsuit. If such a racially or disability-based bias motivates the activity should it nevertheless be protected by the First Amendment? The following case discusses the question:

White v. Lee

United States Court of Appeals, Ninth Circuit
227 F.3d 1214 (2000)

Reinhardt, Circuit Judge:

This case involves the Fair Housing Act, 42 U.S.C. §§ 3601–3631, and the First Amendment. On November 1, 1993 a housing rights advocacy group filed an administrative complaint with an office of the U.S. Department of Housing and Urban Development (HUD) in San Francisco. The complaint alleged that three neighbors in Berkeley opposed the conversion of a motel into a multi-family housing unit because they believed that the project would bring people into the neighborhood who were mentally disabled or disabled through substance abuse. Upon receiving the complaint, the San Francisco HUD office initiated an eight-month investigation into the neighbors' activities and beliefs. During the course of its investigation, HUD officials questioned the neighbors under threat of subpoena about their views and public statements regarding the challenged project; directed them to produce an array of documents and information, including all involved parties' names, addresses, and telephone numbers and all correspondence or other documents relating to their efforts in opposition to the project; informed them and a major metropolitan newspaper that they had violated the Fair Housing Act; and advised them to accept a "conciliation proposal" that required them to cease all litigation and the distribution of "discriminatory" newsletters and flyers. The HUD officials in San Francisco recommended finding that the neighbors had violated the Fair Housing Act, but officials in Washington ultimately concluded that no violation had occurred and that the neighbors had engaged solely in activity protected by the First Amendment.

The three Berkeley neighbors then filed this civil rights action alleging that the investigation conducted by the HUD officials in San Francisco violated their First Amendment rights. The officials argue that they were required by the Fair Housing Act to investigate whether the neighbors had filed a lawsuit in state court with an unlawful discriminatory motive. At the very least, they argue, they are entitled to qualified immunity. The district court denied the officials' motion for summary judgment on the issue of qualified immunity, entered partial summary judgment in favor of the neighbors on the issue of liability, and dismissed as moot the neighbors' claim for declaratory and injunctive relief. Only the issue of damages remains for trial. We affirm the district court in all respects....

On May 12, 1992, a local nonprofit housing developer, Resources for Community Development (RCD), applied for a use permit from Berkeley's Zoning Adjustment Board. RCD sought to convert the Bel Air Motel, a property on University Avenue, to a multi-family housing unit for homeless persons. The use permit required approval by both the Zoning Adjustment Board and the Berkeley City Council.

The plaintiffs lived close to the Bel Air Motel and were opposed to its proposed conversion. They expressed their opposition in a variety of ways. They wrote to the Berkeley City Council, spoke out before the Zoning Adjustment Board and at other public meetings, and published a newsletter with articles critical of the project. The front page of the February 1993 issue of the plaintiffs' newsletter, Flatland News, for example, contained an article titled "City Forcing Bel Air Project Down Our Throats." The plaintiffs discussed their opposition to the project with the local press and attempted to persuade merchants on University Avenue to oppose the Bel Air project also.

The Zoning Adjustment Board granted RCD its use permit on October 1, 1992. An appeal to the Berkeley City Council failed, by a 4–4 vote, in April 1993. That same month, a coalition in which plaintiffs were involved ("the Coalition of Neighborhood Groups Opposing the Bel Air Conversion") filed a lawsuit against Berkeley and RCD in state court....It alleged that one of the Zoning Adjustment Board's members, Linda Maio, was also a member of RCD's board and, because of this conflict of interest, improperly participated in the Zoning Adjustment Board's hearings. On April 19, the coalition moved for a preliminary injunction to prevent the issuance of an effective use permit. The Alameda County Superior Court denied the motion and set the case for trial on November 15, 1993. Although RCD's use permit became effective in May 1993, the developer thereafter experienced difficulty obtaining promised funds for the project from Berkeley and had to seek repeated extensions from other funders.

Marianne Lawless (now deceased) was the executive director of Housing Rights, Inc. ("HRI"), a Berkeley housing rights advocacy group. She had testified at a hearing in support of the Bel Air project. On October 15, 1993, Lawless wrote a letter to the San Francisco Office stating her intention to file a HUD administrative complaint against the plaintiffs. Lawless attached a letter dated October 12 from the executive director of RCD to the Housing and Civil Enforcement Section of the Department of Justice complaining about the plaintiffs' opposition to the Bel Air project. Lawless also attached several flyers and other documents which, she stated, "demonstrate the discriminatory scare tactics used by the opponents."[4]...

The analyst concluded that HUD had jurisdiction and should accept Lawless's complaint for processing, and a supervisor concurred. On October 26, the intake analyst drafted an administrative complaint against the plaintiffs on Form HUD-903. Boxes on the form were checked indicating that HRI had been "[i]ntimidated, interfered [with], or coerced... to keep [HRI] from the full benefit of the Federal Housing Law" and that the plaintiffs had engaged in discrimination on the basis of mental handicap. The complaint included the following statement written on HRI's behalf:

> We are a fair housing agency in the city of Berkeley. As such, one of our missions is to ensure equal opportunities for all persons. The above named respondents have impaired our ability to ensure equal housing by impeding the proposed conversion of the Bel Air Motel to permanently house low-income homeless persons. One of their principal arguments against this project is that it will benefit people that are diagnosed as mentally disabled or disabled through substance abuse. Although the respondents unsuccessfully attempted to obtain a preliminary injunction against the developer acquiring a use permit, they have been given a trial date for November 15, 1993. We believe the above named individuals are blocking the proposed project because they perceive the primary residents of the facility will be the mentally disabled or the disabled through substance abuse.

The San Francisco Office sent this draft complaint to Lawless, she signed it, and the complaint was filed on November 1, 1993.

The San Francisco Office's Investigation

In early November 1993, the San Francisco Office sent letters to White, Deringer, and Graham. The office enclosed HRI's complaint and stated that the plaintiffs could file an answer within ten days. HUD, the letters stated, would "commence an investigation of this complaint, and simultaneously encourage all parties involved to conciliate the matter." If conciliation failed and HUD's investigation produced "evidence to substantiate a finding that there is reasonable cause to believe that you have engaged in an unlawful discriminatory housing practice," HUD would issue a charge against them, at which point they would be exposed to certain penalties—including damages as great as

4. The flyers made a variety of points about the project. One, titled "Who are the Homeless?", showed a pie chart dividing the homeless into three, presumably discrete categories—economic, mentally ill, and substance abusers—and complained about the "inequitable distribution" of Berkeley housing and services for the homeless in poor areas or commercial corridors "with high ethnic concentrations." Another listed projects planned for the area near the intersection of University and Shattuck Avenues, stated that these projects would provide beds for "90 mentally ill and 90 'stabilized' substance abusers," and concluded, "This is commercial suicide! Impacts MUST be assessed!" A third flyer contended that inadequate information had been provided about the Bel Air project for the Berkeley City Council to make a "fair, complete and proper evaluation"; regarding the project's tenant population, it stated, "At least 71% will be homeless, but no details as to mentally ill, substance abusers, dual diagnosis, etc."

$100,000—and could elect to have their case heard by an administrative law judge or referred for trial in U.S. District Court. The plaintiffs filed answers to the complaint on November 12.

Defendant Smith assigned the complaint to defendant Lee to investigate and defendant Zurowski to conciliate. On December 17, 1993, Lawless sent Zurowski a "Proposal for Conciliation" containing the following settlement terms:

> 1) That the above named respondents [White, Deringer, and Graham], and the Neighborhood Groups Opposing the Bel Air Conversion, cease all litigation against Resources for Community Development and the City of Berkeley regarding the development of the Bel Air Motel; and
>
> 2) That the above named respondents, and the Neighborhood Groups Opposing the Bel Air Conversion, cease publication of discriminatory statements (including articles in the CNA Newsletter) and fliers about the potential residents of the Bel Air project. Zurowski relayed these proposed terms to the plaintiffs. According to a declaration by the attorney then representing the plaintiffs, David Bryden, Zurowski told him "that the proposed settlement was a good one because my clients had, in fact, engaged in discriminatory actions in violation of the Fair Housing Act—I recall him telling me that HUD had evidence of a flyer which demonstrated such a violation—and that I should be relieved that my clients would not also have to pay damages to the complainant."

On January 12, 1994, Lee drafted and Smith reviewed and signed, on behalf of the San Francisco Office's compliance director, a letter to the three plaintiffs. It stated that the San Francisco Office was investigating HRI's complaint and that it was HUD policy "to secure the voluntary cooperation of all persons in the collection of information during the investigation." The letter continued:

> When access to premises, records, documents, individuals and other possible sources of information and evidence which may be necessary for the furtherance of the investigation is not provided, the Department may issue subpoenas to compel such access, production or testimony. Any person who willfully fails or neglects to attend and testify or to answer any lawful inquiry or to produce records, documents or other evidence in obedience to a subpoena "shall be fined not more than $100,000 or imprisoned not more than one year, or both."

Attached to the letter was an "Attachment of Request to Produce Written Responses" listing ten items. This request was extremely broad. It directed the plaintiffs to submit, inter alia, the name and contact information of any person "who was involved in or witnessed the act(s) alleged on the complaint form"; "a copy of any documents or the contents of any file in your control concerning the Bel Air Motel conversion"; all correspondence with or minutes or reports generated by the Council of Neighborhoods Association regarding the Bel Air project; and all literature, posters, newsletters, and flyers about the project. On January 18, the plaintiffs, through their attorney, stated that they did not have some of the documents sought and that they refused to provide the others. HUD did not take any further action to obtain these documents from the plaintiffs.

On February 1, Smith told the plaintiffs' attorney Bryden that HUD would issue a subpoena to compel the plaintiffs' testimony if they refused to be interviewed by Lee. Bryden agreed that Lee could interview the plaintiffs by telephone. The interview took place on February 7 and lasted for about one hour. Lee asked the plaintiffs why they were opposed to the Bel Air project and what statements they had made about the project to the public. Lee later testified in a deposition that Smith had directed him to ask the plaintiffs these questions, which Lee had considered irregular and beyond the scope of a routine FHA investigation.

On February 8, pursuant to Lee's request, Bryden sent Lee a memorandum from the Berkeley City Manager stating that Zoning Adjustment Board member Linda Maio had a conflict of interest on the RCD matter. Sometime during the investigation, Smith also became aware that there was reason to believe that Maio had a conflict of interest....

The plaintiffs filed their complaint in May 1995. They alleged that defendants Gillespie, Smith, Lee, Zurowski, and Phillips investigated and harassed them solely because of the exercise of their First Amendment rights to free speech and to petition the government for a redress of grievances....

Although the HUD officials frame this case in terms of a complex doctrinal debate involving *Noerr-Pennington* immunity and its labor law permutation, we find it to be, at heart, quite simple. In opposing their local government's approval of the Bel Air project, White, Deringer, and Graham engaged in activity paradigmatically protected by the First Amendment. The HUD officials' eight-month investigation into the plaintiffs' activities and beliefs chilled the exercise of their First Amendment rights....

The Speech....

The right to expressive association includes the right to pursue, as a group, discriminatory policies that are antithetical to the concept of equality for all persons. The First Amendment also guarantees the right "to petition the Government for a redress of grievances."...

It is important to emphasize that a person's speech or petitioning activity is not removed from the ambit of First Amendment protection simply because it advocates an unlawful act. The First Amendment does not permit government "to forbid or proscribe advocacy of the use of force or of law violation except where such advocacy is directed to inciting or producing imminent lawless action and is likely to incite or produce such action." Brandenburg v. Ohio, 395 U.S. 444, 447 (1969)....

We need not decide whether the plaintiffs' primary objective—the defeat of the proposed conversion of the Bel Air motel—would have involved an unlawful act. The mere fact that citizens urge their government to adopt measures that may be unlawful does not deprive the speech involved of its First Amendment protection....

The Chill

The investigation by the HUD officials unquestionably chilled the plaintiffs' exercise of their First Amendment rights. It is true that the agency did not ban or seize the plaintiffs' materials, and officials in Washington ultimately decided not to pursue either criminal or civil sanctions against them.... Informal measures, such as "the threat of invoking legal sanctions and other means of coercion, persuasion, and intimidation," can violate the First Amendment also.

The FHA as a Justification

The HUD officials argue that their actions constituted lawful efforts to enforce the Fair Housing Act (FHA).... The FHA prohibits, among other things, owners and landlords from refusing to sell or rent housing because of race, color, religion, sex, handicap, familial status, or national origin. § 3604. The FHA also makes it unlawful "to coerce, intimidate, threaten, or interfere with any person in the exercise or enjoyment of...any right granted or protected by section 3603, 3604, 3605, or 3606 of this title." Id. at §§ 3617, 3602(f)....

We have applied § 3617 broadly to cover a variety of practices that have the effect of interfering with the exercise of fair housing rights protected by the FHA. See United States v. City of Hayward, 36 F.3d 832, 835 (9th Cir.1994) (" 'Interference' ranges from racially motivated firebombings, to exclusionary zoning, and insurance redlining.") (citations omitted). In theory, § 3617 could be interpreted even more broadly, so that a wide range of speech regarding the housing rights of others could be investigated and sanctioned. One person's persuasive editorial on a zoning dispute, for instance, might well "interfere" with another person's ability to secure housing. So construed, however, § 3617 would quickly run afoul of the First Amendment principles discussed above.

For this reason, other courts have recognized that a speaker's advocacy of his views, however "ill-advised, uninformed, and even distasteful," can amount to a violation of § 3617 of the FHA only in the event that the advocacy is directed to inciting or producing imminent violence and is likely in fact to do so. We agree. See Michigan Protection & Advocacy Serv., Inc. v. Babin, 799 F. Supp. 695, 720 (E.D.Mich.1992), aff'd, 18 F.3d 337 (6th Cir.1994)....

Noerr-Pennington immunity

The Supreme Court has described the right to petition as "among the most precious of the liberties safeguarded by the Bill of Rights" and "intimately connected, both in origin and in purpose, with the other First Amendment rights of free speech and free press."...The Court has further established that the right to petition extends to all departments of the government, including the executive department, the legislature, agencies, and the courts. California Motor Transport involved *Noerr-Pennington* immunity, a doctrine initially promulgated "to protect efforts to influence legislative or executive action from liability under the Sherman Act." Oregon Natural Resources Council v. Mohla, 944 F.2d 531, 533 (9th Cir.1991) (citing *Noerr*, 365 U.S. 127; United Mine Workers v. Pennington, 381 U.S. 657 (1965)). While the *Noerr-Pennington* doctrine originally arose in the antitrust context, it is based on and implements the First Amendment right to petition and therefore...applies equally in all contexts....The Noerr-Pennington doctrine ensures that those who petition the government for redress of grievances remain immune from liability for statutory violations, notwithstanding the fact that their activity might otherwise be proscribed by the statute involved....

The HUD officials completely failed to satisfy this threshold requirement. From the time they initiated their investigation until the time they submitted their final report to the Washington office, the officials made little or no effort to investigate the basis for the plaintiffs' suit. Instead, their investigation focused almost exclusively on what the officials considered to be the plaintiffs' discriminatory speech. Director Gillespie's two-page, single-spaced letter of July 1994 broadly asserted HUD's purported jurisdiction to investigate "speech advocating illegal acts" and cited reprovingly the plaintiffs' "news articles which referenced the mental disability" of the Bel Air project's intended residents; it did not, however, mention the plaintiffs' lawsuit once. Likewise, investigator Smith did not ask the plaintiffs any questions about the lawsuit during his interviews. Most striking, the officials completed and submitted to HUD headquarters a final investigative report that failed to include any information about the plaintiffs' lawsuit more substantial than what was set forth in HRI's complaint....

[T]he HUD officials argue that a person would violate the FHA if he brought "an unsuccessful state court action to deter another person, or group of persons, from exercising their federally protected rights—e.g. to keep them from moving into the neighborhood." Because the plaintiffs ultimately lost their state-court lawsuit, the officials argue that they acted properly in investigating the plaintiffs' opposition to the Bel Air project to determine whether they had filed that action with a discriminatory motive....

We hold that in this case the unconstitutionality of each of the HUD officials' actions was apparent at the time they acted. The plaintiffs' claim is founded on bedrock First Amendment principles and legal rules that this court and the Supreme Court have applied for decades, if not centuries. In 1993 and 1994, reasonable government officials would have known that they could not conduct an eight-month investigation into the vocal but entirely peaceful opposition of residents to a housing project proposed for their neighborhood, or into their efforts to persuade the appropriate government agencies of their point of view. They would also have known that accusations of law-breaking, threatened subpoenas, improper broad demands for documents and information, and admonishments to cease nonfrivolous litigation and the publication of "discriminatory" statements would chill "uninhibited, robust, and wide-open" debate on public issues....

The officials argue that they were required by statutes and regulations to serve HRI's complaint on the plaintiffs, conduct an investigation, and attempt to resolve it through conciliation. The fact that an investigation may have been initiated pursuant to statutory and regulatory authority does not, however, entitle the defendants to qualified immunity regarding the extent of the investigation and the manner in which it was conducted....

It was also clearly established that the *Noerr-Pennington* doctrine sharply limited the officials' ability to treat the plaintiffs' state-court lawsuit as a possible violation of law. Controlling case law had made clear that the doctrine was not limited to the antitrust context, and that the officials had a duty to first determine that the plaintiffs' suit—the only conceivable FHA violation alleged in HRI's administrative complaint—was objectively baseless before proceeding with a potentially chilling investigation into the plaintiffs' indisputably protected speech and other petitioning activity.

The HUD officials—or, to be more specific, their counsel from the U.S. Department of Justice—contend that they will face the specter of "personal financial ruin" in the event that they are denied qualified immunity...To the extent that HUD is genuinely concerned about the inhibiting effect that the threat of personal liability will have on its future operations, it may indemnify its employees as permitted by law. We would, in fact, be most surprised if the agency did not do so in this case....AFFIRMED

* * *

Notes and Comments

1. Why does the court adopt *Brandenburg* as the standard, interpreting the government's concern to be that the protestors may incite public officials, including judges, to violate the Fair Housing Act? Isn't the real objection that the protestors are using "traditional speech rights" to violate the rights of the homeless and disabled? Is not the court's ruling inconsistent with the employment discrimination cases finding "traditional protected speech" to constitute gender harassment under the federal civil rights Act? See *Meritor Sav. Bank v. Vinson*, 477 U.S. 57 (1986). When should anti-discrimination doctrine trump free speech rights and when should the opposite prevail? Is violence the proper dividing line?

2. Actually, an 8-month HUD investigation may be the fast-track and the HUD office should have been applauded for its efficiency as well as it's good faith. James A. Kushner, *Federal Enforcement and Judicial Review of the Fair Housing Amendments Act of 1988*, 3 Hous. Pol'y Debate 537 (1992); *HUD Responds to Federal Panel's Recommendation on Fair Housing Enforcement* 7 Fair Hous.-Fair Lending (P-H) ¶ 10.6 (1992) (Administrative Conference found failure of HUD to meet 100-day investigation period in 75% of cases).

3. Under the ruling would there be any liability if white supremacists picket and march in front of the home of an Asian, Latino, or African-American family that moves to an historically white neighborhood? How could you distinguish the case for the United States Supreme Court's endorsement of harassment and interference laws? Michael P. Seng, *Hate Speech and Enforcement of the Fair Housing Laws*, 29 J. Marshall L. Rev. 409 (1996); Mary C. Lee, Note, *The Conflict Between "Fair Housing" and Free Speech*, 4 Wm. & Mary Bill Rts. J. 1223 (1996).

4. In response to the Berkeley controversy, HUD issued regulations restricting the ability of investigations based on traditional expressive activities and restricting HUD investigations to interference involving violence. *See* HUD Guidelines, Substantive and Procedural Limitations on Filing and Investigating Fair Housing Act Complaints that May Implicate the First Amendment, Fair-Hous.-Fair Lending (West) ¶ 5345 (Sept. 2, 1994). Was HUD's interpretation too deferential to its critics? Was the Clinton White House and Justice Department overwhelmed by the joint and concurrent assaults of the segregationists, anarchists, libertarians, real estate lobby (includes the bulk of the top ten PACs—political action campaign fund raising organizations), and the ACLU?

Chapter 7

The Taking of Property Through Regulation

> Flying southeast over the countryside from Frankfurt to Munich, the triumph of the German city is visible. In corridors that could have been developed with thousands of one-family houses, there is forest (almost invariably without the second homes which mar Northern California) and farm land (with few farmhouses because farmers live in small villages and commute to their farms). There are no billboards even along the ribbons of the Autobahn. All of this has been achieved with minimal public intervention because private landowners have no right to build in undeveloped areas.
>
> George Lefcoe, *The Right to Develop Land: The German and Dutch Experience,* 56 Or. L. Rev. 31, 46 (1977)

The issue in American land use law that draws the most scholarly and judicial attention is the question of takings. A taking defines the limits of regulation, separating excessive regulation from the difficult to identify valid exercise of police powers. In *Pennsylvania Coal Co. v. Mahon*, 260 U.S. 393 (1922), Justice Oliver Wendell Holmes, Jr. established the model for today's taking doctrine: regulation that goes too far constitutes a taking.

The Fifth Amendment provides that private property may only be taken for a public purpose, contemplating public infrastructure projects being the building of roads, canals, dams, schools, or parks, as well as the water, power, sewage, and solid waste or flood control project. In stark contrast to the *Mahon* test that appears to question any regulation, the public purpose clause has been consistently interpreted to give broad authority to acquire land for the public interest. *Hawaii Hous. Auth. v. Midkiff*, 467 U.S. 229 (1984) (acquisition to break up large landholdings). Private property may be purchased to revitalize the community to remove blight under urban renewal and other redevelopment strategies even where the redeveloper is a private corporation or the land is sold to private parties. *Berman v. Parker*, 348 U.S. 26 (1954). The doctrine supports the use of eminent domain to build public or government-supported affordable housing, or even market priced housing as well as sports stadia, tourist-oriented commercial and recreational developments, or high-tech business incubation parks and other economic development initiatives. Early on, the United States Supreme Court ruled that the Fifth Amendment's requirements were applicable to the states as well as the federal government despite the Bill of Rights, or the first ten amendments, establishing a limit solely on the federal government. *Chicago, B. & Q. R.R. v. Chicago*, 166 U.S. 226 (1897). The provision, like others including the First Amendment's freedom of speech or the Fourth Amendment's limits on search and seizure, are incorporated into the Fourteenth Amendment pursuant to the doctrine of selective incorporation whereby the Supreme Court by majority vote can declare both elements of the Bill of Rights and indeed other unenumerated rights fundamental to the American scheme of justice. *Duncan v. Louisiana*, 391 U.S. 145 (1968).

The Supreme Court has not limited the ability to regulate in the definition of public purpose or the compensation clause, which has generally required payment at some measure of fair market value, whether it be the value of the property in terms of a sale price or a reasonable rental value in the case of temporary excessive regulations, such as where overly restrictive zoning is enforced for a period of years until modified or invalidated. *First English Evangelical Lutheran Church v. County of Los Angeles*, 482 U.S. 304 (1987). The difficult question remains how to distinguish the illegitimate regulation that goes too far from one that fills the needs generated by considerations of health, safety, welfare, or aesthetics. There exists debate among the scholars over the original intent of the framers. Some argue that the colonial understanding of eminent domain was limited to the outright acquisition of property and was never intended to interfere with public regulation. Compare Fred Bosselman, *et al.*, The Takings Issue: A Study of the Constitutional Limits of Governmental Authority to Regulate the Use of Privately-Owned Land Without Paying Compensation to the Owners (1973) (only appropriation of property intended), *accord* Hart, *Land Use Law in the Early Republic and the Original Meaning of the Takings Clause*, 94 Nw. U.L. Rev. 1099 (2000) *with* Kris W. Kobach, *The Origins of Regulatory Takings: Setting the Record Straight*, 1996 Utah L. Rev. 1211 (arguing diminution of value excessive regulatory taking not inconsistent with early historical record). Thus the rule should follow that like all regulation, land use regulations should be judged under the general standard of reasonableness and nonarbitrariness. This standard would ask, as in the case of zoning, whether it is debatable to a reasonable legislator that the regulation might serve police power interests of health, safety, welfare, or morals. *Village of Euclid v. Ambler Realty Co.*, 272 U.S. 365 (1926). Nevertheless, and scholarship aside, the Supreme Court has consistently adhered to Justice Holmes' subjective notion of definition by a majority finding of excessiveness.

The Supreme Court had followed a course of looking for *Mahon*'s excessiveness by looking at an array of considerations under what it refers to as a multi-factor ad hoc balancing test. This test, described in *Penn Central Transportation Co. v. City of New York*, 438 U.S. 104 (1978), looks to the character of the regulation and the effect of the regulation in monetary terms. The Court looks to see if the character of the regulation is nuisance abatement-like and thus likely to be upheld, or is the regulation designed to exact a public benefit, the cost or which should be more fairly apportioned among the community, or whether the reasonable investment-backed expectations of the landowner have been thwarted and whether the owner has been left with a reasonable economic use under the regulation. This multi-factor balancing test is subjective, particularly when regulating to protect sensitive ecological resources, and the results of litigation typically unpredictable. Unpredictability is bad for legislators as it exposes the city to liability for both takings damages and generous attorney's fees, threatens the environment as policymakers must compromise and stop short of fully exercising regulatory authority for fear of liability, and not appreciated by developers who depend on predictability. The unpredictability does generate more lawyer work and litigation and some attorneys for landowners have become adept at not simply winning but utilizing the litigation strategy to obtain extraordinary concessions, either in obtaining more intensive development or reducing the exactions or other conditions typically imposed on development. In some cases, and in some jurisdictions, the subjective law has resulted in the validation of the most extensive forms of regulation.

A change in the Court's direction came in the case of a city's authorization for the placement of cable television wiring on private buildings. In *Loretto v. Teleprompter*

Manhattan CATV Corp., 458 U.S. 419 (1982), the Court cut out from the balancing test the set of takings cases that involved a physical occupation. This would include cases of trespass, such as flooding, or other public act that generates permanent or temporary non-emergency access by government or the public. Instead, the Court announced a near categorical rule characterizing such physical invasions as compensable takings.

The Court subsequently took another class of takings (discussed in Chapter 4), the excessive permit condition, and established the *Dolan* test that there must be (1) an essential nexus between the condition and a legitimate state interest, that is that the condition substantially advance a health, safety, welfare, or morals concern, (2) using an individualized determination, the government must be able to demonstrate the existence of (3) rough proportionality between the need for the condition generated by the proposal and the nature and extent of the condition.

In *Lucas v. South Carolina Coastal Council*, 505 U.S. 1003 (1992), the Supreme Court ruled that where a regulation denied the landowner all economic use that the regulation was presumptively a taking. Although the Court may have intended to take another, and ostensibly, the remaining body of takings claims out of the ad hoc standard, it stopped short of making the *Lucas* standard as categorical as the physical occupation rule. The decision contained a significant exception that the doctrine would not apply to rights that were not contained within the landowner's title. For example, regulation that would abate, avoid, or mitigate a nuisance would not constitute a compensable taking. *Tahoe-Sierra Preservation Council v. Tahoe Regional Planning Agency*, 216 F.3d 764 (9th Cir. 2000), *aff'd*, 122 S. Ct. 1465 (2002) (sustaining moratorium). In addition, where land is subject to other encumbrances, whether in the title such as an express or implied easement, or under a public trust doctrine, no compensatory taking would occur. *Stevens v. City of Cannon Beach*, 854 P.2d 449 (1993), *cert. denied*. 510 U.S. 1207 (1994) (under doctrine of custom, ocean front property owners' property interests never included development rights interfering with public's use of dry sand area in city, thus denial of permit to build seawall not a taking). The public trust doctrine is a state constitutional doctrine that defines public access rights typically to coastal areas or along waterways and lakes. The doctrine, although quite different in different states, might guarantee public access to the ocean and beaches. This access right applies whether the beach is in public or private ownership and regulation that enforces or assures exercise of such rights would not constitute a taking. Jack H. Archer & Terrance W. Stone, *The Interaction of the Public Trust and the Takings Doctrines: Protecting Wetlands and Critical Coastal Areas*, 20 Vt. L. Rev. 81 (1995). Thus, in growth management regulation, or regulation affecting sensitive ecological systems, there remain significant questions about the nature of nuisance, public trust, and other property law doctrines that might affect the definition of excessive regulation. William W. Fisher, III, *The Trouble with Lucas*, 45 Stan. L. Rev. 1393 (1993). It appears that the Court has substituted one form of confusion for the previous unpredictable ad hoc balancing model or analysis. Perhaps the value of the current doctrine is to intimidate all the actors: regulators take a bit less than they want, environmentalists must seek compromise, and developers are eager to sit down early and enter into negotiated development agreements that promise predictability as an alternative to potential for delay and expense inherent to litigation.

In *Palazzolo v. Rhode Island*, 533 U.S. 606 (2001), the Court announced that in cases where regulation fails to destroy economic value under *Lucas*, that the court is to apply the multi-factor ad hoc and unpredictable *Penn Central* balancing test.

The Court of Appeals for the Federal Circuit that hears federal agency takings claims has made some interesting rulings that raise significant issues not resolved by the Supreme Court.

Courts have repeatedly ruled that the entire parcel is to be viewed to determine land value and regulatory impact rather than merely the heavily regulated segment or a portion of the parcel rendered undevelopable. *Keystone Bituminous Coal Ass'n v. DeBenedictis*, 480 U.S. 470 (1987); *Penn Cent. Transp. Co. v. New York*, 438 U.S. 104 (1978). In *Loveladies Harbor, Inc. v. United States*, 28 F.3d 1171 (Fed. Cir. 1994), the developer, sought both a fill permit from the Corps of Engineers which regulates wetlands, and a similar permit from the New Jersey Department of Environmental Protection. The developer sought to develop a 12.5 acre parcel for 35 single-family homes, one acre of which had already been filled. The parcel was part of a 51-acre parcel owned by the developer and the developer had agreed to dedicate the development rights on the remaining 38.5 acres in exchange for the state permit based on ecological impact. The 51 acre parcel had originally been a part of a 250 acre parcel. The developer had already developed 199 acres of the original parcel. The Corps of Engineers denied the federal fill permit. *Loveladies* raises the issue of what denominator to use in order to compute an owner's loss. If the court uses the original 250 acre parcel the loss is slight compared to using a smaller parcel and concluding a more complete taking. The Federal Circuit ruled that the 12.5 acre parcel was the correct denominator and thereby concluded that the permit denial constituted a substantial destruction of the parcel's value.

In *Florida Rock Indus. v. United States*, 18 F.3d 1560 (Fed. Cir. 1994), *cert. denied*, 513 U.S. 1109 (1995), the Federal Circuit reviewed the Corps of Engineers' refusal to issue a permit to mine limestone beneath a tract of wetlands. The court found that the permit denial constituted less than a total loss of the value of the property. Nevertheless, the court appeared to apply *Lucas* given the substantial loss of investment-backed expectations in exploiting the mineral rights. It is certainly an open question whether the Supreme Court will follow either *Loveladies* or *Florida Rock*. *Loveladies* and *Florida Rock* would seem to make sense in refusing to ignore what might constitute a 99 percent loss of value. However, under the Court's ruling in *Palazzolo*, in the absence of a total loss, the courts should have applied the *Penn Central* balancing test.

Finally, *Lucas* may be interpreted by some as an invitation to landowners to partition a parcel of property to leave an unproductive portion of the land in separate ownership to set up the possibility of a taking claim. Courts have not yet ruled on such an arguably bad faith use of takings litigation.

Sponsored by landowner organizations and very conservative private property advocates, numerous proposals have emerged to pass legislation at the federal and state level that would require compensation of landowners for regulation that merely reduced the value of their land. This legislation would cripple attempts to regulate to protect the environment, conserve resources, and assure sufficient infrastructure to accommodate growth. Oregon's recently passed Measure 7 (reprinted below) reflects that movement and would dismantle Portland's forward looking urban planning initiatives such as the urban growth boundary. *See e.g.* Omnibus Property Rights Act of 1995, S. 605, 104th Cong., 1st Sess. (taking on 20 percent devaluation by regulation in proposed legislation); Fla. Stat. Ann. §70.001 (inordinately burdens precluding economic use); Tex. Gov't Code Ann. §§2007.001 to 2007.045 (takings impact statement on 25 percent diminution allowing damages and regulation invalidation). *See generally* Robert H.

Freilich & RoxAnne Doyle, *Taking Legislation: Misguided and Dangerous*, 46 Land Use L. & Zoning Dig. 3 (Oct. 1994).

The following excerpt contrasts the evolution of American takings doctrine with that of Switzerland:

Enrico Riva, *Regulatory Takings in American Law and "Material Expropriation" in Swiss Law—A Comparison of the Applicable Standards,*

16 Urban Lawyer 425 (1984)

There are several reasons for comparing this subject under American and Swiss law. The underlying political systems are very similar: a union of formerly independent states (in Switzerland they are called cantons), which still retain considerable legislative and governmental powers; a three-branch federal government of limited powers; and a cherished array of individual liberties. The constitutions of both countries have an express "taking clause" (a provision ordering compensation for takings of private property). In both countries the doctrine of regulatory takings is a product of case law, not of statutory law. While this may seem natural for the United States, it is not for Switzerland. Under both systems the most difficult issues are found in the distinction between harmless regulations of property and takings requiring compensation. It is interesting that the United States Supreme Court as well as that of Switzerland has declared its inability to develop a manageable formula for this distinction....

Unlike the taking clause of the United States Constitution, its Swiss equivalent (article 22ter, section 3) makes a clear distinction between condemnation of property by the power of eminent domain and takings occurring as a result of governmental regulation. Stated differently, the Swiss constitution requires compensation expressly for both eminent domain *and* regulatory takings. The technical term for a condemnation of property rights in Swiss law is "formal expropriation" (*formelle Enteignung, expropriation formelle*). It is characterized by a forced transfer of title (be it a fee simple or a lesser property interest) from a private owner to the government in a formal proceeding. The purposes allowing the exercise of the power of eminent domain are limited to those expressly mentioned in the statute. The procedure has been regulated by the confederation and the cantons in special statutes. The regulatory taking, on the other hand, is called "material expropriation" *(materielle Enteignung, expropriation materielle)*. This term reflects the fact that there is no formal transfer of title, but that the effects caused by the regulation are materially the same as in a case of formal condemnation. The expression "material expropriation" will be used here as the Swiss equivalent of the American "regulatory taking."...

The city of Solothurn had enacted a zoning plan for the purpose of assuring the future construction of a sports center. By a special statutory provision, the plan entitled the city, for a period of ten years, to condemn the necessary land by exercise of the power of eminent domain, while it barred private landowners for the same period from constructing any building on that land. The restriction, therefore, did not operate on the present, but on the future use of the property. The attack on the plan succeeded when the supreme court declared it a violation of the guarantee of property. The court held that a case of material expropriation did not arise only when the challenged regulation deprived the owner of a present lawful use, but also when it impaired another, presumably future, use in a sensitive way, imposing on a single person or on a few persons an excessive sacrifice for the common good. The challenged plan fell under the latter category....

The *Barret*[28] case, decided in 1965, brought the last doctrinal change to the law of material expropriation. A zoning ordinance, enacted by the Canton of Neuchatel for the municipality of Bevaix and providing for severe building restrictions, was challenged by several landowners. The plaintiffs alleged a violation of due process and of the compensation requirement. The court upheld the ordinance against the due process attack and reserved the compensation issue for a subsequent cantonal proceeding. Without apparent reason, it then went on in an extensive dictum to redefine completely the notion of material expropriation. Referring to the distinction between present and future uses, the court said that both had to be protected....At the same time, however, the court declared that not all possible uses arising in the future could be considered: "Only those deserve protection which, regarding the circumstances, appear as very likely in the near future." The court then said that it wanted to distinguish two situations of material expropriation. If there is a deprivation of an "essential right arising from the property," each person affected is entitled to compensation. In the case of a less intrusive but still considerable restriction of property rights, compensation is due only if a single person or very few persons are affected in a way violating the principle of equal protection.

The impact of the new doctrine was twofold. On the one hand, it extended the protection accorded to property rights by recognizing that some restrictions of present and future uses are so harsh that they constitute a taking regardless of the number of persons affected by them. Theoretically at least, the connotation of singling out," contained in the prior formula for all cases of material expropriation was abandoned. On the other hand, the new doctrine limited the range of protected future uses in a rather drastic way. Henceforth, the mere possibility of a future better use of the property would no longer be protected against governmental interference; protection presupposed a certain likelihood of actualization. The approach taken in *Barret* has been cast in a formula and is now quoted by the court almost ritualistically.[31]

Before considering the practical application of the *Barret* formula, it should be noted that, in Switzerland, the protection against regulatory takings, and accordingly judicial review, is assured in two distinct stages. First, a regulatory measure affecting property rights has to meet certain well-defined standards of legality, which bear a close relation to substantive due process in American law. Unlike compensation, this requirement is not peculiar to regulations of property; it is a prerequisite for all governmental actions affecting individual rights. Legality requires that a restriction of property rights rests on statutory authority and on a valid public interest. Only the

---

28. 91 BG I 329 (1965, *Barret*).

31. The formula reads (as quoted from 105 BG Ia 330, 339 (1979, *Meier*), translation by the author):

> There is a restriction on the property equal to an expropriation if the present or a prospective future use of the property is denied to the owner or limited in a way which is especially grave because it deprives him of an essential right arising from the property. In the case of a less intrusive restriction there is, nevertheless, material expropriation if a single owner or a few owners are so affected that their sacrifice for the community, if not compensated, seems unacceptable and not compatible with the equal protection of the laws. In both cases the possibility of a future better use of the property is taken into consideration only if it appeared at the decisive moment that this use was very likely to be realized in the near future.

means necessary and appropriate for the accomplishment of the intended purpose may be used. In addition, the public need for the regulation must outweigh the burden imposed on the private property owners (so-called requirement of proportionality). If a regulation is challenged and if the court finds that there is a violation of one of these standards, the regulation is declared *void*. Second, a measure affecting property rights, but unobjectionable under the principles of legality mentioned above, may still be challenged as having the effect of a material expropriation. The relief sought under this title is not invalidation, but *compensation*.

Therefore, cases involving property regulations quite often reach the court, and even the supreme court, twice. A first attack is directed against an alleged lack of statutory authority, public interest or proportionality. If the regulation is upheld, the Owner sues the government for payment of compensation. It must, however, be stressed that an affected owner may waive his right to contest the legitimacy of the regulatory measure without losing his compensation claim.

The *Barret* Formula Applied

As evidenced by the preceding explanation, the *Barret* formula, with its general, indefinite terms (essential right, especially grave, unacceptable sacrifice), is by no means a workable test for regulatory takings. It resembles more a statutory rule summarizing the doctrinal underpinnings of the compensation principle. Three cases may illustrate how the Swiss supreme court proceeds when it applies the formula to an actual controversy. It will then be easier to identify the taking tests used in Swiss law.

Lausanne-Boissonnet

The first case, decided in 1971, involved a downzoning in a residential area of the city of Lausanne. A municipal zoning ordinance, enacted in 1942, classed the Boissonnet-quarter in the so-called peripheral zone, allowing the construction of medium-size buildings (maximum measurement on any side of twenty-five meters and maximum height of four stories) and not defining a specific use. Despite this zoning, in the early sixties the area still had the character of a residential neighborhood, dominated by small buildings, mostly one-family houses. At the request of the majority of the landowners, who wanted to preserve the existing residential patterns the city of Lausanne changed the zoning ordinance in 1963. The Boissonnet quarter was classed in the "villa zone," which allows only residential use and limits the construction to villas of two-and-one-half stories, not occupying more than one-sixth the surface of each parcel and respecting certain setback lines.

Two landowners challenged the new zoning for violation of due process without success. Consequently they filed an action against the city of Lausanne, asking for compensation for regulatory taking. The state courts denied compensation and the owners took an appeal to the supreme court.

Evidence showed that the plaintiffs had acquired their parcels, each with a house erected around 1930, in 1948 and in 1951. The purchase prices paid by them were lower than the value of the land as considered under the possibility of larger constructions allowed by the zoning ordinance of 1942. One owner had enlarged and refurbished her house in 1962. The new ordinance reduced the potential *building volume* by two-thirds, but the *value diminution* of the land did not exceed 20 percent.

In its opinion, the court first quoted the *Barret* formula and observed that the landowners had not been deprived of the *present* use of their property. The inquiry then turned to the restriction of the *future* uses, actually represented by the construction options under the former zoning ordinance. The court briefly remarked that there had been no intention by the plaintiffs to make use of these options. On the contrary, the refurbishing of one villa in 1962 gave evidence of the intention to maintain the present situation. But the question whether under such circumstances the future use would very likely be realized in the near future was expressly left open because the court held that there was *no deprivation of essential right inherent in the property.* The rationale for this holding was the following: First, the options left to the landowners under the new zoning were "far from negligible." The owners could transform and enlarge their homes; both plaintiffs even had the option of erecting a second zone-conforming building on their premises. The potential return on investment was, therefore, considerable. Second, the downzoning produced important benefits for all landowners in that they were assured the character of the neighborhood would be preserved. Third, for twenty years almost none of the landowners had taken advantage of the options opened up by the 1942 zoning. The new ordinance did no more than affirm an existing situation. An option that had not been utilized for such a long period could not be qualified as essential.

Having eliminated the first of the two eventualities established by the *Barret* formula (deprivation of an essential property right), the court passed to the second: "special sacrifice." The court observed that thirty-two landowners were likewise affected by the new zoning, and that an adjoining area already had been regulated in the same way. Considering these factual circumstances, the court held that the plaintiffs had not suffered an unacceptable sacrifice for the common good. Since both eventualities of a material expropriation were absent, no compensation was due for the losses the rezoning of 1963 had inflicted on the plaintiffs.[47]...

Zizers

The second case discussed here was decided in 1979. It was without a doubt a landmark because it resolved one of the major pending issues in Swiss land use law. The issue arose when zoning statutes began to provide for special agricultural zones, excluding from these areas the construction of new buildings except for agricultural use. The question of whether the deprivation of the previously existing building option did constitute a material expropriation was the crucial point for the success of these land planning efforts....

The *Zizers* case is a prominent example of the many cases generated by the application of the water protection act. The plaintiffs were owners of land in the municipality of Zizers (Canton of Grisons), situated outside of the building zone established by the municipal zoning ordinance of 1965. The land was zoned as a "residual area" (*uebriges Gemeindegebiet*) and was, therefore, basically reserved for agricultural uses and agricultural buildings. But the ordinance provided that other buildings could be permitted under certain circumstances.[58] In the immediate vicinity of the parcels owned by the plaintiffs, a few houses had been built before 1971 on the basis of this provision. In 1974, the plaintiffs applied for a building permit for two one-family houses on their

47. In a concluding dictum the court observed that, on the basis of the purchase prices paid by the plaintiffs for their land, the new zoning had not actually caused them a loss, but had only deprived them of a gain. Had there been a material expropriation, the question would still arise whether compensation is due for this kind of prejudice.

58. The main prerequisite for obtaining a building permit in the "residual area" is normally that all costs for the equipment of the land (roads, fresh water supply, sewerage) are paid by the landowners or the developers. This was true for the Zizers ordinance.

land. The municipality of Zizers denied the application on the grounds that article 20 of the water protection act of 1971 had abrogated the option in the municipal zoning ordinance of 1965 for land zoned as a "residual area," to erect non-agricultural buildings. The supreme court confirmed this position.

The plaintiffs then sued the municipality of Zizers for compensation. Turned down by the state courts, they appealed to the supreme court. In the first part of its opinion, the court addressed the basic question presented by the case: Could the suppression of the building option for land located outside of a formal building zone, as it had been established by article 20 of the new water protection act, actually generate a compensation duty? The cantonal court had answered the question in the affirmative, arguing that the purpose of the act was to protect the public health through control of water pollution, with the result that no compensation was due for losses incurred by landowners. The supreme court ruled out this solution. It observed that the act, besides its purpose of health protection, also pursued evident objectives of general welfare, especially land planning, and that it therefore could not be considered as a mere regulation of noxious uses. The court nevertheless held that, as a general rule, article 20 did not effect a material expropriation. The reason for this holding was found in the power of the federal legislature to define the contents of property. This power, the court noted, is not limited to the regulation of the private aspects of property. It also includes public aspects, so the legislature must consider different interests of equal weight, expressly recognized by the constitution in the fields of land planning, protection of water and environment in general, as well as conservation of the forests. Assessing these different interests, the legislature was allowed to abrogate, without violating the guarantee of property, the building option which thus far had existed in rural areas. As the court stated it, the legislature had not eliminated an essential right inherent in the property. But the court also made the express reservation that, in the process of determining the boundaries between building and nonbuilding zones, some owners could be affected in a way requiring compensation.

The rest of the opinion turned on the question of whether such an exceptional situation of material expropriation was present in the case at bar. First, on the basis of the *Barret* formula, the court determined the plaintiffs had not been deprived of a prospective use, likely to be realized in the near future, at the time the new water pollution act took effect. Evidence showed that the land was not ready for construction in 1971, although a fresh water Supply and a sewer had been built privately before 1971. The road system was insufficient, and the shape of the single parcels, still used for agricultural purposes, was not suitable for construction. Moreover, the zoning of the land as a "residual area," instead of its inclusion in the formal building zone, showed the intention of the municipality of Zizers to retain control over the future development and excluded certitude about the granting of a building permit. Second, the court determined the plaintiffs had not suffered a special sacrifice, stating that the plaintiffs were not treated differently from any other landowner in the "residual area" now subject to the restriction of the water protection act.

Orbe

This third, quite recent, case[71] is presented here because it provides the only instance of a so-called special sacrifice held by the supreme court since the proclamation of the *Barret* formu1a. In 1977, the city of Orbe (Canton of Vaud) enacted a zoning ordinance

71. 107 BG Ib 380 (1981, *Kocher*).

for a part of its territory. Although the ordinance comprised a larger area, one of its main purposes was to protect from construction a hill that offers a splendid view of the medieval town and the plain of Orbe. While it contained general building provisions and fixed setback lines applicable to all parcels, it specifically limited the building area for two pieces of land extending from the top of the hill down the plain. Construction was restricted to a small area in the plain.

One landowner, having challenged the ordinance without success under the aspect of due process, filed an action for compensation. The case eventually reached the supreme court, where it was under the traditional guidelines. The court found that the plaintiff clearly had not been deprived of an essential right arising from the property. Before the enactment of the 1977 zoning law, the land was already classed in the "villa zone," which limits construction to one residential home on a certain size parcel. The new ordinance neither prohibited this right nor limited the maximum volume.

The court held, however, that the zoning ordinance imposed a special sacrifice on the landowner that could not be justified without compensation. The court compared the situation of the plaintiff with the other landowners and found that the ordinance affected the latter only minimally, but severely restricted the plaintiff. Not only did the ordinance prescribe where to put a future building (which it failed to do for the other parcels), but it placed the building on the least favorable spot, thereby considerably reducing the value of the land. The court also stressed the fact that the ordinance was intended to give a benefit to the public by imposing, not formally but in its effect, a negative easement on the plaintiff's land....

In a recent decision[123] the court has held that the deprivation of the building option can be a taking only if the land had already attained such a degree of development under the aspects of zoning and equipment, that the owners would have been able to realize a construction without involving the public authorities. Obviously, the precedents have greatly reduced the potential for successful compensation claims. Today, only severe downzonings of land situated within a formal building zone or of land especially suitable for construction or other exceptional grounds can raise the question of a material expropriation....

Two conclusions may be drawn from these findings. First, two national courts, working independently but in comparable cultural environments, have reached, in a series of precedents embracing more than one century, similar results for the problem of regulatory takings. This fact evidences the soundness of the judicial answer; one may even argue that there is a certain degree of "objective fairness" in it.

Second, the "multi-factor analysis" engaged in by the courts, actually not more than shorthand for a very complicated and sometimes even contradictory approach to the problem, seems to be the only possible way of coping with the taking issue. There is no single, comprehensive test for the distinction of the two kinds of regulations. If there were, the courts would have found it. Any further search for it is illusion.

* * *

Notes and Comments

1. Contrast the Swiss and American standards. Do they suggest that European and American definitions of property rights are evolving toward the same end? What might that end be? Or are there substantial differences in the systems?

---

123. 106 BG Ia 369 (1980, *Baumberger*).

The following excerpt contrasts a jurisdiction that may place more emphasis on the public communitarian good as compared to the individual interests of the property owner, the case of The Netherlands:

George Lefcoe, *When Governments Become Land Developers: Notes on the Public-Sector Experience in the Netherlands and California*,

51 Southern California Law Review 165 (1978)

.... *The Status of Private Landowners and Developers in the Netherlands*

a. *Developers:* In a country that wanted to encourage development by private landowners, it seems logical to assume that the building process would be made easy for them. If for some reason the government needed a few sites itself, it would compensate private land investors more than adequately for the risks they had assumed. But where, as in the Netherlands, municipalities are accustomed to developing, one might expect that property owners of exurban land would enjoy no right whatsoever to urbanize their sites and receive in eminent domain proceedings only present use, and not any "hope" value for their sites.

On these assumptions the land investor in the Netherlands seems to be protected to a far greater extent than might have been presumed. Legally, the owner has a good claim to a building permit as long as what he proposes to build is consistent with the local government's land use destination plan (*bestemmingsplan*) for the area. The *bestemmingsplan* contains policy guidelines applicable to the development of an area, as well as a map much like our zoning maps. Unlike our zoning laws it is both proscriptive and prescriptive. It outlaws certain activities in certain zones as we do, but it also prescribes in great detail precisely what should be built in the as yet unbuilt areas. If an owner cannot construct in accordance with the plan, and the locality must acquire the site, he is compensated on the basis of fair market value that takes account of the site's potential value, and not only its value as the owner has used it prior to public acquisition.

As is so often the case, local practice may and often does depart substantially from these property-protective norms. Reading the *bestemmingsplan* map, a house builder can discern that portion of an area reserved for one-family detached housing of a luxury type. Suppose he sets about trying to purchase the land scheduled for this development. If its ownership is divided, and it is held by a number of small farmers, he may be able to acquire most—but not quite all—of the site so delineated. In the United States we have no requirement that in an R-l single-family residential zone the developer must acquire *all* contiguous R-l parcels in order to build on any of them. In the Netherlands, however, it is a prerogative of the locality to impose such a requirement.

Buying land is not easy for the homebuilder in Holland. All of these purchases, had they been made by the municipality, would have been made entirely in cash. Because farmers know that the government is always their potential buyer, the private developer will have to pay a premium if he wants to buy on an installment plan. Moreover, unless the homebuilding firm is very solvent, it will not be able to raise the cash required. If a builder were lucky enough to find an institutional lender—an insurance company or a bank—willing to finance the purchase, he might well be forced to yield, as part of the loan agreement, a significant percentage of any future profits he might realize from development.

Moreover, cities have the option of requiring as a condition to building anything that the developer build *all* of what the plan requires. Even assuming that the homebuilder pays what he must to acquire all the contiguous R-l sites, he likely cannot proceed to develop as of right. Although destination plans (*bestemmingsplannen*) may be promulgated for vast areas or tiny ones, most will contain some provision for row houses, garden apartments, and government-subsidized, low-rent units. Should the plan designate such uses, the community is free to insist that no developer may pick off the most lucrative parts of the area development plan—luxury housing or a regional shopping center—and build for just those uses. When they require building in conformity with "the plan," the Dutch mean "the *entire* plan." A locality may permit private builders to develop portions of the plan, but they are also empowered to insist on the developer's building all or none of what the plan prescribes—from nursery schools to cemeteries.

For this reason homebuilders are justifiably cautious in their land dealings. Most of them eschew purchases within the boundaries of the larger cities. These are the jurisdictions with the most active real estate departments. They are also the ones that tend to insist that developers buying the most lucrative development sites must subsidize sites for "social" housing in one way or another. Consequently, homebuilders prefer dealing in smaller, more conservative municipalities.

Many homebuilders feel that if they did not engage in the risky business of acquiring land for development, they would have absolutely no leverage to use in negotiating for building contracts with the municipality and would therefore lose the steady stream of projects they need to meet their payrolls and preserve their ties with subcontractors and suppliers. Owning land is no assurance of the right to develop it. A developer may be forced to convey prime vacant land to a municipality at a price far lower than he paid for it, for the sole purpose of receiving from the municipality a contract entitling him to develop a portion of the site for the luxury houses he wants to build. For the same reasons, when a town's real estate department wants to take advantage of a particularly good buy and doesn't have the cash for it, it will have little difficulty finding a private homebuilder to make the purchase.

b. *Landowners:* The position of the farmer-landowner under Dutch expropriation law is not as precarious as that of the homebuilder under the national physical planning laws. But under neither is the farmer's position ideal. Although the owner is entitled to fair market value for his land, market value is difficult to determine in those municipalities where the city is the predominant owner. The city sells its parcels only after they have been developed, so these sale prices have little relevance in determining the value of predeveloped land. Because the city has a monopoly on the planning power (to control who builds what, where, and how), the city also has the effective means of restraining private purchases of predeveloped land.

Earlier it was noted that the private land owner is entitled not just to present use value but also to prospective use value consistent with the plan. This means that each owner is entitled to the average land price of all parcels included within the *bestemmingsplan*. Those whose sites are marked for lucrative development receive exactly the same compensation as those whose farms are scheduled for social housing, rights-of-way, or parks. This assures fairness among individual landowners, but it often disappoints owners with sites particularly well-suited to intensive and profitable development. A bill pending in Parliament favored by the Labour Party, would go a step further and establish the present use value as the norm for compensation.

Dutch compensation law favors the exurban or predevelopment land owner in several respects. It requires that, prior to instituting expropriation proceedings, the municipality negotiate in good faith to acquire the site by voluntary agreement. All but ten percent of government acquisitions are voluntary. Severance damages (the damages that arise when the city takes only part of an owner's holdings in such a way as to render less valuable the part not taken) are awarded as a matter of course. There are substantial recoveries for personal expenses that result from forced relocation. If the municipality can find a comparable site elsewhere, the court-appointed master who sets compensation may determine whether the preferred site is truly suitable to the condemnee's needs. Should the master determine it to be so, compensation is based on the assumption that the owner is relocating there. No additional compensation is granted should the owner decline the site and incur greater actual costs in moving elsewhere.

Dutch tax law favors the farmer in that capital gains earned by anyone not professionally engaged in the land business go untaxed. This is true whether the sale is voluntary or by expropriation, and whether the purchaser is a municipality or a private party. A further tax advantage is that farms are exempt from property taxation. This advantage is mitigated by the fact that the property tax is not an important one in the Netherlands, and farmers more than make up for this exemption in the special assessments they must pay to the local water boards that manage flood control systems on a district basis.

Sometimes a landowner at the urban fringe is damaged by a locality's planning decisions even though his land is not taken. A number of property-regulating laws, enacted pursuant to the general principle that there should be "equality of citizens with respect to taxes and rates," contain vaguely worded provisions concerning compensation for those who might be specially, substantially, and directly damaged thereby. It is seldom clear, however, whether such provisions are meant to permit, encourage, or require compensation.[223]

Of the hundred or so "inverse condemnation" cases lodged with the Crown, only a handful have resulted in compensation awards' being granted. Most of the denials of claims are accompanied by explanations that damage must be different in degree from that suffered by other owners in the planned area, that property owners should expect some amount of change when urbanization comes, and that the individuals have no right to rely on present traffic patterns or customers (as when a nonconforming trailer park was ordered shut).

Among the few claimants awarded compensation was the owner of a greenhouse who was forced to relocate after a twenty-story building had been constructed in such a way as to prevent the sun from reaching his greenhouses. This was probably not an early strike for solar energy or even a preservation of "ancient lights." More likely, it was one more expression of public policy against "scale enlargement," a Dutch norm in favor of

223. The Physical Planning Act of 1962, art. 49, reads as follows:

> If and insofar as it appears that an interested party incurs or shall incur a loss in consequence of the provisions of the *bestemmingsplan* and such loss should reasonably not, or not fully be borne by him, and its compensation has not or not entirely been guaranteed by purchase, expropriation, or otherwise, the municipality shall at his request allow him compensation to be fixed in reason. Such compensation may take the form of money or otherwise. Appeals may be lodged with Us [The Crown] against a decision to refuse or award compensation as mentioned in the previous paragraph within one month of the day on which the copy of the decision was sent off. The appeal shall include the reasons on which it was based.

When this provision was debated in Parliament, some members thought it should speak of *schadevergoeding* or indemnification—making whole the property owner. Others advocated only the payment of *tegemoetkoming*, a term which means "to meet half way" or "to accommodate." Neither position prevailed, and the act remains ambiguous as to the owner's entitlement, if any.

keeping all buildings on a human and familiar scale; the Dutch prefer the cozy to the monumental and usually express that preference through strict design review. But from time to time high-rise buildings have gone up, although not without protests. This case may cause one to ask whether it takes not only a substantial, peculiar, and direct diminution in value, but also a diminution caused by a particularly unpopular form of building to justify awards in special damage situations.

"Inverse condemnation" has a special relationship to municipal land development. Most construction in previously unbuilt areas throws "externalities," which are unpleasant and sometimes quite costly, onto neighboring properties. In an ideal universe justice would seem to require that those imposing the burden pay the bill or at least part of it—as accommodation if not as indemnification. It is apparent why this redistribution would be so difficult to arrange in the United States where so many private owners develop land. But in the Netherlands where Dutch municipalities can, if they choose, dominate the process of land development from beginning to end, a case could be made for holding that city governments be asked to anticipate the losses to adjoining property owners that urban development might bring about, in order to encourage the cities to take steps to minimize or prevent such losses. Where municipalities do the developing, any legitimate damage claims could be met from the price the city realizes from its development efforts.

In addition to an appeal on grounds of inverse condemnation, the individual property owner threatened by a *bestemmingsplan* can delay the plan for several years by appealing it to the Crown. In practice this means waiting until the provincial government has reviewed and approved it, and then petitioning the Council of State and the Cabinet to review the case. Roughly 10 to 15% of all *bestemmingsplannen* are appealed, often successfully. Pending appeal, the municipality cannot utilize its powers of expropriation to acquire land covered by the *bestemmingsplan*. By threatening such appeal, some landowners have been able to obtain better negotiated prices from municipalities—or so it is rumored....

* * *

Notes and Comments

1. Developers and regulators may be more alike regardless of the country but the end result may differ dramatically based on the national and local political environment and the acceptability of that regime to its population.

The following excerpt offers an alternative view from the Italian experience:

Nico Calavita, *Urbanization, Public Control of Land Use and Private Ownership of Land: The Development of Italian Planning Law,*

16 Urban Lawyer 459 (1984)

In Italy, the social pressure for land-use reform has come from the labor movement. The resulting laws enacted have attempted to recapture unearned increments in land value and put the government in charge of the land market, while the courts have generally ruled in favor of property rights. The particular nature of the Italian situation is due, at least in part, to a conflict between a developing urban-industrial society's need for urban planning and the interests of the ruling party, whose power rests, to a large extent, on real estate, development and speculative interests....

The Constitutional Framework

The Italian and American Constitutions represent two basically different approaches to the problem of the relationship between the state and the individual. The American Constitution stresses the protection of the individual from the state interference in the economic sphere. Property rights, in particular, are seen as something which the government should not only recognize but also protect, as in the provisions which prohibit the taking of private property for public use without just compensation, require equal protection under the law and prohibit deprivation of property without due process.

The Italian Constitution, enacted in 1947, is influenced by a tradition in which state regulation of economic activities was considered a legitimate function of political activity. The state, instead of being perceived as that evil power from which the individual is to be protected, becomes the benevolent collective that assists the individual in the realization of social rights, such as family life, medical care, education, work and social security. The right to private property is not included among the "fundamental rights," such as the right to work, but rather, appears under the title addressing "economic relationships." Furthermore, its limitations are spelled out: "Private property is recognized and guaranteed by law, which determines the methods of its acquisition and enjoyment and the limitations designed to assure its social functioning and render it accessible to all. It has been noted that, in Italy, "planning is in a sense institutionalized by the Constitution." Article 41, for example, while stating that private initiative is free, adds that "the law determines the appropriate programs and controls in order that public and private economic activity may be directed and coordinated toward social ends."

The Italian Constitution, then, provides a framework within which an effective land-use control system might be established. However, the political and social conditions of postwar Italy have made impossible the passage of planning legislation which could seize the opportunities offered by the Constitution. When planning laws have been passed, they have usually reflected the explosive political conditions under which they were enacted, and the Constitutional Court has struck down important portions of those laws, usually those very elements that were especially controversial.

Planning laws have been found unconstitutional because compensation to be paid for land expropriated for public use was negligible. Often associated with the compensation rationale was the fact that limitations imposed on the use of property were considered so restrictive as to be expropriative in nature. These attitudes of the Constitutional Court toward compensation and regulation were established in the period from 1956 (the year in which the Court was established) to the mid-sixties.

Compensation

The compensation question is extremely important to Italy, where the government has increasingly become engaged in land-banking, thus expropriating large quantities of land. When faced with the question of the constitutionality of parameters established by various laws to determine compensation for land expropriated for public use, the Constitutional Court has maintained that the Constitution, imbued with ample objectives of social progress, did not intend to base compensation on market value. In its first decision on the issue, the Court was called to decide on the constitutionality of land-reform laws which made possible the expropriation of thousands of acres of *latifundia*, to be distributed to landless farmers, at below-market levels. The Court found the land-reform laws constitutional because:

> Compensation…means the maximum contribution and reparation that, in the context of the goals of the public interest, the public administration can guarantee to the private interest…To the legislator is attributed discretionary power; which however finds always a limitation, that the need for compensation cannot be considered satisfied with dispositions that would result in purely apparent or symbolic compensation.

But what constitutes "symbolic compensation" is definitely a question of degree. Thus, the principle established by the Constitutional Court has relative and not absolute value, and it can be employed to sustain—as the Court has done in subsequent decisions-different propositions on the legitimacy of the compensation measures… [T]he Court has struck down important aspects of planning laws because it found their compensation parameters unconstitutional. The Court, while not reneging on the position taken in 1957 that compensation can be based on lower than market value, seems to have become less concerned with whether proposed compensation measures represent symbolic compensation and more with whether they constitute "adequate" or "serious" compensation.

Regulation

Until the mid-sixties, Italian jurisprudence had not established a clear and definite approach to the constitutional problems raised by the regulation of private property. As late as 1965, the *Corte di Cassazione* ruled that limitations on the use of property that would eliminate the right of development were permissible because "the modern conception of property rights considers them subordinate to social and collective interests, in accordance with Article 42 of the Constitution."

In 1966 and 1968 the Constitutional Court issued two landmark decisions that embodied two different approaches to the problems of regulation. The 1966 case declared unconstitutional military servitudes because they imposed limitations that were expropriative in nature, even though the owner was left with title and possession. Noting that Article 41 of the constitution recognizes and protects private property, the Court went on to say that:

> The logic of the system makes [it] necessary to consider that violations of property rights would exist not only in those cases when a total or partial transfer of the right would be effectuated, but also in those cases when, even though the title would remain intact, the property right would be eliminated without compensation.

The Court, however, anticipating the 1968 decision, introduced the notion that for some categories of property, identifiable a priori because of intrinsic characteristics that would directly affect a public interest, regulations could not be considered expropriative.

With the 1968 decision, this philosophy was confirmed and expanded. The occasions was provided by the question of the constitutionality of a 1939 law which had intended to protect and preserve areas that presented unique scenic or historic and artistic characteristics. The Court maintained that the properties to be protected "constitute a category that is originally of public interest…and the administration acting in accordance with the law does not modify their pre-existent situation, but shows the correspondence between their concrete qualities and the normative precepts." Thus, for particular categories of properties which *ab origine* present those characteristics that the legislator intended to preserve, Article 42 does not mandate compensation when the law imposes restrictions which aim to insure their social function. The Italian Constitutional Court, then, separates properties into two categories: those that are imbued with a public purpose, which can be regulated without fear of inverse condemnation, and all others, which can be regulated only to a certain extent, beyond which taking will occur....

Clearly the Italian Constitution does not accord property owners the same type of protection guaranteed by the American Constitution, but sees private property as "functional" to the achievement of social ends. Thus, the Constitutional Court can approve compensation at lower than market value (although the Court seems increasingly concerned that it be close to market value), and preservation of scenic and artistic properties without compensation. Properties subjected to urban planning regulations, however, seem to be accorded the same type of protection accorded to American owners, namely, that "if regulation goes too far, it will be recognized as a taking." As a result, the Constitutional Court has struck down planning legislation considered confiscatory....

Law 167 of 1962

The passage of Law 167, containing important provisions for the acquisition of areas needed for low-cost housing at below-market value, was made possible by significant and sudden economic and political shifts that took place in the period from 1959–1963. During this time, high levels of economic growth were achieved and a condition of near full employment created. Scarcity of labor, especially in the advanced sectors of the economy, created the conditions for a successful wave of strikes, with an increase in wages of 80 percent, between 1958 and 1964. The working class had become a force to be reckoned with at both the economic and the political levels....

Law 167's main goal was to promote the construction of low-cost housing neighborhoods on land close to already urbanized areas. For the first time, provisions for areas for low-cost housing were to be an integral part of the long-range planning process. According to Law 167, each locality would prepare its own development plan for low-cost housing and would be allowed to acquire up to 50 percent of the land necessary to meet the projected low-cost housing needs for a ten-year period.

With Law 167, localities were provided with the mechanisms necessary to develop a land-banking program and could, therefore, become directly involved in development activities without waiting for private initiative. One of the drawbacks of land-banking, however, has always been the high cost of the land involved. To ameliorate this problem and to avoid higher prices that would result from the adoption of a housing plan, compensation to property owners was to be based on the market value of land two years before the plan s approval. Thus it was possible that property expropriated during the last year of the ten-year plan would be compensated at values established twelve years earlier.

It was probably this eventuality that led the Constitutional Court to declare, in an eight-to-seven decision, that the compensation as envisioned by Law 167 was "uncertain and aleatory" and subject "to the influence of perturbatory elements," such as an inflationary period, which could lead to negligible compensation and was, hence, incompatible with Article 42 of the Constitution. The Court stated also that Article 42 of the Constitution, although is it does not ensure that compensation be equal to market value, guarantees "a compensation not purely symbolic...but...adequate of correspondent to the maximum value that can be allowed in the balancing of the public with the private interest.

Legislation was passed immediately to fill the gap resulting from the Constitutional Court decision. This time, compensation was to be based on the famous Law of Naples of 1885 that had been found constitutional by the Court. This law based compensation on the average of the market value of the ten years preceding the expropriation date. As a result, localities could still obtain land at below-market values and this power, coupled with the others offered by Law 167, offered the opportunity for the public sector to manage a sizeable portion of urban development in Italian cities. Those opportunities, while seized by some municipalities, were neglected by others. Southern Italian cities, generally strongholds of the DC, preferred to continue the ad hoc approach to development that had benefitted local bosses. Some cities of the North and Center, instead, made the low-cost housing areas as large as allowed by Law 167 and located them in a desirable areas which, under market conditions, would have been developed for expensive housing. Their efforts, however, were hampered by inadequate financing provisions. Almost a decade and additional legislation were necessary to put the low-cost housing areas into full use.

The "Bridging" Act of 1967

After the initial flurry of reforms accompanying the entrance of the Socialists into the government, the Christian Democrats became increasingly reluctant to introduce new reforms, including a new urbanistic law. The impasse was broken in 1966 as a result of the political scandal that surrounded the famous landslide in Agrigento (Sicily), where thousands of people lost their homes because their buildings had been built in an unsafe location. The indignation of the entire country prompted the government to pass Law No. 765, also known as the Bridging Act," as a transition or "bridge" toward the long-awaited new urbanistic law.

Law 765 provided modifications and additions to the earlier 1942 Urbanistic Law. Most importantly, it strongly promoted the application of the law. To force localities to prepare Master Plans, Law 765 strictly limited development in towns and cities without a Master Plan (909 percent in 1967) and forbade development, in the absence of a Master Plan, in towns of historical, artistic or environmental importance. Building permits were now necessary for any activity and were subordinated to one of the following: (a) the existence of infrastructure, (b) a capital program on the part of the municipality to provide the infrastructure within the following three years, or (c) the commitment of the developer to build the infrastructures with the development. In any case, the developer was to pay for the on-site infrastructures and their connection to the municipal network.

The Bridging Act finally established "urbanistic standards" by requiring that Master Plans reserve enough land (18 square meters per person minimum) in appropriate locations for the provision of schools, parks, fire stations and other public facilities and services. Developers, who in the past had built without giving much consideration to the need for facilities and services, were now required to participate in the provision of those facilities through mandatory contributions or land dedications. By requiring a building permit for any development and by tying together development to the timely provision for infrastructures and facilities, the Bridging Act had finally provided Italian cities with the tools necessary to control urban growth.[58]

However, a major problem which had lain dormant in the 1942 Urbanistic Law was brought to the fore by the proliferation of plans generated by the Bridging Act. Under

58. The beneficial effects of the law were not felt for a long time. Its passage exacted a political price in the form of a year's moratorium before the law became operative. A wild stampede for building permits ensued for a total of eight million rooms, resulting in further intensification of urban chaos.

the 1942 Law, Master Plans combined the land-use plan and zoning, making them legally binding, had an unlimited time frame, and indicated precisely the location and acreage of all land use, including public use. The owners of the areas reserved for public use in the Master Plans could not use their land and had to wait for an indefinite time for acquisition. The already bankrupt municipalities were unable to acquire, en masse, all those areas.

Property owners took the matter to court and the question of the constitutionality of land-use designations[59] reached the Constitutional Court in 1968. In the famous decision No. *55*, the Court decided that a "taking" had occurred because an immediate limitation on the use of a property without a definite time schedule for public acquisition must be considered expropriative in nature.

The alternatives left to the legislature after this decision were to allow private development in areas designated for public use in the Master Plans (a solution which would have rendered the plans meaningless), or to provide the municipalities with the means necessary to acquire the areas. Parliament refused to consider either of these alternatives; instead, it passed, with exceptional rapidity, Law No. 1187 of 1969, known also, perhaps not too elegantly, as the "Plug Law," which gave validity to Master Plans for five more years. The legislature made clear its intent that "no indemnity shall be paid for limitations and constraints which result from the passage of Master Plans." Furthermore, it was made clear that new legislation would be passed in the future which would alter the regime of land ownership so as to eliminate the constitutional problems raised by decision No. *55*....

The Housing Reform Act of 1971 (Law No. 865)

The late sixties were a period of economic growth and increased mass migration to the major cities of the industrial North. Law 167 had yet to make a significant contribution to the provision of low-cost housing and the Bridging Act was still in its infancy and could not positively affect the orderly development of urban areas. Lack of affordable housing, inadequate mass transit, schools, recreational facilities, health care and other social services finally led to an explosion of latent social tensions, both in the cities and in the factories. At first, protests were decentralized, spontaneous and autonomous from political organizations. Rent increases and a lack of affordable housing pushed renters into organizing at the neighborhood and block levels and protesting rent and utility increases by withholding payments, demonstrations and "squatting" in empty apartments. University students, objecting to the condition of Italian universities, also supported the housing protest. In the factories, strikes, rallies and sit-downs of union and non-union workers alike were frequent....

Urban planning regulations do not involve direct control of the market and will eventually be accepted, albeit grudgingly, by development interests. However, measures that limit or eliminate windfalls on land transactions are perceived as an infringement

---

59. This question might have become relevant in the U.S. where, historically, the Master Plan has been indicative only, while zoning has carried the force of the law. Zoning is supposed to be based on the Master Plan but the two documents have generally gone their separate ways. Recently, however, an increasing number of states have imposed a consistency requirement, i.e., that land use regulations must be consistent with the Master Plan. As may be expected from the Italian experience, one of the concerns raised by the consistency requirements is "whether planning designations, in and of themselves, can effect a taking private property for public use without just compensation and be the basis for a suit in inverse condemnation....

on property rights, and will always be bitterly opposed by proprietary interests and their political representatives. Thus, in the fall of 1969, a tug-of-war began between reformist and conservative forces, as demonstrations and general strikes on one side were met with bitter resistance on the other. The government, confronted with the strongest and sharpest upsurge of working-class demands of the postwar period, fell twice, first in February and then in July of 1970. Finally, a full year after the beginning of the struggle, in a period of relative political peace and after long and difficult negotiations, the Housing Reform Act (No. 865) was passed in October, 1971. The law's principal purpose was creation of conditions for increased production of affordable housing. It included provision for the reform of the institutions involved in the construction of public and subsidized housing and of the disbursement of additional funds for housing construction. Most importantly, Law 865 made it possible for localities to expropriate up to 90 percent of land indicated for development in the Master Plans at lower than market rate. Compensation was to be based on the average agricultural value of land in the surrounding region used to grow the same crop grown on the owner's land. For properties located within the already urbanized areas, compensation was calculated by multiplying the average agricultural value by a coefficient which could very from 1.1 to 5, depending on the location of the property within the urbanized area and size of the town.

While progressive in its intent, Law 865, from a constitutional point of view, was a poor law, perhaps reflecting the political conditions under which it was passed. Obviously discriminatory, it created a dual land market: one for the private sector, in which private owners could reap full development value of their land, and another for areas to be acquired by the public sector on the basis of agricultural value. Also, total discretion was left to localities in the exercise of their power of eminent domain for development purposes. This could lead to a situation where one locality could take control of up to 90 percent of its development areas while an adjoining locality could leave all development areas in the hands of the private sector. The constitutionality of the use of agricultural value as the basis for compensation for land to be expropriated was questioned by several courts. For example, the Appellate Court of Turin found that "reference to agricultural value... has no relationship to the real value of urban land," and referred the question of the constitutionality of the compensation mechanism to the Constitutional Court. But the Constitutional Court apparently preferred to wait for the new planning law, which was expected to establish a new regime of land ownership. This law, it should be remembered, had become necessary because of the Constitutional Court's 1968 ruling, which invalidated the public land-use designation of Master Plans....

Law No. 10 of 1977

In 1973, the Partito Comunista Italiano (PCI) launched the idea of the "historic compromise," an alliance between the Italian Catholic and Communist forces to solve the complex problems of Italian society. After the electoral gains in the 1975 municipal and 1976 parliamentary elections, the PCI, "while not represented in the cabinet, wielded enough votes to hold the shaky DC government in its hands." This power, however, was wielded only on rare occasions: the PCI was eager to show its moderation and malleability, its capacity to compromise; only then the DC could, perhaps allow it to participate in the government. The long-awaited new planning law, which was going to solve the problems of all preceding planning legislation, was passed in 1977 under these political circumstances (Law No.10). It should not be surprising, then, that the law was equivocal. It simultaneously attempted to make the changes necessary to solve the constitutional problems of preceding legislation, while resisting any substantial change to the status quo.

The attempt to change the regime of land ownership is found in Article 1 of Law 10, which establishes that any development requires a "concession" to be granted by the mayor. Prior to the enactment of Law 10, the mayor—in accordance with the 1942 Urbanistic Law—granted a "licence" to develop. This license was traditionally considered an administrative authorization, and act that removed a limitation imposed by the existing norms to the exercise of the right to develop.

The concession, instead, was intended to assign the right to develop in exchange for a sum of money that should represent the economic equivalent of the gain to be made by the granting of the concession. The law, however, did not affirm explicitly that the *jus aedificandi* had been separated from the right to own property. To make things worse, the law established that the concession was due under the conditions specified by the law, making it, in fact, another administrative decision. This lack of discretionality led some observers to conclude, even before the law was passed, that the proposed concession had the same function as the old license and the regime of land ownership had not been changed. Immediately after the passage of the law, the INU pointed out that the concession was inherent to land ownership, because it was reserved for property owners, was irrevocable, and could be passed to new buyers of land.

Other commentators, while agreeing that the discretionality of the concessions was severely limited, emphasized that it should be considered in connection with the new planning requirements established by Law 10 strictly limiting property owners freedom to develop.[70] With Law 10, development is allowed only in areas included in three-to-five year Implementations Programs. When a concession is granted, a property owner has three years to complete the development. Property owners included in the implementation area have to develop their land; otherwise, the locality will expropriate the land.

Compensation, in eminent domain cases, continued to be based on agricultural value, as established by Law 865 of 1971, except that in already urbanized areas the coefficient was increased, to vary from two to ten (Article 14). To obtain a concession, property owners have to pay a development charge and urbanization costs.[72] The development charge can very from 5 to 20 percent of construction costs. The construction costs are established every year by the minister of Public Works, while the regions determine the percentage to be applied, depending on the type of construction and the location of the building. The regions also establish parameters to guide localities in determining the infrastructure and service costs to be charged to developers. The parameters

70. ...Cutrera maintained that the nationalization of development rights was contained *implicitly* in Law 10 because (1) the intent of the law was to eliminate the problems caused by the 1968 declaration of unconstitutionality of public land use designations. Parliament refused to consider compensation as a possible alternative; (2) in localities without Master Plans, no development is allowed (Article 5), indicating that, before the establishment of plans, no right to develop exists. Only after the various planning steps have been completed—with the concession being the last step—is the right to develop transferred from the public administration to the property owner.

72. There are interesting similarities between Law 10 of 1977 and the British Town and Country Planning Act of 1947. The most obvious are: (1) development can take place only where established by a public authority; (2) permission for development is to be based on a Development/Master Plan and stages thereof; and (3) permission to develop requires the payment of a development charge.

At this point the similarities end, for while in the English system the development charge was to be equal to the increase in value due to developmental potential, in the Italian system the concession to develop is granted upon payment of the infrastructure costs and a percentage of the construction costs.

are developed by the regions on the basis of size, growth rate and location of the town. Also, to eliminate the Law 865 problem of giving localities total discretion in utilization of expropriation powers for development purposes, Law 10 established that implementation programs should contain a minimum percentage (40) of the areas to be utilized for cooperatives, and subsidized and public housing....

In January of 1980, in a seven-to-six decision, the Constitutional Court denied that Law 10 had nationalized development rights:

> [Although the law left to the]...public authority every determination on the whether, the how and also the when of development, the new rigidity of the system does not legitimate the assertion that the *jus aedificandi* is no more inherent to the right of ownership... [I]n the areas designated for private development it is the property owner who develops and, concurring all other conditions, he has the right to obtain the concession, which is transferable with the ownership of the area, and is irrevocable, with the exception of the circumstances provided for by the law. Therefore, the concession is not different from the old license, because it has the purpose of ascertaining the existence of the conditions envisaged by the regulation to exercise the right [to develop].

Furthermore, the Constitutional Court continued, if development rights had been nationalized, then compensation would be based on agricultural value, regardless of location, while Article 14 of Law 10 provided that the agricultural value be multiplied by a coefficient for parcels within urbanized areas. By declaring that development rights had not been nationalized, it was almost automatic for the Court to declare unconstitutional the agricultural value criteria used to establish compensation for property owners whose land was to be expropriated. Such criteria, according to the Court, had no relationship to the actual value of the land and could lead to negligible compensation.

This decision caused an uproar in all sectors of Italian society. Newspapers, magazines, journals, special monographs all reacted to the news of the decision. Some argued that the Constitutional Court had no choice but to declare the law unconstitutional, regardless of the consequences. The fault lay with Parliament, which could not come up with a clear law. Others viewed the decision as a sham, politically inspired, as the Constitutional Court had again taken the side of property owners.

The major point that the critics of the Court made is that, with Law 10, the *jus aediflcandi* had been separated from the right of ownership de facto. Master plans establish if *where, how* and *at what densities* development is allowed, while the multi-year Implementation Programs indicate *when* development is to take place. Only those owners whose property is included in the three-to-five year Implementation Programs can ask the concession to develop. Thus, property owners have no remaining *choice,* let alone a *right,* regarding development. It is for these reasons, these critics of the Court's decision maintain, that the structure of property rights had been profoundly modified by Law 10.

Another aspect of the Court's decision needs to be analyzed, because of its grave implications for future legislative attempts toward windfalls recapture. Law 10 had established the payment of a development charge to accompany the concession in an attempt to recapture windfalls and mitigate the differences between property owners allowed to develop in the open market and those to be expropriated. The Court dismissed this attempt very quickly because "it would be extremely difficult for the adopted system to be able to eliminate the passing down of the development charge to the home-buyer." The Court's reasoning seems to be based on the "simply pass it on" theory, which assumes that taxes on gains in property values will be passed on to buyers of property. Such a theory, while enjoying "remarkable popular credibility," is almost universally denigrated by tax experts. The Court's position, while based on a shaky assumption, practically destroys any attempt at eliminating unearned increments in urban areas, short of generalized expropriation of all developable land, a solution politically and financially problematic.

The declaration of unconstitutionality of the compensation mechanisms envisioned by Law 10 implied the paralysis of government activities in the provision of areas for infrastructures, facilities and low-cost housing. To avoid this, Parliament passed a law which maintained the mechanisms for compensation declared unconstitutional by the Court, except that compensation so established should be considered partial payment. The balance would be established in accordance with a "substitutive law to be issued within one year from the passage of this law." In 1981 and 1982, laws were passed which extended the validity of that law for another year, respectively. Parliament has also postponed addressing the question of the public land-use designations reopened with Decision No. 5/1980. If development rights have not been nationalized, then those designations remain unconstitutional. Almost fifteen years after the other famous decision, the problem remains unresolved....

Attempts to deal with the land value problem in Italy have included land banking, a development charge, and the establishment of the principle of the concession that, it was thought, would nationalize development rights. But the Constitutional Court's decisions have struck a blow to these attempts. The *jus aedificandi* is still inherent to private property, leaving unresolved the public land use designation problem. Compensation to be paid to owners expropriated in the carrying-out of land banking programs has been declared unconstitutional, while localities do not have the financial capability to buy land in large quantities at or close to market value, and the development charge represents only a small percentage of the windfall profit. The land values problem, essential for the establishment of an "effective and acceptable land-use system," has not been solved.

* * *

[Editor's note. Italian law now provides for low-cost housing site acquisition at market value as housing and not at agricultural prices.]

The German law of regulatory takings offers an another alternative model:

Katharina Richter, *Compensable Regulation in the Federal Republic of Germany,*

5 Arizona Journal of International and Comparative Law 34 (1988)...

Zoning and *Bebauungspläne* [binding development plan] are effective land use control instruments used to implement the planning goals of a community. Once fixed, they establish property use rights, obligations, and expectations. Both zoning ordinances and *Bebauungspläne* are stabilizing forces designed to prevent haphazard development, and are relied upon by citizens in their residential, commercial, and industrial location decisions and investments. The planning needs and goals of a community, however, change over time, requiring changes in established land use regulations. Because rezonings, changes in *Bebauungspläne*, or any new land use restrictions affect existing property rights, communities continually run the risk that the new regulation will be challenged as a taking of private property....

The Constitution of the Federal Republic of Germany is called the Basic Law or *Grundgesetz* (GG). One of the basic rights explicitly guaranteed by the *Grundgesetz* is the right of property. Article 14 of the *Grundgesetz* states:

> 1. Property and the right of inheritance are guaranteed. Their content and limits shall be determined by the laws.
>
> 2. Property imposes duties. Its use should also serve the public weal.
>
> 3. Expropriation shall be permitted only in the public weal. It may be effected only by or pursuant to a law which shall provide for the nature and extent of the compensation. Such compensation shall be determined by establishing an equitable balance between the public interests and the interests of those affected. In case of dispute regarding the amount of compensation, recourse may be had to the ordinary courts.

Although the *Grundgesetz* is less than 40 years old, its basic provisions had been included in the Frankfurter Reichs Constitution of 1849 and the Weimar Constitution of 1919.

GG art. 14 § 3 enumerates the preconditions for a constitutional taking of property. Thus, a taking is permitted only if it occurs:

- for a public purpose;
- pursuant to a law (i.e., eminent domain or planning damages statute); and
- after an equitable weighing of public and private interests.

While, on the one hand, GG art. 14 guarantees private. property rights, it also specifically imposes a public duty incident to property ownership. The *Sozialbindung des Eigentums* theory (literally the social duty, or binding nature of property ownership theory), expressed in GG art. 14 § 2, statutorily recognizes the fact that property arrangements are inextricably related to broader social policies and that property ownership carries with it public responsibilities as well as private rights. Under the *Sozialbindung* theory, the individual property owner must accept restrictions on private property rights without compensation.

The *Sozialbindung* concept is very similar to the "general welfare" concept in U.S. taking law. Both theories have been used to broaden the scope of the police power. . . .

Unlike regulatory taking law in the United States which has been. almost exclusively established through, case law, in the FRG several. statutory provisions require compensation (*Planungsentschädigung*) for regulatory interference with property rights. BauGB §§ 39–44 require damages for a loss or reduction of the value of property resulting from local land use decisions which fall short of an actual physical taking of property. . . .

BauGB § 40 requires compensation whenever a use designated in a *Bebauungsplan* primarily serves a public purpose. Pursuant to BauGB § 40, a landowner may demand outright purchase of the property by the government (essentially a statutory form of inverse condemnation), or he may ask for compensation commensurate with the amount of interference with his private property tights. Compensation is paid for downzonings to any use which predominantly serves a public purpose. The provision, however, also includes use designations for the benefit of "special groups" such as the elderly and the mentally retarded. Listed in BauGB § 40, for example, are such uses as playing fields and playgrounds, streets and pedestrian ways, open space, parks, environmentally sensitive areas, public housing, municipal garages and parking lots, and other public or semipublic uses.

It is not necessary that a municipality actually implement the uses indicated in the *Bebauungsplan*. Implementation of such uses would in most cases require the exercise of eminent domain, e.g., for the construction of a public street. BauGB § 40 requires compensation for loss of value due to the mere designation of the use in the *Bebauungsplan*. However, actual purchase by the municipality is not required until it becomes "economically unreasonable" for the landowner to retain possession of the property, either as a nonconforming use or some other use permitted under the new designation....

BauGB § 42 is the most important of the planning compensation provisions (*Planungsentschädigung*) in the BauGB. That section requires compensation for any substantial diminution in property value which may occur when a new *Bebauungsplan*, or an amendment to or revision of an existing *Bebauungsplan*, changes or prohibits a previously permitted use....

If the property is developed, adoption or amendment of the *Bebauungsplan* creates a legal nonconforming use. Similar to regulation of nonconforming uses in the United States, German land use law limits nonconforming uses to the scope and intensity of the use as it existed at the time the new regulations were adopted. Particularly for landowners of commercial or industrial property, who no longer are able to expand their facilities, such restrictions often result in a loss of property value. Pursuant to BauGB § 42, a landowner may demand compensation for interference with established uses only if the new restrictions prevent or substantially impair continuance of the use or the economic value of the land associated with the use.

In contrast to U.S. zoning law under which a property owner has no vested right to a specific zoning classification, interference with the potential uses of vacant property in the FRG is also compensable under BauGB § 42. Compensation can be required for property damages resulting from a legally permitted but previously unrealized land use. Damages, however, are payable for interference with a previously permitted use only if the property owner (1) is, in fact, in a position to develop the property and (2) has a present right to a building permit at the time the land use category was changed. However, a building permit may only be obtained if the property is buildable land (Bauland), which means that the property has been subdivided and all improvements such as sewer availability, streets, and utilities are already in place. Thus, unimproved property (Rohbauland) would not be eligible for damages pursuant to BauGB § 42.

BauGB § 123 states that both improvement of land and provision of the required infrastructure are tasks of the municipality. Absent clear evidence of bad faith on the part of the municipality, however, a landowner does not have a legal right to require improvement of his property. Thus, by delaying the decision to form an improvement district for a particular area, a municipality can control the timing of development. However, municipalities can also (and sometimes do) delay construction of improvements in order to minimize future damages claims.

Prior to 1977, the BauGB did not limit the time period during which an owner could delay development of his land and still retain an indefinite right to compensation for a downzoning of his property. In 1976, however, in order to reduce the potential liability. of municipalities for planning damages, the federal legislature, the Bundestag, adopted legislation which limits a landowner's right to compensation for planning damages to seven years. Effective January I , 1977, the owner of a vacant or underdeveloped parcel of land is given seven years to develop the property in conformance with the legally permitted use. If within those seven years the municipality changes or prohibits the use, the landowner may claim compensatory damages pursuant to BauGB § 42.

The amount of compensation is measured by the difference in value of the property before and after the new regulation becomes effective. Valuation is not based on the actual use of the property at the time the regulation takes effect, but rather on the value of the permitted use under the previously existing use category. After seven years, compensation will be paid only for unreasonable interference with the actual, established use of the property. However, compensation is payable only when, within the seven-year period, (1) the landowner requested a building permit to which he would have a present legal right under the previous zoning, (2) the landowner actually intended and was financially able to develop the property, and (3) the municipality denied the permit on the ground that the use no longer was permitted.

The seven-year statute of limitations applies only when a present right to develop the property existed. BauGB § 42 specifically applies to restrictions on a previously permitted use. As discussed above, only improved parcels can provide a basis for a legal right to a building permit. Thus, even permitted uses are not protected by BauGB § 42 on unimproved parcels, and a municipality may downzone such property without fearing that payment of compensation will be required.

BauGB § 42 does not compensate for all diminution of property value where a new land use regulation restricts or eliminates the potential uses of a property. Compensation is paid only for a substantial loss of property value. Substantial loss is measured by looking to the value of the entire property including all parcels which comprise the economic unit of ownership. This is similar to the rule, expressed by the United States Supreme Court in *Penn Central*, that a court must look to the parcel as a whole to determine whether a taking has occurred.

The value before and after the taking is determined through appraisal of the property by an administrative appraisal committee pursuant to BauGB §§ 192–193. Although there are no definite guidelines, a 10 percent reduction in value may already be viewed as substantial. The committee appraises the property based on its fair market value in the community where the property is located. Merely because a property has been downzoned to a less intensive use category does not necessarily mean the property has incurred a loss in value; conversely, a rezoning to a more intensive use may actually reduce rather than increase the value of the property. For example, if a *Bebauungsplan* calls for multifamily, high-rise development on a parcel, the value of the property will increase only if there is a demand for such housing. Where there is only a demand for low-rise housing, a high-rise residential designation can substantially reduce the value of the property, thus giving rise to a claim for damages.

Within the boundaries of a *Bebauungsplan*, a landowner has a compensable property right in the continuance of the land use designation, not only on his own property, but also on adjacent properties as well. BauGB § 42 may also apply to compensate a landowner for a change in the land use designation on a neighboring property if such change reduces the value of his own land. For example, if in a *Bebauungsplan* the municipality designates residential uses adjacent to an industrial area, the owner of the industrial parcel may be required to meet certain noise or pollution standards which would not be required had the adjacent land also been designated as industrial rather than residential. If the damages suffered are substantial, the owner has a compensable claim against the municipality....

During the 1970s, the FRG experienced a huge construction boom, and local governments were unable to develop and adopt land use plans to keep up with the demand for improved, developable land. Many local jurisdictions, therefore, encouraged and cooperated with developers and landowners, who hired private firms to perform all necessary planning and engineering studies for the adoption of a *Bebauungsplan*.

Numerous *Bebauungspläne* begun in the euphoria of the rapidly expanding German economy of the 1970s are now viewed as overly ambitious and environmentally insensitive; both economic expansion and population growth slowed significantly in the 1980s, while environmental movements which seek to conserve the land in its present form grew rapidly. Thus, many privately financed *Bebauungspläne* have not been adopted by the city councils which often view the protection of the environment as more important than municipal growth. As a result, substantial pre-development costs incurred in the 1970s are not compensable pursuant to BauGB § 39; aggrieved landowners must look elsewhere to obtain compensation for their loss....

As a solution to the taking problem, [American] states should explore the advantages of adopting statutory compensatory regulations. By compensating the landowner for any damages to property value resulting from the restriction, state and local governments would be able to adopt restrictive, but necessary and beneficial, land use regulations, without the necessity of outright acquisition through eminent domain.

A possible model for compensatory regulation is provided by the ALI *Model Land Development Code* § 9-112(3). That section provides that if a court finds a taking of property through overregulation, "the court shall retain jurisdiction if it further determines that the limitation on development could be lawfully imposed if compensation were paid." The provision for compensation under the ALI *Model Code*, does not, however, resolve the problems of compensation for (1) pre-development expenses where no vested right exists; (2) loss of property value because a plan designates portions of the property as open space, public easements, rights-of-way, or for some other public purpose; or (3) loss of value of vacant land which has been legally downzoned where no vested right exists to development under the previous zoning. Provisions for compensating such damages should be included in any compensable regulations scheme....

* * *

The following is Oregon's Measure Seven, an initiative-adopted law, temporarily halted by a state court. The measure would offer compensation to regulated landowners. Does Measure 7 threaten Oregon's growth management scheme?

State of Oregon
Measure 7

Proposed by initiative petition to be voted on at the General Election
November 7, 2000

Amends Constitution: Requires Payment to Landowner if Government Regulation Reduces Property Value

RESULT OF "YES" VOTE: "Yes" vote requires state, local government pay property owner if law, regulation reduces property value.

RESULT OF "NO" VOTE: "No" vote rejects requiring government pay compensation if law or regulation reduces property value.

Summary: Amends Constitution. Oregon Constitution prohibits taking private property for public use without just compensation. Oregon Supreme Court has not required compensation when property value merely reduced. Measure requires state, local governments pay landowner amount of reduction in market value if law, regulation reduces property value. Compensation required if owner must act to protect certain natural resource, cultural values or low income housing. Exemption for historically recognized nuisance laws or if owner sells alcohol, pornography, operates casino. Applies if regulation adopted after owner acquires property.

Estimate of Financial Impact: Direct costs to the state are estimated to be $1.6 billion per year. Local government direct costs are estimated to be $3.8 billion per year. There is no state or local government revenue impact.

Be it Enacted by the People of the State of Oregon:

The Constitution of the State of Oregon is Amended by Adding the Following Subsections to Section 18 of Article I:

(a) If the state, a political subdivision of the state, or a local government passes or enforces a regulation that restricts the use of private real property, and the restriction has the effect of reducing the value of a property upon which the restriction is imposed; the property owner shall be paid just compensation equal to the reduction in the fair market value of the property.

(b) For purposes of this section, adoption or enforcement of historically and commonly recognized nuisance laws shall not be deemed to have caused a reduction in the value of a property. The phrase "historically and commonly recognized nuisance laws" shall be narrowly construed in favor of a finding that just compensation is required under this section.

(c) A regulating entity may impose, to the minimum extent required, a regulation to implement a requirement of federal law without payment of compensation under this section. Nothing in this 2000 Amendment shall require compensation due to a government regulation prohibiting the use of a property for the purpose of selling pornography, performing nude dancing, selling alcoholic beverages or other controlled substances, or operating a casino or gaming parlor.

(d) Compensation shall be due the property owner if the regulation was adopted, first enforced or applied after the current owner of the property became the owner, and continues to apply to the property 90 days after the owner applies for compensation under this section.

(e) Definitions: For purposes of this section, "regulation" shall include any law, rule, ordinance, resolution, goal, or other enforceable enactment of government; "real property" shall include any structure built or sited on the property, aggregate and other removable minerals, and any forest product or other crop grown on the property; "reduction in the fair market value" shall mean the difference in the fair market value of the property before and after application of the regulation, and shall include the net cost to the landowner of an affirmative obligation to protect, provide, or preserve wildlife habitat, natural areas, wetlands, ecosystems, scenery, open space, historical, archaeological or cultural resources, or low income housing; and "just compensation" shall include, if a claim for compensation is denied or not fully paid within 90 days of filing, reasonable attorney fees and expenses necessary to collect the compensation.

(f) If any phrase, clause, or part of this section is found to be invalid by a court of competent jurisdiction, the remaining phrases, clauses and parts shall remain in full force and effect.

* * *

Notes and Comments

1. The Initiative process originally designed as a means for the people to wrest political control from vested monied interests may today be a tool of the vested monied interests. See Edward J. Sullivan, *Measure 7 and the Politics of Land-Use Planning in Oregon*, 53 Land Use L. & Zoning Dig. (Jun. 2001) (arguing that few eligible voted and there was no campaign to inform the public that Oregon's forward-thinking planning was in jeopardy, and most voters voted their pocketbook with images that their land might increase in value and the state might take it away by regulation). The measure has been temporarily derailed by a trial judge, finding the initiative covered too many subject matters, *McCall v. Kitzhaber*, No. 00C20156 (Or. Cir. Ct., Marion Cty. Feb. 21, 2001) (preliminary injunction made permanent), Los Angeles Times, Feb. 23, 2001, 2001 WESTLAW 2463924, but the question is before the state's supreme court. Associated Press, May 16, 2001 (Oregon Supreme Court grants expedited appeal bypassing the intermediate appellate court, in WESTLAW). In the meantime, the Oregon Supreme Court has approved a ballot initiative measure, No. 112, that would repeal Measure 7. *Hunnicutt v. Myers*, 41 P.3d 402 (Or. 2002)

In addition to the laws of the different nations, there also exists a body of international law that is typically applied by international tribunals and in the resolution of international disputes:

Jon A. Stanley, Comment, *Keeping Big Brother Out of Our Backyard: Regulatory Takings as in International Law and Compared to American Fifth Amendment Jurisprudence,*

15 Emory International Law Review 349 (2001)

It is a well recognized rule in international law that the property of aliens cannot be taken, whether for public purposes or not, without adequate compensation. Violations of this rule are referred to as "expropriations." The principle of expropriations in international law evokes certain conceptual similarities to Fifth Amendment jurisprudence in the United States. The question that arises under both paradigms is to what extent, if any, may a government effectively devalue property by regulation before it amounts to a compensable taking. While the United States Supreme Court has held that a government regulation completely devaluating property constitutes a taking pursuant to the Constitution, international law is much more ambiguous on this matter. I will argue in this Comment that while regulatory takings do exist in international law, they currently have a much higher threshold than their American counterparts. This threshold must be lowered and better defined, in order to adequately protect the rights of alien claimants....

Takings in International Law

The widely recognized rule of international law is that property of aliens cannot normally [be] taken, whether for public purposes or not, without adequate compensation. Section 712 of The Restatement (Third) of the Foreign Relations of the United States reads:

> A state is responsible under international law for injury resulting from:

(1) a taking by the state of the property of a national of another state that

(a) is not for a public purpose, or

(b) is discriminatory, or

(c) is not accompanied by provision for just compensation;

For compensation to be just under this Subsection, it must, in the absence of exceptional circumstances, be in an amount equivalent to the value of the property taken and be paid at the time of taking, or within a reasonable time thereafter with interest from the date of taking, and in a form economically usable by the foreign national....[27]

The language of the Restatement itself reflects a remarkable similarity to that of the Fifth Amendment of the United States Constitution which states, "nor shall private property be taken for public use, without just compensation." These linguistic similarities suggest that the international takings law has been influenced to a certain degree by Fifth Amendment jurisprudence....

Formal or de jure expropriations occur when a state explicitly affects the legal title of the property, effectively seizing it in an outright manner.... Formal expropriations are relatively rare in international law.

A taking may still occur in international law in the absence of a formal decree, where the respondent state may specifically disclaim any such intention. Instead, a taking is carried out de facto by successive encroachments upon management and ownership rights. The recognition of de facto takings is a long-standing principle of international law. Christie asserts: "[I]nterference with an alien's property may amount to expropriation even when no explicit attempt is made to affect the legal title to the property, and even though the respondent state may specifically disclaim any such intention." Accordingly, in one of the Iran-U.S. Claims Tribunal's earliest cases... the judges suggested in dictum that "unreasonable interference" is sufficient to constitute an expropriation. Other awards by the Tribunal have described the standard as requiring an "interfer[ence]... to such an extent that [the property] rights are rendered so useless that they must be deemed to have been expropriated." The threshold of interference in terms of extent and duration in de facto expropriation analysis will be paramount in defining the scope of regulatory takings in international law....

International law precedent has firmly established that formal transfer of title of the property of an alien is not required to establish an expropriation. In theory, the showing of sufficient "interference" caused by government action will be construed by courts as a de facto taking. However, in practice, this showing may be close to impossible in certain circumstances. The question that arises is whether state regulations amounting to interference with the title of property owned by aliens may amount to a de facto taking....

Discussion and analysis of regulatory takings has been much less prevalent in the international context than in the United States. This dearth of scholarly attention is evidenced in the Restatement's tenuous and cursory discussion concerning regulatory takings. Accordingly, Dolzer observes that, "It is a curious phenomenon that so much ink has been spilled in this context (analysis of regulatory takings) within national orders, and yet so little writing exists in the corresponding sphere of international law...."

27. Restatement (Third) of Foreign Relations Law of the United States § 712 (1987).

Nevertheless, the principle of regulatory takings does in fact exist in international law....

[T]here are relatively few international cases which have dealt specifically with regulatory takings, and as a result even fewer secondary commentaries on the issue. However, a survey of international expropriation jurisprudence and accompanying commentary reveals that there is an element of consistency among courts and tribunals as to a line between legitimate regulation and compensable takings.

The threshold at which a state regulation may deprive an alien of his property before it amounts to a compensable taking does not correspond with the Supreme Court's current interpretation of the Fifth Amendment, in contrast to the position taken by the Restatement. "In general, the line in international law is similar to that drawn in United States jurisprudence for purposes of the Fifth and Fourteenth Amendments to the Constitution in determining whether there has been a taking requiring compensation." International courts and tribunals have afforded states a large, and almost impenetrable, amount of deference in applying their "police powers."

The result is a legal system in which states must do very little to justify their regulations, leaving alien claimants with a nearly insurmountable uphill battle. This is illustrated by the vast majority of claims for compensation that are denied. As a result, some commentators believe that certain classifications of legislation are per se immune from expropriation claims. Wagner claims that, "[a]nti-trust, consumer protection, securities, environmental protection, land planning and other legislation are non-compensable takings." These conclusions are misguided and seek to undermine the notion of property as a human right. Despite the current status of regulatory takings in international law, expropriation jurisprudence has provided a framework in which expropriations can be constructively inferred from substantial interference without the transfer of legal title. Furthermore, international courts and tribunals have repeatedly upheld the notion that, given the right circumstances, state legislation is capable of surpassing the current line between police power and expropriation, and giving rise to a compensable taking.

Factors in Defining the Threshold of Regulatory Takings in International Law....

Consistent with U.S. domestic terminology, "police power" refers to the state's right to promote a recognized "social purpose" or the "general welfare" by regulation. The notion that exercise of the state's police powers normally will not create a right to compensation has been widely accepted in international law. "[T]he existence of generally recognized considerations of the public health, safety, morals, or welfare will normally lead to a conclusion that there has been no 'taking.'' However, this does not mean that all regulations fall within a state's police powers....

Despite the fact that courts and tribunals have afforded states "extensive discretion," in their application of police powers, they have noted that states are still subject to certain limitations. For example,..."[a]n expropriation, the only purpose of which would have been to avoid contractual obligations of the state or of an entity controlled by it, could not, nevertheless, be considered as lawful under international law." Thus, in theory, a state regulation may rise to the level of a violation of international law in a number of ways, including by exceeding the state's police power.

Another constraint on state regulations is the "non-discrimination rule." Simply put, the non-discrimination rule holds states liable for legislation that disproportionately affects aliens....The Restatement also recognizes the non-discrimination rule: "One test suggested for determining whether regulation and taxation programs are intended to achieve expropriation is whether they are applied only to alien enterprises." ...

International courts and tribunals do not apply the non-discrimination rule as a per se bar. Like the police power, a certain amount of deference is given to the state's economic sovereignty and its policy priorities. Justification for differential treatment between foreigners and nationals is likely to be "rather easily available. In fact, international courts and tribunals have been reluctant to assume discrimination in cases where there is differential treatment of various persons, or class of owners....

Certain courts, tribunals, and commentators have limited regulatory takings analysis to two factors: police power and non-discrimination. Aldrich claims that, according to the Iran-U.S. Claims Tribunal's view of international law, "[l]iability does not arise from actions that are nondiscriminatory and are within the commonly accepted taxation and police powers of the states." ...

There is significant evidence that international law has considered the duration of the alleged deprivation of property in deciding whether or not a compensable taking has occurred. The Restatement contends that "[a] temporary deprivation of control, as by a freezing of assets under the International Emergency Economic Powers Act is probably not a taking but may become one if deprivation is for an extended or indefinite period."[145] ...

A prime example where the temporal factor has played a central role in regulatory takings is the case of *Hauer v. Land Rheinland-Pfalz*.[147] Hauer was a German winegrower. Under German law, the planting of new vines required a state permit. Hauer was denied such a permit. While the case was being appealed, the European Economic Community adopted an order prohibiting the first-time planting of the type of vine which the claimant was planning on growing, for two years. The Court of Justice of the European Communities found no violation of Hauer's property rights, emphasizing in particular that the EEC order was to be valid only for a transitory period of two or three years. The Hauer case illustrates that the temporal component of the taking may play a substantial role in determining whether a claimant's property rights have been adequately deprived as to warrant compensation....

Property in the Context of Human Rights

A survey of the nature and composition of current regulatory takings analysis suggests that situations might arise in which an alien's property rights are infringed upon, and go uncompensated. As property rights are increasingly recognized as a human right, current regulatory takings analysis appears to be inconsistent with fundamental human rights principles. These human rights principles call for a reformed test that achieves a more equitable balance between state sovereignty and the human rights of the claimant.

Article 1 of the First Additional Protocol to the European Convention for the Protection of Human Rights and Fundamental Freedoms firmly establishes a right to property. "Every natural or legal person is entitled to the peaceful enjoyment or his possessions. No one shall be deprived of his possessions. No one shall be deprived of his possessions except in the public interest and subject to the conditions provided for by

145. Restatement (Third) of the Foreign Relations Law of the United States § 712 cmt. 6. The International Emergency Economic Powers Act is codified at 50 U.S.C. § 1701 (1998).

147. Case 44/79, Hauer v. Land Rheinland-Pfalz, 1979 E.C.R. 3727, 3 C.M.L.R. 42 (1980).

law by the general principles of international law." However, Article 1 of the Protocol also acknowledges the police power of the states, as a limiting provision on the rights of the individual. "The preceeding provisions shall not, however, in any way impair the right of the state to enforce such laws as it deems necessary to control the use of property in accordance with the general interest or to secure the payment of taxes or other contributions or penalties." Although the two provisions in Article 1 of the First Additional Protocol resemble components of contemporary U.S. regulatory takings analysis in form, they have been applied differently....

While both American and international law have afforded deference to the government in determining whether a regulation is a legitimate exercise of police power, the U.S. Supreme Court has considered it just one of three factors of a "balancing test." In contrast, international courts and tribunals have given much more weight to the police power component as compared to other factors. The "balancing tests" employed by the Supreme Court in *Penn Central*...essentially balance[s] the public benefit gained by the regulation against the private loss from the regulation of private property. Currently, international courts and tribunals appear to have significantly tipped the scales in favor of state interests, essentially disregarding private concerns once a legitimate exercise of police power has been determined....

* * *

Notes and Comments

1. Mr. Stanley believes that *Lucas* and American takings doctrine is more protective of property rights than international law and advocates extension of the American model. What would be the impact of such adoption? For additional analysis of takings under international law, see George C. Christie, *What Constitutes a Taking of Property Under International Law?*, 38 Brit. Y. B. Int'l L. 307, 307 (1962).

Chapter 8

The First Amendment: Freedom of Expression and Religion Limits on the Exercise of Land Use Regulatory Power

> [W]hile the entertainment afforded by a nude ballet at Lincoln Center to those who can pay the price may differ vastly in content (as viewed by judges) or in quality (as viewed by critics), it may not differ in substance from the dance viewed by the person who, having worked overtime for the necessary wherewithal, wants some "entertainment" with his beer or shot of rye.
>
> Salem Inn, Inc. v. Frank, 501 F.2d 18, 21 (2d Cir. 1974) (Oakes, J.)

The American constitutional experience is unique and on no subject richer than in interpreting the evolving doctrines of separation of church and state, freedom to practice one's religion, and the central subject of the First Amendment, the greatest right and precondition for a democratic free people, freedom of expression.

An overview of the developed religion jurisprudence will be presented later in this chapter. The freedom of speech has evolved through various periods of the Supreme Court's history, through different economic, political, cultural experiences. Regulation of speech was very different during the First World War and the Red Scare of a communist takeover for the next generation, through post-World War II liberalism, into a period when the composition of the United States Supreme Court reflected extremely conservative presidential appointments. As a result, the first amendment jurisprudence may be described as a rich tapestry or perhaps more correctly, a crazy quilt. Erwin Chemerinsky, Constitutional Law Ch. 11 (2d ed. 2002); Laurence H. Tribe, American Constitutional Law 789 (2d ed. 1988).

In what might be referred to as the classic period of the Court, roughly from the 1950's until the 1970's, the Court developed a general philosophy about speech and a set of principles that allowed courts to protect the larger part of expression and objectively assign burdens of proof. For example, if the regulation was tied to the content of the speech, the Court would look to a series of tests for different types of speech to determine if the speech was protected or subject to regulation. These tests included definitions of obscenity, *Miller v. California*, 413 U.S. 15 (1973), defamation, *New York Times v. Sullivan*, 376 U.S. 254 (1964), the advocacy of illegal activity, *Brandenburg v. Ohio*, 395 U.S. 444 (1969), fighting words, *Chaplinsky v. New Hampshire*, 315 U.S. 568 (1942), and commercial speech. *Virginia State Bd. of Pharmacy v. Virginia Citizens Consumer Council, Inc.*, 425 U.S. 748 (1976). The model allowed a regime of harsh censorship over pornography and other forms of expression touching on America's puritanical streak, or perhaps the timidity of politicians to offend the politically well-organized religious right.

Where regulations were directed, not at the content of speech, but simply the question of the appropriate time, place, and manner of content-protected expression, the Court has allowed reasonable rules that leave open alternative channels of communication, and are narrowly tailored, that is, regulate no more than necessary to achieve a substantial state interest. *Heffron v. International Soc'y for Krishna Consciousness, Inc.*, 452 U.S. 640, 648 (1981). These rules would include requirements for parade permits, loudspeakers, and the accommodation of traffic. *Kovacs v. Cooper*, 336 U.S. 77 (1949).

In recent years the Supreme Court has generated a wide array of freedom of expression rulings that are frequently speech protective but sometimes decidedly not. Sometimes the Court adheres to the classic doctrine but almost as frequently has modified traditional doctrine and analytical models.

For example, instead of asking under earlier doctrine if there was a clear or present danger, or whether the message regulated was defamatory or obscene, today's Court may as likely simply apply equal protection-like doctrine and demand that regulation of protected speech serve a compelling state interest. *Texas v. Johnson*, 491 U.S. 397 (1989). Under this analysis, speech that is protected under the classic doctrine can be regulated if the Court majority concludes that a compelling state interest supports the restriction. *Denver Area Educ. Telecomm. Consortium, Inc. v. FCC*, 518 U.S. 727 (1996).

Similarly, the regulation of time, place, and manner, and the definition of content-neutrality have undergone transformation that blurs the protective doctrine. For example, in *FCC v. Pacifica Foundation*, 438 U.S. 726 (1978), the Court reviewed a policy of the communications regulatory agency that prohibited the planned broadcasting of indecent "words," at least during hours when children might be expected to be in the audience. The case presented several problems to a more conservative Court applying classic doctrine. The Court did not wish to decide the case under the question of whether the material was protected speech as the case involved an extremely tame and tasteful monologue of the comedian George Karlin discussing what he referred to as the "7 dirty words," and the doctrine would automatically find protection as the piece in no way met the strict requirements of the definition of obscenity. Alternatively, the Court could not sustain the regulation, even though the sanction was limited to the threat that the subsequent relicensing proceedings would consider the violation, as a time, place, and manner rule as the sanction was clearly based on the content of the speech. Thus, what the Court did was to recast the time, place, manner test from one that insisted on content-neutrality, to one that now only asked if the regulation was message or viewpoint-biased. *City of Cincinnati v. Discovery Network, Inc.*, 507 U.S. 410 (1993); *FCC v. Pacifica Found.*, *supra*. The Court is now allowing regulation based on the content of even protected speech. In essence the Court has folded content-based regulation and time, place, and manner context regulation into one model that provides deference unless the regulation is viewpoint-based and the Court applies strict scrutiny. *Perry Educ. Ass'n v. Perry Local Educators Ass'n*, 460 U.S. 37 (1983).

On other occasions, the Court will return to its more classical roots and decide cases based on the classic system of the classification of forum. *Id.* If a public forum, *Boos v.*

Barry, 485 U.S. 312 (1988), where speech is historically allowed, such as a park, or sidewalk, or if the government has opened up a publicly owned forum for public expressive access to be a "designated public forum," such as a theater or school that rents out access to the general public, *Lamb's Chapel v. Center Moriches Union Free School Dist.*, 508 U.S. 384 (1993), then the Court applies the time, place, and manner test. Where publicly owned land has not been opened up so as to invite the public to engage in expressive behavior, such as in a jail, office building, or airport, the regulation must be simply reasonable and viewpoint-neutral. *Perry Educ. Ass'n, supra.*

The *Pacifica* ruling suffers from another modification from the classic expression rules in that it allows what is undisputably a vague regulation. *Kolender v. Lawson*, 461 U.S. 352 (1983). What is the meaning of "indecent" The Court has long required the invalidation of regulations that either extend beyond what is subject to regulation and sweep into protected speech so as to be overbroad, *Secretary of State v. J.H. Munson Co.*, 467 U.S. 947 (1984); *Broaderick v. Oklahoma*, 413 U.S. 601 (1973) (substantial overbreadth); Richard Fallon, Jr., *Making Sense of Overbreadth*, 100 Yale L.J. 853 (1991), or regulations that are so vague that speakers must guess at the meaning. *Connally v. General Const. Co.*, 269 U.S. 385, 391 (1926). In *Cohen v. California*, 403 U.S. 15 (1971), the Court reviewed a prosecution of a young man who wore a jacket in a courthouse that displayed a simple yet poignant protest of the Viet Nam War: "Fuck the Draft," where the state considered the conduct disorderly. In invalidating the application of the law, the Court recognized that "one man's vulgarity is another's lyric." This simple principle appears lost in the Court's rulings on matters relating to sex. Indeed, never having announced the principle, it nevertheless appears that politically motivated speech receives greater protection than restraints on pornographic or indecent speech. Yet in *United States v. O'Brien*, 391 U.S. 367 (1968), the Court upheld the validity of a federal statute that criminalized the knowing destruction of a draft card against one who burned his draft card as an expression of opposition to the Viet Nam War. In another variation of the theme, the Court in *O'Brien* developed the doctrine that it would allow regulation even where it directly interfered with otherwise protected speech where the government's interest was unrelated to the suppression of speech. This principle, for example, allows the Court to refuse to protect nude dancing despite it being anything but nonexpressive, because the government is pursuing a moral interest separate from speech suppression. *Erie v. Pap's A.M.*, 529 U.S. 277 (2000). By comparison, in *Texas v. Johnson*, *supra*, The Court invalidated a law criminalizing the desecration of the national flag. The defect, according to the Court, is that the government's interest is solely directed to limit a form of expression. There is simply no interest unrelated to the suppression of expression.

There also exist the highly protected rights against the interference with freedom of association, *NAACP v. Alabama ex rel. Patterson*, 357 U.S. 449 (1958), and the presumptively invalid prior restraint: regulations that prevent speech or publication from being uttered or published, *New York Times v. United States*, 403 U.S. 713 (1971); *Near v. Minnesota*, 203 U.S. 697 (1931), as compared to traditional regulation that punishes unprotected speech. Condemned under the prior restraint doctrine, would be licenses and fees for the privilege of engaging in protected expression (subject to the reasonable time, place, manner type permit rules), *Lovell v. City of Griffin*, 303 U.S. 444 (1938), most official censorship, subject to the limited and rigidly restricted permissible censorship authorized in the case of publicly displayed films. *See Friedman v. Maryland*, 380 U.S. 51 (1965).

Adult Entertainment

One application of freedom of expression in the land use context is the treatment of what is one's immoral behavior but another's adult entertainment. The following decision comes from Australia:

City of Camberwell v. Cherry Nicholson

Supreme Court of Victoria
1988 VIC LEXIS 580; BC8800482
2 December 1988

Ormiston, J.

HIS HONOUR: This is an appeal on a question of law from a decision of the Administrative Appeals Tribunal which was constituted by three members of the Planning Division of that Tribunal. By that decision the Tribunal allowed an appeal by the present respondent, Miss Cherry Nicholson, from a determination of the responsible authority, the City of Camberwell, the present appellant, refusing to grant a permit under the Town and Country Planning Act 1961 to use certain Victorian buildings at *265–267* Canterbury Road for the purpose of a brothel.... [T]he right of appeal to this Court is confined to questions of law and permits a review only of relevant legal issues and does not entitle the Court to review the evidence so as to substitute its decision for that of the Tribunal, whether on questions of fact or as to the exercise of the relevant discretions. Parliament has entrusted to the Administrative Appeals Tribunal the final decision on these critical questions of fact and as to the manner in which the powers and discretions granted to responsible authorities under the relevant planning legislation should be implemented. My task is to determine only whether the Tribunal has formed a mistaken view as to the relevant law or whether its conclusion is such that no body could properly reach if it correctly understood that law.

The facts which I shall outline come largely from the Tribunal's reasons and some maps and other evidentiary material adduced before the Tribunal. The premises for which a permit was directed to be issued is a two-storeyed Victorian terrace, with veranda and balcony, situated in Canterbury at No. 267 Canterbury Road, a busy suburban main road running approximately east and west. No. 267 is on the north side of the road, in a mixed shopping and commercial area, just to the east of a railway overpass. The northern end of the site touches on the railway reservation, but it is about 100 metres east of the overpass on Canterbury Road. Between the overpass and the premises are an electrical contractor, a car repair workshop and a landscape garden, and to the east, likewise on the northern side of the road, is a large factory, restaurant premises, two shops, an engineering works and some show rooms. On the opposite, that is the southern side of Canterbury Road, there is an advertising agency on the corner of Wattle Valley Road, which extends directly to the south and is an almost entirely residential Street apart from two buildings at the northern end. To the east on the southern side of Canterbury Road there is a dentist, display rooms and a meeting room, and thereafter an almost entirely residential development extends both to the east and south down nearby Willandra Avenue. To the south-west on the north-west corner of the intersection of Wattle Valley Road and Canterbury Road is an imposing three-storey Victorian boarding house called Canterbury Mansions, in which some 42 people live. The west side of this building also faces onto a popular shopping street

6. Free City of Christiana. 800 squatters have successfully occupied Copenhagen, Denmark's former military base.

known as Maling Road, which has a number of small shops which extend in a southwesterly direction, so that the backs of the shops on the north-west side of the Street follow roughly the direction of the railway line. The zoning of the area for town planning purposes was then controlled by the Melbourne Metropolitan Planning Scheme ("MMPS"). On the north side of Canterbury Road the relevant area, including No. 267, was in a light industrial zone save that a strip of twenty metres next to the road was included in a proposed road widening reservation. The buildings on the south side of the road opposite No. 267 to the east of Wattle Valley Road were contained in the Camberwell Service Business Zone for about forty metres to the east of the advertising agency and from that point further east the area is within the "Camberwell Residential Zone". The area to the west of Wattle Valley Road, including the Maling Road shopping centre, is in a zone called the "Camberwell Urban Conservation-Business Zone". The distance of forty metres is significant as CL25(5) of the MMPS requires that a brothel be situated more than forty metres from any part of the Camberwell Residential Zone. That requirement was satisfied, as was the requirement of §52 of the Prostitution Regulation Act 1986 to the effect that a brothel shall not be situated within 200 metres of a kindergarten or school. The Tribunal visited the area for the purpose of inspecting the proposed brothel and its environs and reached a number of conclusions particularly as to its visual prominence, a matter argued by the parties to be of significance. After concluding that the western building, No. 265 Canterbury Road, also the subject of the application, was reasonably prominent from Wattle Valley Road, they found that No. 267 was not prominent from that road or at least it was visible only from its northern end. Moreover they held that it was not prominent from Maling Road or from Canterbury Road when viewed from west or east, in part because No. 267 is set back a little from the Street frontage. Of course the building is visible from the front of Canterbury Mansions which is the closest building to be used for residential purposes. The Tribunal also reached the conclusion that for a four room brothel there would be ample parking available in the evenings in Canterbury Road and, if necessary, in the northern part of Wattle Valley Road or in a car park apparently being constructed immediately behind Canterbury Mansions...The premises are owned by a company, Hermitage Holdings Pty. Ltd., of which Anthony John Ward and Cynthia Louise Ward are directors, but, as is not uncommon, the application for the permit was not made by that company but by the respondent, Miss Nicholson, who was said to be the person who would manage the premises if a permit were granted. Application was made by her to the City of Camberwell as the responsible authority on 17th February 1987. It was necessary to apply for permission because the land was zoned both in a light industrial zone and in a road widening reserve and, so far as the light industrial zone was concerned, this particular use was what has come to be called a "Column Four" use under the MMPS, that is, a use for which a permit must be sought before the land can be so used. The council of that municipality required her to advertise the application pursuant to §l8B of the Town and Country Planning Act 1961 and as a result some 1,984 objections and three petitions were received, all opposing the use of the premises as a brothel....

After a preliminary hearing the appeal came on before the Planning Division of the Tribunal which consisted of a Senior Presiding Member, Miss Angela H. Smith, and two members Mr. WN Wilkinson and Ms. Janet Dore. The then appellant, Miss Nicholson was represented by counsel as were the City of Camberwell and a group of some 93 objectors, while a smaller group of objectors appeared in person. After an extensive hearing over three days, during which a large number of witnesses including expert witnesses were called, the appeal was eventually allowed on 29th January 1988. [T]he Tribunal directed that a permit issue for a brothel at No. 267 Canterbury Road but subject to a substantial number of conditions, among other things, prohibiting the use of advertising signs and external lighting (without permission of the council), confining the number of prostitutes working there to no more than four, limiting the hours of operation to the period from 7.00 p.m. to 4.00 a.m. each night and restricting access to entry down a drive and through the rear door of the premises. The permit directed to be issued was limited to use for a period of three years from the date of its issue. In substance the Tribunal, after considering a number of issues relating to the prominence of the building and its proximity to residential zones and uses, the proximity to the Maling Road shopping centre, the impact upon what is called "pedestrian amenity," compliance with statutory requirements, the effect on the traffic and parking, and the significance of community opposition and what was described as a "perception of incompatibility," held that a brothel limited in size and with limited hours of operation "would not have.an unacceptable impact upon the amenity of the neighbourhood and in particular upon the residences in the northern section of Wattle Valley Road, Canterbury Mansions and the residences in Canterbury Road east of Willandra Avenue."...

Some seven grounds of appeal were relied upon in the summons but counsel for the appellant reformulated them into four grounds in a form with which counsel for the respondent did not seriously disagree. The first of those reformulated grounds which were drawn from grounds 3(1) and 5(2) of the summons took the following form:—"That the Tribunal erred in that it was influenced by evidence and material heard in other brothel cases and did not disclose that evidence and material to the parties in the present case or give them an opportunity to comment on or respond to that evidence and material."...Most of the hearing before the Tribunal was taken up with evidence and discussion directed to the issue as to what impact the proposed brothel was likely to have on the neighbourhood surrounding No. 267 Canterbury Road, that is on what is called the amenity of that area, and in particular as to the effect of the proposed use on the residents of Canterbury Mansions and of the nearby streets and upon pedestrians and motorists who use Canterbury Road. There was also extensive argument as to what was called the perception of incompatibility felt by the objectors and other residents resulting from the introduction of a brothel into the area. Among the witnesses called were two town planning consultants called on each side, as well as a number of objectors, one of whom had lived close to three brothels or massage parlours in Fitzroy before moving to Canterbury. The arguments advanced on each side also relied heavily on various decisions which had been given by the Tribunal and more particularly by its predecessor the Planning Appeals Board in relation to the grant of permits for brothels both after the passing in 1984 of certain amendments to the Town and Country Planning Act 1961 and also after the proclamation of certain provisions of the Prostitution Regulation Act 1986. In those decisions, some of which have been reported in various series of reports of planning cases and some of which have not been reported, there were wise opinions expressed as to the likely effect of the introduction of brothels.

Counsel for the plaintiff in supporting this ground drew attention to three particular instances which he claimed showed that the Tribunal had relied upon evidence given to that Tribunal and to other members of the Tribunal and the former Board and which he claimed was relied upon by the Tribunal without informing the parties, and in particular the appellant and the objectors, of its intention to do so. It is necessary to repeat part of the Tribunal's reasoning in order to see the way in which this other material was used by it.

In the first place the appellant relied upon a number of passages in that part of the decision which dealt with the consequence of the proposed brothel's proximity to residential uses and zones. Towards the end of its reasoning on this issue it said: "It has generally been accepted by this Tribunal and its predecessor, the Planning Appeals Board, that brothels with planning permits do not as a rule cause amenity problems if appropriately located. Distinctions have often been drawn between massage parlours of the past which could attract noisy drunken disorderly groups, and those operating with permits under current planning controls." In Janice Stebbing and Maria Mat-mo v City of Mordialloc, Woodlands Golf Club and Ors 5 PABR 226, the Board said: "In saying that, the Board needs to restate its oft repeated conclusions (see for instance Michelle Brooke v City of Brighton (1985) 4 PABR 50, and Clarke v City of Fitzroy, Appeal No. P86/0425, Unreported determination dated 14 August 1986) that persons attending brothels seem not to be rowdy, dangerous or even obtrusive but rather they seem to be more furtive wishing to enter and leave the brothel (and the area within which it is located) without being seen." While we accept the submission of Mr. DC. Wilson, that noisy behaviour can be associated with a brothel with a planning permit, we think that its impact very much depends upon the size and character of the brothel, its location and the quality of management. In this instance, we are satisfied that a brothel of limited size in this location with limited hours should not cause unacceptable detriment to the amenity of the locality." On this issue, therefore, the Tribunal concluded that proximity to residential uses and zones was not such as to justify refusal of a permit for a brothel which was of limited size and operated during restricted hours. They nevertheless imposed a condition for three years and stated that, if unacceptable amenity problems arose, the permit would not be renewed.

The second example relied upon of the use of evidence and material from other cases appears on p.9 of the Tribunal's reasons in the course of its consideration of the impact on "pedestrian amenity." There was argument as to a possible conflict between the users of the brothel and school children going to and from Strathcona Girls School situated approximately 1 kilometre south of the premises, for it was alleged that the brothel would attract undesirable people to the area. The Tribunal stated:—"The limitation to evening hours will remove this potential conflict. In any event, we have heard no evidence in this or any other appeal to enable us to conclude that the establishment of a brothel does, or does not, increase the potential for such undesirable conduct to occur. I should add that the Tribunal said that as a result of their inspections of the area they thought it unlikely that children from the school would come as far north as Canterbury Road as they could take a short cut to the Canterbury Station off Maling Road.

The third passage relied upon by the appellant to support this first ground occurred in that part of the Tribunal's reasoning which dealt with community opposition and the perception of incompatibility. After discussing the extent of opposition reflected by the number of objections made to the proposed permit and discussing a number of reported and unreported decisions of the Tribunal and the previous Board touching directly and indirectly on the issue, it concluded (at p.13):—"In summary then, we consider that local perceptions of incompatibility should be treated cautiously where the Tribunal believes on the basis of its experience in other appeals that those perceptions are unlikely to be translated into concrete amenity impacts on the surrounding land". (Emphasis added)...

When the matter came on before the Tribunal no specific allegation at all was made as to the unsuitability either of Miss Nicholson or of any of the directors of the company which owned the premises, and, in particular, of a Mr. Ward, a director who apparently was present throughout the hearing.

* * *

Notes and Comments

1. In Victoria, a brothel is just a business and the land use appears likely to be treated in a neutral and detached manner just as any other land use permit for a use potentially inconsistent with a district's character.

Renton demonstrates the United States Supreme Court's approach to adult entertainment, which can be singled out for extraordinary regulation, including a definition of permissible entertainment that would appear to stop far short of brothels and sex. Indeed, the definition of obscenity set out in *Miller v. California*, 413 U.S. 15 (1973), (1) whether the average person, applying contemporary community standards, would find that the work, taken as a whole, appeals to the prurient interest; (2) whether the work depicts or describes, in a patently offensive way, sexual conduct specifically defined by the applicable state law; and (3) whether the work, taken as a whole, lacks serious literary, artistic, political, or scientific value presents another, albeit vague standard for what speech may be published. Movies, books, magazines, and computer generation may be prohibited. In *City of Erie v. PAP's A.M.*, 529 U.S. 277 (2000), upholding ordinances barring public nudity as applied to all or partially nude dancing demonstrates even greater deference for local regulatory control:

City of Renton v. Playtime Theaters, Inc.

475 U.S. 41 (1985)

JUSTICE REHNQUIST delivered the opinion of the Court....

In May 1980, the Mayor of Renton, a city of approximately 32,000 people located just south of Seattle, suggested to the Renton City Council that it consider the advisability of enacting zoning legislation dealing with adult entertainment uses. No such uses existed in the city at that time. Upon the Mayor's suggestion, the City Council referred the matter to the City's Planning and Development Committee. The Committee held public hearings, reviewed the experiences of Seattle and other cities, and received a report from the City Attorney's Office advising as to developments in other cities....

In April 1981, acting on the basis of the Planning and Development Committee's recommendation, the City Council enacted Ordinance No. 3526. The ordinance prohibited any "adult motion picture theater" from locating within 1000 feet of any residential zone, single- or multiple-family dwelling, church, or park, and within one mile of any school. The term "adult motion picture theater" was defined as "[a]n enclosed building used for presenting motion picture films, video cassettes, cable television, or any other such visual media, distinguished or characteri[zed] by an emphasis on matter depicting, describing or relating to 'specified sexual activities' or 'specified anatomical areas'...for observation by patrons therein."

In early 1982, respondents acquired two existing theaters in downtown Renton, with the intention of using them to exhibit feature-length adult films. The theaters were located within the area proscribed by Ordinance No. 3526. At about the same time, respondents filed the previously mentioned lawsuit challenging the ordinance on First and Fourteenth Amendment grounds, and seeking declaratory and injunctive relief. While the federal action was pending, the City Council amended the ordinance in several respects, adding a statement of reasons for its enactment and reducing the minimum distance from any school to 1000 feet....The Renton ordinance...does not ban adult theaters altogether, but merely provides that such theaters may not be located within 1000 feet of any residential zone, single- or multiple-family dwelling, church, park, or school. The ordinance is therefore properly analyzed as a form of time, place, and manner regulation.

Describing the ordinance as a time, place, and manner regulation is, of course, only the first step in our inquiry. This Court has long held that regulations enacted for the purpose of restraining speech on the basis of its content presumptively violate the First Amendment. On the other hand, so-called "content-neutral" time, place, and manner regulations are acceptable so long as they are designed to serve a substantial governmental interest and do not unreasonably limit alternative avenues of communication....

At first glance, the Renton ordinance...does not appear to fit neatly into either the "content-based" or the "content-neutral" category. To be sure, the ordinance treats theaters that specialize in adult films differently from other kinds of theaters. Nevertheless, as the District Court concluded, the Renton ordinance is aimed not at the *content* of the films shown at "adult motion picture theatres," but rather at the *secondary effects* of such theaters on the surrounding community. The District Court found that the City Council's "*predominate* concerns" were with the secondary effects of adult theaters, and not with the content of adult films themselves....

It is a familiar principle of constitutional law that this Court will not strike down an otherwise constitutional statute on the basis of an alleged illicit legislative motive....

...What motivates one legislator to make a speech about a statute is not necessarily what motivates scores of others to enact it, and the stakes are sufficiently high for us to eschew guesswork.

The District Court's finding as to "predominate" intent, left undisturbed by the Court of Appeals, is more than adequate to establish that the city's pursuit of its zoning interests here was unrelated to the suppression of free expression. The ordinance by its terms is designed to prevent crime, protect the city's retail trade, maintain property values, and generally "protec[t] and preserv[e] the quality of [the city's] neighborhoods, commercial districts, and the quality of urban life," not to suppress the expression of unpopular views. As JUSTICE POWELL observed in *American Mini Theatres*, "[i]f [the city] had been concerned with restricting the message purveyed by adult theaters, it would have tried to close them or restrict their number rather than circumscribe their choice as to location." In short, the Renton ordinance is completely consistent with our definition of "content-neutral" speech regulations as those that "are *justified* without reference to the content of the regulated speech." The ordinance does not contravene the fundamental principle that underlies our concern about "content-based" speech regulations: that "government may not grant the use of a forum to people whose views it finds acceptable, but deny use to those wishing to express less favored or more controversial views."...

The appropriate inquiry in this case, then, is whether the Renton ordinance is designed to serve a substantial governmental interest and allows for reasonable alternative avenues of communication. It is clear that the ordinance meets such a standard....

The Court of Appeals ruled, however, that because the Renton ordinance was enacted without the benefit of studies specifically relating to "the particular problems or needs of Renton," the city's justifications for the ordinance were "conclusory and speculative." We think the Court of Appeals imposed on the city an unnecessarily rigid burden of proof. The record in this case reveals that Renton relied heavily on the experience of, and studies produced by, the city of Seattle. In Seattle, as in Renton, the adult theater zoning ordinance was aimed at preventing the secondary effects caused by the presence of even one such theater in a given neighborhood. The opinion of the Supreme Court of Washington in *Northend Cinema*, which was before the Renton City Council when it enacted the ordinance in question here, described Seattle's experience as follows:

The amendments to the City's zoning code which are at issue here are the culmination of a long period of study and discussion of the problems of adult movie theaters in residential areas of the City....[T]he City's Department of Community Development made a study of the need for zoning controls of adult theaters....The study analyzed the City's zoning scheme, comprehensive plan, and land uses around existing adult motion picture theaters....

[T]he [trial] court heard extensive testimony regarding the history and purpose of these ordinances. It heard expert testimony on the adverse effects of the presence of adult motion picture theaters on neighborhood children and community improvement efforts. The court's detailed findings, which include a finding that the location of adult theaters has a harmful effect on the area and contribute to neighborhood blight, are supported by substantial evidence in the record. The record is replete with testimony regarding the effects of adult movie theater locations on residential neighborhoods.

We hold that Renton was entitled to rely on the experiences of Seattle and other cities, and in particular on the "detailed findings" summarized in the Washington

Supreme Court's *Northend Cinema* opinion, in enacting its adult theater zoning ordinance. The First Amendment does not require a city, before enacting such an ordinance, to conduct new studies or produce evidence independent of that already generated by other cities, so long as whatever evidence the city relies upon is reasonably believed to be relevant to the problem that the city addresses. That was the case here. Nor is our holding affected by the fact that Seattle ultimately chose a different method of adult theater zoning than that chosen by Renton, since Seattle's choice of a different remedy to combat the secondary effects of adult theaters does not call into question either Seattle's identification of those secondary effects or the relevance of Seattle's experience to Renton.

We also find no constitutional defect in the method chosen by Renton to further its substantial interests. Cities may regulate adult theaters by dispersing them, as in Detroit, or by effectively concentrating them, as in Renton. "It is not our function to appraise the wisdom of [the city's] decision to require adult theaters to be separated rather than concentrated in the same areas.... [T]he city must be allowed a reasonable opportunity to experiment with solutions to admittedly serious problems."...

Finally, turning to the question whether the Renton ordinance allows for reasonable alternative avenues of communication, we note that the ordinance leaves some 520 acres, or more than five percent of the entire land area of Renton, open to use as adult theater sites. The District Court found, and the Court of Appeals did not dispute the finding, that the 520 acres of land consists of "[a]mple, accessible real estate," including "acreage in all stages of development from raw land to developed, industrial, warehouse, office, and shopping space that is criss-crossed by freeways, highways, and roads." Respondents argue, however, that some of the land in question is already occupied by existing businesses, that "practically none" of the undeveloped land is currently for sale or lease, and that in general there are no "commercially viable" adult theater sites within the 520 acres left open by the Renton ordinance.... In our view, the First Amendment requires only that Renton refrain from effectively denying respondents a reasonable opportunity to open and operate an adult theater within the city, and the ordinance before us easily meets this requirement....

JUSTICE BRENNAN, with whom JUSTICE MARSHALL joins, dissenting....

The District Court found that the ordinance left 520 acres in Renton available for adult theater sites, an area comprising about five percent of the city. However, the Court of Appeals found that because much of this land was already occupied, "[l]imiting adult theater uses to these areas is a substantial restriction on speech." Many "available" sites are also largely unsuited for use by movie theaters....

Despite the evidence in the record, the Court reasons that time fact "[t]hat respondents must fend for themselves in the real estate market, on an equal footing with other prospective purchasers and lessees, does not give rise to a First Amendment violation." However, respondents are not on equal footing with other prospective purchasers and lessees, but must conduct business under severe restrictions not imposed upon other establishments. The Court also argues that the First Amendment does not compel "the government to ensure that adult theaters, or any other kinds of speech-related businesses for that matter, will be able to obtain sites at bargain prices." However, respondents do not ask Renton to guarantee low-price sites for their businesses, but seek only a reasonable opportunity to operate adult theaters in the city. By denying them this opportunity, Renton can effectively ban a form of protected speech from its borders.

* * *

Notes and Comments

1. *Secondary Effects.* The Court in *Renton* avoided the application of traditional First Amendment doctrine, adopting a theory that the city was not restricting expressive activities because of their content but rather was utilizing zoning to prevent "secondary effects" of the theaters. Under this theory, police powers may be exercised to avoid crime, acts of moral turpitude, or neighborhood deterioration despite the "mere" incidental burden on expression. Because under *Renton* the community is not responsible for any study of these secondary effects, it appears that the Court actually is applying the most deferential of scrutiny levels typically applied in social and economic regulation reviewed under equal protection and substantive due process. For example, could a city prohibit a march because of the "secondary effects" in the form of huge costs of cleanup and policing together with the disruption of the primary use of streets and parks? Could a speaker be silenced because of the "secondary effect" fear that members of the audience would become violent or because groups that engage in violence and property destruction may demonstrate? *See* Boos v. Barry, 485 U.S. 312 (1988) (refusal to extend the "secondary effects" doctrine to classic political speech). In holding that the secondary effect may not be the impact of the speaker on the audience, has *Boos* halted extension of the secondary effects, demonstrating that the doctrine has been fashioned to solely relate to adult zoning, allowing content-based discrimination against first amendment-protected non-obscene expression?

2. Was now Chief Justice Rehnquist being honest when he stated in *Renton* that "the Renton ordinance is aimed not at the *content* of the films shown at "adult motion picture theatres," but rather at the *secondary effects* of such theaters on the surrounding community?" Or when he states "The ordinance by its terms is designed to prevent crime, protect the city's retail trade, maintain property values, and generally "protec[t] and preserv[e] the quality of [the city's] neighborhoods, commercial districts, and the quality of urban life," not to suppress the expression of unpopular views?"

3. Is the ordinance a suppression of speech or a reasonable accommodation? Can exhibitors compete in industrial areas with industrial rents? What if the economics of the genre requires old obsolescent theaters to allow a profitable enterprise?

4. How should the operation of a website where viewers could observe people living in a house be treated, particularly where activities may on occasion be R or X-rated? *Voyeur Dorm, L.C. v. City of Tampa*, 121 F. Supp. 2d 1373 (M.D. Fla. 2000) (classified as adult use not permitted in a residence zone), *rev'd*, 265 F.3d 1232 (11th Cir. 2001) (ordinance not intended to cover E-commerce, only where customers in attendance), *cert. denied*, 122 S. Ct. 1172 (2002).

Religion

The law of separation of church under the establishment clause of the First Amendment is in flux as the composition of the Court changes and the Court searches for a unified understanding of the appropriate doctrine. Under the classic *Lemon* test, the

Court searched for a primary secular purpose, that the activity or regulation not have the primary effect of advancing or restricting religion, and that the measure not generate excessive entanglement between church and state. *Lemon v. Kurtzman*, 403 U.S. 602 (1971). Recent cases have diminished the importance of excessive entanglement—a central problem as the Court allows religious groups to come to the legislative trough and lobby legislation and money as any citizen may. *See Agostino v. Felton*, 521 U.S. 203 (1997). The cases have also limited *Lemon* to questions of private and religious school aid. In other cases the Court looks to whether an activity such as a prayer at a school even such as a sporting event *Santa Fe Indep. School Dist. v. Doe*, 530 U.S. 290 (2000) (invalidating student chaplain public address delivered pre-football game payer) or graduation (*Lee v. Weisman*, 505 U.S. 577 (1992)) is likely to have a coercive effect on students likely to be present. In others the Court seems to be looking for whether the government action suggests endorsement of a particular faith, such as by placement of a religious symbol at a religious holiday. *Allegheny County v. Greater Pittsburgh ACLU*, 492 U.S. 573 (1989) (no stand alone nativity scene at courthouse but allowing a more ecumenical display of a menorah, Christmas tree, and liberty memorial). In other cases a contingent of the Court have been willing to allow that which is traditional or historically permissible to define the limits of the clause, such as official celebration of holidays and other ceremonial and symbolic references to religion. *Lynch v. Donnelly*, 465 U.S. 668 (1984) (nativity scene in Christmas display approved).

The law of freedom of religion from the standpoint of the free exercise clause is in a state of disarray and is likely to undergo alteration as the Supreme Court reviews claims and undergoes anticipated personnel changes. The classic interpretation is the test under *Sherbert v. Verner*, 374 U.S. 398 (1963), where the Court applied its strictest scrutiny standard of requiring a compelling state interest and no less restrictive alternative in cases where state law interferes or coerces a religious adherent to avoid the practice of a sacrament or tenet that one holds as central to one's religion. In a classic application, *Wisconsin v. Yoder*, 406 U.S. 205 (1972), the Court held that compulsory education laws requiring school attendance until age 16 were unconstitutional as applied to Amish who reject public school education after age 14, believing that only early education supportive of the agrarian lifestyle was permitted as an obligation of faith.

Although the classic *Sherbert* test as applied in *Yoder* is preserved in narrow cases such as *Sherbert*, where state unemployment benefits had been denied a worker who refused to work on the Sabbath. The test also survives where legislation or government policy targets a specific religious practice. In *Church of the Lukumi Babalu Aye, Inc. v. City of Hialeah*, 508 U.S. 520 (1993), the Court invalidated an ordinance prohibiting ritual animal killing because it was targeted at a religious sect that sacrificed animals.

In the bulk of free exercise conflicts, religious adherents complain about neutral government regulation that impacts on their faith, be it compulsory education laws, store closing hours, or prison hair length standards. In *Employment Division v. Smith*, 494 U.S. 872 (1990), the Court ruled that *Sherbert* no longer applied to regulation of general applicability and that only the legislature could grant religious exemptions. The extraordinary curtailment of religious liberty is definitely a function of the fact that in *Smith* the religious adherents wished to have their religious-based use of a substance classified as a narcotic. The drug element is likely responsible for the Court's overreaction in eliminating the free exercise clause as a source of significant enforceable rights.

The *Smith* ruling contained one additional and significant exception from the devolution principle. The Court will apply the strict scrutiny of *Sherbert* where the claimant can identify an additional fundamental right that is impinged upon along with free exercise of religion. To explain this hybrid principle, the Court pointed to *Yoder*. The Court was clearly not comfortable overruling *Yoder* so instead it created a theory which would be quite unrecognizable to Chief Justice Warren Burger, the author of *Yoder*, that *Yoder* was not a pure free exercise case. Rather, the *Smith* ruling concludes, it was a combination of free exercise and the fundamental right of the parent to direct the upbringing and education of their children that explained the *Yoder* ruling.

Congress was literally shocked by the breadth and rationale of the *Smith* Court and promptly enacted the Religious Freedom Restoration Act of 1993, Pub. L. No. 103-141, 107 Stat. 1488 (1994) (codified at 42 U.S.C. §2000bb-1) ("RFRA"), that specifically reinstituted the *Sherbert* strict scrutiny test in all religious freedom claims.

The validity of the law was raised in a challenge by a church that wanted religious exemption from an historic preservation ordinance. The Supreme Court ruled that RFRA was an attempt of Congress to reinterpret the free exercise in a different manner from the Supreme Court and thus the law was an unconstitutional violation of the separation of powers as only the Court may interpret the Constitution. Ostensibly, the Court's ruling in *City of Boerne v. Flores*, 521 U.S. 507 (1997), invalidating RFRA, as applied to the states, appears to give the green light on historic preservation policy. Congress responded with passage of the Religious Land Use and Institutionalized Persons Act of 2000 (RLUIPA), Pub. L. No. 106-274, 114 Stat. 803, *codified at* 42 U.S.C.A. §§2000cc (Supp. 2001) (imposing identical burdens to RFRA, but limiting applicability to (1) recipients of federal financial assistance, and (2) the activity affects commerce, or where the activity is the result of a local ordinance or statutory scheme granting discretion to make an individualized assessment and discretionary approval of the proposed use. *See* Roman Storzer & Anthony Picarello, Jr., *The Religious Land Use and Institutionalized Persons Act of 2000: A Constitutional Response to Unconstitutional Zoning Practices*, 9 Geo. Mason L. Rev. 929 (2001); Evan Shapiro, Comment, *The Religious Land Use and Institutionalized Persons Act: An Analysis Under the Commerce Clause*, 76 Wash. L. Rev. 1255 (2001) (arguing unconstitutionality as unrelated to interstate commerce or economic activity, and not addressing Section 5 of the Fourteenth Amendment). The following ruling demonstrates how the religious freedom issues can arise in the context of historic preservation of older church buildings:

Church Protection

First Covenant Church of Seattle v. City of Seattle

120 Wash.2d 203, 840 P.2d 174
Supreme Court of Washington, En Banc
Nov. 20, 1992

Dore, Chief Justice....

First Covenant owns the church located at Pike and Bellevue Streets in Seattle. First Covenant uses its church exclusively for religious purposes. The City of Seattle adopted the Landmarks Preservation Ordinance to:

> designate, preserve, [and] protect,...improvements and objects which reflect significant elements of the City's cultural, aesthetic, social, economic, political, architectural, engineering, historic or other heritage....

Seattle Municipal Code (SMC) 25.12.020(B) (1977)...In April 1981, the Board adopted controls to preserve the exterior of the church....

On September 17, 1985, the city council adopted ordinance 112425, which designated First Covenant's church a landmark. The designation ordinance requires that First Covenant get a certificate of approval before it makes certain alterations to the church's exterior. It also provides that:

> [N]othing herein shall prevent any alteration of the exterior when such alterations are necessitated by changes in liturgy, it being understood that the owner is the exclusive authority on liturgy and is the decisive party in determining what architectural changes are appropriate to the liturgy....

First Covenant filed a declaratory judgment action in January 1986. It sought a judgment that the "religious freedom provisions" of the state constitution prohibited application of the Landmarks Preservation Ordinance to active churches and that application of the Landmarks Preservation Ordinance to its church was void.

First Covenant and the City both filed for summary judgment on the free exercise issues....

Language in the *Smith I* and *Smith II* opinions suggests that the *Smith II* rule applies only to free exercise challenges to criminal prohibitions. Other federal and state courts, however, have specifically rejected this argument and concluded that the Smith II holding is not limited to criminal cases. The rule of *Smith II* applies in both civil and criminal cases and may apply in this case if the City's preservation ordinances are neutral and generally applicable.

Smith II states that the "right of free exercise does not relieve an individual of the obligation to comply with a 'valid and neutral law of general applicability....'" First Covenant and the CLS contend that the City's Landmarks Preservation Ordinances are not neutral or generally applicable because the sites, improvements, and objects they govern are arbitrarily selected, and the selection process requires individual evaluation of each building, site, or improvement....

The designation criteria of SMC 25.12 is neutral. It applies to "[a]n object, site or improvement which is more than twenty-five (25) years old" and meets the designation criteria. SMC 25.12.350....Designation ordinance 112425, however, is not neutral. It alludes to religious facilities in the two references to "liturgy". Because the Landmarks Preservation Ordinances specifically refer to religious facilities, they are not "neutral."

The landmark ordinances must also be "generally applicable" laws. Justice Scalia contrasted "generally applicable" tax laws with statutes that contain "a system of individualized exceptions", that "create...a mechanism for individualized exemptions" or that lend themselves to "individualized governmental assessment" of the conduct governed. The landmark ordinances at issue here are unlike a general tax law because they invite individualized assessments of the subject property and the owner's use of such property, and contain mechanisms for individualized exceptions....The City's Landmarks Preservation Ordinance is not generally applicable....

The rule in *Smith II* also does not apply because First Covenant's claim presents a "hybrid situation". The cases upon which the Supreme Court relied when it formulated the "hybrid claim" exception, as well as other authority, support the view that a "hybrid" case is one in which a single claim encompasses several protected interests. The Church's claim is "hybrid" because designation not only violates First Covenant's right to freely exercise religion, it infringes on First Covenant's rights to free speech.

"Speech" includes nonverbal conduct if the conduct is "sufficiently imbued with elements of communication." There must be "[an] intent to convey a particularized message" and a great "likelihood... that the message would be understood by those who view it.'"

First Covenant claims, and no one disputes, that its church building itself "is an expression of Christian belief and message" and that conveying religious beliefs is part of the building's function. First Covenant reasons that when the State controls the architectural "proclamation" of religious belief inherent in its church's exterior it effectively burdens religious speech. We agree with First Covenant's reasoning. The relationship between theological doctrine and architectural design is well recognized. The exterior and the interior of the structure are inextricably related. When, as in this case, both are "freighted with religious meaning" that would be understood by those who view it, then the regulation of the church's exterior impermissibly infringes on the religious organization's right to free exercise and free speech....

Applying the Sherbert "compelling interest" test, we address the church's contention that subjecting it to the controls of the Landmarks Preservation Ordinance burdens its right to freely exercise religion.... The First Amendment absolutely protects the freedom to believe, but conduct, even when religiously motivated, is not totally free of government regulation.

Government regulation is constitutional either if it does not infringe constitutional rights of free exercise, or if any burden on free exercise, direct or indirect, is justified by a compelling state interest in the regulation of subject matter within the State's power to regulate. The party who alleges that state action restrains his free exercise of religion must "show the coercive effect of the enactment as it operates against him in the practice of his religion." If a party establishes such an infringement on his right to free exercise, the Court will subject the infringement to strict scrutiny. The State then must establish that some compelling state interest justifies the infringement and that the enactment is the least restrictive means to achieve the State's end.

The City's ordinances, as this court held earlier, impermissibly burden First Covenant's right to free exercise in two ways. The ordinances burden free exercise "administratively" because they require that First Covenant seek the approval of a government body before it alter the exterior of its house of worship, whether or not the alteration is for a religious reason. Further, they burden First Covenant financially, because they reduce the value of the Church's property by almost half.

The City urges that the "liturgy exemption" alleviates any burden on the exercise of religion. We do not believe that the exemption cures either the "administrative" or the financial infringements of First Covenant's right to free exercise.

First, the plain and ordinary meaning of the term "liturgy", which we employ absent a statutory definition of that term, does not provide a workable standard that protects the constitutional rights of the church. "Liturgy" is a "rite or series of rites, observances, or procedures prescribed for public worship in the Christian church in accordance with authorized or standard form." "Liturgy" essentially refers to prescribed conduct that occurs within the structure. The liturgy-focused exemption in this case is constitutionally infirm because it allows the City to control any nonliturgical elements of religious conduct that require architectural change. Further, as we previously observed:

> Would a wider door to permit access by handicapped parishioners comprise a liturgical change? Although...widening the door does not relate directly to the rites or procedures of worship in the church, it does facilitate the ability of disabled persons to participate in religious services and activities. The anomalies created by the liturgy exception are cumbersome and would result in...delays in carrying out routine church work.

Secondly, adopting the City's interpretation of the phrase "necessitated by changes in liturgy" as meaning "for religious purposes" does not resolve the ambiguity. The City still has the right to determine what is or what is not for a religious purpose and it acknowledged at argument that it reserved the right to determine if the 'religious purpose' claim was bona fide....

Finally, the liturgy exemption does not mitigate the financial burden that designation imposes on First Covenant. Regardless of how the exemption is construed, the Church suffers the same dramatic depreciation in the value of its property and principal asset. In sum, the liturgy exemption does not cure the infringement of free exercise by the Landmarks Preservation Ordinance....

We hold that the City's interest in preservation of esthetic and historic structures is not compelling and it does not justify the infringement of First Covenant's right to freely exercise religion. The possible loss of significant architectural elements is a price we must accept to guarantee the paramount right of religious freedom....

Washington, like all the states, may provide greater protection for individual rights, based on its "'sovereign right to adopt in its own Constitution individual liberties more expansive than those conferred by the Federal Constitution.'"...

Article 1, section 11, of the Washington State Constitution provides that:

> Absolute freedom of conscience in all matters of religious sentiment, belief, and worship, shall be guaranteed to every individual, and no one shall be molested or disturbed in person or property on account of religion; but the liberty of conscience hereby secured shall not be so construed as to excuse acts of licentiousness or justify practices inconsistent with the peace and safety of the state.

The first amendment to the United States Constitution provides in part: Congress shall make no law respecting an establishment of religion, or prohibiting the free exercise thereof....

The language of our state constitution is significantly different and stronger than the federal constitution. The First Amendment limits government action that "prohibits" free exercise. Our state provision "absolutely" protects freedom of worship and bars conduct that merely "disturbs" another on the basis of religion. Any action that is not licentious or inconsistent with the "peace and safety" of the state is "guaranteed" protection.

Our state constitutional and common law history support a broader reading of article 1, section 11, than of the First Amendment....

Finally, the majority in *Smith II* accepts the fact that its rule places minority religions at a disadvantage. Our court, conversely, has rejected the idea that a political majority may control a minority's right of free exercise through the political process....

We conclude that imposing the City's Landmarks Preservation Ordinance on First Covenant's church violates First Covenant's right to free exercise of religion under article 1, section 11 of our state constitution....

Dolliver, Justice (dissenting)....

The Landmarks Preservation Ordinance and its implementing ordinance, like the criminal prohibition against peyote use in *Smith II*, are neutral, generally applicable laws which do not involve other constitutional protections. The ordinances apply neutrally and generally to protect an object, site or improvement which is more than 25 years old and which "has significant character, interest or value, as part of the development, heritage or cultural characteristics of the City, state, or nation." While the landmark ordinances will affect many religious buildings because of their social and cultural importance, this does not demonstrate a lack of neutrality or general applicability. Indeed, the majority admits the designation criteria in the Landmarks Preservation Ordinance are neutral.

The majority, however, asserts the implementing ordinance's two references to "liturgy", which provide an exemption for religiously motivated exterior changes, transform the otherwise neutral ordinance into a non-neutral one. The irony, even the perversity, of this position is apparent. The Court in *Smith II* recognized the role the political process could and has played by providing exemptions in generally applicable laws for religiously motivated practices. *Smith II*. Particularly, the Court endorsed legislatures which had made, even though it was not constitutionally required, "nondiscriminatory religious-practice exemption[s]" in their criminal drug laws for "sacramental peyote use." *Smith II*. In this case, the Landmarks Preservation Ordinance makes no reference to religious facilities. Only the implementing ordinance, which must necessarily focus on the designated church site, is deemed not neutral because of its exception for liturgically required exterior changes. Yet, the majority uses this exemption as the reason the landmark ordinances fail the neutrality test! Incredible. This is bootstrapping of the most egregious nature....

* * *

Notes and Comments

1. Is *First Covenant* consistent with *Smith*? Does it appear to be a parody demonstrating the *Smith* deficiencies? Could a community ever regulate the height of a steeple or exterior facade design? Could a house of worship in an historic district be required to conform to a uniform materials code? *First Covenant* does demonstrate that state courts may be more amenable to individual rights claims than some federal courts. Chapter 15 includes a discussion of how church politics led to California authorizing local religion-affiliated entities exemption from historic preservation laws.

2. How would *First Covenant* be resolved under RLUIPA? In *C.L.U.B. v. City of Chicago*, 157 F. Supp. 2d 903 (N.D. Ill. 2001), the court sustained a scheme allowing a church as of right in residential districts but requiring a special use permit in business and commercial districts. The court summarily rejected the reasoning of *First Covenant* that the church construction is somehow protected by freedom of expression. Although the churches claimed that the zoning scheme violated RLUIPA, the court found that the amended zoning scheme established no expressive burden on religion requiring strict scrutiny. Does the ruling suggest that traditional special exception review of church siting is consistent with the law?

In addition to zoning problems in tension with the free exercise and obligation to separate church and state, there is also the possibility that communities may discriminate against churches that do not represent mainstream popular local religions:

Islamic Center of Mississippi, Inc. v. City of Starkville, Mississippi

840 F.2d 293
United States Court of Appeals, Fifth Circuit
March 23, 1988.

Alvin B. Rubin, Circuit Judge:

The first amendment to the Constitution begins: "Congress shall make no law respecting an establishment of religion, or prohibiting the free exercise thereof." These provisions, made applicable to the states by the due process clause of the fourteenth amendment, forbid government to burden the free exercise of any religion or to favor one religion over another.

The zoning ordinance of the City of Starkville, Mississippi, prohibits the use of buildings as churches in all of the areas within the city limits near the campus of the University of Mississippi unless an exception is granted by the City Board of Aldermen. There is no church in any part of the City in which churches are permitted as of right. The Islamic Center, which owns a building situated in a residential area immediately adjacent to property being used as a church by another faith, challenges the Board's refusal to permit it to use its property for public worship services. While the city ordinance restricts the use of any property in this type of residential area or in the City's commercial district as a church, 25 churches, all Christian, are located in similarly regulated areas. Sixteen of these churches occupied their present sites before the ordinance became effective, and nine moved in thereafter with the benefit of an exception. Only the Islamic Center has ever been denied an exception. Because the City has failed to establish that the Board of Aldermen based its denial of an exception to the Islamic Center on a sufficient reason or that it has not favored Christian churches over Muslim mosques, we hold the Board's action violates the free exercise of religion clause.

Part of the campus of Mississippi State University, at which 11,663 students are enrolled, is within the eastern section of the city limits of the City of Starkville, Mississippi, and the remainder of the University campus is east of the City, which has a resident population of 15,169, only slightly more than the student population. Among the students at the University are a small number of Muslims, about 15 to 18 families, 35 to 50 individuals. The Muslim faith is demanding for the pious, requiring five prayers a day on a schedule fixed by the solar calendar: before sunrise, at noon, before sunset, after sunset, and when night has fallen. While the City urges that public performance of these prayers is not necessary, one of the few primary duties of the faithful Muslim is to say prayers at the prescribed times, preferably in a mosque or *masjid,* a place of prostration. Friday is a holy day, much like Sunday to Christians or Saturday to Jews, and all Muslim males should attend prayer in the mosque, where the imam, the religious leader, leads the prayers and delivers a midday sermon.

There was no mosque at the University, so in 1977 the Muslim students formed the Islamic Center of Mississippi, Inc., to provide group worship opportunities to Muslim students and the few Muslim faculty members. In 1982, still lacking an established place for worship, members of the Islamic Center appointed a search committee to locate a building that they could use as a mosque. Because few of the Muslim students had cars, the committee sought a site within walking distance of the campus.

The search committee first located a building that might be suitable for Muslim worship at 212 South Nash Street, in Starkville. Knowing of the City's zoning ordinance, the chairman of the search committee, Mohamed Shwehdi, wrote to Larry Bell, the City's building codes official and its liaison representative with the Planning Commission, about the site. Bell told Shwehdi that the location would not be approved because of inadequate parking. The committee then wrote again, proposing a building at 525 University Drive, which appeared to have adequate space for parking and was located across the street from a church. The Planning Commission rejected the committee's request for permission to use this site because of the heavy traffic on University Drive. Shwehdi conferred with Bell informally from time to time about other sites. Bell informed him on each occasion that the site would not pass Planning Commission muster, so the Committee did not seek approval of these locations. In April, 1983, the Committee made its third written request, this time for permission to use property at the corner of Jarnigan Street and Lumas Drive, across the street from a church. Again Bell told Shwehdi that the use of this location for a church would not be approved because it created too much traffic congestion. The Islamic Center's proposal of a site at 523 University Drive met the same reception.

Shwehdi then met with Bell and the Planning Commission and asked "exactly where we can locate." Bell did not testify at the trial, but Shwehdi testified that at this meeting Shwehdi suggested a house situated at 204 Herbert Street, which is only slightly more than one block from the University campus. He testified that Bell responded, "excellent location. If you can buy it," believing that the property was not for sale. According to Shwehdi, the Commissioners agreed that if the Islamic Center could purchase the Herbert Street property and supply the parking the city ordinance required, they would recommend that the Board of Aldermen approve the site. Representatives of the Islamic Center sought out the owner and bought the property in September, 1983.

Pursuant to Bell's instructions, the Islamic Center then prepared a schematic drawing showing the location of the existing structure at 204 Herbert Street and the proposed parking area, 18 spaces. Shwehdi submitted this to the Planning Commission, which recommended approval. Shwehdi then went to the City office to obtain a building permit to make the necessary improvements. The person who issued permits at first refused his request because the building was not approved for congregational worship. Bell and the city electrical inspector instructed her to issue the permit, so she did, designating the use as "commercial," but the next day she telephoned Shwehdi and told him to return the permit. She then changed the specified use to "residential."

The City's zoning ordinance requires final approval by the Board of Aldermen of the use of property for a church when that use requires an exception to the provisions of the ordinance. Consequently, the Planning Commission submitted its recommendation to the Board for approval. On November 22, 1983, Shwehdi received a telephone call from a reporter who worked for a television station, informing him that the Board of Aldermen would consider the Islamic Center's request that evening and that, because of neighborhood opposition, the Board would likely reject the recommendation.

Shwehdi therefore attended the meeting. Bell recommended that the Board grant the exception, but a neighborhood resident, representing property owners in the area, spoke in opposition. According to the minutes of the meeting, the resident based his opposition on "congestion, parking, and traffic problems" in the neighborhood. The Board then voted unanimously to deny the exception without, so far as its minutes show, giving any reasons. Shwehdi asked to be heard, and the Board permitted him to make a statement, but this did not alter the Board's decision. The City did not communicate further with the Islamic Center, but thereafter the City's fire and electrical inspection officers inspected the building and approved its conformity with their requirements for a place for worship.

The Islamic Center made the proposed renovations to the Herbert Street building and began to use it as both a student residence and a place for worship. Seven months later, in June, 1984, City Manager P.C. McLaurin, Jr., wrote to Shwehdi stating that the neighbors were complaining about the use of the Herbert Street property. The Muslims received this letter immediately after Ramadan, the holiest month of the year in the Muslim calendar and the time of greatest activity at the Herbert Street Center. Shwehdi testified without contradiction that, in a conference with him and another member of the Islamic Center, McLaurin suggested that the Muslims "cool it down, be quite [sic].... He advised [them] to promote a good relation to the neighbors too."

On October 31, 1984, thirteen months after the Islamic Center had purchased the Herbert Street property and eleven months after the Muslims had completed both the renovations and the installation of off-street parking and started to gather for worship, the City ordered the Islamic Center to stop holding worship services there. After this suit was filed, however, the City agreed to permit continued use of the Center for worship until the case is decided.

City Manager McLaurin described the neighborhood surrounding 204 Herbert Street as "a residential area undergoing a considerable amount of stress at the moment in the sense that you have had a transition from single family homes... into multi-family, apartment development, duplexes, tri-plexes, this type of thing. Some would say a downgrading of the area." A commercial purveyor of take-out pizza and about 100 units of student housing are located in the vicinity.

The building at 204 Herbert Street is a modest frame structure that was used as a single-family residence before the Islamic Center bought it. A photograph introduced in evidence shows that it is a low-cost one-story residence and its exterior is in a poor state of repair. The Muslims presently use part of the building for worship services and part for housing students. Members enter through the rear door.

Next door to the Islamic Center is an impressive brick two-story building, graced by stately white columns and a broad veranda, once occupied as a fraternity house. This is now Maranatha House, a residence and worship center for a Pentecostal Christian denomination. Five more churches lie within a quarter mile of these two religious centers.

It is not clear from the record when the Maranatha House group began to occupy its Herbert Street property. While City officials have treated its use as if it were grandfathered in as a nonconforming use when the City adopted its original zoning ordinance in 1969, Pete Melby, a neighborhood resident who was called as a witness by the City, testified that the A.T.O. fraternity, not a church, occupied the building in 1969 when the original ordinance went into effect. Melby sought to distinguish Maranatha House on a basis not urged by the City: it is not a church because "it says on the sign" that Maranatha House is a student organization. However, worship services take place at Maranatha House on a regular basis. Indeed, the most heavily attended services at Maranatha House attract more than twice as many persons as the most heavily attended services at the Islamic Center.

Maranatha House has only eight off-street parking spaces, while the Islamic Center provides eighteen off-street parking spaces for its smaller group. All of the Islamic Center congregants who have cars park in the parking spaces provided. Because Maranatha House has insufficient parking spaces, many persons who come to its services park on the streets and sometimes block the Islamic Center driveway.

The Muslim worship ceremony is not obtrusive. As the district court found, noise from services is not audible outside the Islamic Center, and neither singing nor amplified preaching occurs during the service. In contrast, the district court found, noise is often a problem during Maranatha House services due to the size of the congregation, which includes about one hundred members, the playing of tambourines and other instruments, and the use of amplifiers and loudspeakers in the course of preaching and singing.

The City adopted its zoning ordinance in 1969 and amended it in 1982. The earlier ordinance is not in the record, so we cannot determine the changes made by the 1982 amendment, but as amended, it provides for 14 types of districts. Five areas are classified R-E, Residential Estate Districts. The ordinance expressly permits property in R-E districts to be used as churches, but none of the City's 26 churches is located in any such district. Four of the five R-E districts are located at the western or northern edges of the City, all beyond easy walking distance of the University campus. The R-E district nearest the university is three miles away.

Until this action came to trial, the City had never interpreted the ordinance as permitting churches to be located anywhere except in an R-E district unless the Board granted an exception. At trial, however, City Manager McLaurin, based on his intention as one of the three persons who had prepared the ordinance, testified that he now interpreted it to allow churches in the C-3 Central Business District. While the district court accepted that nunc pro tunc interpretation, it does not conform to the ordinance, which provides that no use of property other than the types specified as "permitted" or "permitted as an exception" shall be allowed. The statement of uses permitted in R-E districts specifies that property may be used as a "church, but not including missions or revival tents." The "uses permitted" clause for C-3 districts, however, does not mention churches but only "[p]laces of amusement and assembly." Churches are not even mentioned in the C-3 "exceptions" clause, although residences are. On the other hand, the ordinance states that in R-1 Residential Districts churches are permitted as an exception, suggesting inferentially that they are not permitted in the C-3 district even as an exception.

The heaviest concentration of churches in Starkville is on the east side of the City, near the University campus. The land in the five R-E districts is largely undeveloped and includes considerable farm land. The part of the University campus beyond the city limits, however, is bordered on the east side, the side away from the City, by an unzoned county area in which some churches are located.

Excluding Maranatha House and the Islamic Center, 25 churches are located in the City. When the original zoning ordinance was adopted in 1969, sixteen were already established in areas zoned against such use, but a prior-existing-use clause in the ordinance allowed these to remain. Since 1969, nine churches have applied for permits, or exceptions, to allow their location in areas zoned against church use, and the Board has granted every one of the nine. In response to an interrogatory, "Have you ever denied a zoning exception to a religious group, except the plaintiff's association?" the City answered categorically, "No." The nine churches granted exceptions, the sixteen churches established before the 1969 ordinance, and Maranatha House all serve as worship centers for Christian denominations.

The Islamic Center contends that the zoning ordinance is invalid on its face because it forces Muslims to worship in the least acceptable parts of the City or in the county outside the City's boundaries, that the City's action in denying it an exception violates its members' right to free exercise of their religion, and that the Board's action was arbitrary, thus denying it and its members due process.

The City maintains that the ordinance does not inhibit the free exercise of religion because churches may be built either in the R-E districts or outside the city limits. It maintains that the Board's refusal to grant an exception for the Herbert Street location is based on a secular purpose, visiting only an incidental burden on religion. College View Street, which intersects with Herbert Street, is a main traffic artery to and from the University. It is 24 feet wide. Four-way stop signs mark the intersection of Herbert and College View. College View dead-ends at Nash Street, one block to the west of the intersection. An enormous amount of traffic turns onto Herbert Street from College View to gain access to U.S. Highway 82, which is located one long block to the north of the intersection. There are no sidewalks on Herbert Street, and on-street parking is not permitted. The Chief of City Police described the intersection of College View Drive and Herbert Street as a "hot spot" for accidents. A member of the Board of Aldermen testified that the Board denied the exception for the Islamic Center because of concerns about traffic congestion and neighborhood safety.

In the part of its opinion entitled "Conclusions of Law," the district court stated that "congregational prayer for Muslims is desirable, but not mandatory. The city ordinance...does not infringe upon an individual's right or ability to turn toward Mecca and pray at the specified times during each day." The court also observed, "The Starkville city ordinance does not preclude students from purchasing cars and driving to a worship site located in an R-E district or walking to a site located in the Oktibbeha County section of land which is adjacent to the MSU campus' [sic] eastern boundary." This land is, of course, outside the Starkville city limits. The court dwelt upon whether...the City might be held liable in damages for the acts of its agents, but the Islamic Center had dropped any claim for damages before trial and asked only for a declaratory judgment and that the City and its officers be enjoined from interfering with the use of the Herbert Street property as a mosque. Finally, the court concluded, "Standing alone, the denial of the Herbert Street zoning application is not enough upon which to base an inference of discrimination....The actions of the Board were supported by valid traffic considerations, and there is no evidence to suggest that it improperly considered plaintiffs' religion in reaching its decision." Therefore the ordinance did not infringe upon the Islamic students' right to free exercise of religion. The district court then held the zoning ordinance had not violated substantive due process because it was a legitimate exercise of the City's police power, not clearly arbitrary or unreasonable and having a substantial relation to the public safety or general welfare.

Regulatory statutes or ordinances that affect religious activity are constitutional so long as they impose no undue burden on the ability of the church or its members to carry out the observances of their faith. The district court's opinion and the City's brief both suggest that application of the zoning ordinance to the Islamic Center places no burden on it or its members because they can establish a mosque within walking distance of the campus outside the city limits or buy cars and ride to more distant places within the City. The suggestion is reminiscent of Anatole France's comment on the majestic equality of the law that forbids all men, the rich as well as the poor, to sleep under bridges, to beg in the streets, and to steal bread. Laws that make churches, synagogues, and mosques accessible only to those affluent enough to travel by private automobile obviously burden the exercise of religion by the poor, a class that includes many students. And a city may not escape the constitutional protection afforded against its actions by protesting that those who seek an activity it forbids may find it elsewhere. By making a mosque relatively inaccessible within the city limits to Muslims who lack automobile transportation, the City burdens their exercise of their religion.

The Constitution does not, however, forbid all governmental regulation that imposes an incidental burden on worship by making the free exercise of religion more difficult or more expensive. The government may subject individuals and religious organizations to religiously neutral regulation exercised for a secular governmental purpose, such as fire inspection, building, and zoning regulations. Once it has been established that an ordinance burdens religious exercise, however, the government must offer evidence of an overriding interest to justify its application of the ordinance....

The assembly of a community of believers is an integral part of most religious faiths, certainly of the Muslim. The assembly of those bound by common beliefs and observances not only serves to create a sense of community among the members through the shared expression of their beliefs, it also communicates to outsiders the church's identity as a group devoted to a common ideal. By group worship, each worshipper communicates to outsiders the identity of the group and his own identity as a member of it, a form of self-expression. Ritual preserves, evidences, and perpetuates faith. If government exercises its power to affect group worship, it must demonstrate at least that the burden imposed serves an important government purpose and also that this purpose could not be accompanied by a means less burdensome to the exercise of religion....

The burden placed on relatively impecunious Muslim students by the Starkville ordinance is more than incidental, and the ordinance leaves no practical alternatives for establishing a mosque in the city limits. There is no other place in the City within reasonable distance from the campus where the students may establish a place of worship, and the ordinance forbids the use of property they already own for worship services.

The City's approval of applications for zoning exceptions by other churches suggests that it did not treat all applicants alike. This undermines the City's contention that the Board denied a zoning exception to the Muslims solely for the purposes of traffic control and public safety.

The City has never enforced its ordinance against Maranatha House, with a membership twice as large as the Islamic Center, even though its services are audible from the street, it has only half as many parking spaces as the Islamic Center, and it is located on the same allegedly congested street next door to the Islamic Center. The City has not apparently interfered with parking of cars on the street by those attending Maranatha House, although it argues that on-street parking is not permitted on Herbert Street.

While lines must be drawn at some point, and, when traffic is congested, a few more cars may aggravate a bad situation, just as a final straw may break a camel's back, the City has advanced no rational basis other than neighborhood opposition to show why the exception granted all other religious centers was denied the Islamic Center. As the Supreme Court observed in *City of Cleburne v. Cleburne Living Center,* an equal protection case, neighbors' negative attitudes or fears, unsubstantiated by factors properly cognizable in a zoning proceeding, are not a permissible basis for treating a home for the mentally retarded differently from other group or multi-unit housing institutions. There is even less justification for differentiating between familiar and unfamiliar religions. "Private biases may be outside the reach of the law, but the law cannot, directly or indirectly, give them effect."

Professor Laurie Reynolds has suggested that courts should require that ordinances requiring special use permits or exceptions for the use of property as churches contain specific, religiously neutral standards to reduce the likelihood of abuse and to require uniformity in the allocation of burdens on religious applicants. It is not necessary for us to go so far. The record makes it clear that the City did not act in a religiously neutral manner when it rejected an exception for the Islamic Center....

For these reasons the judgment is REVERSED. This Court declares the ordinance unconstitutional as applied to the Islamic Center and enjoins the City of Starkville from enforcing the ordinance against the use of the property at 204 Herbert Street for public worship.

* * *

Notes and Comments

1. Judge Rubin's opinion is largely based on a pre-*Smith* free exercise analysis. Would the result remain the same if the court used an equal protection religion-based discrimination claim? Chapter 12 discusses discrimination in the land use regulatory system.

Chapter 9

Other Models for Land Use Decisionmaking: Alternatives to Contemporary Administrative and Legislative Zoning and Judicial Review

> Land is a commodity that justifies as much or a greater degree of public overview and private accountability as does telephone service, or the sale of liquor, or wharfingering. Perhaps the time has come to replace exotic proposals with some old-fashioned ideas that have been applied for generations to the regulation of transactions in other commodities far less affected with the public interest than is land.
>
> Richard F. Babcock, Billboards, Glass Houses and the Law 178 (1977)

This chapter addresses some of the larger concerns and criticism about land use control systems. Those on the development side often criticize the extraordinary discretion of the regulators, the political nature of planning controls, the cost of bureaucratic delay, and the rigid, typically low density zoning that prevents the development of anything but traditional suburban subdivisions typically marketed exclusively to the affluent. Advocates for the poor or the environment would argue that the political system is dominated by suburban home building development interests and the current systems fail to generate an adequate supply of affordable housing that is accessible to employment, shopping, health care, and recreation and fails to assure a pattern of development that is the least damaging to the environment.

In the United States, the specter of litigation always hangs over development projects and the added expense of litigation and the delays it engenders create another official bureaucratic level of development review. There is always the danger that litigation can result in a ruling or settlement that may not satisfy the interests of the parties much less the interest of those who are not participants such as environmentalists or the poor. Litigation may also discourage regulators from aggressively protecting the public interest for fear of litigation and exposure to extensive liability should a court conclude that growth management exceeds the police power or constitutes a taking.

Ballot Box Zoning

One alternative policy that appears to be gaining in popularity is "ballot box zoning." Citizens are increasingly going to the initiative and referendum election machinery available in many states. Rezoning and replanning may be carried out through a popular vote on an initiative measure placed on the ballot through a petition drive. *DeVita v. County of Napa*, 889 P.2d 1019 (Cal. 1995). This process can take development authority away from the planning boards and legislative bodies. In other instances, voters have gone to the referendum process, requiring certain controversial developments, such as a land fill or sports stadium, or simply a zone change to be submitted to the voters. *Fritz v. City of Kingman*, 957 P.2d 337 (Ariz. 1998). Under such a scheme, legislation to become effective must be submitted to a public vote following the public approval process or zone amendment. While the initiative or referendum empowers the voting majority and can result in significant enhanced protection for the environment, there is a price. The initiative as well as the referendum vote may not reflect rational scientific planning that should be the basis for land use planning decisions. The majority may have a narrow interest as well. Down-zoning or zoning amendments to thwart higher density development may exacerbate the problem of suburban sprawl sending growth leapfrogging to the next jurisdiction amenable to growth, and may discourage the development of affordable housing. There exists some evidence suggesting that ballot box zoning imposes additional costs on development. *See* Samuel R. Staley, *Ballot-Box Zoning, Transaction Costs, and Urban Growth*, 67 J. Am. Plan. Ass'n 25 (2001) (election-generated growth controls carry negative impacts of higher costs). Despite the inherent opportunity for irrational decisionmaking, the institution has been endorsed by the United States Supreme Court. In *City of Eastlake v. Forest City Enterprises, Inc.*, 426 U.S. 668 (1976), the Court upheld an Ohio town charter that required a 55 percent referendum vote as a condition for a zone change. The tension between developers and environmentalists is likely to generate ever-wider uses of the initiative and referendum processes where powerful groups are unable to capture the official planning process. Developers are also using the process as in Oregon where conservative landowners groups successfully enacted Measure 7 that requires compensation for any devaluation of property values, a measure that would scuttle the state's forward looking smart growth planning initiative such as the use of urban growth boundaries. Measure 7 is set out in Chapter 7. As a strategy, all groups may look to the initiative and referenda ballot box zoning option, yet it has a potential downside that must be seriously considered before its endorsement as an improved form of planning and development control. Homeowners may seek to insulate themselves from growth, density, and the poor, developers may seek a free hand with development and a reduced infrastructure finance burden. Environmentalists may seek protection of specific ecosystems and habitats and ignore the larger regional environmental needs of increasing access and revitalizing declining urban areas. *See* Daniel Selmi, *Reconsidering the Use of Direct Democracy in Making Land Use Decisions*, 19 UCLA J. Envtl. L. & Pol'y 293 (2001/2002) (criticizing the application of *Eastlake* to individual lot rezoning, but endorsing the mechanism for certain policy issues).

Private Regulation

Another obvious alternative to public planning authority would be the utilization of private land contracts or restrictive covenants that would limit the use and intensity of land, taking precedence over inconsistent and often less restrictive zoning or planning permission. These covenants, typically in the form of subdivision covenants, conditions, and regulations (CC & Rs), have proven effective in maintaining the residential, usually single-family detached or condominium communities that have been the target of such covenants. It is likely, however, that those neighborhoods were immune from unfriendly rezoning because of the political power held by homeowner associations, particularly in the American suburban setting. The transaction costs involved in an attempt to reform the design of urban planning through grass roots contractual negotiations appear problematic. Given the likely opposition to the underlying planning principles in a community where the political process has failed to apply such principles, voluntary regulation may be an oxymoron. *See generally* Robert C. Ellickson, *Alternatives to Zoning: Covenants, Nuisance Rules, and Fines as Land Use Controls*, 40 U. Chi. L. Rev. 681 (1973).

Alternative Dispute Resolution

Although not a dramatic replacement of the regulatory system, communities are increasingly utilizing systems of alternative dispute resolution in place of both litigation and a portion of the administrative approval process. Systems of mediation, where a neutral individual works with the parties to find compromise, or arbitration, where the dispute is submitted for a binding decision have long been evolving as an alternative to post-administrative litigation disputes. Increasingly, communities and developers have utilized the development agreement to avoid administrative and litigation disputes. A regulating body and a landowner can through contract spell out the allowable regulation and nature of the development and resolve issues of project conditions, and other infrastructure financing obligations. Fla. Stat. Ann. §§ 163.3223 to 163.3235 (enabling legislation); *Midway Orchards v. County of Butte*, 269 Cal. Rptr. 796 (Ct. App. 1990) (development agreement legislative and filing of referendum petition prevents agreement from becoming effective); David L. Callies, *Developers' Agreements and Planning Gain*, 17 Urb. Law. 599 (1985). While development agreements are a good system to avoid conflicts arising from changing regulations and changing political climates, they do run the risk that what might not be contained in those contracts are adequate provisions to protect the environment, serve the poor, and achieve the optimal planning result. Of course, alternative dispute mechanisms may result in decisions made in a vacuum with the interests of parties not before the mediator or arbitrator not adequately voiced and there is always the possibility that the compromise will fail to meet legal obligations.

British Columbia, Canada has extensively included alternative dispute resolution in its growth management program:

Jeffrey Patterson, *Testing the Partnership Model of Growth Management*,

7 Pacific Rim Law and Policy Journal 721 (1998)

A decade in which regional planning in B.C. lacked authority if not legitimacy gave planners ample opportunity to consider the model of regional planning and growth management that was most appropriate for B.C. and the Lower Mainland. The formal demise of regional planning in 1983 and the previous demise of the LMRPB [predecessor regional planning board] in favour of more de-centralized regional planning by the then four regional districts in the Lower Mainland had made planners and municipal administrators keenly aware of both the potential opposition to imposition of the regional will over local municipalities and the importance of links between the minority municipalities and provincial government, certainly in the GVRD [Greater Vancouver Regional District]. Sentiment was moving towards a model of regional planning that placed greater emphasis on consensus and consensual processes. These were the only forms of planning—loosely defined—that could occur from 1983 to 1995. The Minister after 1993, Darlene Marzari, her ministry (Municipal Affairs) and Lower Mainland officials resolved that a "made-in-B.C." model of regional planning and growth management, a model that addressed and accommodated the fierce localism rampant in local municipalities, would have to be developed. "Growth management" was judged to be preferable to "planning." Local municipalities were responsible for adopting Official Community Plans ("OCP's"), the primary land use planning instrument in B.C., and jealously guarded the planning label.

The model adopted differs from those of other jurisdictions in several respects. The provincial government plays a more minor role than in many other growth management jurisdictions, although its role in delineating agricultural lands and, as is described below, in articulating the regional transportation system, have nevertheless made it more than a minor player in growth management. Further, regional strategic plans, when prepared, must meet the objectives and substantive expectations set forth in detail in the Growth Management Act.

More importantly, regional districts are not able to dictate overall growth management priorities in the face of conflict between the regional strategic plan and the regional context statements of local municipalities. Both parties are bound by the results of one of three binding dispute resolution processes. The minister chooses one of three mechanisms should the parties not be able to agree on one at the pre-resolution stage.

Following the overall regional district model in which the provision of specific services is dependent on the mutual agreement of member municipalities and the board's directors, B.C.'s Growth Strategies Act is largely enabling in character. The Minister of Municipal Affairs may require the preparation of a regional strategic plan. In contrast, under Washington State's 1990 Growth Management Act, plans are mandatory in the largest and fastest growing counties. Also, under the 1973 Oregon Land Conservation and Development Act, growth management is mandatory throughout the state, including the jurisdiction of Metro Portland area established in 1992....

Three municipalities had reservations to the "Livable Region Strategy Plan." Agreements were signed between the three municipalities and the GVRD to mitigate the import of the disagreements until at least after the submission of Regional Context Statements required to be submitted in February 1998. The City of Surrey and the District of Langley expressed concern that the regional strategy plan would impinge on the prerogative of local municipalities over land use decisions in their municipalities. Side agreements with both municipalities enabling adoption of the regional strategy plan clarified that the OCP's and related zoning powers stemming therefrom were the only statutory authority for development. Any challenge to the OCP's of the two municipalities would, of course, have to await a dispute resolution mechanism that might follow the Regional Context Statement submissions in 1998 should they be in conflict with the plan.

The potential disputes between the GVRD and local municipalities present a major challenge to the growth management strategy plan. In the case of Langley District and Surrey, the projected trend population for the two municipalities for 2021 is 175,000 greater than under the strategic plan. Following the trend line would presumably result in increased auto and less transit travel than projected in the plan. It would also potentially undercut the wisdom of the immense transit projects currently planned for the coming decade and place additional burdens on bridge capacity.

The potential challenge to the growth strategy plan will test the resolve of both the provincial government and the directors of the GVRD, the local politicians of the member municipalities. While only a few municipalities are currently challenging the principles underlying the regional strategic plan, the majority of directors appear reluctant to interfere in each other's land use decisions. For instance, in September 1997, the GVRD approved extension of trunk sewer facilities, one of the services for which the regional district is responsible, to serve a part of the suburb of Langley not yet considered ready for development despite recommendations to the contrary from both regional planners and the ALC and despite a requirement in the Growth Strategies Act that requires that all works and services undertaken by a regional district after adoption of a regional growth strategy be consistent with the regional growth strategy. Responding angrily to the planners' report, the mayor of Langley with strong support from the mayor of neighbouring Surrey again reiterated that land use regulation was a municipal, not a regional, function. The chair of the GVRD's strategic planning committee and mayor of Delta, Beth Johnson, indicated that she was concerned that directors had not yet confronted the issue of denying services as a way of forcing urban development in desirable directions....

* * *

Notes and Comments

1. For a discussion of alternative dispute mechanisms in land use practice, see Jonathan M. Davidson & Susan L. Trevarthen, *Land Use Mediation: Another Smart Growth Alternative*, 33 Urb. Law. 704 (2001); Edith M. Netter, *Using Mediation to Resolve Land Use Disputes*, 15 Zoning & Plan. L. Rep. 25, 27–28 (Apr. 1992). *See generally* Lawrence Susskind, Using Assisted Negotiation to Settle Land Use Disputes: A Guidebook for Public Officials (1999); Lawrence Susskind, Mieke van der Wansem & Armand Ciccarelli, Mediating Land Use Disputes: Pros and Cons (2000) (endorsing mediation and describing alternative models compared through anecdotal analysis and vague, typically unquantified comparisons of cases).

2. States are increasingly providing for special masters, mediation, and arbitration, as alternatives to litigation. Fla. Rev. Stat. §70.51. *See also* Barbara McAdoo & Larry Bakken, *Mediation in Public Interest Law*, 22 Urb. Law. 179 (1990).

The following article, although it is focused on international business transactions, stresses the importance of understanding the laws of trading partner nations and the anticipation of disputes through appreciation of choice of law, choice of forum, and choice of litigation or alternative dispute resolution techniques:

Donald C. Dowling, Jr., *Forum Shopping and Other Reflections on Litigation Involving U.S. and European Businesses,*

7 Pace International Law Review 465 (1995)

When U.S. lawyers say they practice "international law," they usually mean "international transactional law." These lawyers help set up international deals. But just as domestic business deals give rise to disputes that wind up in litigation, international business deals which go sour often find their way into tribunals such as courts and the arbitration process. A key part of international law practice is resolving international disputes.

U.S. lawyers, more so than their European counterparts, draw a sharp distinction between transactional and litigation practice. However, an understanding of international business dispute resolution is essential for structuring successful international deals. You cannot set up a deal properly if you do not plan for what will happen if the deal goes bad....

[T]ransactional lawyers representing U.S. companies with international business interests need to be able to spot and address international dispute resolution issues....

Working a forum selection clause into an international contract is perhaps the most important example of how international litigation issues fit into international transactional practice. The transaction lawyer who negotiated an original contract and its forum selection clause often has a greater impact on the outcome of an after-arising dispute than does the litigation attorney who ends up handling the case.

The drafter of a forum selection clause must distinguish choice of law from choice of forum location, and must distinguish both of these from choice of forum type. Choice of law is simply the choice of which legal system will govern the contract. Usually this is the legal system of one of the parties's home countries, but the parties can also designate a third countries' legal system, or even a private legal structure which is not tied to any one government.

Surprisingly, contract drafters often inadvertently truncate the choice of forum location and choice of law issues designating one without mentioning the other. Analytically, choice of forum location is an issue entirely separate from choice of law. Often as a means of compromise, parties which distinguish these issues will stipulate that one party's national law applies to a contract, while the other party's national courts will serve as the site for litigation arising out of the deal.

The third issue related to choice of law and choice of forum location is choice of forum type. At its most basic, this is the question of "to arbitrate or to litigate?" Deciding between arbitration and litigation depends on many factors: a party's assessment at the transaction stage of who is most likely to initiate proceedings in the event of a dispute; how trustworthy are the courts in the respective parties' jurisdictions; and how enforceable a court award would be against the other side.

Common justifications for arbitration such as speed and cost-savings are largely illusory in today's environment. The reality of scheduling international arbitrations, especially those with panels of three arbitrators, can lead to delays similar to those inherent in court proceedings. Also, complex business arbitrations involving U.S. parties can be as expensive as court proceedings....

Yet international arbitration has two important advantages which keep it at the forefront of dispute resolution options in international deals. First is neutrality. Arbitration is a natural middle ground: A foreign adversary's local courts usually appear biased, and your country's courts usually appear just as biased to your adversary. International arbitration associations especially those not based in either party's country, generally do not play favorites. Parties to a deal can also select both a site and a language for an arbitration proceeding which favors neither side.

Perhaps most important, arbitrations are, believe it or not, more readily enforceable abroad than court awards. As a practical matter, a U.S. party which gets a judgment in a U.S. court against a European defendant which does not have sufficient assets in the U.S. will end up re-litigating in a European court, in order to get the Europeans to enforce the judgment against the defendants' European assets. Enforcing an arbitration award within a New York Convention country, on the other hand, is much simpler....

When the claimant bringing the dispute is based in the U.S. and has U.S. counsel, that party almost always favors U.S. courts. The chief reason is the fabled "home court advantage." Although statistics are hard to come by, experience, both personal and by reading enough reported case decisions, shows that judges in every country do indeed tend to favor local parties over foreigners....

However, this factor should not overwhelm the other issues in play, especially when a U.S.-based company has a substantial presence in the adversary's forum, and is to that extent effectively local....

A key choice of law factor is the applicable legal systems' substantive laws governing the actual dispute. Too often U.S. parties and their lawyers reflexively decide that U.S. law is inherently better for U.S. clients. But conceptually, every time U.S. law differs from a foreign doctrine, there is a 50% chance that the foreign rule will be better for the U.S. client. An informed choice of law decision is therefore impossible before researching both legal systems' applicable rules. A knee-jerk preference for U.S. law can be a real disservice to clients.

Additionally, having the "home court advantage" and even winning a judgment are meaningless, if the judgment will not be enforceable against the defendant's assets.... a lawyer should not let that advantage lure the client away from its real, ultimate goal: collecting a judgment.

A vast gulf separates U.S. pretrial procedures from those of the rest of the world. Ironically, while U.S. business people often complain about the expense of domestic U.S. litigation, once an international dispute actually arises, these same American executives often feel more comfortable in U.S. courts precisely because they offer more elaborate pre-trial discovery procedures. Yet the very availability of broad U.S. discovery gives rise to European businesses' healthy aversion to U.S. courts....

> U.S.-style procedural rules, the absence of which U.S. litigants tend to criticize in European courts, are precisely those considered to be the most outrageous by European litigants in U.S. courts. Europeans are wary of U.S. jury trials because of the wide discrepancies in awards between [European] Community and U.S. jurisdictions. In civil law countries, juries do not participate in civil or commercial matters....

Notwithstanding all the foregoing, quite often U.S. parties to international deals end up litigating international disputes in U.S. courts. While many aspects of these cases are identical to domestic business litigation, certain key procedural issues take on special importance in the international context, particularly service of process, personal jurisdiction, discovery, and enforcement of foreign judgments.

Domestically, service of process is usually a relatively simple issue which paralegals and court personnel handle without the need for much attention from lawyers. However, in international-context litigation, service of process is far more complex, because service on a foreign defendant involves sovereignty and international diplomacy. By effecting service abroad, the forum country performs an act with legal effect inside the recipient country's national borders. Service of U.S. process on European parties requires special attention.

I recently worked on a case in which our client was an English defendant sued in a Tennessee federal court. A solid argument existed that the service of process was technically improper, so we challenged it. But our Tennessee local counsel asked us several times why we were expending so much legal time, effort, and expense on a service of process issue likely to be resolved against us. Indeed, because domestic service of process deficiencies are usually curable, domestic service technicalities often are not worth expensive collateral litigation. However, the analysis is quite different in the foreign context. Many U.S. judgments against foreign defendants have been rendered unenforceable due to service of process defects established in foreign courts at the enforcement stage. Defendants who neglect to preserve their service challenges at the outset can later be held to have waived these potentially-dispositive defenses.

The first question regarding how to perfect service of process abroad is whether the defendant's country is one of the 30 signatories to the Hague Service Convention. Each Hague Service Convention country designates a "Central Authority," through which a party from abroad seeking service must transmit judicial documents. The country's Central Authority itself takes care of service. This circumvents the diplomatic breach-of-sovereignty concern. Under the Hague Service Convention, the defendant's countries' own officials serve process, after finding out what a foreign lawsuit is all about.

However, while the Convention is theoretically "mandatory" in signatory countries, there exist certain procedures which effectively streamline the Convention and allow a few simplified service routes entirely short-circuiting the Central Authority.

Service of process in countries which have not ratified the Hague Service Convention requires research into these countries' specific national laws. The usual procedure is to serve "letters rogatory," which in this context means a formal request for service to the proper foreign official. This procedure, which must be followed in Switzerland, can take a lot of time and be quite frustrating, as when foreign functionaries reject pleadings due to technical or de minimus violations. The U.S. Department of State is helpful in researching foreign service matters and it publishes detailed papers on specific topics like "Judicial Assistance in Switzerland."...

A unique treaty called the Brussels Convention controls questions of jurisdiction among the courts of the European Union member states. If you win a lawsuit in Denmark against a Greek defendant, it is the Brussels Convention which will allow you to execute your judgment in Greece. The raison d'etre of the European Union is to encourage the free movement of goods, services, and capital among the member states. The idea behind the Brussels Convention is the concomitant goal of encouraging the free movement of judgments.

Technically the Brussels Convention is not a European Union instrument; it is an entirely separate international treaty which exists as a parallel universe to the European Union treaties themselves. But all the European Union member states ratified the Brussels Convention, and it is adjudicated by the European Union's Court of Justice.

The Brussels Convention's Article 26 states "a judgment given in a Contracting State shall be recognized in the other Contracting States without any special procedure being required." However, even inter-European Union judgments will not be respected if: they are contrary to public policy in the enforcing state; there was a service of process problem and a default judgment was entered; or the judgment is irreconcilable with a prior judgment....

* * *

Alternative Development Approval Processes

In *Fasano v. Board of County Commissioners*, 507 P.2d 23 (Or. 1973), the Oregon Supreme Court transformed the state's zoning system through converting the character of a parcel rezoning from a legislative matter to one that is administrative. Lost is the presumption of legislative validity that typically applies to rezoning decisions. Oregon requires that there be an administrative record and that substantial evidence in the record support nonarbitrary findings that would support the rezoning decision. In addition the standard will require consistency with the comprehensive plan and a demonstration of need for the change. *Fasano* on first look appears to present an improvement over the excessively deferential and political legislative judgement. The downside is that by reclassifying the rezoning as administrative, the initiative and referendum systems are no longer applicable and voters may no longer act as a direct limit on zoning decisions. Many planners believe that moving the planning and development decisions away from the political arena to a system with experienced planning hearing officers is a more fair and more efficient system. As with the case of other alternative dispute mechanisms, there is the possibility that the appointment or political process will capture the reformed system with pro-development or pro-environment agendas. Lawyers tend to prefer the litigation process with promise of protecting ultimate rights through the protections of due process and multiple appeals, the perceived more objective and less political judicial bench officers, not to mention the availability of generous attorney's fees.

Another alternative to traditional planning is the enhanced reliance on citizen participation from the affected community, a more bottom-up planning process. Archon Fung, *Beyond and Below the New Urbanism: Citizen Participation and Responsive Spatial Reconstruction*, 28 B.C. Envtl. Aff. L. Rev. 615 (2001) (charging New Urbanism with imposing a design rather than reacting to community-based design). There appears no reason why New Urbanism would offer less democracy in undertaking planning. There are a multitude of New Urbanist variations in terms of architecture, materials, density, and community design. New Urbanists would argue that "design" is exactly what has been missing from comprehensive planning and project design.

Deregulation

A principle proposal of theoretical land economists is deregulation, converting the regulatory system to one that is more market based. One proposal that has received extensive discussion is the deregulation of land development through the elimination of zoning. The next excerpt argues that zoning is dangerous:

Norman Karlin, *Zoning and Other Land Use Controls: From the Supply Side*,

12 Southwestern University Law Review 561 (1981), *reprinted in* Resolving the Housing Crisis: Government Policy, Decontrol, and the Public Interest (M.B. Johnson ed. Ballinger Publ. 1982)

In California, the prices of homes have doubled, tripled, and even quadrupled within the past six years. Rents have increased at a similar pace, and early in 1980 the vacancy rate was placed at less than one percent. Inflation may have contributed to this phenomenon but cannot fully account for it. The main cause is a shrinking supply of housing relative to demand. Because there are no real shortages of labor, material, or land, had market forces been permitted to operate without restraint, the supply of housing would have kept up with demand. Instead, supply and demand notions were shelved for political decisions to "manage and control growth"—euphemisms for regulations that artificially and deliberately limited the construction of housing. Given a growing demand for housing of all kinds, a policy decision to limit the supply must inevitably drive prices upward. In California, the limitations were great. It was predictable that price increases for homes and rentals would be correspondingly great.

The most effective way of limiting the supply of housing is to give to government a general power to control the use of land. Two notions ostensibly distinguish such a grant from aspects of tyranny: first, a semantic switch in which the word *regulation* is substituted for the word *control,* and second, a requirement in the enabling legislation that the "regulation" be fairly done. The process is called *zoning.* Its stated purpose is regulation that would separate incompatible land uses and protect against present and anticipated environmental harms. But whatever its stated purpose, zoning functions censoriously by imposing and legitimizing prior restraints on the use of land. As a result, genuine monopoly effects are created—less production of housing and prices influenced upward. For all potential buyers, there is a reduction in real income. For those on the lower end of the income scale, there is an infelicitous redistribution of wealth and welfare. With housing at a higher price, fewer are able to buy. Thus, those who advocate land use controls, for whatever reason, are prima facie promoting exclusionary practices that discriminate against and disproportionately burden the poor. Operatively, zoning laws reduce the cost of discrimination, thereby encouraging its use. Through zoning laws, government has, in fact, become the sponsor of exclusion and discrimination and the instrument through which supply is curtailed and price increased.

These effects have been well documented and need not be reviewed here. What perhaps ought to be emphasized is that the stated objectives have been inundated by the reality of predictable events. Why are the law and those engaged in the legal process unable to deal with the serious dislocations and distortions in population distribution and resource allocation that have resulted? The problem is that, given the current state of the law and the incentive structure it generates, any significant change is unlikely. Thus, housing will be kept in relatively short supply, prices will remain artificially high, and entry to the housing market will be restricted to the more affluent and the more preferred. Every so often, a municipality will dramatically overreach itself in passing a zoning law, and a court will invalidate the law. Then a relatively few additional housing units will be made available, and that will be the end of the matter. The overall effect will be trivial. By making minor changes in the ordinance, the municipality will have been forced to yield only slightly. Zoning ordinances alone, or when coupled with subdivision regulations and a high standard building code, can protect what a municipality identifies as its interests with great precision. This protection can always be mounted within the settled law of reasonable regulation and what constitutes a not-unreasonable exercise of the police power. There is no need to exclude all apartments, establish oversized lots, or require areas of open space. What are considered reasonable restrictions, with interesting amenities as provided for in subdivision regulations and high standard building codes, will result in a desired population growth and mix that will not alter what the community regards as its essential character. If that is not enough, the desired effect can certainly be obtained by adding environmental controls.

For the most part, builders and users of property finally accept what they are given. Builders, for example, work within a time limit. They pay for mortgage commitments, which are usually of a fixed duration. The money is nonrefundable, and if the commitment is not used the money is forfeited. Almost any zoning board, planning commission, board of trustees, or village attorney can, in one way or another, sufficiently delay a case to jeopardize a commitment. Furthermore, the parties are required to exhaust all administrative remedies before proceeding to court. This is a lengthy, costly, and often confusing process. For the most part, those who oppose land use control measures capitulate sooner or later. Given the high costs, actual litigation is effectively discouraged. The most important factor, however, in the decision to yield is the knowledge that a court will interfere only in cases of blatant abuse—those situations which it considers to be beyond reasonableness. But that, of course, is not where the significant action is. By then it is too late. Thus, the effects of land use controls will continue unabated. Land use will be improperly allocated and limited, prices will rise, and entry will be restricted.

It cannot be emphasized too strongly that the zoning, not simply the abuse, produces the distorting effects. The failure to distinguish between these two factors, and the tendency to focus solely on the abuse, have hidden the real problem created by the land use control ordinance—the arbitrary curtailment of the supply of housing units, which significantly limits access to the housing market....

* * *

The next excerpt argues that the theoretical model put forth by Professor Karlin is proven by the Houston experience:

Bernard H. Siegan, *Non-Zoning is the Best Zoning*,

31 California Western Law Review 127 (1994)...

People ask, "Do you know what happens if a state planning committee moves to the desert?" The answer is, "First, nothing happens. Then there will be a shortage of sand."

The great lesson of our times is that the forces of production, conservation and creativity exist principally in the marketplace and not in government. True, private entrepreneurs act largely in their self-interest, but probably no more so than government officials, and the endeavors of entrepreneurs in the economic area are much more directed to the general public welfare.

Indeed, most ex-communist nations, as well as many other countries, are eagerly seeking to privatize and deregulate. Nevertheless, although the world trend is away from regulation, Houston considers imposing a powerful new level of government controls. To be sure, zoning in Houston will not bring about a communist economy, but it will greatly reduce the many benefits of free enterprise....

Houston's proposed zoning ordinance provides for eight base zoning districts that entitle an owner whose proposed structure meets the requirements of a district to obtain a building permit as a matter of right. But many owners will not be so lucky. Their properties will not be zoned for the use they desire, and they will have to seek special dispensation from the zoning authorities. This will be quite difficult because the ordinance prescribes a complex procedure for securing zoning amendments and special permissions....

Reflect on what an owner must do to obtain a PUD under Houston's proposed zoning ordinance. The owner must file an application detailing the contemplated development to the planning director. It will then be reviewed by the planning staff and considered at a public hearing by the Planning and Zoning Commission. After this hearing the Commission will submit a recommendation to the city council which must thereafter conduct its own public hearing.

If, at this second public hearing, new information is presented that was not considered by the Planning and Zoning Commission, the city council may refer the application back to the Commission for reconsideration at another public hearing. Thereafter, the city council must hold still another public hearing subsequent to which it must make a final decision by majority vote. However, if the PUD comprehends an amendment of the zoning map, which is often likely to be the case, and 20% of adjoining owners protest, approval requires a three-quarters vote of all members of the city council—a very difficult requirement to meet.

To succeed an owner will require the services of attorneys, probably a planner, an architect to prepare drawings—and plenty of luck and fortitude. If the city rejects the project, all of the preparatory work and fees will have been wasted. The process is a very expensive ordeal that may take many months or even years. These costs will be excessive for many would-be developers and they will not undertake such projects.

As this illustration reveals, the zoning process is very time-consuming and costly to the public. Before recessionary conditions occurred, the city council of San Diego set aside two-thirds of its meeting time to land use matters. Because zoning controversies occupy a great amount of time, city councils and their staffs devote much less time than they should to many other major local concerns.

These public hearings bring theater to land use. Participants at the hearings include the owner and his agents, of course, and often a great many others, including the neighbors, the local civic or homeowners groups, political organizations, the school and park boards, the chamber of commerce and labor groups. Many times, the media will express its opinions on the project. A large variety of interests except probably those who will directly benefit from the development, such as potential homeowners, tenants, and shoppers may enter the fray. Each side will have no difficulty in producing a planner to prove "conclusively" that its position is the only correct one.

How it will come out will depend on who are or what is best able to influence or pressure the city council. Members of the city council can be expected to act in their own self-interest—they usually are not given to self immolation.

By contrast, consider the outcome in Houston under its present land use system. There usually will be no public hearings. The site in question will in all likelihood be developed for the uses that society values the most, thereby satisfying the predominant consumer demand. A developer will erect those structures that he believes will bring the greatest return. Thus, if he believes that a demand exists for apartments, he will build apartments; if the demand is for office space, he will erect these kinds of units. Since most developers obtain most or much of their funds from lenders, it can be expected that the latter will participate in development decisions. Of course, builders and lenders go astray, but their decisions are much more likely to succeed in the market than decisions made for political reasons.

The modern world demands a high degree of expertise. Why then are we so willing to allow inexperienced and untrained people to have a major voice in the development of the land? If the experts in this field are the builders and the developers, why, paradoxically, does zoning require them to submit their proposals for final decision to politicians whose expertise usually is in other areas?

Nor should society give an important role to those who have no stake in the success of a venture and may even prefer its demise. I have attended zoning hearings where home owners, who had no training or experience in land development or real estate construction, condemned complex plans prepared by highly skilled specialists. Worst of all, local authorities weigh such comments heavily because they emanate from sources with a powerful weapon: the ability to vote them out of office.

The zoning experience of this nation has revealed that, frequently city councils try to upgrade proposed developments. I refer to what has been called the "Mercedes" approach. Builders who seek to erect moderate cost housing projects are often hampered by the local residents and officials who understandably want more luxurious structures in their communities and more affluent residents. At times, the real objective is to exclude minorities. The result is that either a "Volkswagen" level of development is prohibited or it must be elevated to a "Mercedes" status to obtain zoning approval. Of course, most people would rather have an expensive Mercedes than an inexpensive Volkswagen. But where will the poorer people live? Aren't we fortunate that zoning does not control automobile production?

Developers may seek to pass on the cost of upgrading the project by raising prices or rents. If market conditions do not allow for such increases, the projects become economically infeasible and are not erected. And this, of course, brings joy to the people who never wanted the project.

Another possibility is that the developer will compensate for the added expense by reducing the quantity or quality of some amenities. He may attempt to offset the cost of required park dedications, special architectural treatment, special recreational facilities, or lower density by, say, lessening the quality of the windows, doors, plumbing, heating, fixtures, etc. He may reduce the amount of insulation and soundproofing. As a result, a purchaser or renter obtains a less desirable structure....

Consider, for example, the factors an apartment builder must evaluate to succeed. Apartment buildings do get built with many amenities not required by government in both zoned and nonzoned areas. The decision as to what should be included as part of the building is invariably a difficult one for a builder due to the financial limitations of any project, a situation which anyone who has ever built a home should understand. He must determine the quality of the refrigerators, air-conditioning, stoves, windows, light fixtures, and dozens of other items. He cannot possibly install the best of each, and must forego the installation of many amenities. This would be necessary even if he were erecting a super-luxury building. The decision as to what is installed and what is omitted will be based on an evaluation of the rental market; he will do those things within the limits of his budget that will cause his apartments to rent better.

No such limitations confine the public regulators. They make decisions for a large variety of reasons, and consumer satisfaction or economic efficiency is rarely a primary one, for there is little they can personally gain from encouraging either....

Zoning has been a colossal flop because it is supposed to do things it cannot do. What, for instance, is the "right" mix of homes and apartments? How much industry is "too much?" Where is business to be allowed, and what kinds? Is there some objective measurement available to determine the "best" use of some or all of the land, of growth and anti-growth proposals, and whether the land is better suited for open space, mobile homes, industry or the housing of people? Should the land be developed with one, two or four housing units to the acre?

Typically, zoners and planners confront Herculean problems in determining land use. Questions of compatibility, desirability, economic feasibility, property values, existing uses, adjoining and nearby uses, traffic, topography, utilities, schools, future growth, conservation, and environment have to be considered for countless locations covering hundreds of square miles. Yet to determine just economic feasibility for a certain use at any one site for any one period of time would require a professional market survey costing thousands of dollars and taking months to complete.

Planners confront serious problems in evaluating the present and forecasting the future, whether it be on a micro or macro level. With respect to zoning, overruling market-based decisions on land use would seem to require economic expertise that relatively few planners or politicians can be expected to possess. They are far less knowledgeable than the developers and lenders in using and developing land. Zoning experience is replete with instances where planners classified land either to allow uses unacceptable in the market or to deny uses eagerly sought in the market....

This desire to control extensively economic activity is an application of the master plan mentality that is totally discredited in the former communist nations which had long experienced it. Government planning was a major factor in the economic collapse of these countries....

The most recent national attack on zoning occurred in July 1991, when the Commission on Regulatory Barriers to Affordable Housing, appointed by then-Department of Housing and Urban Development Secretary Jack Kemp, concluded that excessive and unnecessary local government regulation (including zoning) caused substantial increases in housing prices. Kemp charged that local regulation was denying many the American dream of home ownership.

Anthony Downs, a member of the commission and senior fellow at Brookings Institute, estimated "probably well over half of the cost of building new housing in the average U.S. community is a direct result of local government regulations rather than of any minimum requirements truly necessary for the occupants' health and safety."...

Large size dwelling units. Developers want to build houses or apartments containing, say, one thousand square feet per unit, but the zoning ordinance requires twelve to fifteen hundred square feet. Again, this requirement reduces availability of housing for lower income groups. Growth controls—The NIMBY approach. NIMBY stands for "not in my backyard." Now that I live in the area, build a barrier so no one else can get in. Cities have used zoning to reduce production, increasing land and property prices and lowering the availability of housing and commercial and industrial facilities....

First, zoning increases prices. The absence of zoning has enabled Houston to keep rents and housing prices relatively low. Houston's rents have been far less than Dallas' because of the absence of zoning.

Second, zoning wastes land. Zoning usually increases the land area required for building. Bigger lots consume considerably more land for housing and urban purposes, reducing the supply for other uses, such as farming and grazing....

Third, zoning stifles competition. By limiting development, regulation reduces competition and the creativity, ingenuity, and productivity that go with it. In zoned cities, these talents are often spent in persuading or outmaneuvering the zoning authorities. By contrast, competition thrives in Houston. One result is that Houston is probably the best provider of housing of any major city in the world.

Fourth, zoning eliminates smaller developers. Zoning causes us to lose the talents of small and moderate sized developers. The smaller builders do not have the resources to pay for zoning experts, zoning attorneys, and the cost of keeping the land vacant and unproductive while the zoners meditate. This leaves the market limited to only "the big guys" with the big resources, who, as a result, are often quite satisfied with zoning.

Fifth, zoning promotes politics and graft. Politics in Houston at the present time isn't exactly a minor industry. But with zoning, it will boom. The largest political contributors in zoned cities frequently are developers who require approval for their projects....

Finally, zoning curtails development. As a negative device, zoning has curtailed growth and development, reducing construction activity, business, employment and real estate and other tax collections....

On November 2, 1993, the voters of Houston rejected for the third time in its history the adoption of a zoning ordinance, leaving Houston as the only major city in the nation without zoning....

* * *

Notes and Comments

1. *See also* Robert C. Ellickson, *Alternatives to Zoning: Covenants, Nuisance Rules, and Fines as Land Use Controls*, 40 U. Chi. L. Rev. 681 (1973); Douglas W. Kmiec, *Deregulating Land Use: An Alternative Free Enterprise Development System*, 130 U. Pa. L. Rev. 28 (1981).

The following excerpt presents a different view of deregulation:

Jane E. Larson, *Free Markets Deep in the Heart of Texas*,

84 Georgetown Law Journal 179 (2000)....

In recent decades, the debate over land use regulation has been reinvigorated. Other progressive-era expansions of market regulation have been accepted (perhaps grudgingly) as necessary to a complex and pluralistic society, but the very idea of land use regulation continues to be challenged on both legal and public policy grounds. Although much of this political and scholarly debate focuses on zoning, it also extends to planning, building and housing codes, and infrastructure requirements.

Libertarians resist government control of land use as unwarranted intrusion into the realm of private property. Market advocates resist land use regulation (as they resist other forms of economic regulation), claiming that it interferes with the optimal allocation of a scarce resource-physical space for human habitation in densely settled places. Critics from the left have joined the chorus, coining the term "exclusionary zoning" to describe the ways in which land use regulatory powers, when placed in the hands of parochial local governments, have worked to segregate communities along racial and economic lines, further worsening housing problems for the poor.

The most recent free market attack on land use regulation cites the lack of affordable housing for lower-income people as evidence of the need for more "efficient" allocation of land resources. Free market proponents offer the huge and unmet demand for affordable housing for low- and moderate-income households as evidence of the pernicious consequences of too much regulation, rather than as an indication of a market failure that justifies government intervention. Further, zoning opponents long have argued that land use regulation inhibits the development of affordable housing. In an extension of this claim, one economist argues that homelessness in New York City could be solved by lifting building and housing codes, as well as zoning, density, and other land use restrictions, in order to permit the poor to buy whatever housing they can afford. The Dickensian slum, symbol to an earlier generation of the moral poverty of a society that tolerated such physical deprivation, has now been reinterpreted as the symbol of the liberated (if limited) purchasing power of the most deprived.

Market advocates triumphantly point to the city of Houston, Texas to counter the argument that lack of zoning will lead to slum-like conditions. Houston is unique among American municipalities: it is unplanned and the largest unzoned city in the country. Bernard Siegan, who first brought Houston's alternative urban land use approach to the attention of the scholarly community, contends that although most people consider zoning to be an essential element of municipal order, Houston's very existence proves that the market can distribute physical space efficiently and equitably. In other words, a liveable city that relies largely on market mechanisms for land use management suggests a viable alternative to government regulation. Thus, if there are pragmatic or political reasons to prefer the market, Houston just might prove the case for the market model.

Despite Siegan's claims, however, Houston is not a good example of a free market in land use. Houston has unregulated land use practices at only a superficial level. Although the city has no planning agency and no zoning ordinance, it has adopted a range of other governmental land use regulations, including controls on lot sizes, business placement, and setback requirements. Siegan's impressionistic observation—that Houston looks and works much like a zoned city—was based merely on his conclusions about the "feel" of the place after many of these land use regulations had come into effect (and were shaping the city's configuration and function). Given this fact, the example of Houston hardly proves his claim—that land use planning is irrelevant to urban geography, affordability, or quality of life.

Yet the market approach remains attractive to academics and politicians alike. Thus Siegan's search for a naturally occurring case study of a free market in land use remains an important item on the scholarly agenda. We already have considerable experience with the quality of life in regulated communities, but we lack similar depth and richness of data about the consequences of proposed free market alternatives. In the often heated debate over how best to manage land in complex, interdependent settings, it has been difficult without such empirical evidence of "livability" to decide between the arguments supporting free market theories and the arguments supporting government regulation....

[A] better example than Houston of an unregulated land market exists. In the unincorporated areas of the Texas counties that border Mexico, there are no zoning laws.

And, in contrast to Houston, until recently there were no subdivision and infrastructure requirements nor government provision of basic public services. To this day, there are no building or housing codes, no growth controls, and no planning mechanisms. As market advocates would predict, land and housing in these counties are extraordinarily inexpensive. Housing and environmental conditions, however, are deplorable....

Within Texas, more than a third of a million people live in these settlements. In sharp contrast to unzoned but regulated Houston, the unregulated colonias lack the "basics" that residents of other jurisdictions take for granted: safe drinking water, sewers for carrying away human waste, and housing with minimally adequate wiring, plumbing, and construction. Elsewhere in the world, the health and safety risks and severe environmental degradation endemic to such shantytown settlements are well known. Main Street America, however, has not typically contemplated such Third World problems. Defenders of markets and regulation alike claim that their preferred policy approach best promotes decent and affordable housing for the poor. The colonias, products of a regime that allocates land uses according to a market rather than a regulatory logic, thus offer an opportunity to compare "livability" outcomes under these competing approaches....

A web of circumstances—historical, geophysical, and political—contribute to the colonias' lack of clean water. A large number of colonia households are not connected to public water supplies, in part because the El Paso water utility declared a moratorium in 1979 on extending city water lines outside of the city limits. The utility defended this policy as a protection of land values and the tax base within the city and as a means to restrict development outside of the city. The moratorium succeeded in cutting off tens of thousands of households from a basic public service, but failed to prevent haphazard rural development; since the early 1980s, the El Paso County colonias have grown at an explosive rate.

The only alternatives to public water for colonia residents are private well water and purchased or borrowed water.... According to Eva Galvan of Las Colonias del Paso outside of El Paso: "We have to bring water to bathe, wash dishes, for the bathrooms, to cook—it's so much trouble to get water. We try to go twice a week, but sometimes it's impossible when the car isn't working."...

As an alternative to purchased or borrowed water, many colonia residents dig private wells. Well water causes more health problems than it solves, however, because the groundwater throughout El Paso County is dangerously contaminated by human, animal, and industrial wastes....

The issue of unsafe drinking water exemplifies a much broader problem of inadequate infrastructure that sets the colonias apart even from substandard housing occupied by other very poor people in this country. Most Texas colonias also lack access to sanitary sewers for the disposal of human waste, or well-paved roads with adequate storm drainage systems. Some settlements do not have electricity, trash collection, streetlights, or street addresses.

Virtually all colonia residents must create a private sanitary sewage system. Widespread reliance on improvised sewage disposal systems has polluted the groundwater throughout the county: untreated human waste seeps into the soil, eventually reaching the underground water table and contaminating the well water source for colonia households....

Private waste disposal alternatives include open pit cesspools in the back yard, septic tanks, or outhouses. Where waste is not fully contained, it contaminates not only the ground water but also the soil; as residents walk from their yards into their houses, they carry waste-contaminated soil on their feet....

Not surprisingly, this mingling of water and waste creates significant public health risks. Texas colonias persistently fear an outbreak of cholera, which is spread by human waste contamination of water or food....

Lesser illnesses and symptoms associated with the lack of a clean water supply are also endemic in the colonias, including severe skin rashes, yeast infections, numerous insect bites, diarrhea, and vomiting. El Paso County records almost four times the national rate of salmonella dysentery cases. The Hepatitis A rate in El Paso County has been as high as five times that of the rest of the United States. A 1988 health survey in the San Elizario area found that more than sixty-six percent of the population tested had been infected with Hepatitis A at some time in their lives, probably as a result of widespread contamination of drinking water. Another study in a single El Paso County colonia found that thirty-five percent of all children aged eight years or older had been exposed to Hepatitis A, and that by the age of thirty-five, up to ninety percent of the residents had contracted the disease. The rate of tuberculosis in El Paso County fluctuates between 1.5 and three times the average U.S. rate. An emerging problem is an alarming increase in the rate of drug-resistant tuberculosis cases. Mosquitoes breeding in the standing water and open sewage canals (aguas negras) of the border carry encephalitis, and, more recently, the virus that causes dengue fever, a painful and sometimes fatal viral disease....

Basic infrastructure for dense residential habitation requires sewers not only for human waste disposal, but for draining off rainwater to prevent flooding. The lack of adequate flood drainage is also a serious problem in Texas colonias. In regulated communities, flood-prone land is not zoned for development. Under a free market regime, however, the most vulnerable land is simply cheaper, and the people who build there are those who cannot afford anything else. With even a little rain, the dirt tracks that typically form roads in the colonias, and the dirt yards that surround virtually all trailers and houses, become mud, with large pools of standing water blocking access. Flooding also invades the interiors of colonia homes.

The lack of storm sewers exacerbates problems caused by the lack of sanitary sewers. Floods wash out septic tanks, cesspools, trash piles, and backyard outhouses, turning the pools of standing rainwater collected around houses into a soup of organic and fecal waste. To avoid the hazards of flooding and consequent health risks, residents are often forced to prop up their houses on concrete blocks and drop wooden pallets onto the ground to create walkways through the mud.

Colonia building standards are equally poor. Homes in these subdivisions are a collection of concrete-block bungalows, trailers, shacks, and an occasional conventional frame house. Construction usually is substandard, violating even the minimum habitability standards imposed elsewhere by building and housing codes. Decrepit trailers, shacks made of wood slats, tin, or cardboard nailed onto scavenged pallets, and condemned homes moved from the city are common sights.

The best built homes in the colonias are small bungalows of two to four rooms, constructed of concrete block. Although such houses look neat from the outside, inside it is not unusual to find no floors, walls, or ceilings. In addition, only half of colonia homes in one recent study had indoor toilet facilities. In one-room shacks, walls are frequently built of cardboard or of wood slats covered with plastic sheeting....

Improvisational housing construction methods are common to colonia homebuilders. Houses may be built, for example, from garage doors recovered from city houses under renovation, which are then hammered onto a simple wooden frame to make walls. Fences may be built from pallets, bedsprings, or stacks of used tires. Roofs may be constructed from more garage doors, sheets of plywood, or planks covered with plastic sheeting. Old carpets and plastic sheets pressed directly into the earth can create a floor, and carpet scraps tacked to the walls may insulate the house for warmth and quiet.

Electricity is widely available in the semirural areas, allowing colonia residents to heat homes and cook food using space heaters and electric stoves, if they own these appliances. Indoor kitchens are not as common as electrical hookups, however, and in many El Paso County colonias an outside kitchen is placed in the yard....

Where electricity is not available, propane fuel is commonly used for heating and cooking. Sometimes more primitive means are used, including gas-fired campstoves, improvised oil can stoves, or open cook fires, all of which create significant fire danger. Even where electricity is available, residents may not be able to afford the cost of connecting their homes to the power supply....In houses without electricity, televisions may be wired to the car batteries for power, and kerosene lanterns, candles, oil lamps, or flashlights may be wired to the walls as a means of lighting.

This admirable ingenuity and commitment to self-help homebuilding has a dark side. No building codes apply to the construction of colonia housing, making nonstandard and unsafe wiring, plumbing, and construction the rule rather than the exception. Moreover, because of the common practice of incremental self-help construction, a colonia family may live in overcrowded, unfinished, indeed unsafe surroundings for many years....

Despite relative powerlesness, El Paso County tentatively began to use its authority to exert more direct control over colonia growth in 1986. Relying first on its power to enforce sewage standards (a power unused since it was first granted in 1979), the county began to exact fees from developers as they sold lots to pay for the county to inspect septic tank installations and lot sizes. In 1987, as evidence of groundwater and well contamination in the colonias mounted, the county began to consider tougher sewage regulations. Developers opposed the proposal, making the argument that higher standards were "arbitrary and will hurt the poor." Due in part to political pressures, it took until May 1990 for the county commissioners to adopt model subdivision rules. Under the rules, developers of residential subdivisions with tracts of five acres or less outside the boundary of any incorporated municipality in El Paso County were required to: (1) provide drinking water by connecting each subdivision to a central water supply or by drilling wells that will yield potable water; and (2) provide sewage lines or adequate septic tanks. The new regulations also imposed street paving and flood hazard prevention requirements.

The new subdivision rules applied only to colonias platted after May 1990. The "grandfathering" of subdivisions platted before the effective date created a vast loophole that threatened to undermine the effectiveness of this regulatory victory. Moreover, before the new regulations went into effect, the county subdivided and approved more than half a million undeveloped lots....

The available information about colonia residents contradicts many assumptions about poor Mexican-Americans at the border: almost all adult household heads are workers, homeowners, living in families with children, and either U.S. citizens or legal residents. Yet colonia residents live in housing that is more crowded, has fewer amenities, and is less valued than housing in nearby regulated jurisdictions.

Most men living in the colonias work as laborers, although a smaller number describe themselves as farmer-ranchers or skilled craftsmen. Among laborers and craftsmen the most common occupations are construction and factory work. Many other colonia residents, including women, work as janitors, maids, or restaurant workers. In general, employment problems among adult colonia residents are severe, with high rates of job instability....

* * *

Notes and Comments

1. Professor Larsen proposes (1) Regularize land title held under contract for deed into mortgages; (2) Make credit available at market rates to low-income households for land purchase and home construction, and also for home improvement; (3) Adopt policies supporting self-help housing and abandon current "no-growth" policies directed at colonias; (4) Delegate general ordinance-making powers to counties; (5) Enact minimal but appropriate land use regulations that apply both to new and existing housing in the colonias; (6) Mandate extension of municipal water and sewer service to high-density population areas in unincorporated areas outside of city limits; and (7) Extend the franchise in local government elections to noncitizen permanent residents.

2. Every initiative to improve the quality of life in the Colonias involves government subsidies and increased traditional regulation, particularly through subdivision controls. Does the experience suggest that deregulation is a poor policy, at least in low income communities? Why have no "free market" solutions emerged? Might Professor Siegan argue that if El Paso was deregulated, the housing opportunities would expand, reducing demand for Colonias space and developers in the Colonias would be forced by the market to compete with better planned and built communities?

3. For an argument by a New Urbanist architect that zoning threatens the ability to bring out the vitality of neighborhoods, albeit without an exploration of the potential negative impacts of deregulation, see Joseph Hanania, *Creating a City that Never Sleeps*, Los Angeles Times, Nov. 5, 1996.

4. What proposals would you advance for reforming the planning and zoning process? Deregulation, conversion to administrative processes, a wider use of contractual regulation, ballot box zoning, greater local autonomy over development or less? Would specific state standards provide communities with a clear obligation and direction towards comprehensive planning? Should there be federal planning legislation requiring state legislation to meet minimum standards for comprehensiveness to assure a better economy, efficient transportation and access, and the reduction of national resource consumption patterns?

Chapter 10

Growth Management

They paved paradise And put up a parking lot.
With a pink hotel, a boutique And a swinging hot spot.
Don't it always seem to go?
That you don't know what you've got Till it's gone.
They paved paradise
And put up a parking lot....

Joni Mitchell, *Big Yellow Taxi* (1970)

Towards Smart Growth

The central issue in urban planning is how best to plan for the future. Managing growth is about planning for infrastructure necessary to accommodate anticipated growth and designing an urban form that most effectively serves the needs of residents. In the United States the debate has moved to "smart growth," an acknowledgment that all growth is not good. Growth may be smart or dumb and "smart growth"seeks to encourage the smart kind. This may simply take the form of subsidizing infrastructure facilities such as roads, sewers, and water only where they are consistent with a planned high density area and thus discouraging non-urban sprawl development on the urban fringe that would tend to raise the cost of services and generate traffic congestion on non-urban roads. Growth management touches on critical issues in regional planning, that of balancing growth and the need for housing, the provision of access by automobiles, pedestrians, transit, and other mobility options, and the design of urban spaces to generate attractive pedestrian areas and liveable communities. Sprawl carries not only additional facilities and service costs, it imposes additional consequences. Patrick Gallagher, *The Environmental, Social, and Cultural Impacts of Sprawl*, 15 Nat. Resources & Env't 219 (2001).

In the next excerpt, Professor Stearns describes growth management approaches in Santiago and the State of Washington. She notes, in an earlier portion of her article, that by the year 2025, thirty cities will reach populations in excess of 10 million, seven will have populations in excess of 20 million. Four out of five "megacities" are in developing countries, with New York and Los Angeles the only such cities located in the U.S. By 2050, Pakistan with a 41 percent birth rate will surpass the United States as the third most populous nation.

Worldwide statistics on population suggest that growth management is not just a problem in America, it is the central problem of developing nations, and requires renewed attention within the European community where quality urban planning has long been assumed.

This search for smart growth has followed a generation of largely isolated suburban efforts to restrict the pace and design of their development.

Communities have utilized moratoria, whereby a freeze on new permits is imposed for a limited periods, to permit comprehensive replanning of the community's design or the rebuilding of facilities necessary to accommodate growth.

More permanent systems were implemented in a few jurisdictions that set a pace of development by setting a cap or annual permit allotment. In the leading case in the United States, *Construction Industry Association v. City of Petaluma*, 522 F.2d 897 (9th Cir. 1975), the United States Court of Appeals for the Ninth Circuit, the intermediate appellate federal court, sustained the city's use of permit caps, generally allowing 500 dwelling units year, a rate in line with the earlier average annual growth, over a record where the city did not rigidly control growth, exempted small developments, and appeared to provide incentives to develop affordable housing.

In a sophisticated variation, the Town of Ramapo, New York devised a system allowing development permission only where city services had been extended to the district or where the owner was willing to finance service extension. The system known as timed sequential zoning, simply added the facilities timing element to the traditional zoning considerations of use, height, and parcel bulk coverage. *Golden v. Planning Bd. of Ramapo*, 285 N.E.2d 291 (N.Y.), *appeal dismissed*, 409 U.S. 1003 (1972).

Portland is best known for its innovative urban planning which is symbolized by the placing of urban fringe nonurbanized land such as agricultural and lumbering beyond urbanization. These "urban growth boundaries," although controversial, where part of a state-wide mandated planning system, are credited with making the greatest inroads to urban sprawl and simultaneously encouraging urban infill and the revitalization of declining central cities. *Cf. 1000 Friends of Oregon v. WASCO County Court*, 703 P.2d 207 (Or. 1985) (discussing urban growth boundaries).

One of the unfortunate impacts of any system that attempts to restrict the pace or extent of growth is a rise in the cost of housing. Builders may opt for higher profit more expensive homes where permits are restricted, and a revitalizing city can generate higher rents as housing is converted to higher income use and neighborhoods are "gentrified, displacing the poor to overcrowded expensive shelter. In some communities, rigid growth controls can exacerbate both economic and racial segregation as those of modest incomes have difficulty locating affordable housing outside the traditional same-race neighborhoods or the "other side of the tracks." Matthew E. Kahn, *Does Sprawl Reduce the Black/White Housing Consumption Gap?*, 12 Hous. Pol'y Debate 77 (2001).

The ultimate question, one ostensibly separate from issues of livability and access, is the question of environmental quality. What are the impacts on our environment from internal combustion engines, where growth means increasing dependence on oil and energy production. American development invariably means air conditioning and expensive utilities when better architectural design could require less energy, planned open spaces utilizing water reclamation, could reduce water consumption and the cost of living, and better integration of housing with opportunities for walking and the use of transit could translate into public policy that does not threaten the environment as well as the economy.

The next excerpt describes two different growth management systems:

Janet Ellen Stearns, Urban Growth: A Global Challenge,

8 Journal of Affordable Housing and Community Development Law 140 (1999)

...To provide a specific context for a discussion of urban growth, this article will examine in some detail recent growth-management efforts in Seattle, Washington, and Santiago, Chile. Although neither of these cities is among the largest in the world, each is representative of rapid growth and thus demonstrates some of the similarities and differences in approaches used on two continents. The political and technical shortcomings with traditional [American-model] growth-management programs used in Chile are highlighted and lessons that may be extended to other under-developed countries.

The Need for Controls

Seattle, Washington, is located in the northwest United States and has a population of 516,000. It is the center of a region, known as Puget Sound, that grew by 18 percent between 1980 and 1990. During the same time period, the state's population increased by 20 percent, twice as fast as the rest of the United States. By 1996 the state's population was roughly 5.5 million. Much of this growth was due to migration from other parts of the United States in response to employment opportunities offered by companies such as Boeing and Microsoft. In addition, the natural beauty and quality of life of the region attracted residents, particularly from California. The impact of this population growth, combining worsening traffic congestion with exploding skylines, turned the citizens of Washington state into "true believers" in growth management. By 1990 the state legislature responded with the Growth Management Act, which was substantially revised in the 1991 legislative session to the current law (GMA).

Santiago, the largest city in Chile, has similarly experienced rapid growth in recent times. The city has a population of roughly 5 million people, as compared to a national population of 14.6 million. As is true for other parts of Latin America, much of the population increase is due to a high birth rate (22 percent) combined with dramatic shifts away from rural to urban communities. Whereas the total population of Latin America doubled between 1950 and 1980, the urban population quadrupled. In Chile 85 percent of the population currently lives in urban centers; nearly 60 percent of the population is located in only three metropolitan areas. This urbanization led to an explosion of new construction and traffic congestion, similar to that in Seattle.

As a result of a combination of geographic and environmental factors, the city has also confronted smog on a level most comparable with Los Angeles; the severity of the situation has prompted more sensitive monitoring of air quality. Now, when air quality is determined to be above 200 points, the government can restrict the use of certain vehicles and suspend operation of polluting industries. It is anticipated that special restrictions will be in effect more than sixty days a year. This smog, which portends serious health problems for the city's residents, is probably the most concrete example of inadequate urban planning.

In 1975 the Chilean government adopted a General Law of Urbanism and Construction (LUC) that outlines certain activities related to growth management. However, implementation of these policies was put on hold for a decade, probably as a result of more pressing national needs in a time of political and economic unrest in the country. In 1985 the government again focused on growth management, with a report outlining the national urban development policy and setting forth the importance of increased planning. Only since 1990 has the country and its various regions begun to take planning seriously. In 1996 a nationwide master plan for urban transit was adopted.

Enactment of Controls: The Law and Planning Process

Washington's growth management act (GMA) is one of nine such statutes in the United States. The law establishes thirteen statewide goals but does not implement statewide planning and regulation. Rather, in what has been called a "bottom up" approach, counties and local governments are primarily responsible for these tasks. The GMA requires that counties and cities engage in a series of tasks, in the following order:

(1) Designate and protect natural resource lands (agriculture, timber, and mineral lands) and critical areas (wetlands, potable water aquifer recharge areas, fish and wildlife habitat, frequently flooded areas, and geological hazardous areas);

(2) Develop countywide plans, and for the counties of King, Snohomish, and Pierce (the Puget Sound area), a multicounty plan;

(3) Identify urban growth areas within each county, in which future development will be concentrated;

(4) Adopt comprehensive plans for counties and cities, subject to the limits and requirements of the GMA; and

(5) Enact development regulations consistent with the GMA and with public participation requirements.

The state does not retain any control over the review or approval of these plans or regulations. In addition, the GMA requires that transportation and other public facilities be available "concurrently" with all new development, and authorizes cities and counties to use innovative land-use techniques and impact fees in their development regulations.

Consistent with the requirements of the GMA, the City of Seattle embarked on a comprehensive planning process that resulted in the adoption of a plan in July 1994, and development regulations in December 1994. The city plan called for focusing future growth in forty designated urban villages, which were to prepare their own individual neighborhood-based plans. Again, this entire process was quite decentralized and largely driven by the interplay of city planning officials, community groups, and citizen participation in public hearings.

Chile's LUC tackled the growth management problem during a similar time period as the GMA, but the LUC clearly used a "top-down" planning process. This arrangement reflects the allocation of power in the country's constitution. The country is divided into thirteen regions; the regions are subdivided into provinces, which are further divided into municipalities. Chile's president has the authority to select the head of the region and the governor of the province, and they serve at his discretion. Only the mayors of the municipality, and the corresponding municipal councils, are popularly elected. A separate law defines the duties of each level of government and specifies how differences among them are to be resolved. In general, the national government retains far more authority and control than is the case in the United States.

The LUC required a classification of urban and rural land and prescribed ranges of appropriate population densities for the urban areas. The LUC also set a requirement of concurrency, whereby developers of urban land were required to pay for certain infrastructure costs. The LUC identified basic services needed for quality of life in each urban area (i.e., health, education, culture, green areas, and sports) and established minimum standards for the provision of these services. In addition, the LUC outlined a policy of planning and regulation that included regional, interurban, and urban planning; the regional plans require national approval, while the urban and interurban plans are reviewed only at the county level.

Finally, the LUC called for public participation in the planning process. Interestingly, the law concedes that this participation is not feasible at the regional or interurban levels, but only at the urban or sector level. The law is quite specific that these are merely consultations and are not decisive.

Following the enactment of this law, a regional planning process was undertaken. The Urban Plan for Santiago was adopted in January of 1996.

The Mechanism for Changing and Challenging Controls

The GMA enacted a dispute resolution system that was intended to reduce pressure on the Washington state superior court system. The Act created three administrative review boards known as growth management hearing boards, with jurisdiction divided by geographical region. As mentioned above, the state government retained little oversight control in the implementation of the GMA, so the hearing appeals boards were delegated the task of interpreting and resolving challenges under the law. Appeals may be taken from the decisions of the appeals boards to the superior court. Additionally, the governor has authority to sanction cities or counties that fail to comply with the GMA by withholding certain state revenues, as well as abrogating rights to GMA-related funding and assistance. To date, these sanctions have not been used.

Chile's LUC, through its very centralized process, allows the state to retain significantly more control over the process and outcome of the growth management process. Avenues for challenging decisions and enforcing judgments are limited. The law does set forth a system of "multas," or fines for sanctions, as well as civil and criminal penalties. Any person may make a complaint to the regional secretary of housing and urban development. Either this secretary or the director of municipal public works may bring a legal action before local courts. This framework for sanctions seems to envision penalties for acts or omissions under the law, but it does not establish any system for challenging or debating policy decisions.

In addition to these sanctions, other legal remedies exist. Claims for civil and criminal matters can be brought before the judicial branch. In order to challenge laws on constitutional grounds, a case must be initiated before the national constitutional court. This occurred in April 1997 when certain provisions of the LUC requiring developer exactions were unsuccessfully challenged as a "taking" under the Chilean constitution. The court ultimately rejected these claims, finding that the exactions were reasonable requirements of the urbanization program and consistent with the constitutional protections of private property.

Growth Management in Seattle and Santiago: An Evaluation....

Scope of Planning Process

Both communities have planning processes focused on what can be called traditional criteria. The focus of the GMA is clearly on land use planning and environmental impacts, with some attention to affordable housing. This may be appropriate for a community like Seattle. Such a city is representative of much of the United States, where the goals of the planning process are to shift development to less populated areas rather than to control overall population growth.

Santiago likewise has focused its planning efforts on the impacts of development on environmental conditions such as traffic and smog. Its planning initiatives have not confronted more difficult societal problems of education, job training, and population control. Like many developing countries, Chile must consider ways to integrate a wider agenda into its land-use planning processes; without understanding the forces impacting on the growth of the cities, policymakers will be unsuccessful in enacting successful controls. Given its overall population growth and the limited economic opportunities outside a few metropolitan areas, Chile needs to embark on a broader planning process. Tackling population planning is difficult in a country that has a constitution protecting the rights of the unborn. The Catholic church maintains a strong influence throughout Latin America in laws and attitudes that impact abortion and contraception....

Implementation and Follow-Up

As discussed above, an effective growth management strategy must include enforceable "carrots and sticks." Incentives must exist, whether they be financial or land use, such as density bonuses or transferable development rights, that help to bring opponents to the table in support of the plan and its goals. When these incentives fail, appropriate legal remedies must be in place to require the necessary parties to comply....

The GMA has relegated incentives and enforcement to the local level and to the regional hearing boards by not providing for any statewide oversight of the growth-management process. The LUC, although providing for fines for noncompliance, similarly fails to create an effective system of remedies. Redress to the judicial system is not an effective avenue for airing policy differences or enforcing compliance. Creating models for such review is essential for developing and nondeveloping countries attempting to implement growth-management programs....

* * *

Notes and Comments

1. Professor Stearns attended the United Nations Habitat II conference in Istanbul in 1996, designed to establish strategies and solutions for the problems of global urbanization. Her article describes the components of generated policies yet rather than a blueprint for growth management policy, the generated principles appear to be more a laundry list of concerns that are individually vague and as a collection appear incomprehensible. The U.N.-sponsored conference failed to generate a treaty or other agreement.

2. For a discussion of the problems of urban sprawl in Great Britain, see Pat Thomas, *Urban Sprawl: The English Dilemma*, 15 Nat. Resources & Env't 252 (2001) (noting the need for spatial density and the conflicting English desire for privacy and spatial autonomy).

3. For a discussion of the unique growth planning problems of places with huge immigration, see Rachelle Alterman, *Israel: Land Use Law in the Face of a Rapid-Growth*

Crisis: The Case of Mass-Immigration to Israel in the 1990s, 3 Wash. U. J. L. & Pol'y 773 (2000).

In the following excerpt, growth management is challenged to include the central city and its revitalization as a fundamental component of urban growth management:

James A. Kushner, *Growth Management and the City*,

12 Yale Law & Policy Review 68 (1994)

...During the last three decades, American urban growth policy was directed to suburban growth. Government encouraged the exodus from the metropolis through: deep subsidies for highways, utilities, and open space; housing finance, particularly in the form of tax deductions for mortgage interest and real property taxes; and subsidized Veteran's Administration loans and Federal Housing Administration mortgage insurance. Leaving the city in search of suburban values, the affluent were followed by industry in search of suburban campus locations, retail establishments favoring the mall, and restaurants and entertainment in search of safe locations. Thus, the economic base from which taxes are generated to fund public services was transferred to the suburbs.

Despite notable symbolic, often exciting, urban renewal projects, the suburban growth explosion left distinct patterns of systemic poverty in the cities. These patterns include: racial segregation, burgeoning crime, inadequate transit systems, decaying neighborhoods and housing stock, declining school systems, inadequate job training, high unemployment, rapid population expansion, minimal employment creation, and inadequate systems of public safety and health. America's urban streets and parks are often unsafe and urban transit systems, bridges, water and sewer lines, and public buildings need extensive rebuilding. The situation requires both massive reallocation of the tax base and an escalation in taxing and spending on public works, human services, and job creation rivaling the scale of the New Deal....

Urban growth management is the essence of public urban planning. As practiced in the United States, growth management is reflected in limits on development, typically controlled by zoning, infrastructure capacity, and development timing. Commencing in the 1970s, suburban and rural communities on the outer fringe of development realized that rapid urbanization was outstripping their ability to provide supporting infrastructure, and that developers seeking cheaper rural sites often posed a serious environmental threat to communities.

Growth management must address the form of the developed city rather than simply a restraint on the pace and extent of development. Cities must assure a viable economic base to offer accessible employment and a source of revenue to support needed services and security and a pattern of housing and transportation affordable to its citizens offering an improved standard of living....

Zoning of the undeveloped suburban fringe generally restricts construction to single family homes on generous lots to avoid both street congestion and the exhaustion of the community's capacity to provide schools, water, and sewer service....

Existing growth management systems focus on timing and infrastructure capacity *without considering the ultimate community design and function*. Most communities prefer the sprawl-type development pattern of single family homes on tree-lined boulevards, primarily motivated by anticipated increases in property values. These low density projects usually accelerate sprawl and foreclose the possibility of efficient transit alternatives to automobile travel. In addition, low density projects increase per-dwelling infrastructure costs and result in higher home prices. This increases housing costs and results in economic segregation, confining those on limited incomes to central cities with declining tax bases and deteriorating infrastructure.

Communities typically and parochially fail to address the needs of the entire regional area. These needs include more efficient patterns of development served by transit to and from high density residential areas....

Existing growth management systems tend to generate growth in neighboring communities, thereby exacerbating regional sprawl. Local governments often suppress the pace of development within their own communities, protecting the available capacities of schools, roads, and other essential supporting services. Ironically, growth management schemes designed to avoid suburban low density sprawl thus generate the precise sprawl they were designed to prevent. Additionally, the dispersion of overall regional development patterns may be exacerbated by growth management systems because development sometimes leapfrogs to adjacent and non-adjacent communities that are more accommodating to growth....

Growth management systems fail to coordinate employment development with housing and transit planning so as to ensure access to employment. One tragic effect of post-World War II urban development is the pattern of locating jobs within a suburban belt, while low-income workers—a group disproportionately composed of racial minorities—are housed in distant metropolitan central cities. Low-income workers often lack reliable automobiles that will allow access to their jobs. In addition, public transportation is either unavailable or grossly inconvenient, and suburban rail systems are often prohibitively costly to ride....

* * *

Notes and Comments

1. In studying urban statistics, former Albuquerque Mayor David Rusk has identified a community's relative elasticity. Communities with annexed suburbs or a consolidated region were elastic and thriving, while inelastic central cities were unable to offer a defense to urban sprawl. David Rusk, Inside Game Outside Game: Winning Strategies for Saving Urban America (1999).

2. On the Critical role of job accessibility in welfare reform, see Nicole Stelle Garnett, *The Road from Welfare to Work: Informal Transportation and the Urban Poor*, 38 Harv. J. Legis. 173 (2001).

The following excerpt compares The American growth management experience with that of Berlin and Stockholm:

James A. Kushner, A Tale of Three Cities: Land Development and Planning for Growth in Stockholm, Berlin, and Los Angeles,

25 Urb. Law. 197 (1993)

The most profound component of planning and community development policy is the relationship between transportation and housing. Where transportation needs are inadequately planned for, the result may be highway congestion, air pollution, the social and economic cost of the inefficient or nonexistent home-to-work commute, and the deterioration of neighborhoods and housing stock where long commutes or inaccessibility generates weak demand for housing and community commercial establishments. Alternatively, coordination between trains, fixed rail, buses, or other forms of public transportation and housing and employment centers can reduce automobile dependency, congestion, and air pollution while enhancing the communities' economic base by providing greater open space as housing patterns attain greater density, generating high demand for accessible housing stock, thereby assuring housing and neighborhood maintenance and conservation.

Stockholm has long pursued development and redevelopment policies to assure the availability and dependency upon public transportation. Automobile ownership and dependency is discouraged in Sweden through high automobile purchase and operating costs, which reflect a high level of taxation. Sweden also restricts the expansion and development of highways and urban parking facilities. The early stages of Stockholm's suburban development were located along existing railways. In 1941, Stockholm established a policy to allow development along the line of the proposed underground subway. The centerpiece of Stockholm's planning policy is that each developed neighborhood be adequately served by either train, subway, or bus transportation. Even Stockholm's modern suburban regional shopping centers are all served by underground subway as well as by highways.

Berlin presents another dramatic contrast to Los Angeles, with one of the world's best transit systems on which riders enjoy inexpensive and efficient subway and bus systems... serving both the western and previously East German sections of the city. West German housing and transportation consistency, unlike the planning principle-based Swedish consistency, is more the result of World War II. Due to the absence of autobahns and the fact that few Germans could afford automobiles, post-war housing was built at medium or high density to take advantage of commuter rail and street car lines. Although post-war Germany has accommodated private development to a greater extent than Sweden, West German planning policy has generally prohibited the wholesale development of suburban land unserved by public transport. Although planning policy in the predecessor DDR was not as clear, due to cost and unavailability of automobiles, an essential assumption of East German and East Berlin planning was economic dependency upon mass transportation. The outer belt of East Berlin, however, is a highway rather than the S-Bahn and U-Bahn subways or train system. Indeed, the appearance of consistent application of land-use planning principles in the Federal Republic may also reflect the process assumption of the critical post-war need for efficient mass transportation. In contrast to both Sweden and much of the United States, West Germany generally lacks clear statutory mandated planning criteria.

Both Stockholm and Berlin face major challenges in the future. As Sweden proceeds toward membership in the Common Market, there will be pressure to increase economic growth and investment and simultaneously reduce the former dominant socialist policies of state provision of the vast array of social and economic services. The high tax levels necessary to fund deep social subsidies will discourage investment and reduce Swedish exports. This could translate into a reduction in the role of public transportation and increased dependency on private automobile transportation in Sweden and the outer suburban ring of Stockholm. While Stockholm's supply of developable land has been exhausted, the city has looked to redevelopment projects that will support mass transportation projects. Yet, there is a tradition of public transportation dependency in Stockholm, just as in Berlin.

A reunified Germany also faces a great challenge with the inexorable rush to develop the previously undeveloped eastern sector of Berlin and redevelop its largely antiquated housing stock. Former DDR and East Berlin officials, in embracing a free market ideology, may be disinclined to adopt the previous West Berlin policy of coordinating housing, employment, and transportation policies as the East rushes toward growth and illusive economic security.

Anyone who has visited Los Angeles carries a vivid memory of an ill-planned city. Endless freeways and surface streets clogged with single passenger automobiles, stinging eyes, and choking lungs hungry for fresh air is the result of consumer demand and market response that delivers the preferred single-family detached home. The fiscally motivated public control of land development that prefers tax revenues from concentrated, albeit low density, development in the form of as many housing units and as much square footage for commercial and industrial development as can be accommodated and the virtual absence of controls to assure that housing is developed in a pattern to assure the feasibility of public transportation results in automobile dependence.

Los Angeles represents an extreme example of the American antithesis of planning whereby the built environment is not defined by policies of public growth management. This American phenomenon, whereby private development aspirations prevail over complex public planning principles and administrative processes, is the result of schizophrenia over private enterprise and the interplay with public regulation. This tension, or confusion, generally results in allowing developers to build whatever is politically feasible and often reflects the significant influence of private developer political campaign contributions. The absence of sound consistent planning also reflects the political bifurcation of public planning responsibility whereby the governmental agencies responsible for land development are separate from agencies concerned both with transportation and housing finance. Fundamental to the automobile-dependent sprawl development pattern is the traditional extraordinary capture of the American political system by those who profit from the automobile, including road builders, banks, automobile manufacturers, tire manufacturers, parts manufacturers, oil companies, automobile insurance companies and even automobile clubs that assist drivers with road service and travel assistance.

In recent years, Los Angeles has experimented with modest initiatives designed to reduce the lack of coordination between housing and transportation. For example, Los Angeles may require developers to pay fees to help mitigate the cost of transportation facilities and services including transit subsidy and street improvements. Such ordinances are at best symbolic where much of the city is already built and the attempted mitigation is minimal. The generated fees only superficially assist in reducing infrastructure expansion cost. Such impact fees merely seek contribution of money rather than providing affirmative planning policy and controls to assure that future development is coordinated with public mass transit. Indeed, development may simply fund road improvement costs which may generate a development pattern upon which automobile dependency is assured and transportation alternatives precluded.

In 1986, Los Angeles County, which is responsible for controlling major development in the vast undeveloped ex urban areas of Los Angeles beyond the Los Angeles city geographical boundaries, adopted an amendment to the county's General Plan which seeks to assure that future development will not generate increased traffic congestion. In the United States, the federal government exercises virtually no control over land use other than through the management of federal lands, with each state enjoying land planning and control authority. As a general pattern, this authority has been delegated to local towns, cities, and counties. This bifurcation or balkanization of planning responsibility makes coordination of development and transportation planning virtually impossible in most urban areas as America's cities are typically composites of often more than one hundred separate and autonomous districts. Absent regional government consolidation, individual units of local government are more competitors than partners as they seek to augment their own economic development and tax base. Communities are unable and unwilling to place regional land-use and environmental concerns ahead of parochial interests.

California attempts to guide this planning process through legislation requiring so called comprehensive planning. Pursuant to that delegation, Los Angeles County adopted, albeit reluctantly, in response to a court ruling, a computerized system for linking development to infrastructure capacity.[24] The development monitoring system utilizes the county's street computer model to project the impact from proposed and cumulative development in the form of trip generation to assess whether intersection congestion will exceed a set maximum. Where the system discloses that the standard will be violated in that the current development pattern is at capacity, the developer must either scale back the size of the development or make contributions toward traffic improvements that will bring the effect of the project within the maximum congestion standard.

There is no guarantee under this system, however, that development will be coordinated with the extension of realistic public transportation or that the pattern of community development will be modified from that of automobile dependency. In addition, the system fails to take into account the impact on congestion within the state's interstate limited access freeway system which represents the greatest of congestion problems.

Urban Sprawl

Urban Sprawl, sometimes called "Los Angelization," reflects a pattern of virtual nonexistent regulatory urban boundaries—where developers are free to leap frog out from developed to less expensive land on the community's fringe. This pattern is very costly as the premature extension of roads, schools, and utilities renders the provision of public safety and other services far more costly. The community is unable to enjoy the economies of scale presented from concentrated development, resulting in the escalation of the price of close-in developable land which discourages in-fill development and encourages further sprawl-type development. The process may also cost the community dearly in both the tax revenue that would have been generated by such projects and, of greater significance, in the population density necessary to support mass transit. The resulting sprawl pattern is typically based on private automobile transport and its concomitant urban disadvantages.

The population within the metropolitan area of Stockholm's twenty-two municipalities is 1.5 million, while the population of Stockholm is 670,000. Stockholm, except for those cities lacking the potential for sprawl due to natural urban boundaries, is in the best position to plan against premature urban expansion due to the long-standing city policy of holding title to all developable suburban land. In addition, Sweden, in part,

---

24. 1 James A. Kushner, Subdivision Law and Growth Management §2:21 (2d ed. 2001); James A. Kushner, *The Development Monitoring System (DMS): Computer Technology for Subdivision Review and Growth Management*, 11 Zoning & Plan. L. Rep. 33 (1988).

controls growth so effectively because it has practically eliminated development as a matter of right. Despite such control capacity, Stockholm may permit ill-planned, premature growth, as may cities without such ownership, should its regulatory and political system embrace greater free market concepts in pursuit of future growth.

Berlin, due to its unique status as a town surrounded by the DDR, had no opportunity for sprawl prior to reunification. As in the case of transportation coordination, Berlin may now face market demands for economic and population growth from patterns of rapid immigration, increasing birth rates, and long-denied modern development in the former eastern Federal Republic. The German constitutional court has foreclosed policies of long-term land acquisition and land banking for future development patterned on the Swedish model. Private developers have responded with purchase of large tracts of marginal agricultural land on the outskirts of growing cities, a phenomenon likely to be repeated around a reunified Berlin. Berlin, like Stockholm, can avoid rapid sprawl by continuing its adherence to its ostensible policies of conditioning urban development on the availability of mass transportation to serve the proposed development. Yet, the principal limitations on suburban sprawl and the prevention of premature suburbs under German law are the requirements of costly, detailed plans prepared in advance of new development, restriction on the conversion of land suited for agricultural use unless absolutely needed for other uses, and the requirement of the preservation of landscapes adjoining population concentration areas. German land is further classified as built-up areas called Innenbereich, or land outside such areas called Aussenbereich, with development permits available only in the Innenbereich districts. German control of development has been successful in preserving the ex urban countryside and wooded regions from the single family vacation home sprawl that mars much of the American countryside....

The pattern of urban sprawl and automobile dependency has rendered widespread use of mass transportation nearly unattainable in Los Angeles. Most of the recently developed transit systems in America were developed on the basis of grossly exaggerated forecasts of ridership and grossly underestimated system costs....

Professor Lefcoe suggests that the relative development patterns of compact German and Swedish villages as compared to the scattered form of Los Angeles may simply reflect centuries of land traditions. Just as the American Midwest's rural belt was composed of separate, scattered family farms, the German tradition of more than a thousand years consisted of vibrant villages serving as the residence for community farm owners and workers, the close-in farms resulting in a tight greenbelt around urban centers. As such, cities are built on old ideals while city planners, planning theory, and technique have made far less of a mark on our comparative urban landscapes....

One might speculate on the future. If Stockholm shifts towards a more free market model, market demand for suburban living, recreational homes, and a lifestyle of the upper classes, Stockholm could face suburban low-density, automobile-dependent congested sprawl and "Los Angelization." Berlin is in crisis as its once natural boundary has been demolished and is the target of extraordinary development pressure to convert into the image of other sprawling German cities. Although Los Angeles would benefit from the rigid planning principles of Stockholm, it may be inexorably altering its current community design to reflect the Swedish model, not by government controlling development, but because the demands of the market for better designed, more affordable, and more accessible communities may be shaping the future pattern of urban development....

* * *

Urban Growth Boundaries

The following excerpt describes Portland's growth management system that features urban growth boundaries and targeting growth toward transit stops:

Stephanie Yu, Note, The Smart Growth Revolution: Loudoun County, Virginia and Lessons To Learn,

7 Environmental Lawyer 379 (2001)

....By 1999, Portland's estimated population surpassed 500,000, increasing approximately 3.6% since the 1990 U.S. Census. The real surge in Portland's population, however, occurred between 1980 and 1990, when the population increased from 366,383 to 486,083 (a 32% increase). Observers have commented that it is the success of the city's early growth control planning that attracted, rather than discouraged, newcomers to the city.

1. Smart Growth Initiatives and Tools

Oregon is a pioneer in enacting effective legislation to limit urban sprawl. In 1973, the state legislature, with Senate Bill 100 ("SB 100" or "Act"), mandated that cities and counties create laws to limit sprawl and protect farms, forests and other open space. At the time, few states had comprehensive state-wide land use planning laws, and Oregon's Act "inspire[d] and justif[ied] similar programs elsewhere." The Act created the Department of Land Conservation and Development, which is run by its Commission ("LCDC"). The Act also required every city and county to draft and adopt a comprehensive plan that complies with the goals the LCDC has established, such as encouraging citizen involvement in growth planning, conserving forest lands, and providing housing for state residents. Additionally, each city needed to "[e]nact land use regulations to implement their comprehensive plans." The laws mandated by the Act have proven effective. For example, before enacting the laws, Oregon had been losing 30,000 acres of farmland per year; currently, the state is losing only 2,000 acres a year. Consequently, many municipal leaders, members of the media and conservation groups have recognized Oregon as successful in employing smart growth techniques to control sprawl.

In Portland, state law provides that land use is governed by a regional planning authority, the Metropolitan Service District ("Metro"). Metro adopted its Comprehensive Plan to comply with the Act in 1980 and employs the city's zoning code as the plan's major implementation tool. In conformance with the statewide goal of providing an "efficient transition from rural to urban land use," the Portland City Council created Urban Growth Boundaries ("UGBs") that confine development to designated areas. This technique increases density in one part of the municipality while maintaining farmland and rural space. Public services are then limited within the UGB, "encouraging further urban development within its boundaries." UGBs are intended to manage, not stifle, growth. In conforming with the UGB, some of Portland's zoning ordinances remained the same, while the City Council downzoned many other parts of the city to restrict their uses.

Overcoming Legal Issues

A crucial legal hurdle for SB 100 concerned the extent to which comprehensive plans controlled zoning laws. The same year that the legislature enacted SB 100, the Oregon

Supreme Court determined that zoning ordinances must comply with the comprehensive plan for a particular locality. Only zoning ordinances more liberal than the comprehensive plans, however, are considered inconsistent; a city or county is free to enact zoning ordinances that are more restrictive than the applicable comprehensive plan requires. Furthermore, the Act's passage requires land use and zoning laws to comply with the state's mandatory goals.

Controversies concerning the comprehensive plans did not abate once the courts determined the validity and scope of SB 100. The most specific challenges to Portland's smart growth plan were brought before the Land Use Board of Appeals ("LUBA"), which the Oregon Legislative Assembly created to conserve judicial resources by centralizing the review of land use disputes in the state. LUBA possesses the "exclusive jurisdiction to review any land use decision of a local government, special district or a state agency."

Many of the petitions filed with LUBA have concerned the Metropolitan Portland UGB. Landowners who owned outside of the UGB or city limits and sought to develop their land were deprived of public services, such as water. Such landowners petitioned to have the UGB amended to include or annex their land. LUBA's decisions, however, interpreted the UGB as an inflexible barrier: most of the property lying outside the UGB would remain rural, with little hope for annexation or zoning variances. Conversely, the LUBA decisions often held that land within the UGB, although designated as urban or future urban land, must conform with the current zoning regulation, even if the urban land designation is changed. In situations where the Portland city council granted zoning variances to provide for higher-density development, neighboring landowners filed suit, claiming inconsistent and biased application of the relevant laws on variances; however, these lawsuits generally failed as well. Lawsuits related to zoning and land use concerning UGBs in the Portland area continue to be abundant, but the LUBA decisions more often than not support the control of growth.

In addition to the complaints brought before LUBA, land use-related lawsuits premised on the theory of an unconstitutional taking by the government continue to flourish. Governments are rarely required to compensate private individuals if the value of their land is reduced due to a zoning ordinance, provided that the zoning ordinance is reasonably related to a legitimate public purpose. When local governments consider amending the zoning law, the governing body is not required to show "either [a] public need or a comparison with other available property" as "a specific and independent prerequisite." Such factors are merely relevant in changing the zoning ordinance, thereby allowing the local government much discretion. Furthermore, compensation to landowners is not required when the property value is merely reduced and does not deny the landowner substantial beneficial use of the property.

Ultimately, where regulations controlling urban growth are concerned, Oregon citizens have tried to circumvent the judicial system by organizing ballot measures. Most recently, on November 7, 2000, Oregon citizens voted on a ballot measure that proposed a constitutional amendment that required state and local governments to compensate landowners in an amount "equal to the reduction in the fair market value of the property" if the property's value was merely reduced due to a government-imposed restriction by regulation. In a repudiation of smart growth values and goals, the measure passed with 54% of the vote.

* * *

Notes and Comments

1. For a description of Tennessee's growth management plan utilizing urban growth boundaries, see Michael J. Stewart, *Growth and its Implications: An Evaluation of Tennessee's Growth Management Plan*, 67 Tenn. L. Rev. 983 (2000).

Korea has utilized urban growth boundaries. The following excerpt describes the design and impact of the boundaries.

Chang-Hee Christine Bae, *Korea's Greenbelts: Impacts and Options for Change*,

7 Pacific Rim Law & Policy Journal 479 (1998)

Korea's Greenbelt[25] policy has been in place since 1971. Although amended several times in minor ways over the years, and attacked from many quarters in the recent past, the policy remains entrenched as the key element in Korea's land use controls. Controlled by the Ministry of Construction and Transportation—with management by local governments—it stands as a prime example of top-down, centralized physical planning. It has made the life of local government officials much more difficult as they have had to cope with the pressures of rapid population growth and economic expansion in the face of severe land supply constraints. The moves toward increasing local autonomy in recent years have barely affected Greenbelt strategies. Moreover, they have caused severe adverse effects on land and housing values, aggravating Korea's already serious housing problems. Furthermore, restrictions on development and use have violated the property rights of Greenbelt residents (and landowners)....

Although the designation of Seoul's Greenbelt occurred in 1971, seven years earlier the Korean Planners Association proposed the Capital Region Urban Plan, which included a Greenbelt combined with satellite towns along radial corridors and a development corridor between Seoul and Incheon. These ideas borrowed heavily from the United Kingdom and Japan: from the Greater London Plan of 1944 came the Greenbelt and the formation of satellite towns, and from the National Capital Region Development Plan for Tokyo of 1958 came the development axis concept (Tokyo-Yokohama). A subsequent Master Plan prepared by the Seoul City Government in 1976 suggested a Greenbelt approximately ten kilometers-wide, beginning fifteen kilometers from City Hall.

The Greenbelt was finally introduced in 1971 as an important component of the 1972–81 National Comprehensive Physical Plan. The Greenbelt was created by the Town Planning Act ("TPA") of January 1971, which adopted the term "Development Restriction Zone" rather than Greenbelt. The impetus for the TPA was personal intervention by President Park on his New Year visit to Seoul City Hall in January 1970. The Greenbelt was designated and implemented at the end of July 1971.

The Greenbelt reflected many objectives: to slow down population growth and industrial concentration in Seoul; to prevent contiguous metropolitan sprawl merging Seoul with the cities of Incheon, Suwon, and Euijeongbu; to prevent expansion to the north because of the security and military risks associated with development too near to North Korea; and to develop an environmental protection area by reserving regional

25. Although this paper uses the more popular term "Greenbelt," the official name for the Greenbelts in Korea is Development Restriction Zones (*Gaebal Jehan Guyuk*).

open spaces such as national and regional parks, mountains and river banks, agricultural land, and later the Han River catchment area. The boundaries were based on political decisions, however, and not as outcomes of land use surveys.

The Seoul Greenbelt developed in four phases, each expanding the area. The first phase of the Greenbelt designated an area fifteen kilometers away from City Hall with a band width of between one and nine kilometers. The Greenbelt encircled the city with the exception of several corridors. The north-west zone, although already densely developed, was included within the Greenbelt because of its proximity to North Korea. The area of the initial Belt was 463.8 square kilometers....

In the country as a whole, there are fourteen Greenbelts affecting thirty-three cities established in the 1971–87 period. Greenbelt area totals 5397.1 square kilometers, or 5.4 percent of South Korea's land area (located around major cities, Do (provincial) capitals, industrial cities, and cities located close to preservation areas). In fact, the share of national territory devoted to the Greenbelts is currently a little larger than the share devoted to urban development (4.7 percent). Approximately four-fifths (79.6 percent) of the Greenbelts' land area is owned privately. Although Seoul's was by far the largest, substantial Greenbelts exist around some of the other cities, such as Pusan, Kwangju, Daegu and Daejon. About 964,475 people (more than 2 percent of the total population) live inside the Greenbelts.

While the proportions vary from case to case, most of the Greenbelt land consists of mountains and forests (60 percent nationwide), leaving much of the rest as farmland (27 percent). Only 3.6 percent of the combined land uses are residential. Other minor uses include airports or air bases, transportation facilities (e.g., rail freight yards), cemeteries and recreational facilities (e.g., golf courses, community parks). Recent Greenbelt regulations focus on private property rights, oftentimes exempting central government agencies, especially where national security is concerned.

Objectives of Metropolitan Seoul's Greenbelt

There have been at least seven major objectives in establishing and maintaining the Greenbelt around Seoul, although their relative importance has changed over time. A first, dominant objective was to strictly control development in the northern parts of Seoul for national security reasons. South Koreans have perceived intermittent threats of invasion from the North and have avoided allowing too many people to settle close to the Demilitarized Zone ("DMZ"). However, within the last few years, land scarcity has resulted in new development north of the Han River and beyond the Greenbelt, especially at Ilsan New Town, located within the boundaries of Goyang City.

A second objective, quite important in the early years, was to use the Greenbelt regulations as instruments for eliminating illegal suburban shantytowns around Seoul.

Third, in common with all Greenbelts and urban growth boundaries around the world, South Korea wanted to discourage urban sprawl. However, the eventual scale of the Greenbelt resulted in the establishment of new and the expansion of existing settlements at considerable distances from Seoul (e.g., Ansan). To the extent that some of these settlements functioned as dormitory towns, the sequelae were additional transportation costs and congestion.

A fourth objective, somewhat similar to the third, was to use the Greenbelt as an instrument for harmonizing metropolitan growth by controlling growth within the Greenbelt and promoting suburban and exurban growth beyond the Greenbelt via the development of planned satellite towns.

A fifth objective was to control land speculation within the metropolitan region by extending Greenbelt status to a much larger land area. In fact, this discouraged land speculation only in the short run. In the long run, as shown by the upward trends in land and housing prices, speculative activity in the land and housing markets increased strongly, both at core sites on non-Greenbelt land and in areas beyond the Greenbelt.

Between 1974 and 1989, housing prices in Korea increased at an annual rate of 17.1 percent, while the consumer price index ("CPI") rose at a rate of 11 percent per annum. Land prices increased at an annual growth rate of 19.2 percent in Korea and 24.2 percent in Seoul. Land prices rose much faster than other goods due to a chronic undersupply of urban land for development. The share of city land available for residential use fell from 11.5 percent to 8.9 percent. Although other factors created the under-supply, particularly the government's monopoly power over urban land, the developing land shortage resulting from the creation of Greenbelts severely exacerbated the problem. Korea's sixth objective in creating Greenbelts was to protect agricultural land. Like people in other newly industrialized countries, Koreans have a nostalgic view of farmers and rural life. They rationalize the protection of high-cost agriculture (especially rice farming) in terms of "food security," an attempt to link agricultural protection to national security while disregarding the ease of access to the diversity of supply on the world food market.

A final objective, shared with other countries using Greenbelts, was environmental and natural resource protection. This objective explains the expansion of the Greenbelt area, especially the inclusion of the Han River catchment area in the third designation. This objective has gained importance in recent years, as environmental awareness in South Korea has increased as wealth has expanded. However, as the later discussion about Pusan will show, sound environmental strategies within the Greenbelt have not been consistently pursued.

Kang argues, with some justification, that the Korean Greenbelts have failed to achieve their key objectives. Urban sprawl was not prevented, but merely pushed farther out beyond the Greenbelt boundaries. The natural environment was not protected because of the proliferation of illegal activities, the lack of a natural environmental preservation strategy for Greenbelt lands, the use of the Greenbelt as a dumping ground for locally undesirable land uses ("LULU's"), and the construction of public agency facilities.

There has never been a serious attempt to apply environmental criteria to the location of public facilities within the Greenbelts. Industrial facilities, landfills, and military bases have been placed in the Greenbelts with little regard for environmental preservation. As evident in conversion of United States' military bases, military bases generate large amounts of hazardous wastes and soil contamination. Actually, there was probably a net loss in agricultural land, because the Greenbelts did not stop development. Instead, they promoted development farther out at somewhat lower densities than would have prevailed in the absence of the Greenbelts.

Kang's views are partially supported by a recent survey of different interest groups. Of five groups (Greenbelt residents, other residents, experts (typically professors), members of environmental groups, and government officials), only about 50 percent of the government officials believe that the Greenbelts prevent sprawl (while the other groups fall in the range of 19 to 29 percent, with the experts the most pessimistic). Only the environmentalists (67 percent) and the experts (52 percent) think that the Greenbelt preserves the natural environment. Yet the so-called informed groups (experts, environmentalists and government officials) all believe that the Greenbelts are worthwhile; on the other hand, 55 percent of Greenbelt residents and 27 percent of other residents believe that they contribute nothing....

Seoul's Greenbelt Compared with London and Tokyo

A comparison of Seoul's experiences with those of London (an even earlier Greenbelt example) and Tokyo (where the Greenbelt was abandoned) is useful in pointing out alternative directions for the future of the Greenbelt in Seoul. Bae argued for following Tokyo's example of greater suburban growth, and suggested that more development could be directed to the Controlled Development Area in the Southwest of Seoul (around Suwon and Incheon), established in the 1986 Master Plan of Capital Region Development. On the other hand, following London's example, the need for environmental protection (specifically with respect to water quality) could be met by extending the Greenbelt into the Nature Preservation Area to the East. As a step in this direction, over 2000 square kilometers upstream of the Paldang reservoir were declared as another Environmental Protection Zone in 1990.

Bae also suggested that Seoul's development problems mirror those faced decades ago by London and Tokyo, a potential ill omen for the future. "Urban congestion was seriously discussed in the late 1930s in London, [it] paralyzed Tokyo in the mid-1950s and [it] brought painful problems to Seoul in the 1980s. From this it seems that in terms of development Seoul is about half a century behind London and a quarter of a century behind Tokyo."

Despite having a population much larger than London and catching up on Tokyo, the total area of the Seoul built-up area is quite small, only 457 square kilometers, compared with a London built-up area of 1310 square kilometers and a Tokyo built-up area of 1005 square kilometers. Also, the area of Seoul's satellite towns of 354 square kilometers is small compared to London's Urban Islands of 831 square kilometers and Tokyo's Greenbelt suburban area of 941 square kilometers. The early designation of the Greenbelt in Seoul has limited the area available for suburban development in both the built-up area and the satellite towns. Problems have followed from the prevention of development in the closest and most suitable land around Seoul.

London's Greenbelt grew from a width of eight kilometers in Abercrombie's Greater London Plan of 1944 to eleven to sixteen kilometers in the Plans of the early 1950s, to thirty kilometers in the 1960s and 1970s, returning to a more reasonable twenty to twenty-five kilometers in the 1980s. Although pressures for release of Greenbelt land continued, the Greenbelt Circular 14/84 of 1984 reaffirmed the concept of the Greenbelt and argued that its boundaries should not be breached except "in exceptional circumstances." Rural preservation objectives were introduced in 1988. By 1990, the Greenbelts had expanded to 1.55 million hectares, 12 percent of England's land area and double the 1979 area. A Planning Policy Guidance Note on Greenbelts, published in January 1995, added to earlier objectives the goal of making positive use of the Greenbelts, for example, as a recreational resource. Support for the Greenbelts remained as strong as ever.

Tokyo, on the other hand, abandoned its Greenbelt and the land was developed as moderate income suburbs. An interesting question is why the Greenbelt concept worked in Korea, but came under unbearable pressure in Japan. A probable explanation is that Japanese law protects private development rights much better than Korean law. Parkland per capita in Tokyo is only 10 percent of that in London. By 1990, Seoul's density in the built-up area surrounded by the Greenbelt had reached 28,000 people per square mile and there were less than forty square kilometers of land remaining for development. Bae concluded that following a London Greenbelt strategy would save 60 percent of the likely land consumption resulting from a Tokyo strategy, but he may have underestimated the far suburb and exurban development; the high density and lack of land provide pressure to relax Greenbelt restrictions.

England's Greenbelt policies have not been beyond criticism. Land values have increased two-and-a-half times faster than the consumer price index. Another study estimated that 3 percent of GNP is consumed in maintaining the London Greenbelt and that new homeowners pay more than $500 per year more in mortgaging servicing costs than if the Greenbelt did not exist. While they have constrained the physical expansion of cities, they have not stopped their functional expansion in the form of multi-nucleated settlements; this results in a high degree of inter-urban commuting through the Greenbelts with higher travel costs and more air pollution. The displacement of contiguous development has led, in some cases, to the preservation of poor quality land on the urban fringes at the cost of development in rural landscapes. In-fill development ("town cramming") has been associated with the loss of urban open space. Development restrictions have limited the ability of farmers to diversify out of excess capacity crops into more productive activities (e.g., market gardening structures on the urban fringe). Finally, landholders in the Greenbelt have no incentive to maintain their land because a degraded landscape will more likely receive planning permission to develop—hence the emergence of unsightly "brown" landscapes. Although there are counter-arguments to some of these criticisms, they illustrate that even in England, where Greenbelts originated and where they continue to receive substantial public support, they remain a mixed blessing....

Comparison with the Washington State Growth Management Act ("GMA")

...First, the Korean approach is much more top-down, with most of the decisions dictated by the central government, particularly the Ministry of Construction and Transportation. In Washington State, although the State requires urban jurisdictions in urban counties to adopt an urban growth boundary and other growth management measures, local governments have considerable latitude. In Korea, on the other hand, local governments cannot act freely in the green areas surrounding their jurisdictions. This difference, in part, reflects not only the very recent shift toward a more democratic structure in Korea, but also the fact that attempted development of a higher degree of local autonomy is incomplete.

Second, the urban growth boundary concept is not the same as a Greenbelt. In the former, the aim is to concentrate new development via infill, redevelopment, and other strategies inside the boundary; in the latter, development is not only allowed but may be actively promoted beyond the outer boundaries of the Greenbelt. This distinction has been obvious in the Korean case because of the secular pressures of urbanization that have made suburban and exurban development unavoidable.

Third, the fact that the Growth Management Act was passed only in 1990, and that many of the plans adopted by local governments have yet to be implemented, means that it is premature to evaluate its impact. The results of Korea's 26-year-old Greenbelt policy are transparent, although the extent to which the responsibility of some of its effects (e.g., rising land prices) are to be shared with other influences (e.g., the slow release of land for development by the government under its Land Readjustment Program) remains controversial.

Fourth, although the land uses spared from development (e.g., forests and agricultural land) are similar in the two cases, preservation of the natural environment is a more dominant objective in Washington. Although this goal has recently received more attention in Korea, it remains of secondary concern. In fact, in many locations, environmental conditions within the Greenbelts have been allowed to deteriorate through neglect.

Fifth, South Korea and the United States differ in their needs for monitoring and enforcement. The land use zoning and building permit processes have been in place for so long in the United States and are so widely accepted that there are almost no violations. In Korea, on the other hand, partly because of severe restrictions on development, attempts to build illegal structures and facilities have been frequent and the authorities have had to be vigilant to keep these in check....

Obstacles to Reform

Many obstacles prevent reforming the Greenbelts. An important one is that Korea has shared in the increasing interest and concern about environmental problems that have swept the world in the past two or three decades; as a result, the environmental rationale appears stronger now than when the first Greenbelt was established in 1971.

Another obstacle is the "floodgates" argument. Government officials fear that if they make some significant concessions, then the whole Greenbelt policy would collapse. One must also contend with legal and constitutional barriers. In May 1990, the Korean Supreme Court decided against compensation for Greenbelt owners, on the ground that it was not in the public interest. The issue before the Korean Supreme Court was whether Article 21, Sections 1 and 2 of the Urban Planning Act were in violation of the Korean Constitution. The Court ruled that it was in the public interest to prevent uncontrolled growth of urban areas and to preserve the national environment as a healthy living environment. "In line with that public interest, it is acceptable that the landowner suffer personal losses and therefore the Act, which precludes compensation, is not unconstitutional."

However, some strong winds push for change. The increasing agitation of the residents and landowners continues to find a receptive ear among some politicians. Another, potentially more important political force is the growing autonomy of the local governments that either have or are near Greenbelts and may have different views about preserving them than the central government.

A third political consideration is the origin of Seoul's Greenbelt as an authoritarian decision (by President Park) so that undermining it could be considered a strike for democracy. Urban economists and other urban analysts are beginning to critique the Greenbelts on the ground that they are inconsistent with the "highest and best use" of land principle. This argument has gained strength as the population pressures around the large cities have raised the potential value of land in appropriate parts of the Greenbelts....

A longer-term consideration is that the land shortage problem in South Korea may eventually be relieved when and if reunification takes place. Although there is widespread agreement that this will happen, uncertainty about its timing makes it a difficult factor to consider in deliberations about modifying the Greenbelt.

Violations constitute another obstacle, in that they harden the government's resolve to punish violators. Relaxing the restrictions in a major way would be tantamount to a confession by he government that Greenbelt residents and landowners had merit. Enforcement measures have been somewhat successful, although violations do occur extremely frequently. One-half of Korean Greenbelt survey respondents admitted to violations, as opposed to 1.5 percent in the United Kingdom....

Korea's Greenbelts policy has been in place for twenty-seven years and is ingrained in the national psyche; preserving the Greenbelt becomes a mantra. The perception is that major changes would result in big winners and big losers, a policy maker's nightmare. Yet the prospect of substantial land value increases after Greenbelt deregulation suggests that there are prospects for developing a win-win strategy. The land price within Greenbelts may be as little as 10 percent of the price of any available land in the central core of the city. Abolishing the Greenbelt, however, would not necessarily result in a price increase sufficient to bring the value up to that of the ex ante non-Greenbelt land prices. Much depends on the price elasticity of the demand for land, the area of the Greenbelt relative to the urbanized area, the amount of developable land still available, whether the Greenbelt were to be abandoned as a whole or partially, and many other reasons. The land price would increase substantially, though, perhaps by 50 percent.

People in government, academic, and environmentalist circles commonly argue against relaxing Greenbelt controls because "speculators" (i.e., the absentee landowners) would reap windfall gains. Many of the natives would receive minimal benefits because their land holdings are small and usually have structures in place. Yet these arguments suffer if there is a potent public interest in releasing Greenbelt land. In fact, a cross-subsidy scheme could likely be devised to approximate a win-win solution.[83]

The tax yields could not only buttress the general revenues of government, both central and local, but more importantly could provide funds to supply the natives with much needed community services to satisfy their demands for neighborhood upgrading. In addition, housing consumers would gain substantially from the leveling off of land prices. The main losers would be the environmental groups who would protest the loss to development of open space and natural resources, but as suggested earlier, environmental preservation goals are more of an excuse than an operational rationale for the Greenbelts.

This solution may not be practical. The government of Korea has little experience with, or appetite for, cross-subsidy schemes. On the other hand, the principle of public-private profit sharing has been established for a long time, even in land markets (i.e. the well-known Land Readjustment Program[84]). Another practical difficulty is that many purchasers of land report artificial prices (often 50 to 80 percent of the price paid) as a tax avoidance tactic. This would undermine the cross-subsidy concept, and the problem might even get worse if such a scheme were implemented.

An alternative to this market-oriented, cross-subsidy solution might be a five-fold approach:

---

83. The essence of such a scheme would involve imposing a special tax on the windfall profits of the speculators and providing subsidies to the natives, but still leaving speculators with a healthy capital gain. The tax would have to be at a higher rate than either the Development Gains Charge, which taxes 50% percent of the land value increase above the amount invested on projects larger than 3300 square meters, or the Excess Profits Tax on Land, which also taxes 50% of any imputed increase in land values above the national average land price.

84. The essence of the Land Readjustment Program is that developers hand over a proportion of their land for public use in return for government investments in infrastructure that raise the value of their remaining land. However, land readjustment fell out of favor in the 1980s because of the perception that too much profit was being made.

1. Transfer responsibility for the Greenbelts to local governments, allowing them to take into account local land and housing market considerations;

2. Readjust the boundaries, allowing some development to take place where land pressures are most acute or where environmental quality goals are not violated;

3. Widen the range of land uses permitted to reduce development restrictions and potential property value losses;

4. Draw a distinction, with respect to environmental quality goals, between activities that pollute and those that do not, and allow the development of a wider range of the latter type of activities; and,

5. Introduce a system of transferable development rights ("TDR's") to allow the natives to exchange their land, especially if located in environmentally sensitive areas, for developable land outside the Greenbelt.

This approach might be politically acceptable because out of all the interested groups, only a slight majority of the Greenbelt residents (51 percent) would abolish the Greenbelt altogether. Apart from the general population who are split on all alternatives, the other groups (experts, environmentalists and officials) would maintain the current Greenbelts with some mitigating actions to relieve its inconveniences to the natives....

* * *

Notes and Comments

1. Is the Korean Greenbelt like the Green Heart in the Netherlands? (See Chapter 5). Is the "green belt" a myth perhaps bigger than life, whereby preservation of such resources take on theological tones?

British Columbia utilizes urban growth boundaries:

Jeffrey Patterson, *Testing the Partnership Model of Growth Management,*

7 Pacific Rim Law and Policy Journal 721 (1998)

[A] major development...is the establishment of a growth management planning regime to assure that urban development in [British Columbia] B.C.'s regions occurs in accordance with best practices principles established by provincial government legislation. While growth management has brought new life into planning in other jurisdictions, especially in the United States where the prerogatives of local officials continue to be subject to more onerous takings precedents, its primary contributions in B.C. have been to discipline the behaviour of local municipalities, and promote settlement dispute mechanisms and local cooperation among those municipalities and the regional districts that supply regional services.

Growth management, as used herein, has as its objective the promotion of human settlements that are socially, economically, and environmentally healthy. Growth management attempts to make efficient use of public facilities and services, land, and other natural resources. It is generally perceived as avoiding urban sprawl and ensuring that development takes place where adequate community infrastructure and facilities exist or can be provided in a timely, economic, and efficient manner. Growth management is also viewed as encouraging settlement patterns that minimize the use of automobiles and encourage walking, bicycling, and the use of public transit. Other objectives of growth management include: 1) efficient movement of people and goods; 2) protection of environmentally sensitive areas; 3) maintenance of the integrity of a secure and productive resource base; 4) mitigation and prevention of air, land, and water pollution; 5) adequate, affordable and appropriate housing; and 6) promotion of the efficient use and conservation of energy....

In any case, growth management appears to have managed to gain the allegiance of significant local interests. The real estate development industry supports a growth management regime because it provides development rules understood by all parties. Downtown business interests support it for providing a context for accommodating growth. Environmentalists support it because growth management typically provides an opportunity for mitigating the effects of pollution and for protecting ecologically sensitive areas. Agriculturists have often supported it because it may be used to protect agricultural productivity, as well as to protect agriculture from the burden of taxation based on current use value. Significantly, the recent evolution of urban planning towards growth management often involves extensive intra-regional municipal co-operation, as well as the intrusion of senior government jurisdictions in limiting the latitude often previously provided local governments in planning land uses within their jurisdictions....

B.C. officially abandoned regional planning with Bill 9 in 1983, which abolishes planning as a function of regional districts. "Growth management" represents a limited re-authorisation of regional planning.... Second and related, this limited authorization places particular emphasis on mechanisms designed to reconcile the requirements of regional growth management strategies and the autonomy of local Official Community Plans ("OCP's"). B.C.'s growth management legislation represents a departure from the hierarchical regime imposed in other jurisdictions beginning with the State of Oregon's Senate Bill 100 in 1973. For example, regional district boards may not impose their views on constituent municipalities. Disagreements are settled by one of three dispute settlement mechanisms. All parties are subject to the results of this arbitration process....

The Lower Mainland is divided into two regional districts. The more populous of the two is the Greater Vancouver Regional District ("GVRD"). Consisting of 2,910 square kilometres, 1,990 square kilometres of which is organised into twenty municipalities, the GVRD, which also currently coincides with the Vancouver Census Metropolitan Area ("CMA"), had a population of 1.83 million in 1996. The Fraser Valley Regional District ("FVRD") occupies most of the remainder of the Lower Mainland and contained six municipalities with a total area of 1,070 square kilometres and a population of 215,000 in 1996....

Growth management, of course, takes place in the context of political and social systems. Despite an increasingly common North American culture, Canada and the United States differ substantially politically and socially, and the differences impinge critically on planning practice and urban development.

The federal systems of Canada and the United States have diverged considerably in their evolution....

Total Canadian federal government expenditures, including transfers to other government levels, were less than forty-eight percent of the government sector in 1995. The U.S. federal government is responsible for nearly sixty-five percent of total spending by the government sector. That provinces possess sole jurisdiction over natural resources within their boundaries further aggrandises provincial powers.

One practical result of this division of powers is that Canada has neither possessed a national road network, such as that in the United States, nor had a system of federal subsidies for municipal expressways. Fewer municipal expressways and less suburban sprawl relative to American cities may be a positive consequence.

As most students of political science are aware, Canada's federal and provincial governments possess unitary cabinet governments made up of the dominant party (almost always) or parties (sometimes) in federal Parliament and provincial legislatures. This system contrasts with decentralised power centres and the complex checks and balances in the U.S. federal and state governments. While cabinet government allows the legislative majority to govern with few daily checks, the system itself may be prone to instability. The differences between Canadian political parties appear to be greater than for their U.S. cousins.... B.C.'s political parties have historically maintained radically different views of planning and development. It may be observed that the fortunes of planning in B.C. have historically tended to reflect the views and fortunes of the party in power.

Provincial politics in B.C. have been dominated by a deep left-right schism for over half a century. The NDP, a loose amalgamation of the trade union movement and progressives, has governed since 1991, having briefly governed previously from 1972 to 1975. A right of centre coalition has governed for most of the modern period (1943 through 1972 and 1975 through 1991). As will be noted below, the current brand of growth management in B.C. owes itself to the views and composition of the current provincial government, as well as to B.C.'s political culture.

Canadian municipal affairs are entirely a provincial responsibility....

[T]he provincial government has generally played a heavy hand in municipal administration. B.C. has chosen to intrude in local government affairs by manipulating the functions and powers of local governments rather than by creating or destroying local jurisdictions. It has also generally chosen to either administer additional functions directly or to create special commissions or boards, including provincial Crown agencies, to carry out specific functions. Thus, BC Transit supplies transit services throughout the province.... Property tax assessment is carried out by the B.C. Assessment Authority. The Municipal Finance Authority ("MFA") has been delegated responsibility for approving and issuing debentures to finance local capital debt everywhere outside the City of Vancouver. The provincial Agricultural Land Commission ("ALC") has established Agricultural Land Reserves ("ALR") across B.C., and a more recently established commission performs the same function with respect to forest harvesting licences....

The B.C. Legislature adopted the Growth Management Act in June 1995. GVRD directors confirmed the "Livable Region Strategic Plan" ("LRSP"), its regional growth strategy plan, whose formulation preceded the Act by several years, in January 1996. The twenty municipalities of Greater Vancouver, all of which approved the plan in principle, had until February 1998 to adopt "regional context statements" bringing Official Community Plans ("OCP's") into conformity with the regional growth strategy, or indicating how they intend to do so. The Fraser Valley Regional District ("FVRD") is in the process of developing a regional strategic growth management plan for the upper reaches of the Lower Mainland.

B.C.'s growth management is divided into three components. The first, consists of a series of policies and measures designed to preserve agricultural and other green spaces throughout the Lower Mainland. An Agricultural Land Reserve establishing limits to urban growth is the centrepiece of this set of policies. The second consists of the various plans and measures established under the auspices of the Growth Management Act. The two principal measures are the LRSP and a related component, Transport 2021, developed jointly by the GVRD and the provincial government, and adopted by the GVRD in 1993. The third component is the set of provincial measures implemented in support of the regional growth management plan. As explained above, successive B.C. governments have manipulated the municipal context to achieve provincial objectives. Two critical institutions in this respect are the Crown agencies ("Crowns") BC Transit, which provides public transit services across B.C.; and the Transportation Finance Authority ("TFA"), a Crown agency responsible for financing provincial highways....

The Agricultural Land Commission Act was passed in late 1972.... Local government is integral to the work of the commission to the extent that each regional district is required to file a land reserve plan and bylaw with the Commission. Such a bylaw need not have the support of each municipal member of a regional district, although it would not be possible to pass a bylaw without the approval of a majority of regional district directors....

The overall record is nevertheless usually regarded as a successful one. In the early 1980s, Ontario lost nearly seventeen thousand hectares of farmland to urban development, while British Columbia lost only twelve hundred. In comparison, California reportedly loses twenty thousand hectares [10,000 square meters or 2.471 acres] annually. The program compares favourably with that in the State of Oregon, one of two U.S. states whose approach resembles B.C.'s, and which is generally regarded to possess a successful program as well. Oregon has established a target of six percent losses from 1970 to 2010. At the current rate of loss, even ignoring additions to ALR lands, B.C. will have experienced a 4.5 percent loss from 1975 to 2010. Losses, mostly in the FVRD, have been about double this rate in the Lower Mainland. The program has been especially successful in defining lands excluded from urban development in the GVRD....

Right-to-farming legislation, which protects ALR farms from municipal regulations as long as operations conform to accepted industry norms, was passed in 1995....

The ALR provides a "line in the sand" which urban centres may not transgress. It does little to promote efficient or any other form of urban growth. Some observers have even asserted that the ALR has prevented the development of more efficient urban forms. Nor has it necessarily placed severe limits on urban growth. Over nineteen percent of a GVRD that was then half its area was classed as vacant in 1979. This proportion decreased to twelve percent (16,070 hectares) by 1996. An average of slightly more than six hundred hectares per year was lost to urban growth through the period from 1979 to 1996. Extension of the rate of loss of vacant and developable land into the future indicates that vacant land in the pre-1990 GVRD would be exhausted in about twenty years. It would take considerably longer, perhaps upwards to four times as long, to occupy completely the vacant land in the larger GVRD that includes the Langley municipalities, Maple Ridge and Pitt Meadows which were added in the 1990s. About eighteen percent of the current GVRD was classed as vacant in 1996.

While there was a tendency towards denser development with contemporary growth pressures and following enactment of the Agricultural Land Commission Act, the availability of suitable vacant, developable land outside both the ALR and the "green zone" on the urban fringe made possible continued development of low-density single family homes. Over eighty-five percent of increased residential land use in the older GVRD from 1979 to 1996 was classed as single family/duplex, although this represents a significant decrease from the ninety-four percent in 1979. Over ninety percent of residential land use in the enlarged GVRD in 1996 was single family/duplex in 1996....

A fiscal concern is the road and utility infrastructure required to serve the new population. Notably, travel grew faster than population from 1985 to 1992. While population increased by twenty-one percent from 1985 to 1992, rush hour trips increased by thirty-seven percent. The transit share of rush hour trips decreased from 11.2 to 9.9 percent. Transit's share of trips to downtown Vancouver decreased from thirty-five to thirty-one percent, while automobile dependence for work trips increased. Suburb to suburb rush hour trips increased by four percentage points to sixty-four percent. Suburb to downtown trips decreased by almost three points to twelve percent of total rush hour trips. People travelled further and longer. Average trip length increased by twelve percent to fourteen kilometres Average trip speed decreased by seven percent to 34.7 kilometres per hour, and average trip time increased by twenty percent to twenty-four minutes....

Two documents, the "Livable Region Strategy Plan" and "Transport 2021," currently contain the GVRD's substantive growth management policies. The former is deliberately brief. The GVRD focused its efforts on gaining approval by all twenty local municipalities of a structure of land use, transportation facilities, and municipal targets for both ground-oriented housing and apartments and for employment. In addition, the plan contains a summary of principles protecting the green zone, supporting the public's strong desire for communities with a wider range of opportunities for daily life, achieving a compact metropolitan region, and increasing transportation choice. Underlying the substance of the strategy plan is the funnelling of a substantial portion of incremental population growth to a Growth Concentration Area and the development of sub-regional employment and commercial centres on a scale sufficient that they may be effectively served by public transit.

The strategy plan focuses on altering trends prevailing over the decade of the 1980s and very early 1990s. The plan envisages directing fourteen percent of the projected regional population (410,000 population and forty percent of projected growth from 1991 to 2021) from the fringe areas of Richmond, the southern parts of Delta and Surrey, the Langleys and communities in the FVRD to the Growth Concentration Area containing Vancouver and the suburban municipalities of Burnaby, Coquitlam, New Westminster, Ports Coquitlam, and Moody, as well as the northern parts of Delta and Surrey. The expectation is that this will be accomplished by local municipalities either decreasing or increasing, as the case may be, land available for development per their OCP's....

The companion piece, Transport 2021, documents the erosion of public transit use and the connection between increased automobile reliance and not only sparser residential settlement, but also decentralization of employment. Regional sub-centres would theoretically allow a large enough agglomeration of destinations that could be effectively served by enhanced public transit. A transportation demand management ("TDM") strategy consisting of high occupancy vehicle ("HOV") lanes, tolls, and parking and regional gasoline taxes is considered to be an essential component of the overall strategy, as well as a source of financing for infrastructure development. Growth concentration, also supported by TDM, is viewed as critical in creating threshold residential densities that could be more effectively served by major new light rail transit ("LRT") facilities.

Models developed by the GVRD's transport planning organization indicate that the residence shifts proposed would have significant impacts on the performance of the transport system. Total distances travelled by all vehicles would increase by fifty-five percent from 1991 levels, but be seventeen percent less than trend projections. The number of transit passengers would increase sixty-two percent over the projected trend line number and two to three times 1991 levels, thus justifying the spending of nearly an additional $200 million annually to amortize new transit capital investments to build new LRT lines and increase the size of the bus fleet....

Transit ridership is lower and has decreased significantly relative to other Canadian systems from1986 (a peak year for transit ridership in Canada) to 1994. While the number of riders per capita decreased by an average of twenty-six percent for Calgary, Montreal, Ottawa, and Toronto, riders per capita decreased by thirty-five percent for Vancouver. Vancouver's ridership decreased from fifty percent of the average of the other four cities in 1986 to forty-four percent in 1994. Ridership was thirty-eight percent greater than for Calgary in 1986, but three percent less in 1994. Equipment shortages and low service levels are frequently viewed as a major reason for low ridership in Vancouver....

In addition to transportation projects, the provincial government's designation of sites for parks and wildlife habitat conservation, as well as agricultural and forestry zoning have been critical in supplying the "green necklace" that has been the fabric providing the pattern and bounds of local urban development....

Beginning with ALR zoning in the mid-1970s, but likely stemming as well from the shortage of land connected to the geography of its region, Greater Vancouver transformed itself from a largely single family, low-density city to a denser city region containing a wider mix of housing types. The number of hectares used per thousand total population decreased from seventy-two in 1966 to fifty-eight in 1986, shortly prior to the discontinuation of Environment Canada's Lands Directorate and its land use monitoring system. Hectares consumed per thousand population change from 1966 to 1986 was thirty-four in Vancouver and twenty-seven and thirty-five respectively in Toronto and Montreal. However, it was forty-seven in Ottawa-Hull, fifty-one in Quebec, fifty-nine in Edmonton, forty-three in Calgary and ninety-five in Winnipeg. Vancouver began to more closely resemble its larger urban cousins in central Canada in this two decade period. The proportion of population living in town homes and apartments is today far greater than for its urban cousins in the Pacific Northwest: fifty-one percent in Vancouver; and twenty-one percent in Portland and Seattle. Perhaps as a result of the ALR, approximately thirty-five percent of new urban development from 1979 to 1996 stemmed from conversion of rural residential uses rather than from development of vacant and undeveloped land. Vancouver was also transformed from a city heavily dependent on exploitation of B.C.'s resources to a diverse centre of finance and business services. These are the kinds of changes that lead to the success of growth management strategies. Greater Vancouver has already made considerable progress in these areas. Its development industry is a leader in denser residential development and developing difficult sites....

GVRD and provincial officials will readily admit that the most successful of the three prongs underlying growth management in the Lower Mainland is the "top down" agricultural zoning of the ALC. The recent agreement on transport governance and funding will hopefully overcome shortcomings in transport supply and co-ordination. The strategy plan approved by the GVRD in 1996 acknowledges the impact of the trends and development prevailing from the mid-1960s to the early 1990s. It proposes that they be altered, principally by concentrating up to eighty percent of growth from 1991 to 2021 in a Growth Concentration Area consisting of the Burrard Peninsula and the sectors of Delta and Surrey closest to the Fraser River.

The full extent of divisions inside the GVRD and its board and their potential impact on the ultimate successful implementation of the LRSP have likewise not been fully explored. While there is danger in focusing too extensively on media events, there is a real possibility that divisions in the region that seem to have been intensified subsequent to the adoption of the LRSP in early 1996 are fully capable of derailing the entire initiative. These divisions pit the municipalities south of the Fraser River against those of the Burrard Peninsula, up-valley municipalities, including the FVRD, and those that are more auto dependent against those that will receive the bulk of benefits from planned transit investments over the next decade. The divisions are to some extent fiscally driven. The developing municipalities have low non-residential assessment bases. For instance, Vancouver derives only forty-one percent of property tax revenues from residential taxes, while residential assessment generates seventy percent of tax revenues in Langley and Surrey. Both of the latter are also dependent on the continued flow of development cost charges associated with new development to pay for new capital facilities benefiting their entire jurisdictions, as well as the new subdivisions associated with the special levies. They are systems heavily dependent on new development to sustain their community plans. Diverting development to a Growth Concentration Area may ultimately undercut these plans and visions.

* * *

Notes and Comments

1. It appears that federal highway funding policies may have a greater impact on metropolitan growth patterns than other influences. Should the United States continue with policies of devolution of transportation program responsibilities to the state or regional level?

2. How should the rapid decline of suburban to downtown commuting destinations and the dramatic rise of suburb to suburb commutes influence transportation planning?

3. How could Vancouver correct the inequities and impacts of targeting new development to infill districts when suburban communities depend on impact fees from new development to provide its essential facilities?

Transit Villages: Integration of Land Use Planning with Transportation Planning

Growth management and smart growth in regional planning involve not just the balancing of growth with the need for housing. Rational growth management policies include the integration of transportation, the improvement of environmental quality, the maintenance and revitalization of neighborhoods, and planning for economic development. The following excerpt focuses on integration of growth management with transportation planning:

Voula Mega, *The Concept and Civilization of an Eco-society: Dilemmas, Innovations, and Urban Dramas,*

in Cities and the Environment: New Approaches for Eco-societies 47 (Edited by Takashi Inoguchi, Edward Newman, and Glen Paoletto 1999)

. . . . Cities compete with each other to gain environmental credentials. It is a healthy battle when translated from words into deeds. Many cities declare themselves "Green City" or "Sustainable City." Leicester was the first British city to be given the status of Environment City and is trying to become a national and international model of excellence. Leicester Environment City is assisted by the Business Sector Network to bring together ideas from the city's commercial sector and provide assistance to businesses, while Environ, a nonprofit-making company, has been set up to provide local organizations with access to environmental audits and advice. The city is also worth mentioning for other achievements, for instance, its achievement of solidarity through the harmonious coexistence of various ethnic groups. Indeed, sustainability means the integration of cities as places of culture and citizenship.

In Germany, environmental awareness has often been linked to socio-economic change, first and foremost in the cities which have been the scene of many socio-political transformations. Urban ecology in Berlin—often called the "recycled city"—is an important element for the "renaissance" under way in the city. The often derelict space adjoining the former wall became, once again, a central space for creation and innovation. In Kreuzberg, Block 103 is an interesting example, highlighting links between social well-being and environmental upgrading. Former squatters of the block have been given the opportunity to own the space they occupied and, at the same time, they have been trained to convert the houses into ecological modern buildings. Special emphasis has been placed on energy, water, green spaces, and new materials and techniques. Another complex has been the field of innovation for alternative water systems. The project emphasizes the learning and communication process and allows 50 per cent savings on water, while the residents' association participates in the technological monitoring.

Progress towards sustainable energy consumption and production patterns can be crystallized if there is efficient and increasing use of renewable energy resources (solar, wind, water, biomass), more environmentally sound fuels, and innovation in local energy provision, such as decentralized heat and sewerage plants. The mini-centre for the co-generation of electricity and heating in Milan tries to develop specific scientific and engineering knowledge in a local context and stimulate the interest of potential users. The introduction of photovoltaic cells for combined production of electric and thermal energy is also gaining ground in Mediterranean cities. In the German Lander, energy-saving measures include the introduction of an "energy pass" to optimize the energy conditions of houses. Energy budgets highlight the large share of transport in energy consumption and indicate where improvements are necessary.

Concerning waste management, it has been suggested that the term be replaced with "resource management." Reconsideration of the urban metabolism puts increasing emphasis on waste prevention before the waste is generated, even if investments still concentrate on the recycling end. Once generated, waste has to be considered as a resource. Everywhere, innovative actions are being taken for the prevention of industrial waste and the avoidance, reuse, and recycling of domestic waste. In Parma, plastic waste is being transformed into building materials and in Rimini, organic waste from hotels into agricultural compost. Each citizen contributing to the latter highly environmental process is rewarded with a plant. An eco-station has been created and its management has been entrusted to former drug addicts. The municipality of Oeiras, in the metropolitan area of Lisbon, set up a programme for backyard composting of organic waste aiming at dramatically reducing the amount of waste the municipal services collect, transport, process, and dispose of. It gives inhabitants the possibility of producing a high-quality fertilizer for their gardens and increases people's awareness of urban environmental problems.

All over Europe, cities are becoming laboratories of ecological innovation, with high experimental value. The Understenshöjden ecological village in Stockholm is a good example of improving urban metabolism, with ecological self-building and local participation with the design. Schwabach, a small, self-sufficient German city, offers an example of the efforts to implement an urban ecology planning strategy. The city has been selected by the Federal Ministry because of its unified, dynamic local government and its ecological achievements, especially in waste management. The basic principles are that nothing is impossible and everybody has to participate. The pilot study aims to introduce ecological concepts and actions to a normal city, under normal conditions and with normal funds. After the study, the city council issued guidelines for action and translated them into a concrete programme in its 1993–2003 Model Urban Development Strategy, leading to Schwabach Ecological City.

Environmental problems in European metropolitan areas do not come just from production; they also come from consumption and from traffic. Transport policies are being accused of leading to an unsustainable future. Traffic congestion represents a loss of 3 per cent of GDP in the countries of the European Union, and traffic infrastructure covers 10–15 per cent of the urban space. Mobility has long been regarded as a cardinal urban value, but "mobility at any price" can no longer serve the objectives of urban quality of life. Replacing the focus on accessibility seems a possible alternative. The distinction between access and mobility is not a trivial one. Unlike sheer mobility, access means not only getting people where they need to go, but also getting to them what they need, and new information technologies may play a major role in that process. Traffic provisions are like arteries: they should facilitate the flow of vitality and not dominate the body of the city. The urban renaissance of spaces and functions is best illustrated by efforts to decrease unsustainable mobility, thus favouring public transport over the private car and giving priority to the pedestrian and the bicycle.

The private car is considered to be the single most destructive factor for cities. According to the European Commission, a "car-free city" could be composed of various small units, accessible on foot from one end to the other, separated by green spaces and united by high-speed public transport. The car-free city seems to be not only ecologically efficient, but also even economically efficient, as it appears to be two to five times less costly. In such a city, enterprise has new local challenges to meet, as job creation is essential for the self-sufficiency of each small urban unit. The city of Amsterdam, following the example of cities such as Bologna, conducted a referendum on the restriction of the private car and organized the conference "Car-Free Cities?" in 1994. On that occasion, the Car-Free Cities Club was launched by cities committed to promoting policies discouraging the use of private cars. The European Foundation's study on transport and public spaces also highlights the passage from car-occupied spaces to citizen-occupied spaces.

The human leg is the only sustainable means of transport. A pedestrian-friendly city is more human. Copenhagen has been a pioneer city in recognizing the social value of pedestrian streets. When the main street was pedestrianized in 1962, there was a heated discussion; however, it became a great success almost immediately. Pedestrianization continued over a period of 30 years and the downtown parking policy aimed to remove 2–3 per cent of the parking spaces per year. With the improvement of the public transport system and the enlargement of the bicycle network, more and more space has been taken away from traffic and given to people who started returning to the city centre, leaving behind anonymous peripheries and making it again the centre of gravity and attraction. Experiences abound throughout Europe and expand even in the periphery of cities (Oulu, in Finland, is extending its pedestrian zone, which is proving to be very successful, even in temperatures of—30°C). Italian cities (Perugia, Boizano, Spoleto, Rome) have been pioneers in creating pedestrian cultural environments. In Naples, places like the Piazza del Plebiscito are rediscovering their former splendour after the removal of private cars. And Venice remains the archetype of a car-free city.

Cycling is the only other sustainable mode of transport, after walking. Is it an urban paradox that both walking and cycling have been more developed in northern, rather than in southern, cities, where climate allows more outdoor activities? Is culture stronger than nature and climatic conditions? Amsterdam is the European city with the most elaborate bicycle network, complementing the road and canal routes. A pilot project in Delft indicates that up to 55 per cent of all urban trips may be done by bicycle. In Copenhagen, Münster, Erlangen, and other cities, up to 35 per cent of all transport needs are satisfied by bicycle, while in cities of the former German Democratic Republic, such as Dessau, the use of the bicycle is falling. Cities such as Basle can be traversed and enjoyed by bicycle, while the cities of Zürich and La Rochelle lend bicycles free to citizens and visitors.

A single authority for public transport and private car parking could internalize more equitably the environmental costs of private motoring and improve public transport. In Evora, one of the World Heritage cities, the new traffic plan includes the creation of large car parks outside the city walls, a high-quality public transport system with mini- and microbuses, well adapted to the existing narrow medieval streets, and the creation of pedestrian streets and bicycle paths. In Orvieto, the alternative mobility system has been created out of the need to improve urban life and the will to revitalize the old funicular railway. With the completion of the system, all cars will be parked in large car parks at the foot of the Orvieto hills, the funicular railway will take all passengers to the top of the hill, and a system of minibuses will take them around the city. This system will be completed with the creation of escalators through the rocky caves. The town of 10,000 people is expected to be less affected by the 2 million visitors it receives per year.

In Germany, the concept of "short distances" is gaining ground in many cities. Heidelberg and Freiburg have been pioneers in introducing low-noise vehicles in noise protection districts and eco-tickets for public transport. Clean, silent, fast tramways are gaining acceptance in European cities. Nantes, Grenoble, and Strasbourg introduced from 1985 onwards three technological generations of tram way. In Valencia, the new tramway is called "a tramway named Desire." Moreover, a combination of means is highlighted in many innovative projects. In La Rochelle, a new multi-optional concept (Autoplus) has been introduced through a partnership between municipalities, the semi-public company responsible for public transport, taxi owners, two private bus owners, one ship owner, hotel owners, and a bank. Campaigns have as their objective the limitation of the use of the private car. In Toulouse, the municipality, a semi public enterprise for public transport and the community have created project for the readjustment of the transport services to people's needs.

Fast, clean, comfortable, flexible, easily accessible, and pleasant public transport is a precondition for persuading citizens to use fewer private cars. Examples at the leading edge include experiences from Swiss cities (Zürich, Basle, Berne) and German ones (Freiburg, Bremen, Aachen). Zürich is one of the few cities that have developed a coherent solution to the problem of traffic build-up at intersections. Preserving and upgrading the tram system and rearranging the bus lines were the key elements. The particularity of the system is its ability to deal with each public transport vehicle individually, allowing it to cross intersections without stopping. Deregulation progresses slowly in Europe and subsidies will continue to be needed in order to combat the attractiveness of the private car....

* * *

The following excerpt describes "smart growth," the newest thing in growth management strategies:

Oliver A. Pollard, III, *Smart Growth: The Promise, Politics, and Potential Pitfalls of Emerging Growth Management Strategies,*

19 Virginia Environmental Law Journal 247 (2000)....

"Smart growth" is a relatively new term. It began to be discussed around 1994, and it gained wider currency with the adoption of Maryland Governor Parris Glendening's "Smart Growth and Neighborhood Conservation" initiative in 1997, a package of programs designed to revitalize existing communities, discourage haphazard development, and protect farmland and sensitive environmental areas. In the past few years, smart growth has become a buzzword used in a burgeoning number of articles, reports, conferences, and coalitions, as well as in a host of federal, state, regional, local, and citizen initiatives. Smart growth has reinvigorated growth management discussions, captured politicians' attention, and begun to shape public perceptions of development issues. As a recent National Association of Home Builders' report notes, the smart growth concept has "exploded onto the national consciousness as one of the most critical issues confronting America today."...

The goals of smart growth, in its broadest outlines, largely mirror these recent, comprehensive growth management efforts: to balance economic development and limit sprawl by channeling growth to areas that have already been developed; to revitalize and prevent the decline of existing urban and suburban areas; to promote more compact urban form; to protect open space, farmland, forests, and environmentally sensitive areas from suburban encroachment; to reduce the public cost of providing infrastructure and services to new development by making more efficient use of existing resources; to protect the natural environment; and to provide affordable housing.

Smart growth thus can be viewed as another stage in the evolution of growth management strategies. A far cry from traditional zoning, it shares the objective of comprehensive growth management provisions to shape patterns of growth by affecting the density, location, rate, timing, cost, and quality of development. Nevertheless, smart growth shifts the emphasis of previous growth management efforts in several key areas, and it has the potential to address a more multi-faceted range of issues.

Reduced regulatory emphasis

The first shift in emphasis concerns the role of regulation: smart growth tends to focus less on the need to regulate land use development activity than have previous efforts to guide growth....

Oregon's growth management statute is widely cited as a model It requires all local jurisdictions to adopt land use plans that conform with state goals and standards established by a seven-member Land and Development Commission. Municipalities also must implement regulations, including zoning ordinances, that are consistent with both the state goals and their local land use plan. The Land and Development Commission has the authority to order municipalities to bring their land use plans or regulations into compliance with state goals. A prominent feature of the Oregon model is the requirement that localities identify urban growth boundaries in order to protect rural areas and to promote more compact development. Development is severely limited beyond the growth boundary and encouraged inside its limits.

In contrast, smart growth approaches, at least at this point in the evolution of the concept, do not place as much emphasis on regulation to shape long-term growth patterns. Land use controls, such as zoning codes, and environmental regulations remain important, but smart growth typically seeks to supplement these provisions using incentives rather than additional regulation. The model state smart growth statute is Maryland's Priority Funding Areas Act, which was part of a broader "Smart Growth and Neighborhood Conservation" initiative. This statute does not identify specific measures local governments must adopt. Instead, it targets the flow of state funds for "growth related" projects (such as highways and water and sewer lines) to existing communities and to additional areas where growth is planned as long as these additional areas meet minimum state criteria for average residential density and for provision of public water and sewer. Development is not prohibited outside the designated growth areas, but by limiting state financial assistance outside of these areas, the statute creates a strong incentive for localities to guide growth to existing communities. The premise is that guiding growth to areas with existing infrastructure is more efficient than incurring the expense of building new infrastructure to serve development in outlying areas. In addition, encouraging the revitalization of existing communities both strengthens these communities and reduces pressure on undeveloped areas by providing attractive, alternative places to live and work....

A second, related distinction between smart growth and more traditional growth management approaches is that smart growth focuses more on the role federal, state, and local government policies and practices play in influencing land use development patterns....

Subsidies distort market and individual behavior. There are a host of federal, state, and local public subsidies that arguably have fueled sprawling development for decades, including transportation funding policies that emphasize highway construction; public funding for water and sewer extensions that open new land in outlying areas to development; cash payments and tax breaks to lure new businesses to outlying areas; mortgage policies that subsidize and favor single-family suburban homes; tax deductions for mortgage interest and property taxes; and school construction spending that favors building new schools in new suburban areas over expanding and renovating existing structures.

For example, federal, state, and local government subsidies that encourage automobile usage are estimated to total hundreds of billions of dollars a year, including spending on items such as building and maintaining roads, traffic control, and law and parking enforcement, as well as tax policies such as the oil depletion allowance that lowers gasoline prices. These subsidies influence development patterns by often making it cheaper and easier for people to live further away from where they work, shop, and conduct other activities, thus making development on the fringes of existing communities more affordable. Moreover, subsidies for new roads have made possible the development of many previously inaccessible rural areas. As one commentator has argued, "[f]or at least thirty years, state investments of federal money in the interstate highway system in and around metropolitan areas have played a greater role in the determination of urban form than any regulatory mechanism of any agency." This was no accident. Planners of the Federal Highway Act of 1956 declared that the effect of the massive highway building program would be "to disperse our factories, our stores, our people; in short, to create a revolution in living habits." This is precisely what has occurred.

The smart growth approach seeks to limit or eliminate subsidies that fuel development in outlying areas and undermine existing cities, towns, and suburbs, and to use government expenditures and tax policy to promote more sensible growth patterns in two ways. First, development is guided toward existing communities, encouraging more concentrated, pedestrian- or transit-friendly development within those communities. Measures that promote this objective include providing incentives for infill development, historic preservation, and the development of abandoned industrial sites or "brownfields;" directing government funds for roads, water, sewer, and other infrastructure to existing communities; and allocating a higher percentage of transportation funding to transit, bicycling, and pedestrian projects. Among other things, these measures are designed to reduce the amount of land consumed by development, to reduce the cost of providing infrastructure to new development (to help keep taxes lower), and to reduce the average number of miles people must drive in order to reduce traffic congestion, energy consumption, and air pollution. Second, smart growth investments seek to preserve open space, farmland, and environmental areas through tools such as the purchase of property or development rights, or by providing tax incentives for private donations of agricultural or conservation easements. These measures can preserve important wildlife habitat and historic resources, protect water and air quality, provide recreation opportunities, and help to maintain the economic viability of farming and other components of rural economies....

Unlike more traditional growth management approaches, smart growth targets the governmental regulations that drive sprawl development and revises or streamlines these regulations to make it easier to build more compact, mixed use, pedestrian- and transit-friendly projects. States and localities are increasingly making these changes by exploring and adopting a range of strategies, for example: revising zoning ordinances to permit a mix of residential and commercial uses and a diversity of housing types; streamlining approval processes and offering density bonuses to encourage transit-oriented development; or, changing street standards to encourage walking and bicycling and to reduce the adverse impacts of automobiles on neighborhoods....

More sensible growth patterns are the primary antidote to the environmental damage caused by sprawling development, and a considerable amount of the support smart growth has received is due to its promise to address the environmental costs of sprawl.

Smart growth is also consistent with public concern over the cost of government and the size of taxes. These concerns have often been a major political issue in the United States; most recently, they have been at the forefront of politics since California's Proposition 13 initiated a "taxpayers' revolt" in 1978.

Current patterns of development are increasingly seen as economically wasteful and inefficient. As discussed above, federal, state, and local governments have provided an array of public subsidies that have fueled sprawling development, often drawing investment away from existing cities, towns, and suburbs. Among other things, taxpayers thus are paying for the additional infrastructure (such as road, water, and sewer facilities) and public services (such as education and police and fire protection) that new housing and commercial areas require at the same time that infrastructure for which they have already paid is abandoned or underused. Further, it is increasingly evident that the cost of providing services to far-flung development also drives up taxes since new development often does not generate enough taxes to pay for these services....

A third general source of the appeal of smart growth is that changing demographics and shifts in consumer preferences are transforming the housing market, driving greater demand for the type of more compact, walkable and transit-friendly development that smart growth favors. The fastest growing segment of the population in the United States is the elderly, a trend that is projected to continue for the foreseeable future as the baby boom generation ages and life expectancy continues to expand. There has also been a dramatic rise in single-parent households and in the number of "empty nest" households where children have grown and moved into their own homes. To these segments of the population, dispersed, single-family, automobile-dependent housing with a large lot to maintain is often unappealing As Peter Calthorpe has noted, "Our suburbs are designed around a stereo-typical household which is no longer predominant."

A recent real estate industry report acknowledges these demographic shifts and encourages investment in traditional cities, smaller towns, and better suburbs that offer attractive neighborhoods, retail and office districts that are easily accessible, and transit and other alternatives to driving.]This report concludes that "[s]uccessful metropolitan areas will be those that redevelop and strengthen existing neighborhoods and districts, integrating residential with commercial and residential uses, rather than expanding and diffusing resources outward;" this is precisely the smart growth approach. Although it is important not to overlook the continued appeal of conventional suburban development to many Americans, the strengthening market demand for the broader range of transportation and housing choices that smart growth is designed to provide is a major factor driving support for smart growth approaches...

Despite the popular support smart growth has enjoyed, it will be difficult to make the fundamental changes in deeply entrenched land use and transportation policies, processes, perceptions, and agencies that are necessary to achieve more sensible growth. The inertia of fifty years of land use and transportation policies that have favored scattered development will not be easy to overcome; bureaucracies are resistant to change, and powerful corporate and other financial interests have an enormous stake in continuing current policies and practices.

Efforts to shift decades of transportation policies emphasizing road building offer an instructive example. Congress made fundamental changes to federal transportation law when it adopted the landmark 1991 Intermodal Surface Transportation Efficiency Act (ISTEA). Among other things, ISTEA placed greater emphasis on maintaining the existing transportation system, allowed states to spend a larger share of the federal funds they receive on a broader range of transportation options (such as mass transit), increased local authority over transportation decisions, and dedicated transportation funds to air quality improvements in areas that do not meet the requirements of the Clean Air Act.

As Professor Susan Hanson has concluded, "All this is a far cry from the days, not so long ago, when transportation planning meant highway building." Yet the practical impact of ISTEA has been limited: although some states broadened the focus of their transportation programs as envisioned by these statutes, most have continued to focus on building and expanding roads as the response to their transportation problems and have limited the local role in transportation decisionmaking. When ISTEA was due to be reauthorized, a number of state transportation departments and highway lobbyists attempted to eliminate many of the innovations ISTEA contained and sought to increase funding for road construction. Ultimately, the new transportation law, the Transportation Equity Act for the 21st Century (TEA-21), continued the broadened transportation focus and most of the programs in ISTEA, but it also increased highway funding substantially. Despite improvements, transportation policy reform has progressed slowly in the United States; most states continue to try to build their way out of congestion, and resistance to change remains strong....

* * *

Notes and Comments

1. For a discussion of the legal validity and authority for the adoption of smart growth initiatives, see James A. Kushner, *Smart Growth: Urban Growth Management and Land-Use Regulation Law in America*, 32 Urb. Law. 211 (2000), *reprinted as modified*, Institute on Planning, Zoning & Eminent Domain Ch. 7 (2000). *Compare* Clint Bolick, *Subverting the American Dream: Government Dictated "Smart Growth" is Unwise and Unconstitutional*, 148 U. Pa. L. Rev. 859 (2000) *and* Bernard H. Siegan, *Smart Growth and Other Infirmaties of Land Use Controls*, 38 San Diego L. Rev. 693 (2001) (smart growth would be no zoning) *with* Timothy J. Dowling, *Reflections on Urban Sprawl, Smart Growth, and the Fifth Amendment [Point/Counterpoint]*, 148 U. Pa. L. Rev. 873 (2000) (arguing for broad regulatory authority to control sprawl).

2. *See also* Brenda I. Koerner, *Smart Cities: What Your Hometown Can Learn from Six Success Stories*, U.S. News & World Rep. 26 (Jun. 8, 1998) (describing Vancouver, B.C., Minneapolis, Chattanooga, Curitiba, Brazil, Tilburg, the Netherlands, and Melbourne, Australia).

3. An Outgrowth of Smart Growth is "Smart Lending," the targeting of public investment towards encouraging infill development. Robert W. Burchell & David Listokin, Linking Vision with Capital: Challenges and Operations in Financing Smart Growth (Research Institute for Housing America Rep. No. 01-01 2001); John W. Frece, *Smart Growth: Prioritizing State Investments*, 15 Nat. Res. & Env't 236 (2001).

A principal debate in contemporary urban planning is whether suburban sprawl in the style of Los Angeles and other American cities is more desirable than the alternative of linking residential districts with mass transit to establish "transit villages." The following excerpt describes transit villages:

Robert Cervero, *Growing Smart by Linking Transportation and Urban Development,*

19 Virginia Environmental Law Journal 357 (2000)

Sprawl is like pornography. It is hard to define, but you know it when you see it. Sprawl is the endless expanse of city lights on the horizon a half-hour away from Los Angeles International Airport. It is mile upon mile of ticky-tacky strip-commercial development. It is crawling in traffic on a ten-lane beltway on a Saturday afternoon.

Greater Atlanta is poised to eclipse Los Angeles as the world's most sprawling metropolis. Its land area, which currently stretches some 200 kilometers from end to end, is growing four times faster than its population. Its commutershed—the territory from which workers are drawn—now encompasses four states. The typical Atlantan commutes fifty-five kilometers each day, the farthest in the United States. One Fortune 500 company recently threatened to pull entirely out of the region because of traffic nightmares and a rapidly eroding quality of life. Federal funding for promised highway projects was recently withdrawn because of the region's continuing air pollution problems and failure to adopt a regional plan that conformed to state air quality targets. This was a wakeup call, prompting Georgia Governor Barnes to appoint an all-powerful state authority—the Georgia Regional Transportation Authority (GRTA)—whose principle charge is to reign in sprawl.

The tentacles of sprawl today touch all corners of the globe. In Santiago, Chile, unbridled growth consumes 2000 hectares of land each year, much of it in the fertile Maipo and Mapocho valleys. Resulting losses in vegetation and soil absorption have triggered dust storms and flooding. On Java, Indonesia's most populated island, some 250 square kilometers of farmland, forests, and wetlands are being converted every year to urban uses. A megalopolis of non-stop urbanization is taking form between Jakarta and Surabaya, some 600 kilometers apart....

Two of the most efficient and sustainable cities in the world, Copenhagen and Stockholm, adopted metaphors to articulate and market their visions of the future—the "Finger Plan" in Copenhagen, and a "Planetary Cluster" in the case of Stockholm....

[U]nder smart growth, infrastructure investments are cleverly used to shape and leverage development. This can take the form of extending a rail line to a desired corridor of growth in advance of demand, a practice long employed in Scandinavia and Japan, or withholding public utilities from vulnerable and high-valued areas, like forests, wetlands, and hillsides....

There is no better example of the efficiency and sustainability gains that come from coordinated transportation and land-use planning than Stockholm, Sweden. The last half-century of strategic regional planning has given rise to a regional settlement and commutation pattern that has substantially lowered car-dependency in middle-income suburbs. Stockholm planners have created jobs-housing balance along rail-served axial corridors. This in turn has produced directional-flow balances. During peak hours, fifty-five percent of commuters are typically traveling in one direction on trains and forty-five percent are heading in the other direction. Such balanced directional splits stand in marked contrast to the United States where, because of the lack of any concerted effort to coordinate infrastructure and urban development, trains and buses are often filled in the morning inbound but back-haul three-quarters empty.

Portland aims to follow in the footsteps of rail-shaped European cities like Stockholm. Notably, it has opted to build and expand light-rail transit in lieu of more freeways as a means to channel urbanization and avoid haphazard sprawl. Portland's colorful, vibrant downtown, arguably America's most walkable, has an eighteen-hour, European-like ambience. Ridership on the recently completed western extension to the city of Hillsborough is steadily climbing, growing more rapidly than any transit corridor in the United States. Still, Portland has its nay-sayers, with entire web sites devoted to Portland-bashing (i.e., www.publicpurpose.com). Critics contend that Portland's refrain from road expansion has led to traffic tie-ups that are worsening at a faster clip than in most American cities. In truth, it takes decades for the benefits of smart growth to reveal themselves. If any American city is poised to one day rid itself of sprawl and its ill effects, it is Portland.

Successful integration of "green" transportation investments and sustainable growth patterns can also be found in the developing world, most notably in Curitiba, Brazil. Curitiba, a city of 2.5 million inhabitants in southern Brazil, has taken on the mantle of Latin America's most sustainable metropolis. Through smart urban planning and strong political leadership, Curitiba has built exclusive busways while at the same time channeling urbanization along linear axes served by modern high-speed buses. Along some corridors, elephant-trains of double-articulated buses haul 16,000 passengers per hour, comparable to what much pricier metro-rail systems carry. On a per capita basis, Curitiba is Brazil's second wealthiest city, yet it averages considerably more transit trips than much-bigger Rio and Sao Paulo. It also boasts the cleanest air among any Brazilian city, despite being a provincial capital with a sizable industrial sector. The strong, workable nexus that exists between Curitiba's bus-based transit system and its linear settlement pattern deserves most of the credit....

Besides density and design, diversity in land uses is critical in reducing car dependence. Among Americans who live within a walkable or bikeable distance to work, research shows having in-neighborhood grocery stores and shops increases the odds of commuting by non-motorized transport by seventeen percentage points. Being able to conveniently pick-up items en route to home in the evening makes alternative means of commuting eminently more attractive. Another study of large-scale employment centers across the United States found centers with on-site and nearby retail services averaged relatively high rates of midday walk travel and low rates of drive-alone commuting.

The benefits of well-designed mixed use urban centers most often gets expressed by real estate markets. The Ballston metro station area in Arlington County, Virginia is a case in point. Its relative advantages—Metrorail access, compact development, and integrated land uses—have been translated into a rent premium of over three dollars per square foot (in 1990 dollars) for office space relative to comparable projects in nearby Tysons Corner, one of America's most car-dependent edge cities.

The advantages of developments following the 3 Ds (density, diversity, and smart design) are also underscored by experiences with transit village development. At the Pleasant Hill transit village in the suburbs of the San Francisco Bay Area, nearly half of survey residents get to work by transit each day, compared to 16 percent of those living in the city of Pleasant Hill but who live away from the station. Many self-select to reside near transit nodes for the very purpose of economizing on commuting, sometimes foregoing a second car in return for lower and more convenient commuting costs. Pleasant Hill's success is attributable to three key factors: one, the creation of a good site plan—one that was illustrative, cogent, and market-realistic; second, the existence of a pro-active redevelopment authority that aggressively pursued the plan by incentivizing development and absorbing near-term risks (e.g., by assembling irregular parcels into developable plots; issuing tax-exempt bond financing for supportive infrastructure improvements; and providing direct equity participation in risky real estate ventures); and third, political leadership, which in Pleasant Hill's case involved an elected local official who became the project's political champion.

One policy that stands to make transit-oriented living more attractive is location-efficient mortgages. If transit-oriented living lowers transportation by relieving residents of the need to own a second car, this frees up more earnings for housing consumption. This should be reflected by commercial banks when qualifying applicants for home mortgages. Demonstration programs, cosponsored by Fannie Mae (a federal mortgage insurance agency) and several private banks are currently under way in Chicago, Seattle, and Los Angeles to pilot-test the location-efficient mortgage concept.

Another smart use of urban space is to fill in parking lots that envelop rail transit stations. In contrast to Canada and Europe, many light and heavy rail transit stops in the United States have large supplies of surface parking. The ample parking is a concession to the reality that many Americans will only hop on a train to work if they can conveniently drive to a station. Ironically, these surface parking lots are proving to be a blessing in disguise for they provide large swaths of conveniently located, pre-assembled land with great regional accessibility, courtesy of the nearby transit stop. Additionally, many were originally overbuilt, thanks to generous federal funding for rail development. As areas have matured and surrounding land values have increased, market pressures are prompting U.S. transit agencies to sell at least portions of them off as a means to both create a ridership base and to reap windfalls in the form of value capture (which in Japan is the principle means of financing private suburban railways). Often, the profits earned are more than enough to cover the cost of replacement structured parking, freeing up land for infill development. Surface parking conversion, then, is a back-door form of land-banking, which in many European cities, including Stockholm, has been a principle means of leveraging transit-oriented development.

An important event that has made the retrofitting and adaptive re-use of parking lots possible has been the Federal Transit Administration's revised policy on joint development. In the past, transit agencies who sold off parking lots to private developers would have had to return most of the proceeds to the U.S. Treasury since federal grant monies originally paid for the parking facilities. Under the new ruling, transit agencies can retain all income as long as the resulting real-estate project is transit-supportive in its design and tied to a specific plan aimed at station-area redevelopment. While well intentioned, this is hardly philanthropy on the federal government's part. Encouraging the infill of station-area development is in the direct financial interest of the U.S. Department of Transportation since the addition of new riders will help reduce operating deficits, thus lessening the demand for federal transit operating subsidies.

One of the first places to take advantage of the new federal ruling on joint development is San Jose, California. The city and the Santa Clara Valley Transportation Authority (SCVTA) have joined forces in designing a mid-rise, mixed-use project on the park-and-ride lot at the Ohlone-Chynoweth light rail station. Historically, the region's light-rail system has struggled to build a ridership base in large part because much of its service territory is the Silicon Valley, a landscape of sprawling office campuses and car-oriented shopping plazas. However, as the demand for affordable housing with good access to the Silicon Valley has intensified, local policy-makers have come to the realization that parking-lot infilling was too good of an opportunity to pass up. At the time of project development, only thirty percent of the 1140 original parking spaces at the Ohlone-Chynoweth station were used. Currently, 500 parking spaces are being converted to 195 units of two and three story town homes, a retail plaza, a child-care facility, and a community recreation center. The project was further leveraged by a Livable Communities grant from the Federal Transit Administration along with San Jose's progressive approach to impact fees assessment that allows up to a thirty percent credit to developers who embrace smart growth principles in their project designs.

In Owings Mills, Maryland, a similar effort to re-use station-area parking is underway. Currently, 4000 commuters drop off their cars each day at the Owings Mills light rail station and board trains in the direction of downtown Baltimore. Local planners hope to transform the station area from a car drop-off point to a vibrant urban center. The parking lot represents an unexploited asset—namely, real estate with exceptional regional access. Plans call for transforming the forty-four acre site split by Interstate 795 to a mixed-use urban village featuring professional offices, retail shops, a hotel, housing, and civic facilities. While the immediate area is well developed, including a regional mall and some 2.5 million square feet of office space, it lacks a focal point. Proponents hope that a European-style transit village will finally provide one....

Like rail parking lots, one of the biggest assets of dying shopping centers is their huge amount of pre-assembled real estate. One of the more successful adaptive re-uses of a shopping center and integration with rail transit is The Crossings project in Mountain View, California....

The Crossings is an eighteen-acre compact, mixed-use, and walkable neighborhood near a commuter rail line some thirty miles south of San Francisco. It replaced a slowly dying shopping center and movie theater that were surrounded, in big-box fashion, by a huge, underutilized surface parking lot. The project's 540 housing units have commanded a rent premium, partly because of proximity to rail and partly because of the high-quality urban design. Many well-paid young professionals with jobs in downtown San Francisco and the nearby Silicon Valley have opted to buy into The Crossings, drawn by its ambience and exceptional accessibility to transit. Generous landscaping and public spaces punctuated by an internal pathway network have created a highly attractive urban milieu, notwithstanding residential densities of thirty units per acre, fairly high by suburban California standards. Zero-lot lines and rear-lot parking have allowed such densities to be achieved. As a gateway to the Mount View CalTrain station, The Crossings stands as one of the few transit villages oriented toward commuter rail....

Countries like France, Denmark, and Sweden have held sprawl in check by heavily taxing electricity and petroleum consumption at a rate three to four times higher than in the United States. Besides encouraging the use of smaller cars and appliances, pricing that reflects the scarcity value of resources encourages the commingling of land uses. In Europe, this takes the form of workplaces situated within convenient reach of residences, and in-neighborhood shops and restaurants that reduce the need for gigantic, electricity-hungry refrigerators and freezers.

So far, the city-state of Singapore has made the greatest strides in, to quote many economists, "getting the prices right." There, mandatory in-vehicle debit cards are used to exact congestion tolls from motorists who cross a sensor installed on an overhead gantry. Prices vary by place and time of day according to congestion levels. Singapore has also pioneered a vehicle quota system that requires prospective car buyers to bid for the right to own and register a new car, with the allowable vehicle stock index for any one year tied to island-wide traffic conditions. In 1995, the bid price for a premium luxury car (engine capacity of 2000 cc and above) exceeded $70,000 (U.S.). Vehicle quotas, congestion prices, and an assortment of fees and surtaxes (that add as much as 150% to a car's open market value) have reduced Singapore's annual vehicle population growth from six percent fifteen years ago to under three percent today, a remarkable achievement for a city where per capita incomes have risen faster over the past two decades than virtually anywhere in the world.

Efficient and sustainable growth can be rewarded in many other ways, such as granting credits to impact fees (as practiced in San Jose as well as Orlando and several other U.S. cities), targeting complementary public improvements, fast-tracking development permits, and offering tax concessions. Zurich, Switzerland rewards efficiency by dedicating the majority of road rights-of-way to trams, buses, and bicycles. Advanced monitoring and information technologies have also been used to give preferences to trams and buses at virtually all signalized intersections as well as to provide a continuous flow of information to customers about when transit vehicles are expected to arrive. Minimum-delay, surface-street transit connections have won over most Zurich residents to public transit, producing one of the highest per capita ridership levels in the world. Zurich is also one of the world's wealthiest cities on a per capita basis. Who says compactness, prosperity, and ecological transportation can't go hand in hand?

Many of the strategies and initiatives reviewed in this paper have been roundly criticized by some observers as tantamount to "command and control planning." Clearly, living in compact, mixed-use, easily walkable communities is not for everyone. Middle-class and well-to-do households with several or more children and a preference for privacy and seclusion will continue to reside mostly in the suburbs and beyond. Back-office functions will continue to flock to outlying and far-flung places where real estate prices are cheaper. Big-box retailers and multiplex cinemas will continue sprouting on the outskirts. Smart growth initiatives in no way intervene in such free-market locational choices as long as those making the choice pay something which comes reasonably close to reflecting true social costs. Rather, smart-growth strategies—whether in the form of an infill housing project on a former transit parking lot or an edge city with a balance of jobs-to-housing and roads-to-busways—are mainly about expanding choices and offerings in a free market context. More variety in housing choices, in particular, is an adaptation to the steady growth in single-person households, childless couples, and empty-nesters, many of which prefer in-city, small-lot living in attractive environments that are well-served by public transportation and easy to get around by bike and foot. Variety and choice is something which finds broad political and ideological appeal. It is precisely for this reason that smart-growth will ultimately prevail as a dominant paradigm of community-building in the twenty-first century.

* * *

Notes and Comments

1. Peter Gordon and Harry Richardson argue against the transit village and new urbanism, pointing to market preference and demand, densities too low to economically support as are high-rise high-density development, that future trends and technology suggest a declining need for increased density. Peter Gordon and Harry W. Richardson, *Are Compact Cities a Desirable Planning Goal?*, 63 J. Am. Plan. Ass'n 232 (1997). For a

critique of Gordon and Richardson, see Reid Ewing, *Is Los Angeles-Style Sprawl Desirable?*, 63 J. Am. Plan. Ass'n 107 (1997) (pointing out that very few can afford the suburban estate and the compact city offers an attractive more sustainable alternative, and emphasizing the high costs and adverse effects of urban sprawl).

Anthony Downs, focusing on the significantly lower densities of America's suburbs, is skeptical that transit oriented development is feasible:

> Peter Calthorpe's [New Urbanism Planning Guru] approach to managing urban growth is in no way contradictory to...the new visions posed by this book [pragmatic regional problem solving]. Realistically, it may not be feasible to accommodate all or even most urban growth in the type of transit-oriented developments he advocates. The feasibility of applying them on a large scale is weakened by the high cost of building the rapid-transit links among them that he also advocates. However, his TODs should be viewed as building blocks that could be used to handle some significant part of growth in all the visions described in this book except the unlimited low-density vision.
>
> Anthony Downs, New Visions for Metropolitan America App. C at 227 (1994)

The following excerpt discusses the impact of sprawl on the poor:

James A. Kushner, *Growth for the Twenty-first Century—Tales from Bavaria and the Vienna Woods: Comparative Images of Planning in Munich, Salzburg, Vienna, and the United States,*

29 Urban Lawyer 911 (1998)

Traffic and the Housing-Jobs Mismatch

The American obsession with traffic congestion is due to two major factors. First, except for Boston, Chicago, New York, and Philadelphia, development density has been insufficient to support an efficient public transit system.[109] The resulting pattern of suburban sprawl, combined with the rapidly deteriorating economic life of the central city, generates a perception of public transit as at best inconvenient and at worst dangerous. The few recent experiments with subways and rapid transit lines are interesting and convenient for only a few.[110] The pattern of automobile dependency to get to work, school, market, or recreation generates traffic. The economic relocation of the past decades now finds fewer commuters following freeways or subways lines to the old central business district. Instead most workers live in the suburbs and work in another sub-

---

109. Robert Cervero, *Congestion Relief: The Land Use Alternative*, 10 J. Plan. Educ. & Res. 119, 122, 124 (1991) (transit requires densities of 50 workers per acre or a FAR of 2.0, as compared to average suburban densities of 0.3 to 0.4; 20% increase in floor space for retail use in office buildings generates a 4.5% increase in trips by carpool, vanpool, and transit); Sanjay Jeer, *The Density Issue*, 61 Planning 21 (Jan. 1995) (transit-oriented villages run from nine units per acre for light rail to 30 to typically 40 units per acre in developments served by heavy rail systems).

110. *See* Jose A. Gomez-Ibanez, *Big-City Transit Ridership, Deficits, and Politics: Avoiding Reality in Boston*, 62 J. Am. Plan. Ass'n 30 (Winter 1996) (need for subsidies will escalate to make transit unaffordable unless land-use controls including taxing automobile usage).

urb. This is the problem of what is called the jobs-housing mismatch. Those in the central city lack access to the suburban job site and two-worker families depend on automobiles to make inter-suburban commutes for which public transit is rarely convenient or available. Even if transit is available, jobs are often distant from restaurants and shopping and workers want to go to lunch, stop on the way home for convenience shopping and errands, and enjoy the independence and privacy offered by the private automobile. When employment centers are developed as part of commercial and residential projects, workers need not drive to lunch, and daily automobile trips plummet with trips spread throughout the day, eliminating the need for disruptive alteration of labor practices of business and industry in pursuit of traffic reduction plans.

A few American cities have experimented with mixed use developments. California has enacted legislation establishing a state policy for jobs-housing balance. Transit-linked villages that include residences, commercial uses, recreation, entertainment, and jobs present a popular lifestyle. The result can dramatically reduce automobile usage, producing a personal dividend in allowing a family to rely on at most one automobile with the ability to increase spending for housing and other nontransportation items. Communities may be designed to provide a high level of public safety. Indeed, although it seems counterintuitive, higher density communities are often safer than spread-out cities.[118] Integrating shops and restaurants along residential streets tends to increase pedestrian traffic and public use of streets while reducing criminal activity. In addition, housing costs can be reduced if higher density and fewer parking spaces are traded off for more green space and amenities. Such density is necessary if public transit is to be feasible and if communities are to acquire the excitement and opportunity that city life such as is found in Vienna can offer. Another dividend from transit investment and a policy of transit villages may be urban stability. American cities with well-developed transit systems have experienced a lower level of urban decline since World War II as compared to the average pattern of decline of cities.

European cities have extensive experience with mixed use communities and the results have generated efficient public transit even in outlying recently developed neighborhoods, cleaner air, and a quality of life far greater than that experienced by most Americans. Munich has a significant traffic problem despite its excellent transit program utilizing rapid transit (S-Bahn), subways (U-Bahn), trains, trams, and buses. Some of Munich's earlier mixed-use developments such as Arabella Strasse, built during the 1980s, are successful as housing communities but often failed to abate traffic due to a housing-jobs mismatch. In Arabella Strasse there are 28,000 jobs created but only 5,000 housing units. The low mix of housing to jobs results in most workers having to commute, often by automobile. A mix closer to one for one housing units to jobs would generate a higher transit use and a reduction in automobile trips. Served by bus and two subway stations, the Arabella Strasse project was built at a residential density of forty to sixty dwelling units per acre, which although high by contemporary American standards is low by current German planning ideology and below the 80 dwelling units per acre of the new mixed use development at Berliner Strasse in Munich. Compared to Vienna and Salzburg, Müncheners are experiencing the conversion from a relatively

118. James Gerstenzang, *Cars Make Suburbs Riskier than Cities, Study Says*, Los Angeles Times, Apr. 15, 1996, at A1 (Valley ed.) (more deaths and injuries from cars in suburbs than from guns and drugs in urban settings in study of Pacific Northwest by Alan Thein Durning, titled "The Car and the City," disclosing that urban deaths occurred in 1995 at a rate of 16 per 1,000 residents, while the rate was 19.2 in the suburbs; although crime deaths were 10 per 1,000 in cities, and but 1 of 1,000 in suburbs, driving deaths were 18.2 per 1,000 in suburbs as compared to 6 of 1,000 in urban settings)....

sprawling automobile-dominated pattern of development to one more transit-based, a process likely to be replicated in many American communities.

Newer developments such as Arabella Strasse and Berliner Strasse are attempting to equalize jobs and housing to encourage workers to reside within walking or biking distance. American planning commentators are increasingly encouraging higher density mixed-use projects developed around transit. Increased funding is now available for transit development, including bicycle paths and other alternative modes of transportation from the automobile. Current federal transportation funding encourages automobile and traffic reduction programs by promoting rail transit and encouraging local strategies, including capping parking development, imposing transit subsidy fees on urban development, and providing for an improved pedestrian environment.

Vienna is attempting to provide a healthy jobs-housing mix in both the Danube City and U.N. City ("UNO"-City) projects and appears to have been very successful, as the average Viennese uses public transportation 600 times per year and automobile commuting is only one-third of "journey to work" trips, public transit more than one-third, and nearly one-third are pedestrian and bicycle commuters. Although the Danube City and U.N. City present the archetype of mixed-use, transit-integrated development, Vienna's rigid restriction of view impairment makes higher density development prohibitive in much of the central city.

* * *

Notes and Comments

1. Frustrated motorists are speeding dangerously to make up time lost to congestion with average speeds rising and a huge increase in tickets for speeding more than 100 mph. Richard Marosi, *In Suburbs, Freeway Drivers Hit the Gas—And Get Tickets*, Los Angeles Times, Jun. 4, 2000, at A32.

2. Not only is suburban living more dangerous than an urban existence, it is also less healthy. The Centers for Disease Control reports that serious health risks are faced by those not biking or walking and experiencing a sedentary lifestyle. Evan Halper, *CDC Study on Suburban Life Hits a Nerve*, Los Angeles Times, Jan. 7, 2002, at B4.

3. A California intermediate appellate court refused to invalidate the environmental impact analysis for a monster subdivision containing 22,000 homes containing a population of 60,000 called Newhall Ranch in northern Los Angeles County, for failure to adequately access jobs-housing imbalance. Vega v. County of Los Angeles, No. F036810, 2002 Westlaw 66359 (Cal. Ct. App. Jan. 17, 2002) (not officially published).

What are the transit policies underway in Europe?:

Clay Fong, Comment, *Taking It to the Streets: Western European and American Sustainable Transportation Policy and the Prospects for Community Level Change,*

7 Colorado Journal International Environmental Law and Policy 463 (1996)....

In Western Europe and the United States (US), international agreements and domestic legislation attempt to reduce such costs by fostering strategies that de-emphasize the car and en-courage walking and bicycling.

7. City without Automobiles. Venice, Italy—The world's only car-free city.

The Hutchinson, Minnesota, Light Traffic Project Action Plan is an example of one such program. This program arose from an agreement to develop a sustainable transportation plan by the Government of Finland, the State of Minnesota, and the City of Hutchinson. . . .

Motorization and its concomitant high costs perpetuate social inequity. The benefits of driving are limited to those who can afford vehicles, while those who cannot afford to drive nevertheless must bear the costs of externalities through taxation, noise tolerance, and reduced open space. Emphasizing the automobile as the primary means of transportation also isolates the one-third of Americans who are unable to drive due to age, income, or disability." Access to employment, health care, education, and other necessary services is difficult for those who lack cars. As a matter of public safety, most transportation networks in North America are so biased toward the car that it is physically dangerous to attempt to use alternatives such as bicycling and walking.

One commentator laments. "Squirrel-squashing, land-eating, people-mauling, omnipolluting cars are taking over the planet!" As population growth creates additional transportation demand, these problems will worsen. . . .

Principles of sustainability have been applied in many contexts, and transportation is no exception. Although relating the concept of sustainability to any particular context can sometimes be difficult. Fred A. Reid provides an elegant summation of the relationship between transportation and sustainability: "In the transportation sector, sustainability means lower energy consumption, low cost, and compatibility with sustainable land-use and life-styles. . . .

Rather than just exploring road building, a sustainable approach to transportation assesses planning and zoning, the development of mass and alternate transportation networks, and regulatory-based financial incentives that better reflect the external costs of driving. Perhaps most importantly, a sustainable transportation policy challenges the traditional presumption that building more capacity for cars is the answer to all transportation planning problems.

Sustainable planning and zoning measures relating to transportation include the development of high-density, mixed-use areas. Rather than segregating commercial and residential districts and encouraging urban sprawl patterns, mixed-use areas combine homes and businesses. Residents simply walk or bicycle, rather than drive, to work. Contrary to popular belief, high-density areas are not necessarily more susceptible to problems of crime and squalor. Additionally, mixed-use communities facilitate public transportation development.

Specific examples of this type of development include pedestrian zones, which include roadways converted to pedestrian use, which are currently found in Munich, Germany; Boston, Massachusetts; and Denver and Boulder, Colorado. Pedestrian-oriented commercial areas generate up to twenty-five percent more revenues than spaces developed to encourage automobile use. This financial success is attributable to easier access by foot and public transportation. Additionally, such zones are appealing to shoppers because they offer cultural attractions such as street musicians and other performers.

Curitiba, Brazil, presents one of the best illustrations of this type of pedestrian zone development. Located close to mass transit and residences, one such zone features stores, restaurants, and outer businesses that are open twenty-four hours a day. The city has combined these zones with a highly efficient bus system that carries more passengers than the subway system in Rio, a city six times as large. The integration of mass transit with pedestrian zones in this city of 1.5 million people has created more disposable income for residents due to decreased transportation costs and new markets for locally produced goods such as buses.

In addition to developing pedestrian zones, the construction of mass transit and alternate transportation networks also make mobility more sustainable. Large-scale networks include light rail, subway, and bus systems. More modest efforts include developing park-and-ride lots to supplement existing mass transit and building pedestrian and bicycle routes. Besides building more transit infrastructure, legislatures are developing incentive-based regulations to make transportation more sustainable. These regulations take a "carrot and stick" approach by offering financial rewards to those who reduce their driving or use more efficient vehicles while penalizing unrepentant owners of gas guzzlers.

Incentive-based regulations include gasoline taxes, toll collection, and a variation known as congestion pricing. Congestion pricing schemes essentially employ tolls based on time-of-day use and thereby serve to reduce peak time traffic. Other proposed incentives include "feebates" and pay-at-the-pump auto insurance. Feebates, proposed in both California and Ontario, Canada, encourage the purchase of fuel-efficient vehicles by providing rebates for their buyers, and fees for buyers of low mile-per-gallon cars. These fees subsidize the rebates, creating a system that pays for itself. Pay-at-the-pump insurance, another California proposal, adds an insurance surcharge to each gallon of gas purchased by motorists. Hence, drivers of more efficient cars pay less for insurance.

Increasingly, policymakers around the world are promoting these sustainable transportation measures. In Europe, fuel taxes have reduced driving as they more accurately reflect the costs of gasoline consumption than in the United States. Additionally, European governments often use these taxes as a source of general revenue rather than as funding for additional road expansion....

European Union Efforts

European Union transportation policy is in a state of flux. In the EU, transportation issues are considered part of the larger issue of the urban environment. Many EU policies reflect concern over environmental degradation, economic development, and social costs. Indeed, these concerns are evident in EU transportation policy.

Besides the EU initiative to reduce transportation-related CO_2 emissions, the Dedicated Road Infrastructure for Vehicle Safety in Europe (DRIVE) program strives "to reduce the environmental impact of road transport. The aim...is to increase road safety, ensure better absorption of traffic increases, reduce air pollution and other nuisances and ensure better traffic management. Additionally, the DRIVE program works in cooperation with other projects dedicated to reducing traffic and promoting alternate modes of transportation to the automobile.

In addition, the EU has begun to discuss transportation issues in terms of sustainable mobility These efforts attempt to address environmental harm, set pollution standards, and encourage less ecologically harmful transportation modes. Concerns over increases in individual vehicle ownership and accompanying harms should move these policies forward.

The EU has also been promoting the use of environmental impact assessments (EIAs) in determining the feasibility of road construction projects. These assessments include examinations of the interaction between humans, biological life, and other environmental factors such as water and air quality. However, the development of EIAs and a subsequent comment period do not allow for the levels of public participation mandated by statute in the United States. This will likely undermine the effectiveness of the EU's EIAs.

Financing for the various forms of transportation infrastructure comes from many sources, including the European Regional Development Fund, the European Investment Bank, and the European Community for Steel and Coal. However, most of the EU funds still go to building road expansions....

The passage of the Intermodal Surface Transportation Efficiency Act of 1991 (ISTEA)[63] heralded the start of a new era in American transportation planning. The Act encourages the development of alternatives to simply building more highways and fostering more automobile use. Additionally, it provides a mechanism for communities to fund projects that reduce vehicle-related air pollution, and creates increased opportunities for public participation in the transportation planning process.

ISTEA helps communities comply with provisions of the Clean Air Act by authorizing $6 billion to address problems of traffic and air pollution. Specifically, this appropriation assists communities in funding transportation control measures as defined by the Clean Air Act. These measures can include "programs to limit portions of road surfaces to certain sections of the metropolitan area to the use of non-motorized vehicles or pedestrian use, both as to time and place" as well as "programs to develop bicycle routes and secure storage areas."

The scope of ISTEA projects ranges from the large-scale, such as developing a long-range transportation plan for Washington, D.C., to the small, such as preserving historic train stations. Besides allocating funds for traditional roadway expansions, ISTEA

63. Intermodal Surface Transportation Efficincy Act of 1991, Pub. L. No. 102-240, § 2, 105 Stat. 1914 (1991) (codified at 49 U.S.C. § 101 (1994)) [hereinafter ISTEA].

allows for the expenditure of $58 billion in federal funds for public transit, bicycle, and pedestrian improvements from 1992 to 1997. This sum represents an almost fifty percent annual funding increase for alternative transportation.

The Hutchinson, Minnesota, Light Traffic Project Action Plan

Although sister city projects are not a new innovation, the development of the Hutchinson, Minnesota, Light Traffic Project Action Plan is unique. Rather than simply linking one community with another, this project is an opportunity for a small Minnesota town to take advantage of the expertise of a Finnish governmental agency to develop an improved transportation system. This project intends to "initiate the design of a pilot community for walking, bicycling, and transit—a model of new transportation options and enhanced livability."

Specifically, this project will lead to the construction of an integrated system of bikeways and improvements to road areas and pedestrian crossings, "including the main principles of drainage, lighting, route signing and environmental design."...

Proposed safety education programs in Hutchinson include workshops, exhibitions, and other programs specifically targeted at youth and adult audiences. Besides developing a network of pedestrian and cycling paths, Hutchinson also plans to explore winter maintenance of this network, bicycle parking, and a method for renting and maintaining bicycles....

In terms of economic benefit, a new emphasis on walking and bicycling reduces driving-related externalities in a community. Money previously spent on gasoline will remain in the city and can be used for community investment. Plans for pedestrian and bicycle access will likely lead to increased revenues in Hutchinson's Main Street retail area. But perhaps the most significant economic development benefit comes from the plan making the town more attractive to new business....

As part of the transportation project, Hutchinson police trained 800 children in bicycle safety. At the end of the training, each child received a bicycle helmet, which, along with increasing children's' bicycle safety, became a highly visible symbol of the project throughout the community. Not only did this program help increase awareness of the plan, but it also helped to improve relations between the police department and citizens....

Distinguishing characteristics of the Finnish policy include safety education for cyclists and encouraging bicycle use by constructing cycle and foot paths separate from automobile traffic. A Finnish study determined that the construction of bike paths separated from main roads by a fence or a space of at least a meter resulted in a fourteen percent decrease in accidents and injuries, with the largest decreases affecting cyclists and pedestrians....

* * *

Notes and Comments

1. ISTEA expired at the end of 1997 and was replaced by the Transportation Equity Act (TEA-21), Pub. L. No. 102-240, 105 Stat, 1914 (1998); Dennis C. Gardner, *Transportation Reauthorization: A Summary of the Transportation Equity Act (TEA-21) for the Twenty-First Century*, 30 Urb. Law. 1097 (1998).

2. In addition to conversion to the enhanced density of the transit village, escalating American traffic congestion, according to urban issues Guru Tony Downs, requires po-

litically unpopular policies of altering commuter behavior with ride sharing, transit, travel at nonpeak hours, and raising the costs of solo commuting during peak hours such as with peak-hour road pricing, surcharges on peak-hour long-term parking, and the abolition of free employee parking. Anthony Downs, Stuck in Traffic 164 (1992). Not exactly an optimist, Downs offers his

> advice to American drivers stuck in peak-hour traffic is not merely to get politically involved, but also to learn to enjoy congestion. Get a comfortable, air-conditioned car with a stereo radio, a tape player, a telephone, perhaps a fax machine, and commute with someone who is attractive. Then regard the moments spent stuck in traffic simply as an addition to leisure time.

Landbanking

An alternative strategy for maintaining government control over development and planning is for government to own undeveloped land as has been successfully practiced in Stockholm, described in the excerpt of the comparison of Berlin, Stockholm, and Los Angeles at the beginning of this chapter. The following piece by Professor Roberts discusses land banking within the Swedish planning system:

Neal Alison Roberts, The Reform of Planning Law: A Study of the Legal, Political and Administrative Reform of the British Land-use Planning System

250–261 (1976)

The Example of Swedish Land Storage

There are various possible models available which could change the pattern of land-ownership. Local government's ability to develop land positively could be increased and the transfer of the increase in value due to urbanisation away from the particular owner to either the government or the consumer could be effected....

Sweden has had a system of municipal land-ownership for most of the post-war years. Expressed in its most basic form, the local government simply buys land, holds it, and, after deciding which land will be used for recreation and which for development, sells or leases the land back to the private owner, not at a market price but at a price covering the cost to the authority. In order to obtain financing for the development through the state-guaranteed loan system the developer must not charge more than the land cost him.... Sweden does not have the high density of land-use which, in other countries, so often leads to furious competition for the available land resources. This is because, by European standards, Sweden is relatively sparsely populated. Compared to Britain's 228 people per square kilometre, Sweden has a mere 18 per square kilometre. Although Sweden is highly industrialised, with some 80 per cent of the population living in the cities, it has still used less than 1 per cent of its available space for urbanisation, compared with Britain's use of over 8 per cent of its land.

Another factor to remember about land in Sweden is that, both historically and within the last few decades, land has been viewed differently in Sweden than in the continental or common-law countries. The "right of all men" or right-of-way prerogative, which allows Swedes to walk over all land which is not directly under till or directly attached to a dwelling house, is not an aberration in the Swedish mentality but merely one of the most visible aspects of their different views. Moreover, Sweden has often made fundamental changes in ownership rights (such as eliminating the right of lumber companies to even own land) in order to meet wider social policies. In the last century changes were made to meet the needs of farmers; in this century they have been changed to meet the housing needs of the urbanised industrial population.

The other major point which must be kept in mind is that Sweden has had one political party in power for the entire post-war period. This continued political support has given the policy-makers within the party and the civil service a strong mandate to meet the problems of housing and rational urban development. While the particular goals have changed slowly, for instance from an almost total reliance on communal apartment-style living to a tolerance for single-family dwellings, the controlling political party has remained the same. The political popularity of the Social Democratic Party has allowed them the flexibility to introduce a wide variety of changes in the land and land-financing law, not a few of which might have caused serious controversy in other political climates. The best example of this is perhaps the recently enacted expropriation law, discussed below, the main point of which is to deprive future owners of compensation for their expectation of value due to urbanisation.

The Tools Available

Although the vast majority of the land which comes into public ownership is acquired through ordinary negotiation and purchase, this is only the result of a complicated array of legal and tax mechanisms which make these purchases possible.

First, the government bodies charged with the administration of local development are the kommunes or municipalities, which have been consolidated and strengthened to produce local governments of nearly uniform size and ability. There were 2365 kommunes in the 1940s, the number was reduced by the 1952 boundary reform to 904, and the second wave of reforms in the 1960s and early 1970s further reduced the number to a mere 275 municipal blocs. These units are based on a notion of city regions each with an urban community at its centre. With a minimum population of between 8000 and 10,000 people they are strong enough in terms of resources to carry on a land-buying programme.

The next point is that the income-tax structure of the country itself guarantees the local municipalities an autonomous and self-perpetuating source of funds; property tax constitutes only a small fraction of the municipal tax base. The basic form of tax is on income. The individual files one tax return through one organisation. His tax is made up of two parts: a steeply progressive national-income tax, and a proportional local-revenue tax at a flat rate. This means that each local authority sets its own rate depending on its needs. There is also a national equalising system, based on tax-paying capacity (not total revenue), which brings the resources of the poorer income authorities up to the national average.

This tax system guarantees the local authorities a uniform pool of resources, with no strings attached, for municipal improvement and planning. The first ingredient in land storage, namely how to pay for it, was thus strong from the outset. Combined with a political guideline of buying enough land to cover all projected development for a community for the next ten years, this lays the groundwork for the Swedish idea of community development. In the words of Peter Heimburger of the National Board of Urban Planning, "a good and effective community development implies accordingly that sufficient land is obtainable in the right place at the right moment and at a reasonable price."

The second aspect of tax policy which should be noted was that in 1968 the law concerning capital-gains taxation was changed. Prior to that time, in order to decrease speculation, capital-gains taxes at ordinary income rates had only been charged on profits on land held less than ten years, and gains made from land held longer than that were not taxed at all. In 1968 the rule was changed to provide for taxation of all gains, irrespective of the time the land had been owned. As might be expected, this made landowners in 1967 quite eager to sell prior to the imposition of the tax.

The kommunes also have an entire system of local land-use planning based on negative control. Physical planning in Sweden is done both at the national level in the form of long-range planning and the co-ordination of local efforts, and at the local level. The kommunes develop both master plans of the areas and detailed building plans and town plans. A private party who owns land and seeks to develop it must receive planning permission before he can proceed. These negative controls are further strengthened by a series of levies which allow the kommunes to tax infrastructure costs back to the owners of the benefitted parcels.

This System of negative control has been buttressed by an elaborate system of land acquisition. In 1967 the central government decided to help the kommunes to meet the national goal of ten years worth of stored land, by augmenting their resources. From 1968 onwards the government has made available land-acquisition loans for land destined to be used for residential purposes. These loans are non-secured ten-year arrangements with interest being payable for only the first two years of the term. Starting with only 30 million Sw. Kr. (approximately £3 million) a year in central-government funds the programme is now up to a yearly loan availability of 85 million Sw. Kr. (£8.5 million). The central government controls the use of these funds through a permission system or a ceiling on the amount of municipal borrowing allowed. The central government can allow more borrowing in cases of rapid development and can curtail borrowing in areas which have acquired too much land for their immediate needs. Of course the municipality is always constrained by the fact that the payments on loans are reflected in the local tax rate, and over-investment in land with little return (such as when the kommune only leases its land) will result in an immediate jump in the flat rate.

The kommunes can use their funds, derived either from local income tax or these special funds, to purchase land (without stating its intended use) directly from landowners. Besides this obvious method there are two further devices which make the acquisition process easier. First the kommunes have, in certain circumstances, the right to step into sales which occur in the land market and take the place of the buyer. Under the Pre-emption Act 1967 and regulations therein, all sellers of land must notify the kommune of the intended sale. They keep a record of the sales volume and prices in the local land market, and thus not only have a constant source of knowledge for their own market buying but can also step in and take land on the same terms as the seller was willing to part with it, in all but certain types of transactions which are not covered by the pre-emption (such as very small parcels or transactions between relatives). For instance, if a farmer makes an agreement to sell land to a private builder who is thinking of buying the land and holding it, hoping to get planning permission at some future date, the farmer must record the intended sale with the kommune. The kommune, through its rights under the Pre-emption Act, can then Step in and take the land on the same terms as the farmer was willing to sell it. The farmer would come out the same and the builder would only get his out-of-pocket expenses, but would not receive any compensation for any expectation value the parcel may have had for him.

The second major device which makes acquisition easier is the Swedish Expropriation Law. As early as 1949 the fact that land could be purchased compulsorily for the purpose of storage for a possible future use was specifically laid out in the regulations. A valid purpose under which a kommune could invoke expropriation was "to ensure that land is available on reasonable terms for urban development and otherwise to transfer to municipal ownership undeveloped land for disposal on leasehold tenure."

If the owners were not in a position to exploit the land to conform with the kommune's plans, or if the exploitation would lead to unreasonably high prices for the land, the kommune could purchase the land compulsorily. To give an example: in one area the kommune in its local plans had called for the area north-east of the major city to be used for recreational land with some residential areas. In its dealings with the major landowner to acquire this large parcel the kommune made it known that, although it would have no use for the land for perhaps many years in the future, it still might use its expropriation powers to acquire the land without actually stating what public or private use it might be put to in the future. As might be expected, to avoid the lengthy process of expropriation, the landowner sold the land voluntarily.

The possibility of expropriation and the growth of the amount of land stored by the kommunes provides the backdrop against which the negotiation process could take place with any individual landowner. Since the kommunes hold both the negative control power to say which land can and which cannot be developed, as well as the right to expropriate, they were in a very strong position when bargaining with recalcitrant land owners. Although expropriation is rarely used as the actual method for purchasing land (according to a spokesman for the Ministry of Physical Planning and Local Government, less than 10 per cent of the land bought for storage is acquired through the expropriation mechanism) it is the possibility (or threat) of its use which eases the kommune's task in actually buying the land.

The development of the basis of payment under the expropriation law is an interesting one, for when the cases did get to the special real-estate courts, the level of compensation to the landowner was not supposed to reflect any 'unearned increment', although it was meant to reflect market price and thus expectation value. This obviously ambiguous guideline came to be resolved in favour of the landowner, and, in the words of one government official who worked on the recent expropriation law-reform committee, the courts were very 'generous' to the owners. It came to be the political consensus that the owners were getting in too good a position compared with the municipalities and, as of 1972, an entirely new method of valuation for compensation has been developed. In Sweden, after nearly forty years of Social-Democratic political leadership, the expectation value of a change to urban use has been taken out of the expropriation compensation formula. Although owners are allowed any gains due to expectation up until the fixed date of 1 July 1971, thereafter no increase will be allowed for the owners' hopes of the possibility of development of the property.

The new legislation changes the burden of proof so that it is the owner who must show that his land has increased in value for the particular use it is currently being put to. To do this he cannot give reasons which show an increase in value due to social investment (for example, a subway being constructed nearby) or the possibility of a higher urban use (for example, the fact that neighbouring farm land is now being used for housing). His only method of proving worth is to show that the land's particular use has resulted in higher earnings and thus the land is worth more for that use (for example, if the price of food goes up a farm is worth more). According to Professor Seve Ljungman of the University of Stockholm School of Law, in a personal interview in 1973, the new formula will more or less stabilise the price of land at its current value. Although the new legislation will not decrease the value of land to current landowners, due to the fact that the legislation presupposes land values as of 1971, it will not allow the person who holds land, for say ten years, to benefit from the expectation of change of use generated by future growth. It will only allow adjustments for inflation and actual improvements to the land. The problem is that since the land price should stabilise, this brings into serious doubt the need for the municipality to invest in land prior to the time it is needed at all.

The last major set of mechanisms which must be understood is the way in which the municipalities release the land for urbanisation after storing it for a number of years. The land that is acquired is vacant land purchased at its raw, undeveloped value, and because of the change in the capital-gains law, and the generally low level of land prices, it is acquired at a very low price. Much of the land is acquired for recreational and open-space areas, but as the economy grows the municipality decides where and when the land shall be used for development. The most important point here is that, although there are generalised long-term regional and master plans, the only documents which actually set out the use are detailed town plans and housing plans. These plans deal with immediate plans for urbanisation and, for instance, the five-year rolling housing plan only sets uses that are, in actuality, being contemplated for immediate production. While the municipalities must have some idea of the ten-year future need for land, the five-year dwelling growth plan is the crucial document.

The municipal land can either be sold or leased, but in either case the price takes into account the initial costs of the parcels, the holding costs and the infrastructure costs, but not any increase due to the fact that it has changed use from raw land to land due to be developed. This is, of course, the problematic aspect of the system, because if the market does not locate the better parcels according to price, the allocation mechanism must use political criteria to dispense an item of tremendous economic worth. That is, if it is not the people or organisations with the most money who get the best parcels, they must go to those people or organisations who meet a different standard (such as need, size, social worth, and so on). It is the establishment of those standards in a very political situation which may, as we shall see, lend itself either to abuse or politically correct, but socially inefficient, allocations.

The reason that these low prices for land can be passed on to the eventual resident of either the single-family house or flat is that the central-government loan system of construction finance strictly controls the prices at which development will be financed and thus at which it will be sold. Expressed very simply, the central government guarantees the top 30 per cent of the loans for the purchase of most buildings (the other 'safe' 70 per cent coming from private sources) and those loans are not made on developments which have exceeded certain guidelines for land and construction costs. Since some 90 per cent of all construction is financed through central government, this price control is very effective.

The land-cost increment, in the government finance guidelines, is limited by the price originally paid to the municipality, or, in the case of leases, the cost of the yearly lease payments.

One interesting point to note is the interrelationship between the local taxation system, the central-government land-finance structure, and the local government's land-storage scheme. In order to have income-tax payers to finance local growth and amenity, and in order to meet local demand for housing, local authorities must supply adequate land. However, in order to finance the construction, the municipality has to meet the very low land-price increment in the central government loan scheme. A municipality with a shortage of cheap land would have to sell the land at a price lower than the combined storage and infrastructure costs. In other words the municipalities either have to store enough land to beat the price rise or else subsidise the price of building land itself in order to get housing developments built and financed.

For this system of loan and price control to work, the central government had to ensure that there was a sophisticated mechanism in charge of the valuation side of the production financing. The National Housing Board in Sweden provides this service through a central Stockholm office with some 150 employees, and 450 employees in regional offices. The central government, which ultimately supplies the financing guarantees for development, thus keeps track of local material, labour, and land costs. It develops a series of secret area-cost prototypes for various types of dwelling. The developers must then apply for financing with a given price. The development will not obtain finance if it exceeds the prototype, but it will if it meets it or goes under that price. In 1972 the Housing Board managed to have 32 per cent of the multi-family dwellings that it financed at below prototype costs, with 24 per cent below prototype for single-family dwellings. By not disclosing the method of computation and by not relying on any type of cost-plus-profit formula, the Housing Board kept the costs of housing production at a fairly stable level.

To qualify for this housing and these loans a resident of a community must place his name on a waiting list, either with the various multi-family housing enterprises (or municipal housing co-operatives) or for single-family housing on the municipality waiting list. As housing is produced the earliest name is given the first option on the dwellings produced. The allocation mechanism for newly constructed dwellings is really not a market one at all, but a waiting list. Once a person is selected for a house or a co-operative apartment he must go through the normal problems of finding the down-payment and arranging the financing, but the over-all price will already have been determined within the National Housing Board guide lines.

Most multi-family housing is allocated by a queue system, even to the second or subsequent buyers. Thus, while cooperative owners will receive a return on their capital investment relative to their length of ownership, it is not usually set by the demand for that particular apartment. However, for single-family housing the situation is quite different. The new house-buyer must wait in the queue, and once he has received the right to buy a house he does not get that right again. He pays a price which does not reflect over-all urban demand for single-family housing or land, but one which simply covers the production costs. He can, though, sell his house to a second owner. There is a separate second-owner market for existing privately owned homes and, as could be expected, the prices of these houses, which reflect both over-all demand and particular land location, are considerably higher.

The problem arises that the price differential between the single-family housing production market and the second-owner market is substantial. People with one-quarter to one-third again as much money as their counterparts can buy a home without being in the queue for the requisite five to ten years. It also means that someone who is in the queue and decides he does not want the house the day after he buys it can resell it for a windfall gain of an appreciable amount of money. However, he cannot get a government-financed house twice, so he is permanently in the second-owner market where his 'windfall' is needed to get any type of comparable single-family house.

The Fruits of the Storage System

Sweden has managed to accomplish three major goals through its many-faceted integrated approach to municipal land-buying. First, and most importantly for countries experiencing rapid land-price rises, the price of land through the country has remained remarkably stable. According to Professor Erik Calegrim of the Department of Real Estate Economics at the Royal Institute of Technology in Stockholm, on the whole the levels of land prices throughout Sweden, and even central city land, is only rising somewhere in the region of 5 to 6 per cent per year. These figures were confirmed in interviews. While this is due in part to reforms in taxation, and particularly capital-gains structures, it is due, in no small degree, to the fact that the local governments control a great deal of the land, and thus the market. Secondly, the land-purchasing system has ensured that physical planning on the ground should supply a group of assembled parcels with an adequate infrastructure and that existing private-ownership patterns should not necessarily direct future use. This planning through buying has also ensured that adequate recreational and amenity land will be available within development areas. Thirdly, municipal ownership has allowed the local governments to begin to make decisions regarding the type of community housing and thus social structure desired. A community can be created which can accommodate various types of development to cater for various levels of income, wealth, education and social structure.

These goals were accomplished through a land-storage system which, at least in the communities investigated, paid its own way. In no municipality investigated was the cost of the land-storage policy more than 0.5 to 1 per cent of the total municipal budget. As one development official stated, "even though the community depends on land as long as you buy it as raw farmland, it really only makes up the smallest part of the entire community costs."

[T]he system seems to produce its best results when an element of openness in the allocation (not the acquisition) process is used. The communities who used design competition produced better and cheaper developments, while gaining the added advantages of being free from any commitments for unnecessary development of a certain type.

The Labour Proposals for Land Storage

A scheme similar to the Swedish idea has been proposed at various times by various parties. Most recently, the Town and Country Planning Association proposed that: "The magnitude of the problem of development values is now [1973] such that it demands the creation of a public land bank.... The land must be acquired by the public in advance of development." As might be expected, the Conservative Government which was in power between 1970 and 1974 was not interested in any schemes to transfer land-ownership. There was some emphasis on the taxation of 'windfall' or speculative gains in land with the introduction of the development gains tax idea, later to be implemented by the next government, and pressure was exerted on local authorities to release more land through the development control procedures....

* * *

Chapter 11

Securing a Sufficient Supply of Housing

> The middle-class housing crisis is not new, and there has been no shortage of ideas designed to make the single-family house more affordable. The building industry and generations of architects have dedicated themselves to the task, The results—plastic plumbing, hollow doors, flimsy walls, vinyl cladding—are very clever, but all of them put together do not generate half the savings that can be achieved by allowing a family to own one car fewer. The problem is not one of architecture but of community planning, and as long as we continue to create places where walking, biking, and transit are pointless, we will continue to exacerbate the middle-class housing crisis.
>
> Andrés Duany, Elizabeth Plater-Zyberk & Jeff Speck, Suburban Nation: The Rise of Sprawl and the Decline of the American Dream 57 (2000)

Financing Affordable Housing

The housing problem is two-fold. First there needs to be an adequate supply of housing for all income groups. A community with a shortage of housing for workers is likely to experience high demand, rent escalation, particularly for those of low income, and a difficult time attracting a sufficient workforce to permit continued economic expansion. Similarly, if housing for management and high-skilled workers is in short supply, the impact may be gentrification—the conversion of lower priced neighborhoods to upper income, Keith Aoki, *Race, Space, and Place: The Relation Between Architectural Modernism, Post-Modernism, Urban Planning, and Gentrification*, 20 Fordham Urb. L.J. 699 (1993), the reduction of the supply of affordable housing, or the phenomenon of employers and investors bypassing the community for a more attractive business environment. Equally important is the accessibility of housing to job locations, shopping, health care, and recreation. Where sprawl development separates jobs from housing for workers, communities can experience wage inflation and the inability to acquire a workforce in the very same community that experiences high unemployment and central city urban decay.

The problem of generating an adequate supply of housing affordable to low-wage workers is a most difficult problem in the United States where there does not exist any national or state programs to provide new subsidized or government-assisted housing. The central theoretical problem is the presence of a "subsidy gap." The subsidy gap re-

8. Karl Marx Hof. One kilometer-long social housing in Vienna, Austria, built after World War I remains attractive and accessible.

flects the difference between income available for rent and the actual cost of construction or otherwise providing housing. Charles E. Daye, *et al.* Housing and Community Development 149–160 (3d ed. 1999).

The principal problem is a political one. Most of the nation is well-housed and unwilling to subsidize the poor. Indeed the political environment is much like Victorian England where it was believed that abject poverty was the natural result of an inadequate work ethic rather than the conscious policy of maintaining a low wage scale by generating an overpopulated workforce. Most western European nations set national and local policy to construct and support a substantial supply of social housing, either through direct construction, the provision of housing allowances, or a combination of the two.

The United States during the New Deal embarked on a public housing policy but funding for housing supply expansion has dwindled down to a trickle. Robert W. Burchell & David Listokin, *Influences on United States Housing Policy*, 6 Hous. Pol'y Debate 559 (1995); James E. Wallace, *Financing Affordable Housing in the United States*, 6 Hous. & Pol'y Debate 785 (1995). Under the Ford, Carter, Bush I, Clinton, and Bush II Administrations, housing subsidies represent a symbolic gesture of maintaining a deteriorated and dramatically deteriorating supply of previously built public and government subsidized housing available to but a small portion of the population in need. Peter Salins, *Toward a Permanent Housing Problem*, 85 Pub. Int. 22 (1986). *See also* Peter Dreier, *The New Politics of Housing*, 63 J. Am. Plan. Ass'n 5 (1997). Recent administrations, recognizing the terrible condition of many of the affected neighborhoods, where public housing was concentrated in very low income minority populated inner cities, embarked on a policy of demolishing many of the poorly designed projects and replacing many of the structures with lower density housing to be marketed to the working poor in an effort to revitalize neighborhoods and for the first time attempt to mix income groups within the same housing district. Harry J. Wexler, *Hope VI: Market Means/Public Ends—The Goals, Strategies, and Midterm Lessons of HUD's Urban Revitalization Demonstration Program*, 10 J. Affordable Hous. & Commun. Dev. L. 195 (2001). Ironically, the affluent in America are heavily subsidized as the federal and state income tax systems offer tax shelters, allowing lowered tax payments through programs allowing deductibility of mortgage interest and real property taxes. The tax shelters have grown as consumers seek ever larger loans on more expensive housing under a system that allows borrowers to make larger loans than the housing requires, either in the form of first or second mortgages that permit the wealthy to receive a tax deduction on automobiles, clothing, travel, investments, or other expenditures. *Hearings before the Task Force on Human Resources and Block Grants of the House Budget Comm.*, 97th Cong., 1st Sess. 9 (1981) (testimony of Cushing Dolbeare). *See also* Burchell & Listokin, *supra* at 597 (for 1993, $43 billion in mortgage deductions, and $13 billion for property tax deductions from income tax as compared to roughly $20 billion in annual housing subsidies). The beneficiaries of this system are largely unaware of the operation of the scheme and rarely consider that their message to the government is retain their subsidies but do not support transit or housing for the less affluent.

The following article describes the Swedish housing finance system and offers an interesting contrast to the American system:

Deborah Kenn, *One Nation's Dream, Another's Reality: Housing Justice in Sweden,*

22 Brooklyn J. Int'l L. 63 (1996)

....In 1975, the United Nations assessed the global community's dismal progress in providing housing to its people. Having deemed adequate housing to be an essential for all, the United Nations was appalled by the woefully inadequate national responses to deplorable housing conditions. North America served as a glaring example of misplaced priorities and corrupt social values in which "housing for the needy must take second place to sports arenas or modern speedways." Although much richer in resources than other countries, the United States' lack of a national housing policy fostered an affordable housing crisis. In 1949, the United States legislature began paying lip service to a national policy articulated as providing "a decent home and a suitable living environment for every American family." Despite stated intentions, more than adequate resources, and almost three decades to put these intentions into action, the United States could not claim a comprehensive, working national housing policy. By 1975, the lack of a national housing policy and a widening "affordability gap" between the cost of housing and the ability of people to pay for it led the United Nations to compare the U.S. housing crises to that in developing countries.

In 1996, the crisis deepens. Far from improving the international comparison, the United States maintains an increasingly high level of people living in poverty. In a comparative analysis of eight representative countries undertaken by the U.S. government, the United States exhibited a poverty level double that of other developed countries. In yet another study, international analysts found a 17% poverty rate in the United States, a rate higher than all other countries represented, including Canada, West Germany, Israel, Norway, Sweden, and the United Kingdom. Sweden and Norway had the lowest poverty rates at 5%. When the number of children living in poverty is considered, the United States' poverty level is three times that of other countries surveyed. The United States child poverty rate increased between 1979 and 1986, from 15.6% to 20.4%. In

9. Social Housing. Newly constructed apartments in the forest of Gdynia-Karwiny in Poland.

1991, the number grew to 21.5%, the highest number of children living in poverty in an eighteen country study.

A shameful travesty of justice is perpetrated on low income people in the United States. This travesty appears from the enormous wealth available in the United States and the vastly unequal distribution of that wealth. The United States boasts the highest standard of living among high income nations. High and middle income children in the United States are as disproportionately wealthy in the international sphere as low income children are economically poor. The rich are richer in comparison to other countries and the poor are poorer. While comparable nations address similar inequities with income transfer programs that reduce poverty by as much as 75%, the U.S. government does little to address the problem and accomplishes only a 25% reduction in poverty rates. The United States maintains an alarmingly high poverty rate, both before and after government transfers.

Despite its shamefully high poverty rate, the United States also distinguishes itself among developed countries by committing proportionately fewer resources to providing adequate housing for families living in poverty. In the late 1970s, government investment in housing was 18% higher in the countries of Western Europe than in the United States. Analysis of direct government spending on housing bodes even worse for the United States. The United States holds the distinction of expending an insignificant share of government dollars on housing. In 1980, the percentage of public expenditures dedicated to housing was 0.6 in the United States. For purposes of comparison, the Netherlands spent 7% of its public expenditures on housing in the same year; the United Kingdom, 5%; and Sweden, 3.4%. These comparisons got worse in the 1980s when the U.S. government vastly diminished federal funding for existing affordable housing programs.

It is no surprise that the few federal dollars allocated for the basic necessity of housing have not measurably impacted upon the housing crisis. In 1990, approximately 43% of low-income renters paid more than half of their gross incomes for rent; more than 30% is considered unaffordable. Because almost two-thirds of low-income renters do not receive any government rent subsidy, many low-income households do not have additional resources for their housing costs other than the family budget. As a result, families are unable to feed and clothe themselves properly, and often must choose whether to pay the rent or buy food. Fourteen million households cannot afford a single penny for housing if they are to meet their minimum costs for nonshelter basics such as food, medical care, and clothing. Thus, many families find themselves either completely shut out of housing, or with housing costs so burdensome that basic necessities must be foregone.

The lack of affordable housing in the United States, particularly for low-income households, is caused by a combination of two factors: declining household incomes and sharply rising housing costs. In fact, it has been recognized that "what exists is a fundamental and growing structural gap between incomes and housing costs." For example, from 1970 to 1994, the median income of renter households decreased by 16% to $15,184, while gross rents increased by more than 11% to $403 per month. Furthermore, beginning in the late 1970s and continuing through the early 1990s, the Consumer Price Index (CPI) for housing costs outpaced income. The inability of household income to keep up with escalating housing costs has spawned the affordable housing crisis in the United States today. Estimates show that in order to close the "affordability gap" (the gap between housing cost and income) in the U.S. housing market, $92 billion in funding would be needed annually.

High housing costs, the second key contributor to the affordable housing crisis, can be attributed to a severe shortage in the nation's housing supply. From 1974 to 1994, the number of affordable dwellings has decreased by half in the North east. The total stock of affordable rental housing in the South and West also fell below 1974 levels. According to the Center on Budget and Policy Priorities, in 1985 there were 3.7 million fewer low-rent units than low-income renter households. In 1989, there were 4.1 million fewer low-rent units than low-income renters. The affordable housing stock continues to erode during the 1990s, leaving low-income renters with limited housing choices.

The shortage in the housing market has resulted from a combination of several factors. First, low-income housing production has declined substantially over the past decade. According to the Congressional Budget Office, net new commitments to provide assisted housing averaged less than 10,000 units between 1988 and 1993, down from between 300,000 and 400,000 units in the late 1970s. Given that cutbacks in federal housing programs are on the horizon, the production, and thus the stock of low-cost units will continue to diminish. Moreover, changes in the tax code initiated by the 1986 Tax Reform Act have made investment in rental property less desirable, adding to the lack of low-rent unit production. Finally, state legislation has further decreased the production of affordable housing. Some states require voter approval of low-income housing construction that is publicly financed. Many fear the loss of property values if these units are built in their neighborhoods. Therefore, such legislation gives citizens the ability to block the construction of affordable housing. In many localities this opportunity is eagerly seized.

In addition to the lack of housing unit production, loss of existing units substantially contributes to the housing shortage. For example, condominium conversion and increased gentrification of low-income neighborhoods result in a great loss of low-income housing units. Owner withdrawal of thousands of low-income units built during the 1970s with federal subsidies adds to the shortage. Finally, the abandonment and demolition of run-down housing further contributes to this problem.

As the cost of housing rises due to shortages in housing and other cost-enhancing factors, and the incomes of renters decline, the affordable housing crisis becomes increasingly acute. The impact of the crisis is devastating to low-income people. For those people who somehow secure housing, the rents are increasingly unaffordable, leaving low-income tenants without funds for basic human necessities. For people who cannot secure affordable housing nor continue to pay for unaffordable housing, homelessness results.

In fact, the affordable housing crisis has been recognized as "play[ing] an essential role" in contributing to the onset of homelessness in many Americans' lives. Unable to secure any type of housing due to the affordability problem, increasing numbers of families seek homes in shelters or in the streets. Estimates of the number of homeless individuals in the United States prove difficult to gather due to the nature of the problem. Consequently, the numbers vary from a low of between 192,000 and 350,000 to a high of 1.5 to 3 million. However, as many as 600,000 people remain homeless in America on any given night. Approximately seven million Americans have experienced homelessness at least once in their lives. Families account for 20% of the homeless population and 80% of families that are homeless are headed by a single mother. Children comprise 15% of the homeless population. While homelessness is a devastating experience at any age, it has profound effects upon children. Children whose families cannot afford a home often suffer from malnutrition, perform poorly in school, and have related mental and emotional problems.

The housing affordability crisis not only creates the problem of homelessness, but also results in people being "precariously housed." People who are precariously housed live on the brink of homelessness and are soon to "cross the narrow divide between shelter and the streets." An estimated six million people are precariously housed or "pre-homeless" in the United States. They are often forced to "double up" with friends or relatives which causes overcrowding and substandard living conditions. Moreover, the situation of being precariously housed is often chronic, rather than a passing phase in a family's life. According to one study, "crossing the line between extreme crisis poverty and homelessness has become largely a matter of timing—not when, but how often."

In the current political climate, the crisis will become predictably worse. It doesn't take an alarmist to realize the affordable housing implications of the budget-slashing, program-cutting Republican Congress. Relying on the private, market-driven sector for provision of adequate housing for low income people has not worked. There is no evidence that the private sector will produce affordable housing without government support. Solving the housing affordability crisis will only be possible with significant increases in federal funding....

The initial goal of Swedish housing policy was alleviation of the extreme housing shortage. The large-scale production of housing which was needed could only be accomplished by removing housing distribution from the profit-making vagaries of the capitalist market. Creating a socialist housing market involved curtailing speculation on the cost of land and on the cost of housing on the land. In 1947, legislation gave municipalities the right to expropriate land and to control land sales by a first right of refusal. Municipal land banking provided a generous source of affordable land upon which to build nonmarket housing. Also in 1947, the Building Act legislated municipal control over the location and density of development.

Fueled by national government subsidies and municipal planning, housing development charged ahead. The capitalist system of housing production continued with private enterprise constructing housing. Social democratic principles governed distribution with nonmarket principles dominating the sale and leasing of housing. With cost controls and nonprofit markets in place, the national government committed significant financial resources to housing production, mostly in the form of below-market, fixed-rate loans. More than 90% of all housing built in Sweden since World War II has been funded by state loan subsidies.

The combination of government loans and municipal control of land and development proved a successful formula for curtailing the housing shortage. By the 1960s, Sweden boasted the highest rate of housing development in the world. In 1965, Sweden launched its "Million Dwellings Programme," ambitiously planning to build one million dwellings within ten years. The goal was truly remarkable considering the population of Sweden at the time was 7.5 million people. However, it was not considered enough merely to create dwellings. Those dwellings had to constitute decent, quality housing. Equally as important, they had to be affordable.

While the similar intent expressed in the United States Housing Act of 1949 still remains but a dream, Sweden happily achieved its stated target. By 1975, Sweden gloried in one of the highest ratios of dwellings to inhabitants in the world, at a comfortable 430 dwellings for every 1,000 people. Within its specified ten-year time frame, Sweden reached its aspirations of ending the housing shortage, improving housing conditions, and bringing housing into the realm of affordability. Gone were the days of overcrowded, unhealthy conditions for Sweden's residents. Housing standards now included realistic occupancy limits, adequate sanitation and plumbing, central heating, and modern utilities. Sweden's housing supply, in addition to being in good condition, became affordable to people. A national system of housing allowances guaranteed that a person's contribution to rent would be no more than 25% of their income.

By the mid-1970s, Sweden had declared its housing problems solved. In terms of actual numbers, this proclamation certainly was truthful. In terms of fairness in the distribution of housing, including individual choice of tenure and economic equality in access to different tenures, Sweden still had significant work ahead. During the million dwellings program, construction consisted mainly of public and cooperative housing, which constituted 38% of the housing supply by 1974. The policy objectives expressed in the Housing Act of 1974 reflected an increased need for single family homes, larger apartments in multi-family dwellings, and the availability of both as rentals and cooperatives. Having more choices in types of housing would be meaningless, however, without greater fairness in economic and social benefits among choices. To accomplish this additional objective, financial incentives needed to be distributed in a more equitable manner among tenures. Further, the opportunity for self-determination brought about by tenant management and control of rental housing had to occur.

Having solved the housing shortage, Sweden's attention turned toward housing equity, stressing the importance of economic and social integration of classes in different types of housing tenures. From the start of Sweden's determined housing effort, the ideal of distributive equity in housing was the motivation behind protecting housing distribution from market forces. It would be achieved by increasing the supply and affordability of single family homes and larger apartments in multi-family dwellings. Equalizing costs between rental and ownership posed a challenging task since homeowners enjoyed great tax benefits. Reducing the tax advantages of homeownership was not an option, so increasing the financial benefits for other tenures became the goal. The housing allowance program expanded to meet the needs of distributive equity.

The plan worked. Availability of single family homes with different forms of tenure increased, and equalization of costs became a reality. Within a decade after 1975, rental and cooperative tenures in single family homes rose from 4% to 32%. Total subsidies for homeownership tripled by 1981. There were costs, however. The amount of taxes foregone by government due to homeowners' deductions of mortgage interest from income tax more than quadrupled. In fact, homeowners with the highest incomes enjoyed the greatest financial benefits from the subsidy programs. Conversely, housing allowances which subsidized costs for mostly low-income families slowed in growth after 1975. In 1980, of the total housing subsidies allocated, 63% (including tax deductions) were for homeowners, 8% of the subsidies were for cooperative dwellers, and 28% went to renters. In terms of percentage of people in each tenure who received a housing subsidy, the breakdown was 26% of homeowners, 33% of cooperative dwellers, and 42% of renters.

Unbeknownst to the Social Democratic Party, its developing success in providing all people with a choice of housing tenure would be its temporary undoing. Despite attempts to equalize the attractiveness of the three main housing options, single family and cooperative ownership became overwhelmingly popular. Having achieved homeownership and perceived independence, many people's adherence to the dictates of social democracy lessened and they grew more conservative. The Social Democratic power base became weakest among homeowners....

The Government's Role

Division of Responsibility

The governmental division of labor for affordable housing in Sweden proves extremely efficient. The national government legislates and administers housing policy while regional and local governments implement it. In addition to formulating housing policy, the national government provides the funds for affordable housing production and distribution. At the national level, the Ministry of Housing and Physical Planning administers and coordinates the allocation of funds among regions. There are 24 designated counties with regional governmental entities called County Administrative Boards. The County Boards act as intermediaries between the National Housing Board and municipal governments, overseeing the municipal housing plans. This dominance of regional control proves vastly superior in efficiency, fairness, and effective resource allocation than the city/suburb competition in the United States.

In 1947, national legislation granted municipalities power over the planning, production, and development of housing. With that power came the responsibility to provide adequate and affordable housing for the populations within their jurisdictions. To accomplish these objectives, municipalities were empowered to acquire land, by expropriation if necessary, and to regulate the construction and development of housing on that land. They were also given considerable tax-raising authority. Having broad land use planning control, local governments can lease public land for development, sell it with restrictions, or use public land for development of nonprofit housing. To facilitate the latter option, municipal governments have created municipal housing corporations which develop and manage decent, affordable housing. The municipalities maintain ownership of the self-sustaining, nonprofit housing.

In the Planning and Building Act of 1987, the municipal land use planning powers were expanded and updated. Unlike the United States, where development planning remains practically nonexistent, the 1987 legislation directed each municipality to form a building committee which creates a comprehensive master plan for development of land and buildings. Although housing built under the master plan is funded through the state housing loan program, the master plan does not need national government approval. It does, however, go through an extensive local public review process. The building committee has the final discretion to accept or reject suggestions and objections. Once accepted, the master plan must be adhered to by a developer in order for the developer (private or nonprofit) to receive a state housing subsidy. The developer must also be building on publicly owned land to qualify for a state loan.

Government Spending

The national and municipal governments of Sweden fund affordable housing through three different systems. Sweden has an extensive system of land banking which preserves undeveloped, affordable land for development purposes. The initial outlay of government dollars is spent on land purchases. Next, the government funds affordable housing by providing construction loans. Finally, the national and local governments bankroll housing subsidy programs to make the cost of housing affordable to all individuals and families.

The success of Sweden's national housing policy has been built on the foresight of its land banking program. At the turn of the century, Sweden was already buying undeveloped land with the intent of preserving it for future affordable housing development. In and around the city of Stockholm, a most noteworthy example of land banking, the goal of controlling future development prompted the conservative government to buy up farmland surrounding the city. Continuation of this practice enabled the municipal government to acquire land very inexpensively during the depression of the 1930s. By 1972, the city of Stockholm owned 36% of city land and over 80% of the surrounding land. Throughout Sweden, the design and planning of Stockholm has been duplicated. The beginning of the 1970s saw 75% of all new building in Sweden occurring on municipally-owned land.

Over the years, legislation was enacted to strengthen municipalities' capabilities to buy, sell, and lease land. The Housing Provision and Building Acts of 1947 legitimized land banking by entrusting municipalities with the right of expropriation and the right of first refusal on land for sale. Expropriation rights were strengthened in 1966, and again in 1971. Moreover, in 1968 the price municipalities paid for expropriated land was reduced to the land's value ten years prior to sale. In 1973, municipalities were given the right to expropriate substandard rental housing. If a municipality desires a parcel of land, a private owner must sell it at the market value ten years prior to the time of sale. The expropriation law evidences strong governmental bias in favor of granting the ability to take land and then dispute the price.

Thus, in Sweden, affordable housing begins with governmentally-controlled land costs. Most developable land is removed from the speculative market by the land banking system. Having acquired land at extremely reasonable cost, the municipality can sell it for current value plus the value of any improvements. Or, as is usually the case, it can enter long term leases for the land with developers. By owning vast amounts of developable land, municipalities can control development. Enhancement of this power draws from the municipalities' ownership of nonprofit housing companies and from the legislative requirement that municipal governments create and administer master development plans. State subsidies for development are contingent upon housing developers complying with master plans which give the municipal governments considerable enforcement power.

Municipalities fund the purchase of land in several ways. Since 1966 there has been a national loan program which provides loans for 95% of the site value of acquired property. The National Housing Board assesses site value. In addition, municipal governments have their own sources of revenue, bank loans, and nationally-approved bonds to cover costs of land acquisition. Land banking can be financially self-sustaining. In the early 1960s, Stockholm's aggressive land banking program brought in more rent dollars than it spent. Affordability of housing built on leased land can be maintained by raising rents only for commercially and industrially leased land as land value appreciates. Although financial gains from land development are not available to the building industry in Sweden, valuable incentives exist for construction companies if they follow the rules. They must seek approval for construction from the municipality and follow the master development plan promulgated by municipal governments, as well as comply with all building codes. If they do follow the rules, they profit greatly from the state-subsidized financing of housing construction. The builders benefit from the savings in land cost by the cash flow created for state construction loans. Furthermore, builders gain business from the consistent source of developable land. State financing has accounted for the lion's share of construction since World War II. One hundred percent of the cost of construction of multifamily housing is financed by the national government, as is 72% to 99% of the cost of single-family homes. The state subsidizes rehabilitation as well as new construction and, for the last ten years, has subsidized loans for repairs and maintenance in multifamily housing.

The final way the national and municipal governments in Sweden subsidize housing involves expenditures for housing consumption. Sweden has had a housing allowance system since the 1930s. Currently, the housing allowances are determined based on a formula combining a number of factors, including family size, household income, and housing cost. The housing subsidies operate so that rents never exceed more than 25% of a person's income, and currently assist 26% of all homeowners, 33% of cooperative dwellers, and 42% of all tenants. Middle income families benefit from housing allowances so no stigma attaches to housing subsidization. In addition to direct housing allowances, the national government indirectly subsidizes housing through mortgage interest deductions for homeowners. A closer examination of the forms of housing tenure will illuminate the strengths and problems of each.

Forms of Housing Tenure

Housing tenure in Sweden is a choice between three basic forms. People looking for housing can choose to be renters, cooperative dwellers, or homeowners. The rental sector comprises 43% of the housing market, divided about equally between private and public housing. Homeowners account for 42% of housing consumers and cooperative owners represent 15% of all housing dwellers. . . .

The Potential Problem of Segregation

One other potential problem which lurks on the horizon is segregation of socioeconomic groups. Immigration of refugees from various ethnic backgrounds has steadily increased in Sweden since the 1930s. After World War II, immigrants from other Nordic countries were welcomed in Sweden due to mutual agreements to abolish visa requirements. Although immigrants from Italy, Hungary, and Austria were actively recruited to fill labor needs after World War II, it was not until the 1960s when "[i]mmigrants from outside the Nordic region became a more noticeable feature of Swedish society." The Swedish parliament began to regulate non-Nordic immigration in 1968, requiring work permits, jobs, or refugee status for non-Nordic immigrants entering the country.

By the mid-1970s, the Swedish government began to set policies to avoid segregatory patterns of housing. With the objective of fostering understanding and cooperation among people of different backgrounds, socioeconomic and cultural integration and equality became a priority. Two forms of housing segregation endure in Sweden: ethnic and economic. Economic segregation precipitated by unequal availability of housing across tenure lines has been discussed. As previously discussed, problems of economic segregation were alleviated by increasing the availability of different tenures in homeownership and maintaining housing affordability. Although economic segregation still exists, the high quality of housing for all Swedes mitigates against the development of "slums" for lower income households.

Although the majority of Swedes live in quality housing, ethnic housing segregation still remains a problem. Immigrants comprise 8.5% of the Swedish population, with 5.5% being from other Scandinavian countries. The worst segregation is experienced by the most recent immigrant groups (Chileans, Turks, and Vietnamese) and groups of immigrants exhibiting differences in appearance (Africans, Asians, and Turks) from the Swedes. Nevertheless, this ethnic housing segregation does not seem to result from discriminatory practices, either individual or systemic, but rather appears to be a product of the voluntary settlement patterns of immigrants. In Sweden, opportunities exist to gradually improve one's income and housing. Immigrants can achieve housing equity.

In reality, there is little sign in Sweden of the serious problems experienced in most industrialized countries involving segregation and marginalization of low income people. While there is some economic and ethnic segregation, housing standards still remain acceptable for people with low incomes.

Moreover, the number of people living in poverty is relatively small, and the difference in income level between average income and low income continues to be moderate.

In contrast to Sweden's generally homogenous population, the United States' heterogenous population suffers from housing segregation so severe it has been referred to as "American Apartheid." Deliberate housing segregation of minority groups in central cities has been practiced by federal, state, and local governments on behalf of the American people. The difference in severity of housing segregation and standards between the two countries highlights the inherent racism that precipitates the locational isolation of people who look different than the majority. It becomes difficult not to wonder whether the United States' lack of effective measures to remedy its affordable housing crisis is also a symptom of its racism.

* * *

[Editor's note. Sweden, like most of its European trading partners, is cutting taxes and spending, and housing subsidies are now reserved for only the most needy.]

The following excerpt contrasts the Chinese housing system:

Kam Wing Chan, *Infrastructure Services and Financing in Chinese Cities,*

7 Pacific Rim Law & Policy Journal 503 (1998)

Public Housing Reform Programs

Housing has been another problematic area in Chinese cities. Housing development and reform in China in the 1980s through the early 1990s occurred in two stages. The first stage, from 1981 through 1985, focused primarily on increasing the supply of housing by inviting new sources of finance, including private investment. The second stage launched in 1986 was concerned with the more complicated problem of adjusting rents on the huge stock of public housing, as well as selling off some of its public housing. In 1988 the Leading Group for Housing Reform ("LGHR") of the State Council laid out a plan to commercialize urban housing. Through this plan, the LGHR would disclose the extent of housing subsidies granted to urban employees, reform the investment system so that housing construction is treated as commodity production, set up a house-financing fund, and readjust the production structure to stimulate the development of a real estate market. In 1991 the State Council renewed the reform proposals of 1988, again calling for rent system reforms and the sale of public housing. However, the measures to increase rents made only limited progress. The housing rents accounted for about one percent of the average urban household expenditure in 1994—the same as in 1985.

At the same time, especially in coastal provinces like Guangdong and Fujian, there was no slowdown in sales of public housing at huge discount prices, most of which was below the bottom price of RMBY 120 per square meter proposed by the State Council in 1988. According to the Ministry of Finance, by the end of 1993 about twenty percent of housing stock (including those owned by enterprises) had been sold to individuals. This massive transfer of public property to individuals at bargain prices prompted the State Council in late 1993 to ban the sale of public housing and reassess the program.

Current Situation

Despite the sluggishness of the 1980s reforms, production of urban housing has progressed rapidly, especially in the last three years. The rate went up from just under 200 million square meters in 1989 through 1991 to over 350 million square meters in 1994, and 394 million square meters in 1996. The average per capita urban housing floor area (living area) jumped from 3.6 square meters in 1978 to 6.9 square meters in 1991, and further to 8.5 square meters in 1996. This means that China has already reached its target of eight square meters per capita for the urban population, three years earlier than was planned. However, urban housing is unequally distributed and the allocation system is fraught with problems. As of 1994, 4.4 million households (down from 5.3 million in 1991) were still living on less than four square meters of floor area per capita. This figure, of course, totally excludes the housing needs of the "temporary" population in cities and towns and related problems, an issue that China's government has not yet come to face.

The sale of public housing with partial property rights, banned in 1993, resumed in some cities in the first half of 1994. The current objective is to sell public housing to workers at a "standard price." An official in the Ministry of Finance ("MOF") said that the "standard market price" of a unit consists, on the average, of three roughly equal factors: construction costs, the cost of the land itself, and other infrastructure services (in the form of taxes and fees). A policy promulgated in December 1994 substantially raised the sale prices of the public housing.

Cities are selling off their public housing at varied paces and prices, reflecting differences in location and quality of housing. In Qufu, sales of public housing at an average of RMBY 200 per square meter were well underway in the summer of 1994, and the city expected to sell off all its public housing by the end of 1994. In Qingdao, sales were to begin in late 1994, at the standard price of RMBY 670 per square meter. The program in Guiyang and Anshun in Guizhou began in 1993. The standard price in Guiyang was RMBY 220 in 1994; in Anshun it was RMBY 207 in 1993 and RMBY 460 in 1994. Discounts, typically thirty percent off the standard price in Guiyang, were often given to city residents, existing occupants, and those who paid cash. In the last three years, various initiatives have been tried in different cities. In Guangzhou, owners of public housing who profited from previous discounts have been asked to repay part of the difference. The municipal government also pledged to replace the housing entitlement and assignment policy with an indirect housing subsidy program.

Modest progress has been made in raising the rentals for public housing, at least judging from the experience of cities studied. In 1996, housing accounted for about three percent of the average urban household expenditure. While rents remain low, sale prices are very high relative to incomes. Lump-sum fees and charges levied on new urban housing constitute one factor of the high sale prices. The situation is aggravated by a very rudimentary mortgaging system. Rental public housing is far more tempting than ownership. In the mid-1990s, as a privatized "commodity housing" market started to expand, often beyond the reach of most families, a low-cost housing program (*anju gongcheng*) was initiated to cater to lower income families.

* * *

The following excerpt describes the challenges faced by housing reform in the former Russian republics and federated socialist nations:

Jan van Weesep, *Comment: A Perspective on Housing Privatization in Eastern Europe*,

29 Urban Lawyer 595 (1997)

Since the Profound Political Changes in the late 1980s, the housing systems in Eastern Europe have been thoroughly altered. From largely government-controlled systems, they have become modeled on an extreme concept of market. There were two types of motives driving this transformation. On the one hand, within the countries there was the need to improve housing conditions, that is, to rectify the inequities and inefficiencies that developed under socialist control. On the other hand, there was the need to stop the huge financial hemorrhage that housing represented in government expenditures. This motive was espoused by national governments, but even more forcefully still by outside financial and technical aid organizations such as the World Bank and U.S. Agency for International Development.

Given the economic crises, governments found it impossible to maintain a housing system that cost so much and yielded so little. Prodded on by outside advisors, they decided to rid themselves of the liability that housing represented, and managed to disguise it as an asset to be given away to residents.

Under the previous socialist systems, the allocation of housing had developed from an avowed distribution on the basis of need to one of rewarding privilege. Moreover, in spite of huge subsidies, the quality of housing constructed was generally poor, at least by Western standards, and it deteriorated from there. But privatization has remedied neither of the two problems of inequity and deterioration, nor is it likely to do so in the near future. The systemic changes provided windfalls for some and saddled many others with significant future liabilities. Nor does privatization guarantee a quality housing stock for the future, in spite of the observation that in the West—which provided the model for the new housing systems—homeownership coincides with better quality housing, a sense of community among homeowners, and higher personal wealth. This generalization, however, ignores the ample evidence that where people are pressed into homeownership, neither individual benefits nor positive social effects are likely to result....

[A]t the end of the socialist era in Eastern Europe, the best housing was clearly in use by the elites—political, economic, and social. Single-family housing has replaced social rental units at the top of the housing hierarchy. But much of what was considered the best housing was still part of the social rental sector, which was subsequently privatized. This meant that the better-off were given the opportunity to obtain premium housing at give-away prices, and they enthusiastically took advantage of this. The result has been recreation of the socialist inequality in the evolving private market that will eventually make certain that the gap in housing quality between the rich and poor will be magnified....

The post-1990 housing reforms abolished state ownership of large parts of the housing stock throughout Eastern Europe. By and large, housing was privatized, whereby eventually individual households obtained the title to their dwellings. Ideologically, this transfer suited the desire to create a private market which is supposed to generate social and housing benefits. Practically, since the state was experiencing a grave economic crisis and did not have the funds for maintenance or renovation, privatization appeared to be the only feasible strategy to save the housing stock from complete deterioration. Wholesale privatization was also the advice (or the condition) from the outsiders offering coveted financial and technical aid. Some of the new national leaders accepted the position with enthusiasm. This transfer of future housing costs from the state to individual owners who rarely perceived an alternative option or the risks involved was facilitated by the illusion of obtaining a deep discount of the unit's value, however that was determined. Thus, most East European countries have rapidly been transformed into "nations of homeowners," but with little thought to the consequences when bills for repairs and maintenance come due.

Restitution of ownership rights also contributed to the rapid growth of the private sector in several East European countries. Thus, large parts of the housing stock in older parts of cities reverted to private ownership. New owners, however, rarely had assets to repair the dilapidated buildings. Tenants remained protected from eviction and rent increases were neither feasible nor permitted in most instances. Thus, badly needed repairs and renovation could not be financed from current rental income, nor could owners resort to outside financing since no adequate home-financing system was in place. To date, the banking systems in most of Eastern Europe remain woefully inadequate....

In most countries of Eastern Europe, the privatization of social rental housing is proceeding at a rapid pace. In some, the vast majority of the units has already been sold off. The analogy with similar policies in the 1980s in Great Britain is striking. In but a few years, that country was turned by Prime Minister Margaret Thatcher into a "Nation of Homeowners." The tool was "right to buy" legislation, aided by various coercive measures along with deep subsidies to tenants to buy their public housing units. In some respects, British tenants were "sold" a course of action based upon less than full understanding of the obligations and costs involved. There too, the underlying rational for the government was to rid itself of the burden of housing subsidies by shifting costs to former tenants when they became homeowners. Owners assumed, generally without adequate preparation or awareness, the obligation for all housing costs, including repairs and modernization. In both systems, buying their units could easily lead to impoverishment of those new homeowners without funds to meet future costs and prevent further deterioration of the housing stock....

The only way to achieve progress in the struggle against deterioration of housing and neighborhoods will be by fostering homeowner education, by designing and making

10. Panelized Housing. Recently rehabilitated socialist prefabricated panelized social housing in Prague, Czech Republic is spacious and convenient.

available good mutual management options, and by adopting laws and regulations grounded in public and private contractual principles. In addition, adequate financing must be provided through private financing tools that have been slow to come into effect. Finally, a source of government subsidy will need to be provided to support those whose incomes are lowest, but who must still assume part of the costs of maintenance and repair, either directly or through needed increased rents for landlords....

One of the main motives of government in supporting privatization of housing has been its inability to fund the necessary investment in the housing stock. If the state has been unable to do so, it may be too much to expect of a newly emerging owner class in society, a large proportion of whom are impoverished. The task will be daunting, particularly in a period of transition, when in most of the newly emerging countries (except for the Czech Republic), unemployment is high and inflation is generally in at least double digits....At the moment deterioration proceeds more rapidly than repairs and improvements, and this must change quickly....

* * *

Project Site Selection and Design

A principal charge leveled at the American style of zoning is that local autonomy allows suburban communities to permit only development for the wealthy. Through the use of devices such as permitting only single family detached homes on large lots of a half to five acres of land, the imposition of expensive infrastructure fees or exactions and other growth management strategies, the stark pattern has become known as "exclusionary zoning." In most states, the political environment favors maintaining the status quo, particularly where most voters, including legislators and judges reside in suburbs.

The Pennsylvania Supreme Court, in 1965, suspended the previous near-absolute discretion afforded local zoning policy, and ruled that zoning that seeks to wall out urbanization through excluding certain locally undesirable uses such as modest homes on small lots or apartments fails to act within the authority to legislate for the general welfare. *National Land & Inv. Co. v. Kohn*, 215 A.2d 597 (Pa. 1965). New Jersey was one of several New England states that followed the anti-snob zoning principle, extending it to establish an objective affirmative obligation to plan for all land uses. *Southern Burlington County NAACP v. Township of Mount Laurel*, 336 A.2d 713 (N.J.), *appeal dismissed*, 423 U.S. 808 (1975). Each community was obligated to develop or plan for the development of a fair share of regional housing needs. The New Jersey Legislature passed legislation that enacted the fair share principle and established a state agency to establish numerical planning obligations. *See Hills Dev. Co. v. Township of Bernards*, 510 A.2d 621 (N.J. 1986). Several states followed the Pennsylvania litigation approach where a developer must prove the exclusionary effets of regulatory practices. *Britton v. Town of Chester*, 595 A.2d 492 (N.H. 1991); *Berenson v. Town of New Castle*, 341 N.E.2d 236 (1975). Several other states established administrative machinery that preempts local zoning decisions. Conn. Gen. Stat. § 8-30g; *Mahoney v. Board of Appeals*, 316 N.E.2d 606 (1974), *appeal dismissed*, 420 U.S. 903 (1975); R.I. Gen. Laws §§ 45-53-1 to 45-53-8. The reforms are largely limited to the New England region. Even with the reforms, the result has not changed the general character of the exclusionary suburbs, particularly as there no longer exists any government subsidy programs. The only program that generates new urban affordable housing is a section of the income tax law that provides low income housing tax credits to investors. Janet Stearns, *Low-Income Housing Tax Credit: A Poor Solution to the Housing Crisis*, 6 Yale L. & Pol'y Rev. 203 (1988); James E. Wallace, *Financing Affordable Housing in the United States*, 6 Hous. Pol'y Debate 785 (1995). These low income housing tax credit-financed dwelling units are capped in number by legislation and regulation and unfortunately can be found almost exclusively in traditionally racially and economically-depressed identifiable concentrated areas. Florence Wagman Roisman, *Mandates Unsatisfied: The Low Income Housing Tax Credit Program and the Civil Rights Laws*, 52 U. Miami L. Rev. 1011 (1998). While the motive for replacing direct project subsidies with tax credits was a desire for deregulation and privatization, the segregative impacts of the program were foreseeable and inexorable. For years, the federal housing agency, The Department of Housing and Urban Development, along with local urban housing authorities, have been sued in every region of the country for systematically concentrating all government-subsidized housing into neighborhoods identified as impacted from high concentrations of poverty and typically composed of racial minority groups. James A. Kushner, Fair Housing § 7.02 (2d ed. 1995 & Supp. 2000). The resulting concentration of poverty and stigmatic reputation of the projects have rendered urban rejuvenation ever more difficult. While the growth of minority populations has generated increasing minority presence in older first-tier city suburbs, the affluent, generally white population, has moved beyond that tier, toward the newer and more exclusive edge cities at the urban fringe. Joel Garreau, Edge City: Life on the New Frontier (1988).

While the New England experience has brought national attention to the problem of exclusionary zoning, it has not significantly altered the pattern of urban and suburban development in that region although it has generated affordable housing units that might not have been developed in the suburbs. Several other states have established obligations to plan for affordable housing as part of community planning obligations. Cal. Gov't Code §§65302(c), 65580-65890.5 (housing element); Fla. Stat. Ann. §163.3177(6)(f); Idaho Code §67-6508. Although isolated courts have enforced such requirements, (*see e.g.*, *Building Industry Association of San Diego v. City of Oceanside*, 33 Cal. Rptr. 2d 137 (Ct. App. 1994)), the combination of a lack of government subsidies, unregulated siting of tax credit-financed housing, lack of enforcement of state planning obligations through explicit standards and sanctions, and the political environment of home rule and the desire of the suburbs to avoid uses likely to generate a need for extending municipal services and school capacity, results in a pattern of exclusivity, featuring economic and racial isolation. This is why tax revenue-dependent communities aggressively pursue shopping malls and big-box retailers like Walmart and Home Depot rather than serve the needs of workers.

In *Oceanside*, the voters approved, by initiative, Proposition A. Prop. A established a residential development control system (RDCS) which established annual allotments for dwelling unit development. The allotments were for 1,000 units in year one and 800 thereafter, allowing up to a ten percent adjustment to redress prior year excesses or deficits....

Under Cal. Evid. Code §669.5, because the growth restriction limits residential development, the traditional presumption of validity is reversed placing the burden on the government to justify the constraint as necessary to protect the health, safety, or welfare of the community.

The Court invalidated Proposition A on the basis of conflict with the city's general plan and conflict with three state statutes.

The Oceanside scheme was invalidated because it favored expensive single-family homes and discouraged apartments that required more expensive services and facilities, particularly schools, in a ruling finding the scheme inconsistent with the comprehensive plan's housing element identifying an unmet need for affordable housing.

The proposition was also found to be inconsistent with three statutory provisions contained in the California Government Code, including §65008 that prohibits discrimination against developments intended for those of low or moderate income.

Inconsistency was also found with §65913.1 which requires the zoning of vacant land for residential use with appropriate standards to meet the plan's housing needs. Oceanside was not zoning for apartments which were indirectly being discouraged through the allocation system.

Finally, The court found Prop. A to conflict with §65915 which requires that communities offer density bonuses or an equivalent financial value to developers who construct 25% of units for persons or families of low or moderate income, or 10% of units for lower income households.

A number of local communities sought to remedy the lack of affordable housing. Local government is most commonly facing a series of fiscal crises as the cost of facilities and service delivery escalate and sources of revenue are often politically frozen and frequently declining. As a result, communities have looked to regulatory strategies to generate or encourage affordable housing. Collectively, the strategies are referred to as "inclusionary zoning," because of the way that zoning is being manipulated for the first time to include those previously zoned out of communities. Robert C. Ellickson, *The Irony of "Inclusionary Zoning,"* 54 S. Cal. L. Rev. 1167 (1981); Jennifer M. Morgan, *Zoning for All: Using Inclusionary Zoning Techniques to Promote Affordable Housing*, 44 Emory L.J. 359 (1995). The strategies included mandatory inclusion of lower cost housing, whereby developers were required to include a set percentage of dwelling units that were below market rents or prices. *Home Builders Ass'n v. City of Napa*, 108 Cal. Rptr. 2d 60 (Ct. App. 2001) (sustaining inclusionary zoning ordinance requiring ten percent of all newly constructed units to be affordable), *cert. denied*, 122 S. Ct. 1356 (2002); Jerome G. Rose, *From the Legislatures—The Mandatory Percentage of Moderately Priced Dwelling Ordinance (MPMPD) is the Latest Technique of Inclusionary Zoning*, 3 Real Estate L.J. 176 (1974). Of the few communities that utilized the device, few affordable units were actually generated as the ordinances typically conditioned compliance on the availability of government housing subsidies. Michael Banzhaf, *Are Mandatory Inclusionary Housing Programs Passé? The Orange County Experience*, 13 W. St. U.L. Rev. 473 (1986); Robert A. Johnston, *et al.*, *Selling Zoning: Do Density Bonus Incentives for Moderate-Cost Housing Work?*, 36 Wash. U.J. Urb. & Contemp. L. 45 (1989). As federal subsidies declined, and state efforts to fund housing never materialized, except in New York, and housing responsibilities devolved to local government, the mandatory inclusion was an oxymoron. Rent skewing is one form of subsidy generation that does not entail dependence on government subsidy. Rent skewing involves increasing the rents or prices of the majority of unsubsidized units and using the increment to lower rents for the lower priced units. Although this scheme has on occasion been used privately or in specific development proposals, it has never been enacted as community policy. Theoretically, the system works the same as taxation, yet housing policy students often resist embracing the concept. Perhaps if more revenues were raised and expended locally, citizens would have a greater sense of community and pride. In Istanbul, Turkey, where economic and social conditions have not generated any government housing construction or finance programs, the city government created Ikitelli Başak Şehir Residence, a city within the city for 500,000 occupants, through a system of increasing prices on middle income flats so as to subsidize units for those of lower income and recent immigrants.

Another technique that has the potential for generating some affordable units is a program that swaps the right of the developer to build extra units for an agreement to price a set percentage of units at an affordable level. Jane E. Schukoske, *Housing Linkage: Regulating Development Impact on Housing Costs*, 76 Iowa L. Rev. 1011 (1991). This strategy is seen as a win-win situation as the legislature enacts the authority for the program allowing it to celebrate an effective policy for affordable housing. The local community then bears the responsibility for implementing the program. The density bonus is never mandatory but an option for developers and many developers simply pass up the opportunity. Many developers see the bonus as an insufficient incentive because inclusion may be seen as an interference with market success. Some communities may effectively deny the incentive of the bonus by attaching expensive development exactions or parking requirements to the additional units. Even where such bonus densities are utilized, there can be problems, for affordable housing may be defined as just moderately below market price and thus the poor are not included. In many communities, the city may permit the developer to construct the bonus affordable units at a different site, one that exacerbates the concentration of neighborhoods for the poor, and exclusion from neighborhoods of the affluent.

One strategy suggested by economists was the construction of inexpensive small homes on small lots with a minimum of costly design or construction requirements. The theory was that these "least cost" houses would generate a supply of housing more likely to be affordable to first-time buyers and those in search of affordable housing. *Oakwood at Madison, Inc. v. Township of Madison*, 371 A.2d 1192 (N.J. 1977). The concept was based on the basic econometric housing policy model that posits that as housing is built for the affluent, that the wealthy abandon their prior dwelling which is then available for someone of less income, whose home is in turn handed down ultimately to the poor. Indeed, economists often argue that the current system that subsidizes housing for the affluent but not the poor is the superior system to deliver affordable housing as it creates incentives to expand the housing supply efficiently. Unfortunately, the model does not reflect the dynamics of current housing markets. James A. Kushner, *The Reagan Urban Policy: Centrifugal Force in the Empire*, 2 UCLA J. Envtl. L. & Pol'y 209, 231–241 (1982) ("reverse filtration"). The affluent may no longer prefer a long commute to the suburban fringe and may opt to tear down and replace or to buy a home in a gentrifying neighborhood where the chic are moving in and the poor are being displaced. There also exists a burgeoning demand for more household units as grandparents, parents, and grandchildren all get divorced or choose a singles lifestyle, placing new demands on a limited housing supply. Programs to remove deteriorated housing stock such as urban renewal, code enforcement, or earthquake and other safety compliance standards tend to remove from the market the very housing the economists anticipated for the poor who find themselves squeezed between increasing populations of the poor, minority groups, and new immigrant populations.

The New Jersey Supreme Court, in enforcing its judicially created fair share inclusionary obligation, first experimented with authorizing compliance through constructing least cost housing. *Oakwood at Madison, supra*. However, after seven years the Court confessed error, eliminated the device as a satisfactory implementation tactic, and observed that it had produced no housing stock for the poor, but in fact it allowed the purchasers to benefit from housing inflation as the units rapidly became unaffordable. *Southern Burlington County NAACP v. Township of Mount Laurel* (*Mount Laurel II*), 456 A.2d 390 (N.J. 1983). In many communities, and this is a problem with all suburban inclusionary programs, the beneficiaries of inclusionary strategies may be the friends and relatives of residents or those already working in the community, and the overall regional impact may be increased racial segregation as whites are often the principal beneficiaries of the programs. *In re Township of Warren*, 622 A.2d 1257 (N.J. 1993) (invalidating regional contribution agreements wherein suburbs pay another city to build a portion of their fair share affordable housing obligation). In *Mount Laurel II*, The New Jersey Court suggested utilizing a number of the various strategies, but eschewed reliance on least cost housing.

A program that is becoming more popular is the housing trust fund financed through housing impact fees. Schukoske, *supra*. Developers, particularly of commercial and industrial uses likely to attract lower income workers, are charged an impact fee tied to the square footage of the development. The fees are then deposited into a trust fund used to help underwrite and subsidize new housing units. In the highest court to review housing impact fees, the Ninth Circuit federal court of appeals sustained the Sacramento, California trust fund program, where it was based on a rational formula that did not impose on the developer a burden beyond the impact of the project. *Commercial Builders v. City of Sacramento*, 941 F.2d 872 (9th Cir. 1991).

Apart from the financing and development of an affordable housing program, there are many issues concerning the design of housing. What kinds of neighborhoods are appropriate sites, should poorer and more affluent residents be mixed within the same community? What architectural designs are most practical and efficient? The following except looks at these questions from the Dutch experience:

George Lefcoe, *When Governments Become Land Developers: Notes on the Public-Sector Experience in the Netherlands and California*,

51 Southern California Law Review 165 (1978)

....Dutch localities have had to assume a major role in land development because they have been delegated a primary responsibility for ensuring that there is a sufficient supply of housing for all the population....

The Housing Act of 1901 delegated this responsibility to them by authorizing Dutch cities to promulgate housing plans. For smaller municipalities this meant only the enactment of the sorts of building codes adopted in this country in the early 20th century. But the Housing Act mandated that larger cities prepare housing development plans showing how the community would meet its housing needs. The 1901 law did not force each locality to finance housing for those individuals who could not afford it, but it did call for the cities to take affirmative steps to make sure that what was economically feasible would be built.

The Housing Act of 1901 was also the first modern planning law in the Netherlands, for it authorized cities to prepare expansion plans to show where roads, canals, and squares would be located in newly developing areas. To assure a sufficient supply of developable land for housing, the larger cities began acquiring land. It made little sense to acquire only sites for roads and housing. Shops, schools, and job centers had to be planned and space had to be made available for them as well. Thus, by the 1920's the larger cities were well established in the land development business. During the depression of the 1930's other smaller municipalities entered the market by picking up prime sites at historically low prices.

After World War II, nearly all towns entered the land game. Ninety percent of downtown Rotterdam had been destroyed by bombing, and even those cities with little direct destruction had suffered from years of "deferred maintenance." Building materials were in short supply, and capital was hard to raise. Once the government began allocating materials and borrowing funds for reconstruction, there were severe shortages of construction labor. It became a government policy to subsidize housing for all but the wealthiest, and local governments were delegated the task either of building "social housing" through development subsidiaries or of assisting nonprofit organizations to do the necessary work. The first step was to acquire land so that a steady quantity of sites would be ready for development on schedule. Thus, the Second World War—and the housing shortage it precipitated—can be listed as one more explanation for Dutch municipal land development.

Today the old justifications for government involvement no longer hold. Most of the government land reclamation work has been completed, or will have been completed by the end of the century. Large private firms in the building business are perfectly capable of assuming most of the costs and risks of site preparation. Many of them are international in scope and ownership, and even if there were no development firms with sufficient resources to tackle the larger urban expansion schemes desired by Dutch municipalities, subsidiaries of the major Dutch firms (Philips, Unilever, Royal Dutch Shell, and others) could certainly be organized to meet the need if the financial returns were made promising enough.

As for the housing shortage, its end is in sight. Today the most sizable impediment to increased housing production is the government policy of housing subsidies, a vestige of postwar times. Because so many Dutch people enjoy subsidies of one form or another, they pay rather small percentages of their income for rent—less than 10%. Many prefer to remain in tiny, poorly lit and poorly heated, old-fashioned apartments with less than adequate plumbing, rather than pay 20 to 25% of their incomes (that we in the U.S. regard as normal) for modern unsubsidized housing. Recognizing this, the Dutch government is bent on phasing out most of the subsidies except for those in special need of relief....

....*Amsterdam's Bijlmermeer*

Southeast of Amsterdam in a bucolic field of nearly 4500 acres one comes suddenly upon a neatly arranged series of eleven-story, greyish-white buildings. Some are like S's made with a straightedge, while some are like Washington's Pentagon with one or more sides missing. Known as the *Bijlmermeer*, this complex is Holland's most famous. It may also be its most infamous.

Bijlmermeer as planned would have contained: 2200 acres of residential uses (for 110,000 inhabitants); 620 acres of industrial use; 500 acres for special uses (e.g., shops and parking); and 1100 acres for recreation and open space. Although the housing was to be constructed and managed by a number of nonprofit entities, the city of Amsterdam is the developer-entrepreneur in a project so massive and innovative that it might give pause to even our largest apartment developers.

Amsterdam needed the *Bijlmermeer* to meet the housing commitment it made in the late 1930's when the estimate for the city's population by the year 2000 was 960,000 (a compromise between a predicted low of 900,000 and a high-side estimate of 1,100,000). In 1935 the city's Town Development section in the Public Works Department drew a General Extension Plan for major development south (near Schiphol Airport) and west of the city. These plans were approved by the Crown in 1939, but their realization was postponed during the war.

Since the early 1960's it had been clear that even to house the 1939 population projection for the year 2000, far more space than was planned initially would have to be urbanized. People want larger houses and apartments than were built in 1939. Households are more numerous and are smaller on the average. There are more automobiles and a greater need for more parking space than was contemplated by the 1939 plan. To meet these increased needs the old plan had to be modified.

One of the modifications was the drawing of the southeast extension known as the *Bijlmermeer*. The city was committed to seeing that 100,000 new housing units were built at this locale because there would otherwise be no place to relocate middle-income families displaced by the renewal and rehabilitation efforts in the older parts of the city. Urban renewal in Amsterdam does not mean ripping up all the historic canal houses in favor of high-rises, or evicting tens of thousands of moderate-income families to make way for a smaller population of rich burghers. It means rehabilitating old houses, sometimes tearing down nonbearing walls to enlarge the size of rooms, upgrading the plumbing, or installing central heat. Often, it means providing subsidies so that low-income families can afford the improvements being made, or subsidizing nonprofit or limited dividend societies dedicated to restoring historic houses. But urban renewal also means relieving overcrowding in the old parts of town, and this can only be done humanely if relocation housing is available somewhere in the metropolitan region. The *Bijlmermeer* was planned as one such resource.

The design concept for the *Bijlmermeer* derives from Corbusier as adapted in Holland by Mies van der Rohe. It calls for *strook* (winding strips of housing) with *streaming* (open space) between. By using the high-rise form, it frees larger expanses of open space, which is then available for parks, bike paths, and greenery. Advocates of this type of project contend that these spaces are far more useful than the few square meters of land each unit occupant would have if, say, townhouses of one or two stories were built covering the entire site. By aggregating open space enough land is available to serve the functions open space is designed to serve—aesthetic, recreational, and air purifying. At the same time, population is clustered. This makes it easier to locate shopping facilities and rapid transit connections.

Each high-rise building is long and narrow (one-quarter-mile long), and well-separated from other buildings by open space. Each apartment enjoys the privacy that only comes from having a clear view of the sky, with balconies running the length of the unit on one side. Elevators are spaced to minimize walking distances, and on the first floor there are glass-enclosed galleries running the entire length of the building and connecting it with parking garages. Cars are completely separated from pedestrian walkways, but some unlucky residents may have to walk up as many as four flights of stairs before reaching elevators in the apartment complex. There is enough garage space to accommodate 1.5 cars per unit. All of the first 10,000 units in *Bijlmermeer* are high-rises. The size of apartments varies: two rooms (16%); three rooms (21%); four rooms *(57%);* and five or more rooms (6%). Clearly the apartments were designed to serve the typical Dutch family with one or two children.

Describing the units and the design concept is only preparation for the unhappy admission that, despite the good intentions of the city, *Bijlmermeer*, in the opinion of many Dutch people, is the worst housing in all the Netherlands. One journalist described it as "the greatest and most regrettable urban planning mistake ever begun in the Netherlands." It has been called a high-rise slum where no one is safe in the parking garages at night and where no family that had any choice would elect to live. Despite the fact that the city was responsible for the entire complex, shopping facilities are still woefully inadequate; a car is a necessity because the promised subway to Amsterdam is still several years off. The subway connection and the retail facilities will come—sooner or later. Whether they will come in time to make *Bijlmermeer* attractive to the middle-class Dutch families it was built to accommodate remains to be seen.

Although built for families, *Bijlmermeer* has never appealed to families sufficiently to be filled by them. Rents are extravagantly high—four or five times what people pay in older but otherwise comparable housing in the city. The rent would be beyond the reach of any middle-class family unless they enjoyed a sizable housing subsidy from the central government. Besides the high rents and lack of shopping facilities and public transportation, mothers (only ten percent of the middle-class Dutch mothers work) did not like having their small children playing out of sight all day. They also did not like being isolated in the far reaches of suburbia.

Bijlmermeer survived in its early years because what it lacked in appeal to middle-class families it made up in appeal to young singles. Nearly half of its initial occupants were singles living at two persons per unit, not the three that had been contemplated. Fifty-six percent of the residents were under 39, and there were reportedly 3000 gays among the first 15,000 occupants. These early residents were paying unprecedented percentages of their income for rent. More than half were paying 18 to 25%, and another fifth were paying better that 25% of their earnings—the highest percentages in all of Holland.

Although there is little in the way of empirical analysis on the subject of architecture and family preference, a team of Australian planners provides us with one hypothesis accounting for the popularity of *Bijlmermeer* with young, single people, and its apparent unpopularity with middle-aged, middle-class families. Besides the fact that *Bijlmermeer* was a project of high-rise buildings, its design was sufficiently modernistic to repel persons with conventional taste in architecture. The Australian group studied a number of cluster-housing projects to determine the conditions under which shared open space and unusual house designs could be marketed successfully. They concluded that the professional and managerial classes are more receptive to innovations in housing; the working class consumer who has less confidence in himself and his design judgments generally prefers more conventional styles in housing. So it was in the early days in *Bijlmermeer*.

When the time came in 1970 to build the second phase of the project, an architectural consulting team recommended a shift from the original extension plan that had called for 90% high-rises and 10% garden or low-rise apartments. They recommended instead that as many as 85% of the new units be low-rise and only 15%, or at most 30%, be high-rise. Their recommendations were based on survey data from people in western Amsterdam of the sort that *Bijlmermeer* had been built to lure. The city council paid little attention to this recommendation, concentrating instead on the economics of the project that depended, by this time, on government support to meet the rent levels necessary to bail out the nonprofit housing sponsors that had built *Bijlmermeer's* apartments on land leased from the city. None on the council except the V.V.D. (a liberal party in the 19th century sense of the word *liberal*) wanted to discuss issues of building design and livability. All the others on the council voted to continue with the original, predominantly high-rise plan.

At about the same time, events occurred that no one had contemplated when the original plans for *Bijlmermeer* were first drawn. The former Dutch colonies of Surinam and the Antilles were granted their independence, and large numbers of native colonials elected to migrate to the Netherlands. The new immigrants, especially those coming from Surinam, were poor, ill-educated, and lacked the skills necessary to make a good living in Holland. They came to the large cities, particularly Amsterdam, where the largest single reservoir of public housing was the *Bijlmermeer*. Black-skinned Surinamers and other immigrants constituted 4500 of the 15,000 residents by 1971 and 10,000 of 35,000 by 1975. Increasingly, Surinamers spoke of racial discrimination while the white residents complained of noise, threats of violence, apartment break-ins, and muggings. Many families left, and a good number of all the vacancies in the Netherlands were to be found at the *Bijlmermeer*. Many of those who remained characterized the environment as unsafe, impersonal, and almost jail-like. A ghetto was forming. Fights between police and residents, unheard of elsewhere in the Netherlands, are commonplace at the *Bijlmermeer*, and there is no end in sight.

To some Americans who read this account, the lesson seems a simple one. The *Bijlmermeer* is the Dutch version of Pruitt-Igoe, a high-rise public housing project in St. Louis that was hailed as a marvel of futuristic design when it was first opened in 1955. It was demolished some years later; federal and local authorities could find no way to keep the blighted structure safe for human habitation. Professor Newman, in his analysis of New York City public housing, contends that high-rise structures like *Bijlimermeer* and Pruitt-Igoe contain too much space that is not defensible. This is an insufficient answer, however. When these projects were conceived, they were not planned as high-security fortresses to protect their occupants against criminals living outside the project as well as within it.

The critics of public housing here and in the Netherlands often neglect to ask where an immigrant population like the Surinamers should be housed. If it were not for *Bijlmermeer*, many more immigrants would be crowding into the already densely packed apartments in Amsterdam. Many would be in those deplorable units built to house factory workers in the late 19th century when the North Sea canal was completed. Whatever is wrong with *Bijlmermeer*, it provides far better housing than those 19th century units which lack sunlight, backyards, central heating, and modern plumbing. The first building codes were enacted in Amsterdam in 1906 pursuant to the 1901 Housing Act to make sure that no one would ever build such cramped quarters again for the underprivileged. In 1906 no one was thinking of how the Surinamers would be housed seven decades later. *Bijlmermeer* provided a better answer, however, than most American cities gave when, in their rush to revive their downtown core areas, they displaced thousands of poor people years and sometimes a decade before even a single unit of replacement housing had been opened for occupancy.

This is not to say that high-rises are good for families; almost all authorities agree today that the garden apartment works better for family living—if one-family houses are out of the question. Significantly, the Dutch have decided that in the third segment of *Bijlmermeer* they will eschew high-rise construction. Only 10% of the units will be high-rise, 60% will be four-story walk-up, and 30% will be two-story and one-story garden apartments.

The *Bijlmermeer* experience suggests that when cities act as land developers they take risks in urban design on a scale that no private entrepreneur could assume and stay in business. Sam Lefrak, a New York City apartment entrepreneur, keeps 50,000 apartments occupied and safe, but the design of his buildings pays no tribute to Corbusier or Miles van der Rohe. They are large, plainly built structures, far inferior to *Bijlmermeer* in appearance and function. Public open space is negligible, and pedestrian and vehicular traffic are not separated on the site. Balconies and other frills are kept to a minimum. Additionally, Sam Lefrak or any other private entrepreneur could not offer housing to penniless Puerto Rican immigrants and stay solvent very long. One justification for Amsterdam's continuing with its extension plans is that without projects like the *Bijlmermeer* it has little hope of reducing densities in the old city to facilitate rehabilitating the historic old canal houses and the other quaint, if outmoded, four-story walk-ups of the old city....

* * *

How are neighborhoods designed and chosen for affordable housing development? The following excerpt looks at the question:

James A. Kushner, *A Tale of Three Cities: Land Development and Planning for Growth in Stockholm, Berlin, and Los Angeles,*

25 Urb. Law. 197 (1993)

The treatment of housing affordable to those of low- and moderate-income is also an issue fundamental to urban development policy.

Although Stockholm and Berlin stand in stark contrast to both America's significant rising poverty class and its minority populations of color, they have each, to their credit and economic stability, followed a course of relative class integration. Indeed, in Sweden there does not exist any housing developments designed or marketed only to those of low income. It is Sweden's policy not to segregate by population and to avoid the development of housing for special population groups other than housing for students, the elderly, or the disabled. Although some concentrations of recent ethnic immigrants exist in Stockholm's outer suburbs due to housing cost and availability, the segregation is de minimis in comparison with the United States and seems to disappear as economic parity is attained. The Federal Republic of Germany has experienced some modest concentrations of immigrant workers, but it has occurred mostly in cities such as Hamburg where Germans have left the city for suburban housing tracts. West Berlin is notable for its attractively designed, affordable housing typically built by the nation's top architects and contractors through design competitions. Developments in Berlin are often marked by the juxtaposition and integration of buildings designed by different architects representing radically different exterior design arranged around open spaces. Housing subsidies have been provided virtually universally in Berlin and to all with modest incomes in Stockholm allowing various economic classes to reside in both housing projects and neighborhoods throughout those cities. The result is a more highly educated and better trained work force and metropolitan-wide economic stability in comparison to the American pattern of a burgeoning underclass without access to employment, posing a drain on the national economy and a threat to central city stability of epic proportions.

Both Stockholm and Berlin, however, are facing challenges to their happy status as Sweden and Germany face policies requiring integration of large numbers of foreign workers. Berlin has received large numbers of Eastern European immigrants. Rising levels of violence and racism in both countries have placed those nations at the crossroads America faced at the turn of the century. There are indications that Sweden and Germany may opt for segregation rather than their successful experiments in relative economic integration. Ironically, they may follow the American development pattern which has failed so miserably just as the United States fails to replicate the successful experience of its Swedish and German partners—an experience that may be obligatory for economic competitiveness as well as political and economic stability. Indeed, there has been liberal advocacy in Germany for extending urban boundaries as a means of reducing central city rents and facilitating middle class aspirations for lower density development patterns. Paradoxically, German federal limits on subsidized housing costs requires site selection beyond urban boundaries in the countryside where land is cheap, exacerbating concerns over urban sprawl. . . .

Although there have been experiments with scattered site selection of single family homes and individual rental units under programs of rent supplements and vouchers for the poor, the units were still located in relatively low-to moderate-income housing, central city neighborhoods, housing with only marginally more affluent occupants than those receiving traditional housing subsidies. In a growing number of communities where judicial rulings or legislation have required inclusionary zoning or the inclusion of affordable housing as a condition for developing market rate housing, the typical experience is the construction of a modest, no frills segregated project in or near the more costly development. Only rarely have communities experimented with including dispersed, non-identifiable subsidized units within an upper income or middle class development. America's commitment to class and racial residential separation has profound and grave implications for the nation. Because most services and facilities, including schools, are funded through local property taxes the quality of services often reflects the extent of a community's wealth and tax base. As the white, more affluent classes, along with industry and commercial centers, moved to the suburbs and ex-urban areas, the central cities became unable to supply quality services, safety, adequate education, job training, employment, or efficient transportation. The increasing concentration of fixed-, low-, or no-income people continued to encourage white, middle class, and job flight from the cities. The pattern is ostensibly irreversible absent fundamental political reform. As the voting majority now resides in the suburbs, the political support for urban aid has vanished as America's homeless, unemployed, undereducated, and untrained population was rendered nearly invisible, outside of occasional charitable pleas and news of urban violence. Indeed, American federal policy toward housing subsidies since 1981 has virtually halted the development of new, federally assisted housing and has also halted the dismantlement, demolition, and private sale of marketable government projects.

Ironically, Los Angeles, by comparison with Sweden and Germany, appears able to integrate or at least assimilate unbelievable numbers of foreign immigrants. While racial segregation marks the American urban environment, Stockholm and Berlin experience a rigid class structure despite efforts of government housing policy to generate integration. Ironically, upward class mobility and economic class integration has been a tradition within most of America's middle class neighborhoods despite government policies that tend to segregate.... America, with Los Angeles as a prime example, embarked on a destructive policy of segregation by both race and economic class while Sweden and Germany, as displayed in Stockholm and Berlin, pursued policies of class integration within neighborhoods, development projects, and buildings. Yet, there appears to exist in both Sweden and Germany a rigid unofficial social class structure with minimal upward mobility and minimal social contact as compared to the United States with its official racial and ethnic segregation policies. However, the United States enjoys a far less rigid social and economic class structure as neighborhoods often house a broad range of income groups, albeit in a crazy quilt scheme, which tends to exclude the very poor and the very rich. Swedish and German economic class integration, or more precisely, the absence of a pure poverty underclass, has provided stability to neighborhoods and avoided the pathology of the American city where residents lack access to employment, education, and a safe and decent environment in which to raise the next underclass generation. Anthony Downs has observed that Swedes are motivated by social solidarity. They are willing to sacrifice their own individual welfare, to a great extent to benefit the group as a whole, as compared to America's emphasis on individualism and self-reliance, and he recommends more social solidarity for America. The lack of such solidarity prevents the resolution of America's economic and social ills.

American policies toward affordable housing have traditionally delivered "no frills" housing without amenities, aesthetic charm, or even quality in terms of construction and neighborhood design; the result is disenchantment, alienation, and rapid deterioration. By comparison, the subsidized housing in both Stockholm and Berlin is designed by the finest architects and constructed with the best materials and methods available. The development design policy toward construction and landscaping contributes to widespread positive community attitudes toward protecting and maintaining housing....

* * *

What is the future potential for integrating modern urban forms with the need to provide affordable housing within liveable and accessible neighborhoods. The following excerpt describes the European experience:

Voula Mega, *The Concept and Civilization of an Eco-society: Dilemmas, Innovations, and Urban Dramas,*

in Cities and the Environment: New Approaches for Eco-societies 47 (Edited by Takashi Inoguchi, Edward Newman, and Glen Paoletto 1999)

Cities are becoming increasingly fragmented, a far cry from the European urban archetype or the great urban utopias. The "Balkanization" of the urban fabric—cities torn to pieces—and the cumulative spiral leading to poverty and distress are becoming obstacles to the creation and distribution of urban wealth. Unequal distribution has draining effects on the vitality of urban activities and is a source of both unsustainable lifestyles and obstacles to cultural change. European cities that are showcases of financial power will never become sustainable if they hide social micro-jungles. This is not just the ransom to be paid for success, it is an obstacle to success. Urban renaissance must regenerate all these micro-jungles, their spatial webs and their social fabric. The social city, "the city of solidarity and citizenship," cannot be perceived without equity, otherwise it will be the poly-segmented city (Moss) or the city of forced solidarity (Durkheim). Social justice is a precondition for sustainable wealth. Harvey reminds us that there is nothing more unequal than the equal treatment of unequals.

The spirals of unemployment and exclusion constitute severe problems for cities, threatening to create dual cities. In the 1990s, the European Union has stepped up the pace of its action for the disadvantaged and the excluded. In this vast and vague category, one should include the more than 52 million people (15 per cent of the European Union's population) estimated to live below the poverty line, the 18 million unemployed, and the more than 3 million homeless. Identifying sources of employment in cities is not an easy task. The need is pressing and the achievements not always promising. The European Commission's report on local development and employment initiatives identified urban fields as potential sources for job creation. Services improving everyday life and the quality of the environment, as well as services of leisure and tourism, have an important potential for employment and enterprise creation. Most schemes include training, enhancing the ability for reconversion, professional guidance and orientation.

The improvement of housing environments, the living cells of a city, leads to the coherence of the urban fabric. Mass housing has often created social tensions on the urban fringe. It has often been paternalistic, large, remote, uniform, collective, anonymous, and devoid of management, and it has failed. In many European cities, housing is now beginning to be self-regulated, local, personal, individualized, and proactive, with corporate neighbourhood space and responsive local management. It has to provide proof of vitality of work and enterprise and to allow personal identity. Vibrant local communities are replacing empty or lifeless neighbourhoods. A new human face is judged necessary in most of those built quickly and cheaply after the war as if to house interchangeable people. The Mascagni development in Reggio Emilia shows how a multifunctional urban space can be created from a rigid series of anonymous buildings, a functional marriage between old and new, with integrated public services and schemes to create local business.

In Finland, the Top Toijla project tried to activate and strengthen tenants' potential and engagement for the improvement of the Rautala housing area. Ambitious renewal has been achieved with a modest budget. A "community theatre" has been created to identify and solve problems and nourish visions and actions. In Sweden, the Athena Housing Project in Orebro creates high-quality housing environments. The project group, consisting only of women for the design, building, and ownership of the housing, insists on the role of participation in order to make changes inexpensive. The renewal of the Holly Street Estate in East London provides an interesting example of the transition from derelict, high-rise environments into vibrant mixed neighbourhoods. In Vienna, the Urban Gürtel Plus project aims at improving living and income conditions in the western Gürtel area, where 34 per cent of the population are foreigners. The revitalization of the local economic structures and the creation of 400 new jobs are considered a necessity.

Protecting people and urban spaces is a precondition if cities are to thrive. An innovative integrated approach to fighting graffiti in public spaces has been developed in Maastricht. The project includes extra means to trace offenders, education programmes to improve and redirect the skills of the graffiti "artists," and an anti-graffiti bus with formerly unemployed people specialized in removing graffiti. The city made a wall available to all citizens wishing to express themselves by means of graffiti. Within two years the damage caused by graffiti pollution decreased considerably (by 80–90 per cent, at the railway station). The results of prevention are always hard to prove, but it is clear that graffiti have decreased considerably in Maastricht. Tracing and conditional or alternative punishment have a noticeable effect on preventing recidivism, while there are former offenders who, after their artistic training, have become famous artists. The project is now expanding in the region....

* * *

The following excerpt compares Vienna and Los Angeles in their quest to adequately house their populations:

James A. Kushner, *Growth for the Twenty-First Century—Tales from Bavaria and the Vienna Woods: Comparative Images of Planning in Munich, Salzburg, Vienna, and the United States,*

29 Urban Lawyer 911 (1998)

Unlike the housing policy of the Unites States, which segregates subsidized and public housing in poor, typically minority-segregated neighborhoods with marginal schools and dangerous neighborhoods with few employment opportunities, Austrian and German housing policies call for well-designed projects in stable neighborhoods, often intermixed with market rate housing. In Germany it is even common to integrate subsidized and market rate housing in the same neighborhoods and buildings. The neighborhoods are typically well-served by public transit, close to job centers and shopping, and enjoy significant green spaces and recreational opportunities.

Vienna, has had a long successful experience with social housing. One-quarter of the Vienna population resides in public housing. Recently rehabilitated and quite attractive is the kilometer-long Karl Marx-Hof. Perhaps the first modern planned unit development, Karl Marx-Hof was indeed ahead of its time. With interior courtyards providing lawns, playgrounds, and wading pools, and offering mixed uses such as kindergartens and commercial shops on the first floor, the development offers a sense of community to the small scale mini-blocks. Vienna, a city of 1.7 million is attempting to build 10,000 units of affordable housing a year. By comparison, Los Angeles with a population of nearly 4 million, has recently produced at best 3,000 units per year with not many more units produced in all of Los Angeles County with its nearly 10 million population including the city. As Congress has slashed recent budgets, affordable housing production has been dramatically reduced.

Due to the very deep subsides provided, Munich, a city close in size to Vienna, can produce only about 1,500 units per year. Class variations are reduced in Austria, which enjoys an extensive social security system. Workers pay 30 percent of wages (on top of 20 percent taxes) for social programs, matched by a 30 percent employer contribution, providing comprehensive housing, education, transportation, and health coverage. Germany also provides a high level of social programs. In addition, the populations of Austria and Germany are highly homogeneous, reducing significant objection to the dispersal and integration of social housing within a neighborhoods.

Vienna, unlike Munich, has built higher density, centrally located, urban social housing rather than suburban garden cities, reflecting the desire of the Viennese to spend the evening sitting in a café rather than tending their garden.

The United States embarked on a disastrous path in both segregating projects by race as official government policy and selecting impacted racially and economically segregated sites. Also to blame for America's affordable housing failure is the traditional attitude of Congress in desiring to make public and subsidized housing a sort of temporary shelter that the poor reside in while acquiring education, employment, and wealth on the way toward entrance to the middle class. To encourage that conversion, affordable housing often lacks amenities and design factors that renders the property undesirable.

Austrian and German housing development reflect an understanding that a sense of community calls for compatible and aesthetically pleasing homes and neighborhoods. While German and Austrian social housing often reflects the best in modern architecture and planning design, Vienna is notable in having many projects designed by the nation's greatest artists and architects. The demand for Vienna's public housing has generated long waiting lists and, as in the case of employment, has generated unwritten political patronage preferences. Symbolic of the stability of social housing sites is the opening of a new Ramada Inn hotel on the site of the new Olympic Village social housing project in Munich. The juxtaposition of public housing and quality commercial development is a phenomenon unknown in America.

Residents desire, indeed require, a sense of privacy and dignity. This desire is expressed even in high-density projects by smaller buildings constructed around semi-private interior lawns and playgrounds with close access to parks and recreation. Even in large mixed use projects in Munich, residents will often attempt to chase away any non-residents even from public spaces adjacent to individual home units and buildings. American affordable housing too often has been built with little privacy and no dignity. Affordable housing is seen as a LULU (local undesirable land use) to be excluded, as a land use that reduces neighborhood and community land values and stability, and is opposed by the powerful NIMBY (not in my backyard) lobbies....

* * *

Notes and Comments

1. *A note on optimal community design.* There exists great controversy over normative community design. It is possible to compare the ultra high density apartment blocks as-

sociated with New York and influenced by the designs of Le Corbusier with the more garden suburban village suggested by Lewis Mumford. Jane Jacobs offered a prophetic "muckraking" journalistic critique of modern American architecture and city building. Ms. Jacobs wrote enthusiastically of the benefits of high-density urban life. Jane Jacobs, The Death and Life of Great American Cities (1961). She was speaking of the generous life on the streets that results from multiple around-the-clock pedestrians that bring shopkeepers and cafes outside, discouraging the criminal behavior that quiet low density can promote. At the other extreme is the voice of Oscar Newman, who warns of the dangers of the high density in terms of crime as it relates to livability. Oscar Newman, Defensible Spaces: Crime Prevention Through Urban Design (1972). The message is lower density and defensible areas of personal privacy where the public and other project residents cannot easily roam the community. Picket fences and small gardens, like closing off streets drives down the incidence of street crime. Oscar Newman, Community of Interest (1980). Supporters of Newman's concerns go further and advocate security buildings and gated communities. Gated communities have become very popular in the suburbs. Large walls, gates, and a guarded entry are status symbols that afford residents a sense of security. Gating sends a message to nonresidents that this is not your city or place. They also divide the community, in fact are designed to exclude community life and the creativity and excitement of the commons described by Jane Jacobs. Where residents have legitimate security fears, however, the movement toward security buildings and neighborhoods can hardly be termed irrational. *See also* C. Ray Jeffrey, Crime Prevention Through Environmental Design (1977); Neal Kumar Katyal, *Architecture as Crime Control*, 111 Yale L.J. 1039 (2002); Marlene A. Pontrelli, *Crime Solutions Through Planning and Zoning*, 24 State & Local L. News 16 (ABA State & Local Gov't Section Newsletter No. 2 2001) (crime prevention through environmental design or "CPTED" applied in Tempe, Arizona). Many are looking to gates as both a measure of security and sense of community. Larry Smith, *et al.*, *Gated Communities: Private Solutions or Public Dilemma?*, 29 Urb. Law. 13 (1997); Jill Stewart, *The Next Eden: The Movement into Gated Communities is not About Escape: Its About Building Neighborhoods*, 16 Cal. Law. 39 (Nov. 1996); Joseph Trevino, *Housing Project to be Gated: Safety: Most Residents of Aliso Village Welcome the Plan, Saying it Will Curb Drive-by Shootings. But Some Worry About Access for Emergency Vehicles*, Los Angeles Times, May 11, 1999).

There may be no optimal density level. Some European cities enjoy higher densities without losing livability, offering pedestrians efficient access. At the same time, new urbanist communities reflect the planning and design of many small European towns. As Europe experiences many consumers seeking a traditional American lifestyle based on automobile access to the remote privacy of the suburb, New Urbanism would certainly be a more favorable model than the gated exclusive suburb.

Communities in America are left to design their community under a system that does not include comparisons of alternative community designs. Indeed traditional American zoning very likely set out in law, if not in cement, a design pattern that is neither European nor New Urbanist.

New Urbanism

Recent American urban planning innovation has featured New Urbanism. New Urbanism is a compromise between the neo-traditionalism, reflecting old small town America, and the European urban form of pedestrian-friendly neighborhoods with a mixture of housing types and a town center featuring a mixture of residential and commercial uses:

Eric M. Braun, *Growth Management and New Urbanism: Legal Implications*,

31 Urban Lawyer 817 (1999)

Local governments continue to struggle with growth management techniques designed to minimize urban sprawl, protect natural resources, and enhance the “”liveability” of cities. One such planning technique currently receiving publicity around the nation is “Neotraditional” development or “New Urbanism,” so named because it is intended to reflect development techniques popular prior to World War II. As Jane Jacobs so eloquently observed, in her book The Death and Life of Great American Cities, before Word War II cities developed in a mixed use fashion. Homes were located in or near clusters of retail, office, and manufacturing so that people could live near the places where they worked and shopped. This type of early development resulted from the limited use of automobiles and the relative availability of mass transit (bus, street car, etc.).

In theory, Neotraditional communities are more compact, pedestrian friendly, mixed use communities, that incorporate housing opportunities within walking distance of retail shopping, employment centers, and mass transit nodes. Single family homes are located on small lots and are interspersed among multifamily townhouse and/or apartment developments. Sidewalks are abundant and cul-de-sacs are minimized in favor of short interconnecting “grid pattern” street systems. Residential districts are planned with a variety of housing types designed to appeal to a range of incomes and ages.

With the current backlash against rampant suburbanization and the continuing decline of central cities, elements of New Urbanism are beginning to permeate zoning ordinances in some parts of the country. This emerging trend, however, directly conflicts with current zoning theory and local planning practice. Today’s zoning techniques evolved from the segregation of land uses dating to the 1920s. With the increasing use of zoning after World War II, single family, detached residential developments were often located miles away from employment centers, creating long commutes in single passenger automobiles. These patterns developed from a time when this country was dominated by “dirty” industry, where locating residential development in the vicinity of such employment centers presented real threats to public health, safety, and welfare. While these techniques were acceptable when land was abundant and traffic problems were minimal, as populations increased, suburbanization or “sprawl” caused significant infrastructure problems and degradation of natural resources. Because such problems are becoming the norm among municipalities, local government land planners have begun efforts to inculcate New Urbanism concepts within their zoning ordinances. Conflict, however, is developing due to the stark contrast between New Urbanism’s core theory and prevailing zoning theory.

New Urbanism envisions broad zoning classifications allowing developers flexibility in the types of uses permitted within a proposed development. The result is intended to allow developers to obtain a reasonable return on their investment while affording municipalities greater protection of natural resources and reduced reliance on the use of the automobile. Each Neotraditional development is designed to be a community with distinctive character containing a matrix of uses intended to create a synergistic relationship among residents and businesses. In order to succeed, Neotraditional ordinances must be drafted in a more generalized fashion while being incorporated into existing zoning and planning schemes. The result is often like trying to fit a square peg in a round whole.... Because the heart of New Urbanism requires a broad mix of uses, efforts to utilize Neotraditional zoning may be challenged either for inconsistency with the comprehensive plan or as a violation of the prohibition of spot zoning.

Another conflict that arises as an impediment to the implementation of Neotraditional zoning ordinances is the greater degree of discretion granted to planners in such ordinances. Generally, Neotraditional zoning ordinances are drafted to allow enough flexibility to developers and municipal planners to include a sufficient mix of uses for generating vibrant communities. Due to the breadth of the these ordinances, however, some developers express concern regarding the possibility of conflicting interpretations over time. Because planners often move from town to town, vague design standards can subject developers to inconsistent interpretations of Neotraditional ordinances. Moreover, the resulting discretion afforded to planners during the approval process can lead to arbitrary decisions. This usually arises from the use of broad design standards rather than precise rules for implementing a Neotraditional ordinance. To be legally defensible, a city must develop objective, measurable standards that can be consistently implemented over time. Adequate procedural safeguards must also be instituted to preserve a developer's due process rights....

In addition to the legal impediments to implementing New Urbanism, substantial political impediments exist as well. Despite widespread support among municipal planners, Neotraditional development proposals have been forced to make substantial modifications to satisfy the concerns of nearby "NIMBY" residents. The resulting Neotraditional ordinances function more like traditional subdivision regulations than true Neotraditional zoning ordinances. Many citizens have become so accustomed to suburban developments that they are suspicious of radical new development proposals touting multifamily development and small lot subdivisions interspersed with commercial development. Developers who attempt to utilize these new zoning ordinances may face extensive neighborhood opposition. Although planners and developers argue smaller lots and attached dwellings are offset by greater amounts of open space and park land within these communities, existing homeowners often prefer privacy and exclusivity to neighborhood interaction and pedestrian friendly development patterns. Additional cynicism and skepticism result from the generalized way in which Neotraditional zoning ordinances are drafted and the flexibility that must be incorporated into such ordinances. Because of the recent "strip mall" development patterns throughout the nation, many citizens and local government officials are reluctant to permit retail and commercial development near residential communities. The notion of a neighborhood grocery store with a local pharmacy has been replaced by conglomerations of "co-branded" facilities housing gas stations, convenience stores, and one or more fast food franchises, as well as discount retail strip malls and free-standing mega-drug stores. The resulting cynicism presents a substantial barrier to instituting and developing true Neotraditional developments....

* * *

Notes and Comments

1. The New Urbanism movement has opted for a compromise version, one that would be more attractive to Mumford than Jacobs. The New Urbanism embraces

neo-traditional architecture, emphasizing a modest increase in density, and exchanging unused front and rear yards for porches and green pedestrian spaces leading to a mixed use town center modeled on the literary memory of an American small town. In the optimal new urbanist scenario, transit-oriented development (TOD) town centers would be linked by efficient public transit systems so as to extend the range of pedestrian access. *See also* Jerry Adler & Maggie Malone, *Toppling Towers: The New Urbanism is Transforming Public Housing, Blocks of Giant High-rises Are Coming Down, Replaced by Home-Sweet-Home Townhouses*, Newsweek, Nov. 4, 1996, at 70 (monolithic highrise public housing such as Cabrini-Green, in Chicago, converting projects to new urbanism design); Harry J. Wexler, *Hope VI: Market Means/Public Ends—The Goals, Strategies, and Midterm Lessons of HUD's Urban Revitalization Demonstration Program*, 10 J. Affordable Hous. & Commun. Dev. L. 195 (2001). *Cf.* Susan J. Popkin, *et al.*, The Hidden War: Crime and the Tragedy of Public Housing in Chicago (2000). On the legal questions and debate over the legality of warrantless public housing searches, see Corey Roush, Note, *Warrantless Public Housing Searches: Individual Violations or Community Solutions*, 34 Am. Crim. L. Rev. 261 (1996) .

2. Is New Urbanism adaptable to affordable housing? Is it adaptable to revitalizing central cities? *See* Charles C. Bohl, *New Urbanism and the City: Potential Applications and Implications for Distressed Inner-City Neighborhoods*, 11 Hous. Pol'y Debate 761 (2000) (arguing consistent with revitalization). Doesn't the accessibility, mixed-use, and mixed-income offer the best siting of affordable housing? Canada has developed many New Urbanist projects. A study of the Canadian experience found market success and consumer satisfaction in urban infill projects but less success in the suburban setting. Jill Grant, *Mixed Use in Theory and Practice: Canadian Experience With Implementing a Planning Principle*, 68 J. Am. Plan. Ass'n 1 (2002). The report also found that the New Urbanist design is consistent with considerations of social equity. Can you explain why New Urbanism works better in Canadian cities while its first generation has been more successful in America's suburbs? Perhaps it is simply the cultural and geographical distinction that Canadians are attracted to their urban centers, just as Americans are repelled by most of their cities or most parts of their cities. Are American cities at the zenith of an urban exodus? What is the prognosis for reversing America's urban abandonment? Are there European applications of New Urbanism? While some European cities may be higher density than called for by new urbanism, there is a trend toward automobile-based suburban homes, particularly in prosperous economies such as the Netherlands, Sweden, Great Britain, or Germany, where the suburban wives of commuters are referred to as "Green Widows." Peter Hall points that New Urbanism is essentially Britain's call for "urban renaissance" as to design, but the English policy looks exclusively to brownfield reuse. Peter Hall, *Urban Renaissance/New Urbanism: Two Sides of the Same Coin?*, 66 J. Am. Plan. Ass'n 359 (2000). New urbanism may be a compromise of transit accessibility and pedestrian friendliness, while remaining hospitable to the automobile.

3. For a discussion of the need for, and design of, enabling legislation permitting New Urbanist neo-traditional zoning, see Robert J. Sitkowski, *et al.*, *Enabling Legislation for Traditional Neighborhood Development Regulations*, Land Use L. & Zoning Dig. 3 (Oct. 2001).

The following excerpt describes some of Jane Jacob's observations that have informed New Urbanism and continue to influence today's forward-thinking planners:

Jay Wickersham, *Jane Jacob's Critique of Zoning: From Euclid to Portland and Beyond,*

28 Boston College Environmental Affairs Law Review 547 (2001)....

A city's economic and social vitality and diversity can be strangled or supported by the layout of its streets, parks, and buildings. Jacobs's design orientation, nurtured during her years as a reporter for Architectural Forum, explains the appeal of her writings to architects and urban planners. For Jacobs, physical design matters. In the second section of The Death and Life, she identifies and describes four urban design principles that are preconditions for the creation and preservation of vibrant, diverse cities: (1) high densities of population and activities; (2) mixtures of primary uses; (3) small-scale, pedestrian-friendly blocks and streetscapes; and (4) the retention of old buildings mixed in with new.

For Jacobs, population density is a positive factor in urban residential neighborhoods, as well as in commercial downtowns. At the time that she wrote, urbanists such as Lewis Mumford were arguing for optimum densities comparable to those in the English garden cities, of ten to twenty units per acre, Jacobs, by contrast, supports densities of 100 units per acre and up, like those that characterize such vibrant urban districts as New York's Greenwich Village, Boston's North End, Philadelphia's Rittenhouse Square, and San Francisco's North Beach and Telegraph Hill.

But density must be coupled with variety. Jacobs rejects standardized high-density housing, like New York's Stuyvesant Town, a much-heralded project of high-rise towers in a park-like setting that was developed in the late 1940s by the Metropolitan Life Insurance Company, in favor of the rich mix of housing types found in Greenwich Village: walk-up and elevatored apartment buildings, rowhouses, and even a few one- and two-family houses. And she accepts that encouraging higher densities with lower building heights means construction that covers a higher percentage of the lot, with less open space within development sites.

City vitality also requires a variety of primary uses. "The district... must serve more than one primary function; preferably, more than two." Mixed-use districts that provide housing, offices, shops, and other services, attract a far wider range of people, while spreading out their activities over longer periods of time. Consequently, the streets and sidewalks of mixed-use districts are more active and safer both day and night, while being less congested at peak periods. The most effective mixture of uses are fine-grained: each block should bring together different uses, and not be dominated by a single activity, no matter how thriving.

Mixed-use areas are also more fertile ground for new businesses. Jacobs criticizes the sorting out of functions into single-use districts, including government and cultural centers, because it stifles the cross-fertilization of ideas and experiences that is so important to a city's economic and social health. A failure to bring together all the different activities that make up a city can undermine any sense of shared interests and common purpose. "Without a strong and inclusive central heart," Jacobs argues, "a city tends to become a collection of interests separated from one another."

Jacobs's single most significant contribution to urban planning is her understanding that streets and sidewalks, as much as parks, are the true public spaces of a city. At a time when many planners were arguing that streets were wasteful, and that pedestrians needed to be separated from cars, Jacobs looked closely at how streets and sidewalks are actually used in vibrant urban districts. She concluded that a fine-grained mixture of uses and activities must be supported by a continuous network of small blocks and frequent streets, intensified by siting parks, squares, and public buildings at key locations.

Street traffic is a necessary part of city life, she concludes, so long as one manages the use of those streets to favor buses, taxis, trucks, and pedestrians over private automobiles. Jacobs's suggestion that streets should be redesigned to favor pedestrians over cars is a precursor to current techniques of "traffic calming." And her discussion of how banning cars from New York's Washington Square did not create gridlock, contrary to expectations anticipates the result of the recent demolition of the Embarcadero Freeway along the San Francisco waterfront.

Jacobs was writing just as the historic preservation movement was taking off, yet her arguments for preserving old buildings are primarily economic and social, rather than aesthetic or historical. Part of the physical diversity of a healthy district, she argues, is the retention of old buildings mixed in with the new. Old buildings offer cheap space for new businesses and low-cost housing. They also provide the visual and emotional landmarks that anchor a neighborhood in space and time....

The first strategy is embodied in the model zoning codes being developed by members of the New Urbanist movement, notably the Florida planning firm of Duany Plater-Zyberk & Company. New Urbanist zoning codes began as privately enforced subdivision regulations in places like Seaside, Florida, and Mashpee Commons on Cape Cod. Now they are being adopted in communities across the nation. Oregon has recently issued a new model zoning code, jointly sponsored by the Departments of Land Conservation and Development and Transportation, which incorporates many of these New Urbanist elements and is applicable to all of its towns and small cities. On a smaller scale, many of the urban design principles embodied in New Urbanist codes have been used in special review procedures in New York and other cities since the 1970s.

New Urbanist codes differ from earlier codes in three significant ways. First, these codes are expressed in detailed physical diagrams, as well as words, acknowledging that zoning explicitly regulates physical design. Second, these codes treat the street as a public space—unlike Euclidean zoning, which ignores the street, and conventional subdivision regulations, which treat the street solely as a traffic conduit. And third, although New Urbanist codes have primarily been used to define standards for planned unit developments or other special review procedures, they are increasingly being used to redefine as-of-right zoning rules in an entire district or community.

New Urbanist codes start with the design of the street—the width of travel lanes and sidewalk, the presence of parked cars, and the way that buildings front upon that street. Within urban districts, all streets must have minimum sidewalk widths, and provide on-street parking. Within private building lots, parking must be set back to the side or rear of a building, to preserve the pedestrian character of the street. New Urbanist zoning may also require mandatory shopfronts along the sidewalks in designated retail frontage locations. It may also require that arcades, stoops, or porches provide a human-scaled transitional zone. Special standards are established for civic spaces—parks, greens, and plazas. Standards also allow or encourage special architectural treatments for civic buildings, from government buildings and schools, to religious, cultural, and transportation facilities.

Moving up from the scale of the street to the scale of the district, density and use regulations are significantly relaxed in New Urbanist codes, compared with those in Euclidean zoning. Densities are defined as minimums, but not as maximums. A wide range of residential and commercial uses are allowed in most districts, accompanied by physical constraints intended to ensure a mix of uses.

In existing urban areas, allowing sufficient density is usually not a problem; the challenge raised by Jacobs's principles is ensuring an appropriate mix of uses. As an alternative to the extensive amendments required by a New Urbanist code, Toronto has incentivized mixed use through its definition of "split zones." As an example, one might zone a district with a maximum Floor Area Ratio (FAR) of 5.0, but limit the maximum residential FAR to 4.0 and the maximum commercial FAR to 2.0. In this way, the landowner can only achieve the maximum buildout by providing a mixture of uses. This strongly encourages Jacobs's fine-grained mixture of uses, building by building and block by block, that make lively urban districts, while allowing landowners the flexibility to make choices about use within the framework of the marketplace.

The conservation of older buildings is also an important element of district planning. The challenge is to go beyond the preservation of landmark districts, where there have been notable successes, to a more broad-based set of incentives for reusing older buildings that may not be aesthetically or historically exceptional. New Jersey has recently revised its state building code to make standards more flexible for older buildings. Within the first year of the change, the rehabilitation of older buildings increased eighty-eight percent in Jersey City and sixty percent in Newark....

* * *

Notes and Comments

1. Which groups and entities would likely support new urbanism? Which are likely to provide opposition? Who would likely benefit? Who might be adversely impacted? Are groups who benefit all supporters, or conversely, would opponents benefit?

2. Residents of New Urbanism communities report higher levels of satisfaction, neighborhood interaction and outdoor activities, as compared to traditional subdivisions. Barbara B. Brown & Vivian L. Cropper, *New Urban and Standard Suburban Subdivisions: Evaluating Psychological and Social Goals*, 67 J. Am. Plan. Ass'n 402 (2001).

3. One criticism of New Urbanism is that it is based on the image of a village where citizens are involved in survival, while sustainabilty requires planning on a regional, national, or global scale, and may be in conflict with New Urbanism. Ruth Durack, *Village Vices: The Contradiction of New Urbanism and Sustainability*, Places, Fall 2001, at 64.

4. Another criticism is that New Urbanism imposes a design and thus fails to allow citizen participation to generate a bottom-up plan reflecting community choice. Archon Fung, *Beyond and Below the New Urbanism: Citizen Participation and Responsive Spatial Reconstruction*, 28 B.C. Envtl. Aff. L. Rev. 615 (2001). Communities should not blindly accept a proposal because it is called New Urbanist. But does traffic calming and pedestrianization impose a regime? For New Urbanism to succeed in establishing a heightened sense of community, broad public support following education of the range of alternate design options may be the best planning model. Might the New Urbanism movement generate greater citizen participation and heightened democracy?

Cohousing

The forces that motivate the homeseeking public to prefer gated communities, have also generated a nostalgic desire for a sense of "community." Common interest developments represent a response. Oscar Newman, in Community of Interest 1–17 (1980), describes his view of common interest housing—housing that not only may share ownership of common areas, but is occupied by occupants that share common interests:

> Community of Interest is a concept for creating contemporary physical communities structured around the satisfaction of the shared needs of similar types of residents—needs which can only be met as a consequence of the common geographical location of community members. Community of interest has as its premise the assumption that for most people, at different stages in their lives, there is a need for areas immediately outside their homes which can be used for activities that involve others like themselves—places to play, to gather and gossip, to meet members of the opposite sex....

The following excerpt offers one view of how a community of interest might be designed:

Laura M. Padilla, *Single-Parent Latinas on the Margin: Seeking a Room with a View, Meals, and Built-In Community*,

13 Women's Law Journal 179 (1998)

Cohousing developed out of frustration with limited housing choices. The cohousing concept, known in Danish as *bofaellesskaber*, started in Denmark in 1964 when Jan Gudmand-Hoyer met with a group of friends to discuss alternative housing options. Mr. and Mrs. Gudmand-Hoyer planned to have children, but did not want to raise them in the city. The only housing option which countered the isolation of living in single-family homes, apartments and condominiums, was the row house option. Row houses, however, did not offer common facilities which contribute to the "sense of community" that the Gudmand-Hoyers sought.

Over several months, the Gudmand-Hoyers and friends considered their goals and desires. They wanted the "qualities of a country village," but also wished to remain accessible to "the professional and cultural opportunities" offered by the city. As originally conceived in the 1960s, cohousing residences would be large and private, with walls enclosing the front and back. Likewise, the common house would be virtually hidden from view. Focusing on the importance of cooperation in the home, they decided the housing community should be small enough to allow neighbors to get to know each other and to encourage social interaction.[87]

In 1964, the group purchased some land outside Hareskov and proceeded with design plans. While city officials did not oppose the project, many neighbors did. The opposition's main concern was that the "increased number of children would bring exces-

---

87. Two of Gudmand-Hoyer's main inspirations for the cohousing concept were Thomas More's book, Utopia, and the Doctor's Association Housing of Copenhagen. Utopia described a city of co-operatives not unlike today's cohousing communities, with common facilities. The Doctor's Association Housing, built in 1853, consisted of row houses built on a scale which encouraged neighbor interaction.

11. Housing. Government-subsidized International Building Exhibition housing in the beautiful Tiergarten district in Berlin, Germany.

sive noise to their quiet neighborhood." Even though neighbors ultimately thwarted this project, the cohousing group did not quit. In 1968, Gudmand-Hoyer published an article on cohousing, which generated much interest and support. Times and attitudes had changed from four years earlier and an increasing number of people believed that a "more cooperative living environment would help build a more humane world." Society was certainly more accepting of cohousing and other alternative living arrangements such as "hippie communes."

That same year, Gudmand-Hoyer, Bodil Graae, and the remaining Hareskov families purchased property outside of Jonstrup and Hillerod. Planning and development proceeded and in 1972, twenty-seven families moved into Saettedammen. By 1980, twelve cohousing communities had been built in Denmark and cohousing had evolved into an established housing option....

* * *

Notes and Comments

1. Professor Padilla argues that cohousing is particularly suited to single working Latina women who share a common culture, language, and lifestyle and can share childcare responsibilities. *See also* Delores Hayden, *What Would a Non-Sexist City Be Like? Speculations on Housing, Urban Design, and Human Work*, 5 Signs S170 (1980).

2. Two examples of ["communities of interest"] programs already in place can be found in Los Angeles. The Watts Community Housing Corporation sponsored a housing project for the elderly designed around art. The sponsoring corporation was formed and managed by artists and the project included a community room designed for art projects. Artists and art students served as supervisors for art classes and projects with the residents. [The author served as counsel to WCHC from 1978 to 1980 when WCHC

was represented by Southwestern University's law clinic.] The Exxcel program, on the other hand, combined the need for affordable housing with the need for education. Jean Merl, *EXXCEL Links Home with the School*, L.A. Times, Jun. 22, 1992, §B at 1 (Washington ed.). The project was designed around a community school room where—in exchange for reduced rent for volunteer parents and free housing for university graduate students—tutors and teachers regularly meet with residents to assist with their homework assignments and undertake education enrichment programs. In addition, resident students are rewarded with cash and other prizes for good grades. Successful graduates are offered a college scholarship under the program jointly sponsored by the University of Southern California, the Los Angeles Unified School District, and the private developer. The projects are designed so that only half the units are below-market affordable housing. The projects also include security considerations such as security gates for parking and building entrances, and secured above-ground play areas for children. James A. Kushner, *Growth Management and the City*, 12 Yale Law & Policy Review 68 (1994). The EXXCEL model has been replicated. Bob Pool, *New Apartments Offer Shelter and the ABCs. Housing: New Parkside Complex Provides Tutors, Classrooms and Other Educational Amenities for Low-Income Children*, Los Angeles Times, Nov. 2, 1998.

3. Future retirement communities may cater to special populations or communities of interest, *See e.g.*, Diana Marcum, *A Place for the Gay and Gray*, Los Angeles Times, Oct. 29, 2000, at A24 (first retirement community aimed at homosexuals).

Mark Fenster describes several American cohousing developments and some of the impediments to such development:

Mark Fenster, *Community by Covenant, Process, and Design: Cohousing and the Contemporary Common Interest Community*,

15 Journal of Land Use and Environmental Law 3 (1999)

It seems to me that cohousing is a means for people to make a major step toward community without giving up their privacy, or control over their personal lives....

The common interest community (CIC) is a type of private housing project organized within an association created by either statute or covenants running with the land, whose membership consists of holders of units in the development. It is a central tool of private, commercial housing development, with approximately 205,000 CIC's comprising the residences of forty million Americans in 1998. This prominence has led to the development of a large body of common and statutory law, as well as extensive commentary by advocates and critics who provide vastly different accounts of the social, political, and legal effects of the form. Proponents celebrate the private community by covenant that the CIC form offers, while critics decry the purportedly anti-democratic and coercive effects that the CIC imposes on both its members and on society.

This paper focuses on cohousing, an emerging, small-scale type of residential housing development that illuminates both the theoretical and doctrinal issues in the debates over the CIC. Increasingly popular, cohousing developments are initiated, developed, and managed by residents (occasionally with the assistance of a commercial developer). Cohousing adapts the legal forms of the CIC to a more intensive, deliberative democracy and explicitly strives for a sense of community by neighborhood. With privately owned, individual residences constructed around an extensive "common house" that includes shared cooking, dining, and childcare facilities, cohousing employs participatory management through collective, consensus decision-making.

Cohousing's organizing principle, which operates in residents' active participation in the project's design, development process, and the group's governance, is to resolve competing desires for the inclusivity of community and the exclusivity of privacy. The community serves as the notion of a greater collective "we" that can be invoked while hanging wet clothes on a common line and represents an ongoing goal, something towards which cohousing enables its participants to "make a major step." Privacy, in terms of control over an individual's or family's "private life," as well as a community's collective control over the use of its land, represents the core of selfhood that is continually under threat by the demands of agents external to both the self and to the group, with which the individual most closely identifies. Neither an inclusive public community nor an exclusive privacy is essentially privileged in cohousing. The cohousing movement explicitly attempts to reject the classic isolationism and ideological homogeneity of the American commune, the single family home's private enclave located within wasteful suburban sprawl, and the middle class urban neighborhood that is only drawn together through shared fear of crime and random violence. Cohousing posits a crisis narrative in contemporary housing based upon "[d]ramatic demographic and economic changes" that render "[t]raditional forms of housing" powerless to create and protect those parts of life "that people once took for granted-family, community, a sense of belonging."...

This Article argues, however, that cohousing has not overcome the alienating, older models of property relations through the creation of new legal forms specific to cohousing. Instead, cohousing has proceeded by sometimes adopting, and often adapting, the already existing legal forms of the CIC. Due to the widespread acceptance of these established forms by the disciplinary, regulatory regimes of lending institutions, the common law, and state statutes, cohousing developments have tailored their visions of a new community to the conventions of the widely accepted, decidedly conventional community association, consequently reconfiguring and recreating the CIC as a more participatory neighborhood and democracy....

Originating in Denmark in the 1970s, the cohousing concept was introduced in the United States in 1988 by architects Kathryn McCamant and Charles Durrett through their influential book and presentations on cohousing. Cohousing's design exemplifies the "romantic resurgence" in contemporary architecture that combines nostalgia for an ideal notion of the simple, meaningful, and authentic historical town with modern concepts of progress and modernity, and an increased standard of living. American cohousing has emerged as a viable alternative to the CIC form, which is a mixture of private and common property that is financed, organized, and designed by private developers, sold to individual homeowners with covenants that run with the land, and overseen by a private government. The CIC form itself is the result of a hybrid of utopian ideas about community, a desire for privacy through private property, and a concern with the maintenance of property values. It is the culmination of the movement from early twentieth century "garden cities," through post-war suburbs created by "community builders," and, during the 1960s and 1970s, "new towns" like Columbia, Maryland and Reston, Virginia, to the concurrent boom in condominium building and the rapid expansion of common interest developments in the last two decades.

Proponents stress the design of cohousing's "physical environment" as integral to the support of community ties through the encouragement of social contact. The placement of houses within a site varies widely among groups with some communities, like Muir Commons in Davis, California, utilizing attached townhouse-type units, while others, like Southside Park in Sacramento, California, include detached houses. Regardless of whether individual units are attached, most cohousing sites cluster individual residences more closely than do most CICs. Clustering offers social advantages by increasing human interaction, environmental advantages by minimizing human development on the land and protecting open space, and economic advantages by reducing the infrastructure costs of developing the property and through shared walls, further reducing building costs as well as costs of heating. Nonetheless, cohousing properties are typically more expensive than similarly sized and equipped individual houses, although savings from the energy efficiency of units and the sharing of amenities and equipment with the community may balance the added cost over time.

As the nucleus of community activity, the common house is typically centrally positioned on the property, so residents walk past it frequently and can see it from their individual units. Common houses generally include a large kitchen and dining hall for common meals, a children's playroom, bulletin boards for community announcements, laundry facilities, a meeting room, a lounge, and a craft workshop. Therefore, they provide not only extra rooms that are either left out of or reduced in size in the individual dwellings, but also facilities that will attract activities shared by the entire community. Unlike the clubhouse or community room of the condominium or community association, the common house in cohousing is designed to be open and accessible to all members of the community at all times for a variety of participatory activities....

[C]ohousing's processes of resident development and self-governance sacrifice the efficiency that comes from delegating responsibility of property management and maintenance for an ideal of procedural and substantive democracy that both encourages and demands the participation of members....

[T]he entire development process, from initial group formation through the end of construction, can last between two and eight years. For example, members of the Blueberry Hill group in Vienna, Virginia, who planned to move into their community last year, first began making payments toward securing their site in 1994. In the first stage of the group's planning process interested members paid a $100 fee to participate in regular meetings. Once plans became more definite, they paid $5,000 toward their individual residences and common land. When enough members made the requisite financial contributions, the group began the process of choosing an architect. After zoning for the property was approved, members were required to pay $15,000 over a 21-month period to cover building construction, site work, consultant fees, architectural and engineering costs, legal and county fees, and taxes.

To date, most American cohousing groups have chosen to organize as condominiums, with a minority organizing as cooperatives and subdivisions with community associations. As one how-to guide for cohousing groups describes, "[c]ondominiums are a common legal structure for Cohousing because they are well defined, allowing groups to control common areas and giving individuals title to units. They have the added advantage of being well understood and accepted by the banking industry."...

In some ways, the cooperative form would seem more ideologically amenable to cohousing because it combines the common ownership of the land and improvements (including the common house and residential units) with a shareholder ownership interest and proprietary leases for residents. Cooperatives also allow greater control over the sale of the share interest that residents have in their units. However, outside of financial institutions in the few northeastern states that finance cooperative housing, most banks are unfamiliar with cooperatives and are unwilling to finance such purchases. Furthermore, the Federal National Mortgage Association (FNMA or Fannie Mae), which purchases loans from banks, does not buy co-op loans. Cooperative residents also face joint and several liability for all of the debts of members in the blanket mortgage that the cooperative association takes out. Finally, in some areas co-ops may receive lower appraisals than condominiums because the appraised value may be aligned with rental property....

Doyle Street Cohousing

The Doyle Street cohousing project, completed in April 1992 as the second newly built cohousing project in the United States, inhabits a converted warehouse in Emeryville, California, a city across the bay from San Francisco and next to Oakland. It was developed by a resident group, none of whom previously knew each other, that included a retired professor and his wife, an attorney raising her child alone, a woman raising her granddaughter alone, and a single professional woman. The group developed Doyle Street with the assistance of two parties: the Cohousing Company, a Berkeley-based consulting group which helped to find the then-abandoned warehouse and aided the residents in their self-organization and decision-making processes, and a private local developer with whom the residents formed a limited partnership and who undertook financial responsibility for the project and oversaw the warehouse's renovation.

Organized as a condominium, Doyle Street's two floors include twelve individual units on two levels that range in size from 780 to 1600 square feet. Common facilities on the first floor (including a kitchen and dining room, children's playroom, laundry, and hot tub) total approximately 2000 square feet. The units include high ceilings that enable sleeping lofts in many of the bedrooms, as well as individualized features like fireplaces and skylights. All of the units' front doors open onto a common patio or terrace. The apartments in Doyle Street, located within one of the most expensive real estate markets in the country, are not inexpensive. The most valuable unit in Doyle Street was recently estimated to be worth $275,000....

An...important obstacle to the Doyle Street cohousing project was the creation of contractual agreements that would enable the property relations, design, and decision-making elements of cohousing while still satisfying lending institutions at a time when there were no existing cohousing groups in the United States. In meetings with their attorney and developer, group members attempted to develop a set of management documents concerning community participation, the use of common facilities, and the orientation of new households in the community. As part of the mortgage application process, the residents individually submitted the CC&Rs they created to local banks, who in turn submitted them to the FNMA. As Doyle Street's consultants describe the process, Fannie Mae refused to approve the project because it was "too new and untried" and potentially difficult for a bank to resell in the event of a foreclosure. Fannie Mae's rejection effectively barred lenders from selling Doyle Street mortgages on the secondary mortgage market and led banks to withdraw tentative offers of mortgages to group members. In response, at an emergency group meeting, faced with the possibility of being unable to finance the purchase of their homes, the residents decided to amend the CC&Rs to make no mention of the cohousing nature of the project. Even the legal name was changed to Doyle Street Condominiums [from the original Doyle Street Cohousing Community Association]. While they are free to amend their CC&Rs at any time, at this point, legally, residents have no way to ensure that the project will remain a cohousing community. Although the decision was difficult for the residents, once the changes were made, banks were willing to loan on the project.

[T]he Doyle Street CC&Rs explicitly define a consensus decision-making regime for its condominium association's governance. While the three members of the initial Board of Directors make decisions by a majority vote, once the declarant's voting rights end, the "Appointed Board of Directors" make decisions by consensus. If consensus fails, one member present at the meeting can call for a vote on an issue under discussion. If six members in attendance agree, the group holds a formal vote whose outcome is determined by a majority of the quorum present (as long as no fewer than six eligible voters are in favor of the proposal). Three or more voting members, however, may request that the issue be referred to non-binding mediation. If mediation fails after thirty days, the issue returns to the Board for a majority vote. The CC&Rs also stipulate a specific alternative dispute resolution procedure before parties can formally litigate disputes. Beginning with non-binding mediation, disputants are required to move to non-binding arbitration as a final step before proceeding to formal litigation in court....

EcoVillage Cohousing

In its development process and organizational forms, the EcoVillage Cohousing Cooperative (EVCC) strayed further from the typical condominium/homeowners association model. Completed in August 1997, it is located two miles west of downtown Ithaca, New York. Its land was originally part of a 176-acre parcel of fields, woods, and wetlands owned by EcoVillage at Ithaca (EVI), a nonprofit educational institution with ties to Cornell University....

The "eco-village" concept that EVCC attempts to embody encourages the mixed use of land for domestic, agricultural, and commercial use while limiting the use of power and water. Although consistent with the general concept of cohousing, only a few currently existing cohousing projects in the United States call themselves eco-villages. In the words of one cohousing community member, who suggests making only minor modifications to existing building methods, ecovillages are difficult to create because an "ecologically sound building site" is more expensive to build and more difficult to maintain than a conventional development. In addition, such a project is more likely to meet with resistance from conventional local building codes and departments.

EVCC includes thirty units, all of which are attached duplexes lining a pedestrian walkway the width of a small street. Homes range in size from 922 square feet one-bedrooms to 1642 square feet four-bedrooms, while the majority are 1300 square feet three-bedrooms. The EVCC common house, located at one end of the central walkway, includes a dining area that overlooks the property's pond, restaurant-style kitchen, children's play room, sitting room, private offices, guest room, crafts room, teen room, root cellar, and laundry facilities. The carport is detached from the neighborhood, and includes a wood shop and recycling/storage shed. All of the structures at EVCC are designed to achieve high-energy efficiency through solar power, insulation, and shared hot water. In addition, individual units forego full-sized kitchen appliances and their own laundry facilities under the assumption that residents will take advantage of the facilities at the common house. The basement of the common house includes office space that is part of the proprietary leases of the residents who use the small offices for their businesses. The smallest unit, a one-bedroom, cost $90,000, while the largest and most expensive unit is a four-bedroom, which sold for $155,000.

Residents typically share three meals per week in the common house and each resident helps to prepare a common meal approximately once per month. The common house is also the site of evening events like parties, potlucks, and talks by invited speakers. Residents share the common work of cooking, cleaning, and outdoor maintenance through a rotating "work team" system.

The EVCC resident group is organized as a housing cooperative in which members purchase shares associated with their unit through a proprietary lease. The cooperative acted as its own developer, hiring a private firm as architect and development consultant, and contracting directly with private builders....

The Bylaws also attempt to avoid litigation through the use of alternative dispute resolution. Disputes must first be taken to an internal mediation procedure through a "process committee" appointed by the coop's directors. If this does not bring about a successful resolution, aggrieved parties must agree to "set the matter aside for a period of twenty-four hours of reflection" before the directors submit the dispute to a local dispute resolution center. If this step also fails, then parties may submit the dispute to binding arbitration for money damages only. Unlike Doyle Street, EVCC attempts to foreclose the availability of courts to resolve disputes within the group or between individual residents and the group itself....

The difference between proponents and critics is basic. For contractarians, residents "consent" to the government to which they agree by contract, and that consent should be respected and protected by the state. For communitarians, residents merely "assent" to the contractual arrangement of the CIC, and legislators and the judiciary should not assume their consent, nor should their assent be allowed to create negative externalities for society. By using covenants to bind voluntarily original and future residents to its community and by insuring the presence of both assent and consent through a remarkably active, elaborate, and deliberative contractual negotiation and governing process, however, cohousing should attract both CIC proponents and critics....

Cohousing attempts explicitly to balance the private concerns of the homeowner with the public desires of the community member through the creation of a "commons." Like the private community associations whose corporate forms and legal structure provide part of its legal context, cohousing is legally private to those outside the boundaries of the community. Even a cohousing's "commons" is private. Cohousing as a model of residential development, therefore, does not address the criticisms of CICs as exclusionary "privatopias" that isolate developments from their surrounding communities. Privatopias, critics allege, play on individuals' fears of the encroachment (racial or class) of the inner city in soliciting new residents and develop a local micro-government that implicitly secedes from the municipality and county in which they are located. Cohousing itself is relatively homogeneous in the racial, social, and economic backgrounds of its participants, due at least in part to self-selection and the requirements of available capital, knowledge, and time to participate....

Resident-designed and resident-managed affordable housing has historical precedent. In the first half of the twentieth century, unions in New York used an advantageous state law to establish cooperative housing projects, including five buildings built by the Amalgamated Clothing Workers in the Bronx. During the New Deal, unions and some housing advocates attempted to establish federal legislation enabling the construction of cooperative, low-income housing. Their efforts, tied to the Wagner Public

Housing Act, failed due to the resistance of members of Congress who feared the cost of such projects and the social implications of such a model for housing and due also to lobbying by real estate, business, and banking interests.

Currently, cohousing could be an important part of what affordable housing advocates call a "third sector" of affordable housing creation and maintenance. Third sector housing is owned privately by individuals or non-profit organizations (rather than by the state or city), is "socially oriented" in that its purpose is to serve the social needs of its occupants, and is price-restricted to preserve affordability for future owners or renters. Cohousing attracts "third sector" proponents by encouraging collaboration and by linking renters and/or owners "together in common cause." The same self-creation of community that should attract libertarian and communitarian commentators to cohousing has led one commentator to praise cohousing's "potential to empower women of color, particularly Latinas, [t]hrough the steps of identifying their own needs, planning a community to meet those needs, working with other residents, architects, city governments, contractors, nutritionists, health care professionals and education professionals, and seeing their plans materialize through construction of their own community." ...

As part of the solution for affordable housing, some cohousing groups have included low-cost units within their developments. These include Common Ground in Aspen, Colorado, which is exclusively comprised of permanently affordable units, and Depot Commons in Morgan Hill, California, which includes twelve single-parent families attempting to move off of welfare. Southside Park, in downtown Sacramento, California, included affordable housing as part of a deal with the city to gain approval for its high-density plan of development, and received assistance from the city's housing and redevelopment agency to enable residents to receive low-income housing subsidies. Cohousing not only offers a model for affordable housing developments, it also serves as a model for small-scale, mixed-income urban projects that allow for a mix of diverse groups of individuals....

* * *

Notes and Comments

1. *See also* Kathryn McCamant & Charles Durrett, Cohousing: A Contemporary Approach to Housing Ourselves (1988); Eric Lichtblau, *California and the West—"Cohousing"—Modern Twist to '60s Dream*, Los Angeles Times, Nov. 23, 1998 (Lifestyles).

Common interest communities are not all the same. The following excerpt describes the Disney-developed community of Celebration:

Dana Young, Note, *The Laws of Community: The Normative Implications of Crime, Common Interest Developments, and "Celebration,"*

9 Hastings Women's Law Journal 121 (1998)

Disney's "Celebration"—At The Extreme

The Disney Development Company, a subsidiary of Walt Disney Co., has created a new, somewhat controversial, housing development in Florida called "Celebration."

Having modeled the area after the "American small town," the company claims it will "become an international prototype for communities." The approximately 5,000 acre "town" will have 20,000 residents, a pedestrian-oriented downtown, schools, parks, recreation facilities, and, as a more modern feature, "high-speed interactive communication with everybody else in town." The development has stimulated a great deal of interest. More than 5,000 people entered a drawing that gave priority appointments to buy the first 351 homes and rent the first 270 apartments.

According to some, Celebration "satisfies the growing American hunger for a sense of community" by providing locations where residents can "come together for special events or places where people can casually meet each other during the day." For others, Celebration is more akin to community's evil twin; rather than a system to develop communities, Celebration represents nothing more than a "glamorized comity," with the "absence of a bona fide purpose such as inspired most towns." In the end, its ambition is "no greater than to be like a town." Celebration even has a program called "Celebration Traditions." Since every town should have roots and a historical heritage, Disney has decided to manufacture, or in Disney-speak, "imagineer," their own. Celebration represents the privatization and increased corporate control of whole aspects of the American lifestyle, a bastardization of the term "community."

Much like common interest developments, Celebration functions largely by conformity and control rather than true cultural consensus and community decision-making. Though Celebration will have many of the semblances of a real town, for example, "The Celebration Town Hall," "The Workplace," and "The Institute," there is no real town government. The closest thing to representation in Celebration is membership in the homeowner association. However, even the actions of this homeowner association can be unilaterally overruled by the corporation. The sense of community so often yearned for seems to be ironically misguided in the "pretty calm" and "civic infancy" of Celebration. The longing for a bygone America, "is a yearning for civic maturity" in which the "messy responsibility of democracy held sway, and society worked." Celebration does not offer these attributes.

The more theoretically and analytically coherent communities, such as Native American tribes and cohousing projects, are built by the people within them. The tribal negotiation process takes work; it cannot be bought or canned. This emphasis on sharing, trade-offs, and sacrifice is clearly seen in cohousing projects with tasks such as the rotating responsibility of the communal meal. In a tribal approach, the emphasis on community norms and standards may restrain individual desires. By contrast, the imposed standards in common interest developments and Celebration seem to create only a comfortable, dreamy image of community, without the attendant, yet fulfilling, direct experience of true involvement and participation. In spite of what the Disney developers claim, it may still be that place really does matter, culture has importance, and communities need to evolve idiosyncratically, without corporate control....

* * *

Notes and Comments

1. For an endorsement of common interest communities from the standpoint of security and crime prevention, see Oscar Newman, Community of Interest (1980).

Squatters

The following excerpt looks at the experience of squatting, where the poor take over abandoned or vacant buildings:

Brian Gardiner, Comment, *Squatters' Rights and Adverse Possession: A Search for Equitable Application of Property Laws*,

8 Indiana International and Comparative Law Review 119 (2000)....

According to the United States Census Bureau, the total world population on January 1, 1998, will be 5,886,645,394 people. Using average annual growth rate percentages, the Census Bureau estimates that the world population will be approximately 9,368,223,050 by the year 2050. With this geometric rise in world population, invariably there will be an increase in scarcity and competition for vital resources, including food, fossil fuels, raw materials, shelter, and land. With increasing disparities in wealth and resources between the world's rich and poor, many of the world's citizens will continue to be forced into homelessness. Already, the United Nations (U.N.) estimates that "one hundred million [persons] have no home at all" while "more than one billion persons throughout the world do not reside in adequate housing." An accurate number of currently homeless persons in the United States is difficult to establish; however, numbers range from 350,000 to 3,000,000 persons. In raising the world's consciousness of the condition of the homeless or poorly housed, the U.N. has established the right to housing as an international human right. As of 1994, 129 nations had signed or ratified the International Covenant on Economic, Social, and Cultural Rights, under which states must "retain ultimate responsibility for shortfalls in housing or deteriorating housing conditions." Despite broad declarations by the U.N. and attempted remedies by individual nations, deplorable economic conditions and housing shortages continue to plague the homeless and the under-housed in both developed and least-developed countries (LDCs).

Frequently, the homeless find themselves needing both food and shelter. Thus, squatting on unoccupied lands, buildings, forests, or even garbage dumps becomes an attractive remedy that squatters frequently practice. *Black's Law Dictionary* defines a squatter as:

> [o]ne who settles on another's land, without legal title or authority. A person entering upon lands, not claiming in good faith the right to do so by virtue of any title of his own or by virtue of some agreement with another whom he believes to hold the title. Under former laws, one who settled on public land in order to acquire title to the land.

Traditionally, both governments and citizens have viewed squatters as criminals who take advantage of neglectful municipalities and land owners. The U.N.'s Commission on Human Rights, the Sub-Commission on Prevention of Discrimination and Protection of Minorities issued a report illuminating "Twelve Misconceptions and Misinterpretations of the Right to Housing" and attempting to dispel the notion that "squatters are criminals." The Report found that generally an "impression is created that pavement dwellers are anti-social elements, and that a majority of them are criminally inclined, unemployed and not interested in working." However, many squatters contribute to local economies; for example, the Asia Coalition on Housing Rights found squatters who worked an average of "9.9 hours per day," compared to higher income groups who only worked "7.3 hours per day." Plainly, society should not always view squatters as benevolent revolutionaries fighting for equity and justice; however, there are times when squatters and squatters' movements must be recognized for their noble and courageous efforts in developing efficient uses of property and alleviating one of society's ills.

In several nations, including the United States, Germany, and Great Britain, a squatter may gain legal possession of land through adverse possession. Adverse possession is "[a] method of acquisition of title to real property by possession for a statutory period under certain conditions." Adverse possession generally has five elements that a claimant must establish: the possession must be (1) open, (2) continuous for the statutory period, (3) for the entirety of the area, (4) adverse to the true owner's interests, and (5) notorious. In some jurisdictions, if a squatter or an adverse possessor can establish these elements within the statutory period, then she may take legal and rightful title to the property. The policy supporting adverse possession is that the rule forces landowners to maintain and monitor their land. Moreover, this policy discourages owners from "sleeping" on their property rights for an indefinite period. While squatting problems and adverse possession may often involve private land owners, governments are often large land holders whose interests should be examined. Adverse possession promotes efficient and economic use of land, thereby serving important economic and social ends. However, there are problems associated with adverse possession, including, but not limited to, monitoring problems, safety concerns, and environmental degradation.

Unlike squatters in many Western countries, squatters and the homeless in LDCs often face unclear property rights and inefficient property allocation systems. While both squatters in LDCs and squatters in more-developed nations face severe housing shortages, the squatters in LDCs, with fewer resources and less-developed legal systems at their disposal, face an even steeper climb than their Western counterparts. This note will survey squatting, squatters' rights, and adverse possession from an international perspective....

Great Britain and the Common Law Tradition

Despite squatting's long history, squatting became a significant problem in Great Britain in the late 1960s and 1970s.[70] Because of high property taxes and urban renewal projects, there were many vacant buildings in Great Britain at that time. In 1968, a wave of squatting hit Great Britain as a result of these conditions. The squatters in Britain were not simply homeless persons looking for shelter. Instead, the squatting movement in Great Britain took on a strong political flavor as squatters urged changes in existing property policies. This lower class "revolution" received great public sympathy, which is common in many squatting movements. Nonetheless, in the 1970s, this sympathy waned when some squatters shifted from urban squatting to residential squatting. In this new wave of squatting, a home owner might leave on an extended vacation only to come back and find his home occupied by squatters. Under the Criminal Law Act 1977, "the person who comes back from holiday may use or threaten to use violence to oust

70. ....After World War II, there was a massive squatting movement in London after the government promised "homes fit for heroes," but housing was lacking. Greg Neale, *50 Years on a Squat Fit for Heroes*, Sunday Telegraph (London), Apr. 28, 1996, *available in* 1996 WL 3945816.

squatters found in his home; but the squatters will commit the offence [sic] [of threatening violence without lawful authority] if they retaliate."

As evidence of the strength of the current squatting movement in Great Britain, agencies currently exist that show potential residential squatters a list of vacant houses or buildings. The agencies have photos for the prospective squatters to examine, and they give the squatters instructions to "not cause damage when entering properties and...[to] not change the locks" because if so, "the landlord can do nothing except apply for an eviction order."

In Great Britain, these "commercial squatters" often reflect poorly upon squatters as a whole. In Katherine Bowen's letter to the editor, The Worst Kind of Squatter, she describes the ordeal of having commercial squatters moving into viable "letting retail premises." Commercial squatting has been described as "a highly organised business, with groups now set up to provide information on vacant properties, arrange false leases and keys and even introduce commercial squatters to suppliers of stock, which is often of dubious origin." However, with respect to the commercial and residential squatter, it is sound public policy for governments to differentiate between the squatter who inhabits because of necessity and the squatter who simply is out for profit: public policy should allow residential squatters greater latitude for basic humanitarian reasons.

In 1995, there were an estimated 60,000 squatters in Great Britain. Many of these squatters were among the estimated 700,000 homeless people in Great Britain. Today, these squatters may only be removed after a civil hearing in the British courts at considerable expense to the homeowner. Each year about 10,000 property owners seek expulsion of squatters through the civil courts. Unfortunately, this wave of squatting has also prompted British government officials to enact criminal legislation specifically aimed at the squatters. One anti-squatting provision is found in the Criminal Justice and Public Order Act of 1994. The offense of "aggravated trespass" was specifically aimed at squatters. Under the new laws, a property owner who has a potential squatter problem will "receive a hearing three days after applying to a county court." If the squatters fail to appear, then the squatters "have 24 hours to leave and face up to six months' jail and fines of up to pounds 5,000 if they stay."...

In Great Britain, the statutory period for adverse possession is twelve years under section 15 of the Limitation Act 1980. Interestingly, in *Mount Carmel Inv. Ltd. v. Peter Thurlow Ltd.*, the court held that tacking of claims could exist among squatters: "[i]f a squatter dispossessed another squatter and the first squatter abandoned his claim to possession, the second squatter could obtain title to the land by 12 years' adverse possession by both squatters."[94] Thus, some squatters have had success using the English adverse possession rules. As another example, in 1996, a pair of squatters "earnt Pounds 103,000 from the sale of the Victorian house where they had lived rent-free for 19 years."

It is nearly impossible to evaluate the overall success of the squatters' movement in Great Britain. At minimum, the squatters in Great Britain have raised public awareness of the housing crisis and one potential remedy—squatting. With some unusual but visi-

94. Mount Carmel Inv. Ltd. v. Peter Thurlow Ltd., 3 All E.R. 129 (C.A. 1988). This tacking without privity is not allowed in most jurisdictions in the United States, where clear privity between transferors of adverse possession claims is required. "Tacking occurs whenever the successive occupiers are said to be in 'privity of estate.' Privity of estate is a term that recurs often.... [P]rivity would be satisfied if the relationship between the first and second occupier were: grantor-grantee, landlord-tenant; testator-devisee; decedent-heir; mortgagor-mortgagee."

ble exceptions, liberal squatting in Great Britain seems to have somewhat alleviated the problems associated with homelessness and the housing crisis. Despite the acts criminalizing squatting, Great Britain has a climate generally warmer to the plight of squatters.

Continental Europe and the Civil-Law Tradition: Germany

Like many wealthy western countries, Germany has had its share of squatting problems. Germany also has an established property system that includes rights of adverse possession. The prevalence of squatting in Germany may be attributed to the fact that in 1994 the number of homeless individuals was estimated to be in excess of one million. Some of Germany's homeless problems are due to the reunification of East and West Germany, evidenced by the billions of Deutsche Marks that the West has poured into the East.

The German government has a core of centralized power that is checked by the powers of the individual states. The German Civil Code and basic law provide much of the framework and structure for German governance. The most important laws involving property and adverse possession are found within the German Civil Code, The Third Book: Law of Property. The first section of the Law of Property, entitled "Possession," considers property possession and adverse possession. The second section of the Law of Property contains a provision delineated as Section 900, which states: "[a] person, who is registered in the Land Register as the owner of a piece of land without having obtained ownership, acquires the ownership, if the registration has subsisted for thirty years and he has during this period held the piece of land in his proprietary possession." This thirty-year period in Germany represents a governmental policy that does not promote adverse possession claims. Typically, the shorter the statutory period, the greater the governmental interest in preventing owners from "sleeping" on their property rights, through lack of maintenance, lack of visitation, or a general disregard for their duties. Despite this lengthy statutory requirement for adverse possession (especially when compared to other countries), in one particular squatting situation German authorities found it necessary to compromise and depart from the written civil-law.

In Hamburg, Germany, a group of squatters who were occupying a block of buildings won a fourteen-year battle against the government. This prolonged battle began in October 1981 "when a group of about 100 punks and social revolutionaries occupied a block of empty houses overlooking the harbour and owned by the city." This site was very important to Hamburg city officials because it "is near some of Germany's most exclusive hotels and brothels... [and] city officials feared the squatters would harm tourism." As in Great Britain, the squatters received public support, as illustrated by a demonstration in 1986 when "10,000 supporters of the squatters marched through central Hamburg." However, a year later the German police remained unsuccessful in their attempts to evict the squatters from the group of buildings. Finally, in 1996, the city officials radically changed their policy, and the city government accepted the squatters and decided to take "the decisive step toward permanently ending this difficult conflict."

This reconciliation is quite different from the approach taken by many governments, including jurisdictions within the United States, as local authorities appear quite willing to oppose residential squatters' claims in American cities. In this agreement between the German city and the squatters, the squatters will purchase the buildings for "less than a third of [their] market value." The squatters will shoulder the costs of repairing and renovating the buildings, and they will pay the city one-half of overdue rent and utility bills. This type of compromise should serve as a model to other municipalities around the world as a way of ending potentially violent and expensive conflicts. This type of

12. Free City of Christiana. Mural in the Copenhagen, Denmark squatter community.

compromise produces a win-win result. Hamburg may not have received full market value for its property, but the city was able to avoid costly litigation and/or eviction costs and the associated expenses of housing the evicted squatters. Further, by transferring the property rights to the squatters, the government created a cost-effective remedy to a housing shortage.

Continental Europe and the Civil-Law Tradition: Denmark

Danish legal philosophy has been described as a system "of positivism as well as of realism in the common and commonplace sense." Under this system of "commonplace sense," Denmark has had a long history of promoting efficient use of property. Since 1683, under King Christian V's Danish Code, "*twenty years of possession* is required for prescription." Under this code, "[i]t is up to the user—regardless whether his use is lawful or contrary to other rights—to prove that his prescriptive possession of the property took place during the necessary period of time." If the use of property is for a general purpose "ownership [of the property] is regularly obtained." However, if the use is "directed for a specific purpose" then "an easement is obtained." Although Denmark does not have a long history of squatting problems, this theory of "commonplace sense" and "positivism" has been reflected in the creation of a major squatters' settlement in Copenhagen.

The Free City of Christiana celebrated its twenty-fifth year in 1996. In October 1971, as a response to housing shortages, an abandoned army barracks in the Danish capital of Copenhagen was occupied by 800 squatters. Squatters call Christiana the "free city" because there they are "free of rents, free of taxes, and free of laws imposed by the society." Part of the freedom also included the open sale of drugs and collectivized property. Because of a governmental policy of "tolerance of diverse philosophies and lifestyles," the squatters were able to remain and the "Ministry of Defense even left on the water and electricity."

Although the Christiania experience may seem extreme, it suggests an interesting housing solution for the United States, Europe, and the Soviet states. Due to the end of the Cold War, both East and West have many vacant military complexes. Some of these facilities could be turned over to squatters, homeless persons, and homesteaders for rapid change into low income housing. Transfers of military property could quickly change a remnant of the past into a salient solution to the homeless problem.

Continental Europe and the Civil-Law Tradition: Netherlands

The Netherlands has a long history of squatting and a strong tradition of adverse possession. Supporters of the squatting movement "numbered tens of thousands at its heights in the Sixties." The Dutch squatters' movement "lost much of its strength during the 1980s when many of its members were offered alternative housing over the years." Despite its weakened state, squatting is still a powerful force in the Netherlands. In fact, squatting has been called "lasting evidence of the continuing anarchic youth movement [in the Netherlands]."

The Dutch legal system is considered to "belong to the Romano-Germanic family." The rules for acquisitive prescription of property, i.e., adverse possession, are set out in article 3:99 of the Dutch Civil Code:

> 1. possession; whether there is possession is decided along the lines of generally prevailing views (art. 3:108); 2. possession must have been acquired in good faith. Once a possessor is in good faith, subsequent knowledge will not affect his good faith (3:118 par 2). 3. possession must have been uninterrupted. Loss of possession therefore means that a current prescription-period is terminated.... (art. 3:103). 4. lapse of time: a. a period of three years for non-registered movables...; b. a period of ten years for all other goods.... [immovable goods, real property](art. 3:119).

Despite the seemingly strict rules on prescription, Dutch squatters, particularly in Amsterdam, have had some successes. According to Dutch historian Han Van Der Horst: "[i]n spite of clear legislation to the contrary, tolerance had become second nature for the political leaders in the Netherlands." Edward Soja, professor of urban and regional planning at the University of California, described the squatter movement in Amsterdam as:

> more than just an occupation of abandoned offices, factories, warehouses and some residences. It was a fight for the rights of the city itself, especially for the young and for the poor. Nowhere has this struggle been more successful than in Amsterdam. Nowhere has it been less successful than in Los Angeles.

Squatters in the Netherlands have been successful in part due to compromises by the Dutch government. After the Dutch coronation in 1980, squatters and police often battled. Like the experiences in Great Britain and Germany, these battles "brought a great wave of public sympathy, not for the state's over-reaction but for the young and lawless." After the great squatter battles of 1980, the Dutch government passed "new legislation to tidy up the rules on empty property" that "requir[ed] local authorities to keep a list of empty houses and other buildings which could be converted into homes." The new criminal code also protected property from occupation and "squatters [could] be fined up to $215."

Despite the tightening of laws in the Netherlands, squatters have still enjoyed success. Dutch culture and society emphasize tolerance and compromise, two qualities needed to address homelessness effectively. Nonetheless, as in Germany and other countries, there will always be some problems in the Netherlands related to squatting due to the tension between property rights and adverse possession. But governmental cooperation and public support of squatters in the Netherlands have seemingly reduced the specter of violence in the battle for shelter and land.

United States

English law influences much of the law of adverse possession in the United States. Despite this background, United States adverse possession law has taken on its own unique flavor. This is evidenced by the various statutes of limitations for adverse possession claims that range from five years in California, Idaho, and Montana, to forty years in Iowa.

New York

In the United States, no city has experienced more urban squatting activity than New York City. Within the United States, New York is a relatively old city with diverse regions and many abandoned buildings and factories. New York State's adverse possession law provides that those who openly and hostilely possess land for ten years can request title to that land....

In New York City, the "13th Street squatters" received significant attention because of protests, riots, and subsequent police action. On 13th Street, the squatters claimed title by asserting themselves as the "homesteaders" of abandoned buildings owned by New York City. Many squatters invested money and "sweat equity" in the properties, "controlled them, secured them, and behaved in all ways as owners of the property." In 1995, the radio program "All Things Considered" interviewed one of the 13th Street squatters who estimated that he spent about $6,000 renovating his apartment. The city evicted the squatters to make way for a four million dollar low-income housing project. The squatters protected their squat by creating a "flimsy tangle of bicycle frames and barbed wire welded to the metal stairways." New York City Mayor Rudolf Giuliani justified the eviction based on safety concerns. The squatters claimed adverse possession in excess of the statutory ten-year period because the 13th Street buildings had been vacant since 1984. The failure of the squatters to establish adverse possession claims in court partially rested on their inability to establish tacking for their claims. It was nearly impossible for the squatters to prove that they had continually lived in the building for the required ten-year period. Thus, the squatters lacked the type of documentation required to win their adverse possession suit....

The February 8, 1996 decision in *Walls v. Giuliani*[95] was considered by many to be a victory for the squatters in New York City because the court considered the actual merits of the squatters' case. The case represented a critical decision for squatters because "[t]he ruling left the door open for similar legal challenges to be brought by squatters all over the city." In that case, the court held that the squatters had stated a valid civil rights claim under 42 U.S.C. § 1983 and denied the City's motion to dismiss. Mayor Rudolf Giuliani called the district court's ruling "ideology run amok." The 13th Street squatters' short-lived success came to an end on August 8, 1996, when the New York Supreme Court, Appellate Division, reversed the district court's decision in Walls v. Giuliani.[141] Subsequently, to evict the squatters, the New York Police employed a 50,000 pound

95. 916 F. Supp. 214 (E.D.N.Y. 1996).

141. East 13th St. Homesteaders' Coalition v. New York City Dep't of Hous. Preservation and Dev., 230 A.D.2d 622 (N.Y. App. Div. 1996).

tank-like armored personnel carrier along with fifty policemen. Strangely, despite the city's spirited battles with the residential squatters, New York City allowed and even encouraged small businesses to squat in an abandoned court house. In light of Giuliani's claim of "ideology run amok," this action of allowing commercial squatting can be seen as nothing short of an unconscionable double standard....

California

California is a large and wealthy state with a large and expanding population because of internal growth, domestic migration, and both legal and illegal immigration. The most prevalent squatting problems in California are typically not found within urban environments. California law requires the typical elements for adverse possession: (1) possession must be held either under a claim of right or color of title; (2) possession must be actual, open, and notorious occupation of the property in such a manner as to constitute reasonable notice of that occupation to the record owner; (3) the occupation must be both exclusive and hostile to the title of the true owner; (4) possession must be continuous and uninterrupted for at least five years; and (5) the occupier must pay all taxes assessed against the property during such five-year period. Despite the clear requirements of California's adverse possession law, most of the squatting problems in California stem from abuses of an 1856 property law.

Middle-class neighborhoods in California have been invaded by squatters guided by squatters' agencies. These squatters' agencies have legal standing based upon the "1856 [law designed] to break up Spanish claims to land after California changed hands." This law allows squatters to enter a dwelling "as long as a window or door is open or has been left unlocked[;] they can't break in." Often squatting "agents" will look for foreclosed property and then inform their customers of the ripe pickings. The squatters agree to pay monthly rent to the agents. These housing agents give their customers "four to six months in a house... [and] a three-page disclosure on what [they] do." In many ways, this type of squatting is similar to the squatting promoted by residential squatting agents in the United Kingdom.

One California company, Windsor Pacific, "scours public records for properties in foreclosure or finds homes that are vacant, looks for ways to enter the home, and makes its [adverse] claim. If no one objects to the claim, it rents the home to its customers and may even make an offer to purchase." As of April 1996, this company had thirty-six houses under an alleged claim of adverse possession. Jay E. Orr, the Riverside County Supervising Deputy District Attorney, stated: "[t]hese companies have been allowed to flourish because banks are so far behind on foreclosures." The proprietors of Windsor Pacific ask their "house sitters" to sign a disclosure form that indicates "Windsor Pacific has attempted to file a notice of adverse possession, cleaned the house and re-keyed all locks, and notified the lender it has placed a tenant on the premises." This disclosure states that the tenants are to move out within thirty-days notice, if and when the bank takes title. Many of these squatters are families that became interested in a property because of an advertisement for low rental rates.

Typically, these companies will ask for three months rent up front; therefore, they make money from the house sitters/squatters regardless of the results of their adverse possession claims. These squatters' agencies maintain that they are making legitimate adverse possession claims, but such claims are dubious at best. These companies do not pay property taxes, which would be required for a proper adverse possession claim under California law. Despite the inadequacy of such adverse possession claims, it is still true that this suburban squatting is maximizing the use of land that would otherwise remain vacant for months or years at a time. One squatters' agent, who was facing thirty-six felony counts involving houses, reasoned that he was performing a public service because "[squatting] tells the banks they have to pay attention to their properties and do something with abandoned houses.... It gets banks off the dime." Some law enforcement officials have taken unusual steps in dealing with squatters' agencies like Windsor Pacific. Sheriffs' deputies are now telling renters/house sitters/squatters not to pay rent. Sheriffs' deputies believe that someone has broken into "at least 13 foreclosed homes, cleaned them up, changed the locks and rented them under the name of Windsor Pacific." If this alleged breaking and entering is true, these actions would violate California law even under the 1856 adverse possession statute.... One California couple bid on a $385,000 home only to find that a squatter had moved in the day before. In that case, the purchasers obtained a restraining order that prevented the squatters from remaining in the house, but such a civil action still may take more than one month to settle....

Least Developed Countries: Property Laws and Squatting

Brazil....

In Brazil, conflicts related to squatting occur most often "[w]here land title is not clear and/or government programs provide incentives for invasion." A study commissioned by the National Science Foundation and World Bank study found that violent clashes are often caused by sluggish governmental policies and rising land values. The U.S. State Department, noting the power of the landowners and the ineffectiveness of the government, reported: "[i]n rural areas... landowners [have] often intimidated judges, lawyers, and police with violence and threats of violence." The report points out that violence has intensified "because of the slow progress of the Federal Government toward reaching its goal of granting land tenure certifications to hundreds of thousands of landless families."... Brazilian governmental policies have increased violence by placing incentives and subsidies for land development in certain areas.... Moreover, police and governmental officials have been implicated in much of the violence against the squatters. On August 9, 1995, nine squatters were killed when police opened fire on a squatters' camp. Seven of the nine squatters killed "were shot point-blank in the face, neck, chest, and back." According to the Pastoral Land Commission, the battles over land have "left 74 people dead."...

Malaysia....

In Kuala Lumpur, it is estimated that 226,000 squatters reside in 255 squatter settlements.... The Malaysian government has accepted the reality that squatters and squatters' movements are an integral part of their country. Instead of fighting the squatters, Malaysian officials are taking real and logical steps to assist the squatters: this type of partnership is a model that other LDCs should emulate and follow.

Philippines....

Manila, the capital of the Philippines, contains a very large concentration of squatters. The National Housing Authority estimates that "[a]bout 3.5 million people live in squatter colonies in and around Manila, representing 39 percent of the capital's population." Squatters armed with "rocks, darts, broken bottles and gasoline bombs" have fought police in an attempt to "prevent government wrecking crews from demolishing more than 500 shanties and semi-concrete houses they had built on private property. Many of them have been living in the area for more than a decade." One particular area of Manila has been a hot spot for squatter activity. "Smokey Mountain" is a huge dump sight that houses thousands of squatters and has been described as "a small mound [that] soon spread out of control, sprawling over a nine-acre area and containing 2.2 billion tonnes [sic] of rotting rubbish."... However, the government has treated these squatters poorly as evidenced by its preparation for last year's APEC [Asian Pacific Economic Cooperation] forum: "[h]undreds of squatter shacks [were] bulldozed along the capital's major roads leading from the international airport to the big hotels and convention sites." "Imelda Marcos, widow of former president Ferdinand Marcos, used to call [the bulldozing] beautification...." This "beautification" of Manila left "at least 10,000 of the city's estimated 3 million people homeless.... About 1,000 families were removed from a stretch of land reclaimed from Manila Bay, and 200 more families were left homeless when the bulldozers plowed though the Paco slum." This strategy of "[r]elocating squatters to distant relocation camps [didn't] work; the people return[ed] since there [was] no work there."

* * *

Notes and Comments

1. In Istanbul, most new housing needed for the thousands that daily stream in from the rural districts lacking economic opportuinity is provided through squatting. The squatting in Istanbul, however is a far cry from that described in the literature in developed and developing nations. The squatters in Istanbul have carefully planned and saved and utilize an army of experienced developers and contractors. Under Turkish law, anyone who can put up a one-story structure and place it under roof before sunrise is entitled to title to the land, whether it is owned privately or by the government. Thus, construction goes on throughout the night and owners of vacant developable land often post armed guards each evening. Later, the squatting developer can more leisurely complete the typically multi-floor apartment house. Families often save for years for the construction funds, which is no small undertaking with Turkey's triple digit inflation rate, requiring quarterly rent and salary renegotiation for those with bargaining power.

2. To revitalize the most deteriorating and abandoned neighborhoods in the United States, the federal government and some local governments established programs designed to encourage settlement and rehabilitation. The urban homesteading programs, designed after schemes from the time of the settlement of the country, seek to offer land for settlement. Under the programs houses that had been foreclosed by the United States Department of Housing and Urban Development (HUD) or by local taxing authorities, would basically be given to any who agreed to repair and reside in them for a minimum period. 12 U.S.C. § 1706(e), *repealed in* 1990. Pub. L. No. 101-625, tit. II, § 289(b)(1), 104 Stat. 4128; David P. Varady, Neighborhood Upgrading: A Realistic Assessment (1986). Unfortunately, many of the neighborhoods were so distressed that the incentive was insufficient to attract new urban vitality. William G. Grigsby & Louis Rosenberg, Urban Housing Policy 235-36 (1975) (brightly wrapped package with nothing inside); Joshua A. Newberg, *Anatomy of a Housing Program: Urban Homesteading in Theory and Practice*, 8 J. L. & Pol. 731, 751-52 (1992). Where programs were more successful the homes were often in highly desirable districts undergoing gentrification. The homes were more often occupied by young urban professionals than by groups who typically compete for affordable housing.

3. *Tacheles*. When the Berlin Wall came down, the German rock band *Tacheles*, along with hundreds of roadies, groupies, and artists took over a bombed and partially demolished structure in a not particularly popular district in East Berlin. The neighborhood has miraculously become the center of the trendy Mitte District, the center of Berlin's roaring nightlife. The structure was a turn of the century retail shopping mall, later converted to a cinema. Although the rockers have gone on, the squatters and artists have remained in a building and large parcel of land now referred to as *Tacheles*. With the approval of the City of Berlin, the squatters are planning to redevelop the parcel. Already completed are popular theaters, cafés, and working artist studios. The Duany, Plater-Zyberk, Miami-based New Urbanism architects have been retained, following an Internet design competition, to plan an urban apartment block to include thirty buildings. The project is to be a joint venture between *Tacheles* and an "involuntary" private investor. The power of the squatters is reflected in their success in opposing a proposed east-west road and the delay of a major real estate development, while insisting on preservation of the surviving portion of the structure, for more than a decade—rent free. George Lefcoe, U.S.C. Traveling Land Use Seminar—Berlin 1997 at 2–4 (based on conversations with *Tacheles* planner Toni Pfeiffer).

4. Squatters and performance artists have been permitted to become redevelopers of "Kinetic North" in an abandoned shipbuilding yard in Amsterdam. The development will focus on performance, theater, the arts, and recreation, as well as housing. The project came about without any squatting as the city was anxious to keep the artists in Amsterdam to maintain that city's avante-garde image. Radio Netherlands, Aug. 2001, visited at http://www.rnw.nl/holland/html/kinetic010801.html

Chapter 12

Housing and Land Use Discrimination

> ....[T]he problem with other transit systems is that no matter how much we subsidize them, they remain *mass* transit. The cheapest and most flexible form is buses in special high-occupancy-vehicle lanes. But there is something about buses we hate. "show me a man over thirty who regularly takes the bus, and I will show you a life failure," said one senior mass transit official who obviously wished to remain anonymous. Buses feature the fewest cubic feet of elbow room per passenger of any transportation mode in this century, with the possible exception of the New York-to-Washington air shuttle. Because they have to make so many stops, and frequently have roundabout routes, they are often slower even than bumper-to-bumper traffic. Their ambiance is that of a public washroom. Buses are those contrivances onto which affluent people would like to force everybody else—in order to make it easier for them to drive.
>
> Joel Garreau, Edge City: Life on the New Frontier 130 (1988)

America has had a long and frustrating experience with the search for equal opportunity. James A. Kushner, *Apartheid in America: An Historical and Legal Analysis of Contemporary Racial Residential Segregation in the United States*, 22 How. L.J. 547 (1979), republished as James A. Kushner, Apartheid in America (1980) [hereinafter cited as Apartheid]. Because of the central role played by that nation's judicial system and the centrality of race and gender to the intellectual focus of its university legal academy, the experience rather than requiring institutional memory, is one that has produced a dramatic written record. *E.g.*, Derrick Bell, Racism, and American Law (3d ed. 1992); Jack Greenberg, Race Relations and American Law (1959); Gunner Myrdal, An American Dilemma (1944); Robert C. Weaver, The Negro Ghetto (1948); C. Van Woodward, The Strange Career of Jim Crow (1957). Born as a slave nation, The United States succeeded in dismantling that system, but replacing it with a nearly universal pattern of separate housing and neighborhoods according to skin color with official and unofficial policies of widespread discrimination and segregation in schools, transportation, voting, employment, public accommodations, and the allocation of municipal services on the basis of race. Apartheid, *supra*. Beginning in 1954 with the Supreme Court's condemnation of public school racial segregation, *Brown v. Board of Educ.*, 347 U.S. 483 (1954). America fought an internal civil rights war on inequality. While the courts on occasion established rights or principles that appeared to advance the cause of equality, in the 1960's it was Congress, state, and local legislatures that responded to rational public criticism and enacted broad legislation to desegregate and eradicate racial discrimination in public accommodations, voting, employment, housing, and in the administration of government programs. James A. Kushner, Government Discrimination ch. 7 (1988 & Supp. 2001).

Because of the centrality of discrimination in housing, land use, and development policy to a system of segregation, there exists a rich history of the nature of how government and private practices can generate a divided society. Douglas S. Massey & Nancy A. Denton, American Apartheid: Segregation and the Making of the Underclass (1993). *See also* Apartheid, *supra.* Until 1968, the official government policy at the federal and most state and local levels was one of racial segregation. 42 U.S.C. §§3601-20, 3631 (Title VIII, the Fair Housing Act of 1968). As the urban white populations migrated to the suburbs, blacks were excluded by official policy as housing finance was marked by federal regulation that conditioned the availability of government mortgage insurance and other government assistance on maintaining racially segregated communities through the use of restrictive covenants and equitable servitudes, Apartheid, *supra.* at 16–30, 22 How. L.J. at 562–576, typically binding deed restrictions or subdivision regulations that bound the developers and purchasers of new homes. The federal government regulations undoubtedly also contributed in influencing the nation's customs and beliefs towards race. Separation was favored by many whites and believed essential to the successful operation of the housing market. The inclusion of racial covenants remained industry and the Federal Housing Administration policy after the United States Supreme Court ruled that courts could not enforce private racially restrictive covenants. *Shelley v. Kraemer*, 334 U.S. 1 (1948). Apartheid, *supra.* at 16–19, 22 How. L.J. at 562–566.

Together with the near universal exclusionary zoning of the developing suburbs, Advisory Commission on Regulatory Barriers to Affordable Housing, "Not in My Backyard:" Removing Barriers to Affordable Housing (1991); Lawrence G. Sager, *Tight Little Islands: Exclusionary Zoning, Equal Protection and the Indigent*, 21 Stan. L. Rev. 767 (1969), where housing was produced for the more affluent, pricing out the poor and many workers, racial segregation and discriminatory housing marketing practices generated cities that separated the neighborhoods for people of color from the nearly all-white suburbs. Massey & Denton, *supra.* Policies that subsidized and facilitated suburban growth, including federal highway, utilities, and other grants, as well as federal housing assistance and tax policies attracted whites from the cities. At the same time, housing programs for the poor were targeted at the impacted innercity making neighborhoods less desirable and stable. Apartheid, *supra.* at 30–37, 22 How. L.J. at 576–83. *See also* William M. Rohe & Lance Freeman, *Assisted Housing and Residential Segregation: The Role of Race and Ethnicity in the Siting of Assisted Housing Developments*, 67 J. Am. Plan. Ass'n 279 (2001) (current programs segregative, targeting assisted housing to low-income census tracts). Employment opportunities also relocated from the declining city centers to the suburban fringe industrial and commercial parks. In addition to pervasive private market housing discrimination carried out by sellers, brokers, and housing managers, suburban regulators, when encountering the isolated proposed integrated or subsidized housing project frequently manipulated zoning and development criteria to exclude the development. James A. Kushner, Fair Housing §7.13 (2d ed. 1995 & Supp. 2000). Some communities have employed zoning techniques to expel minority residents that previously resided in the community. *Amen v. City of Dearborn*, 718 F.2d 789 (6th Cir. 1993); *Garrett v. City of Hamtramck*, 335 F. Supp. 16 (E.D. Mich. 1971), *plan ordered*, 357 F. Supp. 925 (E.D. Mich. 1973), *modified*, 503 F.2d 1236 (6th Cir. 1974); Yale Rabin, *Expulsive Zoning: The Inequitable Legacy of Euclid*, in Zoning and the American Dream 122 (Charles M. Haar & Jerold S. Kayden eds. 1989).

The American law of discrimination is an amalgam of constitutional and legislative law. The Supreme Court has interpreted the equal protection clause of the Fourteenth Amendment to prohibit intentional segregation and official discrimination. *Village of Arlington Heights v. Metropolitan Hous. Dev. Corp.*, 429 U.S. 252 (1977). The Court has extended the protections designed to protect freed slaves to also prevent what it perceives to be irrational discrimination on other bases, such as national origin, gender, or even sexual orientation. See e.g., *United States v. Virginia*, 518 U.S. 515 (1996) (greater scrutiny for gender classifications requiring an exceedingly persuasive justification); *Romer v. Evans*, 517 U.S. 620 (1996) (invalidating statewide initiative preempting efforts to legislate against sexual orientation bias); *City of Cleburne v. Cleburne Living Center*, 473 U. S. 432 (1985) (invalidating permit for homes for the disabled where use indistinguishable from permitted uses and law targeted at mentally disabled, in a decision set out below). The United States Supreme Court, despite favorable rulings for a selection of challengers, has evolved to its current conservative ideology, cutting protections against official discrimination more frequently than it advances doctrine. David G. Savage, *United They Sit: Last Term Suggests 5–4 Splits Likely in Areas of Federalism, Civil Rights, Religion*, 87 ABA J. 34 (Sept. 2001). The Supreme Court, in a requirement never established as a condition under any other constitutional provision, only imposes discrimination liability where the challenger can prove that the bias was intentional or purposeful. *Village of Arlington Heights, supra*; *Washington v. Davis*, 426 U.S. 229 (1976). This means that the bulk of discrimination or segregation claims are fruitless as rarely does the law classify on the basis of race. Thus, for example, claims of zoning manipulation may be difficult to prove because actions are cloaked in environmental or planning criteria and the courts are unwilling to base liability on the segregative impact of government programs. The only exceptions are outrageous cases where nothing but racism can explain irrational actions unsupported by believable planning considerations. *E.g., Kennedy Park Homes Ass'n v. City of Lackawanna*, 436 F.2d 108 (2d Cir. 1970).

Legislative enactments, on the other hand, reach many actions that carry a discriminatory or segregative impact, and extend to actions within the private sector. *Huntington Branch NAACP v. Town of Huntington*, 844 F.2d 926 (2d Cir.), *aff'd per curium*, 488 U.S. 15 (1988). There also do not exist more than a few handfulls of experienced attorneys willing to undertake protracted litigation over suburban development. James A. Kushner, *The Fair Housing Amendments Act of 1988: The Second Generation of Fair Housing*, 42 Vand. L. Rev. 1049 (1989). With the loss of urban housing production subsidies, there are simply very few developers interested in developing housing for the poor outside of traditional urban centers where land is usually the cheapest and opposition nonexistent, and thus few ideal litigants to challenge suburban development practice. Benefitting by the long struggle over racial discrimination, most civil rights legislative enactments at the federal level have extended protections to victims on the basis of gender, national origin, religion, disability, and in some instances to families with children and on the basis of marital status. James A. Kushner, Government Discrimination Ch. 7 (1988 & Supp. 2001).

Despite efforts at suing the federal government for segregating public and subsidized housing having generated some programs to upgrade innercity projects, and remedial obligations to locate housing or target housing allowances to suburban locations, the segregated pattern remains intact. Massey & Denton, *supra*. At the same time, the bulk of the suburbs have been built and the exclusionary zoning and other development criteria are in place so that even without future discriminatory or segregative actions the cities and suburbs will remain segregated on the basis of race and wealth.

America's efforts to dismantle segregation have proven somewhat pyrrhic. The school desegregation effort, at first successful in some southern communities, proved not to be the integrative force promised, but instead a powerful contributor to America's segregation. Apartheid, *supra.* at 73–84, 22 How. L.J. at 619–630. As urban schools became mired in litigation, the white residents voted with their feet and moved to the suburban fringe leaving central school districts with a nonintegratable largely minority school population. The United States Supreme Court established virtually insurmountable barriers to litigation seeking to integrate urban and suburban schools. *Milliken v. Bradley*, 418 U.S. 717 (1974). Other efforts to reform the system, such as affirmative action programs to accord greater access opportunities to minorities have been systematically eliminated by a Supreme Court. *Adarand Constructors, Inc. v. Pena*, 515 U.S. 200 (1995); *City of Richmond v. J.A. Croson Co.*, 488 U.S. 469 (1989). Even affirmative action policies designed to prevent the systematic vote dilution of minority groups by provided greater rights of representation in legislative matters has been invalidated by the Court. *Shaw v. Reno*, 509 U.S. 630 (1993). *See also Abrams v. Johnson*, 521 U.S. 74 (1997) (no dilution); *Shaw v. Hunt*, 517 U.S. 899 (1996) (invalidating affirmative effort to assure minority voting power); *Miller v. Johnson*, 515 U.S. 900 (1995) (invalidating scheme). America's segregation has proved largely intractable and is a contributor to the inability to launch initiatives to revitalize its cities. As the wealth and employers move to the suburbs, cities, while facing greater service needs as its population becomes poorer, find their resource and tax base diminishing. Jerry Frug, *The Geography of Community*, 48 Stan. L. Rev. 1047 (1996).

Part of the problem of dismantling America's segregation is that the Court is caught in a parodox. The Court condemns racism and racial discrimination but also embraces what it perceives to be the American exclusionary suburb. *See Village of Belle Terre v. Boraas*, 416 U.S. 1 (1974) (sustaining anti-commune zoning defining family as no more than two unrelated persons).

Has the civil rights revolution in America been a success? On several levels equality has been well-served. First, the enacted laws have been well-publicized and are a part of the American culture. Race discrimination unfortunately continues to be prevalent in the rental housing market and in lending and is also a part of the employment environment albeit on a dramatically reduced basis. The great successes of the era are in eradicating most public accommodations bias and in launching a burgeoning black middle class. Today those with the financial resources and occasionally the willingness to litigate, can live in any chosen neighborhood, and minority students are pursuing higher education in significant numbers. Apart from the continuing legacy of slavery and segregation in the form of market place acts of discrimination, the causes of continuing segregation are both economic and cultural. A significant percentage of minority group members due to poverty, lack adequate access to quality education and employment. In addition, the separation between races has generated fear and distrust in both majority and minority populations. There are many minority group members that choose to reside in a community where their race is culturally dominant. This may be because community resources and social support is available but is also because of perception that the majority community is hostile. There are simply too many stories of drivers, walkers, students or shoppers being subjected to racial profiling and discriminatory treatment. Nevertheless, those who have lived through life in America prior to the implementation of the 1964 Civil Rights Act have witnessed an extraordinary transformation of American life and a dramatic improvement in the status of people of color. That dramatic transformation, however, masks the continuing plight of those who have not benefitted from economic prosperity, those residing in concentrations of poverty removed from access to opportunity; opportunity that is taken for granted as a privilege by most Americans.

The following excerpt describes the American urban race conundrum from the standpoint of regional growth management policy formation:

James A. Kushner, *Growth Management and the City*,

12 Yale Law & Policy Review 68 (1994)

Along with community design, community planning efforts also ignore the need to dismantle entrenched patterns of racial and economic class segregation, particularly in housing. Growth management systems fail to consider race yet contribute to the institutionalization of segregation. Suburban growth management may benefit regulating communities—since effective demand for costly new infrastructure partially abates while prestige and property values increase—but, as "white flight" from the city continues, large minority populations are trapped in a central city without the resources to provide quality schools or full employment.

Race segregation is the only universally consistent principle of American land planning. America's cities have been systematically regulated to establish America's equivalent of apartheid. The federal public housing program was administered on a strictly segregated basis from its inception and despite anti-discrimination legislation and court decisions, the United States Department of Housing and Urban Development continues to administer its programs on a segregated basis. Desegregation remains politically unpopular. HUD and the HUD-funded landlords, developers, and local housing authorities, perpetuate segregation through tenant assignment practices and the universal practice of project site selection for affordable housing. These policies result in the location of all-minority projects within existing minority neighborhoods and in initial single-race occupancy; at best the project may integrate Blacks and Latinos. The most dramatic segregation force was the Federal Housing Administration's single family policy under which the nation's suburbs were developed following World War II. FHA policy required single-race subdivisions, mandating racially restrictive covenants as a condition for the availability of mortgage insurance and lower-than-conventional down payments.

The stark pattern of racial separation also was supported by segregated war housing, urban renewal, and highway development projects that generated white displacement to the suburbs and the relocation of blacks into minority resettlement patterns, together with school assignments on the basis of segregated neighborhood school attendance zones. The ultimate segregative irony is that the landmark decision of *Brown v. Board of Education*, which ordered the desegregation of public school districts, instead effected hyper-segregation by federal courts ignorant of the inevitable white and affluent flight from urban districts. Hypersegregation refers to the pervasive urban geographical pattern of nearly complete racial isolation. The result has been devastating: Because property taxes generated from homes and businesses are the primary source of public school funding, minority urban school districts are unable to finance good schools and unable to cope with the special educational needs and problems of today's urban students. who lack the traditional preparation and familial support provided in suburban districts.

The pattern of apartheid created a segregated central city with limited hope and high unemployment for its inhabitants, which generated potential for civil unrest, increased the lack of public safety, discouraged employment-generating investment, and motivated still more white and middle-class flight. The increasing concentration of an underemployed under-class, and its concomitant expanding prison population, present the greatest security concern of the 1990s.

Controversy over strategies for integration persists. Dismantling the pattern of hyper-segregation is pivotal to restoring a willingness to fund programs for the city. Integration strategies depend upon abating the special economic problems faced by inner-city minorities. Yet, opposition to integration initiatives appears in Black as well as white communities.

Politically feasible urban revival is not going to dismantle the institution of segregation. As current urban policy has a decidedly segregative impact, the issue is whether the city is to become more segregated or a bit less segregated....

* * *

Notes and Comments

1. Although the problem of direct outright discrimination can be significantly reduced or eliminated by administrative testing and judicial or administrative enforcement, James A. Kushner, *The Fair Housing Amendments Act of 1988: The Second Generation of Fair Housing*, 42 Vand. L. Rev. 1049 (1989), the problem of segregation or physical separation of the races poses different and difficult problems. One of the reasons that the problems appears intractable is that, for example, blacks and whites have very different ideas about the nature of integration. While an increasing number of whites express a preference for integrated living, they often have in mind a small percentage of minority group members in the community so that the population may be characterized as diverse. Blacks, for example, however, may define an integrated neighborhood as one which is half white and half minority. This different perception may cause whites to move to distant edge cities and by-pass or leave communities where minority presence becomes significant. This process leads to racial change and often the failure of "integrated" neighborhoods to offer the same generous increases in property values as experienced in the distant suburbs. The search for stability and increasing home equity frequently results in whites leaving neighborhoods and districts where minority occupancy is increasing, fearing that the demographic changes may be a harbinger of the eventual resegregation of the neighborhood into a minority-majority district. Perhaps the most hopeful signs of eventual integration are statistics that demonstrate that the greatest reductions in racial residential segregation have occurred in communities experiencing significant growth and development as minority groups, just as whites, are taking advantage of newer attractive towns and housing developments and the reality that America is becoming a multi-racial, multi-ethnic society. Richard H. Sander, *Housing Segregation and Housing Integration: The Diverging Paths of Urban America*, 52 U. Miami L. Rev. 977 (1998). As America evolves even the definitions of what race or nationality a person might be becomes hopelessly confusing and irrelevant.

2. Municipal services such as transit can be provided on a discriminatory basis, providing superior highly subsidized services to white affluent suburbs. Kevin L. Siegel, *Discrimination in the Funding of Mass Transit Systems: Formulating a Title VI Challenge to the Standardization of the Alameda Contra Costa Transit District as Compared to the Bay Area Rapid Transit District*, 4 Hastings W.-Nw. J. Envt'l L. & Pol'y 107 (1997) (highlighting Los Angeles and San Francisco Bay Area). See the discussion of environmental justice in Chapter 13.

The following excerpt looks at Israel and the presence of discrimination:

Geoffrey Graber, Note, *Choosing the Chosen: The Validity of Racial Restrictions on the Alienation of Property in Israel and the United States*,

73 Southern California Law Review 437 (2000)

Israel is a nation that resists definition. Not by accident, it is both a Jewish state, existing of, by and for the Jewish people, and a liberal-democracy, guaranteeing to all citizens freedom and equality under the law, regardless of race or religion. These two conceptions of the state are not opposites, nor are they synonyms. Instead, they relate to one another as a tension upon which the state of Israel is founded.

It is easier to understand this dual nature of Israel as a Jewish and liberal-democratic state by putting the issue into context. That context is the "Jewish Question." While, the Jewish Question presents itself as a myriad of paradoxes and dilemmas; the present study focuses only on the dimension of Israel as a secular or religious state. That is, does the diaspora, i.e., an existence of profound homelessness, compel the Jews to seek civic, political emancipation, or rather, can the condition of homelessness never truly be solved until the Jews return (t'shuvah) home, i.e., to the Jewish land?

Neither of these "solutions" adequately addresses the condition of homelessness. On the one hand, for very practical reasons, many Jews sought to resolve the Question through a secular path. This approach grew from the failure of assimilation in nineteenth century Europe and culminates in political Zionism: The problem of the Jews can be readily solved through the establishment of their own state. In other words, the solution resides in seizing the reins of political power. But, as Leo Strauss pointed out, this solution was not a solution at all: "The basic idea underlying purely political Zionism was not Zionism at all. It could have been satisfied by a Jewish state anywhere on earth." Pure political Zionism is another expression of assimilation, only at the macro level.

On the other hand, others believed that the Jewish Question could only be solved by returning to Israel, to the Jewish homeland. If so, the Jewish state would have to adopt Hebrew, the language of Judaism. Yet, this view also presented difficulties. To begin with, there was as kind of slippery-slope dilemma: Once a Jewish state becomes the goal, exactly how Jewish does it need to be? Founding the nation in the Biblical homeland and adopting Hebrew may not be enough. Perhaps the state would have to also adopt Jewish law, or Torah, as well. Taken to its very extreme, messianism, the notion of a Jewish state is inseparable from the rebuilding of the Temple and the coming of the Messiah.

The modern state of Israel attempts to strike a balance between these two positions, and thus expresses the tension between them. The Declaration of Independence, dated May 14, 1948, illustrates this tension more vividly than anything else: "We...hereby declare the establishment of a Jewish state in Eretz-Israel....[I]t will ensure complete equality of social and political rights to all its inhabitants irrespective of religion, race or sex; it will guarantee freedom of religion, conscience, language, education and culture." This leaves open the question of whether Israel is a Jewish state, offering equal freedoms and rights to Jews, or a liberal-democratic nation that holds paramount the rights of every individual....

Israel is a common law country modeled on the English parliamentary system. Like the English system, there is no written constitution. Furthermore, Israel's sole legislative body, the Knesset, which is roughly analogous to England's House of Commons, enjoys technical sovereignty. Acts passed by the Knesset are theoretically immune to judicial override. However, it would be inaccurate to portray the Israeli legal system as completely lacking any hint of judicial review....

Without devoting an entire study to the issue, it is fair to say that judicial review in Israel is barred in theory yet prevalent in practice.

On the one hand, some Supreme Court decisions appear to clearly prohibit what we would call judicial review, that is, the practice of striking down a legislative act on the grounds that it conflicts with a law or principle endowed with superior normative power. For instance, in the case of *Rogozinski v. State of Israel*, Justice Berinson stated that the "Knesset as the legislative branch of the state is sovereign and has the power to pass any law it likes."...

On the other hand, there is evidence that something akin to judicial review is practiced in Israel. This begins with the landmark 1948 decision, *Kol Ha'am Co. Ltd. v. Minister of Interior*, where the Court held that although certain principles of civil liberties are not contained in Knesset legislation, those principles nonetheless inform and guide judicial decisions:

> The system of laws under which the political institutions...have been established and function are witness to the fact that this is indeed a state founded on democracy. Moreover, the matters set forth in the Declaration of Independence, especially as regards basing the State "on the foundations of freedom" and securing freedom of conscience mean that Israel is a freedom-loving State. It is true that the Declaration "does not consist of any constitutional law laying down in fact any rule regarding the maintaining or repeal of any ordinances or laws"...but in so far as it "expresses the vision of the people and its faith," we are bound to pay attention to the matters set forth in it when we come to interpret and give meaning to the laws of the State....

This decision makes clear that, from the founding of the State of Israel, the Supreme Court has been willing to "interpret" laws and ordinances in light of higher principles. Although ostensibly an "all-mighty" legislature, the Knesset is hardly afforded that treatment by the Supreme Court. In short, the debate seems to have focused on the nature and extent of judicial review, rather than on its existence. As the Israeli Constitutional scholar Amos Shapira has noted:

> To be sure, in a parliamentary system without a written constitution endowed with a "super law" quality, the legislature is vested with theoretically unlimited legislative powers and may legislate in derogation of basic individual freedoms and rights. It can do this because no constitutional super-norm exists to limit its power. Yet, in practice, the court attributes to the legislature the intention not to deny or restrict any of these fundamental freedoms, except in instances where the court is faced with a clear-cut, explicit legislative decree to the contrary which it cannot explain or interpret away. Every discrepancy or ambiguity which offers an interpretation option is bound to trigger this presumption in favor of human rights and individual freedoms. This, in turn, brings about a restrictive, narrow construction of legislative measures purporting to curtail fundamental freedoms. This libertarian judicial endeavor has been carried out, particularly in recent years, in an unabashed activist drive.

Thus, it seems clear that although Israel is without a constitution, courts do in practice call upon extra-statutory principles in coming to a decision. Those principles, or norms, might derive from the Declaration of Independence, from prior decisions, or from the very history of the Jewish people. At the same time, it is important to keep in mind that these "extra-statutory" principles, that is, unwritten laws, upon which courts might rely, are at present "soft legal principles. That is, in the face of clear legislative language, an Israeli court is bound to uphold the statute even if it conflicts with principles enunciated in prior decisions or the Declaration of Independence....

Although it technically has no legal status, the legal landscape in Israel cannot be understood without considering the Declaration of Independence. As touched on earlier, the Declaration, if nothing else, evidences the deep fissure underlying the State of Israel: between a Jewish state and a secular liberal-democratic nation. More specifically, the Declaration of Independence describes Israel as a "Jewish state in Eretz Israel [the land of Israel]" that "would open its doors to every Jew and grant Jewish people the status of a nation with equal rights among the family of nations." However, it also promised that the new state "would develop the country for the benefit of all its inhabitants, and that it would maintain complete equality of political and social rights of all its citizens, irrespective of race, religion or sex."

The ambiguous legal status of the Declaration of Independence reflects its tension. On the one hand, the Declaration expresses what are seemingly inviolable principles of freedom and equality. Subsequent statutes, court decisions, and executive opinions have made clear that those principles are "not merely a pious statement of intent adopted in the Declaration of Independence." On the other hand, as noted earlier, the Declaration is not afforded formal legal weight, and the principles enshrined in it are frequently subject to limitations when deemed necessary. The circumscribing of these principles no doubt stems in large part from the realities facing a Jewish nation in the midst of hostile neighbors.

The second source of law that should be noted is the statutes and ordinances passed by the Knesset. As mentioned earlier, the Knesset is technically sovereign and cannot be overruled by the courts....

The third source of law, really a subset of the statutes and ordinances passed by the Knesset, is a series of statutes known as the Basic Laws. There are eleven Basic Laws dealing with various issues, among them civil rights (right to dignity and freedom), form of government and land law....

The fourth source of law consists of prior decisions of the court.... Supreme Court decisions bind subsequent decisions.

The millet system serves as the fifth and most unique source of law in Israel. First established by the Ottoman Empire in the Fifteenth Century, the millet system originally granted autonomy to every non-Moslem religious community. The system was left largely intact by the British authorities during the Mandatory period and still endures to this day. In its present form, matters of personal status, that is, marriage and divorce, are within the sole jurisdiction of the respective religious communities. That is, Jews, Moslems, Druse, and Christian denominations have their own courts....

The final source of law is the precedents and legal principles of other common law jurisdictions....

The vast majority of land controlled, in one form or another, by the Israeli government can be divided into two categories: state lands and JNF [Jewish National Fund, the successor company to the former private British landowning company] lands. Under the Basic Law: Israel Lands (1960), none of this land can be permanently transferred: "Lands in Israel of the state, the Development Authority, or the JNF, shall not be transferred by sale or any other manner." ... [T]he government directly owns 75% of the real property in Israel. This property, in turn, is leased out through the Israel Lands Administration (ILA), the governmental body charged with administering all Israel land. As an organ of the state the ILA is legally prohibited from overtly discriminating on the basis of race, religion or sex, and thus leases Israel lands to both Jews and Arabs.

More important for the present study are JNF-controlled lands, which are governed by a restrictive covenant barring Arabs from leasing the land....

The substance of that agreement—the memorandum and articles of incorporation of the new company—constitutes the restrictive covenant governing JNF lands. In particular, the memorandum of the new company approved by the Minister of Justice states that the primary objective of the JNF is:

> purchasing, acquiring by lease or exchange, receiving by lease or in any other way, lands, forests, rights of possession or easements and all other such rights, as well as immovable property of any sort, in the designated area (which includes the State of Israel and any area controlled by the Government of Israel) for the purpose of settling Jews on the said lands and property....

Although the government owns 75% of the land, nearly two-thirds of it is located in the Negev desert, which for all intents and purposes is non-cultivatable. Thus, upon excluding the Negev, which constitutes half of Israel's territory, or roughly 10,100,000 dunams, it turns out that the state owns roughly 5,100,000 dunams while the JNF owns 3,570,000 dunams. In other words, the JNF owns nearly 45% of the cultivatable and urban property in Israel; property that is off-limits to all non-Jews....

It is important to note that considering the JNF restraints on alienation in light of the American experience is not simply academically intriguing. In fact, the Israeli Supreme Court might very well find it necessary to look abroad were it to take up the JNF matter because all of the other sources of law listed above are ambiguous. Clearly, the Declaration of Independence, notwithstanding its questionable legal status, leaves open the question of whether Israel is a liberal-democratic state or Jewish state. The former would compel a court to invalidate the arrangement while the later might allow it to be upheld. The body of statutes coming out of the Knesset is similarly ambiguous. While the legislation accompanying the JNF-government agreement clearly sanctions the restrictions, other statutes appear to recognize an over-arching principle of equality. More to the point, the Kiryat Arba opinion of the Attorney General clearly states that overt discrimination on the part of a governmental body is strictly prohibited. Similar ambiguities run through the case law, with some decisions holding in favor of complete parliamentary sovereignty, while other decisions appear to interpret statutes as narrowly as necessary in order to trigger the strictures of the equality principle.

Thus, it is quite likely that the Israeli Supreme Court might find that the issue falls within a lacuna, or gap, in the law....

The practice of selective enforcement of the common law rule against restraints on alienation in the service of racism began to see an end, at least at a national level, with the landmark case of *Shelley v. Kraemer*.[98] The case grew out of a dispute among home-

98. 334 U.S. 1 (1948).

owners over a private covenant entered into in 1911 restricting the sale of homes in a neighborhood to whites only. When an African-American family (the Shelleys) moved into one of the homes, a white party to the original agreement brought suit to restrain the Shelley family from taking possession of the property. The trial court refused to enforce the covenant on the grounds that it was defective, but the Supreme Court of Missouri, sitting en banc, reversed in favor of the white petitioners. The United States Supreme Court reversed, refusing to allow enforcement of such a covenant on the grounds that the Fourteenth Amendment bars a court from granting relief for the violation of a racially-restrictive covenant. More precisely, the Court held that, first: enforcement by state courts of racially restrictive covenants constitutes state action under the Fourteenth Amendment because "but for the active intervention of the state courts... petitioners would have been free to occupy the properties in question without restraint;" and, second: such enforcement violates the equal protection clause of the Fourteenth Amendment....

[E]ven if the integrationist approach were adopted, it is doubtful whether Israel would witness a massive change in ownership of JNF lands. Many, if not most, Jewish owners of such property might not be willing to sell to Arabs. The ILA, controlled exclusively by Jews, might not be receptive to the idea of leasing to Arabs. And, just as significantly, Arab individuals might very well not be interested in leasing JNF lands, especially urban property, insofar as it is populated by Jews. If the current demographic patterns are any evidence, it would appear that both Arabs and Jews prefer to a large degree to live amongst themselves, in sharply defined communities. In sum, most Israelis, Arab and Jew alike, do not wish to live out the integrationist ideal enshrined in American law....

The integrationist stage of the American experience would require a per se rule against any racial restraints on alienation, similar to that existing in the United States today. This approach would largely resemble the position outlined above with respect to barring any state sponsored racial discrimination. Likewise, however, the Israel-specific concerns raised by that path also bear relevance here. Namely, the peculiar dilemma of the church-and-state issue in Israel (i.e., a Jewish vs. a secular state), counsels caution in taking on a legal problem that may pronounce a decisive judgment one way or the other. Furthermore, other aspects of the Israeli legal system, in particular the millet system, suggest that a total integrationist position is not universally held by Israeli authority.

Also important for the Israeli court in this context, sitting as a common law court, is the fact that the American experience itself lends reasons to reject integrationism, insofar as it does not reflect the most current position among courts, scholars, and perhaps even individual citizens. As intimated earlier, the notion of color-blindness is viewed as ignorance of cultural identity....

* * *

Notes and Comments

1. Mr. Graber's note demonstrates the need to be informed on comparative and international law as courts may be informed by the wisdom and reasoning from a foreign jurisdiction.

2. For discussion of the experiences of poor and minority populations in coexisting and assimilation in urban centers throughout the world, see The Social Sustainability

of Cities: Diversity and the Management of Change (Mario Polèse & Richard Stren eds. 2000).

The following United States Supreme Court decision demonstrates how the Court can be selectively effective in enforcing equal opportunity norms. The case reflects the American equal protection standard in land use as applied to discrimination based on disability. Is disability bias more easily litigated and remedied than racial bias?

City of Cleburne v. Cleburne Living Center, Inc.

United States Supreme Court
473 US. 432 (1985)

JUSTICE WHITE delivered the opinion of the Court.

In July 1980, respondent Jan Hannah purchased a building at 201 Featherston Street in the city of Clebume, Texas, with the intention of leasing it to Cleburne Living Center, Inc. (CLC), for the operation of a group home for the mentally retarded. It was anticipated that the home would house 13 retarded men and women, who would be under the constant supervision of CLC staff members. The house had four bedroom and two baths, with a half bath to be added. CLC planned to comply with all applicable state and federal regulations. The city informed CLC that a special use permit would be required for the operation of a group home at the site, and CLC accordingly submitted a permit application. In response to a subsequent inquiry from CLC, the city explained that under the zoning regulations applicable to the site, a special use permit, renewable annually, was required for the construction of "[h]ospitals for the insane or feeble-minded, or alcoholic *[sic]* or drug addicts, or penal or correctional institutions."[3] The city had determined that the proposed group home should be classified as a "hospital for the feeble-minded." After holding a public hearing on CLC's application, the City Council voted 3 to 1 to deny a special use permit....

---

3. The site of the home is in an area zoned "R-3," an "Apartment House District." Section 8 of the Cleburne zoning ordinance, in pertinent part, allows the following use in an R-3 district:

1. Any use permitted in District R.2.
2. Apartment houses, or multiple dwellings.
3. Boarding and lodging houses.
4. Fraternity or sorority houses and dormitories.
5. Apartment hotels.
6. Hospitals, sanitariums, nursing homes for convalescents or aged, *other than for the* insane or feeble minded or alcoholics or drug addicts.
7. Private clubs or fraternal orders, except those whose chief activity is carried on as a business.
8. Philanthropic or eleemosynary institutions, other than penal institutions.
9. Accessory uses customarily incident to any of the above uses.

Section 16 of the ordinance specifies the uses for which a special use permit is required. These include "[hjospitals for the insane or feeble-minded, or alcoholic *[sic]* or drug addicts, or penal or correctional institutions."

Section 16 provides that a permit for such a use may be issued by "the Governing Body, after public hearing, and after recommendation of the Planning Commission." All special use permits are limited to one year and each applicant is required "to obtain the signatures of the property owners within two hundred (200) feet of the property to be used.

The Equal Protection Clause of the Fourteenth Amendment commands that no State shall "deny to any person within its jurisdiction the equal protection of the laws," which is essentially a direction that all persons similarly situated should be treated alike.... The general rule is that legislation is presumed to be valid and will be sustained if the classification drawn by the statute is rationally related to a legitimate state interest....

The general rule gives way, however, when a statute classifies by race, alienage, or national origin. These factors are so seldom relevant to the achievement of any legitimate state interest that laws grounded in such considerations are deemed to reflect prejudice and antipathy—a view that those in the burdened class are not as worthy or deserving as others. For these reasons and because such discrimination is unlikely to be soon rectified by legislative means, these laws are subjected to strict scrutiny and will be sustained only if they are suitably tailored to serve a compelling state interest.

Legislative classifications based on gender also call for a heightened standard of review....

Against this background, we conclude for several reasons that the Court of Appeals erred in holding mental retardation a quasi-suspect classification calling for a more exacting standard of judicial review than is normally accorded economic and social legislation. First, it is undeniable, and it is not argued otherwise here, that those who are mentally retarded have a reduced ability to cope with and function in the everyday world. Nor are they all cut from the same pattern: as the testimony in this record indicates, they range from those whose disability is not immediately evident to those who must be constantly cared for. They are thus different, immutably so, in relevant respects, and the States interest in dealing with and providing for them is plainly a legitimate one. How this large and diversified group is to be treated under the law is a difficult and often a technical matter, very much a task for legislators guided by qualified professionals and not by the perhaps ill-informed opinions of the judiciary. Heightened scrutiny inevitably involves substantive judgments about legislative decisions, and we doubt that the predicate for such judicial oversight is present where the classification deals with mental retardation.

Second, the distinctive legislative response, both national and state, to the plight of those who are mentally retarded demonstrates not only that they have unique problems, but also that the lawmakers have been addressing their difficulties in a manner that belies a continuing antipathy or prejudice and a corresponding need for more intrusive oversight by the judiciary....

Third, the legislative response, which could hardly have occurred and survived without public support, negates any claim that the mentally retarded are politically powerless in the sense that they have no ability to attract the attention of the lawmakers. Any minority can be said to be powerless to assert direct control over the legislature, but if that were a criterion for higher level scrutiny by the courts, much economic and social legislation would now be suspect.

Fourth, if the large and amorphous class of the mentally retarded were deemed quasi-suspect for the reasons given by the Court of Appeals, it would be difficult to find a principled way to distinguish a variety of other groups who have perhaps immutable disabilities setting them off from others, who cannot themselves mandate the desired legislative responses, and who can claim some degree of prejudice from at least part of the public at large. One need mention in this respect only the aging, the disabled, the mentally ill, and the infirm. We are reluctant to set out on that course, and we decline to do so....

Our refusal to recognize the retarded as a quasi-suspect class does not leave them entirely unprotected from invidious discrimination. To withstand equal protection review, legislation that distinguishes between the mentally retarded and others must be rationally related to a legitimate governmental purpose. This standard, we believe, affords government the latitude necessary both to pursue policies designed to assist the retarded in realizing their full potential, and to freely and efficiently engage in activities that burden the retarded in what is essentially an incidental manner. The State may not rely on a classification whose relationship to an asserted goal is so attenuated as to render the distinction arbitrary or irrational. Furthermore, some objectives—such as "a bare... desire to harm a politically unpopular group,..."—are not legitimate state interests. Beyond that, the mentally retarded, like others, have and retain their substantive constitutional rights in addition to the right to be treated equally by the law.

We turn to the issue of the validity of the zoning ordinance insofar as it requires a special use permit for homes for the mentally retarded. We inquire first whether requiring a special use permit for the Featherston home in the circumstances here deprives respondents of the equal protection of the laws. If it does, there will be no occasion to decide whether the special use permit provision is facially invalid where the mentally retarded are involved, or to put it another way, whether the city may never insist on a special use permit for a home for the mentally retarded in an R-3 zone....

The constitutional issue is clearly posed. The city does not require a special use permit in an R-3 zone for apartment houses, multiple dwellings, boarding and lodging houses, fraternity or sorority houses, dormitories, apartment hotels, hospitals, sanitariums, nursing homes for convalescents or the aged (other than for the insane or feebleminded or alcoholics or drug addicts), private clubs or fraternal orders, and other specified uses. It does, however, insist on a special permit for the Featherston home, and it does so, as the District Court found, because it would be a facility for the mentally retarded. May the city require the permit for this facility when other care and multiple-dwelling facilities are freely permitted?

It is true, as already pointed out, that the mentally retarded as a group are indeed different from others not sharing their misfortune, and in this respect they may be different from those who would occupy other facilities that would be permitted in an R-3 zone without a special permit. But this difference is largely irrelevant unless the Featherston home and those who would occupy it would threaten legitimate interests of the city in a way that other permitted uses such as boarding houses and hospitals would not. Because in purview the record does not reveal any rational basis for believing that the Featherston home would pose any special threat to the city's legitimate interests, we affirm the judgment below insofar as it holds the ordinance invalid as applied in this case.

The District Court found that the City Council's insistence on the permit rested on several factors. First, the Council was concerned with the negative attitude of the majority of property owners located within 200 feet of the Featherston facility, as well as with the fears of elderly residents of the neighborhood. But mere negative attitudes, or fear, unsubstantiated by factors which are properly cognizable in a zoning proceeding, are not permissible bases for treating a home for the mentally retarded differently from apartment houses, multiple dwellings, and the like....

Second, the Council had two objections to the location of the facility. It was concerned that the facility was across the street from a junior high school, and it feared that the students might harass the occupants of the Featherston home. But the school itself is attended by about 30 mentally retarded students, and denying a permit based on such vague, undifferentiated fears is again permitting some portion of the community to validate what would otherwise be an equal protection violation. The other objection to the home's location was that it was located on "a five hundred year flood plain." This concern with the possibility of a flood, however, can hardly be based on a distinction between the Featherston home and, for example, nursing homes, homes for convalescents or the aged, or sanitariums or hospitals, any of which could be located on the Featherston site without obtaining a special use permit. The same may be said of another concern of the Council—doubts about the legal responsibility for actions which the mentally retarded might take. If there is no concern about legal responsibility with respect to other uses that would be permitted in the area, such as boarding and fraternity houses, it is difficult to believe that the groups of mildly or moderately mentally retarded individuals who would live at 201 Featherston would present any different or special hazard.

Fourth, the Council was concerned with the size of the home and the number of people that would occupy it. The District Court found, and the Court of Appeals repeated, that "[i]f the potential residents of the Featherston Street home were not mentally retarded, but the home was the same in all other respects, its use would be permitted under the city's Zoning ordinance." Given this finding, there would be no restrictions on the number of people who could occupy this home as a boarding house, nursing home, family dwelling, fraternity house, or dormitory. The question is whether it is rational to treat the mentally retarded differently. It is true that they suffer disability not shared by others; but why this difference warrants a density regulation that others need not observe is not at all apparent. At least this record does not clarify how, in this connection, the characteristics of the intended occupants of the Featherston home rationally justify denying to those occupants what would be permitted to groups occupying the same site for different purposes....

In the courts below the city also urged that the ordinance is aimed at avoiding concentration of population and at lessening congestion of the streets. These concerns obviously fail to explain why apartment houses, fraternity and sorority houses, hospitals and the like, may freely locate in the area without a permit. So, too, the expressed worry about fire hazards, the serenity of the neighborhood, and the avoidance of danger to other residents fail rationally to justify singling out a home such as 201 Featherston for the special use permit, yet imposing no such restrictions on the many other uses freely permitted in the neighborhood.

The short of it is that requiring the permit in this case appears to us to rest on an irrational prejudice against the mentally retarded, including those who would occupy the Featherston facility and who would live under the closely supervised and highly regulated conditions expressly provided for by state and federal law....

* * *

Notes and Comments

1. How protective is the Court? What if the neighborhood was single-family residential rather than high density, would the Court permit a special use requirement? Could a community exclude group homes for the disabled because they were perceived to be incompatible with a communities definition of a traditional family district. The following case raises the possibility that *Cleburne* is limited to its rather arbitrary facts and does not stand as a principle of inclusion:

Regulation of Occupancy

Village of Belle Terre v. Boraas

United States Supreme Court
416 U.S. 1 (1974)

MR. JUSTICE DOUGLAS delivered the opinion of the Court.

Belle Terre is a village on Long Island's north shore of about 220 homes inhabited by 700 people. Its total land area is less than one square mile. It has restricted land use to one-family dwellings excluding lodging houses, boarding houses, fraternity houses, or multiple-dwelling houses. The word "family" as used in the ordinance means, "[o]ne or more persons related by blood, adoption, or marriage, living and cooking together as a single housekeeping unit, exclusive of household servants. A number of persons but not exceeding two (2) living and cooking together as a single housekeeping unit though not related by blood, adoption, or marriage shall be deemed to constitute a family."

Appellees the Dickmans are owners of a house in the village and leased it in December 1971 for a term of 18 months to Michael Truman. Later Bruce Boraas became a colessee. Then Anne Parish moved into the house along with three others. These six are students at nearby State University at Stony Brook and none is related to the other by blood, adoption, or marriage. When the village served the Dickmans with an "Order to Remedy Violations" of the ordinance, the owners plus three tenants thereupon brought this action under 42 U.S.C. §1983 for an injunction and a judgment declaring the ordinance unconstitutional....

The present ordinance is challenged on several grounds: that it interferes with a person's right to travel; that it interferes with the right to migrate to and settle within a State; that it bars people who are uncongenial to the present residents; that it expresses the social preferences of the residents for groups that will be congenial to them; that social homogeneity is not a legitimate interest of government; that the restriction of those whom the neighbors do not like trenches on the newcomers' rights of privacy; that it is of no rightful concern to villagers whether the residents are married or unmarried; that the ordinance is antithetical to the Nation's experience, ideology, and self-perception as an open, egalitarian, and integrated society.

We find none of these reasons in the record before us. It is not aimed at transients. It involves no procedural disparity inflicted on some but not on others.... It involves no "fundamental" right guaranteed by the Constitution.... We deal with economic and social legislation where legislatures have historically drawn lines which we respect against the charge of violation of the Equal Protection Clause if the law be "'reasonable, not arbitrary'" and bears "a rational relationship to a [permissible] state objective."

It is said, however, that if two unmarried people can constitute a "family," there is no reason why three or four may not. But every line drawn by a legislature leaves some out that might well have been included. That exercise of discretion, however, is a legislative, not a judicial, function.

It is said that the Belle Terre ordinance reeks with an animosity to unmarried couples who live together. There is no evidence to support it; and the provision of the ordinance bringing within the definition of a "family" two unmarried people belies the charge.

The ordinance places no ban on other forms of association, for a "family" may, so far as the ordinance is concerned, entertain whomever it likes.

The regimes of boarding houses, fraternity houses, and the like present urban problems. More people occupy a given space; more cars rather continuously pass by; more cars are parked; noise travels with crowds.

A quiet place where yards are wide, people few, and motor vehicles restricted are legitimate guidelines in a land-use project addressed to family needs. This goal is a permissible one... The police power is not confined to elimination of filth, stench, and unhealthy places. It is ample to lay out zones where family values, youth values, and the blessings of quiet seclusion and clean air make the area a sanctuary for people....

MR. JUSTICE MARSHALL, dissenting....

The instant ordinance discriminates on the basis of... a personal lifestyle choice as to household companions. It permits any number of persons related by blood or marriage, be it two or twenty, to live in a single household, but it limits to two the number of unrelated persons bound by profession, love, friendship, religious or political affiliation, or mere economics who can occupy a single home. Belle Terre imposes upon those who deviate from the community norm in their choice of living companions significantly greater restrictions than are applied to residential groups who are related by blood or marriage, and compose the established order within the community. The village has, in effect, acted to fence out those individuals whose choice of lifestyle differs from that of its current residents....

...The ordinance imposes no restriction whatsoever on the number of persons who may live in a house, as long as they are related by marital or sanguinary bonds—presumably no matter how distant their relationship. Nor does the ordinance restrict the number of income earners who may contribute to rent in such a household, or the number of automobiles that may be maintained by its occupants. In that sense the ordinance is underinclusive. On the other hand, the statute restricts the number of unrelated persons who may live in a home to no more than two. It would therefore prevent three unrelated people from occupying a dwelling even if among them they had but one income and no vehicles. While an extended family of a dozen or more might live in a small bungalow, three elderly and retired persons could not occupy the large manor house next door. Thus the statute is also grossly overinclusive to accomplish its intended purposes....

* * *

Notes and Comments

1. *Belle Terre* may underscore the importance of legislative enactments such as the Fair Housing Act and The Americans with Disabilities Act. These enactments ostensibly place greater burdens on communities than the nonarbitrariness of the equal protection clause. So far the courts have required a much higher level of justification to survive scrutiny and single family districts have not enjoyed judicial immunity. *Cleburne* and *Belle Terre* appear to convey conflicting messages, one of exclusion and one of exclusivity. The *Cleburne* principle is directed to arbitrary standards in a commercial district, allowing similar types of intensive residential and institutional development, while the *Belle Terre* principle deals with a single family American suburb. The questions of how far the principles might be extended or limited was sidetracked by passage of the 1988

Fair Housing Act Amendments, extending Title VIII to cover disability bias, and the Americans With Disabilities Act, Pub. L. No. 101-336, 104 Stat. 327 (1990), prohibiting disability-based discrimination in zoning and land use controls. *See generally Groome Resources Ltd. v. Parish of Jefferson*, 234 F.3d 192 (5th Cir. 2000) (Title VIII preempts blood or marriage limitations in single family district as applied to Alzheimer group home); *Larkin v. Michigan Dep't of Soc. Servs.*, 89 F.3d 285 (6th Cir. 1996) (Title VIII preempts state law regulating group home). *But see Forest City Daly Hous., Inc. v. Town of N. Hempstead*, 175 F.3d 144 (2d Cir. 1999) (rejecting ADA and Title VIII challenge to denial of special use permit in commercial zone absent disparate treatment); *Gamble v. City of Escondido*, 104 F.3d 300 (9th Cir.1997) (sustaining conditional use permit denial for disabled elderly facility in single-family district). *But cf. Toyota Motor Mfg. v. Williams*, 534 U.S. 184 (2002) (narrowly interpreting Americans with Disabilities Act covered disabilities to those that restrict an individual on a permanent or long-term basis from performing tasks of central importance to daily life, here rejecting claim by employee unable to perform certain tasks due to carpal tunnel syndrome).

2. Another problem with the expansion of legislative protections is that there are more demands placed on precious enforcement machinery. More time is now taken up by administrative agencies and the courts with claims from the disability community and the goal of racial integration has been bypassed. James A. Kushner, *Federal Enforcement and Judicial Review of the Fair Housing Amendments Act of 1988*, 3 Hous. Pol'y Debate 537 (1992).

Affirmative Action

The following case involved one of the rare occurrences in history where a community actually sought to be inclusive and integrated. This is what happened when integration met the Reagan Administration Department of Justice. Indeed, Starrett City was the sole reported decision from fair housing litigation efforts of the Reagan Justice Department during his two presidential terms:

United States v. Starrett City Associates

United States Court of Appeals for the Second Circuit
840 F.2d 1096, *cert. denied*, 488 U. S. 946 (1988)

Miner, Circuit Judge:

The United States Attorney General, on behalf of the United States ("the government"), commenced this action under Title VIII of the Civil Rights Act of 1968 ("Fair Housing Act" or "the Act") against defendants-appellants Starrett City Associates, Starrett City, Inc. and Delmar Management Company (collectively, "Starrett") in the United States District Court for the Eastern District of New York (Neaher, J.). The government maintained that Starrett's practices of renting apartments in its Brooklyn housing complex solely on the basis of applicants' race or national origin, and of making apartments unavailable to black and Hispanic applicants that are then made available to white applicants, violate section 804(a), (b), (c) and (d) of the Act, 42 U.S.C. § 3604(a)-(d) (1982).

The parties made cross-motions for summary judgment based on extensive documentary submissions. The district court granted summary judgment in favor of the government and permanently enjoined appellants from discriminating on the basis of race in the rental of apartments. Starrett appeals from this judgment.

Appellants constructed, own and operate "Starrett City," the largest housing development in the nation, consisting of 46 high-rise buildings containing 5,881 apartments in Brooklyn, New York... [The complex had the benefit of state and federal assistance. During its development Starrett City's developer assured the city of New York it] "intended to create a racially integrated community."

Starrett sought to maintain a racial distribution by apartment of 64% white, 22% black and 8% Hispanic at Starrett City. Starrett claims that these racial quotas are necessary to prevent the loss of white tenants, which would transform Starrett City into a predominantly minority complex. Starrett points to the difficulty it has had in attracting an integrated applicant pool from the time Starrett City opened, despite extensive advertising and promotional efforts. Because of these purported difficulties, Starrett adopted a tenanting procedure to promote and maintain the desired racial balance. This procedure has resulted in relatively stable percentages of whites and minorities living at Starrett City between 1975 and the present.

The tenanting procedure requires completion of a preliminary information card stating, *inter alia*, the applicant's race or national origin, family composition, income and employment. The rental office at Starrett City receives and reviews these applications. Those that are found preliminarily eligible, based on family composition, income, employment and size of apartment sought, are placed in "the active file," in which separate records by race are maintained for apartment sizes and income levels. Applicants are told in an acknowledgment letter that no apartments are presently available, but that their applications have been placed in the active file and that they will be notified when a unit becomes available for them. When an apartment becomes available, applicants are selected from the active file for final processing, creating a processed applicant pool. As vacancies arise, applicants of a race or national origin similar to that of the departing tenants are selected from the pool and offered apartments.

In December 1979, a group of black applicants brought an action against Starrett in the United States District Court for the Eastern District of New York. Plaintiffs alleged that Starrett's tenanting procedures violated federal and state law by discriminating against them on the basis of race. The parties stipulated to a settlement in May 1984, and a consent decree was entered subsequently, see *Arthur v. Starrett City Assocs.*, No. 79-CV-3 096, slip op. at 1 (E.D.N.Y. April 2, 1985). The decree provided that Starrett would, depending on apartment availability, make an additional 35 units available each year for a five-year period to black and minority applicants....

Starrett maintained that the tenanting procedures "were adopted at the behest of the [s]tate solely to achieve and maintain integration and were not motivated by racial animus." 660 F. Supp. at 673. To support their position, appellants submitted the written testimony of three housing experts. They described the "white flight" and "tipping" phenomena, in which white residents migrate out of a community as the community becomes poor and the minority population increases, resulting in the transition to a predominantly minority community. Acknowledging that" 'the tipping point for a particular housing development, depending as it does on numerous factors and the uncertainties of human behavior, is difficult to predict with precision,' "one expert stated that the point at which tipping occurs has been estimated at from 1% to 60% minority population, but that the consensus ranged between 10% and 20%. Another expert, who had prepared a report in 1980 on integration at Starrett City for the New York State Division of Housing and Community Renewal, estimated the complex's tipping point at approximately 40% black on a population basis. A third expert, who had been involved in integrated housing ventures since the 1950's, found that a 2:1 white-minority ratio produced successful integration.

The court, however, accepted the government's contention that Starrett's practices of making apartments unavailable for blacks, while reserving them for whites, and conditioning rental to minorities based on a "tipping formula" derived only from race or national origin are clear violations of the Fair Housing Act. The district court found that apartment opportunities for blacks and Hispanics were far fewer "than would be expected if race and national origin were not taken into account," while opportunities for whites were substantially greater than what their application rates projected. Minority applicants waited up to ten times longer than the average white applicant before they were offered an apartment. Further, the court found that appellants' tipping argument was undercut by the "wide elasticity of that standard" and the lack of difficulty they had in increasing their black quota from 21% to 35% "when it became necessary to avoid litigating the private Arthur lawsuit which threatened their unlawful rental practices." The court also found that Starrett violated the Act by making untrue representations of apartment unavailability to qualified minority applicants in order to reserve units for whites. Finally, the court rejected Starrett's claim that the duty imposed upon government to achieve housing integration justified its actions, stating that "[d]efendant cannot arrogate to themselves the powers" of a public housing authority.

The court concluded that Starrett's obligation was "simply and solely to comply with the Fair Housing Act" by treating "black and other minority applicants…on the same basis as whites in seeking available housing at Starrett City." The court noted that Starrett did not dispute any of the operative facts alleged to show violation of the Fair Housing Act. Accordingly, Judge Neaher granted summary judgment for the government, enjoining Starrett from discriminating against applicants on the basis of race and "[requiring [them] to adopt written, objective, uniform, nondiscriminatory tenant selection standards and procedures" subject to the court's approval. The court retained jurisdiction over the parties for three years.…

Title VIII of the Civil Rights Act of 1968 ("Fair Housing Act" or "the Act"), 42 U.S.C. §§3601–3631 (1982), was enacted…"to provide, within constitutional limitations, for fair housing throughout the United States." 42 U.S.C. §3601. Section 3604 of the statute prohibits discrimination because of race, color or national origin in the sale or rental of housing by, *inter alia*: (1) refusing to rent or make available any dwelling, §3604(a); (2) offering discriminatory "terms, conditions or privileges" of rental, §3604(b); (3) making, printing or publishing "any notice, statement, or advertisement…that indicates any preference, limitation, or discrimination based on race, color…or national origin," §3604(c); and (4) representing to any person "that any dwelling is not available for… rental when such dwelling is in fact so available," id. §3604(d).…

Starrett's allocation of public housing facilities on the basis of racial quotas by denying an applicant access to a unit otherwise available solely because of race produces a "discriminatory effect…[that] could hardly be clearer,"…Appellants do not contend that the plain language of section 3604 does not proscribe their practices. Rather, they claim to be "clothed with governmental authority" and thus obligated, under *Otero v. New York City Hous. Auth.*, 484 F.2d 1122 (2d Cir. 1973), to effectuate the purpose of the Fair Housing Act by affirmatively promoting integration and preventing "the reghettoization of a model integrated community."…

First, Starrett City's practices have only the goal of integration maintenance. The quotas already have been in effect for ten years. Appellants predict that their race-conscious tenanting practices must continue for at least fifteen more years, but fail to explain adequately how that approximation was reached. In any event, these practices are far from temporary. Since the goal of integration maintenance is purportedly threatened by the potential for "white flight" on a continuing basis, no definite termination date for Starrett's quotas is perceivable. Second, appellants do not assert, and there is no evidence to show, the existence of prior racial discrimination or discriminatoiy imbalance adversely affecting whites within Starrett City or appellants" other complexes. On the contrary, Starrett City was initiated as an integrated complex, and Starrett's avowed purpose for employing race-based tenanting practices is to maintain that initial integration. Finally, Starrett's quotas do not provide minorities with access to Starrert City, but rather act as a ceiling to their access. Thus, the impact of appellants' practices falls squarely on minorities, for whom Title VIII was intended to open up housing opportunities. Starrett claims that its use of quotas serves to keep the numbers of minorities entering Starrett City low enough to avoid setting off a wave of "white flight." Although the "white flight" phenomenon may be a factor "take[n] into account in the integration equation," *Parent Ass'n of Andrew Jackson High School v. Ambach*, 598 F.2d 705, 720 (2d Cir. 1979), it cannot serve to justify attempts to maintain integration at Starrett City through inflexible racial quotas that are neither temporary in nature nor used to remedy past racial discrimination or imbalance within the complex.

Appellants" reliance on *Otero* is misplaced. In *Otero* the New York City Housing Authority ("NYCHA") relocated over 1800 families in the Lower East Side of Manhattan to make way for the construction of new apartment buildings. Pursuant to its regulations, NYCHA offered the former site occupants first priority of returning to any housing built within the urban renewal area. However, because the response by the largely minority former site residents seeking to return was nearly seven times greater than expected, NYCHA declined to follow its regulation in order to avoid creating a "pocket ghetto" that would "tip" an integrated community towards a predominantly minority community. It instead rented up half of these apartments to non-former site occupants, 88% of whom were white.

In a suit brought by former site occupants who were denied the promised priority, the district court held as a matter of law that "affirmative action to achieve racially balanced communities was not permitted where it would result in depriving minority groups" of public housing, and thus granted summary judgment in favor of plaintiffs. This court reversed the grant of summary judgment, stating that public housing authorities had a federal constitutional and statutory duty "to flulfill, as much as possible, the goal of open, integrated residential housing patterns and to prevent the increase of segregation, in ghettos," but we recognized that "the effect in some instances might be to prevent some members of a racial minority from residing in publicly assisted housing in a particular location."

Otero does not, however, control in this case. The challenge in *Otero* did not involve procedures for the long-term maintenance of specified levels of integration, but rather, the rental of 171 of 360 new apartments to non-former site occupants, predominantly white, although former site residents, largely minority, sought those apartments and were entitled to priority under NYCHA's own regulation. The *Otero* court did not delineate the statutory or constitutional limits on permissible means of integration, but held only that NYCHA's rent-up practice could not be declared invalid as a matter of law under those limits. In fact, the court in *Otero* observed that the use of race conscious tenanting practices might allow landlords "to engage in social engineering, subject only to general undefined control through judicial supervision" and could "constitute a form of unlawful racial discrimination."

It is particularly important to note that the NYCHA action challenged in *Otero* only applied to a single event—the initial rent up of the new complexes—and determined tenancy in the first instance alone. NYCHA sought only to prevent the immediate creation of a "pocket ghetto" in the Lower East Side, which had experienced a steady loss of white population, that would tip the precarious racial balance there, resulting in increased white flight and inevitable "non-white ghettoization of the community." Further, the suspension of NYCHA's regulation did not operate as a strict racial quota, because the former site residents entitled to a rental priority were approximately 40% white. As a one-time measure in response to the special circumstances of the Lower East Side in the early 1970's, the action challenged in *Otero* had an impact on nonwhites as a group far less burdensome or discriminatory than Starrett City's continuing practices.

We do not intend to imply that race is always an inappropriate consideration under Title VIII in efforts to promote integrated housing. We hold only that Title VIII does not allow appellants to use rigid racial quotas of indefinite duration to maintain a fixed level of integration at Starrett City by restricting minority access to scarce and desirable rental accommodations otherwise available to them. We therefore affirm the judgment of the district court.

Jon O. Newman, Circuit Judge, dissenting:

Congress enacted the Fair Housing Act to prohibit racial segregation in housing. Starrett City is one of the most successful examples in the nation of racial integration in housing. I respectfully dissent because I do not believe that Congress intended the Fair Housing Act to prohibit the maintenance of racial integration in private housing.... The complex was originally to have been built as a cooperatively owned housing development by the sponsor of Co-Op City in the Bronx. When financing was not obtained, the project was taken over by the current owner, whose business was rental housing. Because New York City had given the previous developer substantial tax abatements, the City's approval was necessary if Starrett City was to have the benefit of these tax abatements. The prospect of a large, low-income rental housing complex generated considerable political opposition within the City from those who feared that the project would attract only minority tenants. The new owner and the New York State Division of Housing and Community Renewal (DHCR) gave assurances that affirmative steps would be taken to maintain Starrett City as an integrated community. On these assurances, the New York City Board of Estimate approved the construction of Starrett City as a rental development.

At that time, DHCR policy called for an integration goal of 70% majority and 30% minority tenants in state-sponsored projects. The defendants adopted this goal for Starrett City. Since the size of tenants' families varied, the target percentages reflected the anticipated racial distribution of rental units, rather than of persons living in the complex. To reach its target of racial balance, Starrett City explicitly declined to rent on a first-come, first-served basis. Instead, reacting to the fact that Blacks and other minorities applied for apartments at Starrett City in far greater numbers than Whites, the management imposed ceilings on the number of apartments of various sizes that would be rented to Blacks and other minorities. As the number of tenants of each minority reached the ceiling for a particular size of apartment, subsequent applicants from that minority were placed on a waiting list until sufficient vacancies occurred to permit a rental to a member of that minority without exceeding the established ceiling.

As experience with this rental policy developed, Starrett City decided that it would permit the percentage of apartments rented to minorities to move above 30% and to reach approximately 35%. The components of this aggregate figure are 21% Black, 8% Hispanic, 4.5% Oriental, and 2% other or mixed. These figures have been fairly constant since 1976. During that period the minority percentage of the Starrett City population has been approximately 45%....

In my view, the defendants are entitled to prevail simply on the statutory issue to which the Government has limited its lawsuit. Though the terms of the statute literally encompass the defendants' actions, the statute was never intended to apply to such actions. This statute was intended to bar perpetuation of segregation. To apply it to bar maintenance of integration is precisely contrary to the congressional policy "to provide, within constitutional limitations, for fair housing throughout the United States." 42 U.S.C. §3601....

Title VIII bars discriminatory housing practices in order to end segregated housing. Starrett City is not promoting segregated housing. On the contrary, it is maintaining integrated housing. It is surely not within the spirit of the Fair Housing Act to enlist the Act to bar integrated housing. Nor is there any indication that application of the statute toward such a perverse end was within the intent of those who enacted the statute. It is true that there are some statements in the legislative history that broadly condemn discrimination for "any" reason. Senator Mondale, the principal sponsor of Title VIII, said that "we do not see any good reason or justification, in the first place, for permitting discrimination in the sale or rental of housing." But his context, like that in which the entire debate occurred, concerned maintenance of segregation, not integration. His point was that there was no reason for discriminating against a Black who wished to live in a previously all white housing project. He explicitly decried the prospect that "we are going to live separately in white ghettos and Negro ghettos. The purpose of Title VIII, he said, was to replace the ghettos "by truly integrated and balanced living patterns. As he pointed out, "[o]ne of the biggest problems we face is the lack of experience in actually living next to Negroes. Starrett City is committed to the proposition that Blacks and Whites shall live next to each other. A law enacted to enhance the opportunity for people of all races to live next to each other should not be interpreted to prevent a landlord from maintaining one of the most successful integrated housing projects in America.

None of the legislators who enacted Title VIII ever expressed a view on whether they wished to prevent the maintenance of racially balanced housing. Most of those who passed this statute in 1968 probably could not even contemplate a private real estate owner who would deliberately set out to achieve a racially balanced tenant population. Had they thought of such an eventuality, there is not the slightest reason to believe that they would have raised their legislative hands against it.

This Circuit... [held in *Otero*] that the Act was not violated simply because a race-conscious decision had been made in connection with rental policy:

> Congress' desire in providing fair housing throughout the United States was to stem the spread of urban ghettos and to promote open, integrated housing, even though the effect in some instances might be to prevent some members of a racial minority from residing in publicly assisted housing in a particular location.

Once the Court decided that a race-conscious rental policy did not necessarily violate the Act, it then faced the difficult issue in the case—whether the Act imposed an affirmative duty to promote integration of sufficient force to permit the authority to violate its own regulation. On that issue, the Court also ruled in favor of the authority, remanding for a trial at which the defendant could establish that its apprehension concerning a "tipping point" was well founded and that abandonment of its priority policy was necessary to promote integration.

Our case is much easier than *Otero*. Starrett City is not seeking to be released from a commitment it has previously made to any of the applicants for housing. To prevail it need not find in Title VIII some affirmative obligation compelling it to promote integration. It has freely chosen to promote integration and is entitled to prevail unless something in Title VIII forbids its voluntary policy. If anything in Title VIII prohibited race-conscious rental policies adopted to promote integration, *Otero* would have been summarily decided against the defendant....

But even if Title VIII can somehow be construed to make the lawfulness of a race-conscious rental policy that promotes integration turn on the duration of the policy, Starrett City is entitled to a trial so that it can prove its contention that its policy is still needed to maintain integration. In the District Court, the Government, though seeking summary judgment, contested Starrett City's factual contention that a race-conscious rental policy was currently needed to prevent the complex from passing the "tipping point" and becoming segregated. The Government relied on a brief affidavit of a HUD employee, who made primarily the unremarkable observation that it is difficult to predict with any certainty the precise "tipping point" in a particular neighborhood. In opposing summary judgment, Starrett City presented detailed affidavits providing abundant evidence to show that abandonment of its rental policies would cause the complex to pass the "tipping point" and soon become a segregated development. This evidence was solidly based on relevant experience. Several housing developments near Starrett City, operating without a policy of integration maintenance, have become racially segregated, including one across the street from Starrett City.

...Until Congress acts, we should not lend our authority to the result this lawsuit will surely bring about. In the words of Dr. Clark:

> [I]t would be a tragedy of the highest magnitude if this litigation were to lead to the destruction of one of the model integrated communities in the United States.

Because the Fair Housing Act does not require this tragedy to occur, I respectfully dissent.

* * *

Notes and Comments

1. What policies should the federal, state, or local government pursue to achieve a more integrated society? What rights and remedies should be identified by the courts to assure that goal? At the writing of this book there exist numerous incidents such as the rioting generated by warring Pakastani and Northern England youths, demonstrating that non-United States cities are experienced increasing patterns of racial and ethnic separation and escalating racial tensions. What lessons can England and other nations and cities learn from the American experience?

The following excerpt describes Singapore's approach to housing and integration:

Aya Gruber, Recent Development, *Public Housing in Singapore: The Use of Ends-Based Reasoning in the Quest for a Workable System,*

38 Harvard International Law Journal 236 (1997)

Singapore's monumental achievements in public housing have astounded supporters and critics alike. Law Professor W.J.M. Ricquier of the National University of Singapore has stated, "To say that (Singapore's housing) achievements have been Herculean would scarcely be an exaggeration." Many applaud the Singapore government for transforming a tiny, overcrowded, poor, slum-ridden, third world island into a spotless haven for foreign investors within the space of twenty-five years. Today, 86% of Singapore's 2.93 million people reside in Housing and Development Board ("HDB") flats. Eighty-one percent of HDB residents own their flats, leaving only five percent as renters. This public housing scheme is not only impressive, but arguably necessary in an island only 646 square kilometers in size with a resident urban population density of 9200 persons per square kilometer. Given this density, if the government had not imposed high-rise living on its citizens, Singapore's land may not have been able to accommodate its population....

To prevent housing and other problems created by racial division, the government implemented a massive campaign of racial integration. Singapore is an ethnically diverse nation with one dominant ethnic group, the Chinese.[139] Prior to the government's policy of active integration, the different ethnic groups experienced different socioeconomic statuses.[140] The government felt that deliberately manipulating the arrangement of public housing would help achieve racial integration. "One of the main objectives of Singapore's public housing program (was) to bring people of all ethnic groups to live together in a planned environment with the hope of promoting ethnic integration. Apparently, the government succeeded in integrating housing. Surveys show that 53% of Singaporeans believe their present neighborhoods are more integrated than previous ones. The active integration program has not met with universal praise. Many criticize it on the grounds that the uniform housing and mixed environment has destroyed culture. Others simply argue that ethnic separation is maintained on a different level. One commentator noted:

> [I]n a multi-cultural society like Singapore, different ethnic groups maintain and practice their own values and norms, and in some instances the different norms and practices may clash with one another; what is moral or sacred to one group may be despised or taboo to another. Consequently, ethnic boundaries are maintained and the intensity of inter-ethnic interaction is therefore much lower than that of intra-ethnic interaction.

To ensure contentment with public housing, the Singapore government educated its constituents about socialized living. In order to directly communicate social values to the public, the HDB launched Our Home magazine. Our Home magazine now enjoys the largest circulation among all journals in Singapore. The HDB also communicated

---

139. Seventy-eight percent of Singapore's population is Chinese, 14% is Malay, 7% is Indian, and the remaining 1% consists of other groups.

140. The Chinese, like Caucasians in the United States, enjoyed the highest class in society. The Indians were lower-class, but mostly known as urban dwellers. The Malays experienced the lowest status. They were known as "kampong" (village) dwellers.

with the public through several grass roots organizations. In addition, the government began using schools to orient children towards certain social and moral values. The government introduced into all schools a moral education program based on both Confucian ethics and government policy goals "to promote the awareness and the practice of moral and traditional values among Singaporeans." Such propaganda and education programs have not been viewed favorably by all. One critic stated: "Socialization through mass media and the schools has successfully convinced the bulk of the population that there are no alternative methods or policies workable for Singapore's economic survival." This may be viewed as another example of Singapore employing ends-based reasoning. The government used propaganda, a means viewed unfavorably by many, to achieve its housing ends....

On the surface, Singapore's public housing program may seem attractive as a model upon which to base other public housing programs. Singapore has eradicated slums and homelessness and has put spotless high rises where there once was squalor. There are several aspects of the system, however, that make it unattractive as a model of public housing, especially for the United States. First, Singapore's system is the product of a unique legal and political structure. United States legislatures would not likely pass such broad statutes, and United States politicians would not likely make housing a top priority in their political platforms. Singapore's public housing success was also the product of unique economic, social, and demographic conditions that do not currently exist in any other country. Moreover, experts disagree on whether or not Singaporeans are better off with public housing. Finally, and most importantly, the government achieved its housing goals using means many in the United States would find objectionable. In its quest for the perfect public housing regime, the Singapore government subordinated many of the rights and freedoms people in the United States associate with property ownership, rights and freedoms with which most would be reluctant to part.

* * *

The following chapter looks at the various environmental statutes and policies that intersect with the land development process.

Chapter 13

Environmental Protection and Land Use Planning

> To Drive alone, or to ride share,
> That is the question.
> Whether 'tis nobler in the mind to bear
> The jams and delays of outrageous congestion,
> Or to take passengers against a sea of traffic,
> And by ride sharing, end it.
>
> Anthony Downs, Stuck in Traffic 156 (1992)

Sustainability

Although environmental considerations may have affected project review and design prior to the 1970s, the criteria was typically subjective and simply a function of the discretionary zoning or other planning decision. As America became more environmentally aware at the end of the 1960s, Congress and some of the states passed legislation designed to protect the environment. Today some form of environmental review is required for most projects, either because the project involves federal funding or falls within the jurisdiction of federal agencies such as the United States Army Corps of Engineers that traditionally must approve projects affecting wetlands, or because the project is within one of the urbanized states that impose environmental review obligations.

The most important statute was the National Environmental Policy Act of 1969 (NEPA), 42 U.S.C. §§4321–4370d. Although limited in scope as it applied only to federal projects, the law changed the way that reviewing agencies look at development and spawned many state environmental review statutes. The law basically requires that an environmental impact statement must be prepared by the agency that assesses environmental and social impacts of the proposal and alternatives to the project that could reduce adverse impacts. *Hanly v. Mitchell*, 460 F.2d 640 (2d Cir. 1972) (impacts); *National Resources Defense Council v. Morton*, 458 F.2d 827 (D.C. Cir. 1972 (alternatives). Some of the state legislation, like that in California, goes further and requires that the proponent in addition propose mitigation strategies to reduce any unavoidable adverse impacts. *Quail Botanical Gardens Found. v. City of Encinitas*, 35 Cal. Rptr. 2d 470 (Ct. App. 1994); *Cannon v. Murphy*, 600 N.Y.S.2d 965 (Sup. Ct. App. Div. 1993). Canada has also embraced environmental assessment:

> Both provinces and states require some form of environmental assessment. B.C.'s [British Columbia] Environmental Assessment Act provides a legislative framework for review of both major infrastructure and land use projects. Ontario's environmental legislation imposes environmental impact assessment on local government infrastructure, but not land use. Washington's State Environmental Policy Act ("SEPA") imposes environmental impact assessment on local governments, although there are no requirements in Oregon....

Jeffrey Patterson, *Testing the Partnership Model of Growth Management*, 7 Pac. Rim L. & Pol'y J. 721, 747 (1998).

The United States Supreme Court removed much of the heart of the federal law in ruling that the law simply required full disclosure and did not require the court to review the ultimate substantive decisions made regarding the project. *Strycker's Bay Neighborhood Council v. Karlen*, 444 U.S. 223 (1980). Thus, in most cases a federal agency can disclose adverse impacts yet proceed to approve the project. The experience under state environmental impact analysis has been a good deal more protective and the process has contributed to the cancellation or modification of many development proposals that previously would not have been scrutinized. 2 James A. Kushner, Subdivision Law and Growth Management §7:6 (2d ed. 2001); Gail Bowers, *New York's SEQRA in the Courts*, 5 Pace Envtl. L. Rev. 25 (1987); Sean Stuart Varner, Comment, *The California Environmental Quality Act (CEQA) After Two Decades: Relevant Problems and Ideas for Necessary Reform*, 19 Pepp. L. Rev. 1447 (1992). What is most important, however, is that the laws have changed the way agencies review projects. Assessing the various impacts of the projects and looking at alternatives, including a "no-build" alternative, a smaller project, or the phasing of a project over years, are now very much a part of all project review. The law has not, however, had a significant impact on the way communities do comprehensive planning. Even though the development or modification of a comprehensive plan requires environmental impact analysis, communities rarely take a broad look at transportation alternatives and their relation to housing density and sprawl. Community planning typically assumes automobiles and roads. James A. Kushner, *Urban Transportation Planning*, 4 Urb. L. & Pol'y 161 (1981). This failure of the environmental review process to assess and mitigate regional impacts of development has led to the phenomenon that adjacent affected cities or counties may take the lead in challenging projects in nearby communities. It may become common to see central cities challenging the land use planning policies of its surrounding suburban sprawl communities. Even more likely will be suburb against suburb, region or county against region conflicts.

The protection of wetlands has traditionally been the responsibility of the United States Army. Although this may appear strange it is a function of the history of engineering as the military academy at West Point was the sole engineering school in the nation and Congress placed the obligation for the protection of navigable waters, as under the Rivers and Harbors Appropriation Act of 1899, 33 U.S.C. §403, and wetlands, under the Clean Water Act permitting process, 33 U.S.C. §1344(a), with the Army Corps of Engineers. *National Wildlife Fed'n v. Whistler*, 27 F.3d 1341 (8th Cir. 1994). Even state and local projects not involving federal funds or participation where they affect salt or fresh water wetlands require a Corps of Engineers permit. The permit requirement had both a direct environmentally protective effect as decisions were made based upon environmental criteria, and an indirect effect as developers and state and local regulators anticipating federal review were often more likely to impose greater obligations or grant environmentally protective concessions. The experience of the Corps of Engineers protecting wetlands was endangered by the United States Supreme

Court in *Solid Waste Agency of Northern Cook County v. Army Corps of Engineers*, 531 U.S. 159 (2001) , where the conservative Court held that Congress lacked the power to regulate nonnavigable, isolated, intrastate waters, even those that serve as habitat for migratory birds. The Court found the regulation to be not within Congress's Clean Water Act Authority as the wetlands were within states and beyond regulation absent evidence that the wetlands directly affected interstate commerce. *Compare Missouri v. Holland*, 252 U.S. 416 (1920) (sustaining migratory bird protection).

Another significant federal statute is the Endangered Species Act, 16 U.S.C. §§ 1531–44. This law forbids projects that endanger species habitat and has been responsible for halting many projects that threatened rather obscure creatures such as snail darters or owls. The United States Supreme Court sided with conservative Republican administrations in refusing to enforce the Endangered Species Act outside of the fifty American states by holding in *Lujan v. Defenders of Wildlife*, 504 U.S. 555 (1992), that citizens, even if uniquely interested, lacked standing to challenge American funding of international projects that threatened species.

Congress has enacted numerous statutes regulating solid waste disposal, under the Resource Conservation and Recovery Act (RCRA), 42 U.S.C. §§ 6901–6992k, the disposal of toxic waste, including waste treatment, storage, and disposal, Toxic Substances Control Act, Pub. L. No. 94-469, 94th Cong., 2d Sess, 90 Stat. 2003, *codified at* 15 U.S.C. §§ 2601–2692, comprehensively regulating toxic substances, and the availability and contents of pesticides, The Federal Insecticide, Fungicide and Rodentcide Act (FIFRA), ch. 125, 61 Stat. 163 (1947), *amended*, in 1972, by the Federal Environmental Pesticide Control Act, 7 U.S.C. § 136, regulating the sale and distribution of pesticides prohibiting the most toxic of pesticides as well as unregistered pesticides; and the other laws regulating poisons. There also exist mandatory reporting laws, such as the Emergency Planning and Community Right-to-Know Act of 1986 (EPCRA), 42 U.S.C. §§ 11001–11050.

The Federal Government has also enacted legislation dealing with clean water, in the 1972 Federal Water Pollution Control Act Amendments (Clean Water Act), Pub. L. No. 92-500, 86 Stat. 816, *codified at* 33 U.S.C. §§ 1251–1376, establishing a system of standards including the elimination of pollution discharge based on the best economically available technology. The law also established a permit discharge system under Section 402. The 1977 Clean Water Act, Pub. L. No. 95-217, 91 Stat. 1566, allowed certain extensions for compliance and certain waivers. While many of these programs provide standards and offer grants for state and local initiatives for clean water, air, solid and liquid waste disposal, they do not provide machinery for individual project review and approval. The Clean Water Act imposes liability for pollution and may occasionally be responsible for a project denial or modification due to the cumulative impact of projects and activities on a waterway. *Amoco Prod. Co. v. Village of Gambell*, 480 U.S. 531, 542 (1987).

The Clean Air Act, Clean Air Act Amendments of 1970, Pub. L. No. 91-604, 84 Stat. 1676; Arnold W. Reitze, Jr., Air Pollution Control Law: Compliance and Enforcement (2001), is implemented through establishing air quality standards and requiring communities to attain those standards through a combined strategy of transportation initiatives such as high occupancy highway lanes or ridesharing plans and regulating polluting industry. The Clean Air Handbook (Robert J. Martineau, Jr. & David P. Notvello eds. 1998); Stephen E. Roady, *Permitting and Enforcement Under the Clean Air Act Amendments of 1990*, 21 Envtl. L. Rptr. 10178 (1991); Kristen Thall Peters, Legislative Note, *The Clean Air Act and the Amendments of 1990*, 8 Santa Clara Computer & High Tech. L.J. 233 (1992). Compliance is achieved through state-prepared implementation plans and, pursuant to the 1990 Amendments, Pub. L. No. 101-549, 101st Cong., 2d Sess., 104 Stat. 2399, the Environmental Protection Agency (EPA) may impose a plan if the states fail to produce a valid SIP in a timely manner. The laws are typically not focused on individual projects. The Clean Air Act, like the environmental impact laws, can be quite shortsighted in failing to look at regional planning implications. For example, low density suburban sprawl interprets into automobile dependency and adverse air quality implications, while such planning does not run afoul of the law. Similarly, attainment of urban air quality standards may encourage industrial development on the urban fringe, contributing to suburban sprawl and exacerbating access by central city workers and generating more highway automobile travel. Similarly, industry on the fringe allows less urban congestion by trucks and less urban air pollution and thus fringe site location is favored, generating further sprawl.

Another contributor to urban sprawl is the vast accumulation of urban brownfields. Brownfields refers to land that was the site of industrial or other uses, from military bases to gas stations, where chemicals or petroleum products have been spilled, polluting the soil. These brownfields can often spell huge liability for cleanup both for the polluter or for subsequent owners. *New York v. Shore Realty Corp.*, 759 F.2d 1032, 1043-44 (2d Cir. 1985). This exposure to potential liability discourages brownfields cleanup, investment, or reuse, sending developers to the urban fringe where greenfields are available and local politicians are delighted to convert them to brownfields in exchange for tax revenues and local jobs. Under the Comprehensive Environmental Response, Compensation and Liability Act of 1980 (CERCLA), Pub. L. No. 96-510, 91st Cong. 2d Sess., 94 Stat. 2767, *codified at* 42 U.S.C. §§ 9601 to 9675 Congress has established a program to clean up polluted former industrial, military, and other sites. The law, which is popularly known as the "Superfund," was amended by the Superfund Amendments and Reauthorization Act of 1986 (SARA), Pub. L. No. 99-499, 99th Cong. 2d Sess., 100 Stat. 1613, *codified at* 42 U.S.C. §§ 9601–9675, designed to clean up leaking hazardous waste disposal sites. The "superfund" is not super enough to make a significant dent in the accumulated brownfields. Joel B. Eisen, *Brownfields Policies for Sustainable Cities*, 9 Duke Envtl. L. & Pol'y F. 187, 188–189 (1999) (threat of liability discourages use of brownfields in favor of greenfields). Additional federal aid to clean up brownfields to assist private development and provide certain immunity for redevelopers is provided by the Small Business Liability Relief and Brownfields Revitalization Act, Pub. L. No. 107-118 (2002) (H.R. No. 2869 targets incentives to firms of 100 employees or less). *See also* Faith Dylewski, Comment, *Ohio's Brownfield Problem and Possible Solutions: What is Required for a Successful Brownfield Initiative?*, 35 Akron L. Rev. 81 (2001). German brownfields policy, for example, is vastly different as rarely is any development permitted on greenfields and the government is directly involved in subsidizing cleanup efforts. James A. Kushner, *Social Sustainability: Planning for Growth in Distressed Places—the German Experience in Berlin, Wittenberg, and the Ruhr*, 3 Wash. U. J. L. & Pol'y 849 (2000). America by comparison is obsessed with fault and liability and the litigation process, a phenomenon that, along with inexpensive greenfields and welcomming towns on the urban fringe, discourages urban revitalization and fuels suburban sprawl. *Id.*; Eisen, *supra*.

Although more a growth management tool and less of an environmental policy, states have aggressively sought, through taxation preferences, Richard W. Dunford, *A Survey of Property Tax Relief Programs for the Retention of Agriculture and Open Space Lands*, 15 Gonz. L. Rev. 675 (1980), or exemption from nuisance lawsuits, Ariz. Rev. Stat. Ann. § 3-1051, to provide agricultural protection. Rachelle Alterman, *The Challenge of Farmland Preservation: Lessons from a Six-Nation Comparison*, 63 J. Am. Plan. Ass'n 220 (1997); Robert H. Freilich & Linda Kirts Davis, *Saving the Land: The Utiliza-*

tion of Modern Techniques of Growth Management to Preserve Rural and Agricultural America, 13 Urb. Law. 27 (1981). "Right to farm" laws, Randall Wayne Hanna, Comment, *"Right to Farm" Statutes—The Newest Tool in Agricultural Land Preservation*, 10 Fla. St. U.L. Rev. 415 (1982), and deep subsidies in the form of tax forgiveness, Cal. Gov't Code §§ 51200 to 51295 (Williamson Act), have failed to halt the wholesale conversion of urban fringe farmlands to urbanized uses, but they have had some effect in maintaining the attractiveness or profitability of farming and has paradoxically had a greater impact on the environment than most environmental legislation to the extent that farming presents a greenbelt, halting suburbanization and encouraging infill, higher urban density, and urban revitalization. Ironically, farming is typically anything but environmentally friendly as it generates waste, utilizes toxic chemicals and often demands water that comes at great environmental cost, water that becomes a justification for further urbanized sprawl development. In addition, farmland owners in farming districts adjacent to urban communities are often exposed to economic pressure through high land prices offered by developers to sell or become a developer. Paradoxically, American farm prices are low while farm production escalates in hopes of a better environment for foreign trade, including a weaker dollar that would make current prices more attractive to foreign markets. An anonymous English jingle of the 1870s was quoted in Kenneth T. Jackson, Crabgrass Frontier: The Suburbanization of the United States 305 (1985) and captured the farmer's dilemma:

> The richest crop for any field
> Is a crop of bricks for it to yield.
> The richest crop that it can grow,
> Is a crop of houses in a row.

In recent years, environmental theory has shifted to focus on the concept of sustainability. Sim Van Der Ryn & Peter Calthorpe, Sustainable Communities (1986). Sustainability refers to the notion that communities should be self-contained, neither imposing adverse externalities on neighboring communities, nor being excessively dependent on outside resources. Instead of costly and environmentally questionable sewer and disposal systems, sustainability looks to local water purification and sewer treatment, recycling and reuse of the waste materials, the reduction of surface water runoff through capture strategies, and the conversion to bicycles and pedestrianization as compared to the automobile-dominated community. *But see* Sumudu Atapattu, *Sustainable Development, Myth or Reality?: A Survey of Sustainable Development Under International Law and Sri Lankan Law*, 14 Geo. Int'l Envtl. L. Rev. 265 (2001). Similarly architecture, rather than automatically utilizing air conditioning and inexpensive construction techniques, looks more to natural ventilation, porches, and devices such as solar roof panels that can heat water or generate electricity. The following excerpt looks at the path to sustainability that Europe is pursuing more enthusiastically than the United States:

John C. Dernbach, *Sustainable Development as a Framework for National Governance*,

49 Case W. Res. L. Rev. 1 (1998)

In June 1992, at the United Nations Conference on Environment and Development (UNCED) in Rio de Janeiro, the nations of the world agreed to an ambitious and unprecedented global plan of action for addressing the related and growing problems of environmental degradation and poverty. "Humanity stands at a defining moment in history," they stated in Agenda 21, each committing itself to domestic implementation of the Agenda 21 program. Countries also agreed on twenty-seven principles, contained in the Rio Declaration on Environment and Development, to guide their efforts. Agenda 21 and the Rio Declaration embrace "sustainable development," a conceptual framework for achieving economic development that is socially equitable and protective of the natural resource base on which human activity depends. Sustainable development is a response to the deeply held view that environmental degradation is the small price we pay to achieve progress; the price is not small, however, and environmental degradation prevents or threatens social and economic progress. Because of UNCED, sustainable development is also an internationally recognized normative framework for guiding and evaluating the behavior of national governments and other actors.

Yet five years later, in June 1997, the United Nations General Assembly concluded a comprehensive review of progress since UNCED by stating that "overall trends with respect to sustainable development are worse today than they were in 1992." Most countries were able to identify some domestic achievements, and there appeared to be a higher level of public support for sustainable development. In that five-year period, however, few countries adopted or modified laws or policies to change the overall trajectory of their unsustainable development patterns. In addition, their modest actions were dwarfed by growth in the number of people living in poverty around the world and the further deterioration of the global environment. Nations nonetheless reaffirmed their commitment to Agenda 21 and pledged "greater measurable progress in achieving sustainable development" by 2002, when the next comprehensive review is scheduled.

A starting point for making progress, in the United States and other countries, is recognition of the domestic implications of sustainable development. Sustainable development is something of a mystery to domestic policy makers, economists, lawyers and academics, who tend to be separated from their international colleagues by a lack of common language, knowledge and experience. Whatever reasons explain the lack of progress—absence of governmental leadership, political opposition from economic interests representing unsustainable practices, unwillingness to acknowledge the existence of difficult problems—progress can not occur unless we first understand sustainable development....

The basic point of Agenda 21, after all, is action at the national level. Because the framework for governance explains how the reconciliation between environment and development goals should occur, it is also a useful way of understanding what sustainable development means. Although it is not a complete theory for governance, sustainable development would modify both the purposes of national legal systems as well as their means of governance....

To a great extent, domestic acceptance of international norms—whether they are binding or nonbinding under international law—is based on approval or acceptance of the values on which those norms are premised. It is thus generally recognized that domestic implementation of international norms is better achieved through voluntary means than through coercion. Voluntary compliance occurs when states have internalized the norms on which the international rules are based; countries are thus more likely to implement such norms fully and fairly than if they were simply imposed from outside. Norms cannot be internalized unless they are understood.

No such exposition of the sustainable development framework appears in the literature. Instead, the literature tends to view sustainable development primarily in terms of its implications for international law and international institutions. To the extent that it focuses on domestic legal and policy implications, the literature tends to ignore the international texts, bemoan the lack of an accepted definition for sustainable development and then invent a definition or borrow one from another source, or focus only on selected issues. The idea that UNCED created a coherent overall framework for domestic governance has not received serious attention.

The international texts, such as Agenda 21, are important because they have focused international attention on sustainable development, have shaped the meaning of the concept, will continue to shape its meaning, and have begun to make it relevant to national and international decision-making. Because of the political commitment they represent, and their reflection of much of the best current thinking, they deserve consideration in any serious discussion of sustainable development. Indeed, these texts define sustainable development—not in a single sentence but as a bundle of related concepts. It is not possible to select from the bundle certain concepts and describe the result as sustainable development. Nor is it possible to understand the overall framework from even the best discussions of specific issues, such as sustainable forestry or trade....

[S]ustainable development provides a powerful and attractive set of tools for reinvigorating governance. Sustainable development is a pragmatic, coherent and positive response to deteriorating global conditions....The post-World War II development model fails to protect the environment and the natural resources upon which development depends....Sustainable development affirms the importance of social and economic development goals in governance but adds another goal, protection of natural resources and the environment, and emphasizes that these goals must be furthered for the sake of future generations. In addition to environmental protection, sustainable development is also intended to contribute to a more just or equitable social order....

Perhaps the most direct international assertion about development before UNCED is found in the 1986 Declaration on the Right to Development, when the U.N. General Assembly recognized an "inalienable human right" to development. The Declaration describes development as a comprehensive process that involves political freedoms and "equality of opportunity for all in their access to basic resources, education, health services, food, housing, employment and the fair distribution of income." Each human being, the Declaration states, is "entitled to participate in, contribute to, and enjoy economic, social, cultural and political development, in which all human rights and fundamental freedoms can be fully realized." The claim of a right instead of a goal underscores the perceived centrality of development to human dignity and well-being.

The Declaration expressly refers to peace, economic development, social development and supportive national governance as the basic foundations for development. It recognizes that "international peace and security are essential" to development. In addition, it seeks "to promote more rapid development of developing countries," makes several references to economic development or economic rights, and encourages international cooperation for development, although it does not specifically refer to the economic treaties or the institutions they created. The Declaration also emphasizes the realization of human rights as a basic necessity for development, specifically identifying the two human rights covenants. Finally, it acknowledges that states have the primary responsibility for creating conditions favorable to development....

The world's economy "has grown with unprecedented speed" since World War II, and most people have experienced a rise in their standard of living. Yet the traditional development model has foundered for two related reasons: growing poverty and a deteriorating global environment. A growing number of people live in hunger and poverty, and the gap between rich and poor continues to widen. More than a third of the world's population lacks access to a safe water supply. Health risks from the degradation of natural resources and the improper use of chemicals also are increasing. At the beginning of the next century, more than half of the world's population will live in urban areas, and mostly without adequate housing and sanitation.

Unfortunately, the condition of the global environment is also deteriorating. Among other things, we face widespread and even accelerating extinction of plant and animal species, growing emissions of greenhouse gases into the atmosphere, the depletion of fish stocks in oceans throughout the world, loss of farmland and grazing land through overuse and poor practices, and growing and improper use of chemicals. In every region in the world, these conditions are deepening. Despite some positive efforts since UNCED, "the state of the global environment has continued to deteriorate."

These are large, even overwhelming, problems, and they are getting worse. The world's growing population, now estimated at 5.7 billion, will likely level off at about twice its present size, 10 billion, by 2050. In the same period, the global economy will grow to between four and five times its present size. Although current problems are unlikely to become ten times worse by the middle of the 21st century, the basic direction in which conditions are heading is obvious.

These problems are complicated by the increasing globalization of the economy, a phenomenon that has become particularly prominent since UNCED. Globalization is fostered by advances in information technology and transportation as well as treaty-driven trade liberalization over the past several decades. Private transfers of funds from developed countries grew from $44 billion to more than $240 billion between 1990 and 1996. Official development assistance or foreign aid from governments represented more than half of the capital flowing to developing countries at the beginning of this period but less than a fifth at the end. Although the extent to which globalization has penetrated national economies is disputed, its effect has been to facilitate the flow of capital around the world for trade, investment and production. Globalization has greatly contributed to economic and social development in some countries, but other countries and regions are being left behind, further widening the gap between the rich and poor. The influx of investment capital may foster environmental protection in some countries, but international competition for capital may make it even harder for other countries to successfully address environmental degradation and poverty....

Stockholm and After

Environmental protection as an international objective is more recent in origin than development. The first major global conference on the environment, the United Nations Conference on the Human Environment in 1972, grew out of concern for growing environmental degradation around the world. The Stockholm conference, and the preparatory meetings that led to it, produced "a worldwide raising of consciousness" about the environment "for which there appears to be no precedent," reinforced national responsibility for environmental protection, officially recognized the need for cooperative international action and began to bring the environment into the discussion of what development means. The conference also led to the adoption and implementation of environmental laws in many countries, and to a rapid increase in the number and variety of treaties concerning protection of the environment. It did not, however, suggest a way to reconcile development and environment.

The conference produced a declaration of twenty-six principles, known as the Stockholm Declaration, "to inspire and guide the peoples of the world in the preservation and enhancement of the human environment." Perhaps the single most important principle couples the sovereign right of nations to exploit their own resources with responsibility "to ensure that activities within their jurisdiction or control do not cause damage to the environment of other States or of areas beyond the limits of national jurisdiction." This principle asserts both the need for environmentally protective economic development and the interdependence of nations. The Stockholm Declaration also recognizes the relationship between development and environment by stating, among other things, that "[e]conomic and social development is essential for ensuring a favorable living and working environment for man," and that the "environmental policies of all States should enhance and not adversely affect the present or future development potential of developing countries." The Stockholm conference also created a relatively brief action plan. Although it contained a section on development and environment, the plan contained no comprehensive approach to reconciling the two concepts....

The 1992 United Nations Conference on Environment and Development was held as a response to Our Common Future. As its name suggests, UNCED was not just a sequel to the 1972 Stockholm Conference on the Human Environment; it represented a concerted effort to synthesize and integrate environment and development issues. Like Stockholm, Rio's key documents are a statement of principles and a plan of action. For the first time, the international community endorsed sustainable development. Sustainable development changes the prior approach to development, which called for peace and security, economic development, human rights and supportive national governance, by adding a fifth element, protection of the environment. In so doing, it endorsed a framework that could profoundly affect development, particularly economic development.

The delegates to UNCED approved the Rio Declaration on Environment and Development, a statement of twenty-seven principles for sustainable development. One of these principles reflects this synthesis by asserting the importance of equitably fulfilling the "developmental and environmental needs of present and future generations." Some of these principles also are contained, in slightly different form, in the Stockholm Declaration.

More important than the Rio Declaration, however, is Agenda 21, a comprehensive international "plan of action" or blueprint for sustainable development. It represents a broad and detailed commitment by nations around the world to take actions to further sustainable development. Agenda 21 is based to a great extent on the application, in particular contexts, of the principles stated in the Rio Declaration. The Agenda 21 commitment is not binding in international law, but it does represent a political commitment. Agenda 21 meant, and continues to mean, that the real work of UNCED is to occur in each country. The success or failure of UNCED, in short, ultimately depends on implementation of Agenda 21.

Agenda 21 is divided into four sections and a total of forty chapters. The sections concern social and economic issues, conservation and management of natural resources, the role of major groups and the means of implementation. Representative chapters within these sections concern poverty, production and consumption patterns, combating deforestation, management of sewage and solid wastes, the role of nongovernmental organizations, the role of business and industry, science for sustainable development and information for decision-making. Each chapter describes the factual basis for recommended actions, the objective of those actions, the particular activities that governments and others should take and the entities that need to support and fund these activities....

Agenda 21 established a process for reviewing the progress of individual nations in achieving sustainable development. Each year after 1992, the Commission on Sustainable Development (CSD), a newly created entity which is part of the United Nations system, was to review overall implementation of Agenda 21. In addition, Agenda 21 recommended a comprehensive review by the U.N. General Assembly for 1997.

In the years immediately following UNCED, there were separate international conferences on social development, women, population and development, human settlements, food and other issues. Each of them produced reports that, in varying ways, restated or elaborated on themes contained in Agenda 21 or the Rio Declaration. When the General Assembly met in June 1997 to perform the comprehensive five-year review of progress since UNCED, its Programme for the Further Implementation of Agenda 21 incorporated major conclusions from those conferences.

In addition to reaffirming the UNCED commitment to Agenda 21, the 1997 General Assembly meeting slightly modified the process for implementation review. The CSD will continue to meet annually to review progress, but its reviews will focus more on particular issues and less on overall implementation. The next comprehensive General Assembly review is scheduled for 2002.

Fortunately, there is evidence that sustainable development is possible. Pollution-control laws in the United States and other developed countries have made cities more liveable, lakes and rivers more suitable for recreation, workplaces safer and the air healthier—even as the economies of those countries have grown. In addition, many communities and businesses have been able to further environmental protection, social progress and economic development at the same time. Sustainable development requires us to improve upon, and extrapolate from, these experiences....

Treaties can help clarify sustainable development norms. The parties to each treaty meet regularly, often annually, to examine progress in implementation and to identify problems. Many treaties, particularly environmental treaties, authorize the adoption of protocols to specify the legal obligations of countries with much greater particularity than the original convention....

International conferences on various issues also help create consensus on important aspects of sustainable development....

The experience of the European Community as well as federal systems such as the United States can provide some assistance in solving that problem. Among other lessons, the United States and European Community record suggests the value of addressing particular problems through national goals or standards, and of giving lower levels of government some flexibility in establishing the means by which those goals or standards are achieved. Such an approach requires the national government to decide generally what needs to be done and assigns responsibility for determining how to implement national goals or standards within its jurisdiction to lower levels of government....

In addition to moving toward sustainable development on their own, developed countries are urged to provide financial, technical, and other assistance to help developing countries fulfill their sustainable development responsibilities. In Agenda 21, developed countries stated their commitment to contribute 0.7% of their gross domestic product to official development assistance for sustainable development on an annual basis, provide technical assistance, facilitate the use of environmental technologies in developing countries, and help developing countries improve their capacity to govern in a responsible and sustainable manner. In so doing, they agreed to change the purpose of their official assistance from development to sustainable development.

Scientific and technological capacity building, and capacity building for governance, are important needs. Agenda 21 recognizes that the provision of new and more efficient technologies to developing countries is necessary for sustainable development, and it recommends that such technologies be provided on favorable terms....

An effective legal framework is necessary for sustainable development. Agenda 21 calls on governments to adopt and implement laws and policies that successfully guide both private and governmental decisions for sustainable development, and to regularly assess and modify them when appropriate to improve their effectiveness. Governments also should establish strategies to ensure compliance with their laws as well as procedures for judicial and administrative review. These recommendations suggest a two pronged approach. Each country should conduct an ongoing review and classification of existing laws to identify and repeal or modify laws that hinder sustainable development. In addition, countries should adopt laws and policies that are necessary to foster sustainable development. In both cases, they need to make sure that these changes are implemented....

Most, if not all, governments currently have laws and policies that encourage, support or provide incentives for public and private activities that are not sustainable. Before governments even begin to act to foster sustainable development, they need to recognize that they likely have acted in a variety of ways to discourage it. Sustainable development is not possible unless those laws and policies are modified or repealed. Agenda 21 recognizes the existence of such instruments in most countries, particularly in the form of tax incentives and subsidies....

Subsidies are perhaps the most obvious incentive for unsustainable development. Subsidies are measures that reduce costs for producers and consumers below the level they would otherwise pay in the market. Subsidies include direct government expenditures, tax subsidies and the public provision of goods and services below market cost. Governments of developed and developing countries annually provide hundreds of billions of dollars of subsidies for unsustainable energy production, road transport, water use and agriculture. In many countries, subsidies keep energy and water prices artificially low, encouraging inefficiency and waste.

Subsidies also have played a major role in creating and supporting unsustainable land use patterns. Road users pay only 79% of the costs of road infrastructure in the United States, for example, which means that taxpayers pay the rest. Taxpayers thus help subsidize new and improved roads that contribute to suburban sprawl, automobile air pollution and energy consumption....

A system based on goals requires a means for assuring that they are realized. Planning needs to be undertaken to further various goals and to ensure consideration of relationships among goals. Instead of simply responding to each crisis as it comes, the sustainable development goals suggest the importance of looking ahead, deciding what kind of world we want to live in and how to get there. Planning provides the link between goals and results. By considering all aspects of a problem from the beginning, planning makes it more likely that development and environment goals will be reconciled. Planning to prevent problems also is less costly and more effective than the use of regulatory tools to control or clean up problems once they have been created.

For all its strengths, planning also is associated with top-down governance in Soviet-bloc countries by planners who were supposed to have perfect current knowledge and the ability to anticipate all future events. Of course, planners do not have that knowledge or ability, especially for the wide range of matters covered by Agenda 21. Nor is government by planners likely to be democratic. Fortunately, that is not the kind of planning recommended in Agenda 21 and the Rio Declaration....

Agenda 21 recognizes the importance of traditional regulatory approaches to environmental protection because the market, by itself, can not adopt binding limits on individual or corporate behavior. Nor can the market establish the necessary legal procedures for the achievement of social, economic and environmental goals. Traditional means of environmental regulation, which include prohibitions, standard-setting and permit requirements, as well as the necessary administrative and enforcement mechanisms, are thus a necessary part of sustainable development. Regulation also is necessary to ensure that monitoring is conducted and to establish a level playing field for economic competitors. The protection of natural resources and ecological systems is not likely to be effective without regulation....

Taxes are a particularly important tool. While they could be used to raise new revenue, taxes also could be revenue-neutral, shifting taxation toward materials, energy and pollution, and away from labor and investment. A task force in the United States concluded that "no other single policy step could so effectively and at so low a cost move the country toward more efficient—and eventually sustainable—resource use." Denmark, Finland, the Netherlands, and Sweden have begun such a shift in taxation. In addition to reducing pollutants, this approach also might have a small but positive effect on employment, particularly if the social security tax for low-wage workers were reduced....

One particularly ambitious proposal gives a flavor of what such changes could mean. It involves an annual 5% increase in the tax for fossil fuels and certain other natural resources over a 30- to 40-year period. Among other things, such a tax likely would reduce the consumption of energy and certain materials. Because of the gradual increase over an extended period, it also would ease the transition to more efficient use of materials and energy, as well as encourage development of alternatives to fossil fuels....

Property law in many countries has tended to encourage development of land without much consideration of the environment. Sustainable development thus requires changes in many property laws as well as other laws that affect the use of property. The basic challenge is to ensure that property owners are encouraged by law to use their property in a sustainable manner. This type of encouragement would be consistent with broad public participation in sustainable development because property owners, as property owners, would be advancing the work of sustainable development. It also would be consistent with local-level decision-making because property owners usually are situated close to the land they own. Finally, property-owner-based decision-making may yield better results than governmental decision-making because property owners understand conditions on their land better than the government.

Sustainable uses by landowners are most likely to occur, as Agenda 21 recognizes, if the laws relating directly to real property ownership oblige owners to integrate environmental, social and economic considerations into their day-to-day decision-making. A basic fear of property owners is that government action to protect the environment will reduce property value or the uses to which property can be put. Of course, such laws would have to steer clear of constitutional prohibitions against governmental takings of property without compensation. A variety of constitutional mechanisms are available, including disclosure requirements and tradeable use rights, although such mechanisms would need to be tailored to sustainable development. In addition, property tax laws could be written or modified to provide reduced or no property tax for lands that are managed for biodiversity or other sustainable uses. Similarly, a recently adopted Costa Rican law seeks to maintain important ecological services provided by private property left in natural cover by compensating landowners for keeping it in that condition....

Two major concerns remain to be addressed, and they are related. One is that sustainable development lacks sufficient grounding in international law to be taken seriously. The other is that it represents such a major challenge to existing power structures that governments will not allow it to occur. For all its conceptual strengths, the sustainable development framework has some significant weaknesses. It is based primarily on nonbinding legal instruments. The environmental treaties as a whole contain significant gaps and are based on incompletely articulated norms. Furthermore, the framework does not reconcile trade and the environment.... Such agreements are not trivial, but agreements based on treaties are binding in international law and are thus taken more seriously. As a result, the legal force of agreements such as Agenda 21 is not likely to play a major role in any global effort to achieve sustainable development. At best, Agenda 21 and related texts put the conceptual framework into play, making it part of a continuing dialogue in international discussions. Through these discussions, sustainable development is beginning to be incorporated into legal norms. For sustainable development to occur, however, nations must see the framework as sensible or attractive in its own right, wholly apart from its status in international law....

Soft-law sustainable development norms already are being translated into hard international law. For example, the 1995 agreement on straddling and highly migratory fish stocks details the ways in which states should use the precautionary approach to protect fish stocks. By identifying sustainable development as a relevant concept in a recent case, moreover, the International Court of Justice indicated that sustainable development may have legal stature independent of its inclusion in treaties. In addition, some international organizations are incorporating sustainable development concepts into their practices even though the underlying treaty has not changed. The World Bank, for example, has begun to fund projects that foster sustainable development. As these actions become more frequent, the legal and practical differences between sustainable development and the treaty implementation processes shrink....

Public choice theory attempts to understand the ways in which individuals and corporations use government, and particularly legislatures, to further their own ends. By using government to further their particular interests, groups enrich themselves at the expense of unrepresented groups, direct government resources in socially unproductive ways and undermine democratic governance. In many cases, governments or governmental officials are simply corrupt.

As public choice theory indicates, sustainable development will not be realized unless it includes a means of overcoming the power of these interests. National governments already encourage and support unsustainable activities through subsidies and other means. This support is facilitated by separate consideration of environmental and economic issues, by a range of existing laws and practices, and by a tendency to limit environmental protection tools to regulation. These disparities between sustainable development and current practice in individual countries are not substantially challenged by existing treaties. In the case of trade, treaties may even reinforce those disparities. The failure of governments to accomplish much in the first five years after the Earth

Summit surely is due in part to their unwillingness to confront economic interests that these governments both depend on and support. An irony of this conceptual framework, and a potential barrier to its implementation, is that it depends on the same governments that are now contributing to unsustainable development....

We live at a defining moment in human history, as Agenda 21 says, because we have a choice between two paths. Growing poverty, environmental degradation and globalization of the economy call into question not just the purpose and effectiveness of governments but also the kind of world in which we and future generations will live. Sustainable development offers an alternative path that is difficult and challenging but which provides hope for a better world for ourselves and future generations. We can not take the latter path, however, unless we first recognize that we have a choice.

* * *

Notes and Comments

1. What sorts of American planning initiatives are consistent or inconsistent with Agenda 21? Does America's failure to support the Kyoto Accords on global warming suggest a problem in the pursuit of sustainability? David E. Sanger & Alessandra Stanley, *Genoa Summit Meeting: The Overview; Allies Tell Bush They'll Act Alone on Climate Accord*, New York Times, July 22, 2001, §1, at 1; David E. Sanger, *Bush will Continue to Oppose Kyoto Pact on Global Warming*, New York Times, Jun. 12, 2001, §A, at 1. After the War on Terrorism, following September 11, 2001, will the environment become an even lower priority, or will Europe and other regional support for America's undertaking result in America becoming less isolationist and generate support for trade and environmental initiatives of concern to our partners? How might the war affect urban sprawl? There was virtually no truly high-rise development in America since the mid-1990s, having fallen off dramatically since the 1980s. Jesus Sanchez, *Skyscrapers: Downsized by History*, Los Angeles Times, Nov. 12, 1996. Will consumers and developers be even more enthusiastic about bucolic low density lifestyles far from the city center? Describe a program of "smart anti-terrorism."

2. Smart Growth has been criticized as masking the more important and more elusive goal of sustainability. Timothy Beatley & Richard Collins, *Smart Growth and Beyond: Transitioning to a Sustainable Society*, 19 Va. Envtl. L.J. 287, 296–301, 307 (2000) (advocating a steeply progressive tax on consumption, recognizing affluent consumption, such as the impact of vacation homes on sprawl).

3. Sometimes simple solutions are complex. A Simple initiative designed to encourage conservation is a universal metering system for water and sewer use reflecting marginal cost increase of increased usage, as utilized in electrical pricing systems. The problem is that it dramatically increases costs in low-income housing, threatening the viability of the housing stock. Dick Netzer, Michael Schill & Scott Susin, *Changing Water and Sewer Finance: Distributional Impacts and Effects in the Viability of Affordable Housing*, 67 J. Am. Plan. Ass'n 420 (2001) (based on New York experience). Would a simple answer be to offer a subsidized "life-line" rate for consumers of lower income? Utility bills themselves may have a direct and distinct conservation incentive for the poor. Of course the affluent can afford conservation technology such as solar or water-saving appliances and fixtures, and despite pricing problems, are likely to be oblivious to the costs of their lengthy showers.

13. Bio01 Sustainable new city in Malmö, Sweden 2001.

Environmental Racism

A sad confluence of American environmental and civil rights policy has been a pattern of placing the most environmentally degrading activities in communities with the least political power, although this sometimes involves sparse white affluent communities on the urban fringe, it is most commonly lower income communities and communities composed of people of color that are the site for industry, prisons, and uses involving pollution and heavy trucking operations. This pattern has been termed "environmental racism" by its critics. Environmental Protection and Justice (Kenneth A. Manaster ed. 1995); Lynn E. Blais, *Environmental Racism Reconsidered*, 75 N.C. L. Rev. 75 (1996) (arguing that the ostensible pattern of racism is the result of rational and legitimate preferences of individuals); Luke W. Cole, *Remedies for Environmental Racism: A View from the Field*, 90 Mich. L. Rev. 1991 (1992); Robert W. Collin, *Review of the Legal Literature on Environmental Racism, Environmental Equity, and Environmental Justice*, 9 J. Envtl. L. & Litig. 121 (1994). Although environmental racism can be an effective political challenge before local legislatures, it has yet to find broad acceptance in the courts. The principle problem is that the equal protection clause requires proof of purposefulness and will not impose liability simply on the impact of the government action. *Washington v. Davis*, 426 U.S. 229 (1976). Government may argue that it chose the site because land was cheaper or political opposition less. Courts appear to demand that challengers prove that a decision was made on the basis of race, such as a clear admission that siting an activity was designed to expel a racial group from the community. This is obviously a near-impossible burden and any government entity should be able to present their decision-making process in neutral terms. Civil rights activists have advocated use of the Civil Rights laws such as Title VI of the 1964 Civil Rights Act because courts have on occasion allowed proof to be based on the impact rather than the intent of the activity. The environmental community was emboldened when the Clinton Administration Environmental Protection Agency issued regulations establishing an effects test standard in reviewing agency action. 40 C.F.R. § 7.80. The conservative United States Supreme Court may have diminished the effectiveness of these regulations, ruling that the public lacks the right to enforce such regulations. *Alexander v. Sandoval*, 532 U.S. 275 (2001), discussed after the *Camden* case, in refused to allow citizen suits to enforce agency nondiscrimination regulations. Thus, any willingness to enforce the rules must come from the agency itself, an occurrence not expected from the Bush Administration. Although litigation is likely to continue seeking liability under impacts theories under Title VI, 42 U.S.C. § 2000d (1994) or Title VIII, the Fair Housing Act, 42 U.S.C. §§ 3601–20, 3631 (1994 & Supp. I 1995). There is still the likelihood that courts will identify neutral justifications that can overcome disparate impacts of projects or activities.

Too often, poor neighborhoods and the communities occupied with significant populations of people of color, are the selected sites for land uses that bring pollution, commercial and industrial traffic and present a further structural impediment to urban revitalization. Such uses are typically excluded as NIMBYs (Not in My Backyard) by more affluent and politically powerful suburban communities. The following case, authored by a sensitive jurist prior to *Sandoval*, discusses the burdens of proof in environmental justice litigation:

South Camden Citizens in Action v. New Jersey Department of Environmental Protection

United States District Court for the District of New Jersey
145 F. Supp. 2d 446 (2001)

Orlofsky, District Judge

Plaintiffs' application for preliminary injunctive and declaratory relief presents difficult and novel issues arising under Title VI of the Civil Rights Act of 1964, 42 U.S.C. § 2000d, which prohibits discrimination based on race and national origin by recipients of federal funding. At its heart, this dispute centers around the allegedly racially discriminatory siting of an industrial facility in an impoverished neighborhood of Camden, New Jersey, ninety-one % of whose residents are persons of color.

To understand the nature of the issues presented, I shall set forth a brief summary of the operative facts. Plaintiff, South Camden Citizens In Action ("SCCIA"), is an unincorporated community organization, whose members are residents of a neighborhood in Camden, New Jersey, known as "Waterfront South." The individual Plaintiffs are residents of Waterfront South and members of SCCIA. Defendant, the New Jersey Department of Environmental Protection ("NJDEP"), a New Jersey state agency, is responsible for enforcing the environmental laws and regulations of the State of New Jersey, as well as federal law, where applicable. The NJDEP receives federal funding and is thus obliged to conform its operations to the restrictions imposed by Title VI and the regulations which have been promulgated to implement Title VI. Defendant, Robert C. Shinn, Jr. ("Shinn"), is the Commissioner of the NJDEP. Defendant Intervenor, St. Lawrence Cement Co., L.L.C. ("SLC"), manufactures and distributes cement products. SLC has built and proposes to operate a facility in Waterfront South to grind and process granulated blast furnace slag ("GBFS"). SLC sells the ground GBFS as an additive to portland cement.

SLC's proposed facility will emit certain pollutants into the air. These pollutants will include particulate matter (dust), mercury, lead, manganese, nitrogen oxides, carbon monoxide, sulphur oxides and volatile organic compounds. The GBFS will arrive by barge at a Camden port facility. Trucks will then deliver the GBFS to SLC's proposed facility in Waterfront South, a distance of approximately three miles. The GBFS will then be processed and transported back to the port by truck. Annually, there will be approximately 35,000 inbound delivery trucks arriving at SLC's proposed facility and approximately 42,000 outbound truck deliveries departing from the facility. Inbound truck deliveries will occur on about eighty days per year with approximately 500 truck deliveries per day. Outbound truck departures from the SLC facility will occur on approximately 225 days per year, with about 200 trucks departing per day. The contemplated truck routes pass through the Waterfront South Community.

The population of Waterfront South is 2,132, forty-one percent of whom are children. Ninety-one percent of the residents of Waterfront South are persons of color. Specifically, sixty-three percent are African-American, twenty-eight percent are Hispanic, and nine percent are non-Hispanic white. The residents of Waterfront South suffer from a disproportionately high rate of asthma and other respiratory ailments.

The Waterfront South neighborhood is already a popular location for the siting of industrial facilities. It contains the Camden County Municipal Utilities Authority, a sewage treatment plant, the Camden County Resource Recovery facility, a trash-to-steam plant, the Camden Cogen Power Plant, a co-generation plant, and two United States Environmental Protection Agency ("EPA") designated Superfund sites. Four sites within one-half mile of SLC's proposal facility are currently being investigated by the EPA for the possible release of hazardous substances. The NJDEP has also identified fifteen known contaminated sites in the Waterfront South neighborhood.

As described in greater detail in this Court's Findings of Fact and Conclusions of Law set forth below, the NJDEP granted the necessary air permits to SLC to allow its proposed facility to begin operations. In doing so, the NJDEP considered only whether the facility's emissions would exceed technical emissions standards for specific pollutants, especially dust. Indeed, much of what this case is about is what the NJDEP failed to consider. It did not consider the level of ozone generated by the truck traffic to and from the SLC facility, notwithstanding the fact that the Waterfront South community is not currently in compliance with the National Ambient Air Quality Standard ("NAAQS") established by the EPA for ozone levels, nor did it consider the presence of many other pollutants in Waterfront South. It did not consider the pre-existing poor health of the residents of Waterfront South, nor did it consider the cumulative environmental burden already borne by this impoverished community. Finally, and perhaps most importantly, the NJDEP failed to consider the racial and ethnic composition of the population of Waterfront South....

This case presents the novel question of whether a recipient of EPA funding has an obligation under Title VI to consider racially discriminatory disparate impacts when determining whether to issue a permit, in addition to compliance with applicable environmental standards. For the reasons set forth below, I conclude that on the facts of this case, the NJDEP had such an obligation and failed to discharge it....

All entities which receive EPA financial assistance must submit an assurance to the EPA with their application that they will comply with the requirements of EPA's regulations implementing Title VI. 40 C.F.R. § 7.80.[6]...

---

6. 40 C.F.R. § 7.80, provides, in relevant part, as follows:

(a) Assurances—

(1) General. Applicants for EPA assistance shall submit an assurance with their applications stating that, with respect to their programs or activities that receive EPA assistance,

Section 602 of Title VI clearly authorizes federal agencies, such as the EPA, to promulgate regulations implementing Section 601....

Following this general prohibition, the EPA regulations promulgated pursuant to the EPA's authority to implement Title VI, section 602, include the following "specific prohibitions" cited here in relevant part:

> (b) A recipient shall not use criteria or methods of administering its program which have the effect of subjecting individuals to discrimination because of their race, color, national origin, or sex, or have the effect of defeating or substantially impairing accomplishment of the objectives of the program with respect to individuals of a particular race, color, national origin, or sex.
>
> (c) A recipient shall not choose a site or location of a facility that has the purpose or effect of excluding individuals from, denying them the benefits of, or subjecting them to discrimination under any program to which this part applies on the grounds of race, color, or national origin or sex; or with the purpose or effect of defeating or substantially impairing the accomplishment of the objectives of this subpart.
>
> (d) The specific prohibitions of discrimination enumerated above do not limit the general prohibition of § 7.30.

40 C.F.R. § 7.35.

The EPA has specifically interpreted Title VI to prohibit recipients of EPA funding from utilizing "criteria and methods" which have the "purpose or effect" of discrimination against individuals based on their race, color, or national origin. 40 C.F.R. § 7.35(b). Furthermore, the EPA eliminated any possible doubt that its Title VI implementing regulations apply to permitting decisions by recipients, such as the NJDEP, by specifically extending Title VI prohibitions to permitting decisions....

I conclude, therefore, that the application of the burden-shifting analysis to the claim raised by Plaintiffs in this case, which alleges disparate impact on the basis of a permitting decision, in violation of the EPA's Title VI implementing regulations, presents this Court with an issue of first impression....

The basis for Plaintiffs' prima facie case, and the essence of their claim, is their allegation that the NJDEP's decision to permit the construction and operation of the SLC facility in Waterfront South, a neighborhood whose population is overwhelmingly African-American and Hispanic, is already home to a disproportionate number of the state's environmentally hazardous, pollutant-producing facilities, and whose residents already suffer poor health, disparately and adversely affects the residents of that community in violation of Title VI.

It is uncontested that the NJDEP's permitting policy is facially neutral. The NJDEP uses a complicated system, including air dispersion modeling, to predict the level and pattern of pollutant emissions from a proposed facility such as the SLC facility. The NJDEP then compares these results to the federally established NAAQS, set by the EPA, for the particular pollutants which will be produced by the facility. As counsel for the

---

they will comply with the requirements of this Part. Applicants must also submit any other information that the OCR determines is necessary for preaward review. The applicant's acceptance of EPA assistance is an acceptance of the obligation of this assurance and this Part. 40 C.F.R. § 7.80.

NJDEP explained at oral argument, once the NJDEP reaches the conclusion that a proposed facility will be in compliance with the NAAQS, the NJDEP's inquiry into the environmental impacts of the facility stops, and the NJDEP will issue a permit to operate the proposed facility....

Plaintiffs contend that the operation of the proposed facility will adversely impact them in several ways. After reviewing the record, I have determined that the primary adverse impacts of which Plaintiffs complain are impacts to the health of the residents who live in the Waterfront South neighborhood where the proposed SLC facility is located. While Plaintiffs also complain of adverse effects to their quality of life, caused by the noise, vibrations and dirt associated with the truck traffic which will traverse the neighborhood if the facility becomes operational, I have concluded that the record in this case is insufficient to support such a claim. Accordingly, I shall deny Plaintiffs' request for a preliminary injunction to the extent that it is based on the alleged adverse impact of the operation of the SLC facility on Plaintiffs' quality of life.

The operation of the proposed facility will impact the health of the residents of the Waterfront South community in two specific ways. First, particulate matter emitted from the proposed SLC facility will affect respiratory function in the members of the surrounding community, a disproportionate number of whom already suffer from asthma and other respiratory conditions which will be aggravated by the inhalation of particulate matter. Second, the ozone generated by the annual migration of 77,000 trucks making deliveries to and from the SLC facility will impact residents' health because it aggravates respiratory function and causes cancer. The Court has also found that the Waterfront South community in general, and African-American members of the community in particular, already suffer disproportionately high rates of cardiovascular disease and respiratory disease such as asthma.

The question that remains, however, is whether these impacts are sufficiently "adverse" to support a conclusion that Plaintiffs have carried this portion of their burden in making out a prima facie case of disparate impact discrimination under Title VI....

Applying the Third Circuit's disparate impact analysis for Title VI cases, the final element of a plaintiff's *prima facie* case is the demonstration that the alleged adverse disparate impact is causally linked to defendant's facially neutral policy....

In this case, Plaintiffs rely primarily on the Certification of Dr. Gelobter to demonstrate a causal link between the disparity of distribution of industrial, pollutant-producing facilities in New Jersey and the NJDEP's facially neutral permitting policy, which is based exclusively on compliance with the NAAQS. Specifically, Dr. Gelobter undertook a regression analysis of the relationship between EPA-regulated facilities and the percentage of non-whites in a ZIP Code area. The results of the regression analysis indicate that the odds that there is no relationship between the percentage of non-white residents and number of facilities in a ZIP Code area are approximately three in 10 million.

The NJDEP did not brief the issue of causation for the same reason it did not brief the issue of disparity: once the NJDEP decided that the impact of proposed SLC facility would not be "adverse," because the facility's emissions will not cause an exceedence of the PM-10 NAAQS, the NJDEP terminated its analysis of Plaintiffs' disparate impact claim....

SLC contends that based on Dr. Gelobter's analysis, Plaintiffs make an "unsubstantiated leap" to the conclusion that the NJDEP's permitting process is causally linked to the admitted disparity in the distribution of industrial facilities in the State of New Jersey. According to SLC, this Court must reject Dr. Gelobter's data on causation because he failed to consider all of the factors that could account for the siting of industrial facilities in particular areas, such as access to transportation, existing infrastructure, and available labor force. Thus, SLC asserts that "even assuming the statistical evidence that Plaintiffs have produced is accurate, those statistics are not the result of some defect in NJDEP's permitting process, but are rather the result of hundreds, if not thousands, of individual siting decisions made by private entities searching on the basis of sound business principles for the most appropriate locations for their industrial facilities."

I reject SLC's argument for several reasons. First, this Court has already concluded that there is in fact a severe "defect" in the NJDEP's permitting process, namely, that the NJDEP relies exclusively on compliance with environmental regulations such as the NAAQS, without considering its obligations under Title VI, in issuing permits such as those it issued for the proposed SLC facility.

Second, a review of the applicable regulations promulgated by the EPA clearly indicates that the EPA has determined that there is a causal connection between recipients' permitting practices and the distribution of polluting facilities, and enacted the implementing regulations to Title VI to ensure that recipients consider the potential disparate impact of their permitting decisions. In other words, the EPA has acknowledged that because recipients are responsible for permitting, they are also responsible for considering the distribution of the facilities which they permit with respect to the classes protected by the Civil Rights Act of 1964. The regulations therefore support the conclusion that a recipient's permitting decisions are causally linked to the distribution of facilities as a matter of law....

[A]fter the plaintiff establishes a *prima facie* case of disparate impact discrimination, the defendant has the opportunity to rebut the resulting inference of discrimination by showing that it had a "substantial legitimate justification" or a "legitimate nondiscriminatory reason" for its practice.

The NJDEP did not specifically address the issue of justification, again, because it terminated its disparate impact analysis, with the conclusion that the proposed SLC facility would not violate the PM-10 NAAQS and therefore would not "adversely" affect Plaintiffs....

SLC, however, has offered several justifications for the NJDEP's decision. These include: (1) the fact that the proposed SLC facility was in compliance with the NAAQS and all applicable environmental regulations; (2) the fact that SLC and the NJDEP "consulted with the community;" and (3) the fact that the City of Camden "needs the economic and social benefits that come with a renewed industrial presence attuned to its environmental responsibilities."...

In the absence of guiding legal precedent on the question of what constitutes a "substantial legitimate justification" or a "legitimate nondiscriminatory reason" in the context of this case, I shall look to EPA regulations and practice.

According to the Draft Revised Investigation Guidance, once the EPA OCR makes a finding that a proposed facility will have an adverse, disparate impact on the complainants, "[t]he recipient will have the opportunity to 'justify' the decision to issue the permit notwithstanding the adverse disparate impact, based on a substantial, legitimate justification." The Guidance cautions that "determining what constitutes an acceptable justification will necessarily be based on the facts of the case," but states that "generally, the recipient would attempt to show that the challenged activity is reasonably necessary to meet a goal that is legitimate, important, and integral to the recipient's institutional mission." The Guidance identifies the following types of justifications as examples which the EPA might consider substantial and legitimate: (1) a demonstration that the permitting action will provide a public health or environmental benefit to the affected population; (2) a demonstration that the permitting action will have economic benefit, if the benefit is "delivered directly to the affected population." *Id.* In assessing the validity of an economic justification, OCR will consider both the recipient's perspective, and the affected community's perspective, on whether the permitted facility will in fact provide direct economic benefits to the community.

I conclude that the record in the present case is insufficient for me to determine whether the NJDEP can provide a "substantial, legitimate justification," in the context of Title VI analysis, for its permitting decision. SLC did not cite any applicable legal, statutory, or regulatory source to support its conclusion that the NJDEP provided sufficient justification for its decision to permit the SLC facility. Neither the NJDEP nor SLC has addressed the NJDEP's potential justifications with reference to the guidelines suggested by the EPA, which, as I have stated, are the only source this Court can find that specifically addresses a Title VI rebuttal analysis in permitting decisions.

Accordingly, because Defendants have failed to carry their rebuttal burden, Plaintiffs have established a likelihood of success on the merits....

* * *

Notes and Comments

1. In *Alexander v. Sandoval*, 532 U.S. 275 (2001), decided after *South Camden*, the United States Supreme Court ostensibly took the wind out of the environmental justice sails in ruling that citizens lacked a private right of action, or the right to bring lawsuits, to enforce regulations issued by federal agencies under Title VI. The district court reconsidered its ruling in light of *Sandoval* and proceeded to grant the requested preliminary injunction, distinguishing *Sandoval*, finding that ruling to be limited to the holding that Section 602 of Title VI does not *itself* create a private right of action, and noting that *Sandoval* did not invalidate the disparate impact regulations. 145 F. Supp. 2d 505 (D. N.J. 2001). The Third Circuit reversed *South Camden*, holding that EPA regulations are unenforceable through § 1983, and that agencies lack authority to issue regulations authorizing impact-based tests where statutes establish an intent standard. 274 F.3d 771 (3d Cir. 2001).

2. Should the Supreme Court decide to abandon the disparate effects statutory standard or announce a broader extension of *Sandoval*, a theory that might offer an alternative to the disparate impact approach is one based on cases involving municipal service equalization. In a number of cases, first arising in the South, courts condemned obvious racism in the form of cities providing paved streets, sewers, and lighting to white neighborhoods but not black neighborhoods. *Hawkins v. Town of Shaw*, 437 F.2d 1286 (5th Cir. 1971), *aff'd en banc*, 461 F.2d 1171 (5th Cir. 1972). Where evidence demonstrates disparate policies of siting unpopular uses, the equal protection and civil rights statutes may be more effective in combating environmental racism. *See also* Charles M. Haar & Daniel W. Fessler, The Wrong Side of the Tracks (1986) (recommending state law strategies to equalize municipal services). *But cf. Beal v. Lindsay*, 468 F.2d 286 (2d Cir. 1972) (focus on equality of inputs and not results). Does *Beal* suggest that formula-based service funding provided on an equal basis, such as based on the extent of use, would be valid? Under such a formula, well used parks or libraries in affluent neighbor-

hoods would receive greater funding than underused, less attractive facilities in poorer neighborhoods.

3. If the environmental justice movement is ultimately successful, in addition to a reformed permitting process that assures a fair and sensitive evaluation of applications for racial and socioeconomic impacts, will industry and other economic activities be redirected toward the urban fringe? How can environmental justice be achieved without exacerbating urban sprawl?

4. Are environmental justice concerns unique to the United States? How might globalization affect the environment of the world's poor?

Carmen G. Gonzalez, *Beyond Eco-Imperialism: An Environmental Justice Critique of Free Trade,*

78 Denver University Law Review 979 (2001)

As trade ministers from 135 nations gathered in Seattle for the Third Ministerial Conference of the World Trade Organization (WTO) in late November 1999, over 50,000 protesters, including farmers, trade unionists, and environmentalists, joined forces in a raucous demonstration of opposition to the current organization of the global economy. The massive protests, which quickly became known as the "Battle in Seattle," featured teach-ins, rallies, marches and other events designed to draw attention to the WTO's impact on labor, environmental, food safety, human rights and consumer protection measures.

Media coverage of the issues underlying the protests emphasized the WTO's threat to U.S. environmental and labor laws and posited a conflict between developed countries' concerns for workers' rights and environmental protection on the one hand and developing countries' needs for unfettered economic growth on the other. In so doing, the media reports evoked the familiar image of environmentalism as a new form of imperialism, whereby the environmental preferences and priorities of the wealthy countries of the North are imposed on the poor countries of the South. While this carefully constructed media image contains a kernel of truth, it also perpetuates two powerful myths that obscure the relationship among free trade, environmental protection and social justice. The first myth is that environmental protection is a luxury that developing countries can ill afford. The second myth is that industrialized countries have generally played a leadership role in the protection of the global environment. This article attempts to deconstruct these myths in order to critique the environmental consequences of trade liberalization from an environmental justice perspective....

One important element missing in much of the scholarly literature about trade and the environment is a critical assessment of the environmental imperialism claim. To what extent do the North's efforts to integrate environmental protection into the international trade regime constitute an imposition of Northern values and preferences on less powerful nations? This article attempts to address this question by situating it in the larger context of North-South economic relations and by examining how the economic benefits and environmental burdens of liberalized trade are distributed....

The myth that environmental protection is a luxury that developing countries can ill afford rests on the assumption that environmental protection is an obstacle to economic development and is irrelevant to the immediate needs of the poor. This Part critically assesses this myth by contrasting the environmentalism of the rich with the environmentalism of the poor and by examining the impact of environmental degradation on the Southern poor and on the natural resource base required for economic development.

The environmental movement in the United States has long been perceived as white, middle class, suburban, and concerned first and foremost with the protection of parks, wilderness areas and endangered species. The environmental justice movement, which emerged in the 1980's, challenged the priorities of the traditional environmental movement by making an explicit connection between environmental degradation and issues of poverty, racism, and democracy. Environmental justice activists argued that the traditional environmental movement and the government agencies charged with environmental protection had neglected the distributional consequences of environmental degradation and had failed to effectively incorporate in environmental decision-making the communities bearing the greatest environmental risk. As a result, poor people and racial and ethnic minorities suffer disproportionately high levels of exposure to toxic substances while whites residing in more pristine suburban neighborhoods reap the benefits of environmental protection. These allegations were confirmed by studies that found income and racial bias in the siting of hazardous waste facilities and in the enforcement of statutes that set standards for air, water and waste disposal.

The movement to preserve the global environment has likewise been perceived as a Northern, middle class movement concerned primarily with the protection of nature. Northern environmentalists have typically adopted a technocratic approach to environmental protection, emphasizing global management of the environment based on scientific principles while neglecting Southern aspirations for social justice, cultural rights, self-determination and democracy. Southern non-governmental organizations (NGO's) and grassroots movements have challenged the North's technocratic approach by placing environmental issues in the context of international inequality and of the struggle for social justice. Southern environmentalists have charged that Northern development policies and consumption patterns are the primary causes of resource depletion and global pollution and that the world economic order has institutionalized Southern poverty, which places additional stress on the environment. Indeed, one prominent Southern environmentalist has argued that the South is bearing a disproportionate share of the environmental consequences of globalization, and has described this phenomenon as environmental apartheid....

The second myth underlying the media image of environmental imperialism is that the North is a global leader in environmental protection. It follows from this myth that the North's efforts to incorporate environmental protection into the international trade regime are designed to protect the global ecosystem by elevating the environmental standards of developing countries. While the North in general and the United States in particular have made significant progress in the protection of the domestic environment during the last three decades, the North's role with respect to the global environment is far more problematic....

The North, with 20% of the world's population, currently consumes a disproportionate share of the world's resources, including 85% of the world's timber, 75% of its metals, 70% of its energy, and 60% of its food. The United States has the highest per capita consumption levels in the world, but consumption rates in Japan and Western Europe are only slightly less.

Environmentalists have pointed out that the North's consumption patterns can only be maintained through the appropriation of the natural resources (timber, petroleum, metals, agricultural commodities, biodiversity) and waste sinks (forests, waste disposal facilities) of the South. A team of researchers at the Center for Sustainability Studies in Xalapa, Mexico, developed what they call the "ecological footprint" of 52 nations. This term refers to the amount of biologically productive land and water ("natural capital") that each country must either possess or appropriate in order to maintain its level of consumption. The researchers found that the Netherlands, the United States, Belgium, Germany, Switzerland, the United Kingdom, Japan, and Israel were among the highest per capita importers of natural capital. In other words, these countries utilized far more natural capital (both natural resources and waste sinks) than they possessed. The Netherlands, for example, requires a land mass over 17 times its size in order to satisfy the national demand for energy, food and forest products....

The United States has long used trade sanctions to compel other nations to implement environmental conservation measures....

Northern environmentalists argue that many of the environmental harms arising from liberalized trade can be mitigated by ensuring that the costs of resource depletion and pollution are incorporated into product prices. They claim that goods produced under inadequate environmental standards should be viewed as goods being sold for less than their true cost of production, and describe this phenomenon as environmental dumping. Northern environmentalists contend that it is appropriate for governments to respond to environmental dumping by imposing unilateral trade restrictions, such as embargoes, or by equalizing the terms of trade through "countervailing duties" or "antidumping tariffs" on imports from nations with lower environmental standards. Northern environmentalists have also advocated upward harmonization of environmental standards across jurisdictions through multilateral agreements as a more long-term approach to the problem of environmental dumping.

Developing countries have expressed concern that Northern environmentalists' demands for incorporation of environmental costs in product prices are merely disguised protectionist measures designed to maintain the economic dominance of the North by limiting the South's access to Northern markets. Developing countries have condemned unilateral trade restrictions, eco-duties, and international agreements designed to harmonize environmental standards as intrusions on their sovereign resource management and pollution control decisions. Many developing countries view the North's attempt to impose its pollution control and resource conservation standards on the South as paternalistic and hypocritical given the North's historic and ongoing over-exploitation of the planet's resources. Furthermore, the North tends to prioritize longer-term and more global issues, such as ozone depletion, climate change, and biological diversity, and to neglect issues of immediate, local concern to developing countries, such as basic environmental infrastructure (water systems and sewers), the dumping of outmoded technologies and banned products in developing countries (such as pesticides), the hazardous waste trade, poverty, food security and desertification. Confronted with environmental demands from the North that reflect Northern interests and priorities, many developing countries have denounced the North's use of unilateral trade restrictions to promote environmental protection as environmental imperialism.

There are three fundamental flaws in the North's proposals to reconcile free trade and environmental protection. First, these proposals attempt to change the behavior of the South without addressing the far more ecologically damaging behavior of the North. Environmental trade restrictions thereby become yet another tool for dictating the terms of the North's appropriation of the South's natural resources while the root cause of global environmental degradation, the unsustainable consumption of the North, remains un-

14. McDonalds. Signs of globalization in Bodrum, Turkey.

challenged. Second, the North's proposals fail to address the activities of the most powerful actors in international trade, Northern transnational corporations....

While a full discussion of alternative approaches to the trade/environment debate is beyond the scope of this article, several possibilities emerge from the preceding analysis. These alternative approaches can be grouped into two categories. The first category consists of strategies designed to change the behavior of the North and to scale back the North's appropriation of the resources of the South. The second category consists of strategies designed to support local resistance to environmental degradation and to emphasize bottom-up versus top-down analysis and decision-making. The objective of this section is to suggest alternative approaches for future scholarship rather than to undertake a full-blown description and analysis of these approaches....

The first approach is to address the problem of Northern over-consumption. It is the over-consumption of the North that poses the greatest threat to the global environment and imposes environmental costs on the South. Environmental law has traditionally emphasized pollution control and protection of natural resources while ignoring the ultimate cause of pollution and resource degradation: the over-consumption of the planet's resources....

A second approach is to regulate the activities of transnational corporations. Transnational corporations are the key actors in the global economy and the primary beneficiaries of liberalized trade. Transnational corporations control 80% of foreign investment. The vast majority of transnational corporations have parent corporations that are based in the North. However, transnational corporations operate in a wide variety of hazardous and pollution-intensive industries in the South, including mining, petroleum and agribusiness, and their activities have the potential to produce significant impacts on human health and the environment. Transnational corporations also account for a significant volume of international trade. The trade/environment debate should therefore include an analysis of the role of transnational corporations in environmental degradation and of possible strategies to regulate their conduct. Such strategies might include strengthening environmental enforcement capacity in developing countries, regulating the extra-territorial environmental conduct of corporations headquartered in the North, developing multilateral agreements imposing standards of conduct on transnational corporations, and expanding the rights of foreign victims of environmental abuse to sue Northern corporations in Northern courts for acts committed in other countries....

An environmental justice critique of trade liberalization also suggests that it is important to focus on local environmental struggles in order to understand the precise social and economic forces that promote environmental degradation and social injustice and to develop effective policy responses. Top-down solutions driven by the North's environmental and economic agenda exacerbate environmental injustice by reinforcing Northern economic and political dominance and by failing to take into account the needs and priorities of those most affected by environmental degradation.

Finally, it is important to recognize that trade, human rights, and the environment are inextricably intertwined, and that policy proposals to address global environmental degradation must take into account their complex relationship. Northern initiatives to reconcile trade and environmental protection must be carefully scrutinized to ensure that they promote environmental justice and do not become yet another instrument for transferring resources from the South to the North under the guise of environmental protection.

* * *

Notes and Comments

1. With such a dramatic disparity of wealth, is land use in developing southern nations affected? What types of policies are needed to generate economic development and assure that the development is sustainable? Is globalization a threat or an opportunity for the Southern 80 percent?

2. Influential people have advocated that impoverished nations be the site for polluting industry. Robert Bullard, *Anatomy of Environmental Racism and the Environmental Justice Movement*, in Confronting Environmental Racism: Voices from the Grassroots 19–20 (Robert Bullard ed. 1993) (quoting former Treasury Secretary Lawrence Summers, later a World Bank official).

Chapter 14

Redevelopment

> Here are men that alter their neighbor's landmark...
>
> Shoulder the poor aside, conspire to oppress the friendless.
>
> Reap they the field that is none of theirs,
>
> strip they the vineyard wrongfully seized from its owner...
>
> A cry goes up from the city streets,
>
> Where wounded men lie groaning...
>
> Job as cited in Jane Jacobs, The Death and Life of Great American Cities 5 (1961)

Redevelopment in America has historically taken one of two paths. The first and most significant is simply private market activity. At some point land uses cease to be profitable or a district fails to attain or retain significant economic value. At some point the price of the property falls to a point where, along with considerations of desirability of the site, a private developer finds acquisition and reconstruction attractive. There is no need for public intervention except to assure good planning and in the event that redevelopment generates displacement of businesses or those of lower income, to assure proper relocation planning.

In declining central cities, however, there are vast areas in need of revitalization or redevelopment where the price of land will simply not attract private investment because of poor transportation, inaccessibility to community resources such as entertainment, university, or employment centers, the excessive concentration of poverty, or the relative desirability of land on the urban fringe. During the Truman Administration in the late 1940s, Congress established the urban renewal program. 42 U.S.C. §§ 1450–1462 (1958); National Advisory Comm'n on Urban Problems, Building the American City 152–70 (1968) [hereinafter cited as Douglas Commission]. The concept was to identify neighborhoods that were blighted and not responsive to private market intervention. The program operated by federal grants that were used to acquire and clear existing structures, support administration and the installation of infrastructure, making up the cost of the program after recovering the purchase price from a private redeveloper or public entity. Benjamin B. Quinones, *Redevelopment Redefined: Revitalizing the Central City with Resident Control*, 27 U. Mich. J.L. Ref. 689, 700–709 (1994). The United States Supreme Court in *Berman v. Parker*, 348 U.S. 26 (1954), upheld the use of eminent domain power, whereby the government can involuntarily purchase private property for redevelopment. Although the program was designed to redevelop the worst neighborhoods and replace them with new housing, during the Eisenhower Administration in the 1950s, the program was altered to allow the program to be used in the central cities to remove "skid row" districts near the town center where single occupancy housing and the poor resided. Housing for All Under Law 26 n. 129 (R. Fishman ed. 1978); Ashley A. Foard &

Hilbert Fefferman, *Federal Urban Renewal Legislation*, 25 Law & Contemp. Probs. 635, 655 (1960). The program allowed cities to reclaim sections of the center city for tourists, homes for the affluent, and a revitalized commercial downtown. Scott Greer, Urban Renewal and American Cities: The Dilemma of Democratic Intervention (1965). Frequently the complaint was that housing for the poor was removed and not replaced, forcing the poor into older and overcrowded more expensive housing and generating homelessness. Chester W. Hartman, *Relocation: Illusory Promises and No Relief*, 57 Va. L. Rev. 745 (1971). When urban renewal was retargeted to the deteriorated housing districts during the Kennedy and Johnson Administrations in the 1960s, the program was labeled "Negro Removal" due to extensive displacement of blacks and the failure to follow through on promises for affordable housing redevelopment. Martin Anderson, The Federal Bulldozer—A Critical Analysis of Urban Renewal 1949–1962 (1964). Ultimately, the program failed for two reasons. First, the idea of redeveloping a small portion of concentrated poverty district and generating a revitalized city was unrealistic. Secondly, finding private redevelopers of unattractive sites was difficult and the implementation of a project could take 15 years. Douglas Commission, *supra* at 165–167. Redevelopers and cities soon returned to the central business district to utilize the program to provide desirable sites, as in the case of Lincoln Center in New York, or the SouthWest urban renewal project in Washington, D.C., that provided the land for new offices for HUD, the Department of Transportation, The Watergate, and housing for mid-level bureaucrats. In 1974, Congress, at the behest of the Republican Nixon and Ford Administrations, replaced the program with the Housing and Community Development block grant program that provided automatic grant entitlements to communities and allowed local autonomy over program priorities. James A. Kushner, *Litigation Strategies and Judicial Review Under Title I of the Housing and Community Development Act of 1974*, 11 Urb. L. Ann. 37 (1976).

Under the 1974 Community Development Act, all communities with 50,000 populations, and smaller rural communities, would receive an annual grant that could be used according to local priorities, for a range of activities from renewal to recreation. Redevelopment was now discouraged as the federal government would no longer provide additional assistance to cover the cost of relocation and cities were unable to demonstrate adequate replacement housing where redevelopment was targeted at low income residential neighborhoods. Most communities halted all redevelopment because of the cost and time involved and redirected block grant funds to achieve shorter term economic development priorities such as attracting businesses, conventions, and rendering downtowns more attractive to affluent residents. Gentrification became the accepted path to revitalization. The more poor displaced and the greater the presence of the urban affluent, Yuppies (young urban professionals), or Buppies (black urban professionals), the more successful a community development strategy. This is why the poor and the working poor experience great difficulty attempting to acquire affordable decent housing and the ranks of the homeless expand. Although the 1974 law requires that most funds be expended to assist the poor, 42 U.S.C. § 5304(b)(3) (70 percent must benefit low- and moderate-income persons), creative accounting and the absence of any enforcement by HUD have thwarted that legislative intent as enforcement is through mere certification by the recipient with the mere possibility of a HUD audit. 42 U.S.C. § 5304(b). The program requirements often encourage typical low-wage job creation, and often preclude significant economic development initiatives that might have more dramatically benefitted the community, generating greater economic opportunity and jobs. Louise A. Howells, *Looking for the Butterfly Effect: An Analysis of Urban Economic Development Under the Community Development Block Grant Program*, 16 St. Louis U. Pub. L. Rev. 383 (1997). A hotel in the upscale harbor is characterized as economic development and job development benefitting the poor. As cities enjoyed greater autonomy in the expenditure of community development funds, federal funding was retargeted from the poorest neighborhoods under the original urban renewal program, to the targeting of funds to more affluent communities under the theory of triage. Under triage, a practice utilized in emergency medicine, those patients or neighborhoods that need no intervention to survive or who are likely to die regardless of attention are ignored, while scarce resources are targeted to those that can respond from treatment or investment. William C. Baer, *On the Death of Cities*, 45 Pub. Int. 3, 15–17 (1976), *reprinted in* Roger Montgomery & Daniel R. Mandelker, Housing in America 338 (2d ed. 1979). Under triage, poor neighborhoods are ignored and investment targeted to those potentially gentrifying moderate income neighborhoods where some investment may attract private investment.

As the federal government ceased its redevelopment role, states turned to other alternatives such as tax preferences to encourage investment. A very popular device has been the tax increment redevelopment program. Richard F. Dye & David F. Merriman, *The Effects of Tax Increment Financing on Economic Development*, 47 J. Urb. Econ. 306 (2000) (negative growth rate for assessed property value); Catherine Michel, *Brother Can you Spare a Dime: Tax Increment Financing in Indiana*, 71 Ind. L.J. 457 (1996); Todd A. Rogers, *A Dubious Development: Tax Increment Financing and Economically Motivated Condemnation*, 17 Rev. Litig. 145 (1998); Gary P. Winter, *Tax Increment Financing: A Potential Redevelopment Financing Mechanism for New York Municipalities*, 18 Fordham Urb. L.J. 655 (1991). Under TIF, a neighborhood or project area is designated based on the presence of blight as in the federal urban renewal program. The community then sells general obligation redevelopment bonds that are tax free municipal bonds attractive to investors. The proceeds from the bonds are then used to execute the acquisition, clearance, and redevelopment. The project is financed by freezing the amount of real property tax from the project area that is due to the various taxing authorities such as school, college, or utility districts. The redevelopment is taxed based on the value of the redeveloped project and the difference between the new higher tax revenues and the previous amount that is paid out is the increment. The increment is then used to pay off the bond holders as obligations become due with the unspent balance available to make investments in the district in the form of infrastructure, community resources, or even the financing of affordable housing. Of course the attractiveness of the program is based on the assumption that the value of real estate is escalating so as to generate an increment and the availability of sufficient bonding authority. The tax incentives have been so attractive that some communities have sought to exploit the program by creatively by identifying blight in the most affluent of suburbs. George Lefcoe, *Finding the Blight That's Right for California Redevelopment Law*, 52 Hastings L.J. 991 (2001).

The failure of the block grant program, like its predecessor urban renewal program to assist the poor or revitalize the neighborhoods of the poor ultimately led to enactment of the Empowerment Communities and Enterprise Zone program during the Clinton Administration. Omnibus Reconciliation Act of 1993, Pub. L. No. 103-66, §§ 13301–13303, 107 Stat. 312, 543, *codified at* 26 U.S.C. §§ 1391–1397D. The concept was that federal tax obligations of businesses locating in designated zones would be cut to encourage investment and federal grants would be provided to empowerment communities to assist in social as well as physical redevelopment. The concept was popular with Congress as the tax cuts and credits are not shown in the budget and the principal beneficiaries include banks and other investing businesses.

The use of eminent domain power to provide sites for private redevelopment will always be controversial, particularly where residents are displaced to make way for a sports stadium, a bank, or an employment center. The courts have supported the use of eminent domain where it is necessary to attract an employer or to prevent an employer or sports franchise from leaving the community. The benefits of subsidized development or redevelopment have led employers and sports teams to play a game of extortion, negotiating with other cities and frightening local politicians into offering substantial concessions and incentives such as free land, infrastructure, or utilities. The courts have also supported offering various subsidies or incentives to employers to locate in or relocate to a community. In *Poletown Neighborhood Council v. City of Detroit*, 304 N.W.2d 455 (Mich. 1981), the Michigan Supreme Court upheld residential displacement and the use of eminent domain to provide a site for General Motors to avoid their leaving Motown. These subsidies can arguably be characterized as "pirating" and as there do not currently exist any state or federal laws restricting such subsidies, it can be argued that local subsidies designed to attract relocating employers constitutes an interference with interstate commerce. The United States Supreme Court has extended the reach of the commerce clause, authorizing courts to invalidate state and local regulation that carries an anticompetitive impact. *C & A Carbone, Inc. v. Town of Clarkstown*, 511 U.S. 383 (1994). Indeed, the Court has ruled that state subsidies can generate a scheme that discriminates against interstate commerce. *West Lynn Creamery, Inc. v. Healy*, 512 U.S. 186 (1994) (effect of tax on all milk providers and subsidy to in-state dairy farmers constituted discrimination). *See generally* Dan T. Coenen, *Business Subsidies and the Dormant Commerce Clause*, 107 Yale L.J. 965 (1998) (arguing that ordinary business subsidies are constitutional and are suspect only when linked to a particular tax policy, arguing for an unpredictable subjective inquiry into discriminatory impact). Such subsidies may also conflict with international trade obligations as they may provide an unfair advantage in competing with unsubsidized firms in international trade. The United States is a member of The World Trade Organization, whose requirements mirror the prior General Agreement on Tariffs and Trade ("GATT"), an international treaty generally requiring free trade and eliminating discriminatory trade barriers, and is a signer of the Agreements on Subsidies and Countervailing Duties, known as the Uruguay Round Agreements. Ralph H. Folsom, *et al*, International Business Transactions ch. 7 (3d ed. 1995). Under the Uruguay Round Agreements covering subsidies, GATT was most concerned with imports and subsidies providing a competitive advantage. Terrence J. McCartin, *Red, Yellow or Green: GATT 1994's Traffic Light Subsidies Categories*, in Practicing Law Institute, The Commerce Department Speaks on International Trade and Investment 611 (1994), *reprinted in* Folsom, *supra* at 507 (import impacting subsidies are "red light" and prohibited, while research and development is a permitted "green light" subsidy, with the remainder characterized as "yellow light" and actionable where a serious adverse impact is generated). *See also* Jennifer Gilbert, *Selling the City Without Selling Out: New Legislation on Development Incentives Emphasizes Accountability*, 27 Urb. Law. 427, 446 (1995) (arguing that business subsidies are prohibited). Do contemporary American urban "boosterism" and the pirating of employers or sports franchises through lucrative incentives arguably violate the WTO Treaty (formerly GATT)? Anticompetitiveness is an inherent element in land use controls. When a community undertakes a redevelopment project, the redeveloper often enjoys advantages not enjoyed by competitors. Similarly, the zoning process itself can be manipulated or implemented in a way that provides monopoly status to some by denying similar development permission to potential competitors. The United States Supreme Court in *City of Columbia v.Omni Outdoor Advertising, Inc.*, 499 U.S. 365 (1991), ruled that where a state authorizes anticompetitive behavior as in the case of zoning that the entire scheme, regardless how outrageous and anticompetitive, is immune from federal antitrust law. The ruling, although protecting local government from costly litigation and liability exposure, at the same time licenses, facilitates, and encourages the beneficiaries of such anticompetitive power to engage in all forms of corruption of government officials and the planning process. Unfortunately, the victims of the process of subsidizing large manufacturers or "big box" retail stores are long term local merchants no longer able to compete on a level playing field and the residents who may lose the character of their town to the globalized factory outlet/shopping mall/ big box retailer community that is shaping America and beyond.

As many American communities consider the improvement of public transit as an alternative to suburban sprawl, automobiles and massive congestion, transportation improvements offer a wonderful opportunity to undertake redevelopment. As communities pursue smart growth and environmental sustainability, revitalization and redevelopment become critical components. Urban stabilization requires social sustainability, that is, economic and social stability that cannot permit neighborhoods and districts to deteriorate and be abandoned if the community itself is to remain attractive to business and public life.

The following excerpt describes economic development and redevelopment activities in the European community:

Voula Mega, *The Concept and Civilization of an Eco-society: Dilemmas, Innovations, and Urban Dramas,*

in Cities and the Environment: New Approaches for Eco-societies 47 (Edited by Takashi Inoguchi, Edward Newman, and Glen Paoletto 1999)....

Cities are engines and catalysts of economic growth. The global economy is becoming stronger with the strengthening of creative interdependent city economies. The increased importance of urban economic activity in national and world production is a challenge for cities to improve their productivity. Improved macroeconomic management is a necessary, but not sufficient, condition to improving productivity at the city level. The productivity of the urban economy depends greatly on institutions and infrastructures. Deficiencies in information and infrastructures, the heavy cost of inappropriate urban regulatory policies, and financial and technical weaknesses in municipal institutions are important constraints whose cumulative effects drain the potential for urban economic development. Strengthening the management of urban infrastructures, reinforcing the institutional capacity, improving the financial and technical capacity of municipal institutions, and creating an enabling policy environment for more productive urban economies are cardinal common priorities for cities.

With the progressive globalization of the economy and the advancing international division of labour, many European metropolitan cities are becoming control and command centres. Intelligence is the main asset and value, and cities are the places where the world's in visible production chains interlink. Cities are the only places where economic flows can be decoded, condensed, converted, and metabolized; the places where decision-makers and entrepreneurs and citizens congregate. Synergetic effects are much more important than accumulative ones. Competition can no longer be an impediment, it can become an incitement. A diversified urban economic basis is considered to be a must for entrepreneurial flexibility, irregularity, and fragmented demand. The role of enterprises in the shift from goods handling to information handling is essential. Large enterprises may lead to the "edge city," but small and medium-sized enterprises (SMEs) have potential in revitalizing the city which does not accept its urban life being organized around megamalls. Partnerships are linked to a shift in public policies from direct interference to indirect (or conditional) policies (incubation and innovation).

Cities of bits, technoburbs, and business parks are mushrooming throughout Europe and provide some interesting examples of public—private partnerships for turning areas of blight into healthy spaces and areas of positive environmental and economic profit. Stockley Park, a former derelict rubbish tip within the green belt to the west of London, sets an inspiring example. A partnership between the developer, the local authority, and the university created an inter national business park and public parkland including recreational facilities. In exchange for the right to construct the business park over 36 hectares, the developer guaranteed the reclamation of the whole site (140 hectares), removal of groundwater pollution, environmental enhancement, and landscaping. At all stages of the construction of Stockley, local residents were involved in the process through extensive community consultation.

In the Ruhr valley, the IBA Emscher Park has initiated a new era for urban development and ecological renewal. Experts from ten European cities, together with the cities and industries of the Emscher region, work for the modernization of coal-mining settlements and the creation of new housing, the development of fallow land, and the promotion of attractive locations for industry and services. The preservation and reuse of industrial monuments, the landscaping of the Emscher area into a park, the ecological restructuring of the Emscher river, and the protection of the water environment are leading to a healthy space. New dwellings have been created on fallow land using environmentally friendly materials. High-quality locations for industry and services have been given value. Contaminated areas are insulated and reused. "Working in the park" is possible through the enhancement of the quality and attractiveness of the area.

Economic regeneration aims at revitalizing the whole urban fabric, both its software and its hardware. The objectives of the programme to revitalize and regenerate Dublin city centre were to redevelop dilapidated areas, halt population decline, strengthen the area as a centre for business and services, and create a climate of confidence to stimulate and win back investment. In 1986, a survey revealed that out of 1,000 hectares, 66 were underused (derelict buildings, waste ground, and land used as car parks). For over 20 years there had been no new private developments on the quays. The Dublin City Development Plan was published in 1991, after six years of preparation and consideration of 21,000 representations and objections. It provided a framework, but the municipality had limited resources (and powers) to implement a programme of that magnitude. The scale of the programme required action by the government, which reacted with major initiatives, including the designation of assisted development areas, the establishment of the International Financial Services Centre in a derelict dock area, and the creation of the cultural quarter Temple Bar.

The rehabilitation of the commercial and waterfront area of Galway also offers interesting lessons. As economic activities relocated to sites outside the city (or disappeared altogether) a central area was left abandoned and dilapidated, being used for marginal activities (warehousing and open-air parking). The 1986 Urban Renewal Act designated this a priority assisted development area. Economic measures were introduced, promoting rehabilitation as well as new building. The major objective was that any new building should reflect Galway's unique character and atmosphere and promote a mixture of the functions considered essential for the vitality of the city centre. By the end of 1992, all the derelict space had been rehabilitated and a balance created between shops, services, offices, and dwellings. The construction of housing units (much more suited to Irish culture than apartments) on the terrace roof of the city's main shopping centre is a good example of mixed functions within one building.

The conversion of waterfront areas, seasides, and riversides is a major feature of several European cities. As a result of economic and technological reforms over the last few years, city-centre ports have disappeared, leaving behind the husk of an infrastructure in need of a new role. Disused dock buildings are being turned into exhibition halls, shops, craft workshops, and centres for cultural activities. The Salford Quays development on the Manchester Ship Canal came about through the will to turn derelict space into the ultimate leisure area, respecting the environment and promoting culture. In Turku, the metamorphosis of an old industry and harbour area into a new arts centre is an inspiring example. The conversion of the old harbour area in Gothenburg into a mixed-use city, after the closing down of shipyards, transformed the abandoned area of four square kilometres into a multifunctional city through a multi-partnership between the city authorities, the architects, the former shipbuilding companies, and the public. Formerly industrial buildings were given new, intelligent functions....

"Building Eutopia" is a sustainable planning aim; it now embraces the notion of eco-Eutopia. There is a growing consensus about the need for urban mix, reflecting a need for "a little of a city everywhere in the city." The preference for the compact city, as a contrast to the diffuse city, is gaining ground. The dense, compact city has the advantage of integrating structures and providing shorter distances between home and work or leisure. But the compact city might not necessarily be energy-efficient and may not correspond to lifestyle preferences either. Owens suggests that a sustainable urban form on a regional scale would contain many relatively small settlements, some clustered to form larger settlements of 200,000 and more people on the subregional scale. It would consist of compact settlements, probably linear or rectangular in form, where people could both live and work. The interrelated questions of density and compactness have quite interesting contributions to make to reconstruction and sustainability. Reconstruction schemes, more than the Second World War, have destroyed cities. "High density" should be distinguished from "high rise." Correa suggests "high density low rise" as an ideal option.

Preservation versus new development is a Janus-faced dilemma. Most cities give the answer: renewal rather than expansion, consolidation of the urban fabric, and improvement of the suburbs. The "soft urban renewal" in Vienna includes block improvement schemes, enhancement of public spaces, and ecological measures. The social criteria insist on avoiding segregation or gentrification. Soft renewal allows inhabitants to remain in place and enjoy a range of resident-friendly measures. In Barcelona, the rehabilitation of the Ciutat Vella, comprising four quarters in the historic centre, is an unprecedented and unique event, in terms of dimension, timing, and civic spirit. Following the reconciliation of the city with the sea and the creation of the Villa Olimpica, the whole urban fabric is changing, with the gradual injection of improvements. Selective renovation, rehabilitation, construction, pedestrianization, and greening are the visible elements. Civic centres have been created and have become points of multiple encounters and cultural reference. Strong neighbourhood groups have become partners with the authorities and have played a pioneering role in the attribution of new housing and services, the dismantling of unsound activities, and the whole change of social climate.

15. Emsher Park. Former steel mill and brownfields converted to a recreation center and public theme park in Duisberg, Germany.

Cities open to the future cannot be conceived without the regeneration of the suburban areas, the places where one does not know if one is "in" or "out." This entails recreating the economic diversification, the social heterogeneity and cultural diversity in the periphery. In the south of Stockholm, the Huddinge Centrum is a successful experiment in transforming a suburban shopping centre into a town square, focal point, and meeting point for the community. The location, next to the train station, generated the creation of new offices and apartment units and the whole area has been redesigned on the model of the old medieval city of Stockholm. The Donau-City project in Vienna aims to create a new skyline to the north-east, across the River Danube, and a new mixed-use waterside quarter.

Public spaces belong, by definition, equally to everyone. What Koolhas describes as fortresses of freedom have great potential as islands of urbanity in the archipelago of the city. Public space is not just the space "left" after construction; it should be given major importance as a civic space and shaped as a priority. The unification of the archaeological spaces in Athens and their functional and aesthetic links to green spaces is expected to create a high-value public space. Inviting public spaces may foster democracy. In many cases, "standardized" public space cannot meet its challenges of space for "negotiating" democracy, and becomes space of confrontation and of exclusion. Setting up qualitative recommendations for the functional, environmental, cultural, and aesthetic character of the spaces, roads, and pavements, roadside plantations and public lighting is very important in forging cultural identity. In Brussels, the *Manual of Public Spaces* is a good example.

Along with urban planning, structural projects contribute to shaping the image of cities, provide landmarks, and symbolize their dynamic forces. Often, these structural projects are linked to particular events that act as catalysts for the future restructuring of the cities and the regions (EXPOs, Olympic Games, etc.). Other projects, such as "Seine Sud-Est," result from a determined, well-planned effort to re-equilibrate the urban fabric. In order to meet their objectives, the projects must synchronize their long-term potentials for continuity and flexibility. Flexibility is imperative for adapting the project to market fluctuations, while continuity is linked to a vision for the future of the infrastructures. In the most closely studied projects, the trend is towards guaranteeing an optional multiplicity of land use and a good spatial, functional, and economic integration in order to enhance the vitality and livelihood of the whole area. Stable financial structures for the long-term implementation of major projects are of the highest importance, while the cost of land and infrastructures is a key issue for economic equilibrium. Consultation and partnership become important on several levels, vertically and horizontally. The success of the projects greatly depends on a constant and affirmed political determination, withstanding changes in elected representation.

* * *

How does economic development and urban revitalization in Asia differ from America and Europe? The following excerpt discusses development in China:

Mark T. Kremzner, *Managing Urban Land in China: The Emerging Legal Framework and its Role in Development*,

7 Pacific Rim Law & Policy Journal 611 (1998)

...Following Deng Xiaoping's rise to power in the late 1970s, new policies were implemented that altered the course of the nation's economic development path and the way in which rural and urban land was held and managed. The reform of the land management regime has contributed significantly to the nation's economic growth and development. Just as the de-collectivization of rural land led to great increases in agricultural output, so too has urban land reform accelerated the transformation of China's cities and urban economy.

Several paradigms on the role of the state in economic development are described below and will be used as reference points to assess the role of the central state in managing urban land in China. While some of the basic assumptions and analytical methodologies utilized by each paradigm remain open to debate, they do provide a useful means for analyzing the role of the state in promoting and directing development.

The Modernization Paradigm

Efforts by Western social scientists in the early 1950s to identify the reasons why some countries had undergone more rapid industrialization and urbanization than others focused on the conditions and experience of Western Europe and North America. Drawing upon ideas of evolution, modernity (as opposed to traditional values), and social change, modernization theorists conceived of development as an irreversible process whereby countries progress from a backward or undeveloped stage to an advanced or developed stage. In adopting the assumptions of liberal economic thought, the modernization paradigm maintains that free markets optimize efficiency in resource allocation thereby promoting growth. Government involvement in the market place often has been viewed as little more than an interference that distorts prices, hampers transactions and retards growth. For example, in advising China on urban land management reform, the World Bank has called upon the central government to "remove obstacles to market reform and deregulate urban planning."...

The law and development movement currently is experiencing a limited renaissance in China. Law and development scholars and policy analysts from the West and China posit that economic development can be promoted and a socialist market economy established by setting up new rational legal institutions and promulgating comprehensive laws. This view has been embraced by many of China's current leaders, who repeatedly have stated that law is an essential agent in moving China away from a planned economic system and towards a new socialist market economy....

The Dependency Paradigm

The dependency paradigm emerged in reaction to the modernization paradigm and was inspired by classical Marxist thought. Whereas modernization theory explains that development occurs as the result of factors internal to the economy and society of a country, early dependency theorists claimed that underdevelopment is the result of external capitalist forces. Early dependency theories were largely based on a world system perspective that placed the advanced capitalist nations at the core and countries with a colonial legacy or other exploitative history at the periphery. This structure is believed to perpetuate underdevelopment because capital is drawn out of the periphery and accumulates in the core thereby further polarizing the global economy.

Responding to criticisms from both ends of the political spectrum on the lack of empirical rigor in their early work, dependency theorists modified their views in the 1970s and 1980s, Cardoso put forth the notion of "dependent development," which explained that an LDC can develop when mutually advantageous conditions exist for both it and the partnered advanced economy. By contrast, Wallerstein's world systems analysis explained that limited opportunities existed for LDCs to develop. Later dependency scholars utilized these and other theoretical models to demonstrate through numerous empirical studies that direct foreign investment, trade and aid decreased long term growth and increased inequality. In general these studies demonstrated that LDCs became reliant on foreign trade channels and overseas capital sources in the form of bank loans, direct investment, and donor aid. The influential role of foreign capital led to the co-opting or corruption of local elites and domestic institutions, which became instruments to further promote the interests of foreign capital. An alternative view is that dependency relationships are the product of domestic policies and not the result of global structural relationships.

Legal institutions in particular were seen as promoting and enhancing the domination of foreign capital, and thus the law and development movement came under attack for breeding underdevelopment. Imported legal forms were used to legitimate resistance to change and to suppress reformist elements that aimed to raise the economic and social conditions for a broader spectrum of society. While the governing regimes of many LDCs were sufficiently strong to retain political power at home, they remained dependent upon foreign capital and were unable to effectively manage or regulate their national resources or assets. Finally, laws and legal institutions that privatized economic transactions and limited state involvement in commercial affairs were seen as inhibiting the ability of the central state to control private enterprise and foreign capital.

The Statist Paradigm

The statist paradigm holds that the state is a vital factor in promoting development. Statism reversed the negative attitudes towards the state held by modernization and dependency theorists and emphasized the advantages that flow from states that take an active role in formulating and implementing growth strategies. The intellectual roots of the statist paradigm are based in part upon the works of Gerschenkorn, who argued that late developing states needed to intervene more strenuously to ensure rapid industrialization and catch up to advanced economies. A leading reason for this is said to be the inability of the private sector in LDCs to organize and accumulate the capital necessary for building national infrastructure.

Statists have tended to focus their work on identifying those factors that are most critical for achieving swift and sustained growth. The East Asian newly industrialized countries (NICs) have been the center of much attention. Some studies emphasize that the strength of the state is important for bargaining with other states and organizations to improve opportunities for growth, win acceptance for domestic trade and investment policies, and obtain support or aid. Others point to the role of the state in providing and improving infrastructure, encouraging foreign investment, adjusting fiscal flows, and directing funds into targeted industries to enhance growth. Government policies that match domestic resources and production facilities with global markets may also improve growth rates. Finally, the mixture of both import substitution and export production have been shown to yield beneficial industrial diversification and place a nation on a steady path of development.

With respect to land management, statist policies have been employed to improve land for industrial interests, encourage the construction of housing and commercial space, and to promote the growth of the real estate sector. Singapore and Hong Kong have closely controlled land use to guide urban growth, and have regarded urban land management as critical for their socio-economic development. In Taiwan the central government has actively managed the transformation of land from agricultural to industrial purposes through a legal framework. The Taiwan legislature passed laws to regulate the requisition of land from farmers for industrial purposes, bar land speculation, and encourage entrepreneurs to invest in land for industrial purposes. This legal regime led to the establishment of special export processing zones, the hi-tech Hsinchu Science Park, and more than sixty-eight industrial parks....

Classic Marxist doctrine holds that land is not a commodity and has no exchange value, because it exists naturally and is not the product of labor. This notion was the ideological justification for prohibitions on the sale or lease of land during the Maoist era, and the reason why land was transferred free of charge by central planning authorities. For conservative Party ideologues, ideas of land leases and sales of land use rights was antithetical to Marxist-Maoist ideology. Having the state lease land would be tantamount to the state assuming the status of a landlord. The historic mission of the Party had been to guard the population from exploitation by landlords. If the Party condoned the leasing of land by the state and the reappearance of landlordism, it risked forfeiting its legitimacy.

By the mid-1980s, the issue of urban land leasing was being openly debated in academic journals and the media. Reformers justified land leases and the imposition of land use fees by reinterpreting Marx's writings on land rent. They asserted that urban land could have exchange value because of the transformation in its use in an urban economy. Presuming that urban land had value it logically followed, according to some theorists, that the state legitimately could grant rights to use a parcel of land in exchange for payment equivalent to the transformed value. While this would result in the commodification of the use rights to land, its ownership technically would remain under the ownership of the "whole people," or the state. This formulation also proved to be in accord with the final provisions of the then newly promulgated 1986 General Principles of the Civil Law, which holds that the right to use property is one of four constituent elements that comprise property ownership.

The increasing momentum in support of the commodification of land use rights coincided with calls to accord the real estate industry independent status. A number of ministries and agencies lobbied in favor of the real estate industry. Chief among them were the Ministry of Construction ("MOC") and the Ministry of Finance, both of which stood to gain economically and politically from the legalization of real estate markets. By late 1984 the State Planning Commission ("SPC") granted the real estate industry independent status, which led to the creation of new regulatory institutions to oversee construction enterprises, land management agencies, and associated financial and administrative organizations. In 1987 the real estate industry got another boost when it was declared to be a production, as opposed to consumption, based industry. This pronouncement led to an increase in the availability of investment funds for land development and construction projects. The enhanced status of the real estate industry and the government organs that regulated it strengthened the political clout of those favoring the commodification of land use rights.

Encouraging and Guiding Foreign Investment

While the legal framework for the acquisition and transfer of land use rights was a critical step in stimulating foreign investment in urban land development and real estate construction projects, additional measures have been taken to specifically address foreign investment. The State Council Provisional Regulations on the Use of Land for Construction by Sino-Foreign Joint Ventures were an early attempt to ease the way for foreign investors to develop real estate. However, irregular and unpredictable practices coupled with ambivalent central government officials tended to frustrate rather than encourage investment in urban land development and construction during much of the 1980s. Local officials frequently used ad hoc methods in issuing and regulating land use rights, and there were claims that grant fees were determined in an arbitrary manner.

A significant turning point arrived in 1990 with the promulgation by the State Council of the Provisional Administrative Measures Governing Commercial Land Development and Management by Foreign Investors. These Measures were designed explicitly for the purpose of encouraging foreign capital to invest in and improve land sites for the construction of industrial, commercial and residential facilities, thereby boosting local economies. As one Chinese commentator explained, the intent of this type of law was to change the strategy of "building the nest to attract the birds" into "attracting the birds to build the nest." The 1990 Commercial Land Development Measures outline the procedures by which foreigners may acquire from the state granted land use rights to large tracts of land for comprehensive development, which means: leveling, clearing and draining the land; installing utilities, transportation networks and communication facilities; and preparing sites for various types of end users. Upon completion of the work, the land use rights to the improved land may be either held and managed by the foreign investor or assigned. Many provincial and municipal governments have introduced their own versions of comprehensive large tract development legislation.

A similar type of legislation promulgated at the provincial and municipal levels are the procedures for the grant and assignment of land use rights in economic and technological development zones ("ETDZs"). Designed to attract export oriented and high technology firms, ETDZ legislation typically provides greater flexibility on the duration of the grant term, has streamlined procedures and conditions for the assignment of property interests, and in some cases, reduced grant fees. ETDZ development generally has been quite successful in attracting investment. By early 1993, ETDZ development had become so rampant in the coastal provinces that vast areas of prime agricultural land within or near urban areas had been occupied and developed. Investigations by the State Council found that many county and municipal governments, eager to draw in foreign investors, had set up ETDZs without proper authorization from higher level authorities. In mid-1993, the State Council issued a notice calling for limitations upon ETDZ approvals and the strengthening of regulatory oversight by responsible government officials. In 1996 and 1997, the State Council again ordered provincial governments to limit approvals for the development of ETDZs.

A tension exists between providing inducements to investors in the form of decreased taxes and fees while simultaneously maximizing revenue flows to the government and avoiding an overheated economy. This tension tends to unravel in a series of repetitive cycles. Investment activity rises following the implementation of legislation and policies containing incentives for investors, but then contracts after officials impose measures to control the economy or levy new fees. In the early 1990s, the State Council targeted property developers with incentive packages including reduced tax rates and land use fees. Funds poured into urban land development projects, but by 1993 slowed as the central government ordered compliance with the austerity program designed by then Vice Premier Zhu Rongji. Local governments, strapped for cash, levied numerous fees on investors. In Shanghai, for example, government departments in 1995 levied nearly one hundred types of fees on real estate developers. In 1997 the Ministry of Construction, in an attempt to draw in higher levels of foreign investment, called for the elimination of nearly fifty types of fee collections on property development projects.

Foreign capital has played an important, yet not dominant, role in China's real estate and property development industry. By the mid-1990s, approximately one quarter of the 20,000 registered property development enterprises were foreign invested. The amount of foreign funds invested in urban land development projects fluctuates from year to year. However, the proportion of foreign investment in the nation's real estate sector relative to domestic investment rose through the late 1980s, but has held steady through most of the 1990s. In 1992, approximately US $710 million was invested in the urban land development and real estate construction sector, which constituted one quarter of the total amount of funds invested in this sector. In 1994, approximately US $4 billion of foreign funds flowed into urban land development projects, which again represented nearly one quarter of all investment in the urban land development and real estate construction sector. The amount of foreign funds invested in urban land development and real estate relative to all other foreign invested projects rose significantly from the mid-1980s to mid-1990s. However, the distribution of land development and real estate construction projects with foreign investment is uneven and concentrated in a relatively small number of urban centers.

The issue of what role foreign capital ought to play in urban land development is far from settled. While few central or local officials are wholly opposed to foreign investment, most agree that it needs to be limited and properly channeled. The reasons for restricting foreign capital are more often motivated by protectionism than concerns over dependency. For example, some officials in the Ministry of Construction have stated that they would like to curtail the activities of foreign RPDEs so that domestic firms could increase their lead in the real estate industry. Others want to see foreign capital used primarily in land development projects that would result in either the transfer of advanced foreign design know-how and construction technology, or aid in solving the nation's urban housing crisis.

In early 1992, central authorities began demanding local authorities to place strict limits on the construction of buildings with "limited market potential," such as luxury villas and apartments, high class hotels and commercial office buildings, many of which had high vacancy rates. These types of projects were criticized as being non-productive, consumption oriented, lacking overall market value, and of little benefit for national development. They also urged that efforts be made to direct foreign capital into housing and urban renewal projects. In late 1992, the State Council issued a Notice calling for local officials to provide guidance to foreign investors and link the granting of land use rights to projects encouraged by the state. This was followed in mid-1993 by an MOC announcement calling upon all commercial real estate developers to devote at least twenty percent of their annual development budgets for the construction of standard housing, and a joint policy declaration issued by the MOC, SLA, State Tax Administration and the State Administration of Industry and Commerce requiring at least twenty percent of the land area used in commodity housing (*shangpinfang*) to be reserved for the construction of "low profit residential housing" (*weili jumin zhuzhai*). These approaches to solving the shortage of urban housing soon were modified out of concerns that investors would be driven away.

What has evolved over the past few years is a policy and legal framework that provides incentives for investors to construct residential housing, while limiting those projects that do not advance the economic development goals of the country. Thus, the 1995 Real Estate Law calls for the state to adopt preferential tax and other measures to encourage and support real estate development enterprises to develop and build residential buildings. In mid-1995, the State Council issued a Notice on the Strict Control of Luxury Real Estate Development Projects, calling for foreign investment to be directed towards the renovation of older areas within cities and ordinary housing projects. Furthermore, that Notice requires all foreign invested real estate projects involving more than US $30 million to be examined and approved by the State Planning Commission, while projects in excess of US $100 million must be approved by the State Council. As an incentive to increase the stock of "ordinary, standard residential buildings" (*putong, biaozhun zhuzhai*) as opposed to "high class apartments," "villas," or "resorts," the Land VAT Regulations exempt from taxation the amount realized on the "construction and sale of ordinary standard residential buildings" where the added value realized does not exceed twenty percent after the deduction of expenses. At the local level there is also legislation providing foreign investors with incentives to construct ordinary housing and improve urban neighborhoods....

Planning Land Uses for Modern Cities

In the late 1970s and early 1980s, the State Council and State Planning Commission determined that the urban land planning system had to be reformed if the nation's cities were to contribute effectively to the national economic development effort. As a result, city mayors were given responsibilities for overseeing land use planning; laws were introduced establishing a basic organizational framework; urban planning professionals, many who were castigated during the Cultural Revolution, were politically rehabilitated; and the scope of urban planning was broadened, thereby replacing the narrow focus on industrial location which had been the pre-occupation of a generation of economic planners. From the mid-1980s onward, urban planners and municipal officials urged that the nation's cities had to be restructured if China was to compete successfully in the international economy. They recommended relocating manufacturing and warehouse facilities to the urban fringes, reconfiguring central business districts, upgrading infrastructure systems, and separating residential areas from commercial and industrial districts. Similar conclusions and recommendations were reached by the World Bank. According to the World Bank's published report, globally competitive cities in the next century will require "vibrant producers' service sectors," and the transformation of China's urban land use patterns to a knowledge-based economy will "require an accompanying unprecedented revolution in urban land management." To achieve this, the World Bank recommended a series of economic and legal reforms echoing the prescriptions of the law and development movement two decades earlier. To date the restructuring of the urban land planning regime has emphasized a mix of central planning and market measures. The use of law as a tool to bring order to guide land utilization and implement urban plans is widely regarded as critical for the development of modern cities....

Over the past two decades, China has purposely used law as an instrument to transform its economy into one that relies less on central planning and more on market mechanisms. In doing so it has converted urban land from a resource distributed by the state into a commodity that is sold initially by the state and which subsequently may be exchanged through market transactions. Unlike the prescriptions of the modernization paradigm, which call for a reduced state presence in markets, the legal reforms provide for a strong state presence. Thus, the state maintains a monopoly position in the primary market for land use rights and endeavors to manipulate transactions in the secondary market. Under this approach, central authorities have succeeded in collecting large amounts of revenue that have been used to reclaim and develop additional supplies of urban land, build city infrastructure systems and construct housing. These achievements bear some resemblance to the statist oriented development programs instituted in some of the more successful newly industrialized East Asian economies.

In contrast to the statist models, however, the central state in China has had to contend increasingly with the challenges posed by local authorities and commercial interests. Local governments are taking an ever larger share of the revenue obtained from sales of land use rights. Moreover, competition among localities has depressed prices of land use rights in many urban areas. Beyond the sale of land use rights, China's urban land regime also does not correspond closely with the statism model. Local authorities have not consistently enforced the substantive or procedural aspects of the legal framework for land planning promulgated by themselves or central authorities. The lack of local enforcement is a manifestation of local economic development ambitions that do not necessarily coincide with those of the center. Thus, there is a disjuncture between the formal legal framework for land use planning developed by the center and the way land is actually used at the local level. Where land use plans have been effectively carried out, such as in some areas of Shanghai, local rather than central authorities generally have taken the initiative and guided the process.

To some extent the dynamics between central and local authorities are similar to some of the symptoms associated with the dependency paradigm. However, unlike the dependency paradigm where foreign capital is considered to be the primary corrupting agent, local authorities are influenced more by domestic capital and local interests, than by foreign ones. Most investment in China's urban land markets are from domestic sources. While foreign capital is encouraged under the legal framework, local officials frequently give preferential treatment to domestic interests. Thus, for example, the best building sites in a city generally are reserved for local land development and real estate companies. In addition, while local sources of capital are well-known to local Party and government officials, the origin of what is termed "foreign" capital is unclear. This is because of the proliferation of offshore investment companies and trusts by Chinese enterprises and organizations. Finally, foreign investors periodically are faced with the imposition of unofficial fees and charges that tend to negate the advantages offered under the formal legal framework.

In conclusion, the purpose and effect of the reform of the legal framework for managing urban land has been to promote economic development. However, the effectiveness of that framework and the precise character of China's urban development remain an open question.

* * *

The following excerpt looks at economic development planning in Europe and the United States:

James A. Kushner, *Growth for the Twenty-First Century—Tales from Bavaria and the Vienna Woods: Comparative Images of Planning in Munich, Salzburg, Vienna, and the United States*,

29 Urban Lawyer 911 (1998)

....The experience of both European and American cities teaches that economic development, job development, and the prevention of job loss are central to urban survival. The cities of Vienna, Salzburg, and Munich offer three disparate approaches to addressing those concerns.

In their approaches, these European cities have addressed urban physical development in order to assure the infrastructure necessary for growth and stability, together with the need to make their cities attractive to investment and tourism as well as liveable....

Vienna, Salzburg, and Munich are unique when compared to most American towns as they have developed virtually to the limits of their geographical boundaries. Each city has reached its agricultural, rural, scenic greenbelt, and political border limits. Under Austrian and German law, conversion of rural land for urban development is nearly impossible. This growth strategy does not generate the American version of urban sprawl and central city de-stabilization caused when new homes and jobs leave the city for cheaper and more desirable suburban sites converted from agricultural or open space lands. Instead, growth calls for redevelopment of sites within the city and a focus on economic development....

Each of the cities is vigorously pursuing the development of high-tech, low pollution, archetypically computer-based service and manufacturing industries. Each seeks to identify itself as the "Silicon Valley" of its region, a reference to the San Jose, California, community that rapidly grew in the 1970s with computer firms. Silicon Valley slowed its growth in the 1980s, perhaps reflecting the flight of semi-conductor manufacturing from the United States. Yet, due to its powerful computer base, Silicon Valley appears to be thriving once again. Indeed many American communities are in pursuit of the Silicon Valley "high-tech industrial campus" formula....

Vienna's focus recognizes the high cost of its limited available land, its high cost of labor and living, and its need for additional housing.

Salzburg, although without such an exalted geo-economic view as Vienna, is nevertheless seeking to augment its tourist-based economy with high-tech industrial and service company development. Salzburg's approach focuses on a marriage between industry and its technical university. Under the "Techno-Z" (pronounced Techno-Zed) project, industrial parks are being established around the city to provide incubation for the establishment of new companies. The project is underwritten by subsidies from the state and federal government with support by the city in providing development sites. Industrial development is further supported though the provision of industrial infrastructure and advanced telecommunications systems and access to the technical university's supercomputer, and is supported by active participation by the departments, faculty, and students of the technical university.[18] Business incubation programs have proliferated in the United States since the 1980s.[19]

Ironically, high-tech growth in Germany is being stimulated by Silicon Valley firms, and an aggressive advertising campaign to encourage American manufacturing plant development in Germany. Indeed, the European experience is modeled on the American experience in stimulating research parks.

Although high-tech research parks may appear to be a panacea, successful research parks actually raise rents in the region, provide few additional job opportunities for low-skilled members of the work-force, and indeed may cause industrial gentrification whereby successful parks drive up wages in established industrial areas with traditional manufacturing firms unable to raise wages, retain skilled personnel, or remain in business. Germany and Austria should be extending educational training and retraining programs at the very time that EU membership creates pressure to cut back on both taxation and social programs to remain competitive. Germany and Austria are encour-

18. Salzburg Technologiezentrum, The Salzburg Technology Center (Mar. 1989). Salzburg Technology Center ("Techno-Z") was created as a part of the Salzburg Business Settlement Association. Opened in June 1988, Techno-Z has several buildings, each housing or to house a separate concept or division, including a "factory of the future," a "computer and communication technology center," the five university institutes, and the "high-tech development area." The first, the factory, is an array of new enterprises all developing technology to adapt current manufacturing techniques to the future using computers in every step in the manufacturing process. The second, the computer and communication center, is open to new enterprises as well as research and development divisions of existing companies which specialize in microelectronics, computers, communication, and software engineering. The third division, the university, will be the core of Techno-Z. Its role is to serve as an information and technology transfer center, and to provide industry with fresh minds and holistic business advice. The fourth division, the development area, is a site set aside for international companies looking to expand research and development and engineering facilities. This area will be in close proximity to Techno-Z and can benefit from the university's programs and its supercomputer as do all the other divisions of Techno-Z. The Technical University in Berlin is another notable example of a cooperative venture under which state of the art industrial research in a functioning robotics factory within the university with research and production jointly staffed by academics and private sector scientists within a jointly created and funded university.

19. Nancy Rivera Brooks, *They're Fruitful and They're Multiplying*, L.A. Times, Nov. 20, 1995, at D2 (describing the Calstart's Project Hatchery, USC Annenburg Center for Communication's EC2, as well as several inner-city projects, and reporting on 500 incubators in the nation, with a dozen in Southern California, each with public and private participation; noting that 80% of incubation companies that graduate from the programs were still in business after five years, 60% of incubator tenants sell goods and services to other tenants in the same incubator; warning that some incubation projects may be mere ineffectual real estate deals offering at best cheap rents and that incubation has not been successful with retail and business service firms).

aged to extend educational training and retraining programs by EU membership, which also calls for the harmonization of taxation and social programs.[26]

Austrian economic development policy includes a tax policy that encourages investment, and provides for direct subsidies in the form of financing guarantees, direct financing, or state direct participation in development initiatives as an investor. Indeed, as of 1990, 32.8 percent of Austrian firms were state-owned.

Austria also has a markedly different attitude towards protecting the stability of private enterprise from that of the United States. For example, Austria has engaged in significant programs to assist failing businesses including direct investment. Occasionally, in well-publicized situations such as subsidies for AMTRAK and loan guarantees to Lockheed, Chrysler, or New York City, the federal government in the United States has assisted ailing industry. Thus, large and influential employers may enjoy unique special treatment from local government as seen in the case of Detroit displacing Poletown to accommodate the needs of Cadillac and avoid plant relocation to another region. In addition, government-insured loans and modest assistance for small businesses is available.[37] But for the most part, America's capitalistically driven system lets the successful succeed and leaves the not so successful to fail. Frequently, businesses fail or relocate because of the marginal inability to make a profit and meet payroll. Costly assessments or property taxation can encourage business closings. Often communities pay millions to attract particular business, when much more modest programs to assist in the retention of existing business might be effective in ensuring sustainable economic growth.[38]...

University alliances appear to be a part of the necessary infrastructure for bio-tech and high-tech computer industry development.[39] While American cooperation between industry and the university has been slow and the relationship with government often confrontational or competitive, there are signs of increased cooperation and participation. Indeed, high-tech American research parks have enjoyed university subsidies and government subsidies in the form of reduced infrastructure costs and lower property taxes, with land-use policies favoring park development and expansion. High-tech

---

26. EC Treaty calls for the harmonization of taxes, including turnover taxes (a type of sales tax) and excise duties among others required for the functioning of the internal market, art. 99; and the improvement of living standards and working conditions as well as their harmonization. Art. 117, 3 Common Mkt. Rep. (CCH) ¶ 25,400.

37. 15 U.S.C. §§ 631–635 (Small Business Administration loans administered by the Department of Commerce); 42 U.S.C. § 1471 (Farmers Home Administration loans and subsidy programs). There have also existed federal funds for local community development corporations, designed to stimulate economic development in low-income and minority communities....

38. One such more effective program, which would cost less, would be regional tax base equalization, James A. Kushner, *The Reagan Urban Policy: Centrifugal Force in the Empire*, 2 UCLA J. Envtl. L. & Pol'y 209, 230 (1982), which could lower tax burdens on firms in areas in need of an increased tax base by revenue sharing with wealthier areas, and would discourage the relocation of firms to areas with low taxes who receive excessive amounts of revenue in comparison to their required outlay for infrastructure and services.

39. Robert F. Johnston & Christopher G. Edwards, Entrepreneurial Science: New Links Between Corporations, Universities and Government 23 (1987). Corporations are also investing in basic university research, with affiliations allowing academics to conduct basic research which may yield a beneficial result for the sponsoring company and provides a gateway between talented graduate students and company recruiters. Id. at 21. The University of Texas currently sponsors 32 $1 million endowed chairs to attract faculty in microelectronics and technology.... Justin Martin, *A Guide to the Best Cities for Business*, Fortune 97, 98 (Nov. 13, 1995) (High-tech computer industry employers, including Texas Instruments, 3M, Motorola, IBM, Advanced Micro Devices, and Dell Computer, employ about 85,000 people in Austin).

competitiveness reflects significant public investment in research and development. The United States should accelerate the coordination of government, university, and private industry to assure workforce training. As compared to the United States, Germany and Japan each direct a higher percentage of their gross national product to nonmilitary research and development....

While many American cities have pursued the various tax and other development incentives employed by their European counterparts, the target of economic development has rarely been toward the central city. Instead, new commercial and industrial development generally occurs either in the outer suburban ring of urban centers or toward exurban or rural research or industrial parks. Critics of urban competition to lure relocating employers cite expensive incentives reflecting capital investment diverted from renewing infrastructure essential for community stability and economic development. In addition, communities often fail to contractually require accountability by enticed employers to assure that promises are kept and value received for expensive subsidies and other development incentives. Although articulated economic development policy, as reflected in direct federal subsidies in the United States, appears to be largely targeted at urban revitalization, the effect of tax and spending programs is to redirect economic activity to the suburbs and rural areas. Moreover, the incentives have been challenged for their ineffectiveness. Despite the need for education and human and employment development and training, Republican-influenced spending schemes place little value on human development. Instead, urban redevelopment and revitalization programs tend to be capital based, with programs generating structures that are too often useless....

Local and state budgets tend to be haphazard but may include access to below market rate bond lending or local waivers of development fees or costs. Occasionally, as in the case of certain redevelopment projects, the public sector provides infrastructure such as roads, utilities, and side-walks to serve the project. Lower suburban or rural taxation levels, more affordable insurance premiums, and superior transportation access, also play a role in suburban site selection resulting in urban disinvestment. But apart from these incentives, communities are likely to be seen as hostile both to new development and existing employers except where communities are engaged in pirating employers from other regions, scrambling to retain an employer considering emigration to another region, or engaged in a unique project. Although the pirating or poaching of industry is prohibited under some federal programs, like the EU experience, incubation-oriented projects would appear to enjoy legal sanction.

Enterprise and empowerment zones, providing lowered taxes to encourage investment in new business initiatives, have not yet proven to contribute to an increase in overall employment investment. Enterprise zones may simply re-target economic activity to attain program benefits rather than generate new economic activity. The American labor market, marked by high unemployment, poor education and training, and high levels of racial discrimination tends to inhibit investment. Despite the modest enterprise zone initiatives, local communities anticipate a reduction in federal aid for community development and economic development....

Although clearly tied to an economic development strategy, Vienna, Salzburg, and Munich each recently have embarked on planning strategies looking to traditional physical planning. The planning initiatives include traffic and development policies seeking to make the central city more attractive for retail sales, and recreation. Each of the three cities have successfully created extensive automobile-free pedestrian zones. These areas range from complex labyrinthine arcades and alleys in Munich and Salzburg, to permanent plazas in Munich and Vienna patterned on the Old City squares in Salzburg, to the erection of simple barriers in Munich to exclude trucks, cars, and buses, while converting streets to café sites and pedestrian zones.

Salzburg and Munich, despite tourist and retail success through pedestrianization, have not succeeded in establishing any significant night-life in their city centers other than the Munich beer hall culture, which previously existed, and a proliferation of upscale expense account restaurants and eateries associated with beer drinking. Salzburg's historic city center generally shuts down early in the evening and the streets are empty and eerie late at night. Salzburg's success was supported by progressive historic preservation as well as redevelopment policies.

Nevertheless, the downtowns of German cities have remained vital and stable from the increase in pedestrians and their concomitant rise in retail sales. Interestingly, the establishment of pedestrian malls was opposed by shopkeepers. Areas adjacent to pedestrian zones often experience a back-to-the-city movement enhancing stability but may face problems of increased traffic, parking, and displacement of low-and moderate-income housing.

By comparison, Vienna's planning experiment has been a huge success, with the city center populated by tourists as well as residents very late into the evening without a quiet evening in the week. Night clubs, bars, cafes, restaurants, and coffee houses have proliferated, each catering to a different crowd. There are even traditional coffeehouses filled with intellectuals, artists, bohemians, and Viennese who like to rub shoulders with them, and those who simply enjoy reading daily newspapers or playing a game of chess. In addition, there is a lively street life with musicians, young people, and tourists enjoying themselves. The reason for Vienna's triumph and Salzburg and Munich's partial success is not obvious. Indeed public officials, planners, and architects in Vienna profess wonderment at the city's transformation from the quiet burgh of a decade ago....

The juxtaposition of Hans Hollein's ultramodern Haas Building across from St. Stephen's Cathedral on the square with the Ring's grand historicist monuments of the imperial period has changed Vienna's image to one of a city looking toward a glittering future and unafraid to demonstrate that optimism in architecture. Vienna's planned Danube City will completely exclude automobiles from the surface, with all streets, transit, and parking at the subterranean level.

It appears that several factors may have contributed to the results in each of the cities. Munich's emphasis on shops and its rigid laws regulating the hours of public accommodations has restricted its success. In addition, Munich and Salzburg are dispersed communities with night clubs and popular evening recreation establishments located away from the historic districts. By comparison, Vienna appears to enjoy several factors contributing to its central city success: first, the central historic district is very large suggesting more economical rents and enjoying the benefits and attraction power of a multitude of entertainment opportunities. The cumulative effect creates a kind of critical mass of activity not unlike the success of shopping malls containing numerous competitors. Second, Vienna's rigid zoning has precluded the development of a broad pattern of neighborhood pubs and restaurants; some popular clubs are located outside the city centers, each often popular on but one night of the week. Third, Vienna enjoys a superb public transit system enabling the typical non-automobile operating public to get around town. Most Viennese own a transit pass purchased for a few hundred dollars a year; the average Viennese uses public transit 600 times a year. Finally, although Austrians criticize Germans as being excessively orderly, my observations disclose a much higher level of order and obedience to law in Vienna than, for example, Munich. Pedestrians typically wait for green lights, traffic or not, and drivers meticulously obey traffic laws and give the right-of-way to pedestrians and bicyclists. Even graffiti in Vienna is limited to a few forums permitted or ignored by local government such as along the lower path of the Danube Canal. It is easier to find a Benetton store than litter in Vienna. One evening at 1:00 a.m. in the morning after leaving a coffeehouse I heard the familiar sound of breaking glass. But when I found the source, rather than street hooligans it was a cleaning crew sweeping a square and emptying trash containers. By comparison, there is a good bit more graffiti in Munich, and drivers, often crazed from excessive traffic and a lack of parking, are often rude and too often ignore traffic and parking restrictions.

No doubt, the security one feels on the streets of Vienna as compared with the modestly more threatening feel of Salzburg or the post-beer hall happy drunkenness in Munich may be a factor in Vienna's success in establishing the utopian city. Of course all is not perfect and one hears of the rising incidence of crimes and auto theft, occasional late night subway assaults and drug activity; still, for a resident of Los Angeles, Vienna's (and Salzburg and Munich's) crime scene is as quiet as the nicest town or neighborhood in America.

Despite Vienna's dramatic success in "pedestrianization," a number of German cities, including Munich and Nuremberg, view their experiences as positive with increase in urban vitality as well as retail sales. Studies of Copenhagen, Denmark, disclose that pedestrianizing modern shopping malls results in transformation of areas through a variety of stimulating experiences and can contribute significantly to reducing the urban flight of sales and population. Liveable spaces are most successful when they are located at the heart of the city or neighborhood. This is particularly so where, as in Vienna, Salzburg, and Munich, public squares are located at the heart of the most historic buildings, creating the strongest image of the essence of the community. Communities can engage in a wide array of policies to generate a sense of neighborhood. For example, Bremen, a German city, provides lost and stolen unclaimed gaily painted bicycles and lost umbrellas in public places for use by the public to be borrowed and returned after emergency use. Efforts at promoting pedestrian zones, or "traffic calming," where automobiles are slowed and discouraged, such as where streets are shared by both vehicles and pedestrians are called "Woonerf" by the Dutch. Pedestrianization projects are underway in Boston, Boulder, and Seattle, and being considered in the District of Columbia, Portland, Oregon, and in New York City. While the Third Street Promenade in Santa Monica, California, has long been a retail success, other American small town or small neighborhood malls have often proven unsuccessful.[105] If American cities are to enjoy the European model of success, they must provide safe, clean, and efficient public transit. Higher density of residential districts is central to European pedestrianization success. Those in large expensive homes typically remain at home, as compared to the Viennese, who are attracted to cafes, coffeehouses, and a walk in public spaces. Unfortunately, American planning policy during the last generation has been targeted toward discouraging pedestrianization and transit usage while encouraging automobile-dependent transportation.

---

105. *See generally* Kent A. Robertson, *Downtown Redevelopment Strategies in the United States: An End of the Century Assessment*, 61 J. Am. Plan. Ass'n 429 (1995) (recounts early, often failed, malls, the next generation of enclosed malls, and the need for a pervasive pattern of pedestrian-friendly public spaces around high-density residential development and reused public buildings).

Clearly cities must act as a magnet, a place of diversity, creativity, and entertainment that attracts rather than repels people. American standards and needs for emergency vehicle response may impede efforts to expand automobile free zones or neighborhoods as it has generated lower density development on broad avenues inviting automobile usage. Nevertheless, federal funds are available for traffic calming and pedestrianization. Cosmetic changes, however, are not enough to restore many American cities to competitive status as they must systematically address all aspects of their livability as enhancements to livability are but a part of economic redevelopment....

Broad public green spaces mark successful cities like Vienna, Salzburg, and Munich. The Vienna woods along the outskirts of the national capitol of Austria provided the inspiration for Beethoven's Pastoral Symphony and continues to provide a resource and inspiration to the Viennese today. Although the woods comprise the city's largest green space, the city is ringed by park and forest lands including the Langer Tiergarten, a gated public forest land replete with boar, deer and other wildlife and available for hiking and wandering. The city's beautiful Prater Park and numerous smaller parks along the Danube River and canals offer beauty to neighborhoods and ties the city together. The residents of New Danube City and U.N. City enjoy the adjacent Danube recreational island and the Alta Danube green space parks containing forty kilometers of beaches, lake-like water playgrounds, and Doneau Park. Probably half of Vienna is made up of parks and recreational green space.

Visitors to Salzburg may quickly turn to the built environment of the beautiful medieval and baroque center but are not likely to forget the beauty of its surrounding hills and the green space and bike paths along the Salzach River. Anyone who saw *The Sound of Music* knows the home of Maria. The most popular tour in Salzburg visits the movie locations including the monastery and home of the Von Trapps. Extraordinary green space exceeds in size the urbanized portion of Salzburg, which also has beautiful parks and gardens.

To me the best part of Munich is its green spaces. Neighboring parks and more formal gardens are found throughout the city but the gem is the Englisher Gardens and park and forest lands along the Isar River. The garden constitutes the largest urban park in Germany with lakes and meandering criss-crossing walking and bike trails, large commons, lakes, and forests. Most visitors walk in the gardens and are impressed with the beauty and serenity, and possibly have a long beer in one of its gardens. But it takes a bicycle ride or days of hiking to discover its breadth and majesty. The mixed use new community on the site of the redeveloped airport at Reim will allot more than 50 percent of the site for green spaces. Open space is protected in Germany under planning laws rendering the conversion of open space for urbanization, a commonplace process in the United States, nearly impossible. The German and Austrian commitment to open space and dedication to its preservation is a fundamental part of their cultural imperative on a high-density continent. By contrast, the American land ethic has employed the inexhaustible resource of land and the hegemony of individual self-interest within an historically low density nation.

Sadly, American's urban parks have become the scene of crime and a cause for instability. In Los Angeles, green space, despite the large Griffith Park, comprises a very minor use of urban land. More land is directed to automobiles than parks. It appears that neighborhoods are designed without sufficient parks to discourage visits to the neighborhood by residents of other districts. Despite a broad pedestrian zone in the Los Angeles downtown plan, most new urban plazas in the downtown are located outside the zone. Parks and public spaces are designed to allow security surveillance through minimal landscaping while discouraging public use and access.[151] Los Angeles is currently planning four new plazas linked to eight pedestrian friendly streets referred to as "avenidas." It appears that downtown planning and development policy has been controlled by private developers undermining any sense of strategic public planning. Indeed, in the United States, requiring a developer to dedicate a *de minimis* portion of a parcel for recreational use is often treated as an unconstitutional taking of property.

Cities are less attractive to investment and urban residence as suburban green space is often more attractive and typically safer than urban green space. America's cities also tend to place the burden for open space development on private developers and the political process results in an inadequate development of open space and recreational amenities. Even in the most affluent areas there are insufficient playing and practice fields for little league baseball and soccer. The very physical health of our citizens is adversely affected as sports participation is limited to the availability of play areas and limited open space generates less oxygen, aggravating urban air pollution....

* * *

Notes and Comments

1. American planning commentators are increasingly encouraging higher density mixed-use projects developed around transit. Peter Calthorpe, The Next American Metropolis: Ecology, Community, and the American Dream (1993); Anthony Downs, New Visions for Metropolitan America (1994); James A. Kushner, *Growth Management and the City*, 12 Yale L. & Pol'y Rev. 68 (1994); James A. Kushner, *Urban Transportation Planning*, 4 Urb. L. & Pol'y 161 (1981).

2. Many American communities have pursued professional sports franchises as a method of urban revitalization and economic development. Although cities like Baltimore and Cleveland can point to beautiful facilities and a revitalized portion of the central city, the studies of sports stadia indicate clearly that they provide no economic benefit to the city. Indeed they cost the taxpayer dearly in most instances. The big winners tend to be the local newspapers who find that sports enthusiasts are big subscribers. This is why newspapers tend to be the biggest sports boosters. Newspapers are also the

---

151. [Anastasia Loukaitou-Sideris, *Privatization of Public Open Space*, J. Regional Sci., May 1993, at 139, 153–54] (high enclosing walls, blank facades, distancing from street, deemphasis of street-level accesses, and major entrances through parking structures, disconnecting the space from the surrounding city fabric, as segregated as other parts of urban form; inappropriate play spaces for children, no grass for couples to lie on, or large groups to congregate; designers seek to create settings for an exclusive class of user with materials and design to impress and promote the feeling of affluence; design characteristics serve objectives of control, protection, social filtering, image generation, and manipulation of user behavior; security policies of excluding bag-ladies, the homeless, street vendors, musicians and public performances, noisy teenagers and children, picnicking, those with unique attire, or the engaging in expressive activities, policies driven by owners' concern for maintenance, liability, and marketability). *See also* [Witold Rybczynski, City Life 209–210 (1995)] (the popularity of private enclosed American malls is due to their being perceived as public spaces where rules of personal conduct are enforced, like city streets used to be, free of boorish adolescents, noisy drunks, and aggressive panhandlers); [John Pastier, *New Open Space in L.A.*, Landscape Architecture, May 1984, at 42] (Pershing Square, rebuilt for $14.5 million and the downtown's most striking open space, lacks grass and public toilets to discourage the homeless). *Compare* [Jane Jacobs, The Death and Life of Great American Cities 152 (1961)] (the first condition for creating exuberant diversity in city streets and open spaces is multiple use at different times), *with* the frequent dedication of Los Angeles urban open space for lunching professionals).

biggest boosters of growth as new housing spells new subscribers. William Fulton, The Reluctant Metropolis (1997). There exists a controversy over whether public support for sport stadia is a wise investment of local resources or a give-away to team owners and stadium investors. Mark S. Rosentraub, Major League Losers: The Real Costs of Sports and Who is Paying For it (1999) (no benefits in economic growth, jobs, or regional tax base); Mark S. Rosentraub, *Sports, Facilities, Redevelopment, and the Centrality of Downtown Areas: Observations and Lessons from Experiences in a Rustbelt and Sunbelt City*, 10 Marq. Sports L.J. 219 (2000) (economic objectives unsuccessful); Symposium, *In Defense of New Sports Stadiums, Ball Parks, and Arenas*, 10 Marq. Sports L.J. 361 (2000).

3. *Technology Centers*. On technology parks, see generally Michael I. Luger & Harvey A. Goldstein, Technology in the Garden: Research Parks and Regional Economic Development xvi, 19 (1991) (Research Triangle in Durham, North Carolina; Provo to Orem, Utah; Silicon Valley; and Route 128 in Massachusetts described); AnnaLee Saxenian, Regional Advantage: Culture and Competition in Silicon Valley and Route 128 3, 107–10 (1994) (Route 128 around Boston as well as Silicon Valley); Jay Hailey, *Austin: High Tech Mecca*, 54 Urb. Land 62–64 (Apr. 1995) (led by Motorola and Advanced Micro Devices, each with facilities costing over $1 billion and together contributing nearly $30 million annually to the local tax base, the high tech companies of Austin employing 85,000 and working very closely with the University of Texas, and noting that 900 computer-related high-tech employees demand a high quality of life and excellent schools); Richard Rapaport, *Mormon Conquest*, Forbes, Dec. 7, 1992, at 76 (describing Wasatch Front or the Provo to Orem fifty mile research strip linking Brigham Young University, with Novell's WordPerfect in Orem equaling all software sales in the Silicon Valley).

4. On neighborhood economic development, see Florence Contant, Community Development Corporations: An Annotated Bibliography (Council of Planning Librarians Exch. Bib. No. 293 1972); National Housing and Economic Development Law Project, A Lawyer's Manual on Community-Based Development (1974). *See also* Richard D. Marisco, *Fighting Poverty Through Community Empowerment and Economic Development: The Role of Community Reinvestment and Home Mortgage Disclosure Acts*, 12 N.Y.L. Sch. J. Hum. Rts. 281 (1995) (encouraging lender investment).

Mallification

The following excerpt looks at the "mallification" of Europe as it follows the lead of America's shopping mall success:

James A. Kushner, *Social Sustainability: Planning for Growth in Distressed Places—the German Experience in Berlin, Wittenberg, and the Ruhr*,

3 Washington University Journal of Law & Policy 849 (2000)

Central to the region's economic revitalization strategy are commercial and recreational destinations to attract tourists and shoppers. The development of commercial shopping malls reflects the financial success of the American experience. In Oberhausen, on the cleared and cleaned brownfields that had been the site of a former steel mill adjacent to the Gasometer, private developers have built "CentrO," currently Europe's largest shopping mall and recreation facility, with 2.1 million square feet of commercial space, on a 21 acre indoor and outdoor recreation park, containing $2.32 million in landscaping. The outdoor park called "Adventure Island" contains a 75 foot long pirate ship and a pirate fortress-like jungle gym, adjacent to a several story-high pagoda-like structure surrounded by sliding boards. With the recreation park targeted at children, a car park with structures accommodating 10,500 automobiles, its own rail station, a promenade of outdoor restaurants and cafes, a multi-screen Warner Brothers cinema, miles of fast food, typical mall shopping, the complex is popular among young people, generating rising retail sales but escalating automobile trips. The complex contains a 12,000 seat arena and future phases include a world class aquarium, a 60 yacht marina, and 300 to 600 residential apartments. It is the government's policy to only locate shopping facilities on former brownfields, while preserving greenfields.

In Dortmund, an eight story train station is planned with a modern mall and entertainment complex including multiplex movie cinemas, offices, restaurants, and an aquarium, with the structure in the form of a flying saucer from a martian invasion movie. The 150,000 square meter "UFO" (unlimited fun object) project is designed to attract regional shoppers, increase the local tax base, revitalize the largely social housing community north of the station, and support the rejuvenation initiatives for the old downtown area to the south of the station. According to Erik J. Englebrecht of the developer Immobilien Team Consulting GmbH & Co. ("ITC"), Dortmund is one of twenty-six such rail station commercial projects ITC is seeking to develop in Europe, based on the "UFO" design. In Dortmund, the proposed one billion Deutsche Mark "UFO" would have eight levels, 6,200 parking spaces, 50,000 square meters of shopping, and seven thousand square meters of restaurants, and is projected to create 3,000 new jobs. Political acceptance of the design concept remains to be realized.

One might wonder why the current development pattern and planning model in the Ruhr more closely reflects Los Angeles and sprawling Southern California rather than the success of higher density outdoor pedestrian shopping districts so popular in Germany. Although the shopping malls in the Ruhr are transit accessible, the pattern appears to reflect increasing automobile use and dependency. The causes no doubt include a combination of more and better highways, consumer demand for luxury automobiles, and the decline of the age of the planned community in favor of a more market-driven economy, and an environment favoring deregulation. Dortmund has located its mall at the central rail station while Oberhausen's "CentrO" enjoys a local train line and bus service to a station constructed within the "CentrO" complex. Nevertheless, initially sixty percent of "CentrO's" patrons arrived by automobile, increasing in the first year of operation to a dramatic seventy-five percent. That modal split disparity should continue to increase as more housing developments are being located on the outskirts of the region's cities and towns. Even the excellent autobahns,[2] or limited access and typically unlimited speed superhighways, are congested at rush hours, leaving the region's roadways resembling Los Angeles or Istanbul, rather than a picturesque "Romantic Road" through Bavaria. Each of the cities that make up the megalopolis called the

2. [The] autobahn system in the Ruhrgebiet includes a huge grid of five east-west and six north-south autobahns.

Ruhrgebiet have an attractive pedestrian shopping mall, from Essen to Oberhausen, Dortmund, or the "Bermuda Triangle" of shops, restaurants, and pubs in Bochum. The new shopping districts of the Ruhr augment rather than compete with nearby Dusseldorf's sophisticated Konigsallee ("Ko"). New Shopping malls that may enjoy tax and other development incentives enjoy a competitive advantage over traditional small shops and "mallification" could spell a decline for the relatively historic post-World War II rebuilt pedestrian districts. Each of the cities is hoping that the regional malls will generate economic growth and job development, without any destructive competition. While the simultaneous development of a series of malls in the Ruhr has a dramatic impact on the perception of the region's revitalization, the cumulative number of traditional pedestrian shopping districts and modern malls may not be excessive for a regional population in excess of five million.

Indeed, in my travels in Europe during the summer of 1999, I learned that the "mallification" of Europe is well underway. Vienna will be Cineplex Theater central, with shopping malls and the popular factory outlet center the latest strategy for commercial success. Vienna is also rehabilitating and converting three brick gasometers to a shopping center. Prague is planning a number of suburban malls, one larger than CentrO or the Mall of America. In 1998, I visited Istanbul where Akmerkez, the largest and newest mall in Turkey, and a symbol of that beautiful city's modernity, is competing in "the most mall square footage in the world" contest. Berlin is finding that suburban shopping centers on rural sites just beyond the city's borders are attracting customers from higher price, higher rent, well-planned mixed-use transit-accessible shopping districts. Traditional shopping in Berlin, by comparison, has been carefully, and expensively, integrated with public transit and pedestrianized communities. New suburban shopping centers on non-transit served highways, and just beyond Berlin's regulatory authority, however, by offering lower prices, encourage an automobile-based society by offering further incentive to choose a low density suburban lifestyle dependent on automobile usage. The mall is not, however, the universal model for European or German community development. Wittenberg, Germany, is developing a beautiful pedestrianized *Hauptstrasse* (Main Street) in its *Altstadt* or old town, along the successful model of Heidelberg, or the pedestrian shopping district of Cologne. Los Angeles presents a dramatic contrast to the German retail scene. Long the mall capital with continuing astounding success in retail sales and tax generation, Angelenos appear to prefer the traditional main street outdoor pedestrian shopping found in Old Town Pasadena, Santa Monica's Third Street Promenade, Larchmont, Melrose, Montrose, or the Latin flavor of Broadway to the sameness offered by the Gallerias. Ironically, future mall development and redevelopment may seek to create an interior "outdoor" traditional main street layout, with central landscaping and wide sidewalks along storefronts, exchanging food courts for various "outdoor" cafes and sidewalk vendors. Entertainment by street musicians might replace the recorded music often heard at malls.

* * *

Notes and Comments

1. *Cleaning Up Times Square*. For a description of how Mayor Rudolph Giuliani made Times Square a symbol of his leadership, through the private business improvement district, see Josh Getlin, *Ball Has Dropped on Seedy Times Square—Renovation: New Yorkers Agree Area is Now Safer, But they're Torn Over Whether it's Better*, Los Angeles Times, Dec. 30, 1998, at A1. See the discussion of BIDS in Chapter 4.

Urban Redevelopment

The following excerpt takes a critical look at urban revitalization in comparing the Dutch experience with tax-increment financed redevelopment in California:

George Lefcoe, *When Governments Become Land Developers: Notes on the Public-Sector Experience in the Netherlands and California*,

51 Southern California Law Review 165 (1978)

What happens when local governments assume the functions of developing land—of making land ready for subdivisions, shopping centers, and industrial parks? Governments are major land developers in Sweden, the Netherlands, France, the United Kingdom, Australia, and Canada. Governments, acting as land developers, have claimed several benefits.

First, in Sweden the Socialist Party's land development program can be credited with all but eliminating land inflation. In fact, since land development became a "socialized" activity land prices have risen at rates well below the rate of inflation. This achievement should be of special interest to American cities—particularly Los Angeles and Washington, D.C.—where land and housing prices have climbed sharply in recent years.

Second, in most countries where governments are land developers the best vacant sites have usually been reserved not for affluent but for working class or middle-income people, without their being forced to pay exorbitant rents in order to outbid wealthier people for prime locations. Politics has supplanted the market as the land allocator.

Third, when governments profit as land developers development gains go into public coffers to offset the costs of opening up new areas and supplying them with roads and utility services. Simultaneously, these gains are diverted from private landowners who often have done little to merit receiving them, except by agreeing to sell to a developer.

Finally, by engaging actively in the land market, local governments have been able to make space available so that city firms needing to expand would not have to move to the suburbs to find the space they need. Making scarce urban land available has also helped cities lure new industry, offices, and shops.

Despite the apparent achievements of governmental land development, critics of it can fairly dispute each point. First, it can be argued that in Sweden high land prices appear in the tax bills of local citizens instead of showing up in the buyer's purchase price. It is these citizens who must shoulder the heavy costs of buying and holding vast land reserves a decade or longer before the land becomes marketable. Swedish land policy contributes more than a small share toward that country's rate of taxation, and exorbitant tax levels were partly responsible for the Socialist Party, which instituted the land policy, being voted out of office after four decades in power.

Second, in any country where trade unions exercise strong influence over government policy it is not surprising that land policy favors working people. The issue is whether the same ruling coalitions would have done better for their constituents if, instead of entering the land market directly, they had induced private builders, by regulations or otherwise, to reserve the best sites for popularly-priced housing at private, not public expense.

Third, one might argue that, if transferring land gains from private pockets to public coffers is the goal, taxation seems a far better way to do so. The government can tax without putting public money at risk in the land market.

Finally, regarding the use of public land to lure industry, it can be argued that local officials have often proved no match against the representatives of private firms in bargaining over land rents. Where governments are land developers many prosperous firms are able to buy or lease their sites so cheaply that inquiries can be made about the good judgment or even the integrity of local officials. Once a locality does grant land on "give-away" terms, other localities may feel obligated to follow its lead in order to preserve their industrial job bases. Not only do taxpayers suffer, but all the firms that had located in the jurisdiction earlier risk having to compete with newcomers whose rents they have, in effect, subsidized through their own taxes.[13]

Persuaded by the proponents of governmental land development, two U.S. Presidential commissions in the late sixties—one addressing urban problems in general and the other concerned with housing—recommended that local governments emulate the experiences abroad by "land banking," that is, acquiring development land ahead of need. Local governments could then become subdividers and, in accord with each community's schedule for infrastructure, might use the profits of suburbanization to offset the costs of new roads, parks, and schools, and even to subsidize suburban housing for low-income families.

Today, a similar call for public-sector land development is heard from some homebuilders.[16] They see governments' becoming land developers as a way of freeing homebuilders from the increasing pressure of stringent planning controls and high land prices. Though they are a small minority in the industry, these homebuilders are beginning to realize that the landowners is as often their antagonist as their ally. Because land is in short and relatively fixed supply, and planning controls serve further to restrict the effective supply of land, the landowner often enjoys a near-monopoly position vis-a-vis the private land developer and the homebuilder. Small wonder, then, that no less distinguished a lawyer and scholar than Richard Babcock (whose clients include land developers as well as utility companies) has recently argued that land ownership should be subject to the same price and use controls as are other monopolies "affected with a public interest."

---

13. Of necessity, most of the above arguments can be supported, if at all, by nothing more than anecdotal evidence because there is little scientific data on the subject. Even the most deceptively simple questions about land policy that have been subjected to theoretical and empirical investigation yield contradictory findings and become debates about methodology or economic theory. Left only with anecdotal data, astute advocates are usually able to prove whatever they want from any given set of case studies. But, since speculation and anecdote are what is available in this field, the best that can be done is to attempt to be comprehensive in stating the arguments for and against governmental land development, and to increase, as much as is possible, the stock of anecdotal material.

16. *See, e.g.*, E. Eichler & M. Kaplan, The Community Builder 54–79 (1967). It describes James Rouse's efforts as the developer of a private new town, Columbia, Maryland. To acquire the site, he needed to negotiate with many separate owners without their finding out that one developer was trying to purchase so large a contiguous site. He succeeded. Probably no governmental entity in this country could have proceeded without public notice to buy up so vast and widely held a property. But Mr. Rouse has said that a similar effort would be virtually impossible for a developer to repeat. Among his current projects is a shopping mall in Santa Monica, California, which is being financed through tax increment financing by the city of Santa Monica. The city is acquiring the site. As Mr. Rouse might well have predicted, there are holdout landowners whom the city will have to sue in eminent domain.....

These calls for greater local involvement in the land development business sound revolutionary. In the United States we have drawn a line that separates the public from the private realm, and we have placed land developing on the private side of that line. A few state courts have halted public intrusions into private land development. Except in these states, however, the line exists more in rhetoric than in practice.

In fact, our local governments have served as land developers on many occasions. In the Southwest, many of the major cities were once missions and pueblos, laid out and subdivided by early Spanish and Mexican governors. Taos and Santa Fe in New Mexico offer perhaps the best surviving examples of these early plans. In the eastern states, Washington, D.C., Williamsburg, Annapolis, and Savannah were among the publicly developed new towns on the colonial and post-colonial era. During Franklin Roosevelt's tenure, the government built a number of greenbelt towns in Maryland, Ohio, Wisconsin, and New Jersey. And from 1949 to 1973, thousands of American cities renewed their central business districts under the aegis of the federal urban renewal program.

In each of these instances there were special justifications for public involvements. When the colonial towns were built there were not private firms in the United States with the financial capacity and technical ability to build new communities. The Depression-era "planned communities" were prompted by a pressing need to provide jobs for the unemployed at a time when the private sector was ill-disposed to finance massive new work of any sort.

Urban renewal also had to be public, its defenders explained, in order to use the powers of eminent domain to assemble the thousands of individual sites necessary for an area-wide replanning and redesign of streets and utilities. Even if private redevelopers had been granted the power of eminent domain, as are utility companies in some states, few could have absorbed the expenses incident to relocating displaced residents. In addition, private developers would have had to assume property taxes and mortgage interest payments during the long years of planning and processing that accompanied—and nearly destroyed—many renewal projects. Public redevelopment agencies were free of property tax obligations during their holding periods and financed their acquisitions with tax-exempt municipal bonds. Even with these advantages most renewal agencies would have experienced serious financial difficulties had they not also received massive subsidies—direct grants from the federal government and tax forgiveness and financing advantages from state and local governments. New York State's daring entrant into the public-sector land development sweepstakes—the Urban Development Corporation—initiated fifty-four projects, including three new towns and 43,000 housing units, and defaulted on $100 million of notes 7 years after its inception.

Yet, with surprisingly little public attention and virtually no outcry of "socialism," hundreds of California cities, including almost all populous cities, have initiated redevelopment projects in recent years. This has been accomplished through a device knows as "tax increment financing," the essence of which is to use the expected increase in property taxes from a renewal project as a means of financing the project itself. In this way nearly 50,000 acres have been or are being redeveloped for a variety of "private" uses—office towers, industrial parks, housing (from luxury to low-rent), and parking garages—as well as "public" uses—from parks and civic malls to fire stations and schools.

"Tax increment financing" was introduced as one option among many for California cities to meet their matching share contribution under the federal renewal act. Now that the federal renewal program has been terminated, tax increment financing has become the primary financing device for urban renewal in California. Cities are redeveloping twice as much land today without federal renewal subsidies as they did during the 24 years of federal renewal, and with never a default on a renewal authority bond. The interest on these local securities is exempt from federal income tax, which affords the public sector a margin of advantage over strictly private projects whose lenders must pay income taxes on the interest they receive....

Not surprisingly, tax increment financing has its critics, and chief among them are school officials who feel that tax funds are inevitably and wrongfully diverted from school and other taxing districts. For one thing, some of the increase in assessed valuation is attributable not to the redevelopment effort but simply to inflation. For another, some agencies deliberately draw their project boundaries to include sites already scheduled for private upgrading purely to siphon off the increase in value. This increment is then utilized to support redevelopment bonds even though the private project in question was planned to be entirely independent of the redevelopment effort.

The case against tax increment financing derives strength from the fact that redevelopment projects do nothing to increase the *demand* for retail stores, apartments, offices, and the like. Very few people, for instance, will buy more shoes because there are more shoe stores downtown. The agency has increased the *supply* of new buildings at a particular site. But some of this construction would probably have come into existence elsewhere had there been a market to support it. If the "elsewhere" would have been outside the reach of the taxing districts affected, they could not claim any adverse affect directly.

There is always the chance, however, that if jurisdiction *A* builds a facility that would have located itself in jurisdiction *B*, *B* will retaliate. If *B* mounts a successful redevelopment project of its own, schools in *A* might then experience a loss of future revenues, either because the redevelopment project in *A* will falter, or because projects scheduled for *A* will not be built there after all....

The argument for and against governments as land developers has been divided into three parts. The first part concerns the merit in allowing governments to recoup their "loss-leader" expenditures for highways and utilities from shopping centers and industrial parks. A secondary benefit is that governmental land development reduces the incentive for private landed interests to distort public decisions about what types of public works are to be built and where they are to be located. The case *contra* is that governments would end up recouping nothing as land developers because they would do a poor job. Further, if landowners are powerful enough to influence public works decisions, would they not also be powerful enough to influence local governments in buying the wrong land at the wrong time for too high a price?

The second argument concerns the need for public-sector land development to achieve today's planning goals. These goals require that new development be concentrated in medium or high densities in order to avoid the costs of suburban "sprawl." Traditional zoning is negative: it bars owners from developing in such a way as to lower the value of neighboring lands. We have no means, however, of *requiring* private owners to develop according to a community's general plan. If we did, we would be able to compel that newly developed areas be built so as to minimize commuting and maximize the conservation of open space. Zoning ordinances prohibit densities greater than *x* units per acre; they do not require or mandate that no fewer than *x* units be built. The developer is always free to build at less than the prescribed density because the "spillovers" that zoning is designed to handle are those associated with overcrowding and congestion, and not those associated with "sprawl." The only practical means available for securing a concentrated pattern of exurban development is by the government's assuming the role of land developer.

The response to this argument is that if governments were seeking to earn profits as land developers there is no reason to assume that they would behave any differently from the way profit-maximizing firms act in today's market. Governments act as environmental protectors and/or as referees in resolving disputes between land developers and aroused neighborhood defenders. If governments were also land developers in their own right, however, they would be tempted to compromise their role as environmental regulators, especially in applying restraints to their own development activities. Having governments serve as land developers is no assurance of a concentrated pattern of development as long as small, tax-conscious communities can build as they please. If a greater concentration of development is desired, zoning ordinances could be amended accordingly. But the same political forces that bar developers from building at higher densities (which most of them would prefer) would also militate against local governments as developers building at high densities....

Public-Sector Land Development to Facilitate Traditional Public Works Programs

The Case in Favor

Nearly forty percent of the land in most of our cities ultimately comes into one or another of the conventional public uses: roads, schools, parks, and in some cases utilities (water, power, and sewage disposal). Advocates for a larger public role in suburbia have suggested a number of ways in which public works programs would benefit if the government's role were not confined to supplying public works, but were extended to housing, shopping centers, industrial parks, and the like.

Improving the integrity of public works decisions: Roads were built and water lines run, but open space for parks and even adequate sewage treatment facilities were neglected. The growing cities of the South west—Los Angeles is a prime example—are scandalously short of open space. This was partly due to high land prices. It was also due, however, to the political maneuvering of large landholders, the "pioneer" developers of the early 20th century, who realized that they could easily peddle tract lots with less than optimal open space (especially in largely unbuilt areas), but that they could not easily sell subdivided lots that lacked transportation access and water.

The sad history of Wilshire Boulevard illustrates as well as any example the consequence of governance by landowners. Early in the 20th century, Los Angeles city and county officials resolved to convert Wilshire—from downtown west to Santa Monica—into a 20-mile bicycle and pedestrian parkway. In the early 1920's, however, when the City Planning Commission urged the Council to zone Wilshire residential from Westlake to Western Avenues, a 2-mile distance centered approximately 2 miles west of downtown, owners along the street were successful in having the Council impose commercial zoning. The resulting heavy traffic defeated the park or bikeway plans for the eastern portion of Wilshire. Later, when the fate of Wilshire west of Western was put to a vote, the electorate chose to zone it for apartments as opposed to commercial use.

The real "miracle" of the portion of Wilshire known as the Miracle Mile was that the street could become commercial in spite of a referendum to the contrary. Cumulatively, these lot-by-lot variances rendered impracticable the early hope that Wilshire would become an aesthetic parkway and retreat for pedestrians and cyclists from the bustling downtown business district to the Pacific Ocean.

Large landholders influenced not only the type of public works built but also their location. The consequence is that public works are not necessarily located where they will contribute the most to the ultimate users. Nor are they necessarily located where they will enhance the total value of developed land in the community. If the government were the sole entity entitled to develop land, and if the government had the right to acquire land at its improvement value, no private landowner would have an incentive to exert undue influence over the location decisions for public works.

The Case Against

Costly inefficiencies would follow from public-sector land development: Against the notion that governments could have profited from land dealings sufficient to cover the costs of public works, we can set the balance sheets of several contemporary public-sector land development programs, including New York State's Urban Development Corporation and almost all of HUD's new town loan guarantees. Based upon these financial failures, we may ask whether local and state governments might not have lost far more as land developers in the unproven terrain of exurbia than they ever lost in center cities where there were both federal subsidies and large resident and business populations at hand to buy the land the government had to sell.

When government at all levels in the last century tried to assist rail roads through the device of recoupment—by allowing railroads to profit from the enhancement in value of lands adjoining railway routes—the results were financially disastrous. In response, many state constitutional provisions were adopted prohibiting loans and grants to private parties in order to keep governments as far from business entanglements as possible. For governments now to become private land speculators would be contrary to the spirit—if not the letter—of these provisions and would in any event ignore the costly lessons of the past.

In theory, recoupment seems prudent. In practice, the holding costs of land development and its uncertainties doom even some of the most astute entrepreneurs; many real estate investment trusts recently went broke trying their hands at suburban land development. Countless local governments marching into this most risky of markets—the market for developing land—where even the most knowledgeable mortgage lenders fear to tread, might as easily multiply as reduce the costs of highways and other public improvements.

Admittedly, local and state governments would not be burdened with holding costs as steep as those of private land dealers. The two principal costs of holding land for development are property taxes and mortgage interest rates. State and local governments are exempt from property taxes and pay lower interest rates than private borrowers because interest on state securities is exempt from federal income tax.

Nonetheless, the property taxes foregone when governments hold land is a real, though hidden, cost of public-sector land development. When some land is removed from private ownership, other private land holders must make up the deficit. As for the apparently lower interest rates of local securities compared with private mortgage rates, the reason for the gap is that high-bracket taxpayers and institutional investors calculate the value of the tax-exempt feature in buying these securities. Thus, the savings to local and state governments in borrowing costs are offset by losses to the federal treasury. The very existence of these savings would make local governments unfair competitors with private land developers. All else being equal, local governments would be able to buy more land than might prove efficient precisely because their holding costs are artificially low, subsidized as they are by federal taxpayers....

Setting the record straight on private landowners and public works decisions in Southern California: Returning to the second point raised in the initial argument—that private landowners skewed the public works budget in favor of roads and against open space—it will be instructive to consider the case of Los Angeles because it is often characterized as a city with less park land than almost any other city its size. Dwindling property tax rolls and the refusal of local residents to pay for additional parklands are the true reasons that explain why Los Angeles has so few parks. Most of the parks in Los Angeles came by chance or private gift, and much of that land became parkland because it was thought too hilly to develop. The donation by Griffith J. Griffith of 3000 such acres became the largest municipal park in the nation.

In sum, it was no conspiracy of large land holders that kept Los Angeles from acquiring more parklands. If Los Angeles is short of parks, it is simply because of a continuing resistance to park expenditures by taxpayers and voters. To say that there would have been more parkland had governments been the land developers would be to advocate short-circuiting the political process and forcing people to pay indirectly through land development revenues what they would not have approved directly through the legislative or special district process.

The greatest needs for parkland are in the older, central sections of the city, but population densities are so high in these areas that to install a typical neighborhood park would require the dislocation of hundreds of residents....

Of the 872 municipalities in the Netherlands, over 500 follow what the Dutch call an active ground policy, which means that the local government may well be the most active land developer in the jurisdiction. Among these 500 are all the larger municipalities. The best way of estimating the extent to which the local government monopolizes land development is by estimating that portion of all developable land owned by the municipality immediately prior to development. The total amount of land held by the city at any given time would not be a good indicator since some localities sell parcels once they have been readied for development, while others continue to hold title and lease their properties on long-term ground leases. In Rotterdam it is estimated that as much as 75% of all undeveloped land is municipally owned; in Amsterdam, 80%; and in Utrecht, 90%. According to a consultant from the Association of Dutch Municipalities, it is not unusual for a municipality to own 98 to 99% of the undeveloped land within its boundaries.

American scholars seeking to understand why the Dutch view land development as a proper government activity usually come up with three explanations. First, the Netherlands is the most densely populated country in the world except for Hong Kong and Monaco; hence, it became clear quite early that land should be regarded as a scarce resource and potentially a natural monopoly. If key parcels were controlled by a few firms, the latter might collaborate in setting limits on the number of sites to be built upon each year in order to increase their profit margins. Even short of such a conspiracy, government plans for meeting housing needs, especially after World War II, might have been frustrated if building sites were not brought on line as swiftly as housing subsidy funds were appropriated.

To prevent large landholders from manipulating the pace at which land would be released for urbanization, either the land developer would have to be treated as a utility and subjected to rate controls or the government itself would have to become the prime developer. In fact, Dutch municipalities assumed early the tasks of supplying water, gas, and electricity; consequently, the model of a regulated, privately-owned, quasi-public utility was less prevalent in the Netherlands than in this country. Municipalities not actively engaged in the land development business are not simply the smaller ones, for many tiny towns in the *Randstad* do develop land. Rather, they are the small- and medium-sized towns in sparsely populated parts of the country where vacant, developable land is abundant, and where, consequently, the chance of monopoly gain is negligible.

Second, the government has always had a major role in land development due to the high costs of making land ready for development. Physical conditions, especially in the lowlands, make land development both technologically complex and very expensive.[167] Until recently, there were no Dutch building firms with resources sufficient to finance and prepare land development in lowlands areas.

For the city of Amsterdam, public land development is a tradition dating back to the early 17th century when the city council embarked upon a plan for enlarging the old city by the construction of the three great concentric crescent canals. The plan increased the city area from 450 to 1800 acres. Geoffrey Cotterel characterized the plan as "a remarkable mixture of private enterprise and socialism . . . freedom within order."

Cotterel and most other Amsterdam devotees count this early expansion plan as "a triumphant success." But Cotterel also tells us that one burgomaster, Franz Oetgens, and his brother-in-law "could not resist the temptations offered by their knowledge of the expansion plans and they bought up land they knew the city would have to buy." They made for themselves "a quiet 112,000 guilders. In spite of this sad historic footnote, the expansion completed in the last decades of the 17th century would become a precedent cited with pride by 20th century proponents of public-sector land development.

Finally, Dutch localities have had to assume a major role in land development because they have been delegated a primary responsibility for ensuring that there is a sufficient supply of housing for all the population. . . .

---

167. As Professor Ann Louise Strong has explained:

> More than half of the land would be subject to intermittent flooding were it not for dikes and dams. Almost 20 percent of the land has been created from the sea. Water constitutes 16 percent of the Netherland's total area; and much of the water network is man-made. First the Zuyder Zee and now the Rhine-Meuse Delta area are being converted from salt-water bays or estuaries to fresh water lakes. There are enough drainage canals to encircle the earth six times. Amsterdam's shipping channel, linking the Rhine to the sea, is artificial. A national water management program shapes the natural environment of the future by holding back the sea, draining the land, maintaining an adequate fresh-water supply, and creating new land. . . . Urban development on the lowlands (the most heavily populated coastal areas) is expensive and difficult because of soil conditions and the high water table: yet this is where most of it has occurred, largely because of port growth on the estuaries. The peat of the lowlands is from sixty to seventy feet deep, so that construction of roads and buildings requires fill and pilings. Pilings must be sunk through the peat to solid ground, and the height of buildings is restricted. The cost of roads and the cost of public utilities are up to three times greater than those in the south and east of the country where the ground is stable. The old inner section of Rotterdam was built on pilings but was not filled, while newer areas have been filled to raise them above mean sea level and to provide a more solid foundation for building. When the subway was built, it was cheaper to open trenches, let them fill with water, and then sink sections of the subject tunnel rather than to attempt to keep the excavations pumped dry. In Amsterdam the land is filled some six feet, which leaves it below mean sea level but high enough to be removed from the polder management system. The Hague was built on the edge of the coastal dune where accumulated sand provided a higher and more solid foundation.

There are basically four current justifications for government land development in the Netherlands. First, Dutch people enjoy and want one-family houses and gardens, and private cars. If the government permitted private subdividers free reign, the little open space that remains in the populated sections of the country would swiftly be subdivided into low-density Dutch Levittowns.

Second, although many Dutch people benefitting from housing subsidies do not need them, there are still large numbers of poor residents, many of them immigrants from former Dutch colonies, who have housing needs not likely to be met by private developers. By acting as land developers local governments are able to reserve sites for "social" housing while subsidizing the costs of these sites out of sales of land to private builders of luxury "villas."

Third, if the land market were open to private speculators, land inflation would surely ensue in a country as short of land as is the Netherlands. The government prevents this by its direct intervention in the land market. During periods of time when local governments are buying and developing sites, some land inflation is created by the fact that so many sites have been removed from potential development. But as land is released, all land prices will stabilize—or so it is hoped.

Finally, in some parts of the country land is farmed in long and narrow strips parallel to waterways and canals and perpendicular to the main roads. The Dutch are the most efficient of farmers; these slivers yield remarkably well. They are also the most efficient of land users; along the road they have built greenhouses, farm dwellings, shops, and the like. Private tract subdividers try to avoid purchasing the developed portions of the farm along the roadside and attempt instead to buy only the narrow farmed strips that are cheaper to develop because no structures need to be demolished. If this practice were condoned, the resulting land use pattern would be ugly and chaotic. Only government acquisition of all these strips and gores, of road-side greenhouses as well as fanned strips, can result in a reformulation of boundaries suitable to urbanization.[182]...

Utrecht's *Hoog Catherijne*

Almost 10 years ago an American political science professor was able to describe a project in Utrecht, *Hoog Catherijne*, as "Urban Renewal—Utrecht Style." The analogy to urban renewal was apt because the project in question—a huge, multi-use affair in downtown Utrecht—was initiated by a large, private development firm, one of the few in Holland capable of such a venture. The city's role, as in the United States, was strictly as land assembler and infrastructure provider. In fact, the concept for the scheme, as well as the marketing analysis, financing, planning, and construction, were all handled by the developer, Bredero, a vertically integrated real estate holding company.

The relationship between Utrecht officials and the Bredero firm highlights both the strengths and weaknesses of city governments' becoming partners with private firms in redevelopment. On the plus side, the city brings the power of government. In the case of the Utrecht project this involved the power to close and pave a canal. It also included the power to authorize direct access from the central railroad station (one of Holland's

182. Besides acquiring the land and buildings itself, local government has other options. One is to bar private developers from building upon the unbuilt portions of agricultural land unless they include the greenhouses and farm buildings as well. Professor De Haan of Delft University has suggested another option—use of the Land Consolidation Act of 1954. This legislation provides a means for divergent farm properties to be consolidated and rationalized through reparcelling. Consolidation plans require a majority vote of all landowners in the area whose acreage is affected.

most important railroad stations) to the proposed commercial shopping center. The private firm brings its skill in assessing market demands for shops, offices, and apartments; its determination in marketing these facilities; its capacity to tap private capital markets to pay for the construction; and its experience in estimating construction costs and actually putting up the project within the budget.

On the down side, the developer, however magnanimous, is concerned with only the project, except to the extent that properties outside may affect it. If shopowners in the older downtown area will suffer a loss of tenants, the redeveloper has no incentive to save them from such losses. If the officials who negotiate the deal for the city are not themselves of an entrepreneurial bent, they may not be in a particularly good position to assess accurately the impact of the project on adjoining properties. Their judgments are likely to be amateurish, and they will have to depend upon their intuition or upon independent consultants to a greater extent than would any shrewd private shopping center developer.

City officials are seldom in a position to bargain skillfully over the price the city should receive for the land it makes available unless there is active competition for the site. Open bidding is often a poor technique, however, because it can lead to less well-qualified firms' winning the competition on the basis of unrealistic bids.[240] Then, in order to come out ahead, the winner will have to cut corners during construction in ways that only the most knowledgeable construction supervisors could detect. The city, without entrepreneurial competence, will have difficulty policing a developer who deviates from prescribed plans and specifications. Five or ten years after the project is completed, the construction shortcuts may begin to show. By that time any experienced developer caught in this sort of bind would have unloaded its interest in the project.

In other words, only when a city has personnel skilled at developing can it enter into a partnership with a developer on an equal footing, protecting the public interests the city is supposed to protect. Not many city planners can satisfy this test. Many who elect to enter the civil service tend to be risk averse; if they were high rollers, they might not have been inclined to exchange the chance of large gains for the security of a civil service job. It is often true that cities can lure entrepreneurial types, however, once they have entered the development game in a big way; many Dutch cities have employed ex-developers in their real estate departments. Utrecht was not, however, a town with an aggressive, active real estate program.

Utrecht suffered the customary ills of center cities. Its population of 250,000 was being slowly eroded as middle-class residents sought one-family housing in the suburbs; by 1968, more than 500,000 people inhabited the surrounding suburbs. Although Utrecht had annexed some of these areas, it was still lacking the sort of revitalized urban center that might have served as a magnet to reverse its steady, slow decline. Before *Hoog Catherijne* was built, the city was dismal: "Except for one small segment within the 'inner city,' Utrecht's downtown bares a depressing and unattractive quality. The railroad station on the border of the inner city, and the area surrounding it, are a series of grey-looking, poorly designed structures." Utrecht was sometimes characterized as the ugly sister of the *Randstad*—unable to compete with Rotterdam for industrial growth, with Amsterdam as a cultural center, and with The Hague, as a center of government. In prestige office space, high style fashion, or distinguished universities, Utrecht was invariably second, third, or fourth best.

---

240. ....Bredero, one of the few organizations capable of the complex understanding proposed for Utrecht, was without the pressure of competitive bidding, allowing the development of an optimal plan.

This may explain why the Burgomaster was overcome with delight when Bernard deVries, acting for his firm—Bredero—unveiled a plan for a high-rise office quarter, with a subjacent multilevel pedestrian shopping mall to be connected by enclosed walkways both to the railroad station and to luxury apartments, another part of the project. The plan further called for the establishment of an impressive new department store—clearly an invitation to Holland's *Bienkorp*, analogous to the America's Saks Fifth Avenue. This prospect was much like a plan that would lure Bonwit Teller to Bakersfield.

The city government would have to buy the needed land at an estimated—reasonable-cost of 250 million guilders, but the land would be leased for 100 years to Bredero at a price close to the city's debt service on the land purchase. Most of the roads and other infrastructure to be provided by the city would have had to be provided in any event sooner or later. One canal ringing the old city would have to be paved, but traffic experts had recommended paving it even before the deVries proposal. [*Editor's note: the rededication and reopening of the closed canal represents a symbolic expression of Utrecht's public attitude toward preservation and sustainability in the beginning of the 21st century]

The city councilmen were ecstatic when presented with the project. The *wethouder* who was responsible for overseeing the city's planning department was a socialist strongly in favor of the project. He kept his colleagues—both on the municipal executive council and in the city council—in line. The task was made easier by the lack of vocal opposition to any aspect of the plan except for the closing and paving of the canal.

Today the project is completed and, on many counts, it is a great success. It is *the* shopping center for the region; Dutch cities do not allow ruinous competition among shopping centers and will prevent development from emerging in the suburbs that would displace urban retailers. The development has done little, however, to halt the trend to suburbia. Some people criticize the center—a copy of one built in Birmingham, England—for its being so un-Dutch in appearance, scale, and function. It is a project no foreign traveler would find remarkable since there are multi-use renewal projects like it all over the world. That is part of what has aroused its Dutch critics. There is one older retail street in Utrecht lined with small shops along a canal that resembles the pleasant little shopping streets of Amsterdam and The Hague. But it has now been dwarfed by *Hoog Catherijne*, and *Hoog* was not designed to connect to this older street so as to facilitate comparative shopping that might have strengthened sales in the new shops as well as the old.

The government representatives had never studied or discussed the proposal in all its details and ramifications. As noted, the relationship between the new shopping center and the older retail quarter had been insufficiently analyzed. Moreover, the city had no independent expert advice on the project and did overcommit itself financially. It was unable to buy all the required sites on time, and the developer had to finance some of the land acquisition. There are some public facilities in the project—a sports and recreation hall, for instance—but little thought was given to meshing the proposal with the city's future plans for downtown municipal facilities for the simple reason that the city had not developed any detailed plans for the area.

The Bredero firm had been especially welcome because Utrecht lacked the staff capacity to initiate and realize a project of this scope. That is also one of the reasons that the city—its Burgomaster and Wethouders city council and town planning and public works departments—was ill-prepared to evaluate the project in any depth. An irony of public-sector land development is that cities that could not have built on their own have difficulty predicting the effects of private building plans....

* * *

Notes and Comments

1. The canal paved over for the *Hoog Catherijne* is being restored by the city reflecting Utrecht's environmental ideology. This author believes Utrecht to be one of the beautiful cities of the world, containing a delightful old city with tree-lined canals, fascinating museums and encircled by ribbons of parks, bicycle and pedestrian friendly, only minutes from the extreme rural beauty of the Netherlands: Utrecht reflects the classic Dutch city with the charm of Delft without the tourism and extreme tolerance of Amsterdam.

2. For a detailed account of similar efforts in Sweden, Australia, France, Canada, and the United Kingdom, see The Government Land Developers (Neal Roberts ed. 1977).

3. Another private market revitalization technique is the Business Improvement District. Much like a special assessment district used to finance infrastructure, the BID, like the tax-increment financed redevelopment, sells bonds that are retired by annual assessments from business owners in the district. The proceeds can be used for a range of activities from enhanced security over that provided by the police, cleaning and maintenance, the subsidy of valet parking or various cultural programs such as street fairs, farmers markets, or entertainment, as well as public art and traditional aesthetic improvements such as sidewalks, facades, lighting, or public art. See the discussion of BIDs in Chapter 4.

The following describes a more free-market based redevelopment tool:

Jeffrey M. Euston, *Clinton's Empowerment Zones: Hope for the Cities or a Failing Enterprise?*,

2 Kansas Journal of Law & Public Policy 140 (1994)

Congress enacted President Clinton's version of federal enterprise zone legislation in 1993 as part of his deficit reduction package. The program, which creates nine "empowerment zones" and ninety-five "enterprise communities," has won praise from officials in economically depressed areas, where the working poor and the unemployed often find meaningful job opportunities minimal or nonexistent. "The Clinton proposal appears to present a comprehensive approach to urban development," including features that would "nurture the basic human elements needed for development," according to Parker Anderson, the General Manager of the Community Development Department in Los Angeles, where 1992 riots reinforced the need for congressional action....

This notion was embodied in an idea that arose in the late 1970s in Great Britain: the government, by relaxing regulations and offering tax incentives to businesses willing to locate in specific neighborhoods, could foster economic growth in those areas.

The British Origins

Sir Geoffrey Howe, then a member of the British House of Commons, first coined the phrase "enterprise zones" in a 1978 speech. The idea originated from Peter Hall, then a professor at the University of Reading in Great Britain, whose visit to Hong Kong, Singapore, and Taiwan inspired in him an idea for stimulating industry in underpopulated areas of Great Britain. The burgeoning economies he saw in those countries led Hall, a socialist, to believe that the relative absence of government regulation was crucial to fostering enterprise and economic growth.

Britain's Conservative Party took up the cause in the 1979 campaign that culminated in the election of Margaret Thatcher as prime minister. In November 1980, Britain enacted enterprise zone legislation that reduced some local building and property use regulations in targeted areas and broadened Hall's idea to include a reduction in taxes, particularly local property taxes, for up to ten years. The British program was intended to generate activity in industrial areas, and, in contrast to several later U.S. programs, "zones were not seen as tools to revive depressed neighborhoods." Hoping to create, in effect, metropolitan industrial parks, the British program relied primarily on incentives to attract large-scale property developers, such as property tax exemptions for industrial and commercial buildings and tax write-offs for spending on business-related buildings and machinery.

In reviewing Britain's enterprise zones, Hall wrote: "[T]he experiment in practice produced relatively small numbers of really new jobs, and at appreciable—but perhaps not excessive—cost." Accordingly, the Thatcher-led government allowed the program to expire, although the idea lived on in the form of "freeports," which are areas near airports and seaports where businesses receive tax and regulatory relief. Furthermore, the experiment helped prompt the establishment of a uniform business tax rate throughout Britain, eliminating discrepancies among local business property assessments. Enterprise zones resurfaced under Prime Minister John Major, although the government and the European Commission, which also must approve the zones, expressed doubts about the concept as a vehicle for industrial development.

The American Experiment....

Though enterprise zone legislation floundered on the federal level, the idea thrived in the states. More than three dozen states have enacted variations of the enterprise zone concept since the early 1980s, providing evidence of the types of incentives that are the most effective. The package of incentives offered in a zone may emphasize either capital or labor subsidies or some combination of the two. The incentives may be complex or relatively simple.

Capital incentives are those designed to promote investment in business, including tools, machinery, equipment, and physical facilities, whereas labor incentives are designed to encourage businesses to hire workers. In a 1991 comparative analysis of thirty-eight state enterprise zones, Pennsylvania State University professors Rodney A. Erickson and Susan W. Friedman divided the most commonly offered incentives into three general categories:

1. capital incentives, which include property tax credits, franchise tax credits, sales tax credits, investment tax credits, and other significant employer tax credits;
2. labor incentives, which include a credit for each job created, a selective hiring credit requiring either zone residence or some measure of poverty, unemployment, or other disadvantage, a job training tax credit, and a tax credit for employees who work for businesses in the zone; and
3. finance incentives, which include an investment fund associated with the program, preferential treatment for industrial development bond allocation, and any refundable credits.

The analysis did not include capital gains tax exemptions, depreciation allowances, or regulatory relief because few, if any, states offered those incentives. However, many proposals for federal enterprise zone programs have included such incentives, as only the federal government is equipped to offer those sorts of inducements.

All thirty-eight states with enterprise zone programs promoted economic development as a goal, and most included secondary references to health, safety, welfare, or job creation. Few programs, on the other hand, explicitly mentioned neighborhood revitalization, community development, or state and local collaboration as goals.

A 1989 study of enterprise zone legislation in seventeen states found that, generally, two types of programs exist:

1. Those targeting disadvantaged workers. These programs tend to offer the labor-oriented incentives of selective hiring and employee tax credits. States employing these types of programs generally consider an area's poverty level in the process of deciding if the area receives enterprise zone status.
2. Those encouraging economic development investments. These programs, in contrast, tend to offer the financial benefits of investment funds, refundable credits, and, to a lesser extent, investment tax credits. States with these types of programs generally require areas to meet minimum or maximum population levels to qualify as a zone.

The study also revealed that 215 jobs on average were created each year in each of the 350 zones surveyed. Concluding that zones bring jobs to the inner cities, the study found that this was 10% more than the job growth in comparable areas outside zones

An August 1992 HUD report evaluating zones in thirty-five states and Washington, D.C., offered further analysis of job creation in enterprise zones. The study found that 3,172 zones had been formed in twenty-six of the states evaluated. Within these zones, new and existing private businesses had created 663,885 jobs and sparked investments totaling nearly $41 billion by taking advantage of state incentives....

The Arkansas Program

One believer in enterprise zones is President Clinton. In 1983, while governor of Arkansas, Clinton enacted enterprise zone legislation that, by February 1993, had resulted in the creation of 458 zones, second only in number to Louisiana's 1,553. Like many other states, Arkansas enacted a large number of zones in hopes that it would be prepared if Congress passed federal enterprise zone legislation that worked in conjunction with state programs.

Clinton's Arkansas program leaned toward the labor-oriented approach. The program offered a tax credit for each job created, plus a selective hiring credit, a sales tax credit, and preferential treatment for industrial development bond allocation. The state considered levels of unemployment, poverty, and welfare assistance in designating areas that qualified as zones. According to Dave Harrington, Executive Director of the Arkansas Industrial Development Commission, businesses in Arkansas' zones created 30,174 jobs through 1991, although Clinton suggested that the state went too far in granting tax breaks to business....

The New Federal Law

The program enacted by Congress differs considerably from the plan originally proposed by Clinton. The provisions establishing zones on Indian reservations have been dropped from the plan. The new law authorizes the creation of nine empowerment zones (five in large cities, one in a medium-sized city and three in rural communities) and ninety-five enterprise communities (sixty-five urban and thirty rural). The law further requires one of the urban zones to include areas in two states, an eleventh-hour addition to the law by Senator Bill Bradley (D-N.J.), whose state includes the troubled city of Camden, just across the state line from Philadelphia. The law allows cities to propose one zone or as many as three non-contiguous areas, as long as the area covers no more than twenty square miles and the total population of the zone does not exceed 200,000. The area must meet the empowerment zones' poverty criteria, which include a 35% poverty rate for the population of at least half the area's census tracts and at least a 20% poverty rate in all the area's census tracts. Zone designation will be valid for ten years....

* * *

Wilton Hyman, *Empowerment Zones, Enterprise Communities, Black Business, and Unemployment,*

53 Washington University Journal of Urban and Contemporary Law 143 (1998)

The Origin of Enterprise Zones in Britain

Many credit Peter Hall, a British professor of urban planning, with creating the enterprise zone concept. Professor Hall's enterprise zone concept called for reduced governmental regulation within economically depressed urban communities as a means of stimulating economic growth within those areas. With reduced regulation, lower taxes, and other financial incentives for businesses, economic activity would increase due to the reduced cost of operating businesses within those areas. In addition, Hall asserted that enterprise zones would create jobs in two ways. First, Hall theorized that enterprise zones would create low-wage jobs within the zones due to the increasing number of businesses seeking cheap labor. Second, Hall posited that enterprise zones would foster the creation of skilled jobs because new small businesses would evolve into sophisticated enterprises through innovation. In advocating his enterprise zone concept, Hall added a disclaimer that he did not intend for his proposal to be a model strategy for urban development, but, rather, to serve as a last resort for reinvigorating urban areas.

Professor Hall envisioned enterprise zones as being akin to free trade zones and, thus, modeled them after the economically and commercially successful urban plans of Hong Kong and Singapore. However, the British did not intend for their enterprise zones to stimulate economic activity in populated areas. Instead, their intent was to spur economic activity in abandoned industrial areas.

The British created their enterprise zones under the Local Government, Planning and Land Act of 1980. The main purpose of the legislation that created the British enterprise zones was to attract medium- to large-scale capital-intensive industries to abandoned industrial areas that possessed few, if any, residents. This legislation, while not as comprehensive as Hall's proposals, provided for the designation of eleven enterprise zones in 1980 and thirteen zones in 1982. The Act further provided that businesses in these zones would enjoy less-restrictive land use planning regulations, exemption from property taxes and the Development Land Tax for business-use buildings, and the ability to write-off the cost of buildings and equipment within one year of acquisition. The Act made these benefits available in the enterprise zones for ten years from the time of their designation as enterprise zones....

The Empowerment Zones

The Secretary of HUD and the Secretary of the United States Department of Agriculture (USDA) have designated a total of nine empowerment zones, six of which are located in urban areas and three of which are located in rural areas. Businesses that operate in these empowerment zones are eligible for an employment wage credit and increased section 179 first-year depreciation deductions. The empowerment zone employment wage credit provides a tax credit for wages paid to a "qualified zone employee." A qualified zone employee is any person who performs substantially all of his or her services for an employer within the empowerment zone and who has a principal place of residence within the empowerment zone. The credit, which is gradually phased out, is initially equal to twenty percent of qualified zone wages, up to a maximum credit of three thousand dollars per employee. Under the Taxpayer Relief Act of 1997, federally designated empowerment zones are eligible for the wage credit through the year 2007.

The increased section 179 depreciation deductions are allowed if the business is an "enterprise zone business" as defined in section 1397B of the Internal Revenue Code. Under section 179, small businesses can deduct an additional $18,500 in depreciation deductions on depreciable, tangible, personal property when it is purchased and used in the "active conduct... of any trade or business...." The provision is elective and applies only to the first year in which businesses use the property in a trade or business. Businesses that satisfy the requirements of section 1397B can also deduct an additional $20,000 under section 179, allowing them to take up to $38,500 in additional first-year depreciation deductions.

The empowerment zones may also issue tax-exempt facilities bonds, which businesses can use for acquiring or constructing an "enterprise zone facility" and any land "functionally related and subordinate" to the facility. An "enterprise zone facility" is any depreciable, tangible property that has as its principal user an enterprise zone business. In addition, empowerment zones are eligible for EZ/EC Social Service Block Grants in the amount of $40 million for rural empowerment zones and $100 million for urban empowerment zones.

The Enterprise Communities

The Secretaries of HUD and the USDA considered for designation as enterprise communities those areas not selected or designated as empowerment zones. There are a total of ninety-five enterprise communities, sixty-five of which are located in urban areas and thirty of which are located in rural areas. Enterprise communities are not eligible for the employer wage credit or increased section 179 first-year depreciation deductions, but they can issue tax-exempt facilities bonds. Enterprise communities can use the proceeds from these bonds to build and renovate structures for use by businesses operating in the enterprise community. Enterprise communities are also eligible for Social Service Block Grants of $3 million, which they can use to fund activities and projects in their communities....

There is at least one potentially negative effect of the EZ/EC program. By requiring businesses to locate within an economically distressed inner-city community in order to receive the EZ/EC benefits, the federal program creates a bias toward the creation of small-scale traditional line black businesses. This occurs because such businesses are more likely to locate within inner-city areas regardless of the EZ/EC incentives, and because the EZ/ECs do not provide special incentives to encourage the creation of emerging line black businesses that locate outside of EZ/ECs. Thus, the EZ/EC program wastes resources because it targets areas that may lack adequate consumer markets or adequately skilled labor, and because the traditional line businesses that are likely to locate within those areas, even in the absence of EZ/EC incentives, will not provide enough jobs to reduce unemployment significantly....

The present EZ/EC incentive program has the potential to create more small-scale minority-owned businesses within the EZ/ECs, despite the fact that these type of businesses may not have a significant impact on reducing minority unemployment. The federal government should respond to this situation by modifying the current EZ/EC program to allow flexibility in the locations where EZ/EC businesses can operate. The federal government should provide the EZ/EC incentives to businesses located inside and outside of the EZ/ECs, provided that they hire EZ/EC residents....

* * *

Notes and Comments

1. Enterprise zones were targeted to revitalize poor urban districts, yet is subject to criticism as minority business might be better positioned to locate outside declining central city. Dean Edward Blakely criticizes the old and outmoded tools of urban economic revitalization:

> In the cyberspace age, the old tax incentives and such increasingly irrelevant programs as empowerment zones will solve few problems and create many false expectations. It is interesting that such zones are being proposed for minority communities at the very time that location is becoming the least important factor in the new digital economy.

Edward J. Blakely, *Competitive Advantage for the 21st-Century City: Can a Place-Based Approach to Economic Development Survive in a Cyberspace Age?*, 67 J. Am. Plan. Ass'n 133, 139 (2001). Dean Blakely argues that cities must develop knowledge and its human resources and act as an incubator for the creation of ideas that spawn new firms that fit the human resource base. For a contrary view, see Karen Chapple, *Forsight or Farsight?: It's the Regional Economy Stupid*, 67 J. Am. Plan. Ass'n 142 (2001), arguing that place matters more than ever in the New Economy as investment is lured by a sense of "place." For suggestions on improving the EZ program, see Dan Nnamdi Mbulu, *Affordable Housing: How Effective Are Existing Federal Laws in Addressing the Housing Needs of Lower Income Families?*, 8 J. Gender, Soc. Pol'y & L. 387 (2000).

2. For an endorsement of the Enterprise Zone program by that city's mayor, see William Campbell, *Urban Holism: The Empowerment Zone and Economic Development in Atlanta*, 26 Fordham Urb. L.J. 1411 (1999). For a description of the British enterprise zone program, see M.G. Lloyd & R.W. Botham, *The Ideology and Implementation of Enterprise Zones in Britain*, 7 Urb. L. & Pol'y 33 (1985) (rhetoric contradicts program).

3. Another program was the Urban Development Action Grants (UDAGs), which unlike Enterprise Zones (EZs), based on tax cuts, would create jobs at a cost of $6,400 per job, as opposed to $28,800 to $55,300 for jobs created by EZs. The EZs, with a $95 million revenue loss, have no assurance of job creation. James A. Kushner, *The Reagan Urban Policy: Centrifugal Force in the Empire*, 2 UCLA J. Envtl. L. & Pol'y 209, 230 n. 88 (1982). Increased employment, the attraction of new branches, or the creation of businesses, self-sufficiency, better housing, infrastructure improvements, integrated gentrification, and jobs linked to housing, Otto J. Hetzel, *Some Historical Lessons for Implementing the Clin-*

ton Administration's Empowerment Zones and Enterprise Communities Program: Experiences from the Model Cities Program, 26 Urb. Law. 63, 78 (1994), are factors which could be used to grade programs on their effectiveness to ensure sustainability.

Revitalization of Economically Distressed Areas

The following excerpt describes how transit planning can play a central role in converting traditional automobile-dependent communities to transit villages and undertaking significant urban revitalization in the process:

James A. Kushner, *A Comparative Vision of the Convergence of Ecology, Empowerment, and the Quest for a Just Society*,

52 U. Miami L. Rev. 931 (1998)....

A[n] element of sustainable communities and green planning is that a stable city requires that each of its neighborhoods be sustainable and liveable....

By comparison, in the last decade, Los Angeles has spent billions of dollars on expensive transit improvements in subways, guideway trams, fixed-rail trolleys, and light-rail trains running on traditional rail corridors. Of nearly 200 transit stops, not one has been replanned as a transit village with shops, restaurants, housing, parks, offices, and pedestrian zones. Every light-rail transit stop is in a stark industrial district with a parking lot for transit users to switch from train to car for the final drive to a typically suburban single-family subdivision.

It is time that federal transit subsidies be conditioned on integrated land-use replanning around transit stops. A comprehensive plan amendment should include decisions on which stops should be high-density, designed around housing and commercial activity. Other stops should be set aside for lower density around new-urbanism-designed communities with single-family homes on small lots with front porches arranged around a New-England-style village town center. Other stops should emphasize mixed-use industrial employment centers.

For areas not served by fixed-rail transit, transit villages can be planned around quality express bus service that would provide superior service, as compared to lower-density areas that might be served by slower local buses or jitneys. In the inner city, transit villages could be linked with empowerment zones to provide industrial centers, and mixed-use neighborhoods of varying densities, affording vibrant community centers containing restaurants, cafes, stores, entertainment, and housing. The time has come to abandon policies of triage, where neighborhoods containing concentrations of the poor are ignored in favor of more affluent communities.

Additional funding mechanisms available to most communities include redevelopment programs to assemble land, and financing techniques such as tax-increment financed redevelopment that both subsidize the redevelopment process and capture the enhanced tax revenues. These techniques result in increased property values following the redevelopment. The tax increment would allow financing of neighborhood amenities and provide subsidies for generating affordable housing. In addition, impact fees imposed on unsubsidized housing and non-empowerment-zone commercial, industrial, and residential development may be used to fund additional affordable housing that can be integrated with moderate-income housing to avoid restigmatization and resegregation of transit village development. Additionally, such fees may be used to fund job training programs. Congress and local government could also direct community development block grant funding toward transit villages.

In Los Angeles, the Red, Blue, and Green line subway, trolley, and guideway systems, all have stops in lower-income minority communities. With the city's recent empowerment zone approval, those stops would be interesting sites for transit villages. Other nodes within African-American and Latino neighborhoods could be designated as empowerment zone transit villages, served by high-quality express buses and linked to employment, entertainment, commercial, and housing centers. A transit village redevelopment strategy would be further advanced if state and local governments would cooperate in restricting the continued development of inefficient and hyper-subsidized conversion of non-urbanized land to sprawling single-family traditional communities, instead targeting infrastructure subsidies and programs such as Low Income Housing Tax Credit allocations, to transit village zones. Just as state and federal legislation should condition infrastructure and transit subsidies on planning that integrates land use and transit, communities should be obligated to establish urban growth boundaries that could restrict sprawl and encourage economic development within empowerment and transit village zones.

Richard Sander's analysis of census data reports that residential communities that enjoyed the greatest decline in racial segregation were those that had the largest amount of new housing development. Conversely, cities with a stagnant housing market experienced an entrenched pattern of racial segregation. Launching an extensive program of newly constructed villages around transit would create an opportunity...for people of all colors and ethnicities to have some degree of choice in the type of communities in which they would reside. Such a redesigned community development pattern would offer extraordinary opportunity for increased integration, reduced automobile use and dependency, enhanced employment access, the possibility of reconstruction of the city's tax base, and a realistic hope of extending sustainable communities throughout the region....

* * *

Notes and Comments

1. The Transportation Equity Act for the 21st Century (TEA-21), Pub. Law No. 105-178, 112 Stat. 107 (1998), has replaced ISTEA, providing funds for transit, bicycle and other transportation alternatives, and increasing both transit and highway funding. TEA-21 is the largest public works bill in American history. Oliver A. Pollard, III , *Smart Growth: The Promise, Politics, and Potential Pitfalls of Growth Management Strategies*, 19 Va. Envtl L.J. 247 (2000) (despite improvements, transportation policy reform has progressed slowly in the United States; most states continue to try to build their way out of congestion, and resistance to change remains strong); *New ISTEA Strong As Ever, With New Billions to Spend*, 64 Planning 24 (July 1998).

2. *Modal Splits.* John Pucher, *Urban Travel Behavior as the Outcome of Public Policy: The Example of Modal-Split in Western Europe and North America*, 54 J. Am. Plan. Ass'n

509 (1988) (automobile 82.3% of trips in U.S., 47.6% in West Germany, 38.5% in Austria; public transport 3.4% in U.S., 11.4% in West Germany, 38.5% in Austria; bicycle 0.7% in U.S., 9.6% in West Germany, 38.5% in Austria; walking 10.7% in U.S., 30.3% in West Germany, and 31.2% in Austria; recognizing that automobile alternatives reflect not just subsidies, but relative costs and disparate development patterns). *See also* Jurgen Brunsing, *Public Transport and Cycling: Experience of Modal Integration in West Germany*, in The Greening of Urban Transport: Planning for Walking and Cycling in Western Cities 231, 232 (Rodney Tolley ed. 1990) [hereinafter Greening] (in Germany in 1982, 17.1% use bicycle as main means of transport for distances up to three kilometers; 6.8% use public transport, for distances longer than four kilometers; 6.1% use bicycle; and 17.3% use public transport); Robert Cervero & Roger Gorham, *Commuting in Transit Versus Automobile Neighborhoods*, 61 J. Am. Plan. Ass'n 210, 212 (1995) (presently in pre-World War II San Francisco neighborhoods originally designed around transit, 23% of trips made on foot and 22% by transit, while in newer auto-oriented neighborhoods only 9% on foot and 3% by transit); Wulf Hulsmann, *The "Bicycle-Friendly Towns" Project in the Federal Republic of Germany*, in Greening, *supra* at 218 (bicycle accounts for 11% of all journeys in Germany; Rosenheim, Germany, has increased bicycle modal share from 23% to 26%, with 57% of trips on foot, bicycle, or public transit with a proper bicycle promotion policy costing, according to a formula of population divided by 2.5 times DM1,000 or about $300 million for the city and county of Los Angeles); James A. Kushner, *Urban Transportation Planning*, 4 Urb. L. & Pol'y 161 (1981); Gilbert P. Verbit, *The Urban Transportation Problem*, 124 U. Pa. L. Rev. 368 (1975); Joel Walljasper, *Europeans Reclaim Their Cities from the Car*, Toronto Star, July 15, 1993, A25 (Final ed.) (22% of nonpedestrian traffic in Heidelberg by bicycle; Bremen, Heidelberg, and Lubeck in Germany have designated bicycle-only streets); Jay Walljasper, Star Tribune, Apr. 7, 1991, 29A (in Amsterdam, 24% of all urban trips by public transit, 20% walking, and 20% bicycle; West Berlin tripled bicycle usage from 1986 to 1991, accounting for 6% of urban travel, with plans to increase to 12% with new exclusive lanes and traffic "calming" or slowing and reduction techniques). The United States is going in the other direction. Between 1980 and 1990, 22 million new single-occupant drivers were added to the commute (while only 19 million new workers joined the commute during the same period), while transit lost 200,000 riders, 4 million stopped carpooling, and 650,000 stopped walking to work. Department of Transportation, Transportation Statistics: Annual Report 1994 at 53. *See also* Jane Jacobs, The Death and Life of Great American Cities 354 (1961) (95% of travel in Los Angeles by private automobile).

3. *Pedestrianization. See* Rolf Monheim, *Town and Transport Planning and the Development of Retail Trade in Metropolitan Areas of West Germany*, 22 Landscape & Urb. Plan. 121, 130 (1992). *See also* Jonathan Barnett et al., Making Cities Liveable: Lessons for the United States from Europe 6–7 (1980) (report of the Trinational Cities Exchange of the German Marshall Fund of the United States reports U.S. pedestrian schemes stoutly resisted by merchants fearing lack of automobile access, yet evidence of negligible effect on merchants); Rolf Monheim, *The Evaluation and Impact of Pedestrian Areas in The Federal Republic of West Germany*, in The Greening of Urban Transport: Planning for Walking and Cycling in Western Cities 244, 251 (Rodney Tolley ed. 1990) (indicating some reduction in retail sales in adjacent areas).

4. *Public Safety*. Are the suburbs safer than the city? The media and anecdotal evidence suggests emphatically yes. The literature, experts, and statistics suggests the contrary. Jane Jacobs, The Death and Life of Great American Cities (1961); James Gersten-

zang, *Cars Make Suburbs Riskier Than Cities, Study Says*, L.A. Times, Apr. 15, 1996, at A1 (Valley ed.) (reporting that more deaths and injuries resulted from cars in suburbs than from guns and drugs in urban settings; in 1995 in the Pacific Northwest, urban deaths occurred at a rate of 16 per 1,000 residents, while the rate was 19.2 in the suburbs; although crime death rates were 10 per 1,000 in cities and only 1 of 1,000 in suburbs, driving death rates were 18.2 per 1,000 in suburbs as compared to 6 of 1,000 in urban settings); Michael E. Lewyn, *Are Spread Out Cities Really Safer? (Or, is Atlanta Safer than New York?)*, 41 Clev. St. L. Rev. 279 (1993).

The following excerpt looks at American growth policy and American Housing policy:

James A. Kushner, *Growth Management and the City*,

12 Yale Law & Policy Review 68 (1994)

In the past, some neighborhood revitalization has resulted in widespread displacement of the poor to make way for transportation corridor redevelopment. This history also reveals an abandonment of declining inner-city neighborhoods not likely to be stabilized by an infusion of investment. [most American cities address urban decline through a policy of "triage" which serves as a rationale for abandonment, whereby resources are targeted to neighborhoods that would stabilize and generate private investment, ignoring stable neighborhoods and neighborhoods not likely to stabilize despite investment, a strategy based on the model of the medical catastrophe]. For cities to stabilize, it is critical that existing neighborhoods be a part of the rejuvenation. Existing inner-city neighborhoods should be identified for magnet status. In addition, redevelopment planning should accurately include relocation and housing replacement plans. Relocation planning can reflect the enhanced federal statutory standards providing for displacement planning and relocation assistance....

Magnet neighborhoods will require the resumption of an aggressive housing production program patterned on the model of successful middle-class housing initiatives, rather than on the traditional "no-frills" government subsidized housing....

During the 1960s an interesting initiative called Model Cities was developed as part of the "Great Society" program. Originally, the initiative called for a few experimental neighborhoods to receive all existing federal urban aid as well as funds to design new programs aimed at improving neighborhood stability. Often unfairly criticized as ineffective, the program was never launched as designed. Instead, funding was slashed while demand skyrocketed as most members of Congress wanted a handful of Model Neighborhoods for their constituents. Indeed, toward the end of the program, cities were allowed to expand such neighborhoods to cover the entire inner-city, dissipating limited funding and frustrating unrealistic aspirations. The Model Cities program is an example of excessively lofty objectives—legislative goals unattainable due to the legislative authorization, appropriations, and administrative implementation processes.

Had the Model Cities experiments been allowed to occur as originally proposed, they may have resulted in urban successes deserving of replication and continued funding. Instead, the program was conveniently tossed into the failed programs hopper, thus justifying the conservative national agenda for reduced spending on transportation, housing, schools, employment, and justice. The failure of the Model Cities program presents an example of how many government programs have failed to generate their promised goals. This pattern has provided the justification for the conservative agenda of the past generation.

The magnet city proposal should be patterned after the Model Cities Program. Magnet neighborhoods could establish programs to provide a wide array of needed services. Such services could include pre-school Head Start, day-care, after-school sports, and cultural and educational enrichment programs, together with neighborhood security including community policing and health care. Additional programs could include innovative systems of neighborhood government and housing management such as the development of justice centers that utilize alternative dispute resolution. Neighborhoods might engage in buying cooperatives and marketing cooperatives for goods and services produced by residents. Indeed, communities of interest might be designed around a community economic enterprise, with residents contributing their talents. The burgeoning population of female heads of household may require a new type of living arrangement—high-density, transit-served housing with common areas for dining, recreation, and child care....

* * *

Notes and Comments

1. For literature on the model cities program of President Lyndon Johnson's" Great Society," see Demonstration Cities and Metropolitan Development Act of 1966, tit. II, 42 U.S.C. §§3301–3313 (1970). *See* Bernard J. Frieden & Marshall Kaplan, The Politics of Neglect (1975); Charles M. Haar, Between the Idea and the Reality (1975).

2. A criticism of the "Model Cities" program of the author's proposal for magnet neighborhoods based on the positive image and experience of magnet schools, is that goals are too lofty and programs too large. George Lefcoe, The Florine and Ervin Yoder Professor of Real Estate Law of the Law Center at the University of Southern California, in cautioning pursuit of such proposals, warns of the "universal experience with public programs that those with sweeping goals fail more often than those with limited, manageable, objectively verifiable goals and that "even traditional Democrats are embarrassed to advocate bigger government." Letter from George Lefcoe to James A. Kushner (Aug. 17, 1993).

More Revitalization of Economically Distressed Areas

The following excerpt discusses social sustainability and the relationship of revitalizing neighborhoods to economic stability and the achievement of environmental sustainability:

James A. Kushner, Social Sustainability: Planning for Growth in Distressed Places—the German Experience in Berlin, Wittenberg, and the Ruhr,

3 Washington University Journal of Law & Policy 849 (2000)

In the 1990s, environmentalism focused on the notion of sustainable communities To environmentalists, sustainable communities refers to environmental policies of non-degradation and to economic and development decisions that are designed to renew resources, reduce energy and resource consumption, and improve air and water quality. On the regional level, sustainable development calls for transit-oriented development patterns, with increased trips by pedestrians, bicycling and transit users, and a reduced use of automobiles. Sustainable communities envision being able to walk to a village center main street for shopping, along and through attractive parks and pedestrian walkways with bicycle lanes—a community should be linked by transit to other transit villages, some of which are higher density with mixed uses of shops, offices, and housing, with vibrant street and café life, while others are centers of manufacturing and commerce. Within the neighborhood, sustainable development calls for local biological water and sewer treatment as an alternative to giant expensive treatment plants and delivery systems with too frequent environmentally damaging dumping. It calls for community parks which allow more climate-friendly landscaping, recycling of water, and less maintenance, water use, and polluting surface water runoff, as compared to broad private lawns. At the level of the individual home and building, sustainable communities reflects green architecture. Green architecture looks to climate-responsive design, using natural ventilation and lighting with natural light, and using solar power for both heating and the generation of electricity. Green architecture-designed homes and offices can be both efficient and delightful, utilizing materials that provide longer life and less damage to the environment. [A]s a further element of sustainable communities and green planning, a stable city requires that each of its neighborhoods be sustainable and liveable. This notion of sustainability beyond concerns for ecological survival refers to a community's cultural, economic, and spiritual infrastructure, which I refer to as "social sustainability." The social sustainability infrastructure would include the provision of attractive living spaces, access to employment, shopping, and recreation and the aesthetic, cultural, historic, educational, and emotional resources necessary to sustain urban life.

In order to stabilize a declining neighborhood, city, or region, or in order to rejuvenate stagnant communities, there is a need to create an environment that generates both an attraction to investment and a sense of community. This article looks to several communities undergoing urban revival. A key element to their revival is the utilization of projects and activities to create a sense of excitement and optimism among the community's population. This excitement can be generated by activities such as historic preservation, installation of public art, expansion of public squares and gardens, or the development of unique projects reflecting a community's history and offering a recreation experience for residents and tourists. They are the projects that might not appear to be sound financial investments in job creation. Instead, their value is indirectly related to economic development. Projects that can excite local interest, attract tourists, and give an image of an attractive and stimulating destination, make up this infrastructure for redevelopment that I call "social sustainability." For some communities it will reflect the region's cultural and economic history, other's geographic resources, and in still other communities it might relate to sports and recreation as well as arts and entertainment....

Berlin and Social Sustainability: Reinventing a Capital

Berlin has long been a place to view extraordinary things. One could view the architecture of Karl Friedrich Schinkel, the palaces and monuments of Frederick the Great, evidence of the march of the Third Reich, the construction of the Berlin Wall, and one of the world's greatest collection of museums. Without a doubt the most extraordinary sight of our generation has been the fall of the Berlin Wall that separated the West from the communist bloc nations, and the reunification of Germany.

Just when some critics assumed that Berlin would become just another burg, this cosmopolitan capital with a population of 3.5 million in the city, and 7.7 million including the surrounding area, has brought forth another extraordinary feat. I do not suggest that Berlin's pre-reunification repressed economic condition as a walled and not easily accessible community is comparable with the industrial and economic decline of the Ruhr, but the Berlin Wall was a magnet for tourists and Berlin faced a loss of its perceived uniqueness and attractiveness. Following the fall of the wall and the rapid move to German reunification, the German government designated Berlin as the new capital of the combined German nations. That designation launched a mammoth redevelopment, growth, and revitalization process, and is an example of social sustainability.

When I returned to Berlin in the summer of 1997, the middle of the city was one large construction site. Potsdamer Platz, the old center of the Weimar Republic, destroyed in the bombing of World War II, and later no-man's land within the Berlin Wall, was the biggest construction site in Berlin. The collection of cranes, construction equipment, and workers was so immense that the city and the site developers constructed a $3 million building called the Info Box just so that visitors could watch the action. The Info Box replaced the Berlin Wall as the city's top tourist attraction, at least until the opening of the roof of the Reichstag with its futuristic dome, pleasant restaurant, and awesome views of Berlin.

Now almost all of the Friedrichstrasse, the new fashion and stylish office center of the former East Berlin, is completed. The district includes hotels, offices, and expensive shopping arcades. The district also includes many foreign embassies and other buildings and is adjacent to Pariser Platz at the Brandenburg Gate, a short distance from Potsdamer Platz. The fully rehabilitated Reichstag has been completed awaiting final landscaping and construction of the new chancellery complex in front of the Reichstag and along the beautiful Tiergarten, crossing the Spree River at two of its bends. The Lehrter Bahnhof, the new central train station, is adjacent to the Reichstag and the future Chancellery. The multilevel station represents an amazing engineering feat that will bring high speed trains and new subway (U-Bahn) lines to the district. The modern terminal, scheduled for operations in 2004, will allow fast access to all sectors of the city and all regions of Germany.

The latest extraordinary sight in Berlin is the transformation of Potsdamer Platz. By my return to Berlin in March of 1999, but a year and a half since site preparation, seventeen major buildings designed by internationally renowned architects had been completed on the site developed by Daimler-Chrysler. The huge adjacent Helmut Jahn-designed Sony project is nearing completion following a delayed start to permit construction over a new U-Bahn station. Together, the projects will provide an entire city of hotels, residences, and entertainment. Already open is an I-MAX giant screen "3D" (three dimensional) theater, another theater for live productions, a gambling casino, large shopping arcades, and a rather unpretentious Jose Raphael Moneo-designed Hyatt Hotel. The collection of buildings, although some individually have received aesthetic or design criticism, reflect a collection of varying designs....

The Potsdamer Platz development would reflect several decades of large buildings in most major metropolises. The scale of the complex is awesome and the speed of construction quite unbelievable. When I returned to Berlin in July of 1999, Potsdamer Platz, although not designed to recreate the city center, was showing signs of city life. Filled bicycle racks, planted trees, outdoor cafes, and a few precious public spaces, suggesting that with the completion of the Sony Center and other area construction projects the redevelopment will yield a very modern successful city space. Berlin is a city that because of its renewed infrastructure, cultural, historic, and aesthetic treasures, along with great entertainment and a renowned nightlife, is uniquely poised to welcome the 21st Century.

In addition to their redevelopment plan that recalls Germany's post-war reconstruction, Berlin has launched revitalization projects throughout the city, building over 8,000 housing units around Potsdamer Platz, and rehabilitating thousands more throughout the city. In a city already rich in cultural and entertainment resources, the pace of new museum openings and nightlife expansion is staggering. The newly opened Gemäldegalerie in the Kulturforum near Potsdamer Platz, specializing in 13th to 18th Century European painting and the remarkable collection of contemporary art in the beautifully restored and readapted Hamburger Bahnhof (former rail station for trains to Hamburg) join the Pergamon Museum of antiquities as among the world's best museums. There are new office, commercial, and government buildings everywhere one looks. The renewal has in turn triggered the private revitalization of shops, galleries, restaurants, apartments, and offices, in part due to the excitement generated by growth and reunification, and in part reflecting overly generous German tax incentives.

Berlin is also embarking on a plan to expand the former East Berlin Airport at Shoenefeld into a modern regional airport that will accommodate non-stop intercontinental air flight to Berlin. Such airports not only generate tourist development, but broad industries including consulting and technology development and transfer and related service industries that so heavily rely on access to long distance markets. This is very much the Frankfurt experience. Along with its new and reopened rail and subway lines and stations, Berlin's transportation system and accessibility should provide a significant catalyst to the region's continued economic growth and success.

The revitalization effort is not limited to Berlin. Along with massive infrastructure improvements in the former East Germany funded by a ten percent tax surcharge on already high national income taxes, public and private investment efforts are giving a new face to the former socialist nation. In the summer of 1999 I traveled through the former DDR (East Germany) and was astounded at the condition of cities and towns that in 1990 reflected neglect. Dresden is a remarkably and beautifully restored city. Even smaller communities such as Meissen, Torgau, Wittenberg, Dessau, and Magdeburg have had face-lifts that make the communities indistinguishable from West German towns. One piece of evidence of former Socialist rule, however, is the panelized prefabricated large concrete apartment blocks, most already remodeled....

Hellersdorf: Social Sustainability at the neighborhood level

The community of Hellersdorf in Berlin presents a variation of social sustainability at the neighborhood level. Hellersdorf was a socialist suburban village of 130,000 on the northern political boundary of the city of Berlin within the former Eastern sector of the DDR. Hellersdorf was a model of a socialist community lying at the end of a subway line. There was a complete absence of color and foliage in a village of nearly uniform panelized prefabricated drab concrete apartment blocks, each building with at least one flat windowless wall. Hellersdorf also had no city services, not one telephone, and the apartment units, despite being the newest in the former Eastern sector, were, like East Germany itself, deteriorating and in need of major rehabilitation. A pedestrian-friendly village center was non-existent and the community was without cafes, pubs, restaurants, or other entertainment, Hellersdorf lacked the typical community life found in Germany.

Following the fall of the Berlin Wall in 1989, virtually all of Hellersdorf's population migrated to the West in search of better housing and jobs, reducing the community's population from 130,000 to 350. A reunified city of Berlin, along with its private sector developer partner, installed public art, planted 15,000 trees, modified building facades to introduce variation and color in the structures, and brought in top mural artists to paint beautiful varied mural designs on many of the buildings. The panelized housing was rehabilitated and a significant portion privatized with government subsidy available to assist in the purchase of units. The private developer constructed a massive commercial mixed-use project including a multi-screen cinema entertainment complex with offices, shops and restaurants around the transit line. Along with shopping malls and a state of the art entertainment center, the city has new offices, a city hall, a vocational college, and a full service medical clinic. In addition, the private developer purchased 2,500 units of the former social housing, added balconies and remodeled the units for rental at market rate. Although memories and past images persist, with the construction of additional market rate and senior citizen housing units, Hellersdorf has lost any remaining physical stigma and is now the best example of a rehabilitated community of the former DDR. Today, Hellersdorf, with a population of 140,000, has 100 percent occupancy with a waiting list, and each apartment faces an attractive inner courtyard of new landscaping and modern playground and recreation facilities. Hellersdorf has been transformed into a sustainable village. Both Hellersdorf and Berlin are now more stable and each presents a more attractive site for private investment, more secure that public policy will discourage neighborhood disinvestment and abandonment.

Wittenberg: Urban Sustainability

Best known for Martin Luther's posting his 95 Theses that launched the Protestant Reformation, Wittenberg, an industrial town on the beautiful Elbe River in the German State of Saxony found itself on the Eastern side of the wall in the former DDR. Today, Wittenberg has had a major facelift and resembles, at least in its pedestrianized *altstadt* and beautiful gardens, a typical attractive West German town. The former East German towns are identifiable from their former West German neighbors only by the number of Mercedes-Benz automobiles on the street and the "panelized" or "modularized" prefabricated concrete medium density apartment blocks favored by the former Socialist cities. The problem of rejuvenating a community of panelized housing was solved with a theme that may have been inspired by Hellersdorf. Wittenberg brought the whimsical Viennese artist Friedensreich Hundertwasser to recast the community image. Hundertwasser, a renowned, if not critically acclaimed painter, is best known for his zany social housing project in Vienna known as Hundertwasserhaus. The windows appear irregular in the modern fairy tale-like multicolored apartment complex. The irregularly shaped textured facade gives the appearance that the development design is a collaboration between Disney and the Brothers Grimm. Actually the magic of Hundertwasserhaus is that the artistic facade or bodywork is clapped over normal social housing floor-plans. The city of Wittenberg rehabilitated the housing, adding color to the facades and attractively re-landscaped the sites with many newly planted trees. Hundertwasser designed colorful bodyworks as a facelift for an elementary school and kindergarten. Instead of the school being a frightening institution, the whimsical castle looks like a place a child would eagerly explore. The community, just as the neighborhood around Hundertwasserhaus in Vienna, developed a greater sense of community and a heightened sense of civic pride.

The remodeling of the Wittenberg Hundertwasser school, like the installation of public art, is an example of social sustainability—a policy of investing in infrastructure without a direct economic development return. Instead, the investments cumulatively contribute to the enhanced attractiveness of the community for living and investment. Through the modest investment required to enlist an internationally

16. Hellersdorf. Murals mark the revitalized transit village of 140,000 in the former socialist suburb of Berlin, Germany.

renowned artist, Wittenberg has created both distinction and attraction to tourism and economic development—a form of community building. Wittenberg with its historic image is poised to develop a niche as a center of creativity and the arts. With exhibitions and public art activities and the continued rehabilitation of the city and its historic center, Wittenberg finds itself more attractive to investors, tourists, and employment-generating development.

The Ruhr Valley: Regional Social Sustainability

Another area of Germany that has experienced economic and physical decline has been the Ruhrgebiet, or the Ruhr Valley. Germany's Largest industrial region, the Ruhrgebiet, contains a population of nearly 5.8 million in a megalopolis described as a polycentric agglomeration consisting of 11 major cities and 42 smaller communities. The coal industry continues to follow the remaining coal reserves in the north, reserves that are more difficult and expensive to mine. All but one operating steel mill in Duisberg have been closed, dismantled, or sold and transported to a foreign nation.

Except for the affluent city of Dusseldorf, home to many of Germany's large corporate headquarters, banks, and the center for fashion in Germany and Japanese business enterprises in Europe, and the former federal capital of Bonn with its government and private industry headquarters, or the industrial and media city of Cologne, which are in the State of North Rhine-Westphalia, but not a part of the Ruhr. The Ruhr's population is facing high unemployment and the lack of resources to update its cities and revitalize its once flourishing economic base. Unemployment rates in some cities in the Ruhr reached almost 20 percent during the 1980s. By comparison, in 1999, Berlin's unemployment rate was at twenty percent.

The State of North Rhine-Westphalia by establishing five regional universities in the Ruhrgebiet in the 1960s, undertook actions that can be characterized as social sustainability.

Two recent policies mark the efforts of the government to revitalize the economic life of the Ruhrgebiet. A significant problem in the Ruhr is the broad brownfields of polluted water and soil left in the wake of departing coal mining and abandoned steel mills. In 1988, the State of North Rhine-Westphalia, through the Internationale Bauausstellung (International Building Exhibition or "IBA") and its public real estate management arm LEG Landesentwicklungsgessellschaft NRW GmbH ("LEG"), embarked on an aggressive program of revitalization through environmental cleanup and the adaptive reuse of Germany's abandoned manufacturing infrastructure.

The IBA Emscher Park project is a brownfields cleanup program extending throughout the Ruhrgebiet along the Emscher River, a 550 kilometer waterway that has served as an open sewer. The project area is 75 kilometers long and 10 kilometers wide, between Duisberg in the West and Dortmund in the East. In addition to water quality improvement through treatment and toxic cleanup of the abandoned steel mills and mining sites, the state has set out to make the region interesting to visit through preserving and improving its historic industrial infrastructure. The IBA Emscher project in the Ruhr has expended $1.8 Billion over ten years, or nearly four billion Deutsche Marks. A central focus of the IBA projects in the Ruhr has been environmental enhancement. The enhancement has come not just from brownfields cleanup, but innovative planning components: reuse strategies to environmental planning in the landscaping of the various projects. The projects include returning many brownfields to greenfields and creating parks and recreational greenspace, surrounding 10,000 new and rehabilitated housing units of which 75 percent are to be social housing. The project also included a series of 22 business and technology parks as part of the "Working in the Park" portion of the project.

In Duisberg-Nord, the former steel works have been preserved as part of a recreation park called "Landschaftspark" (landscape park). The young and old can climb giant blast furnaces, practice rock climbing, or slide down a chute. A former iron pit and steel works provide outdoor theaters and concert halls, discotheques, restaurants, and cafes. A large gas tank or "gasometer" has been filled with water and a sunken ship for scuba diving. Also part of the overall program, the inner harbor in Duisberg is being rehabilitated as a mixed use and mixed income residential, commercial, and recreational project.

In Essen, another giant industrial works previously known as the Zeche Zollverein has been readapted as the Design Zentrum Nordrhein Westfalen, an art and industrial park. The park includes an exhibition hall of industrial design located in a former boiler house that was remodeled by Sir Norman Foster, the architect of Berlin's Reichstag renovation. The park also offers a gourmet restaurant within one of the preserved Bauhaus buildings, modern at the time of their construction in the 1930s. Other buildings in the coal complex have been readapted as artist studios, with space for design offices and workshops.

In Oberhausen, the largest Gasometer in the world, providing the largest enclosed space in the world, ostensibly excluding domed stadiums, but on a scale with the Cologne Cathedral, has been converted to another exhibition hall with an interior glass elevator. Exterior elevators on the Gasometer lead to extraordinary views of the Ruhr region. The mammoth structure allows the contemplation of art whether it is exhibited within or painted on the exterior of the Gasometer as in the form of a Warhol Campbell Soup can.

In Bochum-Wattenscheid, the Ecotec Technology Park has preserved and renovated factories making up the former Holland Colliery. The colliery has been converted to a business incubation park for environmentally beneficial textile-related research companies.

The "Minister Stein" Service and Industrial Park, in Dortmund Eving, is a coal mine site that has been converted to a business park under another IBA regional project. The mine head structure has been converted to offices and a disco. New buildings, such as a supermarket and a shopping mall have been built using matching brick and were designed to conform to the architecture and materials of the preserved buildings.

In Gelsenkirchen, the IBA's headquarters is located within the buildings of an abandoned coal company. In addition to rehabilitating the beautiful brick structures, the redesign includes preservation of various features of the prior use that now constitute land art. On land adjacent to the headquarters at Wissenschaftspark Gelsenkirchen, IBA has constructed the largest solar building in Germany for the purpose of new energy-related business incubation.

Many of these projects can be criticized on a number of grounds. First, they could not have been undertaken without an enormous public subsidy. The large and influential coal and steel companies have exerted their power to obtain extraordinary subsidies for brownfields cleanup and redevelopment. Equity would argue that polluting companies should have paid for the high cost of cleanup if not redevelopment. American brownfields policy has focused on cleanup, emphasizing strict cleanup liability against polluters. The American system, imposing joint and several strict liability against all polluters can result in large corporations bearing more than their fair share of cleanup liability. Future research might analyze whether the German subsidy or the American tort liability scheme generates the most effective or most efficient revitalization model. It would appear that delays inherent in the administrative and judicially enforced cleanup obligation could not generate the dramatic scale of the revitalization of the Ruhr generated under the German system.

Second, one might challenge the emphasis on the reuse of polluted industrial parks over making the cities of the Ruhr more liveable or targeting subsidies to create the most jobs.

Yet, these projects preserve the region's heritage and history and provide a unique recreational and economic resource. Indeed, the Emscher project presents a bold statement, on a scale with Berlin's urban renewal, that decline is not to be the fate of this resilient nation, not in any district or region.

Another notable project in the region is the adaptive reuse of an abandoned newspaper printing plant in Essen called "Girardet Haus." In the center of an old and formerly depressed industrial-commercial and residential district, the large factory complex was slated by the city for demolition. Instead, a private sector developer purchased the building and had to battle the city to rehabilitate the structures and construct extensions of the existing buildings to house offices, restaurants, cafes, shops, and a hotel along with residential flats. In addition, the building contains a daycare center, a school, and a full service medical clinic complex. The attractive project fits well into the surrounding neighborhood, preserves a significant historic building, and as a result has sparked revitalization of the entire surrounding neighborhood. Girardet Haus makes a powerful argument for transit villages: mixed uses of commercial, recreational, and residential development offering lively pedestrian-friendly spaces and streets, generating a sense of community....

The public sector Ruhr projects ostensibly present a questionable use of taxpayer money based on strictly economic concerns....

The grandiose design of the Ruhrgebiets's dramatic attempt to provide itself an economic, environmental, and aesthetic makeover is probably essential to undo the typically indelible label of "declining region." It is the grandiosity that is an essential element of social sustainability.

What is being accomplished in the Ruhr, as well as in Berlin, Hellersdorf, and Wittenberg, must also be evaluated in social or political terms as well as according to a direct cost-benefit economic analysis. Instead of declining, like so much of America's "Rust Belt," Germany has dramatically addressed revitalization of the former East Germany, and similarly has taken a leadership role in doing some very sophisticated high visibility projects to announce that the Ruhr will not be permitted to continue its decline. The projects may very well succeed in stimulating private sector investment in these historic industrial communities. As an adjunct to these industrial infrastructure reuses, each of the cities, along with professional sports stadia and cultural infrastructure including theaters and museums, is undertaking new housing and housing rehabilitation efforts. With the emphasis of regional and international shopping, each of the cities is looking to enhanced tourism to render the region more attractive to investment and the traditional job creation that in the past has eluded the Ruhr for more attractive locations.

The strategy of the Ruhr provides a great lesson for America's declining industrial belt. Historic preservation is not just about aesthetics and architectural appreciation. Historic preservation is about larger values of optimism in community revitalization, providing diverse cultural environments and generating an environment of attraction for investment, tourists and people in search of a stimulating community with a high quality of life. Communities need to identify and preserve their unique cultural heritage while creating entertaining spaces with specialized museums and parks. This might mean steel mill theme parks in Youngstown, movies and southwest heritage parks and museums in Hollywood, or military theme parks on abandoned bases, and farmers markets in both rural and urban neighborhoods....

The strategy and general ethic of current local German planning is to provide liveable, attractive communities friendly to pedestrians, bicyclists, and the environment. The strategy utilizes mixing offices, recreation, commercial shopping and housing, designed around specialized cultural centers, museums, exhibition halls, indoor and outdoor theaters, restaurants, cafes, and clubs. Safe, attractive, walkable neighborhoods, designed around local cultural and historic resources and accessible by public transit offer a desirable model for many American communities....

Social sustainability should be recognized as a vital non-ecological element to the larger environmental model of sustainability. The fall of the Berlin Wall is important not just as a victory for liberty but as a testament and evidence that what is universally perceived as impossible can in fact become a reality; that anything is possible; that miracles can indeed happen. Berlin's success in rebuilding its divided city on a grand unimaginable scale, stabilizing a community's least attractive and most distressed neighborhoods as in Hellersdorf, or Germany's undertaking to revitalize the former East Germany and the once-flourishing depressed Ruhr, are examples of social sustainability. These miraculously ambitious programs offer adaptable examples of urban revitalization and a promise of hope for the most neglected of neighborhoods.

* * *

Notes and Comments

1. Professor Klaus Kunzmann of the University of Dortmund has put forward seven principles of regional creativity which are necessary to attract development. The seven elements include: (1) a diversified and differentiated set of educational institutions, (2) a diversified system of public and private research and development institutions focusing on research and development, (3) a cultural environment serving a multicultural society, (4) a positive international image, (5) a high quality natural and built environment, (6) a broad information base of print, audio and visual media, and (7) a sociopolitical environment open to innovation. Klaus R. Kunzmann, *Developing the Regional Potential for Creative Response to Structural Change*, in Cities in Competition: Productive and Sustainable Cities for the 21st Century 286, 288 (J. Brotchie, *et al.* eds. 1995). Does the revitalization strategy in the Ruhr meet Professor Kunzmann's criteria?

Professor Kunzmann has appropriately asked whether there exists a set of criteria or conditions for "social sustainability?" Social sustainability, however, represents a subjective requirement that the investment or combination of programs must make an aesthetic and physical impact sufficient to alter both the community image and public perceptions, replacing a sense of hopelessness with a promise of prosperity. Future research might discover models or formulae for social sustainability, but I suspect that as in the case of neighborhood revitalization, the nature and extent of investment necessary to ignite private market investment enthusiasm and confidence is a function of the desirability and accessibility of the location, the conditions of adjacent neighborhoods, the nature of the competing residential and commercial markets, the regional economic conditions, and a bit of coincidence, luck, and the dynamic of chaos theory.

2. Does German planning policy that sets a fundamental goal of spatial-economic policy to reduce regional socioeconomic disparities, targeting programs and taxation to depressed areas account for its bold revitalization initiatives? Would American urban and rural economic revitalization benefit from such a national policy? Would such programs be better established at the federal, state, county, city, or private level?

3. The problem of security and street crime is a significant component in both the decision to live in the city and the planning theory applied in metropolitan areas. Many communities and private, and even public, development are looking to security buildings and gated communities as protection against what is a perceived deterioration in public security. The price of gating, however, is the loss of street life. See the discussion of gating in Chapter 11.

4. Security is an even greater problem for the poor, particularly those residing in public housing projects that are frequently the scene of criminal behavior. Some, including the Clinton administration have advocated warrantless searches to provide protection to the defenseless poor. *See* Corey Roush, Note, *Warrantless Public Housing Searches: Individual Violations or Community Solutions*, 34 Am. Crim. L. Rev. 261 (1996).

5. For a brief discussion of a true redevelopment challenge that will place your community needs in perspective, see Janet E. Stearns, *Rebuilding Afganistan*, 11 J. Affordable Hous. & Community Dev. L. 154 (2002).

Chapter 15

Planning for Beauty and the Protection of Aesthetic Values

> What started out in Europe as an avant-garde political reaction to the horrors of industrialism—Modernism—degenerated, upon reaching America, into dogma and style. The result, visible all over America today, is a public realm almost entirely devoid of buildings that honor or embellish it, and a crippled civic life in which citizens are made to feel worthless. It matters that the junior high school looks like a fertilizer factory, and that the town hall looks like a wholesale beverage warehouse, and that the library looks like a shipping container, and that a hotel looks like a medium security prison because these buildings dishonor the public realm as they dishonor their institutional roles in our lives, and in their design they make civic life impossible.
>
> James Howard Kunstler, Home From Nowhere 40 (1996)

Aesthetics and the City

Although America contains a great number of beautiful communities and historic neighborhoods, most dramatically Washington D.C.'s government district, New Orleans' Vieux Carré, or San Francisco's hilly jewel, Americans are amazed by the bounty of riches that make up historic Europe and many of the old capitals and communities of the other more mature continents. The beauty of the buildings stand as a symbol of the confidence and achievement of those old town and city centers. It is not simply the buildings, there is beauty in the breathtaking way in which architects and city planners laid out streets, parks, squares, and pedestrian paths with generous opportunities for pedestrian's to enjoy their sojourn, avoid the cacophony and polluting noise and emissions of traffic, and stop at cafes and public spaces to prolong or enhance the enjoyment of their trip.

Contrasting most American communities with their European counterparts finds cities designed more for traffic and automobile access than for pedestrians. Attractive walks require creative planning yet rarely offer the satisfaction of a walk abroad. Wide boulevards allow traffic to dominate the experience and there are rarely green spaces that pedestrians can escape to. Zoning has placed houses in one district and shops in another and frequently offices in still another. The office districts typically become empty and dangerous after working hours and the shop districts are usually abandoned after people return to residential districts. European cities have long followed policies of mixed use. Housing over shops in districts with recreation and offices so that there are people returning to the neighborhood as others leave, resulting in a sufficient population to keep streets lively, safe, and attractive to café sitting. When America redevelops city districts it frequently prefers clearance over preservation because it makes redevelopment more efficient, saves money, and offers new occupants the benefits of the latest architectural design. Particularly because of the automobile accessibility brought about by numerous freeway or highway access ramps and a multitude of surface parking lots, cities, with a few notable exceptions, discourage visits by those without business and essential appointments, and encourages flight from the cities to the relatively bucolic suburbs where the sanctuary offered by European town centers is found in the quiet of the residential subdivision, either before the television or in the backyard barbecue during pleasant weather.

What can communities do to create more attractive towns and cities? First, and most important, cities must be planned for pedestrians rather than traffic. This means walkable safe streets with park-like green spaces to break up the monotony and pollution of the traffic accessway, and frequent squares and attractive stopping, shopping, and recreation opportunities. Successful city districts call for quiet residential streets and blocks, and extensive mixed uses, where offices, housing, shops and recreation are planned to complement the physical plan. This pedestrianization of America's cities is a central component in the "New Urbanism," a movement designed to establish neotraditional towns.

Another activity needed to improve the attractiveness of America's towns is to clean up the unsightly appearance to most urban neighborhoods. This effort includes graffiti removal, and the removal of unsightly signs and billboards as well as making facades and sidewalks more aesthetically pleasing. How might Curitiba approach community aesthetics? The City of Hellersdorf in Berlin established a recreational center for community teens focused on the arts, with art and music programs going on in various studios. A private developer engaged in rehabilitation of the town's older housing stock hired artistic youths, previously involved in graffiti, to paint murals on walkways that had previously been the target of taggers.

Another element that makes public spaces more interesting and attractive is the preservation and renovation of older buildings. Although America is relatively youthful compared to its European or Asian counterparts, it nevertheless has a stock of interesting structures representing a panoply of building styles. The experience of most cities demonstrates that the most successful revitalization efforts occur within districts that are historic rather than newly constructed.

One technique used to assure a common aesthetic design in the absence of a large-scale developer imposing an integrated development scheme, is the architectural review ordinance. Under such an ordinance, towns establish a board of review, typically composed of architects, that review all building plans to assure aesthetic compatibility. The effects of such efforts can be seen in Kansas City's Country Club Plaza district that integrates a design that reflects the influence of Seville, Spain, and can be seen in the New Orleans French Quarter. The danger of such democracy in architecture is that committees may often not appreciate the avant garde and architectural review may result in imposed orthodoxy anathema to American individualism.

The Courts in the United States have been deferential to historic preservation, as in the approval of New York's ordinance in *Penn Central Transportation Company v. New York City*, 438 U.S. 104 (1978), sustaining architectural preservation against claims of building owners required to comply with the facade protection law, or New Orleans' efforts in *New Orleans v. Dukes*, 427 U.S. 297 (1976), sustaining restrictions on pushcart

17. Hellersdorf. Public murals convert panelized housing to a public art gallery in Berlin, Germany.

sales while grandfathering long-time vendors to attain an historic image for the district. The courts have also generally supported efforts to eliminate the aesthetic pollution of billboards and other signs. The only exception is that the courts do not tolerate standards that turn on the content of the sign or other regulation. *Metromedia, Inc. v. City of San Diego*, 453 U.S. 490 (1981). *See also City of Cincinnati v. Discovery Network, Inc.*, 507 U.S. 410 (1993), invalidating newsrack ordinance distinguishing between the content of publications.

Another ingredient in community planning that can make communities more attractive is the inclusion of public art. Public museums are wonderful community cultural resources but cities benefit from not restricting art solely to large collections. Many people have experienced the joy and beauty of painted cows in Zurich or Chicago, large bugs in New York, bears in Berlin, or angels in Los Angeles. These temporary public exhibitions, along with such shows as the Botero public sculpture exhibitions in New York and Los Angeles, have a dramatic impact on public excitement and interest in rediscovering urban centers and spaces. In the Netherlands, the City of Utrecht's Maliebaan is a mile-long tree-lined boulevard of modern sculpture. Antwerp has the Middelheim Open-Air Statuary Museum, a fantastic public park containing 300 significant modern sculptures in a setting of forest paths, meadows and lakes. Hellersdorf, a former socialist satellite bedroom suburb of Berlin has been dramatically revitalized through the inclusion of murals on the flat surfaces of panelized housing, the planting of thousands of trees, together with the greening of the city through developing parks. Although investment in aesthetics may appear to be of a lower priority than problems of declining neighborhoods and poverty, like historic preservation and the development of beautiful structures, it can make a substantial contribution toward creating a psychological state of excitement and hopefulness about the future and status of the city. Attracting people back to the cities and attracting business to the city and the region can make urban revitalization a reality. It can be argued that a central role of urban planning regulation is to overcome developer hostility to the inclusion of aesthetic elements

While readings in this chapter discuss many of these strategies of revitalization and development, the following excerpt discusses aesthetic issues in the European setting:

Voula Mega, *The Concept and Civilization of an Eco-society: Dilemmas, Innovations, and Urban Dramas,*

in Cities and the Environment: New Approaches for Eco-societies 47 (Edited by Takashi Inoguchi, Edward Newman, and Glen Paoletto 1999)....

Braudel called cities the "greenhouses of civilization," and Levi Strauss, "objects of nature and subjects of culture." They have unique aesthetics, character, and culture. The notion "Euro-aesthetics" does not exist but might be considered. EFILWC's study on aesthetics and the functionality and desirability of the sustainable city shows a number of ways to understand a city's soul, to appreciate the desires of its citizens, to listen to its heartbeat. The study suggests itineraries that can be metronomes of desire in various cities. From Fornovo di Taro to Poundbury, there is a common quest for urban beauty, the ultimate antidepressant. Long rejected as a sign of frivolity and elitism, concern for the beauty of cities, made up of asymmetries, paradoxes, and contradictions, is returning to the urban stage.

The city is ultimately complex; to intervene in its operation requires an understanding of complexity. It is composed of relationships and conflicts, convergences and divergences, myths and legends, with not additive but synergetic results. Creating the quintessential City Urbane demands both science and art. The art of creating the sustainable city can only produce prototypes. Design involves responsibility for the appearance of a city. It needs strong leaders and enlightened private developers. It should take into consideration efficiency, flexibility, and imagination and deal with land management, building masses, preservation, and enhancement of core urban elements and citizens. Planning should enhance continuity and change, reveal the potential of a city's physical and cultural assets and portray humanistic values. Functional coherence should be achieved through various land uses to make a city more efficient and enhance its aesthetic quality. Landmark projects could become a ferment for the whole urban fabric.

"Building Eutopia" is a sustainable planning aim; it now embraces the notion of eco-Eutopia. There is a growing consensus about the need for urban mix, reflecting a need for "a little of a city everywhere in the city." The preference for the compact city, as a contrast to the diffuse city, is gaining ground. The dense, compact city has the advantage of integrating structures and providing shorter distances between home and work or leisure. But the compact city might not necessarily be energy-efficient and may not correspond to lifestyle preferences either. Owens suggests that a sustainable urban form on a regional scale would contain many relatively small settlements, some clustered to form larger settlements of 200,000 and more people on the subregional scale. It would consist of compact settlements, probably linear or rectangular in form, where people could both live and work. The interrelated questions of density and compactness have quite interesting contributions to make to reconstruction and sustainability. Reconstruction schemes, more than the Second World War, have destroyed cities. "High density" should be distinguished from "high rise." Correa suggests "high density low rise" as an ideal option.

Preservation versus new development is a Janus-faced dilemma. Most cities give the answer: renewal rather than expansion, consolidation of the urban fabric, and improvement of the suburbs. The "soft urban renewal" in Vienna includes block improvement schemes, enhancement of public spaces, and ecological measures. The social criteria insist on avoiding segregation or gentrification. Soft renewal allows inhabitants to remain in place and enjoy a range of resident-friendly measures. In Barcelona, the rehabilitation of the Ciutat Vella, comprising four quarters in the historic centre, is an unprecedented and unique event, in terms of dimension, timing, and civic spirit. Following the reconciliation of the city with the sea and the creation of the Villa Olimpica, the whole urban fabric is changing, with the gradual injection of improvements. Selective renovation, rehabilitation, construction, pedestrianization, and greening are the visible elements. Civic centres have been created and have become points of multiple encounters and cultural reference. Strong neighbourhood groups have become partners with the authorities and have played a pioneering role in the attribution of new housing and services, the dismantling of unsound activities, and the whole change of social climate.

Cities open to the future cannot be conceived without the regeneration of the suburban areas, the places where one does not know if one is "in" or "out." This entails recreating the economic diversification, the social heterogeneity and cultural diversity in the periphery. In the south of Stockholm, the Huddinge Centrum is a successful experiment in transforming a suburban shopping centre into a town square, focal point, and meeting point for the community. The location, next to the train station, generated the creation of new offices and apartment units and the whole area has been redesigned on the model of the old medieval city of Stockholm. The Donau-City project in Vienna aims to create a new skyline to the north-east, across the River Danube, and a new mixed-use waterside quarter.

Public spaces belong, by definition, equally to everyone. What Koolhas describes as fortresses of freedom have great potential as islands of urbanity in the archipelago of the city. Public space is not just the space "left" after construction; it should be given major importance as a civic space and shaped as a priority. The unification of the archaeological spaces in Athens and their functional and aesthetic links to green spaces is expected to create a high-value public space. Inviting public spaces may foster democracy. In many cases, "standardized" public space cannot meet its challenges of space for "negotiating" democracy, and becomes space of confrontation and of exclusion. Setting up qualitative recommendations for the functional, environmental, cultural, and aesthetic character of the spaces, roads, and pavements, roadside plantations and public lighting is very important in forging cultural identity. In Brussels, the *Manual of Public Spaces* is a good example.

Along with urban planning, structural projects contribute to shaping the image of cities, provide landmarks, and symbolize their dynamic forces. Often, these structural projects are linked to particular events that act as catalysts for the future restructuring of the cities and the regions (EXPOs, Olympic Games, etc.). Other projects, such as "Seine Sud-Est," result from a determined, well-planned effort to re-equilibrate the urban fabric. In order to meet their objectives, the projects must synchronize their long-term potentials for continuity and flexibility. Flexibility is imperative for adapting the project to market fluctuations, while continuity is linked to a vision for the future of the infrastructures. In the most closely studied projects, the trend is towards guaranteeing an optional multiplicity of land use and a good spatial, functional, and economic

18. Bears on the Unter der Linden. Exhibition of artist-painted bears in Berlin, Germany in 2001, like the Cows of Zurich and Chicago, Angels in Los Angeles, or insects in New York can create excitement for pedestrians, an acute sense of civic and cultural excitement, and a tourist attraction.

integration in order to enhance the vitality and livelihood of the whole area. Stable financial structures for the long-term implementation of major projects are of the highest importance, while the cost of land and infrastructures is a key issue for economic equilibrium. Consultation and partnership become important on several levels, vertically and horizontally. The success of the projects greatly depends on a constant and affirmed political determination, withstanding changes in elected representation....

* * *

The following excerpt contrasts the beauty and policies undertaken in three disparate communities. Stockholm and Berlin are very old cities reflecting the history of a millennium, while Berlin bears the scars of War and the physical and political separation caused by the Berlin Wall which from 1961 until 1989–1990 divided the socialist eastern portion of the city, a part of the German Democratic Republic, from the western sector under the control of the Federal Republic of Germany and the occupying military powers, Stockholm is pristine and largely survived Europe's modern travails unscarred. Los Angeles, by comparison, is a new city, yet a city containing beautiful architecture, albeit of a typically more recent vintage:

James A. Kushner, *A Tale of Three Cities: Land Development and Planning for Growth in Stockholm, Berlin, and Los Angeles,*

25 Urban Lawyer 197 (1993)

Stockholm, Berlin, and Los Angeles share unique natural beauty. While Stockholm enjoys its islands and archipelago in the Baltic to boast as the world's most beautiful metropolis, Berlin has its beautiful river system, and Los Angeles enjoys the Pacific beaches and the Santa Monica and San Gabriel mountain ranges.

Stockholm also enjoys a most extraordinary man-made beauty in its architecture, parks, castles, and museums that reflect a millennium of development. Its respect for history is reflected in its tree-lined bicycle paths, parkways, boulevards, and parks. The effect of Stockholm's rigid restrictions on building height to preserve views and cityscapes is breathtaking.

Berlin represents a different variety of the city beautiful. The contrast of the contemporary beauty of the capitol of the Third Reich, as reflected in Berlin's neighborhoods, castles, rivers, parks, and museums, and the unique juxtaposition of new and old architecture is remarkable. From Potsdam and Lake Wansee to the Tiergarten, Grunewald Forest, the broad avenues including Kurfurstendamm and Unter den Linden in the old eastern sector with its firmament of museums with every block a picture postcard, Berlin, thought to have originated as a fishing village in 1244, is a jewel of a city. The former West Berlin's housing projects, ninety percent of which include persons receiving government housing subsidy, typically represent the leading architectural achievements of the city with developments representing the Bauhaus design of the 1950s, later modernist design, and now post-modernist, or anti-modernist architecture such as the IBA housing program. East Berlin's modern developments are typically prefabricated with designs rather stark in comparison to the West, yet developments appear livable with well-maintained open space and playgrounds dramatically more attractive than most affordable American housing projects.

The beauty of Los Angeles principally resides not in its few but attractive parks, nor in its eclectic and too often distasteful commercial architecture, which presents a cacophony of Spanish stucco and tile, Beaux Arts, Tudor, Colonial, Victorian, post-modern, and distinctive fast-food, drive-in, car-wash culture structures, but in its stately, affluent residential neighborhoods. Rather than the landmarks and natural beauty of Stockholm or Berlin, except for the striking beauty of its beaches, one is more likely to recall the neon of Hollywood, the glitz of Beverly Hills, and most notably, the more than a quarter of the city directed to freeways, roadways, automobile sales, servicing, parts dealers, and parking structures and lots. By comparison, one-third of Berlin consists of woods, fields, parks, lakes, and rivers. Despite a few isolated examples within separately incorporated suburbs, which have experimented with architectural review regulations, Los Angeles, has generally permitted urban and architectural design to be dictated by the private sector. The development regulations and the redevelopment authorities appear to have been more concerned with boosting density and the height of commercial offices and residential developments than with the appearance of buildings or neighborhoods. Other than very expensive, well-designed luxury property and neighborhoods, most development appears to be designed so as not to present any psychic or aesthetic loss should the city be the locus for an earthquake or tidal wave. Los Angeles appears to be a metaphor for the plastic society of disposable consumer goods; modest housing and neighborhoods once lived in and used to be discarded in favor of new development with little thought toward any policies of neighborhood or architectural survival and revival.

This dramatic contrast between European urban beauty and American individualism is a key factor in generating both popular support for preserving and extending beauty in Stockholm and Berlin and for disinvestment in Los Angeles. As an example of Stockholm's aesthetic commitment, when buildings are demolished, their facades are preserved and warehoused so that new or rehabilitated buildings can utilize the historic and often highly aesthetically pleasing facades.

Professor Lefcoe eschews the aesthete European viewpoint which reflects "traditional" architectural values. Instead, he emphasizes the wonder of the diversity, mobility, and flexibility of Los Angeles. The eclectic architectural and neighborhood design of Los Angeles has allowed class mobility and access as families of immigrants and the working class are able to share quarters and gradually move to more affluent housing and neighborhoods. This is in stark contrast to the rigid stratification of the class structure in both Sweden and Germany. Indeed, by comparison Sweden and Germany are experiencing great difficulty in accommodating, without significant violence, what is, in comparison to Los Angeles, extremely modest numbers of immigrants and refugees.

Although the poor might attack initiatives designed to create the city beautiful in America, by comparing priorities of unmet medical needs, unemployment, and the homeless, the increased cost of development necessary to assure the likelihood and desirability of the city may be essential to maintain the city's economic viability which is, ultimately, the only hope of revitalization and economic opportunity within the inner city. It must be stressed that city beauty does not demand the construction of castles and traditional architecture to accommodate only the affluent. The new residential developments in Stockholm and Berlin demonstrate that attractive neighborhoods and projects designed around inviting and usable open spaces must be built and maintained for those who lack access to the equivalent opportunities generated by the private market. Similarly, Stockholm and Berlin should be very careful not to allow the call for rapid economic growth to take precedence over retention of those cities' commitment to the highest standards of urban design and beauty....

* * *

Architectural Review

In the pursuit of an alternative to the cluttered or ugly neighborhood and perhaps recognizing that American individuality often manifests itself in the eccentric neighbor who prefers Day-glo colors and non-traditional landscaping, Planned communities, including neotraditional or New Urbanism, typically include rigid covenants to protect the neighborhood and streetscape appearance through design standards. Older neighborhoods and affluent suburbs in many urban communities have enacted ordinances to control aesthetics, including the establishment of a committee of architects to approve the design of homes and other buildings for compatibility. Does such an approach generate more beautiful communities, or communities that look more like new edge cities that may tend to look mass produced lacking flair or character? New Urbanism's pioneers seem to be very satisfied with the appearance and design of their communities.

The following case discusses the problem of how far government should go in the pursuit of aesthetic values:

State ex rel. Stoyanoff v. Berkeley

Supreme Court of Missouri
458 S.W.2d 305 (1970)

Pritchard, Commissioner.

. . . . Relators' petition pleads that they applied to appellant Building Commissioner for a building permit to allow them to construct a single family residence in the City of Ladue, and that plans and specifications were submitted for the proposed residence, which was unusual in design, "but complied with all existing building and zoning regulations and ordinances of the City of Ladue, Missouri."

It is further pleaded that relators were refused a building permit for the construction of their proposed residence upon the ground that the permit was not approved by the Architectural Board of the City of Ladue. Ordinance 131, as amended by Ordinance 281 of that city, purports to set up an Architectural Board to approve plans and specifications for buildings and structures erected within the city and in a preamble to "conform to certain minimum architectural standards of appearance and conformity with surrounding structures, and that unsightly, grotesque and unsuitable structures, detrimental to the stability of value and the welfare of surrounding property, structures and residents, and to the general welfare and happiness of the community, be avoided, and that appropriate standards of beauty and conformity be fostered and encouraged." . . .

[T]he City of Ladue constitutes one of the finer suburban residential areas of Metropolitan St. Louis, the homes therein are considerably more expensive than in cities of comparable size, being homes on lots from three fourths of an acre to three or more acres each; that a zoning ordinance was enacted by the city regulating the height, number of stories, size of buildings, percentage of lot occupancy, yard sizes, and the location and use of buildings and land for trade, industry, residence and other purposes; that the zoning regulations were made in accordance with a comprehensive plan "designed to promote the health and general welfare of the residents of the City of Ladue," which in furtherance of said objectives duly enacted said Ordinances numbered 131 and 281. Appellant also asserted in his answer that these ordinances were a reasonable exercise of the city's governmental, legislative and police powers, as determined by its legislative body, and as stated in the above-quoted preamble to the ordinances. It is then pleaded that relators' description of their proposed residence as "unusual in design" is the understatement of the year. It is in fact a monstrosity of grotesque design, which would seriously impair the value of property in the neighborhood.

The affidavit of Harold C. Simon, a developer of residential subdivisions in St. Louis County, is that he is familiar with relators' lot upon which they seek to build a house, and with the surrounding houses in the neighborhood; that the houses therein existent are virtually all two-story houses of conventional architectural design, such as Colonial, French Provincial or English; and that the house which relators propose to construct is of ultramodern design which would clash with and not be in conformity with any other house in the entire neighborhood. It is Mr. Simon's opinion that the design and appearance of relators' proposed residence would have a substantial adverse effect upon the market values of other residential property in the neighborhood, such average market value ranging from $60,000 to $85,000 each.

As a part of the affidavit of Russell H. Riley, consultant for the city planning and engineering firm of Harland Bartholomew & Associates, photographic exhibits of homes surrounding relators' lot were attached. To the south is the conventional frame residence of Mrs. T. R. Collins. To the west is the Colonial two-story frame house of the Lewis family. To the northeast is the large brick English Tudor home of Mrs. Elmer Hubbs. Immediately to the north are the large Colonial homes of Mr. Alex Cornwall and Mr. L. Peter Wetzel. In substance Mr. Riley went on to say that the City of Ladue is one of the finer residential suburbs in the St. Louis area with a minimum of commercial or industrial usage. The development of residences in the city has been primarily by private subdivisions, usually with one main lane or drive leading therein (such as Lorenzo Road Subdivision which runs north off of Ladue Road in which relators' lot is located). The homes are considerably more expensive than average homes found in a city of comparable size. The ordinance which has been adopted by the City of Ladue is typical of those which have been adopted by a number of suburban cities in St. Louis County and in similar cities throughout the United States, the need therefor being based upon the protection of existing property values by preventing the construction of houses that are in complete conflict with the general type of houses in a given area. The intrusion into this neighborhood of relators' unusual, grotesque and nonconforming structure would have a substantial adverse effect on market values of other homes in the immediate area. According to Mr. Riley the standards of Ordinance 131, as amended by Ordinance 281, are usually and customarily applied in city planning work and are: "(1) whether the proposed house meets the customary architectural requirements in appearance and design for a house of the particular type which is proposed (whether it be Colonial, Tudor English, French Provincial, or Modern), (2) whether the proposed house is in general conformity with the style and design of surrounding structures, and (3) whether the proposed house lends itself to the proper architectural development of the City; and that in applying said standards the Architectural Board and its Chairman are to determine whether the proposed house will have an adverse affect on the stability of values in the surrounding area."

Photographic exhibits of relators' proposed residence were also attached to Mr. Riley's affidavit. They show the residence to be of a pyramid shape, with a flat top, and with triangular shaped windows or doors at one or more corners....

Relators' proposed residence does not descend to the "patently offensive character of vehicle graveyards in close proximity to such highways."... Nevertheless, the aesthetic factor to be taken into account by the Architectural Board is not to be considered alone. Along with that inherent factor is the effect that the proposed residence would have upon the property values in the area. In this time of burgeoning urban areas, congested with people and structures, it is certainly in keeping with the ultimate ideal of general welfare that the Architectural Board, in its function, preserve and protect existing areas in which structures of a general conformity of architecture have been erected. The area under consideration is clearly, from the record, a fashionable one.... The beauty of a fashionable residence neighborhood in a city is for the comfort and happiness of the residents, and it sustains in a general way the value of property in the neighborhood....

In the matter of enacting zoning ordinances and the procedures for determining whether any certain proposed structure or use is in compliance with or offends the basic ordinance, it is well settled that courts will not substitute their judgments for the city's legislative body, if the result is not oppressive, arbitrary or unreasonable and does not infringe upon a valid preexisting nonconforming use. The denial by appellant of a building permit for relators' highly modernistic residence in this area where traditional

Colonial, French Provincial and English Tudor styles of architecture are erected does not appear to be arbitrary and unreasonable when the basic purpose to be served is that of the general welfare of persons in the entire community.

In addition to the above-stated purpose in the preamble to Ordinance 131, it establishes an Architectural Board of three members, all of whom must be architects. Meetings of the Board are to be open to the public, and every application for a building permit, except those not affecting the outward appearance of a building, shall be submitted to the Board along with plans, elevations, detail drawings and specifications, before being approved by the Building Commissioner. The Chairman of the Board shall examine the application to determine if it conforms to proper architectural standards in appearance and design and will be in general conformity with the style and design of surrounding structures and conducive to the proper architectural development of the city. If he so finds, he approves and returns the application to the Building Commissioner. If he does not find conformity, or has doubt, a full meeting of the Board is called, with notice of the time and place thereof given to the applicant. The Board shall disapprove the application if it determines the proposed structure will constitute an unsightly, grotesque or unsuitable structure in appearance, detrimental to the welfare of surrounding property or residents. If it cannot make that decision, the application shall be returned to the Building Commissioner either with or without suggestions or recommendations, and if that is done without disapproval, the Building Commissioner may issue the permit. If the Board's disapproval is given and the applicant refuses to comply with recommendations, the Building Commissioner shall refuse the permit. Thereafter provisions are made for an appeal to the Council of the city for review of the decision of the Architectural Board. Ordinance 281 amends Ordinance 131 only with respect to the application initially being submitted to and considered by all members of the Architectural Board....

Ordinances 131 and 281 are sufficient in their general standards calling for a factual determination of the suitability of any proposed structure with reference to the character of the surrounding neighborhood and to the determination of any adverse effect on the general welfare and preservation of property values of the community....

The judgment is reversed.

Per Curium. The foregoing opinion by Pritchard, C., is adopted as the opinion of the Court.

* * *

Note and Comments

1. *Stoyanoff* for some may suggest the image of Malvina Reynold's classic folk song "Little Boxes" in describing American suburban growth as "little boxes on the hillside... And they're all made out of ticky tacky and they all look just the same." Malvina Reynolds, Little Boxes and Other Handmade Songs (copyright 1964 Oak Publications). For others it may represent George Orwell's *1984* in the notion that the government would dictate what your house looks like. Yet many people choose to live in master-planned communities with extensive covenants, conditions and regulations (CC&Rs) that precisely prescribe matters of house colors, landscaping, and uniform exterior or architectural design. Others may advocate architectural review and regulation, be it a uniform architectural design or may it be various architectural designs that are deemed compatible. Others may see a horror in uniformity, as disturbing as the impact of the

ostensible unplanned and aesthetically suspect American metropolis has on the European visitor. Another and unfortunately growing body of people may intellectually rebel against aesthetic regulation yet view a "tragedy of the commons" whereby instead of sharing a community with people who enjoyed a shared view of the beautiful, today's neighborhood occupants have widely disparate views of the house beautiful from day-glow paint colors to architectural or landscaping designs that may have been borrowed from more ancient or distant homelands or that represent a creativity that is at best individually appreciated. Can these varying views be balanced.? Could zoning offer a solution? Would a system of zoning where certain neighborhoods or a town center could be subject to architectural review, but adequate alternative districts to permit pyramids and other lifestyles were retained?

2. Richard Babcock, the dean of the land use bar in the latter part of the 20th Century, offered a warning against too much aesthetic regulation:

> When one embarks on a campaign to make aesthetics a public issue in a democracy, the line between the conservationist and the philistine is narrow. Once we move from the scenery along the public highway to the design of structures we verge on an area where I, for one, would accept the consequences of individual choice—with all its risks—rather than permit a consensus to have the force of law. If it follows that I must defend the most tasteless developer as well as a Frank Lloyd Wright, I accept that burden. Neither I nor my contemporaries should have the power to deny the next generation the right to judge whether our efforts had grace or were ugly.

Richard F. Babcock, Billboards, Glass Houses and the Law 2 (1977). How do you feel about Babcock's position? It touches on a nerve of individualism that marks the American tradition. His warning of making judgment on aesthetics argues for historic preservation over imposing current tastes on the past. Does not Babcock's individualism impose a regime on the community just as surely as aesthetic regulation imposes some standard of beauty on an increasingly diverse community lacking shared aesthetic values?

3. *Architectural Design and Consistency with Renderings. Frankland v. City of Oswego*, 517 P.2d 1042 (Or. 1973), demonstrates a problem with subdivision and other project review alternatives; the final developed project may depart from the description of the project design concept and renderings submitted to support an application. In *Frankland*, the developer constructed large, monolithic apartment houses of uniform height, after having submitted renderings at the preliminary stages of the review process that presented a melange of "garden apartment" buildings varying in height and building shapes with many architectural details and presenting a woodsy appearance that appeared well integrated with the surrounding forest. The Oregon court ruled that the sketches submitted become part of the plan, thus committing the developer to the architectural design and building configuration depicted. *Frankland* would argue for communities enacting aesthetic control ordinances to require that final plans conform with community standards for beauty and good taste as well as representations tendered during the project approval process.

Historic Preservation

Historic preservation can be a very effective strategy in revitalizing neighborhoods and city centers. Where individual structures or districts are listed on the National Reg-

19. Hundertwasser Haus, Vienna, Austria. Social housing with a radical facade designed by the late whimsical Viennese artist Friedensreich Hundertwasser

istry of Historic Structures, under the National Historic Preservation Act, 16 U.S.C. §470, they may not be destroyed or adversely impacted by federally funded projects. Thomas F. King, Federal Planning and Historic Places: The Section 106 Process (2000); Wesley Kobylak, Annotation, *Application and Construction of §106 of the National Historic Preservation Act of 1966 (16 U.S.C.S. §470f) Dealing with Federally Sponsored Projects Which Affect Historic Properties*, 68 ALR Fed. 578 (1984). Historic preservation, however, is largely a function of local law as the states have generally ignored the subject other than to encourage protection through various tax incentive programs. Lawrence Schmidt, *Historic Preservation Law in Maryland*, Md. B.J. 10 (Sept./Oct. 2001); Mark D. Brookstein, Note, *When History is History: Maxwell Street "Integrity," and the Failure of Historic Preservation Law*, 76 Chi.-Kent L. Rev. 1847 (2001). Individual buildings often survive based solely on the political discretion of the local city council. historic preservation most often succeeds in the regulation of historic districts, such as in Annapolis, Charleston, Georgetown, New Orleans, Williamsburg, or the many neighborhood overlay districts that are so frequently seen as linked to generating economic development as more tourists arrive, shopping and nightlife flourish, and property values soar. What laws are required to assure greater protection of historic buildings and structures?

Prague is undoubtedly one of the world's most beautiful cities. While that beauty is reflected in the river, bridges, hills and green spaces, it is a function of the attractive manner that the city is designed, around public spaces, squares, and the natural elements of the community, the principal element of that beauty is its buildings. A millennium of construction in a multitude of styles, the buildings of Prague offer a tourist's dream and an attraction to business. Yet, its socialist government between World War II and the velvet revolution of 1989 to 1990 was unable to support the preservation efforts needed to fully protect its heritage. The following excerpt looks to the laws of the Czech Republic and raises the issue of what form laws must take to assure the preservation of the city beautiful:

Kirby Mitchell, Note, *Rescuing Prague's Past: A Survey of Legislative Attempts at Architectural and Historical Preservation in Prague, Czech Republic,*

24 Ga. J. Int'l & Comp. L. 523 (1995)

Almost alone among European capitals, the Czech city of Prague largely escaped the ravages of World War II, and now stands as perhaps Europe's largest architectural and historical preservation site. The center of Prague is a "solid-five-square-mile treasure" of ancient churches topped with golden spires, picturesque town squares, and a splendid mixture of Art Nouveau, Baroque, and Romanesque buildings. Stovezata Praha, the "City of a Hundred Towers," is considered by many to be the most beautiful capital in Europe.

Today, however, the historic buildings and sites of Prague are in danger due to decades of neglect and pollution under the Communist government. Further, since the "Velvet Revolution" in November 1989, the rush to a market economy and the return of private property rights have added new pressures and concerns for those interested in preserving Prague's architectural heritage.

The impact of privatization and property restitution has been varied. Previously, seventy percent of the nation's monuments and historic buildings were state property. Now many of these properties are being returned to private owners who have obvious interests in the property. However, these properties are also now "vulnerable to the whims of their owners," who may ineptly or inaptly change the appearance or function of the buildings....

Czech governments have passed a myriad of legislation aimed at preserving the historic buildings of Prague. Czech legislation highlighted in this Note includes the Act Concerning Cultural Monuments of 1958, the 1976 Building Act, the Act for State Care of Monuments in 1987, and the 1992 Amendments to these acts....

Prague's Architectural Heritage

Czechs have every reason to be interested in legal protection for the historic buildings of Prague. The first and most obvious reason is the unique architectural heritage represented by Prague's buildings, many of which are considered to be the best specimens in Europe. In the majestic capital of the Czech Republic, a city of 1.2 million inhabitants, "ten centuries of buildings...stand "harmoniously together," displaying an amazing array of architectural styles. Apart from ancient Gothic and Baroque buildings, the city is rich in Art Nouveau, Cubist, Modernist, and Functionalist style buildings, many of which were designed and built in the early 1900s. Among these buildings wind the cobbled streets of Stare Mesto (The Old Town), which is connected to Mala Strana (The Lower Town) by the unparalleled beauty of the 14th century Charles IV bridge and its thirty-one statues. In all, there are 1,431 buildings and sites registered as historic monuments in Prague.

Prague Castle overlooks the city from the hillside of Hradcany. This huge castle, the oldest sections of which date back to the 11th century, has been described as "Versailles, Westminster Abbey, and the Smithsonian all in one," for the castle has long been the "seat of the country's government as well as the center of Czech religious and artistic life."...

Unfortunately there are now as many reasons to be concerned about Prague's historic buildings as there are reasons to be impressed by them. Prague's monuments have been engaged in a battle for survival for decades. Certainly, the simple passage of time explains much of the deterioration. But a number of more disturbing causes have contributed greatly to the accelerated decay of Prague's cultural heritage.

A major cause of deterioration over the past half century is the widespread burning of brown coal. As the most important commodity in the Czech mining industry, cheap brown coal has driven the nation's unrelenting industrialization since the 1940s and still supplies sixty percent of the country's total energy. Czech brown coal is of very poor quality, with a high sulfur and heavy metal content. Its use in plants and factories produces enormous air pollution, particularly near Prague where it is the primary source of energy for many state-operated thermal power plants. Further, Prague is situated in a deep valley, taking on smoke and fumes from steel plants as far away as Western Germany. Adding to this pall are aging coal-fired stoves, the most common means of heating private homes and apartment buildings in the Czech Republic. Thankfully, Prague's air pollution is not as severe today as it was during the 1960s and 1970s, but as recently as 1993 the environmental organization Greenpeace rated Prague the second most polluted city in Europe.

A direct result of this pollution is acid rain which speeds the erosion of Prague's monuments and coats its buildings in soot. Certainly, most Czechs are primarily concerned with the alarming effect this pollution has on their health, but the pollution's impact on Prague's historic monuments corresponds with the dire effects it has on people's health. For example, due to the air pollution and accumulated grime, many of the Charles Bridge's famed statues have been moved into air-conditioned museums and replaced on the Bridge by concrete copies. Coal dust is visible on statues and cathedrals as well as on Prague's drab Communist-built apartment buildings, as the "dirty smoke has democratically painted black streaks on everything."...

[C]hurches and religious buildings, "the best representatives of the millennia of architectural progress," were completely neglected because religion was discouraged and restricted in Communist Czechoslovakia.

The poor quality of building materials and the manner in which they were used on preservation projects added further to the decay. In 1980, paint imported from Finland was used to whitewash buildings near Prague's grandest crossroads, Vaclavske Namesti (Wenseclas Square). Due to a lack of technical expertise, the buildings were in need of repainting only one year later.

Even the greatest of the city's monuments did not escape such harsh treatment. Parts of Prague Castle were subjected to a "Communist-style make-over worse than neglect: Linoleum was laid over parquet, walls of laminated cabinets were shoved next to Renaissance armoires, ceilings were covered with acoustic tile, and air-conditioning ducts were smashed through priceless boiserie."[W]hen the Communists attempted restorations, particularly as they did in rooms used for state occasions, they simply "glopped gold paint over everything."...

Ironically, one of the new problems facing Prague's historic buildings is tourism. The steady flow of foreign sightseers visiting Prague Castle and other historic monuments has been overwhelming. In 1992 (before Czechoslovakia separated into two separate countries), a record eighty-three million visitors came to Czechoslovakia, a twenty-five percent increase from 1991, and nearly three times that of 1989. Four years after the revolution, Prague became the most popular tourist destination in the world....

Thanks to the return of state-owned buildings to private owners, many of Prague's buildings have been greatly improved in the past four years. Hundreds of Prague's buildings are being repainted and renovated for the first time in decades. Unfortunately, however, the Czech legal system does nothing to encourage this restoration, and most of the renovations have been financed through foreign investment under long-term leases. Moreover, in the rush to remake the center of Prague after four decades of stagnation, many of the renovations on historic buildings have been unauthorized and some buildings are being renovated in questionable ways. Zdenek Lukes, an art historian at Prague Castle, says many buildings have become "'stage architecture' with their facades preserved but everything else gutted, because developers don't mind paying the ridiculously low fines for this desecration." Illegally renovating, or even destroying, an historic building in Prague will cost a developer as little as $3,000, with no further consequences.

Current Czech law also lacks any kind of tax incentives for restoration and preservation, and it is not clear whether even the fragile protections given to historic buildings by the Communist government will survive, as there is growing pressure to tear down and redevelop Prague's older buildings in the name of economic development....

Following the revolution, the first legislation dealing with architectural and historic preservation was the brief Act No. 242 of 1992, which went into effect June 1, 1992....

The purpose of two of Act No. 242's amendments is simply to raise the fines contained in the 1987 Act. Since many of the current renovations in Prague are being funded by wealthy foreigners, preservation law needed a more realistic deterrent to building permit violators than fines starting at 1,000 crowns, or approximately thirty U.S. dollars. Thus, Sections 6 and 7 of Act No. 242 raise the fines against individual violators from 1,000 crowns to 10,000 crowns (approx. $300) and from 5,000 crowns (approx. $170) to 50,000 crowns (approx. $1700), respectively, depending on the severity of the violation. Act No. 242 also states that restoration can be undertaken with the authorization of the Czech Ministry of Culture, thereby asserting the Ministry of Culture's control of who can renovate historic buildings as well as what renovation can be done.

Legislative attempts at architectural and historical preservation in Prague since 1958 have not been very successful....

The return of private property rights has largely corrected the problem of the lack of incentives. Thousands of buildings in Prague have been returned to their previous owners through the official policy of restitution. Private owners, now motivated by both personal attachment to historic buildings and economic self-interest have assumed on the responsibility for renovating and maintaining their property.

Perhaps the best current legislative prospect to further encourage these renovations is the introduction of preservation-based tax incentives. In the United States, the federal government has provided tax incentives for the "rehabilitation"[169] of historic buildings since 1976. This "rehabilitation tax credit" has been modified several times since its inception, but currently amounts to twenty percent of the total cost of rehabilitating a historic building.[170] This tax credit has been an effective incentive for investors, as over 23,000 historic buildings have been rehabilitated in the United States since 1976. Currently, there are no tax incentives in the Czech Republic to promote architectural or historic preservation....

Simply declaring a building a protected monument does not make it one. Enacting appropriate legislation to encourage the preservation of Prague's unique architectural heritage will likely be difficult, but this task is well worth the effort.

---

169. Pub. L. No. 94-455, 2124, 90 Stat. 1520, 1916–19 (1976)....

170. Pub. L. No. 97-34, 212(a), 95 Stat. 172, 235–36 (1981)....

* * *

The following excerpt looks at historic preservation issues in the emerging nation of Cambodia in Asia:

William Chapman, *"The Best Laid Schemes...": Land-Use Planning and Historic Preservation in Cambodia,*

7 Pacific Rim Law & Policy Journal 529 (1998)

....Western notions of rational planning, particularly when they lead to restrictive or protective legislation, often do not sit well with developing countries. An impatience with controls and governmental interference—the idea that poor countries do not have the luxury of imposing constraints and, at the same time, should not be forced to shoulder the burdens of cultural and environmental protection—tends to preoccupy countries struggling with the twin problems of poverty and basic economic development. This has certainly been the case with Cambodia, a country that has suffered numerous false-starts in its efforts to join the modern world.

Not surprisingly, land-use planning, and its corollary, historic preservation, are not considered high priorities by most Cambodians. Outside of a few governmental officials who understand the more long-term implications of guided or directed development and the wise management of resources, Cambodian people and outside investors are more concerned with immediate economic needs. Future planning itself is an abstract concept, and protection beyond the desire to preserve the most recognized national symbols, such as the temple ruins at Angkor (also seen widely as a source of economic development in this cash-starved country) is given only lip-service. Most Cambodians want results now and want to experience the economic prosperity shared (at least until very recently) by their Southeast Asian neighbors, especially Thailand, Malaysia and, increasingly, in the last few years, Vietnam....

While officially required by law, permitting and regulation are not consistently applied. Technically all new construction requires a permit. Instituted in 1989, the approval process *theoretically* begins at the lowest level of municipal or provincial government. Cambodia possesses an administrative structure based on French divisions and includes both provincial and municipal levels of government, the former divided as well into districts, and down the scale, into communes, villages and "groups." As a result, a permit for new construction (and, in principle, a substantial rehabilitation of an existing property) begins with the Group Chief, filters up to the Village and Communal Chiefs, and then to the District Committee and Provincial Governor's office for approval. Simple timber and thatch buildings can be approved by the Commune Chief; larger timber buildings (with tile or metal roofs) require the approval of the District Committee. The Provincial Governor must approve all concrete construction. Finally, buildings taller than five stories must be reviewed by the *Comite national de l'amenagment du territoire, d'urbanisme, et de la construction* ("CNATUC") in Phnom Penh. However, there are presently no mechanisms for enforcement, review, dealing with non-compliance or, alternately, recourse for owners in the event of challenges to requests. It is, in reality, a system on paper only.

Only chaos can describe the present state of land utilization and regulation. Whereas in 1990 nearly all lands and buildings were in government ownership or control, now nearly all property is privately held or owned. The government still occupies key buildings in most municipalities, usually administrative buildings built during the French colonial period or just after colonial rule ended. Other buildings satisfy a wide range of purposes, for example, old rows of shop-houses are squatted in by multiple families, a coffin maker is adjacent to a motorcycle repair shop, which is next to a guest house, which is next to a private home, followed by a disco and so on.

Several laws presently pending, and some recently in place, could help improve the regulatory framework for urban development and land-use planning more generally. These regulations include a national urban development, regional development and construction law, known collectively as the CNATUC Law, passed in 1994 but held up in the Council of Ministers awaiting an implementation sub-decree. A second piece of legislation is the 1992 Land Law, which still provides the basic structure for tenure and registration of ownership. Finally, there is the revision of statutes regarding permitting, the process for which still generates much debate.

The CNATUC Law calls for the formation of provincial and, in some cases, municipal planning agencies to oversee construction and land-use regulations. The law intends to promote a balance between urban and rural development, protect private property rights, enforce legislation and promote the growth of tourism. Each province must set up a CNATUC, and each city larger than 20,000 people must establish a *Bureau des Affairs Urbaines* ("BAU"), following the example in Phnom Penh. These are responsible to the governor of each province and include, as with Phnom Penh, both Cambodian professionals and foreign advisors. At the present time, this law has been implemented in only a tentative way in most provinces and municipalities....

While the BAU study makes considerable provision for the recognition of historic structures, the *patrimoine architectural*, there has been little effort to fully integrate measures for protection into the broader urban scheme. In all, approximately 600 buildings have been considered. Of these, thirty-nine are identified as buildings of "exceptional value," seventy-two of "very remarkable value" (*valeur tres remarquable*), and a remaining ninety-one of "remarkable value," for a total of 202 buildings.

Generally, the selected buildings are properties of singular and/or monumental character; some shop-house rows are listed as are a number of traditional wood houses, but these are the exceptions. Most of the designated properties include larger municipal or governmental buildings, *wats* (Buddhist temples), and larger European houses, usually neoclassical in style and of substantial masonry construction. The issue of modified shop-house rows, smaller buildings, and those with alterations that might still be saved is not addressed adequately. Nor, at this point, have sufficient measures been suggested for review and compliance. In essence, the designations are only a wish-list. Moreover, it has been estimated that as many as ten to twenty percent of the structures have been lost or modified beyond recognition even before the list was published.

The BAU approach lacks a broader commitment to preservation and also a means by which historic structures might be safeguarded under the watchful eye of some extra-governmental body, or of a specially-appointed committee. In fact, the proposals omit a public component, so critical to the success of historic preservation efforts in many North American cities. Similarly, suggestions for incentives of various sorts, including grant programs and tax breaks, so successful in other countries, have not been considered. This approach leads to "top-down" planning with little provision for innovation and modification. Preservation is not well integrated into this urban development and land-use plan....

* * *

Notes and Comments

1. Is it terribly "aesthete" to focus on historic preservation when survival issues face poor nations such as Cambodia? Should historic preservation be the obligation of the developed world or the United Nations?

2. Does historic preservation serve economic development goals in a manner to suggest it should be a priority even in the poorest countries?

The following is a typical example of a local American historic preservation ordinance. American communities, however, typically have not enacted any such ordinances:

Carpinteria Municipal Code, Chapter 12.20 Historical Landmarks

12.20.010 Purpose.

The purpose of this chapter is to promote the economic welfare and prosperity of the city by preserving and protecting those places, sites, buildings, structures, works of art and other objects having a special historical or esthetic character or interest, for the use, education and view of the general public and to remind the citizens of this county and visitors from elsewhere of the historical background of the city.

12.20.020 Temporary designation of landmarks by committee

The Santa Barbara County advisory landmark committee, heretofore established by order of the board of supervisors of Santa Barbara County, is authorized and directed to receive and act upon applications to investigate and designate places, sites, buildings, structures, works ofart and other objects within the city as having historic, esthetic or other special character or interest and being worthy of consideration for protection, enhancement or perpetuation as such. Such designation shall remain and be in effect for a period of ninety days only and thereafter shall be of no force and effect, unless prior to the expiration of such period of ninety days, the city council shall have set a date for public hearing, advertised...at least ten days prior to the date set forth such public hearing, and either at such public hearing or after such public hearing, and within the ninety-day period shall have confirmed the action of the Santa Barbara County advisory landmark committee.

12.20.030 Designation of landmarks—Criteria for determination.

In designating any place, site, building, structure, work of art or other object as being of historical, esthetic of other special character or interest and worthy of protection under this chapter, the Santa Barbara County advisory landmark committee and the city council shall be subject to the following express standards:

A. The landmark designated shall have historical, esthetic or special character or interest for the general public and not be limited in interest to a special group of persons.

B. The designation of such landmark shall not require the expenditure of an unreasonable amount of money to carry out the purposes of this chapter.

C. The designation of such landmark shall not infringe upon the right of a private owner thereof to make any and all reasonable uses of such landmark which are not in conflict with the purposes of this chapter.

12.20.040 Designation of landmark

A. The Santa Barbara County advisory landmark committee shall temporarily impose and recommend to the city council for permanent adoption any or all of the following conditions it deems best suited to carry out the purposes of this chapter. Pending action of the city council, such conditions shall remain in effect for a period of ninety days from and after action of the committee. If the city council does not take action upon such conditions, they shall be of no further force and effect after the termination of the such ninety-day period. The city council may set a public hearing to be advertised once in a newspaper of general circulation in the city at least ten days prior to the date of such hearing. At such hearing, the city council may approve, modify or disapprove the designation by the committee and the conditions to be imposed. The action of the city council shall be final and shall take effect immediately.

B. Conditions that may be imposed under this section are as follows:

1. Demolition, removal or destruction, partially or entirely, may be prohibited unless express consent in writing is first had and obtained from the Santa Barbara County advisory landmark committee. Such consent may impose all reasonable conditions deemed appropriate by the committee to accomplish the purposes of this chapter.
2. No alterations, repairs, additions or changes (other than normal maintenance and repair work) shall be made unless and until all plans therefor have first been reviewed by the Santa Barbara County advisory landmark committee and approved or modified, and reasonable conditions imposed as deemed necessary, and that all such work shall be done under the direction and control of the Santa Barbara County advisory landmark committee or other qualified persons designated by it.
3. That only certain specified uses may be made, or that certain specified uses shall be prohibited.
4. That no buildings or structures exposed to public view within a specified distance may be placed, erected, moved in, altered, enlarged or removed (other than normal maintenance and repair work) without approval, with reasonable conditions imposed where deemed necessary by the Santa Barbara County advisory landmark committee, first had and obtained.
5. Other reasonable requirements, restrictions or conditions to meet special or unique circumstances.

12.20.050 Appeals from committee action.

Any interested person may appeal in writing to the city council from any action of the Santa Barbara County advisory landmark committee filed with the city clerk within ten days from the date of such action, and the city council shall set a public hearing, duly advertised once in a newspaper of general circulation in the city at least ten days before the date of such hearing, to consider such appeal, and the city council may confirm, modify or set aside any or all such actions of the Santa Barbara County advisory landmark committee.

12.20.060 Petition for city funds

The Santa Barbara County advisory landmark committee, or other interested persons, may petition the city council for funds necessary to carry out the purposes of this chapter. The city council may expend all reasonable amounts of money needed to carry out the purposes of this chapter or to acquire fee title or such lesser ownership rights or rights of possession or negative easements as it deems necessary or expedient to carry out the purposes of this chapter.

12.20.070 Enforcement by committee authorized—Referral to council.

The Santa Barbara County advisory landmark committee is charged with the responsibility for the enforcement of the provisions of this chapter and all conditions imposed under this chapter. If unable otherwise to obtain compliance with the provisions of this chapter and conditions imposed under this chapter, it may refer the matter to the city council.

12.20.080 Violation deemed unlawful—Penalty.

It is unlawful for any person, firm or corporation to violate any of the provisions of this chapter. Each separate day or any portion thereof on which any violation occurs shall be deemed to constitute a separate offense punishable as provided in this code.

* * *

Note and Comments

1. *The Battle of St. Vibiana's Cathedral.* In Los Angeles, a controversy in the late 1990s over the fate of earthquake damaged St. Vibiana's Cathedral pitted the powerful Archdiocese of Los Angeles led by Cardinal Mahoney and the City against the Los Angeles Conservancy, the local historic preservation organization, led at that time by its President, Katheryn Welch Howe, who happened to be the wife of Mayor Riordan's forward thinking Director of Planning, Con Howe. Larry Gordon, *Conservancy Plays Underdog in Battle to Save Cathedral*, Los Angeles Times, Jun. 10, 1996, § B, at 1. The conservancy, without any meaningful historic preservation legislation was able to save the Spanish style structure through enforcement of the state's environmental impact reporting laws, the court finding a lack of compliance. Larry Gordon & Abigail Goldman, *Study Ordered Before St. Vibiana's Can Be Razed*, Los Angeles Times, Jun. 20, 1996 (demolition halted pending environmental impact assessment under state law); Judi Wilgoven, *Council Acts to Take Church Off Historic Roll*, Los Angeles Times Jun. 19, 1996) (status would have delayed demolition one year). *See also* David J. Cowan, *The De-Listing of Saint Vibiana's Cathedral: How History Was Saved from the Politician's Wreaking Ball*, 19 Los Angeles Law. 68 (Jan. 1997). Although the judicial ruling provided a respite for the preservationists, Tom Gilmore, a private developer dedicated to revitalizing the city's financial district has purchased the cathedral. Joe Mozingo, *Ceremony Marks a Vision of Hope for St. Vibiana's Development: Both Preservationists and City Officials Say Buyer's Plan will Rehabilitate the Old Cathedral's Legacy and Surroundings*, Los Angeles Times, Nov. 3, 1999 (Metro) (purchased by Tom Gilmore for $ 4.6 million); Associated Press, *$ 4 Million Grant to Aid Renovation of St. Vibiana's*, Los Angeles Times, July 21, 2000

(Metro) (announcing state grant to assist development and preservation, the church elected to build a new $ 69.6 million Raphael Moneo-designed cathedral, "Our Lady of the Angels," on a more desirable Temple Street location adjacent to a proposed riverfront park project).

2. *While Preservationists were Celebrating.* Although St. Vibiana's was ostensibly saved, the opposing forces already succeeded in passing state-wide legislation authorizing the exemption of all churches from compliance with historic preservation laws, proving the power of the Gospel. *East Bay Asian Local Dev. v. State*, 13 P.3d 1122 (Cal. 2000), *cert. denied*, 532 U.S. 1008 (2001) (sustaining statute allowing religiously-affiliated organizations to declare themselves exempt from historic landmark regulations under Cal. Gov't Code §§ 25373(d) (counties), 37361(c) (cities).

3. For a comparative study of American state and local historic preservation legislation, see Gregory A. Ashe, *Reflecting the Best of Our Aspirations: Protecting Modern and Post-Modern Architecture*, 15 Cardozo Arts & Ent. L. J. 69 (1997).

4. One problem that needs to be mitigated is gentrification. Historic preservation, where it is tied to neighborhood revitalization, can result in escalating rents and displacement of the poor. While some displacement is unavoidable, programs can be established to include affordable housing within the revitalized historic neighborhood and to assure that those displaced are relocated to acceptable affordable housing. The following excerpt discusses the relationship between historic preservation and the poor and its impact:

Todd Schneider, Note, *From Monuments to Urban Renewal: How Different Philosophies of Historic Preservation Impact the Poor,*

8 Georgetown Journal Poverty Law and Policy 257 (2001)

....The preservation movement arose in Europe at the beginning of the 19th century and then swiftly crossed the Atlantic to America by 1808, when a group of Bostonians failed in their attempt to save the "Old Brick" First Church meetinghouse. It took almost 50 years more for preservation in the United States to move beyond its localized fights to its first nationwide controversy. During the 1850's, the Mount Vernon Ladies Association managed to "save" Mount Vernon by raising private funds across the country over a six-year period, making their effort the first successful large-scale preservation battle.

In doing so, the Association set preservation on its initial course of Monumentalism, which was "historical" preservation. Because Americans had so little history to work from, preservationists soon fixated on the heroes of the young republic. Sites associated with our Founding Fathers (such as Mount Vernon) became sacred. Paradoxically, though, these early preservationists cared far more passionately about the historical significance of the places they saved than the structures associated with the sites. For example, in 1826, locals proposed to tear down the Old State House in Boston (already a century old at the time) and erect a monument to George Washington in its place. Another motivation for this general irreverence for older structures was that Americans, who reveled in the novelty of their country, sought newness in their environment as well. Americans in the first half of the 19th century "recognize[d] how undesirable it [was] to build the tabernacle of our brief lifetimes out of permanent materials,"an attitude highly antithetical to preserving older buildings.

By the 1890's, though, the preservation movement had begun to drift away from its Monumentalist origins. Urban change seemed to be out of control, with entire city blocks being built, torn down and then built up again, all in the space of decades. Living in such a state of flux, people began to cherish older buildings for their sentimental associations and for the islands of continuity they represented in a sea of "progress." A dilemma quickly arose. Should all older buildings be saved, or could preservationists take a more narrowly focused approach that would both assuage urban residents' sense of dislocation and simultaneously allow the forces of progress to build anew?

The answer lay in the philosophy of Aestheticism, which was forcefully propounded by America's first professional preservationist, William Sumner Appleton, Jr. He too assigned value to older structures based on "history," but not as the Monumentalists had defined that term. Instead, he focused on the cultural aspects of the built environment, so that he concentrated on the art-historical and/or archaeological aspects of the many buildings he saved. Appleton's approach greatly expanded the pool of potentially preservable structures, since there were far more buildings of a certain historical style (e.g., Georgian and Federal) than those where George Washington had once slept. Aestheticism also required more hard work from preservationists themselves. Monumentalist preservationists had wasted little effort on restoring historic sites. For Appleton, though, it betrayed Aestheticism's creed to allow artistic works to decay before one's eyes, and as a result, the entire field of restoration architecture began to flourish.

The most important change wrought by Aestheticism, though, related to the post-renovation phase. Adaptive reuse of historic buildings (i.e., transforming them into new homes or businesses) became more commonplace, because Appleton believed that saved structures could be vital parts of their communities' present, as well as their past. In doing so, Aestheticism replaced the house-museum tradition of Monumentalists with a pro-development preservation strategy, a change that expanded preservation's potential basis of support from amateur historians to local chambers of commerce.

Ironically, in this same time period, Congress enacted the first federal preservation legislation, the Antiquities Act of 1906, which, by protecting only "historic landmarks, [and] other objects of historic interest," was a strong affirmation of Monumentalist principles.[25] However, at the local level, Aestheticism soon gained ground, particularly in the establishment of historic districts. Charleston, South Carolina passed the first historic district zoning ordinance in America in 1931, and other Southern cities followed suit. For Aestheticists, these districts represented the ultimate expression of Appleton's curatorial tendencies. Just as paintings of a particular period and place were deliberately hung in the same gallery to heighten visitors' appreciation, so too were historic properties now grouped and exhibited in large-scale, open-air "museums."

At the federal level, the Historic Sites, Buildings and Antiquities Act of 1935[28] also endorsed the establishment of historic districts, but included few mechanisms for achieving this goal. Not until 30 years later, with the passage of the National Historic Preservation Act ("NHPA"),[29] did federal policy clearly embrace Aestheticism by providing governmental protections through the expansion of the National Register of Historic Places and the creation of a review process for federal action that would affect historic properties. This legislation also required that federal agencies make use of historic

25. 16 U.S.C. §§431–433 (West 2000).
28. *See* 16 U.S.C. §§461–467 (West 2000).
29. *See* 16 U.S.C. §470a (West 2000).

buildings to "the maximum extent feasible,"[30] demonstrating that Appleton's adaptive reuse policy had finally gained government acceptance.

Soon after this success, the preservation movement began to shift course yet again. While Appleton had focused on the aesthetic nature of historic neighborhoods, later preservationists expanded his approach to encompass "preservation of the city itself—its mix of economic uses, varied physical and social fabrics and human scale." In other words, preservation became a catalyst for urban renewal, a philosophy that can be characterized as Revitalization.

The federal government began quickly to incorporate this new school of thought into its urban planning. The Neighborhood Redevelopment Program in the 1960's encouraged local authorities to rehabilitate older buildings instead of replacing them. In the 1970's, programs like Urban Homesteading and Neighborhood Housing Services directly linked preservation with low-income housing. More recently, Executive Order 13006 directed federal agencies to locate themselves in downtown areas and to give highest priority to historic districts.

What is most remarkable about Revitalization is its ability to transform a symbol of the decline of America's cities—decaying buildings—into valued assets that can spark neighborhood revitalization. Similarly, some revitalizationists see themselves as engaging in sustainable development, so that the needs of the present are satisfied without compromising the ability of future generations to meet their needs. Preservation helps achieve this goal because rehabilitation of existing buildings leads to conservation of the built environment, instead of consumption of increasingly scarce natural resources for new construction. In fact, rehabilitation work reduces the heavy burden on landfills imposed by demolition and construction....

States have typically mirrored federal preservation policy and its underlying philosophical justifications by establishing their own state registers, preservation acts and tax incentives. Some states have even enshrined preservation in their constitutions as a legitimate governmental function. At the local level, Aestheticism still reigns supreme, in the countless preservation ordinances and their attendant local preservation commissions. These commissions accept or reject modifications to protected historic structures based on overtly aesthetic concerns. Also, they regulate private action far more than any other governmental entity, a power affirmed by the Supreme Court in Penn Central Transportation Co. v. City of New York.[51] Penn Central, which declared preservation a permissible public goal and preservation ordinances such as New York City's appropriate to achieving that goal, is based explicitly on Aestheticist justifications. "[S]tructures with special historic, cultural, or architectural significance enhance the quality of life for all."...[52]

For much of its history, the preservation movement has been "an elite assertiveness of a class- and ethnicity-based traditionalism," blind to the interests of low-income people.... [B]uildings are historical documents, and as such, they have the power to organize our knowledge of our past, and therefore ourselves. So, if the wealthy could control which historic structures were being preserved and how these "saved" buildings were presented to the public, these Monumentalists would also be able to consolidate their own elite status and identity. This phenomenon occurred most strikingly in the

30. 16 U.S.C.S. § 470h-2 (West 2000).
51. *See* 438 U.S. 104 (1978).
52. *Id.* at 108.

South in the 1930's, where preservation often served as a tool for glorifying the Confederate past and its elite.

Such elitism is not just a relic of preservation's dimly lit past. By the 1970's, the New York City Landmarks Preservation Commission had designated 113 buildings, and 105 of these structures had been built by and for the wealthy, "a narrow focus [that] had no relevance for New York's working people, the poor, or people of color." Even today, ethnic heritage is one of the most underrepresented themes for historic resources listed on the National Register. In sum, the elitism of Monumentalists has led to the neglect of the histories of low-income people.

Like any system of aesthetics, Aestheticism has produced a hierarchy of cultural artifacts, with certain objects deemed more "beautiful" than others, and with "beauty" governed by the tastes of the dominant socioeconomic class. It has done so by fetishizing the opulent mansions of the wealthy and by focusing on homes whose architectural styles, such as Queen Anne and Georgian, were originally found primarily in middle and upper income neighborhoods. Conversely, the exclusion of buildings found in low-income neighborhoods from the Aestheticists' regime has implied that low-income communities lack value, aesthetically or otherwise.

More invidious, though, for low-income people is how some Aestheticists, who originally renovated historic properties to improve society's quality of life, now manipulate the preservation movement and its laws to counter perceived threats to their elite, wealthy lifestyles, i.e., low-income neighbors. Such tampering is possible because Aestheticism's curatorial impulses contain an inherent bias towards the status quo. Aestheticists have created preservation commissions across the country that decide, primarily on aesthetic grounds, whether or not property owners will be allowed to make alterations to protected historic structures. This review process, like any bureaucratic endeavor, can be quite time-consuming. Consequently, any proposed modification to a historic neighborhood can be blocked, either fairly or unfairly, through the invocation of preservation's legal protections. Even a former chair of the New York City Landmarks Preservation Commission has complained about the "growing tendency to use designation for purposes outside the law... [such as] to maintain the status quo [or] to prevent development."...

Revitalizationists have been drawn towards preservation-based affordable housing for several reasons. Historic buildings populate many of the neighborhoods most in need of affordable housing. Reuse of existing vacant properties to create units is more likely to receive funding than construction of new housing for the poor. Local building codes often grant more flexibility to rehabilitation of historic structures than construction of new buildings. Also, the housing stock in historic districts is likely to be superior to new construction because older homes are made of brick.

Moreover, affordable housing projects in historic buildings by definition blend in with their surrounding neighborhoods, removing neighbors' fears of potentially unattractive new construction. In fact, the unobtrusiveness of preservation-based housing projects may make them more likely to increase socioeconomic diversity than new construction would because existing residents are less likely to move out of newly renovated neighborhoods.

It is possible that a new housing project could create more housing units than a rehabilitation project would in the same given space, because the new buildings could be larger and taller than their predecessors. But even the federal government has abandoned high density public housing projects in favor of low density designs such as those in typical historic districts. In fact, historic residential neighborhoods commonly possess the infrastructure prized most by low-income residents, including good public transportation, pedestrian access to basic goods and services, and a wide diversity of housing types. These neighborhoods also give residents of affordable housing units "the emotional benefits of a beautiful, stable living environment and a heightened sense of heritage," i.e., the benefits of Aestheticism-based preservation.

The most important reason to use historic properties when creating affordable housing, though, is that, instead of receiving only one federal tax benefit, the Low Income Housing Credit ("LIHC"),[85] affordable housing developers who renovate historic structures can also claim the Rehabilitation Credit ("RC").[86] In fact, developers can often combine both incentives at the state level as well....

Preservation tax incentives have yielded similarly impressive results. Since 1976, the RC has generated more than $19 billion in private investment. Rhode Island has estimated that it received $1.69 in new state tax revenue for every $1.00 of preservation state tax credit, and that the overall benefit to the state was $29 for every public dollar spent.

Concomitant with all this investment has been the large-scale creation of preservation-based jobs. Each rehabilitation project for which the RC is claimed produces on average 39 new jobs, including more than 40,000 in 1998. In fact, "[d]ollar for dollar, historic preservation is one of the highest job-generating economic development options available," creating more jobs per dollar spent than industries such as auto manufacturing, coal mining and oil pumping.

Obviously, rehabilitation work spurs growth in construction jobs, but it also has a significant impact on another major industry, tourism. "Because of historic preservation, and only because of historic preservation, the travel industry is now the single largest industry in Europe, employing nearly 10 percent of the work force...And benefits from tourism have been won without damage to other economic interests. Commercial progress has not ceased in London, Paris, Rome or Madrid, despite their reverence for the past." Similarly, Savannah, Georgia, which has one of the largest urban historic districts in the United States, has seen its heritage tourism industry grow to $650 million annually....

But funneling public and private dollars into rehabilitation work instead of new construction does carry some negative consequences. Rehabilitated office space rents for only 85% or 90% of the price of newly built offices of comparable quality. Also, the expenses for older buildings are a higher percentage of building income than those of newer structures, which means that the financing available to rehabilitation work is not as attractive as that for new construction. It is not even clear, despite some preservationists' strong assertions, whether it is cheaper to rehabilitate older buildings or construct new ones. Also, while it may be true that rehabilitation work generates employment opportunities in neighborhoods with large numbers of unemployed people, there have been no studies as to whether the low-income residents themselves actually receive the benefits of these preservation-based jobs.

Of more concern, though, is how the very success of preservation-based economic development in rundown historic neighborhoods leads to the possibility of gentrifica-

85. *See* I.R.C. §42 (1994).

86. *See id.* §47. The Credit is equal to 20% of "qualified rehabilitation expenditures" spent on a certified historic structure and 10% of the amount spent on a structure first placed in service before 1936.

tion. When historic districts receive landmark designation, they often attract developers, and property prices start to rise. As a result, poorer residents no longer can afford to live in their own neighborhood, and they are forced to move away....

Unsurprisingly, low-income residents today are still reluctant to seek landmark designation for fear of gentrification.

Yet blind opposition to preservation because of its potentially gentrifying effect is not a solution either. Indeed, such resistance "preserves" low-income neighborhoods just as they are, with all their attendant ills. Moreover, gentrification does possess some advantages. New residents add vitality to the community; their improvements to their residences can spur local economic growth, and the newcomers often exhibit political strength on behalf of their neighborhoods. More significantly, low-income neighborhoods are transformed into mixed-income communities. While middle class residents would never allow low-income people to reside in their neighborhoods, upper income people will move into a poor, racially mixed neighborhood if it is located in a historic district.

Furthermore, some Revitalizationists believe that any historical linkage between preservation and gentrification no longer holds true in the modern urban environment. Unlike 30 years ago, upper-income people who move back to the city want to inhabit lofts in converted warehouses, not historic homes already occupied by low-income residents. So, instead of low-income people being displaced, they now gain new neighbors in newly created residential districts....

However, the most critical issue for low-income residents facing gentrification is the sudden increase in their property taxes. When property sales in a neighborhood accelerate and values start to inflate, cities quickly reassess property taxes in hopes of gaining additional revenue. When such reassessment occurs too rapidly, the taxes rise to such a high level that current low-income residents can no longer pay them, forcing many inhabitants to leave their own neighborhoods.

To protect the poor from being taxed out of their homes, municipalities should impose reasonable yearly maximums on property tax increases. Alternatively, authorities could defer any increase until the sale of a property, so that low-income residents would pay higher property taxes only if they decided to cash in on a "hot" property, and not if they wanted to remain in their neighborhood. It must be acknowledged that cities will not often exhibit the restraint required under the above proposals when they are confronted with the possibility of increased revenues from higher property taxes. Therefore, Revitalizationists arguing for a gradualist tax policy need to point out that any short-term gains a city receives from higher property taxes will eventually become insufficient to cover the cost of additional services required to meet the needs of newly homeless ex-residents. Revitalizationists can also analogize the ill effects of gentrification to that of "flipping," a process by which quick property turnover leads to spiraling price increases. Cities willing to impose anti-flip measures should also be willing to take a gradualist approach in historic districts threatened by gentrification. Furthermore, cities such as Cincinnati, Pittsburgh and Savannah have demonstrated that, by using some or all of the above techniques, it is possible to gentrify neighborhoods gradually and positively, with a minimal displacement of the poor....

[T]he idea that the poor "contaminate" historic properties is an outdated belief. Low-income people are not threats to historic districts, nor are preservationists inherently biased against low-income residents. Instead, both groups today can work together to achieve the preservation of historic buildings and the reduction of poverty.

* * *

Notes and Comments

1. *International Gentrification*. Lester Rowntree, *Creating a Sense of Place: The Evolution of Historic Preservation of Salzburg, Austria*, 8 J. Urb. Hist. 61 (1981) (yet experiencing displacement of poor as in the case of preservation of the Marais district of Paris and the Covent Garden neighborhood of London).

2. Historic Preservationists and others have been eyeing America's aging suburbs for historic designation. In some cases unique architectural examples or unique neighborhoods should be protected, but the suburban-subdivision-homes associations-automobile lobby may embrace historic preservation as a technique to preserve the urban sprawl-automobile dependent development patterns and there are many baby boomers who grew up in Levittowns and their progeny and would join a movement to encapsulate romantic memories of the suburban rite of passage. Is there a danger that historic preservation can be used as an ever-more rigid zoning code? Curiously, the preservation movement is as popular as the criticism of "Euclidean" zoning.

Public Art

While many cities lack the resources to consider expending public funds on art, particularly when schools, public safety, libraries, day care, and even street maintenance must take precedence, aesthetic initiatives are still available. Business and city boosters can be encouraged to sponsor public art installation and public art shows. The Los Angeles angels and Berlin Bears were purchased by businesses which paid artists to paint them and following the installation the works were auctioned off to the public. Many will find their way to permanent public art installations while the substantial proceeds from the auctions can be used for charitable purposes or the investment in public art. The city of Hellersdorf in Berlin has established a club for youths that focuses on art and the best artists from the club have been hired by private developers to paint murals on building surfaces that are frequently the target of graffiti taggers. In cities such as Philadelphia, Pennsylvania and Culver City, California, developers of large structures and projects are required to include original artistic elements such as paintings, sculpture or glass in new projects. Cities can establish artistic trusts that can efficiently plan and execute public art plans and programs and those programs can be funded by a fee on new development:

Ehrlich v. City of Culver City

Supreme Court of California
911 P. 2d 429 (1996)

[In the first part of this decision, set out in Chapter 5, the court vacated the imposition of a $280,000 recreational mitigation fee imposed on the developer of 30 condominiums seeking to redevelop a former private tennis club]...[T]he city also required plaintiff to pay an exaction under the city's "art in public places" program. By municipal ordinance, new residential development projects of more than four units, as well as all commercial, industrial, and public building projects with a building valuation exceeding $500,000, are required to provide "art work" (as defined by the ordinance) for the project in an amount equal to 1 percent of the total building valuation, or to pay an equal amount in cash to the city art fund. The city valued plaintiff's project at $3,200,000. He elected initially to pay the fee, which totaled $33,200, but his successor in interest apparently subsequently placed art of his own choosing on the site rather than pay the in-lieu fee.... The site was subsequently developed and residential units were sold to the public....

Under the city's art in public places ordinance, plaintiff could not receive a certificate of occupancy for any of the 30 townhouses in the project until he either paid $32,200 to the city art fund (1 percent of the total building valuation) or contributed an approved work of art of an equivalent value. Under the latter option, the art may either be placed on site, in which case it remains the property of the applicant, or it may be donated to the city for placement elsewhere. Although petitioner initially opted to pay the fee, his successor in interest subsequently placed art of his own choosing on the site and received the 30 certificates of occupancy during the pendency of this action.

Plaintiff contends that the required dedication of art or the cash equivalent thereof constitutes a taking under the *Nollan-Dolan* standards. This follows, he asserts, from the fact that the city made no individualized determination that the art mitigates a need generated by the project.

[W]e agree with the city that the art in public places fee is not a development exaction of the kind subject to the *Nollan-Dolan* takings analysis. As both the trial court and the Court of Appeal concluded, the requirement to provide either art or a cash equivalent thereof is more akin to traditional land use regulations imposing minimal building setbacks, parking and lighting conditions, landscaping requirements, and other design conditions such as color schemes, building materials and architectural amenities. Such aesthetic conditions have long been held to be valid exercises of the city's traditional police power, and do not amount to a taking merely because they might incidentally restrict a use, diminish the value, or impose a cost in connection with the property.... The requirement of providing art in an area of the project reasonably accessible to the public is, like other design and landscaping requirements, a kind of aesthetic control well within the authority of the city to impose....

Lucas, C.J., and George, J., concur.

Dean Kmiec has criticized the *Ehrlich* ruling as follows:

Douglas W. Kmiec, *Inserting the Last Remaining Pieces into the Takings Puzzle,*

38 Wm. & Mary L. Rev. 995 (1997)

No direct support exists in California land-use law, or even in the law of eminent domain for the court's proposition. Quite the contrary, the common law has always been suspicious of imposing affirmative duties generally, let alone affirmative duties that arise by a type of self-imposed adverse possession—hang around long enough as a private tennis court and don't expect to be anything else, ever. Moreover, even if one assumed that the city could ipso facto confiscate the value associated with voluntarily undertaken and unsubsidized private use, it is not abundantly clear how, on remand, the lower court is to calculate this loss of value to the city. The state supreme court speculated that the city's value may be the "additional administrative expenses incurred in predesignating other property within Culver City for recreational use," or then again, maybe the city's value is the "additional costs of attracting the development of comparable private recreational facilities." The state court really did not address this issue, other than to remind the city—and the reviewing lower court now stuck with the problem—that "[t]he determination of such a fee will, of course, require[s]...specific findings supported by substantial evidence."...

The bad news is that the court concluded that the art fee was not an extortionate circumstance. According to the court, the art fee was akin to a "traditional land-use" regulation. This was error. Although it is true that aesthetic regulation has gained greater acceptability in state courts, such regulation often is sustained in relation to manifest harm such as a decline in property value. In addition, the United States Supreme Court in Lucas suggested that special caution be exercised when the police power pursues aesthetic, rather than "core" health and safety purposes. At any rate, it is questionable whether "public art fees" really are the equivalent, as the California Supreme Court claims, to "minimal building setbacks, parking and lighting conditions, [etc.]." Setbacks and parking requirements are allied closely with the negative burdens caused or created by particular development, and thus these "traditional" controls bear little similarity to "art fees." To this Midwesterner at least, it seems extraordinary that any claimed analytical connection could exist between condominium development and a hankering for public art. Courts should willingly listen to the argument, of course, but the fairness called for by the Fifth Amendment suggests that the listening or the scrutiny must be heightened and bound by the state's background property law principles....

* * *

Notes and Comments

1. Should aesthetic judgments, including a community's amenities be left to property professors, neighbors, judges, or left to local and state political discretion? Cities can be drab and ordinary or beautiful, should the United States Supreme Court mandate only the former?

2. For another critique of the *Ehrlich* ruling, see Gideon Kanner *Tennis Anyone? How California Judges Made Land Ransom and Art Censorship Legal*, 25 Real Estate L. J. 214 (1997), at 223–24, Professor Kanner states:

> Ironically,...land redevelopers like Richard Ehrlich should be viewed favorably because they recycle land, as it were, and thus axiomatically avoid the asserted community detriment of using up limited open space. Yet, paradoxically, the *Ehrlich* decision is based on the directly opposite rationale, namely, that the process of land recycling produces a community detriment because it deprives the community of the benefits said to arise from the land's previous uses. In short,...the California Supreme Court created a classic Catch-22: Building homes on vacant land is said to be a detriment because it deprives the community of open space, but rebuilding them on previously developed land is also a detriment because it deprives the community of the benefit conferred by the previous development. Community housing needs thus appear to play no significant role in the court's decision-making calculus.

Is it a valid criticism of *Ehrlich* that the Court ignored the need to encourage urban infill? Whether *Ehrlich* is the proper vehicle, and whether The state court should have discovered this esoteric charge are subject to doubt, but Professor Kanner's implied criticism may be well taken that those responsible for land use policy should look to the practical effects of their labors. Should regulators institute policies that encourage infill and thus urban revitalization rather than continuing to favorably encourage suburban sprawl?

The following is the Los Angeles ordinance establishing it's Art Fee, the vehicle for raising funds for public art, it is typical of the legislation passed by those cities with mandatory public art exaction programs:

Los Angeles City Code, §91.107.4.6 (2000)

91.107.4.6. Arts Development Fee. The owner of a development project for a commercial or industrial building shall be required to pay an arts fee in accordance with the requirements of this section.

91.107.4.6.2. Fee Amount. The Department of Building and Safety shall collect an arts fee in the following amount:

1. Office or research and development. For an office or research and development building, the arts fee shall be $1.57 per square foot.
2. Retail. All retail establishments shall pay an arts fee of $1.31 per square foot.
3. Manufacturing. For a manufacturing building, the arts fee shall be $0.51 per square foot.
4. Warehouse. For a warehouse building, the arts fee shall be $0.39 per square foot.
5. Hotel. For a hotel building, the arts fee shall be $0.52 per square foot.

In no event shall the required arts fee exceed either $1.57 per gross square foot of any structure authorized by the permit or one percent of the valuation of the project designated on the permit, whichever is lower, as determined by the Department of Building and Safety. Where there are combined uses within a development project or portion thereof, the arts fee shall be the sum of the fee requirements of the various uses listed above. The Cultural Affairs Department shall revise the arts fee annually by an amount equal to the Consumer Price Index for Los Angeles as published by the United States Department of Labor. The revised amount shall be submitted to Council for adoption by ordinance.

91.107.4.6.3. Time of Collection [before issuance of building permit for commercial and industrial buildings].

§91.107.4.6.4. Exceptions:

The arts fee required by Section 91.107.4.6 shall not be assessed for the following projects or portions thereof:

1. Any project for which the total value of all construction or work for which the permit is issued is $500,000 or less.
2. The repair, renovation or rehabilitation of a building or structure that does not alter the size or occupancy load of the building.
3. The repair, renovation or rehabilitation of a building or structure for the installation of fire sprinklers pursuant to Division 9.

4. The repair, renovation or rehabilitation of a building or structure that has been made to comply with Division 88 (Earthquake Hazard Reduction in Existing Buildings) subsequent to a citation of noncompliance with Division 88.
5. The repair, renovation or rehabilitation of a building or structure for any handicapped facilities pursuant to this code.
6. All residential buildings or portion thereof. This exception does not include hotels.

91.107.4.6.5. Use of Arts Fees. Any arts fee collected by the Department of Building and Safety shall be deposited in the Arts Development Fee Trust Fund. Any fee paid into this fund may be used only for the purpose of providing cultural and artistic facilities, services and community amenities which will be available to the development project and its future employees. Any cultural and artistic facilities, services and community amenities provided shall comply with the principles and standards set forth in the Cultural Master Plan when adopted.

At or about the time of collection of any fee imposed by this section, the Cultural Affairs Department shall identify the use to which the arts fee is to be put, and if the use is financing public facilities, the facilities shall be identified.

91.107.4.6.6. Projects Covered. In 1988, the city enacted Ordinance 164,243 which states in part:

> "This ordinance is an interim measure while the City of Los Angeles is giving consideration to the enactment of an Arts Development Fee Ordinance. The owners of a development project shall be obligated to pay an Arts Development Fee if such fee is adopted in the future by the city. The fee will not exceed one percent (1%) of the total value of work and construction authorized by the building permit issued to a development project. This fee would be used to provide adequate cultural and artistic facilities, services and community amenities for the project."

By enacting Section 91.107.4.6 (previously Section 91.0304(b)(11)), the City has adopted the Arts Development Fee referred to by Ordinance 164,243. Accordingly, an arts fee shall be paid to the City of Los Angeles by owners of development projects which received building permits between and including January 15, 1989, and the effective date of this section. This arts fee described in this section shall be paid within 60 days of receipt of a request for payment of an arts fee. All exceptions listed in Section 91.107.4.6.4 shall apply to owners of development projects subject to Ordinance 164,243.

The City Clerk shall bill and collect the Arts Development Fee owed by those persons to whom notice was given pursuant to this paragraph for the period January 15, 1989, through May 7, 1991. The amount due shall be paid in full within 60 days of the billing date unless an agreement to pay in installments pursuant to this paragraph is approved by the City Clerk. Persons indebted to the City of Los Angeles for Arts Development Fees may, upon approval by the City Clerk, enter into an agreement with the City of Los Angeles to pay such fees in installments over a period not to exceed one year. The City Clerk shall collect a service fee of $10.00 on each monthly installment to recover the cost to the city of processing installment payments. The Cultural Affairs Department is hereby authorized to negotiate and accept payment in kind for the Arts Development Fee owed by those persons to whom notice was given pursuant to this paragraph for the period January 15, 1989, through May 7, 1991. The Cultural Affairs Department shall provide notice to the City Clerk of the name of the person on whose account such in kind payment was accepted, and whether the in kind payment constitutes payment in full or only a specified portion of the Arts Development Fee owed....

* * *

The following is the Los Angeles ordinance establishing it's Art trust fund designed to disperse the proceeds from the art fee ordinance, typical of the legislation passed by many cities:

Los Angeles Municipal Administrative Code, Article 21 Arts and Cultural Facilities and Services Trust Fund (1990)

Sec. 5.115.4. Creation and Administration of the Fund.

(a) There is hereby created and established within the Treasury of the City of Los Angeles a special fund to be known as the "Arts and Cultural Facilities and Services Trust Fund" (Fund). The Fund shall be administered by the General Manager of the Cultural Affairs Department. Approval of the Mayor and the City Council shall be required for all disbursements from the Fund. All interest and earnings of the Fund shall accrue to the Fund.

Deposits shall be made to the Fund in accordance with the requirements of this article or other requirements adopted by the City Council by ordinance. In the event any money deposited into the Fund is subject to limitations or restrictions as to its use or expenditure, the deposit shall be placed into a separate account within the Fund, shall not be commingled with other monies in the Fund, and no part of such deposits shall be disbursed in violation of such restrictions.

(b) Expenditure from the Fund shall be exclusively for:

(1) acquisition or placement of publicly accessible works of art; (2) acquisition or construction of arts and cultural facilities; (3) the providing of arts and cultural services; (4) restoration or preservation of existing works of art; or, (5) the City's costs of administering the City's Public Works Improvements Arts Program (Program); and provided that the artwork, facility or service has received the prior approval of the Board of Cultural Affairs Commissioners.

(c) For the year commencing with July 1, 1989, and each fiscal year thereafter, an amount from the City General Fund which is equal to the amount which would be derived during that fiscal year from a transient occupancy tax imposed at the rate of one percent (1 %) shall be placed in the Fund, and the City's budget for that fiscal year shall so reflect.

(d) Within three (3) months after the close of each fiscal year, the Cultural Affairs Department shall provide the City Council with a report identifying all income and expenditures to and from the Fund during the prior fiscal year.

* * *

Chapter 33 Art Development Fee Trust Fund

Sec. 5346. Creation and Administration of the Fund.

(a) There is hereby created and established within the Treasury of the City of Los Angeles a special fund to be known as the "Arts Development Fee Trust Fund," hereinafter referred to in this chapter as the "Fund."

(b) All monies received by the Department of Building and Safety pursuant to the Subdivision 91.0304(b)11 of the Los Angeles Municipal Code shall be placed in this Fund. All monies received shall be deposited, invested, accounted for, and expended consistent with Government Code Section 66006. All interest and earnings of the Fund shall accrue to the Fund.

(c) Once each fiscal year, the City Council shall make findings with respect to any portion of the fee remaining unexpended or uncommitted in this Fund five or more years after deposit of the fee. These findings shall identify the purpose to which the fee is to be put and to demonstrate a reasonable relationship between the fee and the purpose for which the fee was charged.

(d) The Cultural Affairs Department shall be responsible for maintaining the records relating to the Fund.

(e) The General Manager of the Cultural Affairs Department is authorized to establish appropriate procedures to carry out the provisions of this chapter.

(f) No appropriation or expenditure may be made from this Fund without the prior approval of the General Manager of the Cultural Affairs Department or a duly authorized representative....

Sec. 22.118 Arts Development Fee Credits.

1. If private facilities, services and community amenities for cultural and artistic purposes are provided in a proposed development project and such facilities, services and community amenities are to be privately owned and maintained.... However, (the City of Los Angeles Cultural Affairs Department must first find that the subject facility, service or community amenity meets the following standards:

(a) that it may he used by the patrons, occupants and owners of the development project; and

(b) that it satisfies the cultural and artistic needs of the development project so as to reduce the need for public cultural and artistic facilities, services and community amenities to serve (the patrons, occupants and owners of the development project.

2. Credits.

(a) Credits shall be granted dollar-for-dollar for any monies paid for the cost of cultural and artistic facilities, services or community amenities provided....

(b) Cultural and artistic facilities are defined as follows:

(i) Exhibit/Performance Space: Public gallery/exhibition space, public performance spaces, public artistic studio spaces, public arts education facilities.

(ii) Sculpture: Free standing, wall supported or suspended, kinetic, electronic or mechanical in material or combination of materials.

(iii) Murals or portable paintings: In any materials or variety of materials, with or without collage or the addition of non-traditional materials and means.

(iv) Earthworks, fireworks, neon, glass, mosaics, photographs, prints, calligraphy, any combination of forms of media, including sound, film, holographic, and video systems, hybrids of any media and new genres.

(v) Standardized fixtures such as grates, street lights, signage, and other design enhancements, as are rendered by an artist for unique or limited editions.

(vi) Similar facilities on culture and the arts as determined by the Cultural Affairs Department.

(c) Cultural and artistic services are defined as follows:

(i) Performing arts: Theatre, dance, music and performance art.

(ii) Literary arts: Poetry readings and story telling.

(iii) Media arts: Film and video, screenings and installations.

(iv) Education: Lectures, presentations and training in and about arts and culture.

(v) Special events: Parades, festivals and celebrations.

(vi) Similar services on culture and the arts as determined approved by the Cultural Affairs Department.

(d) Cultural and artistic community amenities as defined by die Cultural Affairs Department....

§22.118

Administrative Code

(f) The granting of credits shall also be subject to the following conditions:

(i) The private ownership and maintenance *of* the facilities, services and community amenities shall be adequately provided for by written agreement, and

(ii) The facilities, services and community amenities proposed are in substantial compliance with the General Plan, or an arts and cultural master plan developed by the Cultural Affairs Department, and

(iii) The owners of a development project shall guarantee the payment of the arts fee to the satisfaction of the Cultural Affairs Department.

(g) The following facilities, services and community amenities are ineligible costs for a credit provided herein:

(i) Directional elements such as supergraphics, signage, or color coding except where these elements are integral parts of the original work of art.

(ii) Art objects which are mass produced of standard design such as playground equipment, fountains or statuary objects.

(iii) Reproductions, by mechanical or other means, of original works of art, except in cases of film, video, photography, printmaking or other media arts.

(iv) Decorative, ornamental, or functional elements which are designed by the building architect as opposed to an artist commissioned for this design enhancement purpose.

(v) Landscape architecture and landscape gardening except where these elements are designed by the artist and/or are an integral part of the work of art by the artist.

(vi) Services or utilities necessary to operate or maintain the artwork over time.

3. Credits shall be granted dollar-for-dollar as defined in Subsection 2 for any development project subject to a cultural and artistic facility, service or community amenity requirement pursuant to a written agreement with the Community Redevelopment Agency or Rapid Transit District.

* * *

The following case raises the question of whether the artist retains any interest in artworks for which the artist has sold the work or where it had been commissioned in the context of public art:

Richard Serra v. General Services Administration

United States Court of Appeals for the Second Circuit
847 F.2d 1045 (1988)

Jon O. Newman, Circuit Judge....

Richard Serra, a prominent American sculptor, brought the action seeking to bar the United States General Services Administration (GSA) from removing his controversial sculpture "Tilted Arc" from Federal Plaza in lower Manhattan....

In 1979, GSA selected Serra to create an outdoor sculpture to be installed on the plaza adjacent to the federal office complex at 26 Federal Plaza in lower Manhattan (the "Plaza" or "Federal Plaza"). The sculpture was commissioned under GSA's art-in-architecture program pursuant to which one half of one percent of the construction cost of federal buildings is reserved for the funding of artworks by living American artists. Serra is an internationally renowned sculptor, known primarily for his "site-specific" work. According to Serra, a site-specific sculpture "is one which is conceived and created in relation to the particular conditions of a specific site." Site-specific sculpture is meaningful only when displayed in the particular location for which it is created; such works are not intended to be displayed in more than one place. Serra's site-specific works consist primarily of steel plates or "forgings" that are welded together to form large abstract forms. Serra's sculptures have been displayed in many prominent locations throughout the world, including the Tuilleries Gardens in Paris.

In September 1979, Serra signed a contract with GSA setting forth the terms of his commission. The contract provided that Serra would receive a fee of $175,000 for building a sculpture on Federal Plaza. The contract further provided that "all designs, sketches, models, and the work produced under this Agreement...shall be the property of [the United States]." The contract contained no provisions restricting the Government's use of the sculpture after it was purchased.

"Tilted Arc" was completed and installed at Federal Plaza in 1981. The work is an arc of steel 120 feet long, 12 feet tall, and several inches thick. It is fabricated out of Cor-Ten steel, a material designed to oxidize naturally over time. Consequently, the work is now coated with what the artist refers to as "a golden amber patina" and what the sculpture's critics refer to as "rust." The sculpture bisects Federal Plaza. According to Serra, "Tilted Arc" is site-specific: It was designed for the Federal Plaza and is artistically inseparable from its location. Serra maintains that removing "Tilted Arc" to another site will destroy it.

The pigeons had barely begun to roost on "Tilted Arc" before the sculpture became the object of intense public criticism. GSA received hundreds of letters from community residents and federal employees complaining about the sculpture's appearance and its obstruction of Federal Plaza's previously open space. Initially, GSA took the position that critics should give the work time to gain public acceptance. However, when hostility to the work had not abated after several years, GSA agreed to hold a hearing on the possible relocation of the sculpture.

A public hearing was held in March 1985, presided over by William A. Diamond, GSA Regional Administrator. More than 150 persons spoke at the hearing, representing a wide range of constituencies including artists, civic leaders, employees at the Federal Plaza complex, and community residents. In addition, Serra was given the opportunity to state his views on the site-specific nature of "Tilted Arc" and the need to keep it at Federal Plaza. Those urging removal tended to be federal employees and area residents who complained primarily of the obstruction of Federal Plaza and the sculpture's unappealing aesthetic qualities. Those against removal tended to be artists and others from the art world who pointed to the work's significance in 20th Century sculpture and the importance of protecting the artist's freedom of expression....

Following the hearing, Diamond prepared a report in which he recommended to Dwight Ink, Acting Administrator of GSA, that "Tilted Arc" be relocated. Diamond urged primarily that the sculpture obstructed Federal Plaza, preventing the public from using the space for recreation and community events. Additionally, he noted concerns expressed at the hearing regarding potential safety hazards caused by the sculpture and its vulnerability to graffiti. Though Diamond included in the report his opinion that the atmosphere of the Plaza had been "turned into affrontery," [sic] he also stated that "my consideration of the issue of whether to relocate the sculpture would not be in any way based upon the arguments of its beauty, its ugliness, or its place in art history."...

While we agree that artwork, like other non-verbal forms of expression, may under some circumstances constitute speech for First Amendment purposes, we believe that the First Amendment has only limited application in a case like the present one where the artistic expression belongs to the Government rather than a private individual.

"'The purpose of the First Amendment is to protect private expression and nothing in the guarantee precludes the government from controlling its own expression or that of its agents.'" Consequently, the Government may advance or restrict its own speech in a manner that would clearly be forbidden were it regulating the speech of a private citizen.

In this case, the speaker is the United States Government. "Tilted Arc" is entirely owned by the Government and is displayed on Government property. Serra relinquished his own speech rights in the sculpture when he voluntarily sold it to GSA; if he wished to retain some degree of control as to the duration and location of the display of his work, he had the opportunity to bargain for such rights in making the contract for sale of his work. Nothing GSA has done limits the right of any private citizen to say what he pleases, nor has Serra been prevented from making any sculpture or displaying those that he has not sold. Rather, the Government's action in this case is limited to an exercise of discretion with respect to the display of its own property. Though there are conceivably situations in which the Government's exercise of its discretion in this regard could violate the First Amendment rights of the public, nothing GSA has done here encroaches in any way on Serra's or any other individual's right to communicate....

Nor does relocation of "Tilted Arc" preclude Serra from communicating his ideas in other ways. First, Serra has already had six years to convey his message through the sculpture's presence in the Plaza. Since the First Amendment protects the freedom to express one's views, not the freedom to continue speaking forever, the relocation of the sculpture after a lengthy period of initial display does not significantly impair Serra's right to free speech. Second, Serra has not shown that removal of the sculpture creates "any barrier to delivering to the media, or to the public by other means," whatever message he intended to convey with "Tilted Arc."...Notwithstanding that the sculpture is site-specific and may lose its artistic value if relocated, Serra is free to express his artistic and political views through the press and through other means that do not entail obstructing the Plaza.

Finally, the decision to remove "Tilted Arc" was not impermissibly content-based. According to the reports of GSA administrators Diamond and Ink, the primary reason for removal was the fact that the sculpture interfered with the public's use of Federal Plaza. Additionally, GSA was concerned about public safety and graffiti. Both Diamond and Ink expressly represented that they had not based their decisions on the work's artistic merit or its message. We agree with the District Court's assessment that "[t]here is no evidence in the record that GSA's decision to relocate the sculpture was based on the content of its message.... GSA's decision to relocate the structure was undertaken for functional purposes—in order to regain the openness of the plaza."...

To the extent that GSA's decision may have been motivated by the sculpture's lack of aesthetic appeal, the decision was entirely permissible.... *Pico* held that books could be removed from the school library if they were vulgar or educationally unsuitable. Similarly, GSA, which is charged with providing office space for federal employees, may remove from its buildings artworks that it decides are aesthetically unsuitable for particular locations. Moreover, the Supreme Court has consistently recognized that consideration of aesthetics is a legitimate government function that does not render a decision to restrict expression impermissibly content-based.

We recognize that courts considering First Amendment challenges by artists to governmental decisions to remove purchased works of art must proceed with some caution, lest a removal ostensibly based on unsuitable physical characteristics of the work or an unfavorable assessment of its aesthetic appeal camouflage an impermissible condemnation of political viewpoint. At the same time, artists must recognize that overly intrusive judicial restraints upon the prerogatives of government to decide when, where, and whether to display works of art that it has purchased would pose a serious threat to the vigor of such commendable ventures as GSA's art-in-architecture program. Government can be a significant patron of the arts. Its incentive to fulfill that role must not be dampened by unwarranted restrictions on its freedom to decide what to do with art it has purchased. If Serra had presented any facts to create a genuine issue as to whether GSA was removing "Tilted Arc" to condemn a political point of view or otherwise to trench upon First Amendment rights, we would require a trial, just as we did in *Pico*. [Pico v. Board of Education, 457 U.S. 853 (1982) (invalidating content-based book removal from library)]. But he has not done so. In the absence of such facts, his lawsuit is really an invitation to the courts to announce a new rule, without any basis in First Amendment law, that an artist retains a constitutional right to have permanently displayed at the intended site a work of art that he has sold to a government agency. Neither the values of the First Amendment nor the cause of public art would be served by accepting that invitation....

* * *

The following article discusses the larger artistic context for considering the rights of artists in public art displays:

Barbara Hoffman, *Law for Art's Sake in the Public Realm*,

16 Columbia-VLA Journal of Law and the Arts 39 (1991)

Contemporary public art is still in the process of defining its artistic and legal identity. Indeed, the juxtaposition of the terms "public" and "art" is somewhat of a paradox.

"Art" is a product of the artist's individual inquiries and personal vision. It is the epitome of self-expression, which very often challenges conventional wisdom and values. The term "public" implies self-negation—encompassing references to the community and the social order. Hence, the paradox of the term "public art" comes from the linking of the private and the public into a single concept. As such, the difficult task of formulating a general or jurisprudential theory concerning government sponsorship or ownership of art in public fora requires reconciliation, through government institutions and law, of the tension between artistic expression (with its potential for controversy) and government's duty to promote harmony and the public good.

This article examines and discusses existing contemporary legal doctrine and its failure to accommodate or even adequately define the issues and competing values at stake in the context of public art. Such failure may be attributed in part to the fact that neither legal theory nor art policy have been inspired by the vision of, or located in the broader context of, a socio-political public realm.

The expression "public realm" is Hannah Arendt's. It denotes the arena in which members of the public meet, and where competing values, interests, expectations and goals are open for discussion and modification. The notion of such a "public" was also made popular during the 1930s by American sociologists, who viewed the public as a form of social organization capable of transcending barriers between distinct communities and the restraints of existing social norms and achieving unity through critical interaction and discourse. A public is constituted when persons have the ability to speak to each other across divergent cultural boundaries.

The Dilemma of Contemporary Public Art

Before the mid-twentieth century, most public art commissions awarded by the U.S. government could be labeled "public" in the sense that they served commemorative or functional purposes and served to broaden the appeal of public policies and institutions. Art had a role in clarifying, interpreting and reinforcing accepted social, national and civic values through comprehensible forms and symbols. The artist used the imagery, iconography and formal structures that were part of the visual vocabulary of the society....

Richard Serra stated with respect to his site-specific sculpture Titled Arc: "Tilted Arc was constructed so as to engage the public in a dialogue that would perceptually and conceptually enhance its relation to the entire plaza."

The sculpture involves the viewer rationally and emotionally. A multitude of readings is possible....The work, through its location, height, length, horizontality, and lean, grounds one into the physical condition of the place. The viewer becomes aware of himself, his environment, and of his movement through the plaza.

In recent years, no work of art has been the subject of as much intense controversy as Serra's Tilted Arc. As such, Tilted Arc is a good starting point for a discussion of what happens when an art work's passing audience refuses to constitute itself as a public around it. In the case of Tilted Arc, this refusal resulted in the government's decision after four years of acrimonious debate and three days of hearings to relocate Tilted Arc. In his opinion denying Serra's request to enjoin removal of the sculpture, Judge Pollack referred to the writings of Blackstone, an important eighteenth-century English legal scholar, in his criticism of Serra's work, saying, "the sculpture as presently located has features of a purpresture." (A purpresture is defined as "an inclosure by a private person of a part of that which belongs to, and ought to be free and open to the enjoyment of, the public at large.") Legal scholar Duncan Kennedy described Blackstone's Commentaries as an attempt to "naturalize" purely social phenomena. Judge Pollack's reference makes sense only if viewed in that light and arguably reflects the Judge's perception that difficult art imposed on a reluctant public results in a privatization of public space. That perception is a far cry from that of art historian Rosalind Krauss, who sees Serra's work as exemplifying the phenomenology of Maurice Merleau-Ponty, and Tilted Arc in particular, as "lived perspective."

The case of Tilted Arc reminds us that when the interests of the artist and those of a largely uninformed or hostile community collide—however self-evident the moral, social and aesthetic issues in favor of the art work may seem—in practical terms the burden of proof will always fall upon art's defenders. It is clear then that in the face of an antagonistic judicial approach and negative community reaction, public art's defenders must find not only the reasons but the language to make their defense credible and intelligible to those for whom art is at best a decorative amenity and at worst an authoritarian imposition.

The Tilted Arc debate calls forth many of the aesthetic, social and legal questions important to the many controversies concerning the issue of what is appropriate public art. Even such well known artists as George Sugarman, Alexander Calder, Claes Oldenburg and Mark di Suvero have found their works attacked by a vocal segment of the population when the abstract and non-referential nature of their works proved to be a stumbling block to public appreciation. The tensions faced by funders of public art—including simultaneously promoting the arts and responding to public concerns—are heightened when the government is the funder, and tax dollars are used to finance projects that are perceived by certain representatives of the "public" as an artistic hoax, ideologically incorrect, obscene or offensive to civilized society. It is therefore ironic that controversial public art works, such as those by the four above-mentioned artists, often become prized civic icons as public understanding grows and deepens with the passage of time....

The *Serra* decision may be viewed as a paradigm of the conundrum of American public art policy. It further reveals the inadequacy of contemporary legal analysis with respect to constitutional and intellectual property doctrines as applied to artistic expression in the public context.

The decision of the *Serra* court may be faulted not only because it failed to satisfactorily reconcile and balance the various competing interests—as would be appropriate in such a situation where significant First Amendment freedoms are implicated—but also because it failed to provide an analytical framework for future cases, leaving unarticulated the rights, interests and values actually at stake. The court's opinion sheds little light on one of the central legal issues of the case: how strictly should a court scrutinize administrative actions in removing works of art that have been duly commissioned and brought into existence through government-sponsored programs?

In fairness to the court, its decision was made against a background of exceedingly complex and essentially unsettled legal doctrines. The *Serra* court's obligation was to resolve the issues and make a decision properly fitting within established constitutional mandates. To say that, however, is not to say that the court could easily rely on existing precedent, particularly because the issue was not relocation, but destruction of a unique, site-specific work of art. The Supreme Court, unable to articulate any principled line between content regulation and censorship, has provided little guidance in the form of a coherent theory or pragmatic analytical tools to resolve First Amendment claims of this nature. Furthermore, in a case like this, where so many interests and public policies converge, relatively minor differences in the pattern of facts in prior cases deprive these potential precedents of their usefulness. In part, therefore, the *Serra* court opinion reflects the congruence of the legal and socio-political spheres.

In 1979, Serra's sculpture was commissioned as part of the United States General Services Administration's Art-in-Architecture Program. It was to be a permanently installed, site-specific sculpture at Federal Plaza in lower Manhattan. Ten years later, it was removed to storage, after a GSA-appointed panel of experts failed to find a suitable site for relocation. In Serra's unsuccessful effort to enjoin removal of the sculpture in federal district court, he alleged that the GSA's decision to remove his sculpture violated his rights under the Free Speech Clause of the First Amendment, the Due Process Clause of the Fifth Amendment, federal trademark and copyright laws and state-based moral rights. The linchpin for all of Serra's claims was the existence of a cognizable legal relationship between the site and the art work, which would prevent its relocation or removal.

Judge Pollack dismissed, for lack of subject matter jurisdiction, Serra's claims based on breach of contract, federal trademark and copyright statutes and state law. He granted summary judgment to the GSA on Serra's constitutional claims on the grounds that the decision to relocate Tilted Arc was a content-neutral decision made to further the GSA's mission in administering and maintaining federal property and that the hearing before the GSA provided all the process that was due.

Serra's appeal in 1988 presented the question whether the removal and destruction of a government-owned art work from federal property violated the free expression and due process rights of the artist. An eleventh-hour appeal in 1989 based on moral rights doctrine and U.S. adherence to the Berne Convention was subsequently abandoned, based on clear evidence in the Implementation Act itself that "the provisions of the Berne Convention... do not expand or reduce any right of an author of a work... to claim authorship of the work; or to object to any distortion, mutilation, or other modification... that would prejudice the author's honor or reputation."

On appeal, Serra's lawyers argued that "once a medium of expression—be it writing, film, theater, painting or sculpture is publicly installed or displayed, First Amendment rights attach that prohibit the government from removing the expression on the basis of content." They relied on the Supreme Court decision in *Board of Education, Island Trees Union Free School District No. 26 v. Pico*. In *Pico*, the Board of Education ordered removed from its high school libraries nine books said to be "anti-American, anti-Christian, anti-Semitic and just plain filthy." Students brought an action against the Board alleging a violation of their First Amendment rights to receive information and ideas. Justice Brennan, writing for a plurality of the Court, affirmed the opinion of the Second Circuit and remanded the students' challenge to the district court for a determination of whether the book removal was improperly motivated solely to "prescribe what shall be orthodox." Justice Brennan stated that once a book is acquired and placed in a school library, removal by a school board on the basis of objections to the ideas contained in those books violates the First Amendment. Books might be removed, however, if found to be "pervasively vulgar" or because of lack of "educational suitability."

In the *Serra* appeal, Judge Newman, despite the language of his concurring opinion in *Pico*, wrote for a distinguished three-judge panel of the Second Circuit which included the former counsel to the Museum of Modern Art and affirmed Judge Pollack's granting of summary judgment, holding that Richard Serra's First Amendment rights had not been infringed....

20. Hellersdorf. Sculpture marks an interior courtyard at the rehabilitated Berlin, Germany socialist satellite suburb of Hellersdorf

Despite its conclusion that the government had the right to control the art work, the court did consider the possibility that Serra nonetheless retained some First Amendment interest in the continued display of Tilted Arc, although the court declined the opportunity to articulate a theoretical basis for this interest. The court held that the GSA's action was permissible as a time, place and manner restriction....

The *Serra* court's decision reflects current judicial attitude towards First Amendment theory as applied to artistic expression. Unfortunately, the opinion provides little discussion of First Amendment interests or of the objectives of public art policy, nor does it explain why either is served by a rule that practically allows government to remove, relocate or destroy works of art that seemingly offend a vocal segment of the community (unless the government action is based on the art work's political viewpoint). To its credit, the decision does not accord unfettered discretion to government officials in all situations. In addition to the above-mentioned *Pico* limitation imposed on the government as owner of the work, the government must also arguably afford a certain amount of time for the work to gain acceptance, absent a contractual provision to the contrary. (Tilted Arc was removed only after six years of unabated community hostility.) Further, government actions may be subject to a more "exacting" scrutiny in the case where the artist retains ownership of the work, particularly where the government revokes a permit previously granted....

In *Piarowski v. Illinois Community College District 515*,[118] the Seventh Circuit permitted relocation, but not complete removal, of an artist's stained-glass panels in a community college gallery exhibition, deferring to a hostile segment of the public. Judge Posner's description of the work is as follows:

> In the third window another brown woman, also naked except for stockings and also seen from the rear, is crouching in a posture of veneration before a

118. 759 F.2d 625 (7th Cir.), *cert. denied*, 474 U.S. 1007 (1985).

robed white male whose most prominent feature is a grotesquely outsized phallus (erect penis) that the woman is embracing.

For Posner, the art intended no political statement, was not disparaging of women or blacks — the choice of glass color was purely aesthetic—and contained no comment on race or sex relations. Simply put, it was "art for art's sake." Nevertheless, the artist, who was chairman of the art department and also the gallery coordinator, was held to have no First Amendment right to exhibit the allegedly sexually explicit, racially offensive art works in the busiest corridor on the campus when the college had ordered him to move the art to another room in the same building.

In a later article, Judge Posner commented on his decision in *Piarowski*, stating that any rule implying "that the scope of First Amendment protection may be different for works of art than for political or scientific works, is not to everyone's taste." He continued, "A rule that gave privileged status to the flaunting of offensive art—might engender public hostility to art that would be out of all proportion to the benefits in artistic freedom gained."

Sefick v. City of Chicago,[124] is the only case to date in which an artist has successfully prohibited the removal of his work. In that case, the court invalidated on First Amendment grounds the revocation of a permit granted to John Sefick by the city of Chicago to display in the Richard J. Daley Civic Center art work satirizing then-Mayor Bilandic. The court noted that a governmental entity has no obligation to provide a forum for the display of art work, but once it does, constitutional protections apply. The court found that the motivation for the revocation was political and based on content alone. In applying strict scrutiny, the court rejected the city's arguments that it needed to protect a captive audience and that it did not want to appear to sponsor specific views....

It is difficult to draw a bright line between art that communicates political ideas and art that does not. It is also erroneous to distinguish between artistic categories such as "aesthetic," "political" or "erotic." Even the familiar proposition of First Amendment doctrine, that expression has special value in the context of dialogue, does not facilitate any such distinction. As...*Piarowski* show[s], categorizing artistic expression as non-political or political is itself the product of political and ideological choices and often serves merely to legitimize the status quo.

In addition, some forms of contemporary art rebel against traditional measures of artistic quality and seek to escape categorization, while others, such as formalism and abstract expressionism, reject the Platonic ideal of art in order to find reality in what is perceptible to the senses and in art's physical properties. As a consequence, classification or evaluation of such art for legal purposes may be extremely difficult. If the government has the right to define what counts as political speech and to define the manner of expressing that speech, the risk exists that requiring speech to conform to traditionally accepted forms will impose similar constraints on the substance of that speech....

Future public art policies should involve the selection of artists who, while representing myriad voices and visions, share the recognition that to make public art is to enter into dialogue with diverse communities, each of which views the art work, as does the artist, as a quest for and mirror of a public self-identity.

* * *

124. 485 F. Supp. 644 (N.D. Ill.1979).

Notes and Comments

1. Should ownership of the artwork by the government control as in *Serra*? Did not the government own the removed books from the *Pico* library? Is the court struggling to identify viewpoint-based action as the key so as to justify content-based behavior? Any removal of art would be based on appearance and thus content-based. Of course, if removed for a point of view expressed, that would be viewpoint-based. Thus removal of a dark and disturbing exhibition that most of the viewing public finds "revolting," would be content neutral, while removal for a blasphemous, pornographic, or homosexual content or theme would be viewpoint based? Certainly removal for the point of view reflected (anti-Republican, anti-Moslem, anti-American) would be viewpoint-based. This may reflect a false dichotomy as to why was "Tilted Arc" removed? Neutrally, to reclaim public space, or because the majority saw no beauty? Should majority aesthetic judgment trump the minority? Is anti-modernism viewpoint-based?

Nicole B. Wilkes, *Public Responsibilities of Private Owners of Cultural Property: Toward A National Art Preservation Statute,*

24 Columbia-VLA Journal of Law and the Arts 177 (2001)

A tourist walks into a souvenir shop in Florence and buys a plaster replica of Michelangelo's David. When he returns home to the United States, he puts the statue on his desk to inspire him in his creative writing. One night, frustrated and angry at a particularly bad case of writer's block, he smashes the statue into an unsalvageable mess of fragments. Though the writer's act is destructive, it does not implicate any larger cultural or legal concerns. But what if the object was an important Renaissance painting by Fra Angelico instead? Now the writer's act is a cause for serious concern because of the cultural significance of the destroyed work of art.

Intentional "crimes against art" are not as uncommon as some might imagine, and unfortunately such acts are not explicitly addressed by the law. A related problem exists with respect to "crimes of omission" committed by owners of historically significant objects who choose to withhold their treasures from the general public.[2] These phenomena are of heightened concern with respect to private owners of movable art objects, where detection is particularly difficult and the public has no legal recourse. Should owners be able to exercise unbridled power over objects (even if there is a loss to scholarship or art history)? Do private owners of cultural objects have an obligation to the community or the public at large? Traditional conceptions of property rights dictate that "ownership of physical things" is "private and unqualified." However, there is an identifiable public or community-centered interest in certain objects. Even when pieces of art remain in private hands for a substantial period of time, they may eventually reemerge in the public realm via donations to museums and other cultural institutions. In addition, private owners often loan their works for public display. Thus, the line between public and private becomes somewhat blurred with respect to cultural property. The notion of a collective public heritage has previously been identified through statu-

2. The paradigmatic example of such activity is outlined in the case of Dr. Albert Barnes, who acquired a world-renowned collection of French Impressionist and post-Impressionist paintings, and greatly restricted public access until a court order demanded it.

tory models protecting historic buildings, antiquities, and artist's moral rights. However, none of these legal regimes directly protect art objects.

There is a host of empirical evidence suggesting that the general public is concerned about art and cultural heritage. In terms of government policy, the United States established the National Endowment for the Arts as a public agency to fund artistic endeavor and finally joined the 1970 UNESCO Convention. Congress established the National Foundation on Arts and Humanities, thereby "[a]cknowledging that the arts belong to all the people of the United States." The Visual Artists Rights Act of 1990 (VARA) federal moral rights regime and the state art preservation laws in California and Massachusetts provide additional support for an identifiable public interest in art. In particular, the California Art Preservation Act states that "there is a public interest in preserving the integrity of cultural and artistic creations."[12] The same provision is found in the Massachusetts Art Preservation Act.[13]...

According to Professor Monroe E. Price, "it might... be possible to say that there is a public right to share reasonably in the aesthetic value of a work of art."[24] Price advocates more than a general right of access, by indicating that the public should possess "a carefully controlled power to ensure that works are not totally or arbitrarily withheld from public view." As a method of balancing the rights of the public and the rights of private owners, a reasonableness requirement would be attached to the right of access to ensure that the owner is not overburdened with additional costs and diminished enjoyment of his work. In particular, Price proposes that the risk of loss or damage during the period of display would be borne by the museum (or other institution) exhibiting the work and a work could not be borrowed more than once every five years. An additional incentive mechanism could involve granting tax benefits to those owners who loan their artwork to public museums for exhibition....

The concept of a shared cultural heritage for all humanity can be gleaned from the ideals set forth in the preambles to the 1954 Hague Convention for the Protection of Cultural Property in the Event of Armed Conflict and the Convention on the Means of Prohibiting and Preventing the Illicit Import, Export and Transfer of Ownership of Cultural Property, adopted by the United Nations Educational, Scientific, and Cultural Organization in 1970. The same idea is embedded in the UNIDROIT Convention on Stolen or Illegally Exported Cultural Objects, which was completed in Rome in 1995. These international efforts highlight the significance of cultural property for "the advancement of civilization." The Hague Convention Preamble states that "damage to the cultural property of any people whatsoever means damage to the cultural heritage of all mankind." The Preamble to the UNESCO Convention declares that "cultural property is one of the basic elements of civilization and national culture" and that its exchange "increases the knowledge of civilization, enriches the cultural life of all peoples and inspires mutual respect and appreciation among nations." In the same vein, the recent UNIDROIT Convention recognized "the fundamental importance of the protection of cultural heritage and cultural exchanges for promoting understanding between peoples, and the dissemination of culture for the well-being of humanity and the progress of civilization." International recognition of the public value of cultural property accentuates

---

12. Cal. Civ. Code § 989(a), § 987(a) (2000).
13. Mass. Gen. Laws ch. 231, § 85S (2000).
24. Monroe E. Price, *State Arts Councils: Some Items for a New Agenda*, 27 Hastings L.J. 1183, 1188 (1976).

the need for protection and preservation of such property through both legal mechanisms and heightened public awareness.

For the purpose of constructing a legal framework to protect cultural property, the international conventions provide a valuable model for delineating the scope of protection under a proposed statute. These established structures bring us closer to a workable definition of "cultural property." Determining what is "in" and what is "out" is imperative to ensure that any proposed regulation or incentive structure does not creep too far into the realm of private property rights. In addition, any form of government regulation or incentive-based system involves an expenditure of resources. Therefore, a federal program to protect and preserve privately held cultural objects should only be applicable to those objects that sufficiently embody the public interest.

The 1970 UNESCO Convention defines "cultural property" to include:

(a) Rare collections and specimens of fauna, flora, minerals and anatomy, and objects of paleontological interest;

(b) property relating to history, including the history of science and technology and military and social history...;

(c) products of archaeological excavations...

(d) elements of artistic or historical monuments or archaeological sites which have been dismembered;

(e) antiquities more than one hundred years old, such as inscriptions, coins and engraved seals;

(f) objects of ethnological interest;

(g) property of artistic interest...;

(h) rare manuscripts and incunabula, old books, documents and publications of special interest...;

(i) postage, revenue and similar stamps...;

(j) archives, including sound, photographic and cinematographic archives;

(k) articles of furniture more than one hundred years old and old musical instruments....

In his article entitled "Art Destroyed, Sixteen Shocking Case Histories," Avis Berman outlines historic events in which works of art were destroyed by those who owned or had jurisdiction over them." A striking example of purchase for the sake of destruction is outlined in Berman's discussion of a Gustave Courbet painting entitled Return from the Conference, depicting a procession of drunk clerics. The painting overtly communicated Courbet's anticlericalism, resulting in a considerable degree of negative public attention. Courbet was unaffected by the scandal and proceeded to display the painting to the public in his Paris studio and sent it to London for purchase. Although Courbet expected an American financier to acquire the painting, Return from the Conference was eventually sold to a devout Catholic, who purchased it for the express purpose of destroying it.

A relevant case for the protection of works produced by artists who are now deceased involves the art critic John Ruskin and J.M.W. Turner. When Turner died in 1851, he bequeathed all of his unsold works (including 300 oils and 19,000 drawings and watercolors) to the British nation, with Ruskin named as one of the executors of the estate.

Ruskin was horrified when he discovered that erotic drawings of "sailors' women" were part of the Turner bequest. A recently discovered letter indicates that after some deliberation on Ruskin's part, staff members at the National Gallery of Art in London burned the "obscene drawings" in 1858 with Ruskin's approval. The Turner case highlights the extent to which an artist's body of work can be jeopardized when he is no longer capable of exercising control.

The problem of the "pharoic owner" was highlighted recently when Van Gogh's Portrait of Dr. Gachet was unable to be located for display in a traveling exhibition. In the spring of 1990, Ryoei Saito, owner of the Daishowa Paper Manufacturing Company in Japan, paid $82.5 million at auction for Van Gogh's Portrait of Dr. Gachet, the highest price ever paid for a painting. Saito indicated that he would consider cremating the painting with his body to avoid taxes....

The California Art Preservation Act was the first state legislative effort to recognize a public interest in works of art. Alan Sieroty, the former California state senator who sponsored the bill, made the following statement:

To pass this law, you have to get legislators to rethink their concepts of property rights. Property rights are very strong in this country, and that's why we have not adopted art preservation laws. You have to begin to think that maybe the person who created the work of art, and perhaps also the public, retain some interest in seeing that the art is not destroyed, not mutilated, and not changed without the artist's consent. The first impression that members of the judiciary committee had when we presented our bill was "it's mine, I can do anything I want with it, I can cut it up if it's too big for a certain place that I want to put it." California enacted Civil Code § 987 in 1979 and § 989 in 1982. The first bill is a fairly conventional moral rights statute, granting artists a right against anyone who intentionally defaces, mutilates, alters, or destroys their work that qualifies as "fine art." The statute defines fine art as a work of "recognized quality," to be determined by courts through reliance upon "the opinions of artists, art dealers, collectors of fine art, curators of art museums, and other persons involved with the creation or marketing of fine art." In the remedies provision of § 987, the public interest is recognized by requiring that punitive damages recovered by the artist be received by "an organization or organizations engaged in charitable or educational activities involving the fine arts in California." The second bill functioned as an expansion of the law to provide the public with the right to protect certain recognized works of art when the artist is dead or the artist's heirs are not concerned with protection. Civil Code § 989 permits established non-profit arts organizations "acting in the public interest" to "commence an action for injunctive relief to preserve or restore the integrity of a work of fine art" (as defined in the earlier law) from defacement, mutilation, alteration, or destruction. The definition of "fine art" for the purposes of § 989 includes the "recognized quality" provision from § 987, but also requires that the art be "of substantial public interest." The determination of "substantial public interest" is made by the courts in reliance on the opinions of the art community as outlined in the earlier law. Section 989 also provides that site-specific art that "cannot be removed from real property without substantial physical defacement, mutilation, alteration, or destruction" will not be protected under the statute. However, this provision can be circumvented if an arts organization "offers some evidence giving rise to a reasonable likelihood that a work of art can be removed from the real property without substantial physical defacement, mutilation, alteration, or destruction of the work, and is prepared to pay the cost of removal of the work." The public is thereby injected into the preservation equation once again.

According to Sax, § 989 "is plainly meant to protect the public's interest in the art, not merely that of the artist."[103] The communitarian underpinnings of the law were highlighted by then Senator Sieroty in his letter asking the governor to sign the bill: "works of fine art are more than economic commodities and they oftentimes provide our communities with a sense of cohesion and history. The public's interest in preserving important artistic creations should be promoted and our communities should be able to preserve their heritage when it is in jeopardy."

By enacting the Visual Artist's Rights Act of 1990 (VARA),[114] Congress recognized that art is a significant part of our cultural heritage. The statute provides a legal right for contemporary visual artists to protect their works against modification or destruction that would be prejudicial to their historical legacy. Congress anticipated that VARA would "prevent distortions of works that cheat the public of an accurate account of the culture of our time." VARA defines "work of visual art" as: (1) a painting, drawing, print or sculpture, existing in a single copy, in a limited edition of 200 copies or fewer that are signed and consecutively numbered by the author, or, in the case of sculpture, in multiple cast, carved, or fabricated sculptures of 200 or fewer that are consecutively numbered by the author and bear the signature or other identifying mark of the author; or (2) a still photographic image produced for exhibition purposes only, existing in a single copy that is signed by the author, or in a limited edition of 200 copies or fewer that are signed and consecutively numbered by the author.... [118]

Despite the preservation-oriented impulses underlying the law, VARA fails to operate effectively as a preservation statute. By placing enforcement responsibility in the hands of individuals, the communitarian goals of art preservation are ill-served. The public is only represented when the public interest clearly aligns with the individual interest of the artist. Thus, "[p]ublic concern for the preservation of any work goes unheeded unless the artist is willing to pursue protection." In cases of explicit conflict between artists and the public, "a work may become valued by a segment of society, yet remain unprotected because the artist or his heirs are either missing or indifferent to the fate of the work." From this perspective, it becomes clear that artistic creations are not afforded protection of preservation-scope under VARA.

In addition, copyright protection could impede certain works from being publicly displayed or catalogued....

The public trust doctrine has previously been used to promote environmental protection and could be extended to safeguard art objects that are subjected to extensive public use.... When an owner of artwork donates, sells, or loans a work of art to a museum, he impliedly offers his property to the public for educational uses. In the terminology of public dedication law, he is "throwing open" his property to the public for its evident public use, and thus an inference arises that he intends to dedicate the property for those cultural and educational purposes. Since museums may be considered representatives of the public for cultural purposes, once a museum accepts the offer to dedicate, that is, once it agrees to acquire the work, the public interest in that work should be established. [A] public trust would thereafter run with the work, permanently prohibiting the owner from treating it in a manner inconsistent with the public interest....

---

103. [Joseph L. Sax, Playing Darts with a Rembrandt (Ann Arbor: University of Michigan Press, 1999)] at 24.

114. 17 U.S.C. § 101 (1990).

118. 17 U.S.C. § 101 (1995).

The Antiquities Act of 1906 forbids taking any "historic or prehistoric ruin or monument, or any object of antiquity" from federal lands without a permit.... The limitations of the Antiquities Act were somewhat addressed by the passage in 1979 of the Archaeological Resources Protection Act (ARPA), but ARPA still "extends protection only to human-made artifacts (archaeological resources) on federally owned or Indian lands." The private realm is regulated by ARPA only to the extent that it prohibits interstate trafficking of artifacts obtained in violation of state or local law....

International Protection of Monuments and World Cultural Heritage

The principal international instrument for the protection of monuments and sites is the UNESCO Convention for the Protection of the World Cultural and Natural Heritage ("1972 UNESCO Convention"). As a means of protecting monuments and sites of cultural significance, the 1972 UNESCO Convention created a World Heritage Fund, which is financed by contributions from signatory states based on a percentage of their annual UNESCO dues. The funds are then used to provide advice and financing for the preservation of sites of cultural significance. The 1972 UNESCO Convention also established an Intergovernmental Committee for the Protection of the Cultural and Natural Heritage of Outstanding Universal Value, referred to as the World Heritage Committee. One of the primary functions of the World Heritage Committee is to publish a "World Heritage List" composed of properties that have outstanding value as part of the cultural and natural heritage. In 1980, pursuant to United States participation in the 1972 UNESCO Convention, Congress recognized the need to nominate properties of outstanding universal value in the United States to the World Heritage Committee....

Japan maintains a national register of cultural property in order to regulate the export of cultural objects. The United States could also establish a national register, loosely modeled on the National Register of Historic Places, as a communicative device through which the federal government could assert the public interest in preserving culturally significant works of art....

* * *

Notes and Comments

1. Nicole Wilkes advocates legislation that would impose restrictions on neglect, mutilation, alteration and destruction, and provide obligatory public access to private collections, while offering preservation and access tax incentives. Would such restrictions discourage private art collection? Have art collectors learned anything from the Gun lobby? Would regulation including registration or cataloging lead to "politically correct" crusades against pornography whether by the art establishment against William Turner or by local politicians against Robert Maplethorpe or other controversial artists, just as Nazis condemned decadent art?

Final Note

It is the design of these materials to identify and facilitate discussion of a broad array of contemporary and compelling land use issues. It is hoped that they have demonstrated that the experiences of other lands, both rich and poor have important lessons that can inform American Urban policy. Likewise, the American experience, as that of other nations, can offer valuable insights for the formulation of public policy.

Index